HISTORY

OF THE

TOWN OF RYE

NEW HAMPSHIRE

FROM ITS DISCOVERY AND SETTLEMENT
TO DECEMBER 31, 1903

BY

LANGDON B. PARSONS

A HERITAGE CLASSIC

1905

Facsimile Reprint

Published 1992 By
Heritage Books, Inc.
1540-E Pointer Ridge Place
Bowie, Maryland 20716
(301) 390-7709
ISBN 1-55613-668-4

A Complete Catalog Listing Hundreds Of Titles On
Genealogy, History, And Americana
Available Free On Request

Genealogy.

ACKERMAN—AKERMAN.

1. PETER ACKERMAN married, first, Nov. 28, 1779, Rachel Foss, and second, Oct. 19, 1797, widow Charity Locke, sister of his first wife. Children by first wife:

Peter, bapt. Aug., 1782. Joseph, bapt. Aug., 1782. Phineas, bapt. June 22, 1783. John, bapt. Nov. 28, 1785.

Child by second wife:

2. Benjamin M.

2. BENJAMIN M. AKERMAN, son of Peter (1), married for his second wife, March 5, 1821, Sally Philbrick. Children:

Ira, Bartlett, Henry C.

ADAMS.

REV. JOHN W. ADAMS, born May 23, 1832; married, second, Aug. 24, 1858, Lydia M. Trefethen. Pastor of the Methodist church 1857 and 1858. Children by second wife:

Lydia Viola, b. July 8, 1859; m. Oct. 29, 1882, Lewis H. Foss. Wilbur Fisk, b. Nov. 15, 1860. Charles W., b. June 4, 1863. Freddie O., b. March 4, 1871; d. March 7, 1871. Sadie Elvira, b. Aug. 4, 1874; d. Jan. 10, 1878.

OLIVER ADAMS married Mary Jane Foss and had Lorenzo, born Feb. 16, 1856.

ALLEN.

JUDE ALLEN married, first, Jan. 6, 1738, Elizabeth Locke, and second, Oct. 4, 1776, widow Dorcas (Marden) Mow. Children by first wife:

Jude, bapt. Sept. 18, 1743. Nathaniel, bapt. July 12, 1747. Joshua, bapt. Aug. 9, 1761. Salome, b. [1771?]; m. John Brown.

Child by second wife:

Elizabeth Locke, bapt. April 19, 1778; m. Nov. 10, 1803, Simon Locke.

SAMUEL ALLEN married April 8, 1824, Sally Mowe. After his death she married James H. Locke. Child:

Samuel Osborn, b. July 13, 1824; d. Feb. 18, 1848.

AMY.

JOEL AMY married, Jan. 22, 1776, Elizabeth Dowrst, and had Joel, bapt. June 15, 1777.

AYERS.

REV. OLIVER AYERS married Caroline Garland. She died Sept. 23, 1857. Children:

Elizabeth Garland, b. Nov. 5, 1836; m. Warden B. Clapp; d. Sept. 27, 1865. Henry, b. Sept. 7, 1838; m. Sarah Shields. Anna Day, b. Dec. 29, 1841; d. Dec. 29, 1861. Oliver, b. Sept. 25, 1845. Caroline Matilda, b. July 23, 1849.

BALCH.

1. NATHANIEL BALCH married Elizabeth M. Tucker. Resided in Portsmouth. Children:

2. Edward H., m. Julia Bunker 1864; she d. Nov. 24, 1884. Martha C., m. Sept. 24, 1877, Charles E. Trefethern.

2. EDWARD H. BALCH, son of Nathaniel (1), married, 1864, Julia Bunker. Child:

Gracia, b. July 12, 1864; m. Nov. 29, 1882, John H. Jenness; d. Nov. 24, 1887.

BALL.

PETER BALL married Mary Wallis. Children:

Peter. John, m. Brown. Hannah, m. Fields. Susan, m. Trickey. Mary, m. Thomas.

BANFIELD.

CAPT. SAMUEL BANFIELD married Mary Seavey. He died in 1743, and she died in 1753. Child:

Mary, b. 1704; m. Capt. Joseph Langdon; d. Aug. 10, 1753.

BARNARD.

CALVIN BARNARD married Sarah E. Jenness. Children:

Charles, b. April 13, 1768. James.

GENEALOGY. 295

BATCHELDER.

1. JOSIAH BATCHELDER married, first, Abigail Cotton; and probably second, Feb., 1799, Olive Wells. Children by first wife:
    Nathaniel, d. Sept. 3, 1804. Betsey, b. Sept. 14, 1786; m. 1807, Josiah Perkins. Abigail, d. Dec. 20, 1809. Comfort, m. John Lamprey. Sarah, m. Elijah Shaw.
    Children by second wife:
2. Jonathan Cotton, b. Jan. 7, 1800; m. Abigail Varrell. Mary, b. Sept. 15, 1806; m. Jan. 7, 1827, Bradbury C. French.

2. JONATHAN COTTON BATCHELDER, son of Josiah (1), born Jan. 7, 1800; married March 1, 1827, Abigail Varrell. Children:
    Susan, b. July, 1828; m. John M. Davis. John E., b. Jan., 1830. Sarah A., b. Oct., 1832; d. Oct. 10, 1838. Mandana, b. March, 1837; m. Andrew Sides, had one child and was then divorced. Martha Ann, b. Sept. 24, 1838; d. Oct. 1, 1858.

JAMES BATCHELDER married Elizabeth Batchelder. Lived at North Hampton. Children:
    Clara A. James. John, m. Mary Ann Philbrick of Rye. Ambrose. Albert. Warren. Jane, b. May 19, 1819; d. Dec. 20, 1900. Annie, m. George Hill. Almira, b. April 9, 1823; m. Sheridan Jenness. Emily, b. 1830; d. May 21, 1901. May A., b. May 18, 1834.

JOSEPH BATCHELDER married Sarah Philbrick. Lived at North Hampton. She died June 23, 1888. Children:
    Angelina, m. Benjamin P. Philbrick. Clarinda. Amanda, b. Dec. 30, 1829; m. Robert P. Locke.

BENJAMIN D. BATCHELDER married Martha M. Lord. Child:
    Helen W., b. Feb. 1, 1855; m. Edward Taylor.

BATES.

WILLIAM BATES lived at Newcastle and died before 1731. Children:
    Mary, who was living unm. in Rye in 1731. Judith, m. James Marden.

BECK.

JAMES BECK of Portsmouth married Nov. 13, 1794, Deborah Lear. Child:
    John, bapt. Sept. 18, 1798.

JOHN BECK married Sept. 16, 1798, Betsey Odiorne.

BELL.

SHADRACH BELL married Dec., 1739, or Jan., 1740, Grace Tucker. Children:

Margaret, bapt. Feb. 22, 1741. Frederick Morgan, bapt. Nov., 1749.
Three Bell brothers lived in Rye; Samson Bell, who married Elizabeth ———; Thomas, who married Mary ———; and Matthew, who married Dorothy ———.

BERERLAND.

DAVID BERERLAND married and had Margaret, who was baptized in Feb., 1740.

BERRY.

1. JOHN BERRY is said to have been the first settler in Rye or Sandy Beach. He probably was the son of William Berry, one of those sent out by Mason for his plantation, and who was at Portsmouth as early as 1631 (Savage). William Berry died before June, 1654. His widow, Jane, married Nathaniel Drake.

January, 1648-'49, at a town meeting held at Strawberry Bank, "Granted that Wm Berry shall have a lot upon the neck of land upon the South side of the Little River at Sandy Beach."

John Berry married Susannah ———. Children:
2. John, b. Jan. 14, 1659. Elizabeth, m. John Locke.
3. William.
4. James.

2. JOHN BERRY, son of John (1), born Jan. 14, 1659; married Mary ———. Children:

Jonathan, b. Jan. 15, 1693. Ithamar, b. March 5, 1698.

3. WILLIAM BERRY, son of John (1), married July 8, 1678, Judith Locke. Children:

Elizabeth, b. March 16, 1680; d. young.
5. Nehemiah. Elizabeth, b. Oct. 15, 1686, at Newcastle; m. July 24, 1705, Christopher Palmer. Nathaniel, b. Feb. 13, 1689, at Newcastle.
6. Stephen, b. Jan. 18, 1691, at Newcastle.
7. William, b. Nov. 18, 1693, at Newcastle. Jeremiah, b. March 8, 1695, at Newcastle. Frederic, b. Jan. 15, 1699, at Newcastle. Abigail, b. March 15, 1700, at Newcastle. Jane, b. Jan. 26, 1702, at Newcastle.

GENEALOGY.

4. JAMES BERRY, son of John (1), married. Children:
8. Ebenezer.
9. Samuel.

5. NEHEMIAH BERRY, son of William (3), married Sarah ———. Children:

Susanna, b. Aug. 23, 1725; m. Nathan Marden (?). John, b. March 10, 1736; m. July 27, 1757, Betsey Yeaton (?).
10. Jacob, b. July 7, 1738. Hannah, b. Sept. 23, 1740. Nathaniel, bapt. June 1, 1746; d. unm. Dec. 16, 1815.

6. STEPHEN BERRY, son of William (3), born Jan. 18, 1691; married Jan. 4, 1716, Anna, daughter of Thomas Philbrick. Children:

Joseph, b. March 11, 1717. Phebe (or Tryphena), b. Sept. 3, 1719. (Tryphena bapt. Oct. 11, 1719.) Judith, bapt. June 3, 1722. Stephen, bapt. June 14, 1724. Ephraim, b. Oct. 11, 1727. James, b. March 25, 1731.

7. WILLIAM BERRY, son of William (3), born Nov. 18, 1693; married Dec. 21, 1721, Sarah Lane. He lived on the Eliza Ann Walker farm, and died Oct. 8, 1786. She died Jan. 3, 1776. Children:

11. Jeremiah, b. 1721; m. Oct. 3, 1745, Hannah Locke. Widow Eleanor Brackett and widow Dorothy Emerson. Mary, bapt. March 10, 1723; m. March 28, 1745, Jonathan Hobbs.

8. EBENEZER BERRY, son of James (4), married, first, Keziah Merryfield, and second, Mary Kingman. He lived at the Reuel Garland place. Farmer and large landowner. Children by first wife:

Abigail, b. June 21, 1719. Rachel, b. Nov. 13, 1721. Eleanor, b. April 4, 1722. Charity, b. April 4, 1726. Ruth, b. June 4, 1727; d. Sept. 10, 1735. Benjamin, d. Sept. 20, 1735. Keziah, d. Sept. 23, 1735. Ebenezer, d. Nov. 3, 1735.

Children by second wife:
Susannah, b. Dec. 13, 1730; m. Doe.
12. Merrifield, b. Aug. 15, 1733. Simon, b. June 4, 1735.

9. SAMUEL BERRY, son of James (4), married Abigail ———, who died June 19, 1750, aged 75 years. The following children are named in a deed of 1750:

13. Jotham. Rachel, m. June 7, 1733, Hickerson (or Joshua) Foss. Sarah, may have m. in 1751 George Randall. Deborah, may have m. and had a dau., Elizabeth.

10. JACOB BERRY, son of Nehemiah (5), born July 7, 1738; married Rachel Rand; died Dec. 11, 1811. He was a shoemaker by trade. Children:

Isaac, b. April 20, 1767; m. Tarlton; d. of smallpox at Newcastle, where his dau. m. William Amazeen. Richard, bapt. April 26, 1772; m. March 30, 1805, Olive, dau. of William and Mary Holmes, of Portsmouth. Sarah, bapt. Nov. 30, 1777; m. Thomas Sleeper; lived at Nottingham.

11. JEREMIAH BERRY, son of William (7), born in 1721; married first, Oct. 3, 1741, Hannah Locke. She died July 1, 1770, aged 46 years, and he married, second, Sept. 8, 1770, widow Eleanor Brackett. He lived on the Eliza A. Walker farm. Was corporal in Capt. Parsons' Co. in the Revolutionary War, stationed at Newcastle. Children by first wife:

Sarah, b. 1746. Hannah, b. June 28, 1747; m. July 22, 1768, Nathaniel Marden. Sarah, b. July 6, 1749; m. Aaron Jenness. Mary, b. March 24, 1751; m. Jan. 13, 1774, Samuel Dowrst Foss.
14. William, b. April 12, 1753.
Jeremiah, b. April 2, 1755; m. Fanny Hayes. Joses, b. 1757; scalded to death by hot fat.
15. Levi, b. Feb. 29, 1760. Patience, b. Feb. 13, 1762; m. James Seàvey.
16. Solomon, bapt. Nov. 17, 1765.
Children by second wife:
Hannah, bapt. Aug. 21, 1773; m. April 17, 1801, James Locke. Lydia, bapt. Nov. 27, 1776; m. Jan. 20, 1801, William Trefethern, Jr.

12. MERRIFIELD BERRY, son of Ebenezer (8), born Aug. 15, 1733; married, Aug. 17, 1756, Huldah Towle of Hampton. He lived on the Reuel Garland farm, now owned by A. H. Drake. Died May 20, 1817. She died Nov. 9, 1809. Children:

34. James Towle, b. March 15, 1758; m. Hannah Randall. Huldah, b. Oct. 26, 1760; d. about 1776. Olly, b. Sept. 19, 1763; m. June 24, 1786, John Jenness.
17. Ebenezer, b. March 15, 1766. Abigail, b. Dec. 26, 1768; m. Aug. 9, 1787, Edmond Johnson.

13. JOTHAM BERRY, son of Samuel (9); married, first, Nov. 11, 1731, Mary Bates; and second, April 16, 1780, widow Tryphene Sanders. Children:

18. Timothy.
19. Samuel, bapt. April 20, 1741. Rachel, bapt. July 3, 1743; m. Ithamar Mace, or Maj. Hall. Judith, m. Jacob Tibbets. Sarah, m. George Randall. Mary, d. unm.

14. WILLIAM BERRY, son of Jeremiah (11), born April 12, 1753; married, first, Nov. 10, 1774, Love Brackett. She died Jan. 17, 1795, and he married, second, March 6, 1796, Elizabeth Wendell. Children by first wife:

Lydia, b. 1775; m. William Trefethern.
20. Samuel Brackett, b. April 14, 1777; m. Hannah, b. March 25, 1781; m. Dec. 24, 1801, Josiah Marden.
21. Jeremiah, b. Dec. 16, 1783; m. Eleanor, b. April 25, 1786; m. Feb. 18, 1808, James Locke. Love, b. May 17, 1788; m. June 26, 1806, Ebenezer Marden. William, b. Nov. 10, 1790; d. Patty, b. July 21, 1792; m. March 22, 1809, Job Foss.

Children by second wife:
Sarah Wentworth, bapt. Jan. 12, 1797. Dolly, b. May, 1798; d. July 12, 1822. Sarah Sargent, b. Sept. 3, 1799; m. Feb. 17, 1823, Gilman Dearborn; d. May 13, 1877. Eliza, b. Dec., 1806; m. A. K. Warren.

15. LEVI BERRY, son of Jeremiah (11), born Feb. 29, 1760; married, Nov. 13, 1785, Sarah Jenness. Cordwainer. Children:

Mary, b. April 17, 1785; m. March 18, 1803, Alexander Salter. Sally, b. Feb. 8, 1787; m. April 27, 1806, Simon Goss.
22. Joseph Jenness, b. May 17, 1789. Hannah L., b. June 19, 1791; m. Jan. 29, 1810, Joseph Trefethern. Olive, b. June 24, 1793; m. Joseph Locke. Betsey, b. March 24, 1797; m. Oct. 3, 1821, Joseph Berry. Nancy J., b. March 4, 1801; m. May 22, 1825, William Varrell; d. Feb. 19, 1881. Levi, b. Sept. 19, 1804; a cripple; d. Sept. 27, 1873.

16. SOLOMON BERRY, son of Jeremiah (11), bapt. Nov. 17, 1765; married, Oct. 15, 1794, Patty Kate. Children:

Benjamin, m. Brasbridge. Levi, d. unm. Sarah, m. Robert Spencer. Betsey. Lydia. Belinda. Thomas. Mehitable. Keziah, b. Dec. 3, 1815; m. Patrick Ownes, an Irishman.

17. EBENEZER BERRY, son of Merrifield (12), born March 15, 1766; married, Nov. 10, 1786, Polly Garland. "Aunt Polly," as she was called, lived in the old Berry house with her son, Thomas G., who was a prominent merchant in Portsmouth, having early been in the store of his Uncle

William there. He inherited the Colonel Benjamin Garland farm from the heirs of William Garland and lived there until he died. Polly died April 26, 1857. Children:

Thomas Garland, b. Nov. 10, 1786; d. Oct. 21, 1870, at Rye. Ebenezer, bapt. Oct. 11, 1788; d. at New Orleans. Betsey, bapt. Aug. 15, 1790. Charles, b. 1792; followed the sea.

18. TIMOTHY BERRY, son of Jotham (13), married, May 19, 1760, Mary Tucker. Removed to Chichester. Was sergeant in Capt. Joseph Parsons' company in the Revolutionary War, stationed at Newcastle. Children:

Sarah, bapt. 1761; m. first, Joseph Dow, of Seabrook; m. second, —— Lake, of Pittsfield. Susannah, bapt. April 10, 1763; m. April 11, 1811, Richard Fitzgerald, of Portsmouth. Mary, bapt. May 12, 1765; m. Nov. 19, 1784, Edward Varrell. Jotham, bapt. July 24, 1767. Samuel, bapt. Sept., 1769; lost at sea. Mehitable, bapt. Sept. 6, 1772. Mehitable, bapt. Sept. 9, 1775; m. James Lake of Loudon. Joseph. bapt. Sept. 21, 1777; unm.; lost at sea with "Great Sam Foss." A daughter, killed at school, a rock thrown into a tree, coming down upon her head.

19. SAMUEL BERRY, son of Jotham (13), bapt. April 20, 1741; married, first, Aug. 26, 1762, Mary (Molly) Foss, and second, Elizabeth Marden. Served under Capt. Parsons in the Revolutionary War. Children:

Elizabeth, bapt. March 2, 1764; m. Nov. 14, 1782, George Randall. Molly, bapt. Nov. 24, 1765. Molly, bapt. Sept. 13, 1767; m. Sept. 16, 1790, Henry Shapley. Jotham, bapt. Oct. 5, 1769. Timothy, bapt. March 13, 1770.
23. Nathaniel, bapt. Aug. 13, 1775.

20. CAPT. SAMUEL BRACKETT BERRY, son of William (14), born April 14, 1777; married, Feb., 1798, Abigail Webster; died Feb. 3, 1823. She died Sept. 4, 1860. Was captain of a company of light infantry in the War of 1812. Was promoted to major of the 35th Regt. Sept. 19, 1816. Children:

Brackett, b. May 14, 1798; m. —— Carter. A child, d. Nov. 12, 1813. William, b. Aug. 19, 1803; d. March 20, 1877. Charlotte, b. Jan. 20, 1806; m. Oct. 26, 1843, Joseph Caswell; d. April 12, 1884; no children.
24. Samuel C., b. Feb. 23, 1807. Abigail, b. Dec. 18, 1810; m. first, Crummitt White; second, James Brown.

25. Oliver, b. Oct. 29, 1813; m. March 5, 1839, Elizabeth Dalton.
26. Gilman C., b. Dec. 26, 1816. Mary Ann, b. Sept. 26, 1819; m. Robinson F. Berry, and d. at Portsmouth. John, b. April, 1822; m. Sarah A. Shapley. After his death she m. John Grogan.

21. JEREMIAH BERRY, JR., son of William (14), born Dec. 16, 1783; married, June 22, 1808, Sally Foss. Children:

Alfred, b. Oct. 29, 1808; d. May 15, 1828, at Savannah, Ga. Ira, b. June 19, 1810; d. "non compos mentis." Robinson F., b. Sept. 5, 1813; m. his cousin, Mary Ann Berry, and d. June 29, 1864; a dau., Anna B., d. May, 1872. Brackett M., b. Sept. 3, 1816; humpbacked; d. of the rickets, July 20, 1826. Sarah Ann, b. Sept. 30, 1818; m. ——— Anderson.

22. LIEUT. JOSEPH JENNESS BERRY, son of Levi (15), born May 17, 1789; married, first, 1812, Betsey Wedgewood. She died in 1817, and he married, second, in 1818, Hannah W. Locke, who died June 30, 1893, aged 98 years. Farmer, and for a number of years carried the mail between Rye and Portsmouth. He died June 2, 1868. Children by first wife:

Louisa, b. May 24, 1813; m. April 5, 1835, Elvin Locke. Sarah W., b. April 20, 1815; m. July 17, 1834, Leonard Fry of Portsmouth; d. Dec. 3, 1898.

Children by second wife:
Joseph Whidden, b. July 3, 1819; m. first, Nov. 24, 1854, Pamelia Ann Locke; d. Feb. 21, 1886; second, June 1, 1893, Harriet Hodgdon. Abigail, b. May 16, 1823; m. Langley B. Lewis of Portsmouth; d. Sept. 20, 1878. Charles, b. Aug. 15, 1831; d. Sept. 10, 1879, in Washington Ter. Oliver, b. Oct. 3, 1837; d. 1842.
27. Woodbury, b. Aug. 19, 1834.

23. NATHANIEL BERRY, son of Samuel (19), bapt. Aug. 13, 1775; married, first, Feb. 9, 1797, Betsey Lang, and second, Jan. 24, 1806, Esther Hall. She died in 1876, and he died April 19, 1834. Children by first wife:

Molly, b. Feb. 16, 1798; m. first, Oct. 18, 1821, John Mace; second, March 4, 1824, Richard Varrell. Elizabeth Marden, b. Jan. 9, 1800; m. Nov. 26, 1818, Reuben S. Randall. Sally, b. March 30, 1802; m. Oct. 22, 1820, Joseph M. Caswell. Samuel, b. Aug. 10, 1804; d. Oct. 30, 1805.

Children by second wife:
28. Samuel Foss, b. March 10, 1806.

29. Nathaniel Foss, b. June 8, 1808. Betsey M., b. Oct. 4, 1809; m. Oct. 23, 1829, Abraham Matthews. Joseph Hall, b. April 13, 1811. Abigail, b. Nov. 18, 1814. Martha M., b. May 7, 1816; m. John Coney. Clarissa L., b. Sept. 14, 1819. Jotham S., b. Dec. 22, 1821. John W. P., b. Nov. 22, 1823.

24. SAMUEL C. BERRY, son of Samuel Brackett (20), born Feb. 23, 1807; married, first, Sarah M. Norton. She died July 6, 1876, and he married, second, Mary H. Odiorne. A baker by trade, and lived at Portsmouth. Child:

> William H., m. Dec. 29, 1871, Alice J. Walker. Lives at Dorchester, Mass. Child: Flora M., m. Allen G. Bryant of Pittsfield.

25. OLIVER BERRY, son of Samuel Brackett (20), born Oct. 29, 1813; married, March 5, 1839, Elizabeth Dalton. Lived at Kittery. Children, two of whom died of croup and one of scarlet fever:

> Moses Granville. George William, b. Sept., 1849. Martha Ann, b. May 4, 1852. Carrie, b. Aug. 1, 1855.

26. GILMAN C. BERRY, son of Samuel Brackett (20), born Dec. 26, 1816; married, Nov. 28, 1841, Elizabeth J. Caswell, and died April 10, 1894. Children:

> Mary Abby, b. 1842; d. unm. Aug. 25, 1866, aged 24 years, 4 months.
> 30. Gilman Woodbury, b. Jan. 9, 1845. Alice J., b. April, 1847; m. Smith. John O., b. July 13, 1850; m. Nov. 29, 1871, Adelaide French. Florence L., b. July 3, 1855; m. Nov. 25, 1875, Martin H. Rand; one child, a boy; was then divorced, and m. Dec. 30, 1880, W. Salter. Horace A., b. Dec. 29, 1859; d. June 6, 1861.

27. WOODBURY BERRY, son of Joseph Jenness (22), born Aug. 19, 1834; married, Sept. 24, 1863, Maria Adelaide Locke. Children:

> Charles F., b. April 9, 1865. John, b. Oct. 10, 1867. A son, b. Dec. 7, 1871; d. May 22, 1872.

28. SAMUEL FOSS BERRY, son of Nathaniel (23), born March 10, 1806; married, first, March 6, 1836, Mary Caswell of Gosport; and second, Lovina Weeks, who was born Sept., 1821. He died July 1, 1894. Children:

> Linda, b. May 4, 1836; m. Joshua Smith. George W., b. Nov. 2, 1842; m. Alice Willet.
> 31. Joseph William, b. Oct. 27, 1844. Mary Esther, b. April 23, 1846; m. Warren Caswell. Merrilla, b. 1847; d. Oct. 4, 1849. Dennis J., b. Aug. 28, 1850. Merril, b. Oct. 2, 1854; d. Sept. 29, 1857.

GENEALOGY. 303

29. NATHANIEL FOSS BERRY, son of Nathaniel (23), born June 8, 1808; married, in 1827, Rebecca Caswell. Children:

Ann, m. John Chadborn. William C., m. Sally A. Caswell. Nathaniel, m. Jesse Hanson. John W., m. Laura Wilson. Drucilla, m. Daniel Clark. Judith. Harrison, b. June 27, 1840; m. Anna Baker. Lorenzo D. Edwin, m. Anna M. Gove. Winfield S. Millard F. Cordelia F.

30. GILMAN WOODBURY BERRY, son of Gilman C. (26), born Jan., 1845; married, Jan. 4, 1872, Julia A. Butler of Bay View. He was killed at Bay View. Child:

32. Horace B., m. June 30, 1897, Cora B. Caswell.

31. JOSEPH WILLIAM BERRY, son of Samuel Foss (28), born Oct. 27, 1844; married, Dec. 21, 1872, Mary A. Green. He was a carpenter. Served in the War of 1861-'65, Co. K, 13th N. H. Children:

Linden O., b. Nov. 8, 1873; d. Feb. 10, 1875.
33. Rosco, b. July 3, 1876. Blanche, b. May 1, 1879; m. Oct. 19, 1898, Arthur M. Foss. Ruth, b. Feb. 8, 1882. Beatrice, b. Apr. 4, 1884. Alonzo, b. March 29, 1890.

32. HORACE B. BERRY, son of Gilman Woodbury (30), married, June 30, 1897, Cora B. Caswell. Children:

Ralph, b. Jan. 3, 1898. Alice Pearl, b. March 1, 1903.

33. ROSCO BERRY, son of Joseph William (31), born July 3, 1876; married, Oct. 25, 1898, Isabella Walker. Children:

Hilda, Hazel, twins, b. March 13, 1899. Girl.

34. JAMES TOWLE BERRY, son of Merrifield (12), married Hannah Randall, born April 11, 1759. She died May 4, 1826. He died Oct. 29, 1818. Lived at Rye and Moultonborough. Children:

James, b. Feb. 28, 1779; m. Hannah Vittam; then she m. Joseph Locke, 1st. Ebenezer, b. June 23, 1781; m. Sarah Randall, d. of Reuben. Huldah, b. Feb. 4, 1785; m. Dec. 23, 1806, John W. Bean. Joseph, b. Sept. 14, 1787; m. Oct. 3, 1821, Betsey Berry, b. 1797; d. Feb. 24, 1859. Benjamin, b. May 25, 1791; m. Aug. 31, 1815, Nabby F. Locke. John, b. June 2, 1795; m. Mary Adams. Hannah, b. March 8, 1802; m. Sept. 24, 1822, John Foye, Jr.

35. EBENEZER BERRY, son of James Towle (34), born June 23, 1781; married Sarah Randall. Children:

Augusta, m. Edmund Johnson; second, Mary Randall. Sally, m. Seavey Goss. Joseph, m. Deborah Hanscom; second, Mary A. Gorham. Ebenezer, m. Polly Randall. James Towle, m. Malvina Hanscom. Lovina, m. William F. Yeaton.

1. NATHANIEL BERRY, perhaps son of William (3), married Esther ———. Children:
2. Zachariah (?). Esther (?); m. Jan. 13, 1735, Ebenezer Marden.
3. William (?).
4. John, b. March 22, 1725.
5. Nathaniel, b. July 10, 1727; m. Abigail Rand.
6. Thomas (?), b. Feb. 17, 1731.

2. ZACHARIAH BERRY, perhaps son of Nathaniel (1), married Oct. 23, 1734, Charity Webster. Children:
Caleb, bapt. Jan. 9, 1736-'37. Sarah, bapt. Aug. 30, 1741. Frederica A., bapt. June 10, 1744. John, bapt. May 3, 1747.

3. WILLIAM BERRY, perhaps son of Nathaniel (1), married Elizabeth Hobbs, and lived in Greenland. She hung herself with a skein of yarn. Children:
7. Thomas. Mehitable, m. Fabins. Elizabeth, m. Richard Jenness.

4. JOHN BERRY, son of Nathaniel (1), born March 22, 1725; married, May, 1746, Sarah Symes. Children:
Abigail, bapt. Sept. 13, 1747. Samuel Symes, bapt. Jan. 29, 1749. George, bapt. April 28, 1751. Sarah, bapt. Dec. 24, 1752. John, bapt. Aug. 4, 1754. Thomas, bapt. Mar., 1756. Nathaniel, bapt. Feb. 19, 1758. Alexander, bapt. May 4, 1760.

5. NATHANIEL BERRY, son of Nathaniel (1), born July 10, 1727; married, April 21, 1747, Abigail Rand. Children:
Esther, bapt. Nov. 29, 1747. Stephen, bapt. Nov. 6, 1749. Abigail, bapt. Jan. 12, 1752; m. (?) 1763, William ———. Mary, bapt. 1754; m. (?) 1765, George ———. Elizabeth, bapt. Aug. 8, 1756. Nathaniel, bapt. April 23, 1758. Samuel, bapt. May 4, 1760.

6. THOMAS BERRY, perhaps son of Nathaniel (1), born Feb. 17, 1731; married Abigail Lane, who was born Nov. 23, 1734, and died Nov. 20, 1826, at Greenland. Children:

GENEALOGY. 305

Joshua. William, m. Ward. Thomas.
8. Isaiah, b. Apr., 1761. John, m. Drake. Mehitable, m. Thomas Berry. Betsey, m. Brown. Nabby, m. Aug. 29, 1792, Jacob Brown.

7. LIEUT. THOMAS BERRY, son of William (3), married his cousin, Mehitable, daughter of Thomas Berry, and lived in Greenland. Children:

9. Thomas, b. 1779. Nabby, b. Nov., 1801; m. William Brackett. William.

8. ISAIAH BERRY, son of Thomas (6), born April, 1761; married Bathsheba Shaw, who was born Nov. 11, 1760, and died May 17, 1845. He died June 9, 1845. Children:

Joshua, b. March 19, 1786; d. Nov. 16, 1863. Susannah, b. April 11, 1788; d. March, 1789. Isaiah, b. Feb. 10, 1790; d. April 2, 1855.
10. Levi, b. March 26, 1792. Mary, b. July 7, 1794; d. Aug. 30, 1818.
11. William, b. Jan. 8, 1796; m. Olive S. Locke of Rye. Thomas, b. Feb. 9, 1800; d. unm. Jan. 3, 1870. Abigail, b. Jan. 11, 1802; m. Robert Henderson of Portsmouth. Elizabeth, b. July 8, 1804; m. Lane.

9. THOMAS BERRY, son of Thomas (7), born in 1779; married Sarah Lang and lived at Greenland. Children:

Thomas, m. first, April 16, 1828, Lettis Seavey; m. second, Sarah Seavey; d. Jan. 23, 1880. William. Daniel. Elizabeth Lang, m. Shepard.

10. LEVI BERRY, son of Isaiah (8), born March 26, 1792; married, March, 1815, Patience Marden, and lived at Greenland. He died Dec. 1, 1867. She died Feb. 1, 1864. Children:

Abigail, b. Sept. 26, 1815; m. James B. Rand. Nathan, b. Oct. 23, 1818; m. March 4, 1841, Sally J. Chapman. Had a son, George. Oliver, b. April 28, 1821; m. first, Nov. 21, 1848, Abigail Brown; second, Elizabeth Hatch; third, 1869, Jennie Cole.
12. Francis Albert, b. April 3, 1824; m. Feb. 1, 1854, Martha Adeline Brown; d. July 31, 1861.

11. WILLIAM BERRY, son of Isaiah (8), born Jan. 8, 1796; married, March, 1817, Olive Shapley Locke, and lived at Greenland and later at Newington. He died Sept. 14, 1867. She died May 18, 1874. Children:

Mary, b. Aug. 25, 1818; m. June 5, 1835, John Lowe Pickering. Elziabeth, b. June 3, 1821; m. Aug. 28, 1844, Joseph W. Whidden. John Gilman, b. May 8, 1824; d. Feb. 18, 1878. William, b. Feb. 25, 1829. Martha Olivia, b. Nov. 4, 1830; m. Nov. 13, 1858, Robert Manson.

12. FRANCIS ALBERT BERRY, son of Levi (10), born April 3, 1824; married, Feb. 1, 1854, Martha Adeline Brown of Rye, and lived at Greenland. He died July 31, 1861. Children:

> Mary Louise, b. July 19, 1855; m. May, 1873, Millage Berry; lived at Greenland. Charles Edward, b. June 9, 1857; d. June 8, 1859. John Francis, b. Jan. 23, 1859; d. Nov. 30, 1866. Abby Ann, b. March 21, 1861; m. Sept. 3, 1884, Walter S. Littlefield.

JAMES BERRY, son of James Towle, married Hannah Vittam, and after his death she married Joseph Locke. Children:

> Betsey, b. May 23, 1804; m. Sept. 14, 1823, William Goss. James, b. Feb. 18, 1808; m. Polly Keen of Kittery. He was drowned at sea in 1848. Huldah, b. April, 1810; m. Oct. 12, 1828, Stacy Page.

EBENEZER BERRY, married Sarah Randall. Children:

> Augusta, m. first, Edmund Johnson; second, Mark Randall. Sally, m. Seavey Goss. Joseph, m. first, Deborah Hanscom; second, Mary A. Gorham. Ebenezer, m. Polly Randall. James Towle, m. Malvina Hanscom. Lavinia, m. William F. Yeaton.

Nehemiah Berry and Alice Locke, married, March 14, 1705.

Samuel Berry and Joanna Jenness, married, Dec. 27, 1750.

Samuel Berry and Mary Foss, married, Aug. 26, 1762.

Simon Berry and Phebe Moulton, married, Nov. 29, 1757.

Jotham Berry and Tryphena Saunders, married, April 16, 1780.

Samuel Berry and Eliza Marden, married, Nov., 1780.

BICKFORD.

JOSEPH BICKFORD, married, July, 1760, Ruth Rand, and had Joshua, bapt. Nov. 21, 1762.

HENRY B. BICKFORD, born Dec. 5, 1809, of Epsom; married, May 24, 1868, Julia Ann P. Rand. He died June 10,

1889, and had Ethel, born May, 1874, married, Sept. 9, 1903, Frank A. Phillips.

BLACK.

ELISHA BLACK, married, Dec. 11, 1766, Mary Sanders. Children:
Hannah, b. Nov. 3, 1770. Mary, b. Aug. 5, 1773.

BLAISDELL.

ABNER BLAISDELL married Judith Powers. Children: Adelaide, m. George Dexter. Lovina, m. Joseph Currier. John C.

BLAKE.

JOHN BLAKE married, May, 1740, Jemima Locke, and lived at Greenland. Children:
Elisha, bapt. July 3, 1743. John, bapt. Nov. 3, 1745. Mary, bapt. Dec. 13, 1747.

SAMUEL BLAKE married, Nov. 24, 1743, Sarah Libby. Children:
Hepzibah, bapt. Jan. 19, 1746. Mary, bapt. July 20, 1746. Sarah, bapt. Oct. 16, 1748. Samuel, bapt. Sept. 15, 1751. James, bapt. Aug., 1757.

BLUE.

EDWARD BLUE married, Jan. 4, 1753, Mehitable Seavey. Children:
Jonathan, bapt. Jan., 1755. Edward, bapt. May, 1757.

BLUNT.

CAPT. JOHN BLUNT married Hannah Frost (?), and had George F.

BOICE.

JEREMIAH BOICE married, June 30, 1851, A. Mandana Foye, daughter of John. Children:
Alice F., b. Sept. 23, 1854; m. William P. Chandler of Concord. Frank F., b. Feb. 7, 1866; m. July 18, 1899, Martha A. Brown.

FRANK F. BOICE married, July 18, 1889, Martha A. Brown. Children:
Gladys, b. Jan. 16, 1892. Hester, b. Jan. 16, 1895.

BOND.

JOHN BOND married, Aug. 17, 1752, Esther Rand, and had Mary, born July 26, 1753.

BRACKETT.

1. ANTHONY BRACKETT. The name of Brackett was originally Brocket. They came from Wales. Anthony Brackett lived near Salt Water brook in Brackett's lane, and was killed by the Indians; buried on the eastern side of the highway. His will, 1691, proved July, 1692, shows children: Jane Haines and Eleanor Johnson, son John appointed executor, and grandchildren, Keziah Brackett, Rosa Johnson, and Samuel Brackett.

13 Aug., 1649. Granted that Anthony Brackett shall have a lot between Robert Puddington and Wm. Berry at the head of the Sandy Beach Fresh River at the Western branch thereof.

Children:
John, d. 1726.
2. Samuel, b. Dec. 3, 1733. John, unm., would write on birch bark; never worked on the farm or went to school. Mary. Phebe, unm., d. about 1796; very old. Anna. Love, m. March 3, 1748, Joseph Knowles.

SAMUEL BRACKETT, son of Anthony, married Eleanor Dow. He died Oct. 25, 1766. She married, second, J. Berry. Children:
Love, b. Aug. 9, 1758; m. Nov. 10, 1774, William Berry.

BRAGG.

JOHN BRAGG married, June 7, 1796, Amelia Sanders. Children:
Polly, bapt. April 12, 1798; called "Molly," and supported by the town. George, m. Patty L., widow of Simon Dow, and dau. of Dowrst Rand. Henry. Edward.

BROWN.

1. JOHN BROWN. It is said the father of John Brown went from Scotland to England when John was born in 1588 or '89, emigrated in 1635, and is said to have settled

GENEALOGY. 309

in Hampton as early as 1639. In 1651 and 1656 he was one of the selectmen. His wife's name was Sarah. He died Feb. 28, 1687. Children:

Sarah, b. about 1643; m. John Poor; d. Dec. 28, 1678, at Charlestown, Mass. John, d. Aug. 29, 1683.
2. Benjamin, b. about 1647. Elizabeth, m. Isaac Marston; d. Oct. 5, 1689.
3. Jacob, b. 1653. Mary, b. Sept. 13, 1655; m. April 15, 1675, Nathan Parker.
4. Thomas, b. July 14, 1657. Stephen, b. about 1659; killed by Indians at Black Point, June 29, 1677.

2. BENJAMIN BROWN, son of John (1), born about 1647; married Sarah (or Elizabeth?) Brown of Salisbury, Mass. Children:

William, b. June 5, 1680; m. Ann Heath. Sarah, b. Sept. 11, 1681; d. Oct., 1684. Benjamin, b. Dec. 20, 1683; m. Sarah Gove. Elizabeth, b. July 16, 1686; m. Benjamin Green. John, b. March 18, 1688; m. Abigail Johnson. Jacob, b. March, 1691; m. Mary Green. Stephen, b. July 17, 1693; m. Mary Heath. Mary, b. 1696; m. Thomas Cram. Thomas, b. May 21, 1699; m. Mehitabel Towle. Jeremiah, b. Nov. 20, 1701; m. Mary Weare.

3. JACOB BROWN, son of John (1), born in 1653; married Sarah Brooklin of Portsmouth, and lived at Hampton. He died Feb. 13, 1740. Children:

John, b. about 1684; m. Ruth Kelly.
5. Samuel, b. Sept., 1686. Abraham, b. 1688; m. Feb. 6, 1718, Argentine Cram. Joshua, b. April 1, 1691; m. first, Rachel Sanborn; second, Sarah Leavitt. Sarah, b. 1693; m. Philip Griffin. Jacob, b. Dec. 22, 1695; m. Nov. 16, 1721, Joanna Jones. Abigail, b. March 3, 1698; m. first, John Dowst; second, Amos Knowles. Jonathan, b. Feb. 24, 1699-1700; m. first, Feb. 27, 1725, Joanna Abba; second, widow Joanna Brown.
6. Jeremiah, bapt. June 28, 1702.

4. THOMAS BROWN, son of John (1), born July 14, 1657; married Abial, daughter of Joseph Shaw. She died Dec. 25, 1739, and he died June 29, 1744. Children:

Thomas, b. Dec. 14, 1686; m. Dec. 13, 1710, Dorcas Fanning; d. June 7, 1776; lived at Hampton.
7. Joseph, b. Jan. 30, 1689. Sarah, b. April 5, 1691; m. Feb. 6, 1713, Joshua Towle; d. April 29, 1762; lived at Hampton. Elizabeth, b. April 21, 1694; m. Jan. 31, 1723, Solomon Dowst, and lived in Rye. Ebenezer, b. 1696; m. first, Feb. 27, 1724, Moulton; second, Oct. 5,

1753, Mary Flanders; d. Oct. 20, 1780; lived at Kensington. Josiah, b. Feb. 5, 1701; m. first, Jan. 1, 1724, Elizabeth Fellows; second, Dec. 5, 1744, Mary Bradbury; d. Dec. 4, 1790; lived at Kensington.

5. SAMUEL BROWN, son of Jacob (3), born Sept., 1686; married Elizabeth Maloon. Lived on the Brown homestead at Hampton, and died Jan. 14, 1772. Children:

Mehitable, b. 1710; d. unm. May 3, 1790.
8. Stephen, b. 1712; m. Deborah Lucy of N. C. Hannah, b. 1714; m. Jan. 27, 1732, Joshua Amazeen of Newcastle.
9. Zachariah, b. 1716. Sarah, b. 1718; d. unm. Feb. 17, 1769.
10. Samuel, b. Jan. 20, 1720. Elizabeth, b. 1722; m. John Garland of Moultonborough.

6. JEREMIAH BROWN, son of Jacob (3), bapt. June 28, 1702; married Elizabeth Moody. Lived at North Hampton and Saco, where he died about 1780. Children:

Abigail, bapt. Nov. 26, 1727. Clement, bapt. June 22, 1729. Jeremiah, b. 1737. Moody, b. Dec. 20, 1739. Jacob, Amos, and Mary.

7. JOSEPH BROWN, son of Thomas (4), born Jan. 30, 1689; married, about 1715, Elizabeth Moulton. Lived, first, at Hampton, removing to Rye about 1740, where he died Jan. 21, 1760. Children:

Joseph, b. Jan. 2, 1716; d. about 1716. Thomas, b. Aug. 6, 1717.
11. Samuel, b. Nov. 20, 1720.
12. Joseph, b. Dec. 2, 1722.
13. Jonathan, b. Dec. 20, 1724. Elizabeth, b. Aug. 6, 1727; m. Jan. 3, 1754, Simon Garland. Mary, b. July 1, 1732; d. Nov. 12, 1736, at Hampton. Sarah, m. June 20, 1756, Moses Tappan.

8. STEPHEN BROWN, son of Samuel (5), born about 1712; married Deborah Lucy, and died Sept., 1792. He lived at Little River. Children:

Mehitable, bapt. Dec. 22, 1734. Benjamin, bapt. Aug. 22, 1736; m. first, 1761, Elizabeth Batchelder; second, 1768, Mary Page. Nathan, b. Aug. 30, 1738; m. Jane Lamprey of Hampton. Stephen, bapt. Jan. 27, 1740; d. unm. in the French War. Mary, bapt. Oct. 6, 1745. John Lucy, bapt. April 17, 1748; m. Feb. 26, 1769, Mary Godfrey. Jonathan, m. Ann Lapish.

9. ZACHARIAH BROWN, son of Samuel (5), born about 1716; married Ann Leavitt, and died Jan. 31, 1783. Lived at Hampton. Children:

14. Jacob, b. Dec. 8, 1740.
15. Moses, b. Oct. 5, 1742.
16. Simon, b. Aug. 13, 1744. Mary, b. Jan. 31, 1747; d. Aug. 28, 1748. Molly, b. May 12, 1749; m. Jonathan Blake. Sarah, b. June 18, 1752; d. Sept. 10, 1754. Zachariah, b. Nov. 22, 1754; d. Nov. 16, 1755. Anna, b. Dec. 19, 1756; m. John Mobbs Moulton; d. May 23, 1846.
17. Zaccheus, b. March 16, 1759. Sarah, b. June 17, 1761; m. Joseph Knowles.

10. SAMUEL BROWN, son of Samuel (5), born Jan. 20, 1720; married, first, Dec. 2, 1742, Mary Philbrick, and second, March 2, 1757, widow Elizabeth Johnson of Kensington. She died June 30, 1816. Children by first wife:
Samuel, b. Oct. 19, 1743; m. Oct., 1766, Rachel Marston. James, b. July 11, 1745; m. Ann Brown, and removed to Machias, Me. Nathan, b. Jan. 5, 1747; m. Ann Cilley. Jonathan, b. Oct. 29, 1748; d. March 25, 1749. Jonathan, b. Feb. 13, 1750, m. Mary Brown. David, b. Dec. 9, 1751; m. Elizabeth Tilton. Elizabeth, b. Feb. 14, 1754; m. 1776, James Marston. Molly, b. Feb. 29, 1756; m. Josiah Batchelder.
Children by second wife:
Theodore, b. Oct. 30, 1757; m. Sarah Giles. Hannah, b. April 23, 1759; m. 1779, John Taylor. Amos, bapt. Dec. 20, 1761; m. Sarah Philbrick. Betsey, b. March 22, 1764; d. unm. April 20, 1853; three children. Olly, bapt. Dec. 22, 1765; d. Sept. 8, 1766. Daniel, bapt. Aug. 9, 1767; m. Martha Haskell. Olive, bapt. May 7, 1769; m. Joshua Towle. Susannah, bapt. March 31, 1771; m. first, Thomas Nudd; second, Jacob Marston. Anna Sanborn, bapt. July 11, 1773; d. Aug. 29, 1777. Dolly, bapt. Sept. 1, 1776; m. Richard Whittier.

11. SAMUEL BROWN, son of Joseph (7), born Nov. 20, 1720; married, July 18, 1745, Susannah Knowles. Died in 1804. Lived at Rye and Chester. Children:
Mary, b. Apr. 21, 1746. Jonathan, b. Sept. 15, 1747.
18. John, b. Nov. 20, 1760; m. Comfort Jenness; d. Sept. 5, 1822. She d. Oct. 30, 1846.

12. JOSEPH BROWN, son of Joseph (7), born Dec. 2, 1722; married Nov. 27, 1746, Abigail Goss. Children:
19. Richard B., b. Aug. 16, 1748. Elizabeth, b. May, 1750; m. first, Feb. 16, 1769, Jonathan Goss; second, Eleck Lear; lived at Epsom. Abigail, b. April 19, 1752; d. young. Joseph, b. April 5, 1754; m. Abby Doleby; lived at Epsom. Job, b. 1756; m. Dec. 31, 1778, Huldah Page; lived at Gilmanton. Abigail, b. 1758; m. Jan. 20, 1782, Samuel Davis; lived at Epsom. Jonathan, b. 1760, m. Mary Smith. James, b. 1763; m. Hannah Smith. Samuel, b. 1766; m. Mary Morrell.

13. COL. JONATHAN BROWN, son of Joseph (7), born Dec. 20, 1724; married, Jan. 3, 1753, Mary, daughter of John Garland. He died Jan., 1798. Children:

Elizabeth, b. June 21, 1755; m. March 21, 1776, Elijah Locke; lived at Rye, Epsom, and Chichester.
20. Joseph, b. April 27, 1757.
21. John, b. Nov. 13, 1759; m. Feb. 4, 1779, Sarah Allen; d. Jan. 21, 1807; lived at Rye, Epsom, and Chichester. Jonathan, b. April 13, 1762; d. April 15, 1782, of smallpox. Mary, b. Aug. 24, 1766; m. March 16, 1794, Joseph Locke. Abigail, b. July 29, 1769; m. April 5, 1792, Theodore Coffin; d. March 29, 1832; lived at Hampton and Newburyport.

14. JACOB BROWN, son of Zachariah (9), born Dec. 8, 1740; married Hannah Lamprey. Lived at Little River. Children:

Elizabeth, m. Reuben Philbrick. Nabby, m. Benjamin Philbrick. Jacob, m. first, Abigail Lamprey; m. second, Abigail Philbrick. David, m. Ruth Lamprey.

15. MOSES BROWN, son of Zachariah (9), born Oct. 5, 1742; married, Feb. 1, 1773, Elizabeth, daughter of Andrew Mace of Hampton. Children:

Anna Leavitt, b. Nov. 17, 1773; m. Eli Brown. Lydia, b. May 6, 1777; m. Jeremiah Brown. Abigail, b. Nov. 28, 1778; m. James Towle.

16. CAPT. SIMON BROWN, son of Zachariah (9), born Aug. 13, 1744; married Mary, daughter of John Leavitt. Lived at North Hampton. He died July 20, 1831, and she died Sept. 23, 1837. Children:

22. Simon, b. Aug. 14, 1766. Mary, b. Nov. 5, 1768; m. Simon Dearborn; he d. Aug. 19, 1843. Sarah, b. Nov. 30, 1773; m. Capt. Trueworthy Dearborn; lived at Concord.
23. John, b. Sept. 7, 1775.

17. ZACCHEUS BROWN, son of Zachariah (9), born March 16, 1759; married, Oct. 28, 1781, Martha Davidson. Children:

William, b. and d. June 16, 1782. Martha (Patty), b. June, 1783; m. Daniel Lane. Sarah (Sally), b. April 29, 1785; d. May 15, 1785. William, b. Aug. 23, 1786; m. Nancy H. Downing. Sally Leavitt, b. March 30, 1788; m. David Lane. Nancy, b. Sept. 15, 1790; m. Thomas Lane. Abigail, b. Jan. 30, 1793; m. first, Enoch Moore; m. second, Feb. 28, 1839, Capt. Reuben Osgood of Salisbury, Mass. Belinda S., b. June 1, 1802; d. unm., Sept., 1878.

GENEALOGY. 313

18. JOHN BROWN, son of Samuel (11), born Nov. 20, 1760; married, Oct. 25, 1785, Comfort Jenness. He died Sept. 5, 1822; and she died Oct. 30, 1846. He came from Chester. Children:

John Sam Jenness, b. May 10, 1798; d. Sept. 3, 1815. Job, bapt. Aug. 28, 1791; d. young.

19. RICHARD BROWN, son of Joseph (12), born Aug. 16, 1748; married, Jan. 12, 1873, Sarah Jenness. Removed to Epsom. He lived where Samuel Smart resides. Children:

Anna, bapt. June 26, 1774. Abigail, bapt. Oct. 20, 1776. Mercy, bapt. Jan. 23, 1785.

20. JOSEPH BROWN, son of Jonathan (13), born April 27, 1757; married, Dec. 4, 1777, Martha Coffin. He died March 7, 1841. Lived at Boar's Head, North Hampton. Children:

Sarah Hook, b. Nov. 10 or 30, 1778; m. 1799, Nathan Knowles; d. Dec. 22, 1859.
24. Jonathan, b. 1780. Joseph, b. 1782; m. April 26, 1804, Elizabeth Seavey. He was drowned Sept. 10, 1806, and she m. second, Dec. 18, 1809, Richard Jenness. Martha, b. April, 1786; m. Oct., 1809, Daniel P. Dalton; d. July 8, 1854.

21. JOHN BROWN, son of Jonathan (13), born Nov. 13, 1759; married, Feb. 4, 1779, Salome Allen. He died Jan. 21, 1807. Lived at Epsom and Chichester. Children:

25. John, b. Aug. 14.
26. Jonathan, b. June 1, 1782. Joseph, m. March 15, 1810, Rachel Locke; lived at Epsom and Deerfield. Elizabeth, m. Joseph Yeaton; lived at Epsom. Mary, m. Charles Mills; lived at Concord. Jeremiah, m. Mary Ball; lived at Hampton Falls. Sarah, m. Burnham; lived at Epsom.
27. James, b. Nov., 1789.
28. Benjamin. Abigail, b. March 12, 1802; m. Jonathan Philbrick. Josiah, m. Mary Garland; lived at Concord. William, b. Aug. 14, 1796; m. Lucetta Gray; she d. May 11, 1875, aged 90.

22. LIEUT. SIMON BROWN, son of Simon (16), born Aug. 14, 1766; married, first, Aug., 1793, Esther Dalton. She died May 25, 1805, and he married, second, March 16, 1806,

Polly Seavey. She died March 1, 1832, and he died March 4, 1846. Was a member of Capt. James Coleman's company of cavalry in the War of 1812. Children by first wife:

29. Ira, b. May 30, 1795. Henry, b. Jan. 1, 1803; d. Oct. 29, 1805. Eliza, b. Jan. 14, 1805; m. April 21, 1824, Thomas J. Parsons; she d. Dec. 20, 1888, and he d. March 4, 1890.
Children by second wife:
Mary Esther, b. Jan. 5, 1807; m. July 12 or 14, 1831, Jonathan T. Walker. Sarah Ann, b. May 17, 1809; m. Nov. 24, 1831, Thomas Rand; d. June 5, 1891.
30. Simon, b. Sept. 6, 1811.
31. Langdon, b. June 2, 1814.
32. John Henry, b. Feb. 11, 1817. Martha Adeline, b. Jan. 9, 1822; m. Feb. 1, 1854, Francis Albert Berry; he d. July 30, 1861. Lucetta S., b. Dec. 10, 1824; d. Oct. 20, 1850.

23. JOHN BROWN, son of Simon (16), born Sept. 7, 1775; married Polly, died July 20, 1868, daughter of Samuel and Mary (Locke) Jenness. He died Aug. 23, 1825. Lived at North Hampton. Children:

Eliza, b. 1799; m. first, Joseph Ward; second, Nathaniel Batchelder. Mary, b. 1802; d. unm. 1840. Simon, b. Aug., 1804; m. Emily, dau. of Nathaniel Drake. Leonard, b. 1806; m. Lucy Ann Hallett; d. Oct., 1879; lived at New York. Jenness, b. Feb., 1808; m. Lydia Ward of Hampton; she d. Feb., 1876; lived at Newburyport, Mass. John Trueworthy, b. March, 1818; m. widow Eliza G. Wedgewood; d. June, 1869; lived at New York. Jeremiah, b. Sept. 18, 1810; m. Elizabeth Sanborn; d. Feb. 12, 1875; lived at North Hampton. Adeline, b. 1816; m. Abraham Drake; lived at North Hampton.

24. JONATHAN BROWN, son of Joseph (20), born 1780; married, Oct. 7, 1802, Hannah Drake. He died Jan. 31, 1843. Known as "White House Jonathan," his house being the first one painted white in town. He was a member of Capt. James Coleman's company of cavalry in the War of 1812. Children:

33. Joseph Ward, b. May 12, 1804. Sarah Ann, m. Josiah W. Philbrick.
34. Jonathan, b. Feb. 27, 1807. Hannah, m. Joseph B. Dalton; d. Oct. 9, 1850. Martha, m. July 4, 1842, Daniel Dalton; d. Feb. 4, 1866. Data, m. Dec. 22, 1842, Samuel Whidden, 2d, of Portsmouth.

GENEALOGY. 315

25. JOHN BROWN, son of John (21), born Aug. 14, ——;
married, first, July 29, 1802, Sarah Foss; married, second,
April 28, 1807, Nancy Jenness. He died Dec. 10, 1854.
Children by second wife:
35. Ivory, b. Dec. 1, 1808. Mary, b. Dec. 31, 1820; m. John C. Cogswell of Boston. Sally, d. 1833, aged 17.
36. Alfred, b. June 27, 1817; m. Mary A. Clark.

26. JONATHAN BROWN, son of John (21), born June 1,
1782; married, Nov. 5, 1805, Mary, daughter of Joshua
Locke. He died Sept. 18, 1831. Children:
Mary Smith, b. March 6, 1806; m. Nov. 27, 1825, Ebenezer L. Odiorne. Sally, b. May 29, 1808; m. Dec. 25, 1831, John Philbrick. Alfred, b. July 27, 1810. Clarissa, b. Nov. 12, 1812; m. Aug. 4, 1836, Nathan Brown. Almira, b. March 16, 1815; m. Nov., 1838, Jonathan Locke. Rhoda, b. Sept. 10, 1817. Artemissa, b. April 13, 1820; m. May 29, 1842, Daniel Marden. Abigail, b. July 16, 1824; m. Oliver Berry of Greenland. Angelina, b. Jan. 3, 1826; m. James H. Dow. Jonathan Alva, b. April 3, 1830.

27. JAMES BROWN, son of John (21), born Nov., 1789;
married, Dec. 9, 1819, Martha Webster. Children:
37. Elihua, b. April 6, 1822. Rosilla, b. Dec. 7, 1819; d. unm. Dec. 20, 1887.
38. James, b. Jan. 15, 1824.
39. William, b. Nov. 21, 1825. Emeline, b. June 4, 1827; d. Sept. 23, 1838. John A., b. Nov. 20, 1828; d. Jan. 22, 1887.
40. Levi Webster, b. Sept. 7, 1830. Abigail, b. Sept. 12, 1832; m. first, 1854, David Marden; m. second, E. Wolcott. Sarah, b. Feb. 16, 1835; d. July 2, 1848. Sophia, b. June 21, 1841; d. Oct. 27, 1842; scalded with hot water.

28. BENJAMIN BROWN, son of John (21), married,
March 31, 1817, Jane Locke. After his death she married
John Randall of Gosport. Child:
Sarah Ann Brown, *alias* Goss, b. 1817; m. Moses Blake of Hampton.

29. GEN. IRA BROWN, son of Simon (22), born May 30,
1795; married, Sept. 6, 1820, Jane M. Perkins; died July
10, 1845. She died March 3, 1841. A general in the
N. H. state militia. Children:
Emily, b. Dec. 8, 1820; d. May 23, 1841. Sophia, b. Nov. 19, 1822; m. Feb. 20, 1848, Charles C. Rand; d. May 30, 1850. Calvin, b. June 27, 1825; d. March 27, 1831. Eliza Ann, b. Aug. 17, 1827; d.

Oct. 25, 1843. Mary Esther, b. March 10, 1830; d. Dec. 29, 1849.
Semira J., b. Feb. 22, 1833; m. Oct., 1859, George G. Lougee; d.
Oct. 27, 1863; had a dau., Bertha, m. W. H. Hayward. Abby P.,
b. March 19, 1835; unm. Ira Arvin, b. May 27, 1838; d. Sept., 1856,
at Boston, Mass.

30. SIMON BROWN, son of Simon (22), born Sept. 6, 1811; married, Jan. 4, 1837, Mary Seavey. He died March 2, 1882. Lived at Lynn, Mass. She died Aug. 10, 1885. Children:

Annie Mary, b. May 19, 1837; m. Dec. 10, 1868, James J. Grover of Lynn; he d. March 31, 1883; Clara E. A. Augusta, b. Dec. 20, 1840; m. Dec. 14, 1870, William W. Cilley of Lynn.
41. Amos Simon, b. Nov. 10, 1843. Sarah Auzolette, b. May 27, 1846; d. Sept. 27, 1857.

31. LANGDON BROWN, son of Simon (22), born June 2, 1814; married, first, May 30, 1837, Elizabeth Dow; died Oct. 9, 1848; married, second, Augusta Marston of Hampton; died Feb. 8, 1872. He died Jan. 23, 1867. Children by first wife:

Ann Eliza, b. Nov., 1845; m. May 24, 1870, Charles Austin Jenness; d. June 11, 1877. Otis Simon, b. March 21, 1848; d. Dec. 25, 1848.

Children by second wife:
42. George Henry, b. March 8, 1855. John Shirley, b. Aug. 20, 1858; d. Dec. 22, 1859.

32. JOHN HENRY BROWN, son of Simon (22), born Feb. 11, 1817; married, July 27, 1873, widow Mary Abby Davis. He died March 19, 1902. Child:

John Howard, b. Nov. 2, 1877.

33. JOSEPH WARD BROWN, son of Jonathan (24), born May 12, 1804; married, March 24, 1829, Emily Parsons. She died Feb. 15, 1879, and he died March 29, 1883. Farmer and miller. Children:

43. Charles Jonathan, b. Sept. 13, 1829. Abby Ann, b. April 8, 1844; d. Aug. 28, 1858.

34. CAPT. JONATHAN BROWN, son of Jonathan (24), born Feb. 27, 1807; married, Jan. 3, 1832, Almira Parsons. She died April 5, 1871, and he died Oct. 30, 1872. Children:

Martha Hannah, b. April 26, 1832; m. May 25, 1851, Uri H. Jenness; was divorced.
44. Amos Parsons, b. Sept. 24, 1836. Emerett, b. Oct. 16, 1844; m. Jan. 17, 1866, J. Rienza Jenness.

35. IVORY BROWN, son of John (25), born Dec. 1, 1808; married, May 8, 1845, Mary C. Johnson. Children:
Maria, m. Harvey Locke. Sarah Frances, m. April 25, 1867, John Towle Marden. Emma Adeline, b. Dec. 22, 1847; m. Sept. 17, 1871, Frederick Kimball. Harriet Annetta, b. Feb. 20, 1850; m. 1870, Godfrey.

36. ALFRED BROWN, son of John (25), born June 27, 1817; married Mary A. Clark. Children:
George A. Frances A. Norris E. Laura. Herbert W.

37. ELIHUA BROWN, son of James (27), born April 6, 1822; married, 1856, Mehitable Locke. He died Feb. 12, 1859. Child:
Etta, b. Jan. 25, 1857.

38. JAMES BROWN, son of James (27), born Jan. 15, 1824; married, Nov. 2, 1855, Margaret Vercilda, daughter of Charles Green. He died July 11, 1880, and she died June 14, 1897. Children:
Minnie, b. April 19, 1857; m. Alba H. Foss; d. July 22, 1887.
45. George W., b. March 5, 1861; m. 1883, Mary Emma Rand.

39. WILLIAM BROWN, son of James (27), born Nov. 21, 1825; married, Oct. 23, 1851, Henrietta Downs. He died July 11, 1887, and she died Oct. 30, 1896. Children:
Sophia, b. April 28, 1852. Jessie M., b. Oct. 30, 1856; m. April 29, 1877, Charles Julyn. William M., b. July 12, 1859; d. May 5, 1875. Henry J., b. 1862; m. Sept. 26, 1887, widow Fanny Dow, dau. of Wesley Jenness.
46. Frank G., b. July, 1864.

40. LEVI WEBSTER BROWN, son of James (27), born Sept. 7, 1830; married, Oct. 2, 1852, Sarah O. Verrell. Child:
Charles W., b. Jan. 15, 1854; m. Dec., 1883, Maria Groom.

41. AMOS SIMON BROWN, son of Simon (30), born Nov. 10, 1843; married, Sept. 29, 1869, Martha E. Mudge. Lived at Lynn, Mass. Children:
Florence Mudge, b. May 11, 1871; d. June 10, 1885. Ernest Lamper, b. July 29, 1874. Clara Belle, b. Feb. 15, 1876; d. March 10, 1879.

42. GEORGE HENRY BROWN, son of Langdon (31), born March 8, 1855; married, Dec. 21, 1876, Cora J. Moulton. Children:
Shirley, b. May 14, 1880. Alice Eliza, b. Sept. 1, 1887.

43. CHARLES JONATHAN BROWN, son of Joseph Ward (33), born Sept. 13, 1829; married, Nov. 30, 1855, Mary L. Drake. He died Oct. 5, 1893. He was a justice of the peace and a successful school teacher, and did much work in surveying and making wills. Children:
47. Joseph Arthur, b. March 30, 1856. Emily Blanche, b. March 1, 1860; m. Dec. 24, 1884, Charles M. Remick. Abby Parsons, b. Aug. 17, 1864; m. Dec. 4, 1889, Fred D. Parsons. Agnes, b. March 22, 1876.

44. AMOS PARSONS BROWN, son of Jonathan (34), born Sept. 24, 1836; married, first, Oct., 1857, Margaret A. Jenness. She died Nov. 28, 1862, and he married, second, Jan. 27, 1867, Calvinna E. Seavey. Child by first wife:
Luella M., b. Aug. 30, 1858; m. Dec., 1883, Gilman Moulton.
Child by second wife:
Carrie G., b. Dec. 2, 1874; m. April 14, 1895, Walter Woodbury, divorced.

45. GEORGE W. BROWN, son of James (38), born March 5, 1861; married, 1883, Mary Emma Rand. Carpenter. Children:
Ruth Beatrice, b. Sept. 17, 1884. Margaret Medesta, b. Oct. 26, 1886. Norman Howard, b. Dec. 16, 1888. James Webster, b. Nov. 21, 1890. Charles Rand, b. Oct. 16, 1892. Susan Minnie, b. Dec. 22, 1894. Son, b. May 17, 1896; d. Dec. 15, 1897. Helen Vercilda, b. Aug. 16, 1899. Aleck Forbes, b. Oct. 22, 1901.

46. FRANK G. BROWN, son of William (39), born July, 1864; married, July 2, 1893, Hattie W. Dow. Children:
Doris Julyn, b. Dec. 16, 1897. Perley William, b. March 23, 1900. Alan Francis, b. Nov. 10, 1901.

47. JOSEPH ARTHUR BROWN, son of Charles Jonathan (43), born March 30, 1856; married, Nov. 20, 1878, Olive A. Goss. He was a justice of the peace. Children:
Carroll W., b. Sept. 24, 1879. Bessie Marion, b. July 31, 1884. Edna Olive, b. Oct. 24, 1886. Charles O., b. Oct. 29, 1889; d. Feb. 17, 1892. Arthur L., b. Dec. 25, 1891. William Goss, b. Oct. 12, 1895.

GENEALOGY. 319

1. JOHN BROWN married, first, 1796, Mary (Polly) Gould; married, second, Nov. 9, 1839, Polly Rand. Children:
 Polly, b. April, 1799; d. unm. March 27, 1873.
 2. Joseph, b. July 3, 1802.
 3. Daniel, b. May 29, 1808.
 4. Ira, b. Jan. 31, 1811.
 5. Oliver, b. Jan. 31, 1811. John, b. March 13, 1813; m. Mary Ann Jenness. Hannah, b. Nov., 1818; m. Isaac Jenness.

2. JOSEPH BROWN, son of John (1), born July 3, 1802; married, first, Mary Fogg; married, second, Sept. 13, 1843, Mary D. Foss. Children:
 Clara N., b. Sept. 6, 1831; m. William G. Harding. Almira A., b. Dec., 1840; m. Henry Jenness.
 6. Joseph Ira, b. Sept. 17, 1834; m. Feb. 26, 1857, Augusta Anderson.

3. DANIEL BROWN, son of John (1), born May 29, 1808; married Sarah Ann Garland. He died Nov. 12, 1898. Children:
 7. Moses, b. March 23, 1835. Charles Woodbury, b. Sept. 1, 1839; m. widow Lizzie Frost, dau. of Calvin Garland.

4. IRA BROWN, son of John (1), born Jan. 31, 1811; married, Oct. 27, 1834, Hannah Garland. He died, and she married, first, E. S. Wedgewood; second, Alfred G. Jenness. Child:
 Emeline, m. Albert Dana Jenness.

5. OLIVER BROWN, son of John (1), born Jan. 31, 1811; married Elizabeth Marston. Children:
 Mary E., m. John Lamper. ———, m. Charles Lamper.

6. JOSEPH IRA BROWN, son of Joseph (2), born Sept. 17, 1834; married, Feb. 26, 1857, Augusta Anderson. He died July 10, 1898. Children:
 Franklin, b. May 1, 1858.
 8. James Franklin, b. April 2, 1859. Robert William, b. Aug. 28, 1864; d. Oct. 26, 1864. Anna Maria, b. July 4, 1866; m. Alvado Jenness. Clara Emma, b. Oct., 1874.

7. MOSES BROWN, son of Daniel (3), born March 23, 1835; married, Dec. 9, 1869, Henrietta Garland. Children:

Alice S., b. March 30, 1871; m. Nov. 29, 1888, Frank L. Graves; d. Dec. 10, 1893. Mattie, b. July 7, 1872; m. July 18, 1889, Frank F. Boyce. Daniel W., b. July 15, 1874; m. Oct. 21, 1899, Jennie E. Fraser. John W., b. July, 1877. Etta, b. March 10, 1880.

8. JAMES FRANKLIN BROWN, son of Joseph Ira (6), born April 2, 1859; married, Dec. 23, 1890, Geneva Berry. Children:
Daughter, b. March 6, 1899.

JOSEPH BROWN married Abartha Coffin. He lived at Little Boar's Head. Children:
Sarah Hook, b. Nov. 30, 1778; m. 1799, Nathan Knowles; d. Dec. 22, 1859. Jonathan, b. Dec. 24, 1780; m. Oct. 2, 1802, Hannah Drake; d. Jan. 31, 1843. Joseph, b. 1783; m. April 26, 1804, Elizabeth Seavey. He was drowned while coming home from Newcastle, and she afterwards m. Richard Jenness, Jr., Dec. 18, 1809. Martha, b. April, 1786; m. Oct. 2, 1809, Daniel P. Dalton; d. July 8, 1854.

OLIVER BROWN married Lydia Dalton. She married, second, Ezenezer Fogg of North Hampton. Children:
Lydia D., b. March 16, 1836; d. Jan. 28, 1837. Oliver B. Fogg, b. Nov. 27, 1848; m. 1875, Emma, dau. of Elvin Locke.

ALEXANDER BROWN and Polly, daughter of Michael Dalton, married Sept. 2, 1813.

BUNKER.

1. LEMUEL BUNKER married Sally Towle. Children:
2. James, b. April 8, 1802. Belinda, m. Lemuel Locke.

2. JAMES BUNKER, son of Lemuel (1), born April 8, 1802; married, Sept. 27, 1820, Nancy Hobbs. Children:
Mary Ann, b. Dec. 24, 1820; d. unm. Oct. 9, 1878.
3. Lemuel James, b. June, 1823. Belinda, b. Oct. 2, 1827; school teacher; d. unm. Oct. 4, 1884.
4. Oliver Dearborn, b. Oct. 18, 1830. Gardner Towle, b. Nov. 26, 1834; unm.

3. LEMUEL JAMES BUNKER, son of James (2), born June, 1823; married, first, March 7, 1848, Izette S. Garland; married, second, Anna R. Towle. He died Nov. 24, 1893, and she died June 7, 1899. Carpenter. Children by first wife:

GENEALOGY. 321

Julia, b. Feb. 24, 1850; m. 1864, Edward H. Balch. Addie P., m. Oct. 27, 1868, George D. Cotton of North Hampton.
Children by second wife:
Christy Ann, b. March, 1855; d. Aug. 15, 1876. Izette, b. March 21, 1859; d. Oct. 15, 1878. Willie, b. Nov., 1861; an adopted child; m. Cora E. Palmer.

4. OLIVER DEARBORN BUNKER, son of James (2), born Oct. 18, 1830; married Christy Laws of Illinois. Children:

Rosabella, b. Jan. 1, 1859. Sophronie Lillian. Frank, b. May 1 or June 3, 1865.

BREED.

FREDERICK BREED married Ida F. Philbrick June 19, 1884. Children:

Bernice, b. March 15, 1885. Edith, b. Dec. 17, 1887. Ethel, b. Sept. 17, 1889.

CARROLL.

JOHN CARROLL married Oct. 31, 1793, Sally, daughter of Simon Goss. Children:

Richard, bapt. Nov. 25, 1795. Arnold. Polly, bapt. 1802.

CASWELL.

JOHN CASWELL. Lived at Gosport. Children:

John, m. Nov. 2, 1816, Elizabeth G. Locke, and had Rebekah, who m. Nathaniel Berry. William, m. 1817, Catherine E. Marston. Joseph M., m. Oct. 22, 1820, Sally Berry. Asa, m. Mary Marston. Mary, m. March 31, 1817, Isaac Newton. Lemuel.

1. SAMUEL CASWELL married Elizabeth Randall. She died Jan. 4, 1825. Lived at Gosport. Children:

Tamah, b. Nov. 15, 1788; m. Manasseh Dutton, who was a soldier at Fort Constitution.
2. Samuel b. May 8, 1790.
3. Michael, b. Aug. 17, 1792. Nabby, b. June 14, 1795; m. Simon Lamprey.
4. Edward, b. Sept. 14, 1797.
5. William, b. July 17, 1800.

2. SAMUEL CASWELL, son of Samuel (1), born May 8, 1790; married, April 28, 1808, Polly Green. He was lost in the privateer *Portsmouth* in 1814. His widow married, second, Aug. 15, 1819, William Caswell. Children:

6. Richard Green, b. Dec. 5, 1808; m. Anna B. Marden. John, b. July 15, 1811; m. Raynes; one child, John; last seen at Portsmouth. Mary Elizabeth, b. Dec. 3, 1813; d. Jan. 5, 1814.
7. Samuel, b. Jan. 4, 1815.

3. MICHAEL CASWELL, son of Samuel (1), born Aug. 17, 1792; married, Oct. 24, 1816, Dorcas Green. She died April 18, 1887, aged 93 years. Children:

>Thomas Green, b. April 9, 1811. Joseph, b. March 2, 1817; m. Oct. 26, 1843, Charlotte Berry. Charles G., b. Oct. 5, 1819. Asa, b. Nov. 21, 1821; m. Fannie Hildreth; d. Feb. 8, 1885. Emily, b. June 25, 1825; m. Rufus Eastman. Almira, b. Dec. 23, 1827; m. Charles Bird. William, b. Dec. 16, 1833; d. June 7, 1867. Albert M., b. June 25, 1837; m. Mary Page.

4. EDWARD CASWELL, son of Samuel (1), born Sept. 14, 1797; married, first, June 13, 1819, Sarah Frost Locke; married, second, Sally Varrell. Children, both of whom were adopted by Daniel Burleigh of Lee, and took his name:

> Sylvester, m. Abby Locke. Daniel, m. Margaret Locke.

5. WILLIAM CASWELL, son of Samuel (1), born July 17, 1800; married, Aug. 15, 1819, Mary (Polly), widow of his brother Samuel. He died Nov. 20, 1884. Children:

> William, b. Nov. 14, 1819.
8. Mary, b. Feb. 5, 1822. Elizabeth J., b. July 21, 1824; m. Gilman C. Berry; d. March 18, 1887. Lulu Ann, b. Nov. 12, 1828; had a son, Gustavus, b. April, 1846.
9. Warren, b. May 10, 1832. Maria Salter, b. Aug. 9, 1835; m. Swett.

6. RICHARD GREEN CASWELL, son of Samuel (2), born Dec. 5, 1808; married, June 22, 1828, Anna B. Marden. She died Sept. 27, 1893. Fisherman. Children:

> Mary H., b. Dec. 20, 1828; m. Feb. 19, 1850, John Cook Randall.
10. Charles Reuben, b. Feb. 21, 1831. Alfred S., b. April 19, 1833; d. Feb. 6, 1847. Elizabeth A., b. Nov. 12, 1835; m. John Mace. Sarah A., b. Oct. 9, 1838; m. Dec. 4 1856, Gilman N. Varrell. George Brewster, b. 1844; m. Aug., 1882, Mary McGuire of Concord. Was out in the Civil War. Angeline, m. John Pool.
11. Henry N., b. 1845. Clarence Kimball, b. Aug. 10, 1850; m. Nov. 9 1878, Ada Brown of Raymond.
12. Frank O., b. March 31, 1852. Edwin, m. Lucy Hart.

GENEALOGY. 323

7. SAMUEL CASWELL, son of Samuel (2), born Jan. 4, 1815; married Sarah E. Varrell, *alias* Palmer. He died March 3, 1882. Fisherman. Children:

A girl, b. Sept. 20, 1854. Cynthia, b. March, 1857. Sarah, b. April 6, 1862; m. May 22, 1880, Wallace Goss. Samuel, b. Dec. 23, 1859. Letitia, m. Frank Rand of Portsmouth. Rosa, b. April 6, 1862. Gracie. James W., b. June 22, 1867. Amy J., m. Richard F. Varrell.

8. MARY CASWELL, daughter of William (5), born Feb. 5, 1822, and had the following children:

13. John William, b. Oct., 1841. J. Winfield S. Varrell. Greenville, d. in the Civil War. She married, first, June 9, 1850, Benjamin Varrell; second, Clay of Hooksett; and third, Charles Bunton.

9. WARREN CASWELL, son of William (5), born May 10, 1832; married, first, June 26, 1861, Sarah E. Knowles, and second, Mary E. Berry. Children by first wife:

Charles Law, b. Sept. 17, 1865. George, b. Nov. 2, 1868; m. Oct. 28, 1891, Maud I. Gilbert.

Child by second wife:
Ella, b. March 30, 1871; m. Sanborn.

10. CHARLES REUBEN CASWELL, son of Richard Green (6), born Feb. 21, 1831; married, first, Nov. 9, 1853, Mary O. Varrell; second, Sept. 16, 1863, Sarah Robinson. Drowned in his boat, Nov., 1865. Served in the war, 1861-'65. Children:

Horace Washington, b. May 2, 1854. Mary Augusta, b. April 9, 1857.

11. HENRY M. CASWELL, son of Richard Green (6), born 1845; married, March 15, 1871, Lydia C. Randall. Children:

Maud Arabella, b. Sept., 1871. Emma Albertina, b. July, 1874.

12. FRANK O. CASWELL, son of Richard Green (6), born March 31, 1852; married Martha Jane Randall. Children:

Alfred. Arthur, b. 1887. Marion, b. Jan. 3, 1890. Lynden, b. June 30, 1892. Lizzie, b. Nov. 8, 1895. Charles, b. Sept. 12, 1897. Sherman.

13. JOHN WILLIAM CASWELL, son of Mary Caswell (8), born Oct., 1841; married, July 10, 1864, Hattie M. Mat-

324 HISTORY OF RYE.

thews, Portsmouth. Served in the navy during the Civil War. Children:

Ida, b. Aug. 13, 1867; adopted; m. Aug. 13, 1890, John Sweetser of Portsmouth. Hattie, b. Dec. 2, 1868. Ova, b. Jan. 31, 1874; m. Aug. 7, 1895, Flora Frye. Harry, b. June 5, 1879.

1. AUGUSTUS CASWELL married, March 19, 1868, Leila A. Jenness. Enlisted and mustered into service in 1862—in the war 1861-'65. Children:

2. Elmer W., b. Oct. 5, 1868; m. Feb. 14, 1891, Sophia G. Smart. Cora, b. Oct. 1, 1876; m. June 30, 1897, Horace B. Berry.

2. ELMER W. CASWELL, son of Gustavus (1), born Oct. 5, 1868; married, Feb. 14, 1891, Sophia J. Smart. Children:

Ethelyn, b. Feb. 15, 1892. Alvah L., b. July 27, 1893. E. Gay, b. June 28, 1895. Myrtle V., b. Nov. 8, 1899.

CHAMBERLAIN.

WILLIAM CHAMBERLAIN married Nov. 27, 1729, Mary Randall. Children:

Lydia, b. April 3, 1737. Samuel, b. Aug. 18, 1740. William, b. May 17, 1743. Mary, b. July 20, 1746. John, b. July 14, 1749.

CHAPMAN.

JONATHAN CHAPMAN married Mary ———. Child:
Phebe, bapt. April 12, 1752.

JOB CHAPMAN married Rachael Marden of Rye. Lived at North Hampton.

CANNEY.

HERBERT S. CANNEY married Annie Odiorne. Children:
J. Newman, b. Oct. 3, 1895. Son, b. April 20, 1900.

CHESLEY.

1. LIEUT. SIMON CHESLEY, born Oct. 21, 1783; married, April 29, 1807, Olive Elkins; died, July 3, 1851. She died Oct., 1872. Lieutenant in Captain Berry's company of light infantry in the War of 1812. Children:

Samuel, b. June 23, 1807; d. unm. June 14, 1880; fisherman. John, b. Aug. 15, 1809. Eliza B., b. June 28, 1811; m. Dec. 1, 1841, Samuel Coleman of Newburyport. Hannah P., b. Oct. 23, 1813; m. Jan. 11, 1841, James Locke; lived at Seabrook. William E., b. June 11, 1816; d. unm. Nov. 13, 1887.

2. Simon Locke, b. April 1, 1822.

2. SIMON LOCKE CHESLEY, son of Simon (1), born April 1, 1822; married, March 22, 1858, Susan M. Green. Merchant with his brother William, "at the Four Corners." Children:

Frank E., b. Feb. 7, 1860; m. Nov. 27, 1884, Ella Moulton; lives at North Hampton.

3. William Elkins, b. Jan. 24, 1874.

3. WILLIAM E. CHESLEY, son of Simon Locke (2), born Nov., 1874; married, 1898, Susie P. Rand. He died Jan. 7, 1903. Child:

Jackson, b. Sept. 21, 1900.

CHICK.

EVERETT E. CHICK born Jan., 1874; married, Sept. 19, 1899, Annie G. Blake, born July 13, 1878. Children:

Ethel, b. Dec. 6, 1899. Susie, b. June 16, 1901. Ralph E., b. March 9, 1903. Ernest, b. March 24, 1904.

CLARK.

1. JOHN CLARK married, June 19, 1766, Mary Mace. Children:

Joseph. John, bapt. July, 1768. Molly, bapt. July 1, 1770; m. Reuben Dow.

2. Andrew, bapt. April 4, 1773. Deborah. Polly. Edward. Josiah, William.

2. ANDREW CLARK, son of John (1), baptized April 4, 1773; married, Nov 23, 1797, Hannah Remick. She died April 18, 1844. Children:

3. Thomas Remick, b. March, 1799. Betsey, b. Nov. 3, 1801; m. Sept. 20, 1827, John H. Webster.

4. John, b. 1804. Daniel, b. 1806; d. May 2, 1831. Mary A., b. 1808; d. July 1, 1831. Hannah, b. 1809; d. Oct. 3, 1831. Emily, b. 1812; d. June 8, 1831.

3. THOMAS REMICK CLARK, son of Andrew (2), born March, 1799; married, March, 1824, Maria Greenough, born May 19, 1804. Children:

Lucy Ann, b. Sept. 12, 1824; m. March 18, 1856, Joseph S. Foss; she had John, b. Sept. 27, 1851. Hannah, m. David Page. Mary Frances, m. Seth M. Sprague. Daniel, m. Rosella Berry. Charles, m. Josephine. Anna M., b. 1838; m. Oct. 1, 1856, Horace L. Trefethern. Eliza Jane, b. 1840; m. Nathaniel Lear. Amos, m. Anna Kerns. Lyman, m. Louisa Gordon. Levi, m. Mary Hutchins. Oliver, m. Charlotte Trefethern. Albert, m. Anna Merrill. Harriett Augusta, m. July 3, 1866, James M. Haley.

4. JOHN CLARK, son of Andrew (2), born 1804; married, first, Mary Locke; married, second, Adeline Tucker. He died Aug. 8, 1847, and she died March 10, 1899. Child by first wife:

5. Moses, b. 1829.

Children by second wife:
Mary Emily, b. 1835; m. June 18, 1862, Supply F. Trefethern. Abby S., b. Feb. 28, 1843. Clara A., b. Feb. 25, 1846; m. July 30, 1873, Michael Henry Magraw of Portsmouth; d. Feb., 1881.

5. MOSES CLARK, son of John (4), born, 1829; married, Oct. 26, 1858, Susan A. Tucker. Children:

Emmons, b. March 6, 1860. Marcia B., b. Oct. 23, 1863; m. Aug. 6, 1884, Edwin H. Drake. Marietta, b. Sept. 27, 1866; d. Jan. 27, 1887. Charles H., b. Jan. 13, 1870; d. Jan. 13, 1888.

THOMAS CLARK. Children:

Jane, m. Elliot Frost. Susannah, bapt. July 22, 1764. Betsey. William, b. May 11, 1766. Polly. Thomas. Hannah.

CLERK.

SAMUEL CLERK married, March 30, 1758, Hannah Marden. Children:

John, bapt. March 23, 1760. Judith, bapt. July 9, 1769. Olly, bapt. July 9, 1769.

JENNY CLARK, daughter of William, was baptized Oct. 22, 1752.

CLIFFORD.

PETER CLIFFORD married July 25, 1738, Hannah Dolbee, and had Peter, born Sept. 12, 1753.

ABRAHAM CLIFFORD married May, 1746, Abigail Seavey, and had Peter, baptized Sept. 23, 1753.

CLOUGH.

NATHAN CLOUGH married Oct. 29, 1837, Abigail Marden. She died Nov. 19, 1892. He died Jan. 14, 1872. Children: Jane Ann, b. Oct. 24, 1838; m. first, Charles Delancy; m. second, Dec. 1, 1895, Charles H. Rand. Elizabeth Rosamond, b. Feb. 12,. 1841; m. first, Albert Rumery; m. second, Dec. 16, 1880, Charles Lear. Selina, b. Dec. 18, 1842; d. Feb. 21, 1878; partly blind for years. Alvida, b. Oct., 1844; m. Oct. 27, 1874, Oliver Winslow Trefethern. Electa Jane, b. June, 1846; m. Joseph Chapman. Martha Mosher, b. Jan., 1849; d. Aug. 29, 1893. Arabella, b. Feb., 1852; m. Oliver E. Locke; lives at Portsmouth.

GEORGE A. CLOUGH married widow Edith (Varrell) Torrey. Child by first husband:

Willis S., b. May 23, 1895.

Child by second husband:

Mahlon L., b. Feb. 25, 1897.

COFFIN.

NATHANIEL COFFIN married June, 1864, Martha Olive Green. Child:

Ovid G., b. 1865; d. Aug. 21, 1867.

COLEMAN.

NATHANIEL COLEMAN married Aug. 7, 1796, widow Mercy Sanders. Children:

Robert Hodgkins, bapt. Sept. 17, 1797. Nathaniel, bapt. May 5, 1799; m. Philbrick. John. Lydia.(?)

CONNOR.

JOSEPH CONNOR married Jan. 25, 1738, Mary Seavey. Children:

Samuel, bapt. May 24, 1741. Sarah, bapt. June 10, 1744. Benjamin, bapt. Sept. 13, 1747.

COTTON.

THOMAS COTTON. Children:

Adam, bapt. April 30, 1738. Nathaniel, bapt. Aug. 3, 1740; m. Hannah; living in Portsmouth, 1781. Abigail, b. Aug. 28, 1748.

THOMAS COTTON married April 1, 1790, Judith Clark, and had Hannah, baptized July 24, 1791.

DALTON.

REV. TIMOTHY DALTON was born in England, 1577. He came to New England about the year 1637. On his arrival he went to Dedham, Mass., and probably removed to Hampton two years later. He died Oct. 28, 1661, and his widow, Ruth, in 1666. Rev. Timothy was associated with Rev. Mr. Bachiler of Hampton in the work of the ministry, the latter holding the office of pastor, and the former that of teacher, the great age of the pastor being the reason for employing another minister.

1. PHILEMON DALTON, settled in Hampton, brother of Rev. Timothy Dalton, was born about 1590. His wife, Dorothy, was born about 1600. He was fatally injured by the fall of a tree, and died June 4, 1662. His widow afterwards married Godfrey Dearborn. Child:

  2. Samuel, b. about 1629; m. Mehitable Palmer.

2. SAMUEL DALTON, son of Philemon (1), born about 1629; married Mehitable, daughter of Henry Palmer, of Haverhill, Mass. He was a very influential man in town, and held many offices of trust. He died Aug. 22, 1681. His widow married, second, Nov. 26, 1683, Rev. Zechariah Symmes of Bradford, Mass. Children:

  Hannah, b. Jan. 11, 1655; d. unm. Sept. 12, 1674. Samuel, b. Sept. 19, 1656; m. Nov. 23, 1683, Dorothy Swan of Haverhill, Mass. Mehitable, b. Nov. 3, 1658; m. Thomas Philbrick. Elizabeth, b. Feb. 11, 1661. Timothy, b. Jan. 25, 1663; d. Oct. 24, 1681, at Boston.
  3. Philemon, b. Dec. 15, 1664. John, b. Dec. 23, 1666. Caleb, b. April 29, 1668; d. Aug. 29, 1675. Abiah, b. June 3, 1670; d. immediately. ———, b. June 3, 1670; d. immediately. Joseph, b. May 2, 1672, d. April 2, 1673. Abigail, b. Nov. 21, 1673; m. April 24, 1699, Richard Hall. Mary, b. Oct. 31, 1675; m. Joseph Clement. Dorothy, b. Dec. 6, 1677; m. July 23, 1701, Ebenezer Stiles.

3. DEA. PHILEMON DALTON, son of Samuel (2), born Dec. 15, 1664; married, Sept. 25, 1690, Abigail, daughter of Edward Gove. Children:

Hannah, bapt. June 27, 1697; m. John Sargent.
4. Timothy, bapt. June 27, 1697.
5. Samuel, b. July 22, 1694. Philemon, b. Aug. 16, 1697; m. July 15, 1720, Bethia Bridges of Andover, Mass. Abigail, b. Sept. 2, 1699; m. Feb. 23, 1721, Benjamin Carlton. John, b. Feb. 10, 1702; d. Dec. 10, 1717. Sarah, b. April 19, 1704; m. Joseph Towle; d. July, 1779. Jeremiah, b. May 25, 1707; d. Dec. 17, 1707. Michael, b. Feb. 22, 1709; sea captain at Newburyport; father of Hon. Tristram Dalton. Mehitable, b. Sept. 25, 1713; m. Oct. 16, 1728, Benjamin Prescott.

4. TIMOTHY DALTON, son of Philemon (3), bapt. June 27, 1697; married, Feb. 2, 1721, Sarah, daughter of Robert Mason, who came from Boston. Children:

Philemon, b. Jan. 4, 1722; d. May 4, 1722. John, b. March 2, 1723; m. Betsey Norton; she afterwards m. Thomas Jenness. Sarah, b. Dec. 24, 1724; m. Samuel Prescott. Abigail, b. Nov. 9, 1726. Maria, bapt. June 8, 1729. Mehitable, b. Aug. 30, 1730; m. James Batchelder; d. Dec. 22, 1819. Hannah, b. Sept. 13, 1734; m. William Murray.
6 Timothy, b. May 26, 1737. Josiah, b. May 15, 1740; unm.; *non compos mentis*. Michael, b. Nov. 12, 1743; d. aged 21 years.

5. SAMUEL DALTON, son of Philemon (3), born July 22, 1694; married, April 28, 1720, Mary Leavitt. Children:

Mary, b. Feb. 22, 1721; d. May 7, 1721.
7. Benjamin, b. May 9, 1722. Anna, b. Nov. 2, 1723; d. young. Samuel, b. April 5, 1726; m. Sarah Scott. Mary, b. July 2, 1728; d. unm. June 30, 1769. Philemon, b. Jan. 23, 1731. Anna, b. Nov. 2, 1733. Moses, b. June 5, 1736. Jeremiah, b. Dec. 21, 1738. Elizabeth, b. April 1, 1745.

6. TIMOTHY DALTON, son of Timothy (4), born May 26, 1737; married, Dec. 29, 1763, Elizabeth Marden. He was a soldier in the Revolutionary War, and was killed at Ticonderoga. His widow died Aug. 21, 1813, aged 78. Children:

8. Michael, b. Aug. 4, 1764. Mary, b. July 1, 1766; m. Nov. 29, 1791, John Johnson of Wakefield. Ebenezer Marden, b. Oct. 3, 1768; m. May 22, 1796, Love Hobbs; lived at North Hampton. John, b. May 23, 1770; m. Whidden. Esther, b. July 29, 1772; m. 1793, Lieut. Simon Brown.
9. Tristram, b. Feb. 10, 1774. Timothy, b. Nov. 18, 1776; m. Dec. 2, 1804, Nancy Nudd.

7. BENJAMIN DALTON, son of Samuel (5), born May 9, 1722; married Mary, daughter of Capt. Mimowell May of Little Harbor. Children:
10. Michael, b. Nov. 13, 1753. Mary, bapt. June 6, 1756; m. Jeremiah Brown. Sarah, bapt. Aug. 19, 1764; m. Foss.

8. MICHAEL DALTON, son of Timothy (6), born Aug. 4, 1764; married, May 29, 1786, Mary, daughter of Joseph Palmer. Removed to Deerfield. Children:
Mary, d. unm. James, m. Betsey Rand.
11. Joseph, doctor. Michael, m. Martha Wiggin. Elizabeth, m. John Bartlett. Hannah, m. Reuben Sanborn. Lucetta, m. Ward C. Sturtevant of Center Harbor.

9. TRISTRAM DALTON, son of Timothy (6), born Feb. 10, 1774; married, first, Nov. 14, 1798, Dorothy Brown of North Hampton, who died Feb. 14, 1802; married, second, Oct. 7, 1804, Mrs. Huldah (Webber) Cotton, widow of Morris Cotton of North Hampton. Lived at Little River. He died April 3, 1886. Child by first wife:
Benjamin B., b. Jan. 14, 1800; drowned Aug. 23, 1824, at Newburyport.
Children by second wife:
12. Morris Cotton. Lydia, b. Feb. 6, 1813; m. first, July 19, 1835, Oliver Brown; m. second, Dec. 22, 1846, Ebenezer C. Fogg.

10. MICHAEL DALTON, son of Benjamin (7), born Nov. 13, 1753; married Mercy Philbrick. Served as fifer in Capt. Parsons' company at Newcastle. He died Oct. 6, 1846. She died Nov. 19, 1846. Children:
13. Benjamin B., b. 1780. Abigail, b. April 15, 1782; m. Feb. 12, 1799, Moses Shaw; d. March 1, 1869; lived at Hampton.
14. Daniel Philbrick, b. 1785. Mary (Polly), b. 1792; m. Sept. 2, 1813, Alexander Brown.

11. DR. JOSEPH DALTON, son of Michael (8), married Mary Dow Parsons. Lived at Brentwood. Died Dec. 15, 1856. Children:
Mary, m. James Thing; lived at Roxbury, Mass. Charles, m. Maria Prestwick; lived at Bloomington, Ill. Martha D., m. Albert G. Webster; lived at Chicago, Ill. Joseph M., b. June 1, 1835; m. Lydia Glimper; d. April 3, 1886.

GENEALOGY. 331

12. MORRIS COTTON DALTON, son of Tristram (9), married, Jan. 13, 1827, Ursula, daughter of Eben Leavitt. Removed to Acton, Me. Children:
15. Ebenezer Leavitt. Morris Benjamin, m. Lydia Ann Brackett. Tristram S., m. Jennie ———; lived at Boston. Sally W., m. John Hubbard.

13. BENJAMIN B. DALTON, son of Michael (10), born 1780; married, Dec. 3, 1805, Sarah Garland. She died in 1844, aged 63 or 64 years. He died Sept. 10, 1861. Children:
Mary, b. 1806; d. Feb. 20, 1829. Mercy, b. 1808; d. Feb. 28, 1829. Elizabeth, b. June, 1813; m. March 5, 1839, Oliver Berry. Moses, b. Oct. 20, 1815; d. unm. Dec. 14, 1889. Anna Leavitt, b. Sept. 7, 1818; m. first, William S. Garland; second, Jan. 2, 1876, Gardner T. Locke; divorced; d. 1903.

14. DANIEL PHILBRICK DALTON, son of Michael (10), born in 1785; married, Oct. 2, 1809, Patty Brown. He died Sept. 13, 1842. She died July 8, 1854. Children:
16. Joseph Brown, b. 1809.
17. Michael, b. 1812.
18. Daniel, b. July 2, 1814. Louisa, m. June 20, 1837, William B. Leavitt. Elvira, m. July 2, 1845, Edward L. Garland.

15. EBENEZER LEAVITT DALTON, son of Morris Cotton (12), married Elvina Cotton. Child:
George E., m. Jan. 5, 1879, Emma Perkins Jenness.

16. JOSEPH BROWN DALTON, son of Daniel Philbrick (14), born 1809; married, first, March 14, 1833, Hannah Brown; died, Oct. 9, 1850; married, second, Abigail Brown. Children by first wife:
Emily B., b. May, 1835; m. March 7, 1854, David Jenness. Daniel Curtis, b. 1840; d. April 26, 1848.
Child by second wife:
Curtis E., b. Oct. 9, 1850; married 1871.

17. MICHAEL DALTON, son of Daniel Philbrick (14), born 1812; married, April 28, 1839, Elizabeth W. Scammon. Children:
Viana M., b. July (?), 1840; m. Emmons B. Philbrick; d. Nov. 4, 1869. Abby. Mary W., m. Nov. 12, 1867, William Harvey Garland. Clara, m. Jan., 1867, Alonzo Stephens.

18. DANIEL DALTON, son of Daniel Philbrick (14), born July 2, 1814; married, first, July 4, 1842, Martha Brown; died, Feb., 1866; married, second, widow Eliza (Bean) Parsons; married, third, Emily Shapley, who died March 24, 1898. He died July 14, 1888. Children by first wife:

Eliza A., b. Jan., 1844; d. Oct. 8, 1865. Daniel Woodbury, b. May 21, 1849; m. March 19, 1877, Belle O. Lane; divorced.

DAVIDSON.

1. WILLIAM DAVIDSON, married, first, Roberts of Epping; married, second, Abigail, widow of Daniel Philbrick. Children:

2. Josiah. William, m. Sally Blake, and had Patty, who m. Jonathan Locke. John, *non compos mentis;* fell into a well and was drowned.

2. JOSIAH DAVIDSON, son of William (1), married, Oct. 28, 1794, Abigail Shaw. Children:

Newhall, bapt. April 5, 1796. Abigail Taylor, bapt. June 11, 1797. Josiah Marsters, bapt. Feb. 20, 1799. Elias, b. June 4, 1809. William. Nancy.

DAVIS.

1. JOHN DAVIS married Eunice Seavey. She also married Thomas Lake. Children:

2. Ephraim. (?) William, bapt. May 22, 1757. David, bapt. Oct. 21, 1759.
3. Samuel, bapt. Oct., 1761.

2. EPHRAIM DAVIS, son of John (1) (?), married ——. Children:

Samuel, bapt. Dec. 15, 1776. Ephraim, bapt. Aug. 8, 1779.

3. SAMUEL DAVIS, son of John (1), bapt. Oct., 1761; married, Jan. 20, 1782, Abigail Brown. Children:

Betsey, bapt. 1784. Billy, bapt. Oct. 2, 1785.

ROBERT DAVIS, who married Almira Dearborn, and lived at Concord, had Charles A., a physician, who died April, 1863.

DEARBORN.

REUBEN DEARBORN. Children:
Anna, bapt. Nov. 15, 1772. Josiah, bapt. May 23, 1774. Anna, bapt. May 23, 1774. Abigail, bapt. Sept. 15, 1776.

SIMON DEARBORN, son of John and Abigail Dearborn, of Hampton, was born April 28, 1766; married, May, 1787, Mary, daughter of Capt. Simon Brown. Children:
John, b. Nov. 23, 1787; m. Sarah Ward; colonel; fell from a building at Lynn, Mass., and was killed, Sept. 15, 1832. Lucinda, b. May 8, 1790; m. John Hobbs. Henry Washington, bapt. July 19, 1795; d. Jan., 1803. Mary Brown, b. Dec. 27, 1805; m. Samuel Locke; d. Aug., 1872.

CAPT. TRUEWORTHY DEARBORN married Sarah, daughter of Simon and Mary (Leavitt) Brown. Lived at Greenland and at Concord, where he was keeper at the State Prison for many years. Children:
Daniel, physician. Almira, m. first, Robert Davis of Concord; m. second, Asper Evans. Sarah Ann. Caroline. Elizabeth, m. Coffran; d. about 1839; lived at Concord.

MARY ANN ADELINE DEARBORN, daughter of Levi Dearborn, was baptized Oct. 28, 1796.

DELANEY.

CHARLES DELANEY married Jane Ann, daughter of Nathan Clough. Children:
Estelle. Fred. Anna, b. 1867; d. Feb. 15, 1886.

DOLBEE.

1. NICHOLAS DOLBEE married Sarah Smith. He died before 1743. Lived in Rye prior to 1700. Children:
2. John, b. Jan. 23, 1714.
   Israel, b. March 23, 1715; went to Chester and Candia about 1778. Hannah, m. July 25, 1738, Peter Clifford.
4. Jonathan, b. April 17, 1720. Daniel, b. March 17, 1724. Mary, b. April 16, 1726.

2. JOHN DOLBEE, son of Nicholas (1), born Jan. 23, 1714; married, Feb. 24, 1742, Elizabeth Clifford of Hampton Falls. Joiner. Children:

Judith, bapt. May 8, 1743. Eli, bapt. Sept. 9, 1744. Jesse, bapt. Oct. 11, 1747. Isabella, bapt. March 4, 1750.

3. ISRAEL DOLBEE, son of Nicholas (1), born March 23, 1715; married, Nov. 11, 1736, Sarah Lamprey. Children:
Israel, b. Jan. 6, 1737-'38. Hannah, b. March 12, 1741-'42. Daniel, b. Feb. 10, 1745. Sarah, bapt. Nov. 6, 1748.

4. JONATHAN DOLBEE, son of Nicholas (1), born April 17, 1720; married Sarah White. He died March 18, 1761. Children:
Ruth, b. Dec. 2, 1745.
5. Nichols, b. May 8, 1748; m. Mary Randall. Jonathan, b. Aug. 7, 1750. Abigail (?), b. Jan. 5, 1751-'52; d. young. Stephen, b. July 12, 1753. Abigail, b. Dec. 24, 1756; m. March 28, 1780, Joseph Brown. Hannah, b. July 22, 1761; m. Jan. 5, 1784, Samuel Rand.

5. NICHOLS DOLBEE, son of Jonathan (4), born May 8, 1748; married, May 27, 1773. A soldier in the Revolution. Children:
Jonathan, bapt. March 13, 1774. Aston, b. 1776. John, bapt. Aug. 23, 1778; m. Sally Sherburne of Portsmouth; she d. 1819. Patty, b. 1781. Stephen, b. 1783. Molly, bapt. Aug. 13, 1786. Billy, bapt. Dec. 13, 1789. Nicholas, b. 1792; buried at New Rye.

DANIEL DOLBEE, of Chester, married Margaret Haines, May 25, 1767.

DOW.

1. ISAAC DOW, son of Simon and Mehitable (Green) Dow, of Hampton, born Oct., 1701; married Charity Philbrick who was born April 29, 1702, and died June 22, 1771-'72. He died in 1735. "Isaac Dow of Parish of Rye, deeded to Richard Jenness of Rye, land beginning at the lower part of Breakfast hill by the road that goes from Greenland to Lanebeach (Sandy Beach) at a certain rock and pine burch which is the bounds between John Black and said Dow, and to extend from said rock and burch S. W. 90 rods and then near a S. E. point so many rods as will make 20 acres. I bot said tract of Richard Jose or Joice of Portsmouth. Witness Nat Sargent & Joseph Redwood. 1727." Children:

GENEALOGY.

2. Henry, b. Dec. 29, 1729. Mary, b. Sept. 6, 1730; m. Dec. 25, 1750, Capt. Joseph Jenness. Eleanor, b. Dec. 8, 1733; m. first, Samuel Brackett; m. second, Sept. 8, 1771, Jere Berry.

2. HENRY DOW, son of Isaac (1), born Dec. 29, 1729; married Martha Perkins. Children:

Hannah, b. Oct. 15, 1752; m. Aug. 20, 1778, Isaac Jenness.
3. Isaac, b. Dec. 13, 1754.   Martha, b. Oct. 6, 1758; m. June 25, 1778, Joseph Locke; d. Jan. 31, 1792.   Mary, b. Dec. 23, 1761 or '62; m. first, Oct. 25, 1781, John Dowrst; m. second, Benj. Wiggin.
4. James, b. Jan. 8, 1765.

3. ISAAC DOW, son of Henry (2), born Dec. 13, 1754; married, Aug. 21, 1777, Elizabeth Seavey. She died Dec. 17, 1823, aged 67 years. Children:

Patty, b. Oct. 28, 1779; m. Aug. 3, 1796, Amos S. Parsons.
5. Amos, b. 1781.
6. Isaac.
7. Henry, b. 1783.
8. James, b. June 3, 1785.   Betsey, b. 1791; m. John T. Rand; d. March 18, 1834.

4. JAMES DOW, son of Henry (2), born Jan. 8, 1765; married Mary Parsons. She died Dec. 7, 1842. Child:

Martha Leavitt, b. May 12, 1799; m. Aug. 10, 1820, Nathaniel G. Foye; d. Sept. 18, 1885.

5. AMOS DOW, son of Isaac (3), born in 1781; married Lydia Fabens. Children:

Langdon.   Eliza Ann.   Emiline.   Lydia P.   Priscilla.

6. ISAAC DOW, son of Isaac (3), married Lydia Pickering. He died Feb. 25, 1862. Children:

Valentine.   Isaac.   Frances, m. Isaac Brackett.   Martha.   Lydia, m. John Furber.   Eliza Ann, d. unm.

7. HENRY DOW, son of Isaac (3), born in 1783; married Elizabeth Fabens. He died Oct. 18, 1865. Children:

Isaac.   Elizabeth.   Washington.   Jefferson.   Martha.   Hannah. Wallis.

8. JAMES DOW, son of Isaac (3), born June 3, 1785; married, Feb. 6, 1812, Data Drake. He died May 19, 1853. She died April 24, 1848. Children:

Jonathan D., d. in Illinois. Elizabeth, b. 1817; m. May 30, 1837, Langdon Brown; d. Oct. 9, 1848.
9. Albert, b. 1819. Sarah Ann, b. 1821; m. Jan. 1, 1845, Dr. Warren Parsons; d. Nov. 2, 1850. Martha Ann, b. Aug., 1823; d. April 11, 1845.
10. James Henry, b. Oct. 23, 1825. Eli Sawtell, b. 1828; d. Aug. 30, 1858. Cazendana, b. 1830; d. April 5, 1847, aged 17 years. Harriett A., b. 1832; m. Sept. 5, 1855, Levi T. Walker; d. Sept. 1, 1858.

9. ALBERT DOW, son of James (8), born in 1819; married, Nov. 21, 1847, Ann Elizabeth Seavey; died 1854. He died April 10, 1886. Married, second, ———. Child by first wife:

John H., b. 1848; accidentally shot himself dead, July 29, 1865.
Child by second wife:
Mamie, m. Charles Wendell.

10. JAMES HENRY DOW, son of James (8), born Oct. 23, 1825; married, June 5, 1849, Angelina Brown. He died Jan. 20, 1864. Children:

Clara Maria, b. April 5, 1850; m. Nov. 4, 1869, James Alba Rand. A child, b. July 22, 1852. Charles H., b. July 31, 1854; d. March 18, 1869. Flora, b. Jan. 15, 1860; m. Ella F., b. Sept. 12, 1863; d. Feb. 28, 1864.

NOAH DOW, son of Simon and Mary (Lancaster) Dow of Hampton, born May 1, 1736; married Phebe Palmer. Children:

Simon, bapt. Sept., 1762. Daniel, bapt. May 20, 1764. Nathan, bapt. June 26, 1768. Jonathan, bapt. Feb. 21, 1773.

DOWNING.

1. EBENEZER DOWNING, married Abigail Allen. Lived at Newington. Children:

2. Samuel, m. Mary Davis. Abraham, m. Hannah. Sarah, m. Timothy Pettigrew.

2. SAMUEL DOWNING, son of Ebenezer (1), married Mary Davis. Children:

John, m. Lydia Ellsworth; lived at Methuen, Mass.
3. William C., m. Hannah C. Knowles. Sarah, m. James Morris. Emeline, m. George Brown; lived at Newington. Eliza, m. William Fernald.

3. WILLIAM C., son of Samuel (2), married Hannah C. Knowles of Candia. He was a fisherman, and died May 28, 1887. He adopted Harriette Annette, daughter of Ivory and Mary (Johnson) Brown, who was born ———. She married Nov. 20, 1869, Jacob T. Godfrey of Hampton.

Thomas Downing and Martha Norris were married Aug. 14, 1796.

DOWNS.

1. EDWARD DOWNS, married Margaret ————. Children:
2. Henry.
3. Abner.
4. John.
5. Samuel. Margaret, m. Moses Dow. Sally, m. Robert Robinson.

2. HENRY DOWNS, son of Edward (1), married Abigail Bragg. She was born Oct. 17, 1793. Lived at Gosport. Children:

Harriet, b. 1804 (?). Henry, b. 1808 (?); m. Elizabeth P. Foss; d. 1839. John Bragg, b. 1809 (?); m. Nov. 27, 1834, Olive Foss; d. 1888; lived at Gosport. Mark, b. 1816 (?); m. Abigail. Ephraim P., b. Aug. 12, 1819; accidentally shot while gunning. Billy, b. April 24, 1822. Mary, m. Asa Robinson. Eliza, b. March 8, 1826; d. Sept. 26, 1883. Nancy, m. John Lear.

3. ABNER DOWNS, son of Edward (1), married, Oct. 13, 1805, Sally Downs. After his death in 1818, she married, second, Feb. 27, 1821, James Robinson. Children:
6. Abner. Edward, b. 1809. Mary, b. May 11, 1811; m. William Randall; she had before m. John H., b. Jan. 30, 1831, who m. Hannah Jane Foss, and d. 1865. Love, b. 1813; unm.; had Joseph W. Marden, b. Oct. 9, 1830, who d. Jan. 21, 1861.
7. William, b. Dec. 27, 1815; m. Mary Grant; d. Sept., 1882.

4. JOHN DOWNS, son of Edward (1), married, 1815, widow Betsey Matthews. Children:
8. Robert.
9. Edward M., b. June 22, 1818.

5. SAMUEL DOWNS, son of Edward (1), married, Aug. 16, 1814, Betsey, widow of Joseph Tucker. Children:

Betsey, b. Oct. 13, 1818; m. John Whidden. Ann Thomas, b. June 25, 1822; m. Thomas Gammon. Samuel Washington, b. Nov. 30, 1823; d. Dec. 3, 1831. Harry, b. Jan. 19, 1826; m. Adeline Hodgdon. Henrietta, b. April 10, 1828; m. William Brown. Mary Olive, b. June 30, 1831; m. William R. Mace.

6. ABNER DOWNS, son of Abner (3), married, first, ———; married, second, Elizabeth P. (Foss), widow of Henry Downs. While a widow she had Moses Foss, born May 17, 1828, who married Mary Townsend of Rhode Island. Abner Downs was drowned Dec. 30, 1844. Children:

Charles H., b. Jan. 22, 1830; m. Georgie Ann Kean. John L., b. Dec. 7, 1831; m. Susan M. Marston. Solomon F., b. May 8, 1833 or '35; m. Eliza Parson of Gloucester, Mass. Eliza A., b. Oct. 13, 1839; d. Sept., 1883, at Lowell, Mass. Sarah J., b. Sept. 6, 1843; m. Dec. 11, 1866, John Q. A. Ferguson.

7. WILLIAM DOWNS, son of Abner (3), born Dec. 27, 1815; married Mary Grant, and lived at Portsmouth. He died Sept., 1882. Children:

Caroline. James K., m. Holmes. Wallace. Lillian.

8. ROBERT DOWNS, son of John (4), married Huldah Randall. Children:

Frederick. Appia. John Matthews, b. 1852; d. March 24, 1870.

9. EDWARD M. DOWNS, son of John (4), born June 22, 1818; married Mary Abby Lear. She died Dec. 22, 1866, and he died June 10, 1870. Children:

Emma R., b. Dec. 17, 1846; m. Levi W. Marden. Amanda A., b. March 1, 1848; m. June 26, 1870, Augustus Y. Rand; he d. Feb. 27, 1902. Willis A., b. May 10, 1850.
10. Edward N., b. Oct. 30, 1857.

10. EDWARD N. DOWNS, son of Edward M. (9), born Oct. 30, 1857; married, Nov. 24, 1891, Julia M. True. Children:

True J., b. Sept. 1, 1892; d. Sept. 10, 1893. Girl, b. Jan. 7, 1894; d. 1894. John L., b. Aug. 28, 1895. Ralph W., b. Nov. 6, 1896. Dorothy Emma, b. Oct. 23, 1897. George E., b. July 18, 1899.

BENJAMIN DOWNS, married widow Abigail Randall. Lived at Gosport. Children:

Benjamin. William. Abigail. Sally, m. Jarius Towle. Ann, m. Francis Oliver. John Randall, m. Jane Locke. Betsey, m. George S. Randall.

DOWRST.

Solomon, Ozem, and Samuel Dowrst probably were brothers.

SOLOMON DOWRST, married Elizabeth ———, and was living in 1770. Children:

Thomas, b. Aug. 28, 1724; d. Aug. 27, 1735. Samuel, b. March 26, 1726; d. Aug. 19, 1735. Abial, b. Sept. 24, 1728; d. Aug. 24, 1735. Sarah, b. Jan. 19, 1729; m. May 10, 1748, Samuel Rand. Solomon, b. May 23, 1730; d. Nov. 13, 1735. Elizabeth, b. Jan. 11, 1732; d. Nov. 19, 1735. Rachel, b. Aug. 1, 1735; m. July 31, 1754, Benjamin Marden. Rachel's father gave her half of his real estate and buildings in Rye and Portsmouth, and a 30-acre lot in Epsom, of which he was the original proprietor.

SAMUEL DOWRST, married Rachel. Children:

Mary, b. May 8, 1723; m. Jan. 25, 1739, Wallis Foss. Simon, b. Sept. 20, 1730; d. Oct. 26, 1734.

1. OZEM DOWRST, married Elizabeth, daughter of Benjamin Seavey. Children:

Sarah, b. Oct. 23, 1725. John, d. Sept. 13, 1730. Elizabeth, d. Sept. 6, 1730. Comfort, b. Aug. 21, 1731. Mary, b. 1734.
2. Ozem J., b. March, 1737. Abigail, b. 1739. Elizabeth, b. 1744. Did she m. Joel Amy in 1776? Samuel, b. 1749.

2. OZEM J. DOWRST, son of Ozem (1), born March, 1737; married, first, Oct. 29, 1761, Elizabeth Jenness; married, second, Nov. 3, 1796, Martha Webster. Children:

3. John, b. Feb. 22, 1762. Jonathan, b. Dec. 5, 1764; m., and had Samuel Morrill, bapt. Sept. 5, 1790. Sarah, bapt. Nov. 29, 1767; m. Israel Marden. Molly, bapt. June 3, 1770; m. Hobbs. Elizabeth, bapt. June 13, 1773. Betsey. Anna, bapt. June 15, 1777. Lydia, bapt. June 29, 1781.

3. JOHN DOWRST, son of Ozem J. (2), born Feb. 22, 1762; married, Oct. 25, 1781, Mary Dow, and removed to Deerfield. Children:

Martha, b. March 5, 1782; d. Nov. 22. Isaac. Henry.

Samuel Dowrst and Elizabeth Shannon were married Jan. 8, 1754.

DRAKE.

1. JONATHAN DRAKE, son of Col. Abraham and Abigail (Dearborn) Drake, born Jan. 15, 1758; married, Nov. 21, 1782, Sarah, daughter of Lieut. Cotton Ward. She died Dec. 21, 1822. Children:
   Hannah, b. Sept. 16, 1783; m. Oct. 7, 1802, Jonathan Brown.
2. Abraham, b. March 10, 1786. Sarah, b. July 29, 1789; m. June 16, 1807, Amos Seavey; d. April 31, 1874. Data, b. April 15, 1792; m. Feb. 6, 1812, James Dow. Anna, b. Jan. 25, 1796.
3. Jonathan, b. May 18, 1798.
4. Cotton Ward, b. May 28, 1801.
5. John, b. Nov. 20, 1803.

2. ABRAHAM DRAKE, son of Jonathan (1), born March 10, 1786; married, March 21, 1811, Mary Jenness. After his death she married, Aug. 23, 1827, David W. Jenness. He belonged to Capt. Coleman's company of cavalry during the War of 1812. Children:
   A child, d. Jan. 28, 1816. Anna, b. 1813; d. July 19, 1826.
6. Joseph Jenness; b. Dec., 1816. Sarah Ward, b. Feb., 1819; m. April 15, 1841, David A. Jenness; d. May 12, 1881. Abraham, b. 1820; d. Sept. 3, 1826.
7. Oren, b. Jan. 30, 1824.

3. JONATHAN DRAKE, son of Jonathan (1), born May 18, 1798; married, May 14, 1818, Eliza J. Garland. He kept a general store, which was subsequently occupied by Thomas J. Parsons, under the firm name of Seavey & Drake, and was killed by falling from his horse, Jan. 21, 1833. After his death she married, Dec. 28, 1834, Capt. B. W. Marden. Children:
   Amos G. Oliver, b. 1820; d. June 12, 1843. William. Eliza Ann, m. Feb. 5, 1856, Benjamin Jarvis. Gilman J., b. July, 1827. Emeline, m. Richard R. Higgins; d. June 22, 1874, in Boston.

4. DEACON COTTON WARD DRAKE, son of Jonathan (1), born May 28, 1801; married, July 14, 1822, Martha Parsons. She died April 2, 1895. He died Nov. 10, 1880. Children:
   Elizabeth Dow, b. Dec. 21, 1823; m. June 21, 1842, Oliver P. Jenness. Anna, b. May 27, 1827; m. Nov. 27, 1855, Hiram Fuller. Martha Maria, b. Jan. 14, 1830; unm.; deformed; d. Oct. 26, 1870.

8. Charles Abraham, b. Oct. 30, 1832. Mary Letitia, b. Sept. 2, 1835; m. Nov. 30, 1855, Charles J. Brown. Sarah Abigail, b. May 14, 1838; m. Feb. 25, 1862, Dudley Chase Littlefield; lived at Stratham. James McEwen, b. Feb. 19, 1846; m. July 2, 1874, E. Maria Upham of Framingham, Mass.

5. CAPT. JOHN DRAKE, son of Jonathan (1), born Nov. 20, 1803; married, Nov. 22, 1822, Anna S. Parsons. She died Jan. 29, 1891. He died Oct. 29, 1882. Lived at Breakfast Hill. Child:

Sarah Parsons, b. Feb. 2, 1823; m. Feb. 25, 1851, Jacob Marston.

6. JOSEPH JENNESS DRAKE, son of Abraham (2), born Dec., 1816; married, Oct. 12, 1838, Clarissa Knowles. He died June 4, 1897. Children:

Nathan D., b. 1839; d. Feb. 11, 1840, aged one year. Annie D., b. Sept. 26, 1840; m. Oct. 22, 1860, Joseph W. Garland. Mary J., m. Feb. 17, 1870, Alfred V. Seavey; d. 1875. John Harvey, b. 1847; d. Feb. 11, 1848.
9. Abraham J., b. Nov. 4, 1849.
10. Adams Elisha, b. Nov. 4, 1849.
11. John Oren, b. Nov. 14, 1851. Clara Josephine, b. Jan. 3, 1854; m. May, 1877, Alfred V. Seavey. James Buchanan, b. May 16, 1856; d. Oct. 5, 1874. Leonie S., b. Nov. 3, 1862; m. 1889, Blake Rand.

7. OREN DRAKE, son of Abraham (2), born Jan. 30, 1824; married, first, April 2, 1848, Mary A. Odiorne. She died Jan. 2, 1877; and he married, second, Feb. 1, 1880, Izette Trefethern. He died Sept. 25, 1898. Children:

12. Morris A., b. June 23, 1850. Sarah Olive, b. Jan. 2, 1854; m. Nov. 24, 1872, Irvin J. Seavey. Augusta Emma, b. Aug. 7, 1856; m. Nov. 19, 1879, Charles M. Rand.
13. Albert Herman, b. Feb. 21, 1861.

8. CHARLES ABRAHAM DRAKE, son of Cotton Ward (4), born Oct. 30, 1832; married, May 9, 1859, Helen A. Weeks. He was a justice of the peace. Children:

14. Edwin Howard, b. Sept. 5, 1861. Elizabeth Martha, b. Feb. 11, 1864; m. Charles Smith of North Hampton. Kate Augusta, b. Dec. 3, 1866; m. Nov. 28, 1900, Charles F. Patterson, M. D. Percy, b. Dec. 25, 1876; m. Dec. 24, 1901, Minnie E. Wood.

9. ABRAHAM J. DRAKE, son of Joseph Jenness (6), born Nov. 4, 1849; married, Oct. 20, 1870, Emeline A. Philbrick. Child:

Abbott B., b. Nov. 22, 1889.

10. ADAMS ELISHA DRAKE, son of Joseph Jenness (6), born Nov. 4, 1849; married, June 24, 1871, Emma Marden. Children:
> Chester, b. July 25, 1872. Gracie, b. Feb. 11, 1875; m. May 8, 1900, Fred Brown; he d. June 11, 1901. Linden A., b. Feb. 22, 1881; d. April 21, 1881. Marcia, b. April 12, 1882. Annie L., b. March 24, 1887. Merton, b. Aug. 16, 1893.

11. JOHN OREN DRAKE, son of Joseph Jenness (6), born Nov. 14, 1851; married, Aug. 4, 1876, Carrie Dearborn of Hampton, born Aug. 18, 1852. He died Feb. 2, 1901. He was a justice of the peace and notary public. Children:
> Mary, b. March 21, 1879. Jennie, b. July 11, 1883. Evelyn, b. May 29, 1888.

12. MORRIS A. DRAKE, son of Oren (7), born June 23, 1850; married, July 21, 1872, Laura F. Trefethern. Children:
> George Weston, b. Dec. 17, 1872; d. Dec. 20, 1877. Carrie, b. Feb., 1874; m. first, George Foster; second, Aug., 1890, Harry Rand. David T., b. Aug. 28, 1875; m. Alice G. Wilson. Mary, b. Jan. 2, 1877; m. Jan. 1, 1897, George N. Perry. Oren, b. June 8, 1880; m. Feb. 4, 1903, Clara M. Ackerman. Cora, b. Dec. 26, 1884; m. June 17, 1903, Ernest Foss.

13. ALBERT HERMAN DRAKE, son of Oren (7), born Feb. 21, 1861; married, 1883, Emma Holmes. Children:
> Ruth, b. Oct., 1885. Joseph Holmes, b. March 21, 1887. Willard, b. Nov. 9, 1891.

14. EDWIN HOWARD DRAKE, son of Charles Abraham (8), born Sept. 5, 1861; married Marcia B. Clark. Child:
> Helen, b. March 7, 1887.

DRISCO.

THOMAS DRISCO, married, Dec. 6, 1753, Mary Damrell. After his death she married Thomas Remick. Child:
> Robert, bapt. Sept. 29, 1754.

John, son of John Drisco, was baptized Sept., 1756.

EDMUNDS.

1. JOSEPH EDMUNDS, married, Sept. 27, 1753, Ruth Libby. Children:

GENEALOGY.

2. Jonathan. John, m. Rebecca Copp. Polly, m. David Piper. Hannah, m. Benjamin Horn. Jane, d. unm.

2. JONATHAN EDMUNDS, son of Joseph (1), married Catherine Clifford. Children:

Jane, m. James Tuttle; lived at Tuftonborough. Benjamin, m. Hannah Merrill; lived at Portsmouth. Fanny. John, b. Nov. 20, 1790; m. Charlotte Carter. Jonathan, b. Nov. 20, 1790; m. Hannah Fullington.

JONATHAN EDMONDS, married ———. Children:

Erie, b. 1800; m. Hall. William. Samuel. Polly J., m. July 19, 1835, Samuel W. Jenness.

EDWARD EDMONDS, married, Dec. 25, 1744, Susanna Tucker. Children:

Hannah, bapt. June 21, 1747. Thomas, bapt. March 5, 1749. Mehitable, bapt. June 30, 1751. Sarah Rand, bapt. Aug. 25, 1754. Jonathan, bapt. Oct., 1756. Mary, bapt. May 4, 1760. William, bapt. July 3, 1762. Edward, bapt. June 17, 1764. Nathaniel, bapt. Oct. 9, 1768. Elsie, bapt. May 27, 1770. Susannah, bapt. Oct. 4, 1772.

WILLIAM F. ELDRIDGE, married ———. Children:

Roy K. Willie S. Nellie P.

ELKINS.

1. HENRY ELKINS, son of Jonathan and Joanna (Roby) Elkins of Hampton, born March 26, 1708; married, March 25, 1729, Catharine, daughter of Samuel Marston. He died March 27, 1756. Children:

Mary, b. 1731. Mercy, b. 1733. Elizabeth, b. 1734. Hannah, b. Jan., 1737. Henry, b. 1739. Catherine, b. June 20, 1741; m. Paul Smith Marston. Joanna, b. May 14, 1743; m. William Emery; d. March 7, 1822, at Andover, N. H.

2. Samuel, b. Jan. 30, 1745.

2. SAMUEL ELKINS, son of Henry (1), born Jan. 30, 1745; married, June 24, 1773, Olive Marden. She died Dec. 3, 1835, aged 62 years. In 1773 Samuel Elkins bought 20 acres of land of Trustin Coffin Sleeper, consideration ten Spanish milled dollars. Children:

3. Henry, b. April 23, 1775.
4. James, b. May 3, 1777. Samuel, b. May 14, 1779; d. Aug. 11, 1836; unm. at Portsmouth; merchant. Mary, b. June 25, 1781; m. Dec. 10, 1801, Josiah Philbrick of North Hampton. Olly, b. Oct. 3, 1783; m. April 29, 1807, Simon Chesley. Nabby, b. April 18, 1786; m. first, May, 1823, Hartwell Hall; m. second, Simon Brown. William, b. Dec. 21, 1788; d. Oct. 3, 1789.

3. HENRY ELKINS, son of Samuel (2), born April 23, 1775; married, 1806, Mary Webster. Children:
5. Samuel, b. April 8, 1809. Catherine, b. 1813; m. Edward Walcott; d. Aug. 26, 1869.

4. JAMES ELKINS, son of Samuel (2), born May 3, 1777; married, March 7, 1809, Mehitable Rand. Children:
James Seavey, b. Dec. 24, 1809. David, b. Nov. 4, 1812. Moses, b. Feb. 2, 1818.

5. SAMUEL ELKINS, son of Henry (3), born April 8, 1809; married Mary Lord. Children:
George, d. aged 21 years. Levi, b. Jan. 28, 1837; m. Maria Allen.

FINLAYSON.

ARCHIBALD FINLAYSON, married, Aug. 22, 1894, Elizabeth Lord. Electrician. Children:
Mary, b. Dec. 8, 1895. Donnel, b. Sept. 20, 1897.

FITZGERALD.

DANIEL FITZGERALD, married ———. Children:
Molly, bapt. Sept. 21, 1794. Nancy, bapt. Sept. 21, 1794.

FOGG.

OLIVER BROWN FOGG, son of Lydia Dalton Fogg, married Emma A. Locke. Resides in North Hampton. Children:
Alvin, b. June 30, 1875. Bertha Emma.

FOSS.

John Foss was the ancestor of this family. He is said to have arrived at Boston in a British war vessel, from which he jumped overboard and swimming ashore, ran away. He thought of settling at a place called Reid's Temple, but not being pleased with the location, came to Rye, where he was admitted into the family of John Berry, and married his daughter. It is said that twelve children were born to them, one son settling in Maine, near Scarborough, where he was drowned. A John Foss was at Dover in 1665, served on the grand jury in 1688, and died in 1699.

1. JOSHUA FOSS, probably son of John of Rye and Dover, married Sarah Wallis. She was living in 1723. He removed to Barrington, where he died, aged 99 years and six months. Children:

    Thomas.
2. Nathaniel. John, d. Feb. 15, 1731, aged 24 years; buried in the old burying ground near Dr. Patterson's, recently removed.
3. Job.
4. Wallis (?). Jane, m. June 27, 1736, William Palmer. Hannah, m. Aug. 21, 1741, Samuel Saunders.
5. Mark.
6. George (?).

2. NATHANIEL FOSS, son of Joshua (1), married, Oct. 16, 1740, Mary Tucker. Children:

7. Joshua. Mary, bapt. Feb. 2, 1745; m. Samuel Berry. Sarah, bapt. Feb. 20, 1747. William, bapt. April 17, 1748; d. unm.; followed the sea. Olive, bapt. Sept. 5, 1751; had by Richard Rand a dau., Olive, who m. Joseph Locke. Jane, bapt. Dec. 9, 1753; m. Isaac Remick.
8. Nathaniel, bapt. June 17, 1756. Job, bapt. May 13, 1759; lost at sea.
9. Samuel, bapt. July 3, 1762.

3. JOB FOSS, son of Joshua (1), married, Nov. 1, 1750, Sarah Lang. Tame Indian stayed at his house one night and the board to which he was tied caught fire and came near burning a child and the house. Children:

    Sarah, b. Aug. 1, 1751; m. June 6, 1776, Mark Foss; lived at Barrington. Hannah, bapt. Aug. 17, 1775; m. Simon Chapman; lived at Epsom.
10. John, bapt. June, 1757. Dorothy, b. Aug. 14, 1758. Job. bapt. May 13, 1759. Joshua, bapt. Aug. 30, 1761; m. Betsey Hunt. Mary, bapt. Feb. 11, 1764; m. Robert Saunders.
11. Ebenezer, bapt. Sept. 20, 1767; m. Mary Foss. Comfort, bapt. May 17, 1772; m. Richard Lang.

4. WALLIS FOSS, probably son of Joshua (1), married, Jan. 25, 1739, Mary, daughter of Samuel Dowrst; lived near Rye Center. Children:

    Samuel, b. Oct. 25, 1739. John, b. July 7, 1746; d. unm., of lockjaw, aged about 30; lived at Rochester. Elizabeth, bapt. June 26, 1748; unm.; d. at Joseph Goss'. Rachel, b. 1750; m. Nov. 28, 1779, Peter Ackerman; lived at Epsom. Abigail, b. 1752; d. young.

12. Samuel Dowrst, b. 1754. Abigail, b. 1757; m. Reuben Libby; lived at Gorham, Me. Phineas, b. 1759; probably d. young. Mary, b. 1761; probably d. young.

13. Solomon.

5. MARK FOSS, son of Joshua (1), married, Nov. 28, 1745, Amy Thompson. Children:

    Nathaniel, b. 1747. Mark, b. 1749; m. 1776, Sarah, dau. of Job Foss; lived at Barrington. Abigail, b. 1752. John, b. 1755.

6. GEORGE FOSS, probably son of Joshua (1), married, April 3, 1746, Mary Marden. Children:

    Abigail, b. 1750. James. George.

7. JOSHUA FOSS, son of Nathaniel (2), married, Nov. 29, 1762, Rachel Marden. Children:

    Elizabeth, b. 1763; m. Sept. 24, 1789, Jonathan B. Waldron; d. Jan. 5, 1835. Mary, b. 1766; m. Ebenezer Foss; lived at Epsom.

14. William, b. July 12, 1769.

8. NATHANIEL FOSS, son of Nathaniel (2), baptized June 17, 1756; married Mehitable, daughter of Eben Jackson of Portsmouth. She died April 11, 1837, aged 77 years. Children:

    Polly, bapt. March 27, 1791; m. April 4, 1811, Richard Goss. Jane, bapt. Nov. 18, 1792; m. Dec. 24, 1812, Daniel Page of North Hampton; d. April, 1864. Nathaniel, bapt. Dec. 11, 1795; d. March 31, 1817. Samuel, b. May, 1798; d. unm. April 8, 1867; drummer. Patty W., m. first, Jan. 25, 1809, Joseph Mason; m. second, Robinson Foss.

9. SAMUEL FOSS, son of Nathaniel (2), baptized July 3, 1762; married Salome Trefethern. She died April 10, 1851. Children:

    Supply C., m. ———; both were killed by the falling of a house at Dubuque, Iowa. Samuel P., bapt. Dec. 22, 1799.

GENEALOGY. 347

10. JOHN FOSS, son of Job (3), baptized June, 1757; married, March 6, 1783, Sarah Tucker. He died Jan. 1, 1819. Served under Capt. Joseph Parsons in the Revolutionary War. Children:
15. Job, b. 1785.
16. Robinson, b. April 30, 1787. Betsey, b. April 20, 1788; m. William Mathews; d. July 22, 1873. Olive, b. April 20, 1788; m. 1815, Joseph Sheppard. Sarah, m. June 22, 1808, Jeremiah Page, Jr.
17. Richard, b. May 4, 1795. Anna Partridge, m. Jan. .3, 1830, Thomas J. Whidden of Portsmouth.

11. EBENEZER FOSS, son of Job (3), baptized Sept. 20, 1767; married, Nov. 26, 1789, Mary (Molly) Foss. Children:
William, bapt. Oct. 17, 1790. Hannah, bapt. June 3, 1792. Joshua (?).

12. SAMUEL DOWRST FOSS, son of Wallis (4), born in 1754; married, Jan. 13, 1774, Mary Berry. Removed to Rochester. Children:
Wallis, b. Aug. 5, 1775; m. Mary Libby. Samuel, b. July 4, 1777; m. Abigail Reid. Hannah, b. 1779; d. young. Jeremiah Berry, b. 1780; d. 1794. Polly, b. 1783; d. young. Mary, b. Jan. 8, 1785; m. John H. Ham.
18. James Seavey, b. June 22, 1787. Patience, b. 1789; m. first, James Newton; second, Joseph Butler; third, John Smith; lived at Barrington. Sarah, bapt. July 3, 1791; m. Samuel Rand.

13. SOLOMON FOSS, son of Wallis (4), married Jane Remick, who died May 27, 1847. Children:
19. Joseph Remick, b. May 15, 1800. Margaret, b. March, 1803; m. first, Nov. 12, 1822, David Nason; second, Benjamin Marden. Catharine, m. Augustus Warren. Esther J., b. March 5, 1808; m. Nov. 12, 1827, John Jones; d. Jan. 2, 1887. Elizabeth P., b. 1810; m. first, 1828, Henry Downs of Gosport; m. second, Abner Downs. Mary D., b. 1811; m. Joseph Brown. Martha W., m. Paul Peterson. Sarah, m. Joseph W. Pickering. Hannah Jane, m. John H. Downs. Samuel W., b. 1818; m. Aug. 10, 1845, Ursula Ann Locke; and she afterwards m. John S. Goss. Caroline, m. Calvin Garland of North Hampton.

14. WILLIAM FOSS, son of Joshua (7), born July 12, 1769; married, March 11, 1790, Abiel Marden. Children:
Joshua, b. Jan. 21, 1790. Sarah, b. Dec. 3, 1791; d. unm. May 13, 1810.
20. Benjamin Marden, b. April 28, 1794. Rachel, b. Aug. 3, 1795; m. Samuel Shapley.

15. JOB FOSS, son of John (10), born 1785; married, March 22, 1809, Patty Berry. Children:

>Olly, b. 1809; m. first, April 17, 1830, Eli Cole; m. second, Nov. 27, 1834, John Bragg Downs of Gosport; she had before marriage a son, Edward Sargent. Elizabeth, b. May, 1811; m. Thomas Green. Alexander, b. Aug., 1813; d. July 30, 1860. Sally, m. Jacob Waldron. Oliver. Jeremiah, d. young.

16. ROBINSON FOSS, son of John (10), born Aug. 30, 1787; married, first, Nov. 12, 1818, widow Patty Mason. She died April 1, 1828, and he married, second, widow Charlotta Holmes. Was a member of the Alarm List in the War of 1812, under Capt. Jonathan Wedgewood, and died Jan. 1, 1878. Children by first wife:

>Mehitable, b. Feb. 5, 1819; m. Jan. 14, 1841, Joshua M. Foss.
>21. Hardison, b. Jan. 23, 1821.
>Children by second wife:
>22. John Hunt, b. Dec. 9, 1831.
>23. Henry D., b. Sept. 18, 1832.
>24. Daniel Morrison, b. March 10, 1834. Charlotte Drown, b. Oct. 22, 1835; d. Nov. 14, 1837. Robinson T., b. Sept. 22, 1837; d. Dec. 8, 1865.

17. RICHARD FOSS, son of John (10), born May 4, 1795; married, Oct. 17, 1819, Eliza Shapley. He died May 4, 1842. A member of Capt. Samuel Berry's company of light infantry in the War of 1812. Children:

>John Henry, b. March 27, 1820; d. Sept. 7, 1825. Oran, b. Dec. 4, 1822; d. Sept. 13, 1825.
>25. Robert S., b. April 7, 1825.
>26. John Oren, b. Aug. 19, 1830. Eliza Esther, b. July 7, 1832; m. Robert W. Varrell. Chalcedony, b. 1837; m. Nov. 28, 1858, Daniel M. Foss.

18. JAMES SEAVEY FOSS, son of Samuel Dowrst (12), born June 22, 1787; married Sally Hodgdon, and removed to Rochester. Children:

>Abigail M., m. William Buchanan. Richard H., m. Lydia Durgin. Jeremiah B., m. Esther Berry. James N., m. Hannah Jones. Alonzo H., m. Elizabeth W. Davis. Susan H., m. Samuel McClure. Charles B. Mary J. Judith B. Martha A. Caroline M. Harriett N., m. John Varney.

19. JOSEPH REMICK FOSS, son of Solomon (13), born May 15, 1800; married, Dec. 6, 1826, Joanna Seward of Kittery. She died Jan. 21, 1861, aged 51 years. He lived where Charles Lear now resides. Children:

Isaac W., b. Dec. 3, 1827; d. May 12, 1840.
27. Joseph S., b. Oct. 8, 1829. Mary Jane, b. March 20, 1834; m. Sept. 29, 1855, Oliver Adams; lived at Portsmouth. Eliza Ann, b. April 25, 1844; m. Enoch Hutchings of Kittery. Isaac Dallas, b. Feb. 19, 1847; m.

20. BENJAMIN MARDEN FOSS, son of William (14), born April 28, 1794; married, Feb. 17, 1814, Dorcas, daughter of Henry Shapley. Children:

William, b. July 20, 1814; m. Nov. 7, 1834, Caroline Amazeen; lived at Newcastle.
28. Joshua Marden, b. Sept. 7, 1816. Sarah G., b. May 13, 1818; m. Oct. 21, 1841, Augustus White. Mary, b. Dec. 5, 1819; m. Joseph Amazeen.
29. Joel U., b. Dec. 7, 1821; m. Adeline Locke. Almira P., b. 1825; d. Dec. 25, 1866.

21. HARDISON FOSS, son of Robinson (16), born Jan. 23, 1821; married, July 16, 1843, Elvira Holmes, daughter of his stepmother. He died Dec. 15, 1882. Children:

Charlotte M., b. Nov. 11, 1843; m. June 13, 1869, James Seavey.
30. Sylvanus W., b. March 13, 1846. Ezra Drown, b. 1847; d. Feb. 28, 1848. Annie Julia, b. Jan. 24, 1849; m. May 13, 1873, Lewis E. Walker. Ezra H., b. Jan. 2, 1850; d. Jan. 28, 1868. Alice, b. Nov. 27, 1853; m. Feb. 10, 1881, Cotton W. D. Jenness. Susan Minette, b Nov., 1866.
31. Alba H   , b. Feb. 29, 1856.

22. JOHN HUNT FOSS, son of Robinson (16), born Dec. 9, 1831; married, first, Eliza Felker. She died, and he married, second, Augusta Felker. Children:

Charles, b. Nov. 23, 1855. George E., b. Sept. 9, 1859; m. Margaret E. Carter, Sept. 6, 1892, and had Harriet F., b. July 21, 1898. Theodora R., b. Feb. 17, 1903.
Child by second wife:
Lizzie, b. Dec. 5, 1862; m. Hanson Seavey; lived at Portsmouth.

23. HENRY D. FOSS, son of Robinson (16), born Sept. 18, 1832; married, Oct. 5, 1858, Clara A. Matthews. Children:

Henry Herman, b. Aug. 25, 1859; d. July 31, 1862. Lizzie, b. May 28, 1864; d. Nov. 8, 1892, at Boston. Robert, b. Oct. 18, 1869.

24. DANIEL MORRISON FOSS, son of Robinson (16), born March 10, 1834; married, Nov. 28, 1858, Chalcedony Foss. She died May 30, 1889. He served in the navy during the war, 1861-'65. Children:
    Christie, b. Jan. 30, 1859; m. Feb. 14, 1889, George S. Walker.
32. Arthur M., b. Oct. 15, 1868; m. Oct. 19, 1898, Blanche Berry.

25. ROBERT S. FOSS, son of Richard (17), born April 7, 1825; married Ann E. Moulton. He died Oct. 29, 1891. Enlisted and mustered into the service in 1862 in the Civil War. Children:
    Emily Jones, b. Aug. 16, 1852; m. 1884, Joseph W. Rand.
33. Lewis Henry, b. Sept. 19, 1853. Charles Edward, b. July 8, 1856; d. July 17, 1888. Anna Louise, b. Jan. 4, 1858. Ella Mary, b. May 11, 1860.

26. JOHN OREN FOSS, son of Richard (17), born Aug. 19, 1830; married, first, Nov. 10, 1853, Mary J. Green. She died May 11, 1864, and he married, second, May 24, 1866, Amanda Marden. He died Feb. 4, 1903. Children by first wife:
    Charles Henry, b. Nov. 23, 1855; d. June 21, 1861. Willey John, b. Dec. 3, 1857; m. Merrill; d. April 7, 1899. Carrie M., b. Feb. 28, 1860; m. Dec. 28, 1883, Hollis N. Marden. Mabel Jane, b. May 4, 1862; d. Jan. 23, 1876.
    Children by second wife:
    Lizzie Haven, b. Oct. 5, 1866; d. Charles Osmond, b. Sept. 8, 1867; drowned in Parsons' creek, July 4, 1881.
34. Herbert E., b. April 8, 1870; m. 1894, Lottie Odiorne. Edith C., b. May 27, 1873; m. April 9, 1896, Jedediah Rand. Ernest, m. June 17, 1903, Cora W. Drake. Myron.

27. JOSEPH S. FOSS, son of Joseph Remick (19), born Oct. 8, 1829; married, March, 1856, Lucy Ann Clark. She died Sept. 18, 1898. She had before marriage, John Clark, born Sept. 27, 1851. Child:
    Reinza, b. June 11, 1856; d. June 5, 1861.

28: JOSHUA MARDEN FOSS, son of Benjamin Marden (20), born Sept. 7, 1816; married, Jan. 14, 1841, Mehitable Foss. Removed to Haverhill; died July 4, 1901. Children:
    Mary, b. 1846; d. Frank M., b. June 14, 1853.

GENEALOGY.

29. JOEL N. FOSS, son of Benjamin Marden (20), born Dec. 7, 1821; married Adeline Locke. Child:
   Almira Pitman, b. May 26, 1850.

30. SYLVANUS W. FOSS, son of Hardison (21), born March 13, 1846; married, April 3, 1879, Ellen Philbrick. Child:
   Bertha, b. Feb. 27, 1880.

31. ALBA H. FOSS, son of Hardison (21), born Feb., 1856; married, first, Dec. 2, 1883, Minnie Brown. She died July 22, 1887, and he married, second, Nov. 4, 1891, Emma Hoyt. Child by first wife:
   Lena Forbes, b. July 4, 1887.
   Child by second wife:
   Analesa, b. March 26, 1900.

32. ARTHUR M. FOSS, son of Daniel Morrison (24), born Oct. 15, 1868; married, Oct. 19, 1898, Blanche M. Berry. Painter by trade. Children:
   Reginald, b. Dec. 17, 1900. Daughter, b. Sept. 10, 1903.

33. LEWIS HENRY FOSS, son of Robert S. (25), born Sept. 19, 1853; married, March 15, 1881, Lydia Viola Adams. Mason. Children:
   Emma L., b. Oct. 30, 1882.   Alice Adams, b. Sept. 2, 1884.   Mabel Josephine, b. Oct. 5, 1887.

34. HERBERT E. FOSS, son of John Oren (26), born April 8, 1870; married Feb. 5, 1894, Charlotte Odiorne. Child:
   ———, b. Sept. 2, 1894.

1. JOHN FOSS, married Abigail ———. Children:
2. Thomas (?). Abigail, b. Sept., 1731. Zachariah, m. Joanna ———; had Henry.
3. Joshua, b. June 12, 1738; m. John.

2. THOMAS FOSS, son of John (1), married, Sept. 18, 1760, Merribah, daughter of Thomas Rand. Removed to Barrington. Children:
   Hannah, b. Aug. 26, 1761. Merribah.

Hinkson Foss and Rachel Berry were married June 7, 1733.

3. JOSHUA FOSS, son of John (1), born June 12, 1738; married, Sept. 18, 1764, Abigail Locke. Children:
William, b. Oct. 15, 1765. Elizabeth, b. Jan. 22, 1768; m. David Hatch. Joshua, b. March 14, 1770; m. Elizabeth, dau. of Simon Locke; lived at Hollis, Me. David, b. Aug. 9, 1772; lived at Strafford.
4. John, b. Jan. 9, 1775. Job. b. March 22, 1777; m. first, Marden; m. second, widow Tilton; lived at Dover, N. Y.

4. JOHN FOSS, son of Joshua (3), born Jan. 9, 1775; married Elizabeth Titcomb. Removed to Chicago, Ill. Children:
Caroline T., b. 1806; m. Stephen Coffin; lived at Moultonborough. William Ham, b. 1807; m. Mary Drown. Lucinda, m. Hanson Caverly; lived at Bennington. Samuel, m. Eliza Haywood; lived at Chicago, Ill. Abigail, m. Bebee, M. D.; lived in Wisconsin. Robert, m. Harriett Spear; lived at Chicago, Ill. John, m. first, Lydia Troop; m. second, Hannah; lived at Chicago, Ill. Mary, m. Appleton.

FOYE.

JOHN FOYE was at Fort William and Mary (Great Island), Newcastle, from the 18th to the 31st of May, 1708. The Foye family came from the Shoals to Kittery, Me.

1. JOHN FOYE, probably a grandson of the foregoing, had a brother, Joseph, a sister, Betsey, who married a Sheppard, and a sister, Susan, who married Richard Mitchell. John married, first, Hannah Fernald; and second, Lydia Stevens. She died June 17, 1830, aged 94 years. He died Jan. 17, 1818, aged 82 years. Children:
2. John, b. Nov. 6, 1769.
3. Stephen.
4. William. Eunice, m. Benjamin Grace of Kittery; she committed suicide by hanging.

2. JOHN FOYE, son of John (1), born Nov. 6, 1769; married, first, Elizabeth Seavey. She died, and he married, second, Dec. 1, 1805, widow Hannah Rand. She died Feb. 7, 1829, and he married, third, Nov. 5, 1829, widow Martha Odiorne. Was a member of the Alarm List under Capt. Wedgewood during the War of 1812. Children:

Eliza, bapt. Oct. 9, 1796; d. April 16, 1826.
5. Nathaniel Graves, b. Sept. 10, 1798.
6. John, b. July 28, 1800.

3. STEPHEN FOYE, son of John (1), married, April 1, 1804, Hannah N. Mason. Children:

Almira, m. William F. Craig. Hannah J., m. Abel C. Baldwin. Martha T., m. Charles Rozzell. Charles, d. at Boston.

4. WILLIAM FOYE, son of John (1), married, first, Feb. 23, 1795, Hannah Seavey. She died, and he married, second, Nov. 15, 1804, Hannah Rand. He died Aug. 28, 1824, aged 50 years. Children by first wife:

Lydia Stevens, b. March 22, 1795; m. Jan. 7, 1813, Hopley Yeaton. Thomas Fernald, b. Nov. 13, 1796; m. Nov. 28, 1822, Clarissa Willey. Stephen, bapt. May 5, 1799; d. aged four years.
7. William L.

Children by second wife:

Hannah, d. unm. Eunice, m. J. L. Hickerman; d. April 24, 1866; lived at Cincinnati, Ohio. John Oren, m. Mary Cushman. Joseph, became insane and d., 1872, in a Mass. asylum. Eliza Ann, m. John Hodgdon. Apphia, m. Robert Holbrook; he was lost at sea, and she d. Feb. 10, 1873. Stephen. Adeline, m. Gilson.

5. NATHANIEL GRAVES FOYE, son of John (2), born Sept. 10, 1798; married, Aug. 10, 1820, Martha Locke Dow. She died Sept. 18, 1885. He died Jan. 27, 1873. Was a member of Capt. Ephraim Philbrick's company in the war of 1812. Children:

Mary Elizabeth, b. Feb. 25, 1821; m. Dec. 9, 1841, Joseph Disco Jenness. Ann Cecelia, b. April 22, 1822; m. June 7, 1843, Samuel Marden.
8. Orion Leavitt, b. Aug. 9, 1824. Eliza, b. Jan. 25, 1827; d. June 22, 1843. Martha Abby, b. March 10, 1829; d. July 15, 1844. Fidelea E., b. Oct. 13, 1830; d. May 26, 1861.
9. James Nathaniel, b. April 27, 1833. Ellen Ruthdian, b. March 6, 1835; m. Joseph Disco Jenness. Sarah Ann, b. March 25, 1837; d. Aug. 31, 1838. Sophia Jenness, b. March 8, 1839. John Harrison, b. March 6, 1841; member of Co. K, 13th N. H. Vols.; killed in a skirmish near Suffolk, Va.

6. JOHN FOYE, son of John (2), born July 28, 1800; married, Sept. 24, 1822, Hannah Berry. He died Sept. 25, 1884. She died Aug. 27, 1886. Children:

Amos Dolbee, b. April 11, 1823. Hannah Elizabeth, b. June 13, 1825;
d. March 4, 1900. A. Mandana, b. Feb. 18, 1828; m. June 30, 1851,
Jeremiah Boyce; d. Feb. 8, 1866. Ann Mary, b. March 14, 1831;
d. Oct. 29, 1851. John Wesley, b. Oct. 5, 1836; m. March, 1871,
Mary Jane Seavey.

7. WILLIAM L. FOYE, son of William (4), married, first, Nov. 7, 1822, Eunice Weeks. She died, and he married, second, Hannah G. Williams. He died Aug. 3, 1856. Children by first wife:

Mary Hannah, b. 1823; killed, Aug. 6, 1829, by a cart falling on her.
John W. Samuel D., b. June 17, 1827.

Children by second wife:
Josiah W. Mary H., d. July 3, 1862. Luther P. Stephen J.
Thomas F. Eunice A. Isaac and Charles, twins, b. 1842; Charles
m. Hill.

8. ORION LEAVITT FOYE, son of Nathaniel Graves (5), born Aug. 9, 1824; married, Nov. 4, 1852, Sarah Abby (Cotton), widow of Abraham Jenness; died Oct. 5, 1903, aged 79 years. Children:

Morris Cotton, b. Nov. 7, 1853; m. Nellie Clough; merchant in Portsmouth. Eliza Josephine, b. May 25, 1855; m. Nov. 20, 1878, Herman W. Oxford.

9. JAMES NATHANIEL FOYE, son of Nathaniel Graves (5), born April 27, 1833; married Elizabeth Daker of Dixon, Ill. Children:

Edward. Charles. Mattie. Frank Harrison.

FRASER.

JOHN FRASER, married, Sept. 29, 1880, Ella Maria Parsons. Electrician. Children:

Julius Warren, b. Jan. 21, 1882. Frederick John, b. March 25, 1883. Susan Parsons, b. Oct. 4, 1885; d. March 27, 1888. Phillip, b. June 24, 1892; d. 1892.

FRENCH.

1. DAVID FRENCH, married Clara W. Wiggin, 1812. She died June 8, 1828, and he married, second, Susan E. Burley in 1830; she died Jan. 4, 1870; he died Nov. 3, 1862. Lived in Stratham. Children:

2. David J. Otis, m. Mary Marston of North Hampton. Clara P. Martha, b. 1814; m. 1862, Dea. Jonathan Locke of Rye.

2. DAVID J. FRENCH, son of David (1), married ———. Children:

Daniel James. David Alfred. John Otis. Clara Etta. Rachel Emma, m. Jan. 15, 1889, Oris Garland, son of Joseph W. Martha Bell.

BRADBURY C. FRENCH, married, Jan. 7, 1827, Mary Batchelder. Removed to Nottingham. Children:

George B., b. May 11, 1828. Alvin C. M., b. May 4, 1831; d. at sea. Josiah B., b. March 15, 1834; m. Martin of Newcastle. Mary Amanda, b. April 17, 1842.

FROST.

A Frost came from Durham and lived and owned the Stephen Foye farm, subsequently by John S. Odiorne, Thomas R. Clark, and others. He also owned lands at Durham. James Thomas lived with him, and his cousin Olive Thompson, who married Samuel Odiorne.

Aaron, son of Aaron Frost, was baptized Aug. 4, 1771.

FULLER.

1. JAMES FULLER, son of John of Hampton, born March 27, 1679; married Mary ———. Children:

James, b. Dec. 2, 1704.
2. Joseph (?). John, b. March 4, 1711. Mary, b. Aug. 17, 1713. Elizabeth, b. June 28, 1715.
3. Jeremiah, b. Sept. 25, 1717. Lovey, b. May 14, 1721.

2. JOSEPH FULLER, probably son of James (1), married, March 8, 1733, Joanna Seavey. Children:

Elizabeth, b. Sept. 14, 1733; d. young. Joanna, b. Dec. 6, 1734; d. young. Mary, b. 1736. Joanna, b. 1737. Joseph, b. 1738. Elizabeth, b. Sept. 25, 1740. James, b. 1743. Hannah, b. 1747. Rachel, b. 1749. David, b. 1751. Sarah, b. 1753. Olly, b. 1755.

3. JEREMIAH FULLER, son of James (1), born Sept. 25, 1717; married, July 26, 1745, Mary Scadgel. Children:

George, b. May 24, 1746. Richard, b. July 21, 1747. Sarah, b. 1749. Margaret, b. 1751. Christopher, b. 1752. Mary, b. 1754. Deborah, b. 1756. Jane, b. 1757. Jeremiah S., b. 1760.
4. Theodore Atkinson, b. 1762.

4. THEODORE ATKINSON FULLER, son of Jeremiah (3), born 1762; married, first, Nov., 1780, Sarah Abbott. She died, and he married, second, Oct., 1799, Hannah Jenness. Child by first wife:

———, m. Hartshorn.
Children by second wife:
Nancy, m. Joshua Stackford. Joseph, m. Gale.

GARLAND.

1. JOHN GARLAND, probably son of Peter, of England, was here as early as 1652.

In 1650, John Garland with others from Hampton were forbidden from cutting any timber in Exeter, but he had a lot granted him if he stay one year in the town of Exeter. He married, first, Oct. 26, 1652, Elizabeth Chapman; second, 1654, widow Elizabeth Chase, daughter of Thomas Philbrick. He died Jan. 4, 1672, "aged about fifty years." Children by second wife:
2. John, b. March 11, 1655.
3. Jacob, b. Dec. 20, 1656.
4. Peter, b. Nov. 25, 1659.

2. JOHN GARLAND, son of John (1), born March 11, 1655; married, first, Dec. 24, 1673, Elizabeth Robinson, who died April 15, 1715, aged 62 years. He married, second, Sept. 29, 1715, Mary Philbrook of Greenland.

He took the oath of allegiance in December, 1678, in Hampton; was representative to General Assembly in 1693. Impressed as a soldier for 28 days at Oyster river in 1696. Was at Fort William and Mary, Newcastle, in 1708. Children:

Elizabeth, b. July 16, 1674. John, b. Oct. 12, 1675; d. Oct. 6, 1676. Esther, b. April 6, 1679; m. Jan. 12, 1702, William Powell. Peter, b. Dec. 10, 1681; d. Dec. 21, 1755; m. Elizabeth Clifford. Mary, b. March 14, 1683; m. Israel Clifford. Sarah, b. Oct. 18, 1685.

3. JACOB GARLAND, son of John (1), born Dec. 20, 1656; married, June 17, 1682, Rebecca, daughter of Thomas Sears of Newbury, Mass. Lived at Newbury and Hamp-

ton. Took the oath of allegiance in Hampton in 1678. He was one of eight persons sent from Hampton in 1676 to defend the town of Marlborough, Mass. Children:

Jacob, b. Oct. 26, 1682, in Newbury; d. young. Rebecca, b. Dec. 3, 1683, in Newbury; d. young.
5. Jacob, b. July 3, 1686, in Hampton. Mary, b. about 1688; m. Thomas Dearborn. Thomas, b. March 9, 1692; d. young. Tabitha, bapt. Dec. 11, 1698, together with Thomas and Joseph. Joseph, b. Dec. 29, 1697; probably d. young. John, b. Sept. 28, 1700; m. Elizabeth Philbrook. Elizabeth, b. Sept. 28, 1700. Thomas, bapt. Jan. 3, 1702; m.

4. PETER GARLAND, son of John (1), born Nov. 25, 1659; married, first, Elizabeth, who died Feb. 19, 1688, aged 88 years; and he married, second, Sarah, daughter of John Taylor. "Sloop *New Design*, 16 tons, was bought in Boston in 1705 by Peter Garland and Samuel Nudd, mariners, for £106; sailed between Boston and Hampton; had no guns." (Dow.) Children by first wife:

Peter, b. Oct. 4, 1686. Samuel, b. Feb. 2, 1688; shoemaker; lived at Kingston, N. H.
Children by second wife:
6. Jonathan, b. Oct. 28, 1689.
7. John, b. April 13, 1692. James, b. about 1694. Mary, b. Sept. 7, 1699; m. Henry Moulton. Abigail, b. Feb. 25, 1704; m. Worthington Moulton.

5. JACOB GARLAND, son of Jacob (3), born July 3, 1686; married, first, April 28, 1708, Hannah, daughter of Josiah Sanborn; second, Oct. 24, 1723, Sarah, daughter of Abraham Drake. Children by first wife:

Joseph, bapt. May 27, 1711; m. Dec. 3, 1736, Jane Stickney. Rebecca, bapt. Jan. 4, 1713; m. Benjamin Towle. Jacob, bapt. July 21, 1716; m. Hannah ———. Hannah, bapt. June, 1718. Simon, bapt. June 10, 1722; m.; resided at Hampton Falls. Sarah, bapt. June 20, 1725.

6. JONATHAN GARLAND, son of Peter (4), born Oct. 28, 1689; shoemaker; married, Oct. 21, 1714, Rachel, daughter of Dea. Samuel Dow; lived in Hampton. He had a bark mill, currying shop, shoe shop and tan pits. Children:

Samuel, b. Nov. 21, 1716; m. Lydia Moulton. Jonathan, b. July 16, 1719; m. widow Bethia Taylor. Abigail, b. March 6, 1722; m. David Marston. Mary, b. Jan. 20, 1724; d. young. Sarah, b. May 12, 1725; m. Benjamin Tuck. James, b. Nov. 13, 1726; d. July 13, 1750. Rachel, b. May 25, 1729; m. Benjamin Johnson. Anne, b. July 1, 1731; d. Dec. 27, 1735. Joseph, b. May 11, 1734; m. Hannah Marston. Simon, b. Jan. 18, 1736; d. March 3, 1738. Simon, b. Oct. 7, 1738; d. Dec. 2, 1759. Mary, b. April 6, 1741; m. Samuel Blake.

7. JOHN GARLAND, son of Peter (4), born April 13, 1692; married, Jan. 12, 1716, Elizabeth, daughter of John Dearborn. He settled in Rye about 1720, and was living as late as 1752. She died about 1774-'76. He was a large owner of lands in Hampton, Rye, Portsmouth, Nottingham, and Barrington. Was in service at Fort William and Mary, 1708, under the crown. Children:

Peter, b. April 24, 1717; d. June 3, 1729.
8. John, b. May 18, 1719. Sarah, bapt. Jan. 8, 1721; m. Deacon Francis Jenness; lived at Cotton Drake's. Abigail, b. Jan. 11, 1723; m. Nov. 15, 1748, Samuel C. Jenness. Elizabeth, b. March 13, 1724; m. Richard Locke.
9. Simon, b. Jan. 16, 1726; m. Mary, b. April 27, 1728; m. Jan. 3, 1753, Col. Jonathan Brown.
10. Peter, b. July 24, 1732.
11. Benjamin, b. Oct. 29, 1734.

8. JOHN GARLAND, son of John (7), born May 18, 1719; married, Feb. 14, 1744, Mary Rand. Removed to Barrington. Children:

Mary, b. May 21, 1744. John, b. March 27, 1746. Elizabeth, b. March 31, 1748. Olly, b. April 30, 1750. Sarah, b. March 11, 1752. Richard, b. March 11, 1754. Susannah, b. March 22, 1756. Nathaniel, b. Aug. 12, 1758. Abijah, b. July 16, 1760. Abegonia, b. June 17, 1763. Joseph, b. April 12, 1765. Benjamin, b. July 11, 1767.

9. SIMON GARLAND, son of John (7), born Jan. 16, 1726; married, first, Jan. 3, 1754, Elizabeth, daughter of Joseph Brown; second, Dec. 20, 1781, widow Rachel Morrison. The record states of the last marriage that "he took her naked and covered her in presence of Eleanor Berry and Patience Marston." Children by first wife:

Mary, b. 1756; m. John Robie of North Hampton.
12. Simon, b. 1758.
13. Joseph, b. May 6, 1760. Elizabeth, b. 1763.
14. John, b. 1767.

10. PETER GARLAND, son of John (7), born July 24, 1732; married, Sept. 15, 1757, Mary, daughter of Jonathan Leavitt. He was a blacksmith. Peter and Benjamin Garland and Capt. Joseph Parsons, all of Rye, were a committee to get soldiers for the Continental army. He died April 26, 1816. Children:

Mary, b. 1758; d. unm., May 17, 1843. Abigail, b. about 1760; m. 1780, Isaac Lane; lived at Chester. John, b. 1762; d. unm. April 23, 1837.
15. Jonathan, b. Oct. 11, 1764.
16. Levi, b. 1766.
17. Peter, b. July, 1768. Anne or Nancy, b. 1770; m. Nov. 13, 1798, Joseph Smith; lived at Chester.
18. Benjamin, b. 1772. Elizabeth, b. Sept. 28, 1775; d. unm. Jan. 16, 1847. Sarah, b. 1779; m. Dec. 3, 1805, Benjamin Dalton.

11. COL. BENJAMIN GARLAND, son of John (7), born Oct. 29, 1734; married, Dec. 5, 1757, Sarah, daughter of John Jenness. Inn keeper. Lived in the old Thomas G. Berry house, Rye Center, now owned by Richard R. Higgins (1903). Col. Benjamin was a minute man in the Revolutionary War and a large owner of land and property in Rye. When he returned from the war he brought home a black servant called "Black Prince," whom he bought for a keg of rum. He died May 2, 1802, and she died Feb. 18, 1803. Children:

19. John, b. Oct. 4, 1758. Elizabeth, b. Oct., 1760; m. July 17, 1777, Joseph L. Seavey. Abigail, b. March, 1763; m. Aug. 14, 1785, Jonathan Jenness. Sally, b. Oct., 1764; while a child fell in the barn and afterwards died of lockjaw. Benjamin, b. Jan., 1767; insane; d. unm., Jan. 14, 1835.
20. Lieut. Amos, b. May, 1768. Polly or Mary, b. April 27, 1770; m. Nov. 10, 1786, Ebenezer Berry. The same night Thomas G. Berry was born; lived on the Reuel Garland farm; she afterwards refused to live with her husband and he went to New Orleans, and she returned and lived at home. Sarah, b. July, 1772; d. unm. July 4, 1846.
21. William, b. June 10, 1775. Thomas, b. August, 1777; d. young.

12. SIMON GARLAND, son of Simon (9), born 1758; married Abigail Norton and removed to Nottingham. Children:

Simon. Elizabeth, m. John Mack. Joseph, m. Sarah Batchelder.

13. JOSEPH GARLAND, son of Simon (9), born May 6, 1760; married Patience Marston. She died Sept. 9, 1844, aged 83 years. He died March 8, 1846. Children:

John, b. Sept. 26, 1784; d. unm. Oct. 28, 1854. Betsey Godfrey, b. Jan., 1789; d. June, 1791. Mehitable G., b. June 12, 1792; d. April 26, 1873.
22. Joseph, b. May 9, 1805.

14. JOHN GARLAND, son of Simon (9), born 1767; married, Jan. 28, 1790, Abigail Seavey. He died Nov. 6, 1826, and she died March 13, 1851, aged 81 years. Children:

23. Amos Seavey, b. 1789. Betsey Brown, b. 1791; m. 1823, Ephraim Seavey.
24. Simon G., b. Feb. 16, 1793.
25. William Seavey, b. 1800. Mary.

15. JONATHAN GARLAND, son of Peter (10), born Oct. 11, 1764; married, May 14, 1797, Betsey Woodman, who was born Sept. 28, 1773. Children:

Harriett, b. April 13, 1801. Eliza, b. Sept. 4, 1803; m. first, about 1826, Thomas Marden; m. second, June 1, 1853, David Brown of North Hampton. Gilman, b. Aug. 14, 1801; d. young.
26. William Cutler, b. March 3, 1810. Emily, b. Sept. 4, 1806; m. June 6, 1829, Richard Jenness Sleeper.

16. LEVI GARLAND, son of Peter (10), born 1766; married, first, Nov. 24, 1789, Lucy Salter; died Jan. 2, 1814, aged 45 years; married, second, 1814, Nancy Leavitt. He died Feb. 4, 1857. Was a member of Capt. Coleman's cavalry in the War of 1812. Children:

27. Levi, b. June 11, 1793. John Langdon, bapt. April 3, 1795.

17. PETER GARLAND, son of Peter (10), born July, 1768; married, Sept. 30, 1792, Mehitable Seavey. He died July 24, 1804. Children:

Thomas Leavitt, bapt. June 16, 1793; d. Sept., 1796. William, b. Sept. 9, 1795; m. Nabby Knowles; no children. Sally, b. March 24, 1798; m. Jonathan Jenness; d. Nov. 8, 1889. Polly Leavitt, b. Dec. 12, 1799; m. Dec. 19, 1824, Joseph Jenness, Jr.
28. Moses Leavitt, b. March 21, 1801.

18. BENJAMIN GARLAND, son of Peter (10), born 1772; married, May 15, 1803, Fanny Seavey. Children:

Charlotte, b. Aug. 30, 1803; m. 1827, William S. Garland. Data, bapt. July 16, 1809; m. Leonard Lang. Sarah Ann, b. April 12, 1813; m. Daniel Brown. Hannah, b. Dec. 20, 1814; m. first, Oct. 27, 1834, Ira Brown, Jr.; m. second, E. S. Wedgewood; m. third, Alfred G. Jenness; d. Feb. 20, 1889.
29. Moses, b. Jan. 30, 1819.
30. Rufus I., b. July, 1827.

19. JOHN GARLAND, son of Col. Benjamin (11), born Oct. 4, 1758; married, Oct. 18, 1778, Abigail Perkins. He died March 24, 1844. Abigail Perkins was one of seven beautiful daughters. She died June 23, 1844. He lived on the farm now owned and occupied by Reuel Shapley. He with a pair of oxen and some others hauled a load of powder taken from Fort William and Mary by the Continentals to the Fort at Newport, R. I. He was a soldier in the Revolutionary War in Capt. Joseph Parsons' company. Children:

31. John, b. Nov. 23, 1776. Thomas, b. March 3, 1779; d. 1795. Abigail, b. Aug. 14, 1782; m. Aug. 11, 1803, John Wilkes Parsons, M. D. James, b. Nov. 15, 1784; d. unm. July 21, 1850.
32. Benjamin, b. July 30, 1791.
33. Reuel, b. Dec. 31, 1798.

20. LIEUT. AMOS GARLAND, son of Benjamin (11), born May, 1768; married, Nov. 18, 1800, Olive Jenness; died Dec. 16, 1830. He built the Congregational parsonage, and died Feb. 21, 1833. Children:

Eliza J., b. July 1, 1801; m. first, Jonathan Drake; m. second, Benjamin W. Marden. Olive, b. March 25, 1806; m. June 23, 1825, Simon Moulton. Sarah Ann, b. 1811; d. Oct. 11, 1812, aged six months. Caroline, b. Sept., 1816; m. Dec. 23, 1838, Jonathan Dearborn Locke. Sarah Ann, b. June 16, 1815; d. June 25, 1815.

21. WILLIAM GARLAND, son of Benjamin (11), born June 10, 1775; married, July 8, 1806, Elizabeth Howe. Was a merchant in Portsmouth. He died July 31, 1820, and she died Sept. 5, 1866, aged 81 years. Children:

William A., b. May 14, 1807; d. May 25, 1840. Elizabeth H., b. April 9, 1809; m. April 4, 1827, Charles P. Hill. David Howe, b. July 7, 1810; d. Dec. 11, 1838. Alfred B., b. Feb. 25, 1812; d. Jan. 24, 1841 or '42. Caroline P., b. Dec. 11, 1813; m. Nov. 25, 1835, Rev. Oliver Ayer of Plaistow.

34. Thomas Berry, b. Aug. 20, 1817.

22. JOSEPH GARLAND, son of Joseph (13), born May 9, 1805; married Elizabeth H. Garland. She died Dec. 17, 1898. Children:

Elmira, b. June 22, 1838; d. Aug. 31, 1875. Clara D., b. May 22, 1840; m. Thomas Marston, and was divorced; d. Oct. 21, 1866. Alfred Curtis, b. March 12, 1849; insane; d. Dec. 5, 1869. Laura E., b. Dec. 25, 1851; m. Nov. 18, 1869, William S. Brown; lived at Hampton. Emeline A., b. July 14, 1855; d. Jan. 7, 1875.

23. AMOS SEAVEY GARLAND, son of John (14), born 1789; married, Nov. 28, 1816, Martha Seavey. He died Feb. 21, 1843. Children:

Lucinda R., b. Sept., 1817; m. July 3, 1850, Alfred G. Jenness. Mary Patten, b. Feb. 5. Martha, b. Sept., ——; m. June 7, 1843, Alfred G. Jenness.

35. Samuel Patten, b. Feb. 5, 1821. Semira, b. Dec. 23, 1828; d. Nov. 24, 1884. Mary L., b. Nov., 1832. Cilden, b. Aug. 12, 1835; d. at Portsmouth.

24. SIMON G. GARLAND, son of John (14), born Feb. 16, 1793; married, first, Sept. 11, 1825, Mary Ann Garland. She died Oct. 13, 1826, and he married, second, 1829, Sally Knowles. Child by first wife:

Simon Elbridge, b. Nov. 24, 1825.

Children by second wife:

36. Oliver Perry, b. May 26, 1832. Nathan W., b. Feb. 26, 1835; d. Feb. 3, 1836. Orlando, b. May 31, 1837; m. first, Oct. 19, 1862, Elizabeth J. Rand; m. second, Mary Lowe. Mary Ann, b. Aug. 6, 1840; m. Jenness Marden. Horace Woodbury, b. Jan. 6, 1844; m. Dec. 27, 1869, Nettie R. Whidden, b. Oct. 6, 1848, and had Florence W., b. Nov. 12, 1881, and Edna C., b. Nov. 20, 1882; he died in 1901.

25. WILLIAM SEAVEY GARLAND, son of John (14), born 1800; married, first, 1827, Charlotte Garland; died May 11, 1845; married, second, Anna L. Dalton. She died Dec. 25, 1902. Children:

GENEALOGY.

Gideon, b. 1830; d. March 9, 1858. Amos R., b. Aug. 14, 1850; d. Aug. 31, 1869.

26. WILLIAM CUTTER GARLAND, son of Jonathan (15), born March 3, 1810; married, first, Oct., 1834, Mary Marden. She died Feb. 15, 1856, aged 41 years; he married, second, Oct. 21, 1860, Elvira McDaniels. She died July 2, 1884. He died Jan. 15, 1894. Children:

Elizabeth Fidelia, b. April 26, 1835; m. Jan. 31, 1861, Charles Seavey; d. Sept. 16, 1864. William Harvey, b. April 24, 1839; m. Mary Dalton; lived at Gloucester, Mass. Emmons Cutter, b. Oct. 30, 1840; m. Roberts of Maine; she d. March, 1875, leaving a dau. b. Feb., 1875.
37. Charles David, b. Oct. 1, 1849.

27. LEVI GARLAND, son of Levi (16), born June 14, 1793; married, first, Nov. 21, 1811, Polly Perkins; died Jan. 26, 1829; married, second, May 29, 1838, Mary Watson, born Sept., 1799; died April 3, 1892. He died Dec. 11, 1863. Children by first wife:

Lucy Ann, b. Jan. 8, 1812; m. 1832, William Marden; d. Aug. 24, 1870. Mary Jane, b. 1814; d. Nov. 18, 1826. Lucretia Emeline, b. 1815; m. Horatio Hobbs. Sarah Adeline, b. 1816; m. April, 1838, Moses C. Philbrick. Julia H., m. Eben Marden.
38. Edward, b. 1821. Izette, b. 1824; m. Lemuel Bunker; d. March 8, 1850. Polly Jane, b. Sept., 1836; m. John Ira Rand.

28. MOSES LEAVITT GARLAND, son of Peter (17), born March 21, 1801; married, first, July 18, 1822, Lucretia Locke; died Dec. 22, 1869; married, second, Nov. 26, 1871, Nancy, widow of James W. Locke. He died Aug. 24, 1890. Children:

39. Charles, b. Sept. 11, 1822.
40. Gilman, b. Nov. 27, 1825. Mary Abby, b. June 3, 1841; m. Warren Brown of North Hampton. Malvina, b. Dec. 1, 1844.

29. MOSES GARLAND, son of Benjamin (18), born Jan. 30, 1819; married, March 8, 1840, Adeline S. Jenness. Children:

Charlotte Ann, b. June 30, 1840; m. Jan. 31, 1861, Alfred V. Seavey; d. March 10, 1869. Albert W., b. June 19, 1842; d. March 8, 1862. Clara J., b. April 14, 1844; m. Dana Jenness. Irving W., b. Feb. 10 or 16, 1850; m. Dec. 19, 1877, Anna A. Whidden; had Theodata, m. Dec. 6, 1900, Fred L. Cotton of North Hampton. Mariah A., b. Jan. 31, 1854; d. April 17, 1856.

30. RUFUS I. GARLAND, son of Benjamin (18), born July, 1827; married Semira P. Jenness. She died Dec. 22, 1884, and he died Dec. 24, 1891. Children:

    Viennah F., b. May 27, 1852; m. Nov. 11, 1868, Horace S. Brown; lived at North Hampton.
41. Morris Jenness, b. April 30, 1858.

31. JOHN GARLAND, son of John (19), born Nov. 23, 1776; married, Aug. 15, 1799, Elizabeth Parsons. She died Feb. 20, 1843. Children:

    Mary Ann, b. March 25, 1800; m. Simon Garland. Hannah Parsons, b. Aug. 11, 1802; m. May 6, 1824, Reed V. Rand; lived at Portsmouth.
42. Joseph Parsons, b. Dec. 20, 1804.
43. Oliver, b. Nov. 25, 1806. Abigail, b. Jan. 13, 1809; d. Dec. 23, 1828
44. Samuel Parsons, b. April 30, 1811.
45. John Calvin, b. Nov., 1813.
46. David, b. March, 1816. Julia Ann, b. Nov. 4, 1821; m. Dec. 28, 1844, Gardner T. Locke; she d. July 14, 1873.

32. BENJAMIN GARLAND, son of John (19), born July 30, 1791; married Polly Philbrick. Children:

    Mary, b. Sept. 29, 1819; m. George Blaisdell; lived at Epping. Thomas, b. Sept. 13, 1821; m. first, Mary Williams; m. second, Lucy Furber; had Abby A., drowned, July 30, 1873, in Newington Bay; Ann M.; lived at Newmarket. Charles, b. May 13, 1823; m. Lucy F. Dearborn; had Charles Barrows, d. Feb., 1870; lived at Newmarket.

33. REUEL GARLAND, son of John (19), born Dec. 31, 1798; married, June 11, 1826, Patty Locke. Blacksmith and farmer. A member of Capt. Ephraim Philbrick's company in the War of 1812. She died Feb. 17, 1866. He died Aug. 28, 1869. Children:

    Elvira, b. Oct. 23, 1827; m. April 18, 1857, Joseph G. Jenness; d. Oct. 13, 1864. Abigail P., b. Feb. 12, 1832; d. Dec. 22, 1865.
47. Joseph William, b. Sept. 4, 1836. Thomas Reuel, b. Feb. 7, 1839; d. Oct. 9, 1854; accidentally shot himself.

34. THOMAS BERRY GARLAND, son of William (21), born Aug. 20, 1817; married, Dec. 10, 1842, Harriett Kimball of Littleton, Mass. Lived in Dover. Children:

William A., b. Jan. 13, 1844; d. Dec. 1, 1865, at Augusta, Ga. Elizabeth, b. March 30, 1845; m. Feb. 25, 1868, D. Hall Rice of Lowell, Mass.; had Lepine Hall, b. Feb. 22, 1870; William Alfred, b. July 28, 1871; d. Oct. 2, 1871. Alfred Kimball, b. Oct. 24, 1849. Caroline Harwood, b. Jan. 25, 1854. Charles, b. April 16, 1856; d. Aug. 18, 1856.

35. SAMUEL PATTEN GARLAND, son of Amos Seavey (23), born Feb. 5, 1821; married, April 5, 1850, Eliza D. Marston. Children:

Martha H., b. Nov. 18, 1851; d. March 21, 1882. Amos, b. April 7, 1853; m. Ida Mayo. Mary Patten, b. Dec. 22, 1855. Eliza Ella, b. Jan. 12, 1858; m. July 8, 1882, Clarence A. Goss. Sarah L., b. May 9, 1860. Samuel Austin, b. Aug. 11, 1867. Gertrude, b. Feb. 5, 1870.

36. OLIVER PERRY GARLAND, son of Simon G. (24), born May 26, 1832; married Frances Frazier of Gloucester, Mass., who was born in Nova Scotia. She died in 1876. Children:

Melissa, b. July 16, 1859; m. June 29, 1884, Horace Mace. Charles Frost, b. Aug. 8, 1864; d. Lizzie Junkins, b. Nov. 12, 1873; d. Dec. 15, 1876. Fanny E., b. April 16, 1870; m. Sept. 10, 1894, Allen F. Eisiner.

37. CHARLES DAVID GARLAND, son of William Cutter (26), born Oct. 1, 1849; married, Nov. 3, 1869, Eliza J. Garland. Merchant and justice of the peace, West Rye. Children:

Susie Emma, b. Sept. 12, 1873; m. Sept. 12, 1892, Gilman Walker. 48. William E.

38. EDWARD L. GARLAND, son of Levi (27), born 1821; married, July 2, 1845, Elvira Dalton. She died March 18, 1898. He died July 7, 1872. Children:

Mary W., m. April 9, 1866, Samuel G. Smart. Annette. Eliza Jane, b. May 7, 1854; m. Nov. 3, 1869, Charles D. Garland.

39. CHARLES GARLAND, son of Moses Leavitt (28), born Sept. 11, 1822; married Sophia Jenness. Children:

Emma L., b. April 22, 1855. Walter, b. April 27, 1858; died.

40. GILMAN GARLAND, son of Moses Leavitt (28), born Nov. 27, 1825; married Martha J. Jenness. Child:

James Filmore, d.

41. MORRIS JENNESS GARLAND, son of Rufus I. (30), born April 30, 1858; married Emma Manson. Child:
Harold B., b. June 9, 1888.

42. JOSEPH PARSONS GARLAND, son of John (31), born Dec. 20, 1804; married, first, Eunice Kenney; second, widow Leavitt. Lived at Saco, Me. Children:
James. Parsons. Jerome. Elizabeth.

43. OLIVER GARLAND, son of John (31), born Nov. 25, 1806; married Mary Tarleton of Newcastle. He died April 20, 1887. Child:
Leander, b. 1830; m. Yeaton.

44. SAMUEL PARSONS GARLAND, son of John (31), born April 30, 1811; married, first, Hannah Marston; married, second ———. Lived at North Hampton. Children by first wife:
Mary Abby. Sarah Elizabeth. Hannah Jane.
Child by second wife:
George W.

45. JOHN CALVIN GARLAND, son of John (31), born Nov. 26, 1813; married, first, Jan. 4, 1835, Elizabeth Spead; second, Caroline Foss; third, Jan. 19, 1884, Elizabeth Riley. He died April 28, 1889. Farmer. Children:
John Wesley, b. Sept. 2, 1837; d. April 9, 1850. Calvin Thompson, b. June 15, 1839; m. May 21, 1877, Elizabeth M. Evans. Marshall W., b. May 17, 1841; killed in Florida during the Civil War. Charles William, b. April 6, 1843; m. July 12, 1871, Mrs. Helen McKee; residence, Oklahoma. Elizabeth Ann, b. June 17, 1845; m. first, J. C. Frost; second, Woodbury Brown. Henrietta, b. July 15, 1846; m. Dec. 9, 1869, Moses Brown. Abby Annah, b. Aug. 21, 1849; m. Nov. 24, 1868, Nathan Knowles; d. 1895. Franklin, b. 1854; d. 1855.

46. DAVID GARLAND, son of John (31), born March, 1816; married, Oct. 22, 1839, Mary Trickey. He died Oct. 29, 1846, and she married, second, Charles C. Marden, and was divorced. Children:
Augenette, b. Dec. 3, 1841; d. July 29, 1858. Albert Sumner, b. April 9, 1843; m. Anna Streeter; lives at Boston, Mass. Estelle, b. Jan. 2, 1845; m. Jan. 28, 1869, John W. Warner of North Hampton.

GENEALOGY.   367

47. JOSEPH WILLIAM GARLAND, son of Reuel (33), born Sept. 4, 1836; married, Oct. 22, 1860, Anna D. Drake. Children:

Joseph Oris, b. March 26, 1861; m. Jan. 16, 1889, Emma French. Elvira Jenness, b. Nov. 19, 1868; d. Aug. 18, 1872. James Weston, b. May 17, 1871; m. 1893.

48. WILLIAM E. GARLAND, son of Charles David (37), married, Feb. 23, 1899, Ethel M. Locke. Child:

Edna May, b. Sept 20, 1899.

SIMON GARLAND, perhaps son of Simon (12), and Abigail of Nottingham, married Rachel Morrison of Portsmouth. Children:

John, b. 1805; m. Nancy Doe. Samuel, b. 1807; m. Clara Broad. Elizabeth H., b. Sept. 21, 1811; m. Joseph Garland; d. Dec. 17, 1898. Daniel, m. Elizabeth Burnham. David, m. Mary Jane Doe. Mary Caroline.

GATES.

STOVER GATES, of Vermont, married Mrs. Martha (Trefethern), widow of Woodbury Green. Child:

Charles, b. July 21, 1868.

GODFREY.

JOHN GODFREY, married, Nov. 25, 1801, Abigail Seavey. She died Dec. 9, 1819. Children:

Susan, m. first, April 6, 1820, Josiah Knowles; second, Moulton; lived at Tamworth. Anna Brown, bapt. 1806. Abigail, bapt. July 16, 1809. Nancy, m. Abner Moulton. Elizabeth, m. Atwood. John, b. 1816; d. Dec. 29, 1817.

GOSS.

The name appears in various spellings:—Gors, Gaus, Gosse, and Goss. Robert Gosse was of Portsmouth in 1693, and probably was the same Robert who settled at Greenland, near Great Bay.

1. RICHARD Goss, a twin brother of Robert of Greenland, married Martha ―――, she living in 1739. He had 20 acres common land granted to him in 1701. The land is

now (1903) owned by L. B. Parsons and Daniel J. Parsons. Children:
2. Richard. Mary.
3. Jonathan.
4. Thomas. John W.
5. Jethro. Patty, b. 1714; m. Sept. 21, 1738, Josiah Webster; d. Nov. 18, 1798. Margaret. Rachel.

2. RICHARD GOSS, son of Richard (1), married Rachel ————. He died before Aug. 4, 1735; and she married, second, Jan. 6, 1737, Job Chapman. Children:
Abigail, b. Oct. 2, 1724; m. Nov. 27, 1746, Joseph Brown. Margaret, b. Feb. 18, 1731.

3. JONATHAN GOSS, son of Richard (1), married, May 22, 1735, Salome Locke. Children:
Richard, b. Nov. 3, 1738; d. aged about 30 years. Salome, b. Feb. 22, 1741; m. Mark Lang.
6. Jonathan, b. 1743. Joseph, b. 1746; m. Betsey Seavey. Elizabeth, b. 1749.

4. THOMAS GOSS, son of Richard (1), married, Dec. 5, 1736, Mary Hall of Portsmouth. She was born Aug. 24, 1709, and died, Aug. 17, 1802. He lived on what is now the Daniel J. Parsons place, and was drowned by falling off the Newcastle bridge. Children:
Hannah, b. 1740.
7. Nathan, b. Sept., 1741. Mary, b. July, 1743; m. first, Joseph Tarlton; second, Nathaniel Jenness. James, b. Aug. 30, 1745; d. unm. April 11, 1825. Thomas, b. Dec., 1747; m. first, Hannah Black; second, June 28, 1803, Mrs. Elizabeth (Randall) Jenness. Richard, b. Aug. 24, 1750; killed, Oct. 17, 1777, in the Revolution.
8. Elizabeth, b. Dec. 8, 1752.

5. JETHRO GOSS, son of Richard (1), married Esther Rand. Children:
Samuel, b. Aug. 21, 1728; d. Aug. 22, 1735. Esther, b. Feb. 5, 1734; d. Aug. 18, 1735. Levi, b. Feb. 3, 1735; d. Aug. 18, 1735. Sarah, b. June 13, 1736. Mary, b. Aug. 10, 1738; m. Dec. 16, 1757, Thomas Lang.
9. Esther, b. 1741; had a son, Joseph, who m. Hannah Berry. Susannah, b. 1744; m. Joseph Rand.
10. Levi, b. 1747.
Richard, b. 1751.

GENEALOGY.   369

6. JONATHAN GOSS, son of Jonathan (3), born 1743; married, Feb. 16, 1769, Elizabeth Brown. Was in the Revolutionary War under Capt. Parsons, and he sailed in the privateer *Portsmouth* with Samuel Seavey, and was captured, and died of smallpox in Dartmoor prison. Children:
11. Joseph.
12. Jonathan.

7. NATHAN GOSS, son of Thomas (4), born Sept., 1741; married Sarah Johnson. Lived on the Richard P. Goss farm. Was second lieutenant in Capt. Parsons' company in the Revolutionary War; stationed at Newcastle. Children:
13. Gen. Thomas, b. Sept. 16, 1768. Simon, b. 1771; m. April 27, 1806, Sarah Berry; no children. Sally (twin), b. 1775; m. Oct. 31, 1793, John Carroll. Molly (twin), b. 1775; d. young.
14. Richard, b. 1778.

8. ELIZABETH GOSS, daughter of Thomas (4), born Dec. 8, 1752; died Oct. 15, 1828; had two children: Michael D. Goss, born March 20, 1777, and Betsey, born April 7, 1794; died Dec. 5, 1870. Michael and Betty lived in a small one-story house that stood in the field now owned by L. B. Parsons and near his residence.
Michael D. Goss, married, Oct. 21, 1799, Sally Trudy, who was born in Rye, Feb., 1778. He died March 18, 1851. She died Nov. 10, 1851. Children:
Tobias T., b. Feb. 26, 1801; d. Aug. 17, 1824. James, b. March 8, 1805; d. Aug. 17, 1807.
15. James Madison, b. Sept. 5, 1809.

9. ESTHER GOSS, daughter of Jethro (5), born 1741; was unmarried. Had a son, Joseph, born 1768 (baptized 1779), who died April 27, 1795. He married Hannah Berry and had:
16. Joseph, b. June 24, 1795.

10. LEVI GOSS, son of Jethro (5), born 1747; married, Aug. 18, 1767, Sarah Rand. Children:

17. Levi.
18. John. Jethro, m. Nov. 16, 1796, Patty Wells. Joshua.
19. Daniel.

11. JOSEPH GOSS, son of Jonathan (6), married, March 6, 1791, Sally Seavey. Was a member of Capt. E. Philbrick's company in the War of 1812. Removed to Moultonborough. Children:

Jonathan, bapt. Aug. 5, 1792; m. Dec. 20, 1812, Olive Adams. Elizabeth, bapt. Sept. 14, 1794. Seavey, m. Sarah Berry. Helen (adopted).

12. JONATHAN GOSS, son of Jonathan (6), married, Jan. 10, 1796, Patty Davidson. She died May 21, 1843. He died Aug. 29, 1851. Was in Captain Berry's company of light infantry in the War of 1812. Children:

Sarah Blake, b. Sept. 19, 1797; m. Nov. 24, 1825, Daniel Lord, b. Sept. 25, 1797; d. Dec. 13, 1882. William Davidson, b. July 30, 1801; m. Data Mason of Hampton.

13. GEN. THOMAS GOSS, son of Nathan (7), born Sept. 16, 1768; married, first, Dec. 17, 1801, Sarah Marden. She died May 26, 1815 (?), and he married, second, June 2, 1816, Abigail Locke; died Feb. 26, 1881. He was appointed Captain by Gov. Gilman at Exeter July 5, 1794. Appointed Major of the Second Battalion in the first Regiment of Militia of N. H. Dec. 11, 1804. Appointed by Gov. John Langdon, Lieutenant Colonel Commandant of the 35 Regt. in N. H., Feb. 25, 1806. Colonel 35 Regt. 1st Brigade and first Division of Militia in 1810. Brigadier General of the first Brigade of Militia in N. H. 1813. He died Oct. 7, 1857. Children by first wife:

20. William, b. Jan. 21, 1803. Sheridan, b. May 11, 1809; d. Dec. 23, 1813. Sarah Ann, b. April 10, 1815; m. April 26, 1839, Ira Rand.

Child by second wife:
21. John Sheridan, b. Oct. 26, 1817.

14. RICHARD GOSS, son of Nathan (7), born 1778; married, April 4, 1811, Polly Foss. She died April 4, 1811, and he died Feb. 6, 1814. Children:

Nathan, b. Dec. 13, 1811; d. Feb. 27, 1845. Mary Jane, b. Aug. 28, 1814; m. Dec. 20, 1832, Joseph Pickering; d. Nov., 1877; lived at Newington.

15. JAMES MADISON GOSS, grandson of Elizabeth (8), born Sept. 5, 1809; married, April 20, 1834, Lucinda Snow. He died Feb. 21, 1870, and the following year she married Josiah Searcy and died July 3, 1874. Children:

J. Greenville, b. Dec. 28, 1836; drowned, July 16, 1854, at Exeter. Abby Francette, b. Jan. 10, 1842; m. Nov. 3, 1869, John Wallace; lives at Fort Wayne, Ind. Josiah Snow, b. March 14, 1846; d. Jan. 29, 1870.

16. JOSEPH GOSS, grandson of Esther (9), born June 24, 1795; married Eliza Seavey. Children:

Hannah Berry, d. unm. Dec. 21, 1889.
22. Alfred Seavey.
23. Joseph Jackson. Mary Esther, m. Charles Foss of Greenland.

17. LEVI GOSS, son of Levi (10), married, Nov. 15, 1796, Mary Saunders. Children:

Betsey, bapt. July 1, 1798. Nancy, bapt. Jan. 5, 1800.

18. JOHN GOSS, son of Levi (10), married, June 14, 1790, Abigail Randall. Children:

Joshua, bapt. Oct. 18, 1795. Joseph, bapt. Oct. 18, 1795. Daniel, bapt. Aug. 11, 1798.

19. DANIEL GOSS, son of Levi (10), married, first, June 25, 1801, Sarah Mace of Gosport; second, April 6, 1820, Hannah Perkins. Lived where Oren Drake resided. Children by first wife:

Eliza. Daniel James, m. Hannah Leavitt.
Children by second wife:
Sarah Jane, b. March 15, 1821; m. Nathaniel Hanscom. Mary Ann, b. Jan. 24, 1823; m. George Townsend.

20. CAPT. WILLIAM GOSS, son of Thomas (13), born Jan. 21, 1803; married, Sept. 14, 1823, Betsey Berry. She died Jan. 1, 1880. He commanded several schooners plying between Rye and Boston. He died Dec. 14, 1891. Children:

A child, b. 1823; d. Aug. 24, 1825. James W., b. Dec. 23, 1825; m. Harriet Crane; served in the war, 1861-'65; d. Jan. 24, 1888.
24. Otis, b. 1827. Amanda M., b. 1830; unm. Mary C., b. Feb. 29, 1832; unm. Charles Carroll, d. Jan. 25, 1859. Arthur L., m. 1880, Susie Knowlton. Sarah Abbie. Nathan R.

21. JOHN SHERIDAN GOSS, son of Thomas (13), born Oct. 26, 1817; married, Oct. 7, 1855, Sula A., widow of Samuel W. Foss, and daughter of Richard R. Locke. She died July 7, 1894. He died March 12, 1903. Child:
25. Wallace S., b. Dec. 20, 1856.

22. ALFRED SEAVEY GOSS, son of Joseph (16), married, Dec., 1866, Mary Eliza Marden. Child:
Carrie S.

23. JOSEPH JACKSON GOSS, son of Joseph (16), married, Dec. 25, 1868, Eliza A. Marden. He died Nov. 17, 1893. Child:
Nellie A., b. June 19, 1870.

24. OTIS GOSS, son of William (20), born 1827; married, Nov. 12, 1852, Ann M. Locke. Children:
Elzada, b. Oct. 10, 1853. Isabella, b. July 3, 1855. Olive Ann, b. May 10 or 14, 1858; m. Nov. 20, 1878, Arthur Brown.

25. WALLACE S. GOSS, son of John Sheridan (21), born Dec. 20, 1856; married, May 22, 1880, Sarah Caswell, born April 6, 1862. She died Feb. 26, 1896. Children:
John Sterling, b. Dec. 17, 1880; drowned while bathing July 11, 1903. Melville Jewell, b. Oct. 14, 1882. Leon Wallace, b. Nov. 5, 1886. Philip Nathan, b. Jan. 23, 1894; d. Sept. 13, 1894. Elizabeth Amy, b. Feb. 22, 1896.

1. RICHARD PICKERING GOSS, son of Joseph and Mary Jane (Goss) Pickering, assumed the name of Goss. He was born 1833, and married, Oct. 17, 1858, Harriett J. Locke. Children:
2. Clarence A., b. Feb. 11, 1860. Estelle, b. Aug. 16, 1861; m. Feb. 28, 1885, Edward Philbrick. Annie Marie, b. May 19, 1868; d. Oct. 9, 1877. Gilman P., b. June 6, 1870. Erastus, b. Aug. 3, 1872. Walter W., b. Dec. 11, 1875; m. Feb. 14, 1900, Fannie B. Knowles.

2. CLARENCE A. GOSS, son of Richard Pickering (1), born 1859; married, first, Mary Mace, divorced; he married, second, July 8, 1882, Eliza Ella Garland. Children by second wife:

Harriett, b. June 1, 1888. Annie, b. Jan. 26, 1890.

GOTHORPE.

THOMAS GOTHORPE, married, 1889, Lizzie Gomersawl. Electrician. Children:

Sarah Gertrude, b. Oct. 27, 1890. Esther Agatha, b. July 16, 1892. Hilda Gwendoline, b. Oct. 28, 1894.

GOULD.

CHRISTOPHER GOULD, married Waters. Schoolmaster. Children:

Ephraim, m. Oct. 20, 1791, Molly Towle of Epsom; lived at West Rye. Polly, m. John Brown. Ruth. Hannah, m. Rundlet.

GRANT.

CHRISTOPHER G. GRANT, married, Aug. 7, 1870, Elsie C. Locke. Children:

Ella Jane, b. Aug. 12, 1872. Charles Emery, b. Aug., 1877.

GREEN.

1. RICHARD GREEN, married, March 5, 1778, Mary Mow. She died May 14, 1854, aged 96 years. Children:

Richard, b. March 13, 1779; d. March 29, 1806, in the West Indies.
2. John, b. April 2, 1784. Ephraim, b. June 2, 1786; d. at North Hampton. Thomas, b. May 15, 1788; lost in a privateer during the War of 1812. Mary, b. Aug. 5, 1791; m. first, April 28, 1808, Samuel Caswell; second, Aug. 15, 1819, William Caswell. Dorcas Marden, b. Nov. 19, 1793; had a son Thomas, b. before marriage; m. Michael Caswell.
3. Charles, b. March 3, 1795. Samuel Marden, b. May 31, 1799; went to sea. Joseph, b. Aug. 5, 1798; d. aged about 2 years.

2. JOHN GREEN, son of Richard (1), born April 2, 1784, married Abigail Nutter. Lived at Portsmouth. Children:

John. Abigail. Frank. Ephraim, m. Mary White.

3. CHARLES GREEN, son of Richard (1), born March 3, 1795; married, March 23, 1826, Mary Smith Lamprey. She died March 21, 1858. A member of Capt. Berry's company of light infantry in the War of 1812. He died April 22, 1884. Children:

    Vercilda, b. March 9, 1827; m. Dec. 31, 1855, James Brown, Jr.
4. Charles Alpheus, b. Nov. 15, 1829. Mary Jane, b. Feb. 20, '832; m. Nov. 10, 1853, John Oren Foss; d. May 11, 1864. Cyrus Fayette, b. June 23, 1834; d. May 5, 1836. Woodbury C., b. Oct. 19, 1836; m. Jan. 1, 1864, Martha S. Trefethern; d. Sept. 20, 1864. Martha Olive, b. Oct. 4, 1839; m. June, 1864, Nathaniel Coffin.
5. Oren Smith, b. Oct. 23, 1845.

4. CHARLES ALPHEUS GREEN, son of Charles (3), born Nov. 15, 1829; married, Jan. 10, 1856, Lizzie Falls. For many years an engineer on the B. & M. R. R. between Portsmouth and Boston. Lived at Portsmouth. Child:

    Fred Charles, b. 1857; d. 1894.

5. OREN SMITH GREEN, son of Charles (3), born Oct. 23, 1845; married, Oct. 27, 1888, Clara A. Harvey. Children:

    Harry, b. Feb. 16, 1892. Charles Oren, b. May 29, 1893. Marion E., b. Oct. 10, 1895. Kate H., b. April 11, 1899.

Deacon Stephen Green of Hampton Falls and Dolly, daughter of Webster, were married July 20, 1806. Probably lived where J. Jenness Rand resides, and removed to Hampton Falls. Served in Capt. Berry's company in the War of 1812. Children:

    Anna Treadwell. Silas. Izette, m. Batchelder. Elizabeth.

THOMAS L. GREEN, married, first, Elizabeth Foss. She died June 1, 1868; and he married, second, Lizzie A. Ayers. He died Sept. 14, 1893, aged 83 years. Children:

    Thomas Otis, b. Feb. 23, 1834; m. Waldron; d. Feb. 15, 1873. Maria Elizabeth, b. Dec. 9, 1835; m. Richard Hilton; d. July, 1863; Rosilla, b. Nov. 23, 1837; m. James M. Rand. Brackett, b. March 13, 1841; m. Martha S. Rand. Mary Adelaide, b. March 10, 1843 (?); m. Joseph W. Berry. Alonzo, b. Sept., 1850 (?). Sarah W., b. Feb. 5, 1852; d. Jan. 2, 1874.

GROGAN.

JOHN GROGAN, married Sarah A. Shapley. Children: Harriett. Walter. John. Frank. Samuel. Elizabeth. Addie.

GROVER.

1. JOHN GROVER, married ———. Children:
2. John Henry, b. Sept. 22, 1854. Anna. Emma, b. 1863. Ella, b. 1868. Charles C., b. June 14, 1870.

2. JOHN HENRY GROVER, son of John (1), born Sept. 22, 1854; married, June 4, 1887, Malvina B. Jenness. Child: ———, b. Aug. 18, 1888.

HAINES.

Deacon Samuel Haines came in the ship *Angel Gabriel*, which was wrecked at Pemaquid, now Bristol, Me. He was selectman at Portsmouth, 1653-1663, and one of the nine founders of the town, and deacon of the church in 1671.

His son Samuel, born in 1646, married, Jan. 9, 1673, Mary Fifield, and had six children, one of them, William, born Jan. 7, 1679, married Mary Lewis, and had a daughter, Sarah, who married Jonathan Locke, in 1727.

HALE.

BENJAMIN HALE, son of Benjamin, was baptized March, 1741.

HALEY.

1. SAMUEL HALEY, married Love Randall. After his death she married Samuel Robinson. Children:
2. Richard G. Daniel.

2. RICHARD G. HALEY, son of Samuel (1), married Lucy J., daughter of John Randall of Gosport. Children:
Otis F., m. Julia Chauncy.
3. James M. Joseph B., m. Leonora Caswell. Elizabeth M., m. William Phinney.

3. JAMES M. HALEY, son of Richard G. (2), married, July 3, 1866, Harriette A. Clark. Children:
Hattie L. James I.

HALL.

1. JOSEPH HALL, married, first, Aug. 27, 1751, Esther Tucker. She died, and he married, second, widow Mary Rand; third, widow Rachel Mace. He died 1801. Children:

Mary T., b. 1752. Joseph, b. 1754; d. young. Joseph, b. 1755; d. in the Revolutionary army. William Tucker, b. 1757; shot at the beach near "Bass tree" by British gunboats in the Revolutionary War. Sarah, b. 1759. Elizabeth, b. 1761; m. Samuel Smith.

2. Edward, b. 1764. Hannah, b. May 19, 1780; d. unm. May 17, 1839; *"non compos mentis."* Esther, b. Sept. 18, 1781; m. Nathaniel Berry.

2. EDWARD HALL, son of Joseph (1), born 1764; married, April 22, 1784, Sarah Rand, born 1764. Children:

3. Joseph, b. June, 1787. Edward, b. May, 1789; d. unm. at sea, April 10, 1806.
4. Ephraim R., b. Jan. 19, 1793.
5. William, b. Dec. 26, 1795.

3. JOSEPH HALL, son of Edward (2), born June, 1787; married, Nov. 28, 1805, Mary, daughter of George Randall. She died March 19, 1808. He died at sea April 1, 1806. Child:

Joseph, b. April, 1806; d. March 26, 1828.

4. EPHRAIM R. HALL, son of Edward (2), born Jan. 19, 1793; married, March 20, 1817, Nancy Rand. Served in Capt. Samuel Berry's company of light infantry in the War of 1812. Children:

6. William, b. Feb. 28, 1818. Sarah Ann, b. March 15, 1822; m. John Holmes of Portsmouth. Joseph, b. June 14, 1826; d. unm. June 15, 1855, at the almshouse. Mary O., b. May 20, 1834.

5. WILLIAM HALL, son of Edward (2), born Dec. 26, 1795; married, July 10, 1824, Sarah, daughter of Billy Rand. She died Dec. 14, 1885. He died Jan. 29, 1864. Children:

7. Moses, b. 1826.
8. James Moses, b. March, 1828. Charles William, b. Dec. 11, 1830.
9. Levi Wallace, b. June 18, 1839; m. Emily Trefethern. George H., b. 1846; d. Aug. 13, 1854.

6. WILLIAM HALL, son of Ephraim R. (4), born Feb. 28, 1818; married Deborah Pickering of Newington. Children:

Martha Ann. Edward William.

7. MOSES HALL, son of William (5), born 1826; married Grace Harrington of Portsmouth. Children:

Ida. Frank.

8. JAMES MOSES HALL, son of William (5), born March, 1828; married, July 4, 1853, Ann E. Mathes. Children:

Emma. George.

9. LEVI WALLACE HALL, son of William (5), born June 18, 1839; married, April 26, 1863, Lucenna Jane Trefethern. Children:

Alice M., b. Feb., 1866. Herbert C., b. Aug., 1867. A girl, b. March 15, 1871; d. Sept. 26, 1871.

JOHN HALL, of Gosport, married Mary Merrifield of Billingsgate, England. He was drowned, and she married, second, Lepinle and had thirteen children. Children:

Joseph, m. first, Esther Tucker; second, widow Mary (Smith) Rand; third, widow Rachel (Berry) Mace. Betsey, m. Nat Tucker. Sarah, m. first, Sinclair; second, Allen; both Portsmouth sea captains. Edward, d. young.

HAM.

John H. Ham, formerly of Portsmouth, married Molly or Mary Foss; lived on Locke's Neck and owned considerable land there. He died Dec. 25, 1855. She died August 29, 1874, aged 89 years.

HANKIN.

FRED W. HANKIN, born 1874; married, Nov. 18, 1895, Maud G. Walker. Children:

Clyde, b. Jan. 17, 1896. Grace, b. April 15, 1897; d. May 29, 1897. Russell, b. Sept. 14, 1898. Marshall, b. July 12, 1900. Frances, b. March 4, 1903.

HILLS.

CHARLES P. HILLS, married, April 4, 1827, Elizabeth H. Garland. He died Aug. 23, 1829, and she died June 13, 1853. Child:

Elizabeth G., b. April 24, 1828; m. June 9, 1845, Paul A. Stackpole.

HOBBS.

1. MORRIS HOBBS, son of Morris and Sarah (Easton) Hobbs of Hampton, born Jan. 15, 1652; married, June 13, 1678, Sarah, daughter of Benjamin Swett. Children:

Esther, b. April 12, 1679; m. Peter Johnson; d. Aug. 24, 1741. Morris, b. Sept. 13, 1680; m. Theodate Batchelder; d. May 7, 1739. Benjamin, m. Mary (Marston?). Sarah, m. Joseph Towle. Mary, b. March 5, 1687. John, b. Dec. 12, 1688; m. Abigail Dow; d. March 17, 1783.
2. James, b. May 16, 1691. Joseph, b. May 15, 1693; d. probably unm. Dec. 21, 1717. Jonathan, b. Feb. 11, 1695; d. Oct. 20, 1715.

2. JAMES HOBBS, son of Morris (1), born May 16, 1691; married, Jan. 1, 1720, Lucy, daughter of Capt. Jabez Dow. Lived at Little River. He died Jan. 16, 1756. Children:

Esther, b. Oct. 9, 1720; m. Reuben Dearborn.
3. Jonathan, b. April 17, 1722. Sarah, b. April 11, 1724; d. unm., Aug. 17, 1749. James, b. June 6, 1726; Harv. Col. 1748; clergyman; m. Elizabeth Batchelder; d. June 20, 1765. Benjamin, b. April 18, 1728; m. first, Deborah Batchelder; second, Elizabeth Fogg; d. April 22, 1804. Morris, b. June 27, 1730; m. Theodate Page; d. June 20, 1810. Lucy, b. Dec. 14, 1732; m. Daniel Sanborn; d. July 15, 1813. Patience, b. March 10, 1734; m. Simon Lamprey. Comfort, b. March 28, 1736; m. first, John Shepard; second, Benjamin Lamprey; d. April 8, 1830.

3. JONATHAN HOBBS, son of James (2), born April 17, 1722; married, March 28, 1745, Mary (Molly) Berry. He died Jan. 3, 1756. Children:

Huldah, b. Jan. 12, 1746; m. Richard Locke.
4. James, b. Sept. 18, 1748. Lucy, b. Sept. 24, 1752; m. Feb. 7, 1782, Levi Towle, and d. soon after her marriage. Jonathan, b. Oct. 11, 1754; d. unm. Oct. 5, 1815.

4. JAMES HOBBS, son of Jonathan (3), born Sept. 18, 1748; married, Jan. 6, 1774, Mary Towle. Children:

Lucy, b. Nov. 8, 1774; d. March 19, 1776. Molly, b. Nov. 10, 1776; d. Jan. 21, 1788. Jonathan, b. Nov. 8, 1778; d. Dec. 20, 1810. Elizabeth Jenness, b. Sept. 4, 1780; m. Asa Locke. Lucy, b. Sept. 2, 1782; d. Dec. 11, 1785. Nathaniel, b. June 12, 1786; d. Jan. 21, 1788. Nancy, b. July 26, 1789; m. James Bunker. Sally, b. 1793. Perua Junkins, bapt. 1799; d. young.

JOHN W. HOBBS, married Elmira A. Seavey. Children: Nellie, b. July 21, 1868; m. Ralph Walker. Hervey.

HODGDON.

ALEXANDER H. HODGDON, married, July 13, 1871, Anna D., daughter of David A. Jenness. Child:

Mabel H., b. Oct. 4, 1871; m. April 18, 1891, Herbert Perkins.

HOLMES.

1. BENJAMIN HOLMES, married, first, Elizabeth Slooper; second, July 6, 1780, Margaret Holmes; third, Molly Rand. He was drowned about 1800, at London. Children by first wife:

2. Jacob. Shadrach. Isaac. Benjamin, m. Lowd. James, m. Cook.

Children by second wife:
Jotham, *non compos mentis;* Sally, Polly (twins).

Children by third wife:
Isaac. Elizabeth, David (twins). Mesach. Ann. John. Oliver, Mary (twins).

2. JACOB HOLMES, son of Benjamin (1), married, Jan. 20, 1799, Polly Hobbs. Child:

3. Jacob, b. March 8, 1800.

3. JACOB HOLMES, son of Jacob (2), born March 8, 1800; married, first, May 22, 1832, Nancy Lang. She died, and he married, second, Elizabeth Lang; she died May 3, 1842, aged 31 years. Children by first wife:

Charles Edward, b. Sept. 21, 1832; m. Anna Hildreth; two children; lives at Newton, Mass. Sarah Eliza, b. May 20, 1839; m. Charles F. Wilkins.

1. JAMES HOLMES, married Deborah Libby; lived in Portsmouth. Child:

2. William.

2. WILLIAM HOLMES, son of James Holmes and Deborah Libby, born Feb., 1806; married, May, 1828, Mary Rand. Farmer. She died March 24, 1863. He died Feb. 22, 1891. Children:
    Sophia C., b. Aug. 28, 1828; m. Aug. 5, 1855, John Salter Marden; d. Feb. 11, 1885.
  3. Joseph Rand, b. 1830.
  4. William Ira, b. Dec., 1831.

3. JOSEPH RAND HOLMES, son of William (1), born 1830; married Charlotte Seavey. Lived at Portsmouth. Contractor. Child:
    Emma, b. Feb. 19, 1860; m. Albert H. Drake.

4. WILLIAM IRA HOLMES, son of William (1), born Dec. 1831; married, Oct. 28, 1860, Sarah E. Trefethern. She died Aug. 28, 1902. Farmer. He died March 14, 1897. Children:
    Ella, b. 1866; m. April 7, 1888, Everett Odiorne; d. 1903. Ernest, b. May 2, 1872; d. Feb. 18, 1881.

HUNT.

ZEBEDEE HUNT. Children:
    Samuel, bapt. March 2, 1760. ———, b. Nov., 1761. Elizabeth, b. April 10, 1763.

HUTCHINS.

SAMUEL HUTCHINS, married Hannah Seavey. Children:
    John, bapt. March 12, 1769. Samuel, b. May 17, 1772.

Melvin Hutchins (born 1840) and Georgiana Locke married Nov. 25, 1876.

JENNESS.

The progenitor of the numerous and now widely scattered family of Jenness in this country was one Francis Jennings, who at the age of 35 emigrated to New Hampshire from Rye in England, about the year 1665, and took up his abode at Great Island, now Newcastle. The freeman's oath of fidelity was administered to him there, Oct. 2, 1666. For about five years the young man, then unmarried, pursued in Great Island the vocation of a mariner and fisherman. He married Hannah Swaine of Hampton and made his future home in that town. The territory which he took up, and most of which was laid out to him by the town of Hampton in 1675, extended in a strip along the seacoast from Josselyn's or Locke's Neck, in a southerly direction more than half a mile. Francis erected a dwelling house, saw- and grist-mill, and also a bakery, and by means of small boats he distributed his bread all along the coast towns to Boston.

He was denied his proper interest in the commonage, feedage, and sweepage (or the right of mowing grass), in the undivided town lands. In 1707, when he attempted to insist upon these rights before a meeting of the commoners, he was "denied speaking at this meeting." His sons after his death, in 1721, procured acknowledgment of these long-resisted rights.

1. FRANCIS JENNESS, born about 1634, came to Hampton as early as Feb. 15, 1670, when he married, 1671, Hannah, daughter of William Swaine. He married, second, Feb. 4, 1701, widow Salome White of Portsmouth. He died Aug. 27, 1716. Hannah died in 1700. Children by first wife:

    Thomas, b. Feb. 23, 1671; d. Aug. 24, 1696, at Little Harbor. Hannah, b. March 26, 1673; m. Edward Locke.
2. Hezekiah, b. March 30, 1675.
3. John, b. June 14, 1678. Elinor, b. Jan. 30, 1681; m. July 4, 1700, James Berry. Mehitabel, b. 1683; m. Matthias Haines of Portsmouth; d. 1768, aged 85 years.
4. Richard, b. June 8, 1686.

2. HEZEKIAH JENNESS, son of Francis (1), born March 30, 1675; married, May 13, 1697, Ann Folsom of Exeter; settled where Josiah and his son, Lewis L. Perkins, lived. Children:

    Thomas, b. March 10, 1698; m. Elizabeth Norton; removed to Hampton, having exchanged farms with James Perkins. Francis, b. Dec. 30, 1699; m. Sarah Locke. Hezekiah, b. March 8, 1702. Hannah, b. Sept. 30, 1704; m. Oct. 8, 1724, Samuel Langdon, cooper, of Portsmouth; son, Capt. Tobias. Ann, b. Dec. 10, 1706; m. Parker.

5. John, b. April 4, 1709. Mary, b. Jan. 25, 1718; m. Sept. 12, 1735, Job Jenness.

3. JOHN JENNESS, son of Francis (1), born June 14, 1678; married, first, June 25, 1702, Hannah Foss; second, Nov. 25, 1718, Mary Mason of Portsmouth. He was a blacksmith. Children by first wife:

6. John, b. March 16, 1703.
7. Joshua, b. May 14, 1705.
8. William, b. March 28, 1706.
9. Job, b. Oct. 15, 1708. Mark, b. Oct. 12, 1710; m. ———; had Cornelius, bapt. June 5, 1748. Hannah, b. March 7, 1712; m. Woodman. Richard, b. Sept. 25, 1714; m. first, Jan. 13, 1743, Abigail, dau. of Samuel Palmer, d. Sept., 1743; m. second, Sept. 18, 1755, Abigail Rand, d. Jan. 20, 1755, aged 37 years; m. third, Jan. 4, 1774, widow Mary Dalton, d. Sept. 1, 1785.

Children by second wife:
Francis, b. June 7, 1721. Thomas, b. Dec. 16, 1722; m. Feb. 25, 1753, Abigail, dau. of John Moulton; d. Feb. 10, 1793.

10. Nathaniel, b. Aug. 22, 1725.

4. CAPT. RICHARD JENNESS, son of Francis (1), born June 8, 1686; married, Feb. 9, 1710, Mary, daughter of Simon Dow. Lived where Sheridan Jenness resided; died 1769. The territory north of Locke's Neck and Sandy Beach which had hitherto been a part of Newcastle was erected into a distinct town by the name of the Parish of Rye. This new parish being declared entitled to representation in the Provincial Assembly, the first member returned by it to the house of representatives was Captain Richard Jenness. Children:

Sarah, b. March 6, 1711; m. Marston of North Hampton. Mary, b. Dec. 27, 1712; m. Joshua Weeks of Greenland. Hannah, b. July 4, 1714; m. 1730, Joseph Locke.

11. Francis, b. Dec. 1, 1715.
12. Richard, b. June 28, 1718. Simon, b. March 1, 1720; imbecile. Jonathan, b. Oct. 15, 1721; d. young.
13. Samuel, b. May 19, 1724.
14. Joseph, b. Feb. 28, 1727.

5. JOHN JENNESS, son of Hezekiah (2), born April 4, 1709; married, Nov. 30, 1732, Elizabeth Seavey; died Feb. 14, 1745. Children:

GENEALOGY. 383

Elizabeth, b. April 4, 1734; m. Jonathan Towle, Jr. Sarah, b. April 25, 1736; m. Dec. 5, 1757, Col. Benjamin Garland. Mary, b. Aug. 5, 1738; d. unm. Hannah, b. March 29, 1741; m. March 4, 1764, Enoch Hardy. Anna.

6. JOHN JENNESS, son of John (3), born March 16, 1703; married, 1725, Lucy, daughter of Bonus Norton of Hampton. Lived at Rochester. Children:

Lucy, b. Feb. 25, 1728; m. John Place.
15. Paul, b. 1727. David, ran away with a woman; d. at Philadelphia. John, m. McNeil; lived in Vt. Mary, m. Benjamin Hurd.

7. JOSHUA JENNESS, son of John (3), born May 14, 1705; married, first, Nov. 16, 1732, Hannah Langhorn, who died Jan. 10, 1785, aged 75 years 10 months; he married, second, Mary Jenness. Said to have been partially insane. Lived in the field by Brown's grist-mill. Children by first wife:

Anna, b. Aug. 8, 1733 (?); m. Hardy. Sarah, b. Jan. 30, 1736. Hannah, b. Jan. 30, 1737; unm. in 1771. Joshua, b. April 2, 1739; d. April 6, 1785. Deliverance, b. Jan. 14, 1741; unm. in 1771. Elizabeth, b. 1744; m. Taylor. Mary, b. 1747; m. Morrill; lived at Salisbury. Hezekiah, b. 1749; d. Oct. 31, 1770; aged 21 years.

8. WILLIAM JENNESS, son of John (3), born March 28, 1706; married Sarah Locke. Children:

William. Moses. Aaron, may have m. Sarah Berry and had: Jeremiah, William, Aaron, and Levi. David.

9. JOB JENNESS, son of John (3), born Oct. 15, 1708; married, Sept. 12, 1735, Mary, daughter of Hezekiah Jenness. Children:

Hezekiah, b. Aug. 26, 1736. Job, unm., d. Nov. 15, 1777, in the army. Betsey, b. 1738; m. first, Thomas Rand; second, Jonathan Woodman. Anna, b. 1750; unm.
16. Richard, b. Dec. 8, 1751. John, unm., d. in the army. Hannah, m. Woodman. Samuel. Comfort, b. 1760; m. John Brown.

10. CAPT. NATHANIEL JENNESS, son of John (3), born Aug. 22, 1725; married, first, Dec. 27, 1749, Hannah, daughter of Simon Dow; second, March 8 or 28, 1771, widow Mary Tarlton; third, Oct. 21, 1781, widow Mary Wedgewood. Children by first wife:

Simon, went to England, having written over the fireplace, "you shall see my face no more." Mary, b. 1750; m. Nathaniel Foss; lived at Barrington. Jonathan, unm., d. at Boston in the army.
17. John, b. 1752.
18. Noah, b. 1755 (March 2, 1762 ?). Hannah, b. 1757; d. young.
19. Nathaniel, b. 1760. Patty. Hannah, b. 1765; m. Sept., 1799, Theodore Fuller. James, unm., drowned, aged about 24 years.
Children by second wife:
Joseph Tarleton, b. 1772; unm.
20. Thomas, b. Dec. 8, 1774.
21. Richard, b. 1775. Betty, b. 1777; m. Reuben Philbrick. Molly, b. June, 1778; m. March 31, 1800, Eliphalet Sleeper.

11. FRANCIS JENNESS, son of Richard (4), born Dec. 1, 1715; married Sarah, daughter of John Garland. Children:

Elizabeth, b. Sept. 9, 1741.
22. Jonathan, b. Jan. 25, 1743.
23. Isaac, b. Dec. 30, 1744. Mary, b. Feb. 22, 1746. Sarah, b. April 7, 1749; m. Lieut. Richard Brown.
24. John, b. 1751.
25. Francis, b. 1753. Abigail, b. 1761.

12. ESQUIRE RICHARD JENNESS, son of Richard (4), born June 28, 1718; married, second, widow Abigail (Coffin) Sleeper. He was a large landowner and lived opposite Joseph G. Jenness. Justice of the peace and member of the house of representatives. He died in 1782. Children by first wife:

26 Richard, b. 1746.
27. Thomas, b. 1748.
28. Simon, b. 1751. Elizabeth, b. 1753; m. 1784, Enoch Burbank. Levi, b. 1756; d. young. Anna, b. 1759; unm.
Children by second wife:
29. Jonathan, b. 1760.
30. Benjamin, b. 1763.

13. ESQUIRE SAMUEL JENNESS, son of Richard (4), born May 19, 1724; married, first, Nov. 15, 1748, Abigail, daughter of John Garland; second, widow Elizabeth Shapley. Children by first wife:

Mary, b. 1749.
31. Samuel, b. 1752.
32. Peter, b. 1755.

33. Levi, b. 1757. Mary, b. 1758; m. Samuel Drake, Hampton. Elizabeth, b. 1761; m. Nathaniel Drake, North Hampton. John, b. 1763; m. first, Page; second, Batchelder; lived at Pittsfield. Child by second wife: Abigail, b. 1769; m. John Locke.

14. CAPT. JOSEPH JENNESS, son of Richard (4), born Feb. 28, 1727; married, first, Dec. 25, 1750, Mary Dow, born Sept. 6, 1730; second, widow Anna Parker of Portsmouth, born in 1739. He died in 1815. He was captain of the Second Independent Company of Infantry in 1744. Children:

34. Isaac, b. 1751. Mary, bapt. Jan. 18, 1752; d. of throat distemper.
35. Richard, b. Dec. 24, 1757.
36. Jonathan, b. July 25, 1760. Sarah, b. May 11, 1764; m. Levi Berry.
37. Joseph, b. Feb. 12, 1771.

15. PAUL JENNESS, born 1727; married Caturah Dame. Lived at Rochester. Children:

Jacob, d. aged about 21 years. Isaac, b. 1781; m. first, Mercy Wentworth; second, Judith Sanborn. Betsey, m. David Jenness.

16. RICHARD JENNESS, son of Job (9), born Dec. 8, 1751; married, July 23, 1778, Mary Page of North Hampton. He was killed by lightning. Children:

Polly, b. April, 1779; m. Moses Lowe; lived at Canaan.
38. John, b. April 7, 1781. William, b. Feb. 26, 1783; d. unm. Oct. 22, 1851. Job, b. Feb. 26, 1786; m. Phebe Dow of Seabrook. Stephen, m. Mary Witchen; lived at Canaan.

17. LIEUT. JOHN JENNESS, son of Nathaniel (10), born 1752; married Dec. 23, 1777, Sarah Randall. Lived at Moultonborough. Served in the Revolutionary War under Captain Parsons. Children:

Sarah, b. 1777; m. Clemmens. Olly, b. 1778. Hannah, b. 1779. John, d. young. Abigail, bapt. July 23, 1786; m. Abraham Clemmens. Peter Mitchell, bapt. Dec. 7, 1788.
39. John, bapt. May 12, 1793.

18. NOAH JENNESS, son of Nathaniel (10), born 1755, or March 2, 1762; married, Jan. 25, 1784, widow Elizabeth Randall, born Feb. 27, 1755. She died Jan. 25, 1784, and he died Oct. 17, 1801. Children:

40. Simon, b. May 19, 1785. Joses, b. Jan. 10, 1787; removed to Edgecomb, Me., in 1807. Betsey, b. June 24, 1794; d. Aug. 22, 1811. Polly, b. March 27, 1797; d. June 9, 1824.

19. NATHANIEL JENNESS, son of Nathaniel (10), born 1760; married, Oct. 21, 1781, Mary Wedgewood. Children:

41. David Wedgewood, b. Jan. 12, 1782. Polly, b. Dec., 1785.
42. Jonathan, b. Nov. 1, 1792. Nancy, b. Jan. 12, 1795; m. Col. Simon Jenness. Clarissa, b. May, 1800; m. Dec. 31, 1818, Samuel Jenness, Jr.

20. THOMAS JENNESS, son of Nathaniel (10), born Dec. 8, 1774; married, May 16, 1799, Sarah Page of North Hampton, born Aug. 30, 1781. He died Nov., 1851. Children:

Alice (?). Fanny, b. May 18, 1800; m. Samuel Towle. Jonathan, b. April 26, 1802; m. first, Martha Philbrick; second, Catherine Clapp; lived at Hampton. Joseph Tarleton, b. April 15, 1804; m. first, Elizabeth Varrell; second, Esther Jones (?). James, b. June 11, 1806; m. Lucinda Davis. Simon, b. Aug. 30, 1811; m. Miralda Fox. Polly, b. Aug. 7, 1815; m. Dearborn Batchelder. Abigail, b. Jan. 24, 1820; m. Dearborn Batchelder.

21. RICHARD JENNESS, son of Nathaniel (10), born 1775; married, Aug. 2, 1819, Caroline Rand. Children:

Andrew Jackson, b. 1815, before m.; d. Feb 11, 1882.
43. Amos J., b. Aug. 1, 1819. Sarah Ann, b. 1825; m. Dec. 29, 1842, William Wait, Jr.; lived in Boston.
44. Nathaniel, b. Jan. 2, 1827.

22. JONATHAN JENNESS, son of Francis (11), born Jan. 25, 1743; married Jan. 9, 1779, Olive Cate. Lived at Northwood. Children:

Sally, b. 1779; m. Thomas Demeritt. Olive, m. Joel B. Virgin. Betsey, m. Paul Hanson.

23. ISAAC JENNESS, son of Francis (11), born Dec. 30, 1744; married, July 10, 1770, Mercy Haines. Lived at Newmarket. Children:

Joseph, b. 1772. Francis, b. 1774. Molly, b. 1777. Sally, b. 1779. John.

24. DEACON JOHN JENNESS, son of Francis (11), born 1751; married, July 5, 1774, Elizabeth Cate of Portsmouth. Lived at Strafford. Children:

Abigail, b. 1779. William, b. 1780; m. Olive Johnson. Charlotte, m. Hall. Peter, m. Hall. John, m. Johnson.

25. FRANCIS JENNESS, son of Francis (11), born 1753; married Batchelder. Lived at Newmarket. Children: Data, b. 1780. Nancy, b. 1781. Sally, b. 1783. Hall Jackson.

26. JUDGE RICHARD JENNESS, son of Richard (12), born 1746; married, first, Betsey Berry. She died in 1773, and he married, second, Feb. 22, 1774, Hannah Seavey. Lived at Deerfield. Children by first wife:

45. Thomas. Anna, d. unm. Nancy, d. unm.
Children by second wife:
Amos. Richard, m. Hannah Emerson; removed to Vermont. Joseph, m. first, Betsey True; second, widow Sally Nye. Woodbury, m. Pillsbury of Candia; removed to Vermont.
46. Benjamin. Betsey, m. David French. Polly, m. Benning Sanborn. Hannah, m. Josiah Butler.

27. THOMAS JENNESS, son of Richard (12), born 1748; married, Jan. 31, 1775, Sarah Yeaton. Children:

Polly or Olly, b. 1775; m. Rev. ——— Remington. Thomas, m. Moore. Richard. Jonathan, m. French. Sally, m. Gate Cilley. Patty, m. Phineous Colby. Simon. John.

28. SIMON JENNESS, son of Richard (12), born 1751; married, June 24, 1773, Olive Shapley. He died April 27, 1798. Children:

Olive, b. 1776; m. Lieut. Amos Garland. Alexander Shapley, b. 1778; d. March, 1799. Anna or Nancy, b. July 21, 1780; m. April 28, 1807, John Brown. Betsey, b. 1782; d. July 20, 1789, of St. Vitus' dance. Abigail, bapt. Nov. 13, 1785. Simon, bapt. March 15, 1787; d. young.
47. Simon, b. Nov. 18, 1792.

29. JONATHAN JENNESS, son of Richard (12), born 1760; married, Aug. 14, 1785, Abigail Garland. Lived at Deerfield. Children:

Elizabeth, b. 1786; m. Nathaniel White; d. Sept. 11, 1866; aged 80 years. Benjamin Garland, bapt. Oct. 12, 1788. Polly, b. 1790; m. 1816, David Wedgewood. Jonathan, d. unm. William, m. Mary J. Saunders.

30. BENJAMIN JENNESS, son of Richard (12), born 1763; married, March 11, 1787, Martha Seavey. He died Feb. 8, 1824; and she died May 27, 1830. Children:
- Polly, b. Oct. 9, 1788; d. June 15, 1789. Polly, b. Oct. 9, 1790; d. Jan. 29, 1803. Richard, b. Sept. 4, 1794; d. Sept. 25, 1794. Nabby Coffin, b. Feb. 7, 1797; d. Jan. 28, 1816.
- 48. Amos Seavey, b. Oct. 3, 1801.

31. SAMUEL JENNESS, son of Samuel (13), born 1752; married, March 26, 1775, Mary Locke. Lived at North Hampton. Children:
- Jeremiah, b. 1776; m. Mary Hobbs. Polly, m. John Brown.

32. PETER JENNESS, son of Samuel (13), born 1755; married, Dec. 26, 1782, Abigail Drake. Children:
- Molly, bapt. Aug. 12, 1787; m. May 19, 1807, David W. Jenness. Abigail, b. 1791; m. June 30, 1814, Jonathan Jenness, 3d; d. Nov. 17, 1818.
- 49. Samuel, b. Sept. 14, 1794. Nancy, b. 1795; m. June 23, 1814, Simon Jenness.

33. LEVI JENNESS, son of Samuel (13), born 1757; married, first, Sarah Dearborn; second, Nov. 17, 1785, Elizabeth Wallis. Children by second wife:
- 50. Samuel Wallis, b. June 17, 1787. Levi, b. Jan. 4, 1790; d. unm. 1813. Sarah Dearborn, b. June, 1792; m. May 2, 1816, Benjamin Jenness. Martha Wallis, b. Oct. 8, 1795; m. April 15, 1819, Samuel Chapman, Jr., of North Hampton.
- 51. Josiah, b. April 15, 1797.

34. ISAAC JENNESS, son of Joseph (14), born 1751; married, Aug. 20, 1777, Hannah Dow. She died April 20, 1840, and he died Dec. 6, 1841. Children:
- Mary, b. Feb. 20, 1780; m. Nathan Brown. Hannah, b. Dec. 27, 1782; d. 1862.
- 52. Henry, b. April 7, 1786. Joseph, b. June 11, 1790; d. Feb. 10, 1875.

35. RICHARD JENNESS, son of Joseph (14), born Dec. 24, 1757; married Mary Coffin. Lived at Derry. Children:
- Sarah, b. Aug. 24, 1782. Joseph, b. June 18, 1786; m. Drake.

36. JONATHAN JENNESS, son of Joseph (14), born July 25, 1760; married Abigail Locke. Children:

Polly, b. May 15, 1785; m. James Marden; d. Oct. 15, 1853. Nabby, b. May 9, 1789; d. July 10, 1789.
53. Jonathan, b. May 29, 1791.
54. Joseph, b. July 27, 1795. Abigail L., b. April 3, 1801; m. Dec. 31, 1826, Jonathan Palmer of Kensington; d. April, 1867. Emily, b. March 24, 1807; m. Samuel H. Rand; d. Aug. 15, 1866.

37. LIEUT. JOSEPH JENNESS, son of Joseph (14), born Feb. 12, 1771; married, first, Feb. 22, 1791, Anna Yeaton; second, Dec. 8, 1801, Sarah Philbrick; third, Dec. 8, 1809, Betsey Philbrick; fourth, Aug., 1817, Anna Knox, who was born in Ossipee. Lieut. Jenness was a member of the Alarm List in the War of 1812, serving under Capt. Jonathan Wedgewood. He died Sept. 13, 1845. Children by first wife:

55. Benjamin, b. June 19, 1791. Mary, b. June 19, 1793; m. first, March 21, 1811, Abraham Drake; second, Aug. 23, 1827, David W. Jenness; d. Oct. 28, 1885. Sarah Taylor, b. 1795; m. May 2, 1811, David W. Jenness.

Child by second wife:
56. Reuben Philbrick, b. Dec. 2, 1807.

Child by third wife:
Anna Yeaton, b. July 14, 1813; m. Obed Rand.

Children by fourth wife:
Joseph Disco, b. Sept. 30, 1818; m. first, Mary E. Foye; second, Helen Foye. Elizabeth, b. Sept. 7, 1820; m. March 11, 1844, William J. Rand; d. March 15, 1901.
57. Sheridan, b. May 12, 1824.

38. JOHN JENNESS, son of Richard (16), born April 7, 1781; married, Nov. 17, 1808, Lydia Rollins. He died Jan. 28, 1855. Children:

58. Job, b. July 14, 1811.
59. John. Mary, m. Francis Sweeney. Louisa, m. Newell Clifford.
60. Jonathan Rollins. Sarah Ann, m. William Pope; d. May, 1862. Lydia A., m. William Gordon. Olive C. Lucy Jane, m. Alexander Stephens.
61. Wesley, b. April 10, 1831. Levi, went to California.

39. JOHN JENNESS, son of John (17), baptized May 12, 1793; married Hannah Webster. He died in 1823. Children:

Albert, b. 1817; m. widow Sarah Dodd; removed to Palmyra, Ill. John, b. March 20, 1820; removed to Palmyra, Ill. Elizabeth, b. July, 1821; m. William Stackpole; lived at Dixon, Ill.

40. SIMON JENNESS, son of Noah (18), born May 19, 1785; married, Nov. 23, 1815, Nancy Sleeper. Children:

> Alfred G., b. March 12, 1818; m. first, Martha A. Garland; second, July 3, 1850, Lucinda Garland; third, widow Hannah Wedgewood. Eliza Ann, b. 1820; d. Aug. 18, 1826.

41. DAVID WEDGEWOOD JENNESS, son of Nathaniel (19), born Jan. 12, 1782; married, first, May 19, 1807, Molly Jenness; second, May 2, 1811, Elizabeth Locke; third, June 16, 1816, Sarah T. Jenness; fourth, Aug. 23, 1827, Mary, widow of Abraham Drake; she died Oct. 28, 1885. He served in Capt. Samuel Berry's company of light infantry in the War of 1812. Children by third wife:

> Mary Ann, b. March 13, 1819; m. Aug. 13, 1833, Hezekiah Lamprey; d. March 8, 1881. Clarissa, b. Dec. 7, 1821; m. James P. Jenness.
>
> Children by fourth wife:
>
> Abram, b. Aug. 23, 1828; m. April 15, 1849, Sarah Cotton. David, b. July 5, 1833, m. March 7, 1854, Emily Dalton; d. Oct. 27, 1901; was a member of the state senate and legislature.

42. JONATHAN JENNESS, son of Nathaniel (19), born Nov. 1, 1792; married, March 28, 1816, Sarah Garland. Child:

> 62. Gilman Harrison (adopted), b. Sept., 1839.

43. AMOS J. JENNESS, son of Richard (21), born Aug. 1, 1819; married, Nov. 8, 1849, Mary Jane Locke of Seabrook. He died June 1, 1902. Children:

> Eliza P., b. March 20, 1851; m. first, Richard Fogg; second, Woodbury Philbrick; third, James Barton. Frank P. Cora Belle, b. Dec. 15, 1857; m. Edwin Walker; divorced. Abbott C., b. 1861; d. June 18, 1863.

44. NATHANIEL JENNESS, son of Richard (21), born Jan. 2, 1827; married, Aug. 25, 1862, Rozanna Sweeney. Child:

> Carrie M., b. June 2, 1867; m. James Reynolds.

45. THOMAS JENNESS, son of Richard (26), married Deborah Sanborn. He died in 1836. Lived at Deerfield. Children:

GENEALOGY. 391

Deborah, m. Horatio Cilley. John S., b. 1794; d. unm. Sept., 1867.
Thomas, m. Polly True. Peter, m. Sally True. Anna, m. Judge
Ira St. Clair. Richard, b. April 21, 1801; m. Caroline McClintock; d. Feb. 2, 1872. Betsey, m. Samuel Whidden. Horace.
Benning W. Sally, m. Dearborn. Matilda, d. unm.

46. BENJAMIN JENNESS, son of Richard (26), married Sarah Dowrst. Lived at Deerfield. Children:

Dowrst, m. Stearns. Josiah. Langdon, m. Clark. Elizabeth, m.
Bradbury Cilley. Benjamin, lived at Manchester.

47. COL. SIMON JENNESS, son of Simon (28), born Nov. 18, 1792; married, June 23, 1814, Nancy Jenness. He died Dec. 3, 1870, and she died Feb. 18, 1876. Was a member of Capt. Samuel B. Berry's company of light infantry in the War of 1812. Children:

63. David A., b. Aug. 26, 1814. Adeline S., b. Oct. 27, 1820; m. Feb. 15, 1840, Moses Garland.
64. Levi Woodbury, b. April 24, 1824. Sophia, b. Aug. 6, 1826; m. Charles Garland. Semira, b. Aug. 6, 1826; m. Rufus I. Garland.

48. AMOS SEAVEY JENNESS, son of Benjamin (30), born Oct. 3, 1801; married Sarah Ann Locke. He died March 30, 1886. She died Dec. 17, 1889, aged 90 years. Lived at Breakfast Hill. Children:

65. William Benjamin, b. May 29, 1819. Abby Coffin, b. Sept. 10, 1821; m. first, Feb. 7, 1870, Simon Ordiorne; second, Christopher Moor.
66. Joseph G., b. March 21, 1825. Martha Seavey, b. Aug. 17, 1829; m. Feb. 23, 1851, Albion D. Parsons.

49. CAPT. SAMUEL JENNESS, son of Peter (32), born Sept. 14, 1794; married Dec. 31, 1818, Clarissa Jenness. She died Aug. 14, 1842. Children:

67. Oliver Peter, b. Jan., 1820.
68. Nathaniel Gilbert, b. Nov., 1823. Mary Abby, b. June 3, 1826; m. William B. Jenness. Emeline, b. Oct., 1829. Rosamond, b. April 1832; m. Charles Rand. Samuel Alba, b. Oct., 1834; m. Wilson.

50. SAMUEL WALLIS JENNESS, son of Levi (33), born June 17, 1787; married, first, March 1, 1810, Abigail Perkins; second, 1835, Polly Edmonds; third, Feb., 1861, Sarah S. Randall. Children by first wife:

Warren, b. Oct. 31, 1810; m. Mary Richardson. Levi, b. Oct., 1813. m. Lydia Hart. Elizabeth, b. July 10, 1816; m. first, Oct., 1838, Frederick Colcord; second, Jeremiah Dudley. James Perkins, b. Oct. 12, 1818; m. first, Clarissa Jenness; second, Dec. 3, 1843, Elizabeth Jenness. Sarah A., b. June 14, 1826; m. Yeaton Jenness. Martha J., b. Oct. 13, 1828; m. Gilman Garland. Samuel W., b. Jan. 4, 1823; m. May 13, 1847, Eliza Colcord; she d. May 31, 1901; had Alice J., b. May 1, 1856, who m. Oct. 2, 1876, Charles Whidden.

51. JOSIAH JENNESS, son of Levi (33), born Aug. 15, 1797; married, Jan. 7, 1822, Huldah Perkins. Resided and built the house now occupied by Mr. Goodwin before removing to the beach. Children:

Eliza, m. John C. Philbrick. Fidelia, d. June 10, 1833; aged about two years.

52. HENRY JENNESS, son of Isaac (34), born April 7, 1786; married, Aug. 5, 1813, Charlotte Lamprey. He died March 11, 1869. Children:

69. Isaac, b. March, 1814.
70. Simon Lamprey, b. Feb., 1816.
71. Henry, b. Dec. 24, 1825.
72. Joseph Jerome, b. May 1, 1828. Mary Ann, m. John Brown.

53. JONATHAN JENNESS, son of Jonathan (36), born May 29, 1791; married, June 30, 1814, Abigail Jenness. She died Oct. 17, 1818, and he died July 12, 1870. Child:

Oliver Peter, d. Oct. 3, 1818.

54. JOSEPH JENNESS, son of Jonathan (36), born July 27, 1795; married, Dec. 19, 1819, Polly Garland. Child:

Uri Harvey, b. July 10, 1827 or '28; m. first, May 25, 1851, Martha Hannah Browne; second, Feb. 23, 1890, Sarah Garland.

55. BENJAMIN JENNESS, son of Joseph (37), born June 19, 1791; married, first, May 2, 1816, Sarah Dearborn Jenness; second, Dorothy Brown. He died Aug. 4, 1875. Children:

Joseph, b. Oct. 3, 1816. Edwin, b. Sept. 8, 1818. Yeaton, b. Aug. 14, 1820; m. Sarah A. Jenness. Elizabeth, b. March 24, 1823; m. Nathan Brown. Levi, b. Feb. 20, 1825; d. Jan. 24, 1826. Benjamin Leavitt, b. April 24, 1828. Levi M., b. May 13, 1830. Nathan Brown, b. March 4, 1832.

GENEALOGY. 393

73. Albert Dana, b. April 7, 1834. Joseph B., b. May 11, 1836. Sarah M., b. Dec., 1841. Warren, b. March 1, 1846; d. July 30, 1846.

56. REUBEN PHILBRICK JENNESS, son of Joseph (37), born Dec. 2, 1807; married, Oct. 5, 1834, Mary Knowles. He died June 17, 1862, and she died April 9, 1895. Children:

Sarah P., b. Nov. 25, 1835; m. Nov. 15, 1859, Richard L. Locke. Margaret Ann, b. April 11, 1838; m. Oct., 1857, Amos P. Brown; d. Nov. 18, 1862. Mary Abby, b. March 18, 1841; d. unm., Dec. 13, 1897.

57. SHERIDAN JENNESS, son of Joseph (37), born May 12, 1824; married Almira Batchelder. He died Dec. 10, 1888, and she died July 19, 1900. Children:

Susan M., b. Jan. 6, 1851; m. Nov. 5, 1868, Horace Sawyer. Alice, b. Sept. 16, 1857; unm.

58. JOB JENNESS, son of John (38), born July 14, 1811; married Keziah Wilson. He was proprietor of the Ocean House, the first hotel built at "Jenness Beach." She died Jan. 19, 1879, and he died Feb. 29, 1888. Children:

74. Job Rienza. Charles W., b. 1852; m. Feb. 8, 1875, widow Mary Butler Crouse; d. Jan. 29, 1897.

59. JOHN JENNESS, son of John (38), married Salome Wilson. Lived at Methuen, Mass. Child:

Lyndon Y., m.; lives in Florida.

60. JONATHAN ROLLINS JENNESS, son of John (38), married Sarah E. Marston. He died April 17, 1852, and she married, July 1, 1853, Adna Brown. Child:

Henry.

61. WESLEY JENNESS, son of John (38), born April 10, 1831; married, Oct., 1853, Harriett Mow. Children:

Fanny Wesley, b. Aug. 10, 1855; m. first, Dec. 24, 1873, George E. Dow; second, Sept. 26, 1887, Henry Brown. Archie Linden, b. April 30, 1862; m. Feb. 8, 1882, Lizzie B. Shaw; had Linden, b. April 16, 1886; Harry B.; David W.; Frank A., b. March 16, 1890; Jennie, b. Feb. 17, 1892.

62. GILMAN HARRISON JENNESS, adopted son of Jonathan (42), born Sept., 1839; married, first Eliza True

Leavitt; second, Elmira Newell of New Jersey. Children by first wife:

    Charles Leavitt, m. Edwin Jewell, b. April 26, 1865. Frank Benning, b. May 30, 1869; m. Dec. 19, 1899, Mrs. Cora D. Willson, dau. of Geo. H. Babbitt of Bellows Falls, Vt.

Child by second wife:

    Harrison N., b. May 7, 1889.

63. DAVID A. JENNESS, son of Simon (52), born Aug. 26, 1814; married, April 15, 1841, Sarah W. Drake. He died March 28, 1869, and she died May 12, 1881. Children:

    Emery Curtis, b. June 3, 1842; m. Dec. 3, 1871, Ellen A. Rand. Harriett O., b. March 5, 1844; m. March 20, 1864, James W. Marden; d. Aug. 18, 1900. Anna Drake, b. Jan. 31, 1846; m. July 13, 1871, Alexander H. Hodgdon.

64. LEVI WOODBURY JENNESS, son of Simon (47), born April 24, 1824; married Emeline S. Locke. He died Jan. 9, 1852, and she died Feb. 1, 1890. Child:

    Woodbury L., b. June 8, 1851; m. Mary Davis Poole; had one child, Gertrude; m. Nov. 28, 1901, Frank Cousins.

65. WILLIAM BENJAMIN JENNESS, son of Amos Seavey, (48), born May 29, 1819; married, Dec. 25, 1844, Mary Abby Jenness. Children:

    Clara Ann, b. June 17, 1845; m. Aug., 1866, Clarence B. Mason; divorced; m. second, John Simmons. Louis Wentworth, b. June 7, 1848; d. April 12, 1880, at Epping; fell from a team and was run over. Flora May, b. Nov. 5, 1858; m. July 25, 1875, Samuel Pike.

66. JOSEPH G. JENNESS, son of Amos Seavey (48), born March 21, 1825; married, first, April 18, 1857, Elvira Garland; second, widow Marden. Child by first wife:

    George M., b. Jan. 28, 1864; d. July 16, 1884.

Child by second wife:

    Josephine G., b. Aug. 15, 1889.

67. OLIVER PETER JENNESS, son of Samuel (49), born Jan., 1820; married, June 21, 1842, Elizabeth Dow Drake. She died May 11, 1888, and he died March 10, 1897. Children:

75. Charles Austin, b. Dec. 30, 1843. Cotton Ward Drake, b. Aug., 1849; m. Feb. 10, 1881, Alice Foss; d. Jan. 21, 1897.

68. NATHANIEL GILBERT JENNESS, son of Samuel (49), born Nov., 1823; married, April 11, 1848, Emeline Lang. He died March 12, 1897. Children:
76. Otis Simpson, b. 1849. Clara Emma, b. Dec. 17, 1856; unm.

69. ISAAC JENNESS, son of Henry (52), born March, 1814; married, March, 1833, Hannah Brown. He died March 19, 1899. Children:
Martha Jane, b. Oct. 13, 1834; m. March 24, 1854, Martin V. Sleeper. Hezekiah A., b. March 28, 1838; m. Oct. 5, 1861, Sarah J. Foster. Sarah E., b. Jan. 24, 1842; m. Feb. 2, 1855, Calvin Barnard. Nettie, b. Oct. 18, 1845; m. John Blaisdell. Corasanda, b. June 21, 1848. Ellen F., b. Dec. 15, 1850; m. John Hobbs. Melissa, b. April 6, 1853; m. Frank Philbrick. Emily A., b. Sept. 18, 1855; m. William Smart. Ida V., b. April 15, 1859; m. Baker. Malvina, b. April 19, 1863; m. June 4, 1887, John Grover.

70. SIMON LAMPREY JENNESS, son of Henry (52), born Feb., 1816; married Mary E., widow of Simon F. Tarlton. Removed to Hampton in 1832. Children:
Frank Towle, b. Sept. 21, 1845; m. Ida Dunbrack of Rye. Abbott Brown, b. Dec. 30, 1847; m. May 25, 1876, Zipporah J., dau. of Edward Shaw. Emma E., b. 1850; d. Feb. 12, 1851. Annie May (adopted), b. Nov., 1854; m. Fred B. Dunbar.

71. HENRY JENNESS, son of Henry (52), born Dec. 24, 1825; married, first, Mary Page; second, Rebecca J. Rowe. Children:
Herman, m. Lydia Philbrick.
77. Alvato, m. Annie M. Brown. John, m. Nov. 29, 1882, Grace Balch. Willis. Carrie.

72. JOSEPH JEROME JENNESS, son of Henry (52), born May 1, 1828; married, first, Martha A. Folsom; second, Page. Children by first wife:
Emma C., b. Aug. 24, 1851; m. Currier; d. Jan. 24, 1887. Mary Anna, b. Feb. 9, 1853; m. George Page. Sarah, b. Aug., 1855; m. Frank Rand.

73. ALBERT DANA JENNESS, son of Benjamin (55), born April 7, 1834; married, first, Oct. 23, 1855, Emeline Brown; second, April 14, 1863, Clara J. Garland. Children:

Elmer M., b. June 22, 1866; d. Nov. 15, 1878. Willard M., b. Sept. 17, 1871; m. Oct. 30, 1901, Emily Wharton, b. July 12, 1877, and had Olivian Mildred, b. April 22, 1903. Arthur A., b. June 18, 1882.

74. JOB RIENZA JENNESS, son of Job (58), married, first, May 10, 1860, Sarah Emeline Perkins; second June 9, 1865, Emerett A. Brown. He died Feb. 3, 1872. Children:

Emma Perkins, b. Aug. 31, 1861; m. Jan. 5, 1879, George E. Dalton. Ida M., b. March, 1867; m. Oct. 6, 1897, Hervey C. Moulton. Etta, b. Oct., 1868; m. 1890, Clarence F. Bickford.

75. CHARLES AUSTIN JENNESS, son of Oliver Peter (67), born Dec. 30, 1843; married, first, May 24, 1870, Ann Eliza Brown; second, Jan. 21, 1880, Hattie B. Weeks. Child by first wife:

Howard L., b. June 4, 1874; d. Feb. 29, 1876.

Children by second wife:

Fannie Weeks, b. March 28, 1885. Herbert Leon, b. June 25, 1887. Thornton W., b. May 20, 1889.

76. OTIS SIMPSON JENNESS, son of Nathaniel Gilbert (68), born 1849; married, March 30, 1875, Anna P. Marston. Children:

Edith Maud, b. Sept. 22, 1875; m. Charles J. Lasbury. Edgar, b. Feb. 18, 1877. Ethel, b. April 11, 1882.

77. ALVATO JENNESS, son of Henry (71), married Emira M. Brown. Child:

A son, b. March 25, 1897.

1. FRANCIS JENNESS, perhaps son of John (3), and Mary (Mason) Jenness, married Sarah Locke. Children:

Joseph, m. French; lived at Epping.
2. John Bean. Sarah, m. Norris of Epping. ———, m. John Pike of Epping. Lydia, m. Jeremiah Elkins. Abigail.

2. JOHN BEAN JENNESS, son of Francis (1), married, June 24, 1786, Olive Berry. He came from Epping and lived with his uncle, "tanner" Richard Jenness, who gave him his farm. Children:

3. Richard, b. Jan. 19, 1787.
4. John, b. March 8, 1790. Olive, b. 1794; m. Oct., 1812, Benning Leavitt.

3. RICHARD JENNESS, son of John Bean (2), born Jan. 19, 1787; married, first, Dec. 18, 1809, widow Betsey Brown; second, widow Betsey B. Folsom. Children:
5. Lowell, b. March 11, 1813. Langdon Seavey, b. Nov. 25, 1815; d. unm., Aug. 2, 1873.
6. Oliver, b. March 30, 1818. Elizabeth Howe, b. July 6, 1820; had Lula A., who m. Augustus Caswell. Rufus Kittridge, b. Oct. 27, 1822.
7. Richard, b. July 13, 1825.

4. JOHN JENNESS, son of John Bean (2), born March 8, 1790; married, Dec. 25, 1816, Hannah Wedgewood. Children:
8. David Wedgewood, b. 1817. George Washington, b. May 13, 1827; m. July 28, 1873, Elvira Moulton of North Hampton; d. Feb. 15, 1887.

5. LOWELL JENNESS, son of Richard (3), born March 11, 1813; married, Oct. 19, 1845, Ann L. Folsom. Lived at Portsmouth. He died in 1895. Children:
Albert Jewell, b. Nov. 4, 1846; d. Feb., 1851. Albion Jewell, b. Nov. 4, 1846. Clarence Albert; m.; died.

6. OLIVER JENNESS, son of Richard (3), born March 30, 1818; married Dec. 24, 1842, Sidney Seavey. He died Feb. 9, 1896. Blacksmith by trade. Children:
Minerva S., b. May 9, 1844; m. Aug. 31, Charles E. Wentworth. Rufus O., b. Oct. 25, 1846; d. Nov. 30, 1900. John W., b. April 17, 1850. Florence A., b. Sept. 1, 1863; unm.

7. RICHARD JENNESS, son of Richard (3), born July 13, 1825; married, Dec. 29, 1866, Sarah B. Page, born Jan. 29, 1846. He died Dec. 5, 1885. Children:
Charles Moore, b. March 29, 1867. Ivan Douglass, b. Oct. 29, 1868.

8. DAVID WEDGEWOOD JENNESS, son of John (4), born 1817; married, April 28, 1839, Abigail Knowles. She died Feb. 9, 1888. Child:
9. John Leroy, b. Dec. 4, 1842.

9. JOHN LEROY JENNESS, son of David Wedgewood (8), born Dec. 4, 1842; married, Dec. 24, 1868, Hattie E. Cunningham. Lives at Lynn, Mass. Child:

Nellie M., b. Aug. 28, 1869; m.

Benjamin Jenness married Hannah ————. Joined the church in 1764, and resided at the Center. Children:

John, b. 1763. Benjamin, b. 1765. Joanna.

JOHN W. JENNESS, grandson of Isaac (69), born Feb. 25, 1868; married March 4, 1891, Florence W. Farrell. She was born in 1869. Children:

Morris, b. June 4, 1892. Ervin, b. June 2, 1895.

JOHNSON.

1. PETER JOHNSON, son of Peter and great-grandson of Edmund, who settled at Hampton in 1639, was born July 11, 1714; married, April 19, 1737, Sarah, daughter of Simon Dow. Children, all baptized at Hampton:

Esther, bapt. May 13, 1739. Ruth, bapt. Oct. 7, 1739.
2. Peter, bapt. Feb. 28, 1742. Sarah, bapt. April 29, 1744; m. Nathan Goss. Simon, bapt. Dec. 22, 1745; m. Deliverance Knowles of Chester; d. 1813. May, bapt. July 24, 1748; unm.; deranged.

2. PETER JOHNSON, son of Peter (1), bapt. Feb. 28, 1742; married, Sept. 18, 1767, Mary Yeaton. Served as drummer in Capt. Parsons' company in the Revolutionary War. Children:

Sally, d. unm., aged 21 years.
3. Peter, b. Aug. 6, 1770.
4. Edmond.

3. PETER JOHNSON, son of Peter (2), born Aug. 6, 1770; married, Nov. 26, 1801, Abigail D., daughter of John Batchelder. She died Feb. 4, 1816, and he died May 4, 1834. Children:

Abigail D., b. 1802; d. Feb. 5, 1816. Sally, b. Oct. 12, 1803; m. Jonathan Perkins; d. March 19, 1872.
5. John Batchelder, b. Aug. 7, 1806. Mary C., b. May 21, 1812; m. May 8, 1845, Ivory Brown; had before m. Maria L.

4. EDMUND JOHNSON, son of Peter (2), married, first, Aug. 9, 1789, Abigail Berry. She died Feb. 28, 1808, and he married, second, E. Black; third, Eliza Stearns. Children by first wife:

Mary, bapt. Jan. 30, 1791. Sally, bapt. Oct. 9, 1791; m. first, William Randall; second, George Randall of Newcastle. Edmund, bapt. Oct. 9, ——; d. young. Simon, bapt. July 14, 1793; m. Adeline Drake of Newcastle; went out West. Edmund, bapt. Sept. 18, 1796; m. first, Augusta Berry, d. Oct. 10, 18—, in the U. S. navy.

6. John Greenleaf.

Child by second wife:

Mary, m. John Brown of Lexington, Mass.; three children.

5. JOHN BATCHELDER JOHNSON, son of Peter (3), born Aug. 7, 1806; married Mary Folsom, born 1810; died Dec. 16, 1883. He died Nov. 11, 1890. Children:

John B., b. May, 1834; enlisted in U. S. army. Richard Mentor, b. Nov. 28, 1836. Sarah. Gilman W., b. 1843; m. 1874, Mary Mow; she d. Dec., 1885. Charles DeWitt Clinton, m. Lizzie ———. Charlotte, m. first, ———; second, Charles Lang of Portsmouth. Martha J., m. Nov., 1872, Albert Frank Libby.

7. Albert M., b. Nov. 19, 1853.

6. JOHN GREENLEAF JOHNSON, son of Edmund (4), married, July 13, 1822, Sally B. Mace. She afterwards married, Feb. 8, 1827, Ithamar Mace. Children:

John Edward, b. 1823; was drowned with his son John; his other son, Greenleaf, d. Aug. 17, 1880, aged 31 years, at Bay Port, Fla. Abby S., b. Jan. 20, 1825; m. first, Nathaniel Mace; second, David Remick.

7. ALBERT M. JOHNSON, son of John Batchelder (5), born Nov. 19, 1853; married Mary F. Mace. Children:

Minnie Addie, b. April 20, 1881. John Batchelder, b. Nov. 7, 1883. Ada May, b. April 16, 1886. Charles Clinton, b. March 1, 1890. Burleigh Albert, b. Oct. 22, 1892.

Edward Johnson and Sarah Allard were married Feb. 25, 1743.

Charles Johnson of Sweden married, 1874, first, Annie ————; second, 1885, Annie Swinson. Children by first wife:

Henry, b. 1887; m. Edward S., b. 1880; soldier in the Spanish-American War.
Child by second wife:
Fred, b. 1886.

JONES.

JOHN JONES, an Irishman, married, Aug. 27, 1733, Anna Webster. Children:
William, b. June 7, 1735. Sarah, b. April 23, 1737. Mary, b. Nov. 1740; d. Nov., 1740. Anna, b. Nov. 19, 1741; unm.; insane and supported by the town; d. Nov. 8, 1806. Catherine, b. April 15, 1743. Susannah, b. Oct. 17, 1745. Olly, b. 1747. John, b. March 17, 1748. Olly, bapt. 1752. Abiah, b. May 4, 1753. Mary, b. 1756.

1. JOHN WILLIAM JONES, married Margaret Brewster, an Irish woman. She afterwards married Reuben Moulton. Children:
Margaret, b. 1766; m. Simon Lamper.
2. William. Joseph.

2. WILLIAM JONES, son of John William (1), married, June 16, 1796, Sarah Moulton. Children:
3. John. Joseph, drowned with William Walker, May 3, 1831.

3. JOHN JONES, son of William (2), married, Nov. 12, 1827, Esther Y. Foss. Children:
Cyrus ., m. Mary Towle.
4. Charles W.

4. CHARLES W. JONES, son of John (3), married Abbie Towle. Children:
Fannie E., b. 1872; m. first, April, 1895, Harold A. Michie; second, April 29, 1899, Robert J. Rawding.

HIRAM JONES married Martha S. Leavitt. He committed suicide, and Sept. 15, 1861, his widow married Frank Jones of Portsmouth. Child:
Emma I., b. Nov. 27, 1855; m. Charles A. Sinclair of Littleton.

SAMUEL JACKSON JONES married Elizabeth G. Locke. Children:
Montrose, b. May, 1856. Son, b. May 12, 1868.

GENEALOGY. 401

JONATHAN JONES married Caroline Warren. Children:
———, b. Dec. 15, 1865. ———, b. Aug. 26, 1867. ———, b. June 26, 1869.

KATE.

Frances, daughter of Daniel Kate, was baptized Oct. 14, 1792.

Joseph Kate of Nottingham and Prudence Marden of Portsmouth were married May 7, 1789.

Richard Kate of Barrington and Polly Rand were married Nov. 16, 1790.

KEEN.

WILLIAM KEEN, born Feb. 12, 1792; married, March 3, 1840, Harriett Rand, born Sept. 14, 1810. Children:

Georgianna, b. July 16, 1836; m. June 29, 1843, Charles H. Downes. Harriett Elizabeth, b. Nov. 9, 1840; m. Dec. 25, 1856, Warren W. Keen.

WARREN W. KEEN married Dec. 25, 1856, Harriett Elizabeth Keen. Children:

Hattie G., b. Sept. 26, 1859. Carrie M., b. Dec., 1861. Nellie W., b. May, 1863. Addie P., b. Dec., 1865. Henry H., b. Feb., 1867. Emogene, b. 1868.

KIMBALL.

HEZEKIAH KIMBALL, married Hannah Philbrick. Children:

Susan, m. Franklin Heald. Fabins, went out West. Charles, lived at Washington, D. C. Scott, d. Feb., 1876, at Malden, Mass. Lafayette, m. Feb. 25, 1849, Mary Grover; lived at Gilford, Me.

KINGMAN.

WILLIAM KINGMAN, married, first, Mary ———; second, Aug. 19, 1747, Elizabeth Webster. Removed to Barrington and was driven back by Indians. After living here for a time he returned to Barrington and found everything just as it had been left. He had a sister Mary, who married Henry Seavey Sept. 18, 1740. Children by first wife:

Elijah, b. Aug. 5, 1743. Ruth, b. Oct. 11, 1745.

Children by second wife:
John, bapt. May 22, 1748; m. Dolly Waterhouse; had Jeremiah and a dau. Olive, bapt. July 8, 1753. A daughter.

KNOWLES.

1. EZEKIEL KNOWLES, son of John and Susanna, of Hampton, was born June 29, 1687; married, Jan. 31, 1712, Mary, daughter of David Wedgwood. Children:
   Hannah, b. March 1, 1713. Nathan, bapt. May 27, 1716; m. Mary, b. Nov. 2, 1718; m. John Lane; d. 1787.
2. Amos, b. Nov. 4, 1722. David, b. Sept. 1, 1725; m. Deborah Palmer, lived at North Hampton.

2. AMOS KNOWLES, son of Ezekiel (1), born Nov. 4, 1722; married, Oct. 11, 1744, Libby. Children:
3. Nathan, b. 1745. Lydia, b. 1747. Ezekiel, b. 1749. Isaac, b. 1751.
4. Amos, b. 1755. Elizabeth, b. 1755; d. young. John, b. 1759. Elizabeth, b. 1761; m. Benjamin Palmer. David, b. 1764. Seth, b. 1766.

3. NATHAN KNOWLES, son of Amos (2), born 1745; married Hannah Clifford. He died Jan. 19, 1820. Children:
   John Clifford, b. 1768; d. unm. Nov. 7, 1837.
5. Nathan (twin), b. 1775. Ezekiel, b. 1777. Hannah, b. 1782; m. Theodore Coffin.

4. AMOS KNOWLES, son of Amos (2), born 1755; married Betsey Palmer. Children:
   John. David. Ezekiel, m. Betsey Clifford. Isaac, m. Locke of Epsom. Lydia, m. Joseph Morse. Seth, m. Emerson. Betsey, m. Judkins. Amos, m. Dolly Quimby. Nathan, m. Hannah Clifford.

5. NATHAN KNOWLES, son of Nathan (3), born 1775; married, Nov. 10, 1799, Sarah Hook Brown. Served in Captain Coleman's company of cavalry in the War of 1812. He died Oct. 17, 1863. Children:
   Patty B., b. July 28, 1800; m. Dec., 1818, Joseph Philbrick, Jr. John Langdon, b. Aug. 14, 1804; d. Jan. 22, 1806. Sarah L., b. April 29, 1807; m. June, 1829, Simon Garland. Hannah, b. Nov. 12, 1808; m. Nov. 28, 1833, Joseph Locke.

6. John, b. Feb. 9, 1811. Mary, b. Jan. 9, 1814; m. Nov., 1834, Reuben P. Jenness. Abigail, b. Feb. 4, 1817; m. April 28, 1839, David W. Jenness. Clarissa, b. April 15, 1818; m. Oct. 11, 1839, Joseph J. Drake.

6. JOHN KNOWLES, son of Nathan (5), born Feb. 9, 1811; married, May 25, 1834, Nancy Lane, daughter of John Lane and Sarah Dow. She was born Dec. 13, 1811, and is still living (1903), the oldest person in town. Children:

Sarah Elizabeth, b. July, 1834; m. June 26, 1861, Warren Caswell; d. Aug. 2, 1866.
7. Charles Nathan, b. June 30, 1839.

7. CHARLES NATHAN KNOWLES, son of John (6), born June 30, 1839; married, Nov. 24, 1868, Anna A. Garland. She died Oct. 24, 1894. Children:

Lizzie Abby, b. Oct. 6, 1871; m. Oct. 5, 1890, Fred A. Brown. Annie, b. Jan. 30, 1874; m. April 18, 1897, Frank M. Pierce. Clinta Cleveland, b. Dec. 11, 1882.

1. SIMON KNOWLES, son of ————, married Deliverance ————. Child:
2. Joseph, b. Dec. 13, 1727.

2. JOSEPH KNOWLES, son of Simon (1), born Dec. 13, 1727; married, March 3, 1748, Love Brackett. He died Nov. 7, 1823. Children:

Simon, b. May 16, 1748; m. Feb. 8, 1779, widow Esther Yeaton.
3. Samuel, b. Oct. 27, 1749. Deliverance, b. Oct. 26, 1751; m. first, Simon Johnson; second, Benjamin Marden. Love, b. Aug. 26, 1754. Rachel, b. Jan. 8, 1756. Joseph, b. June 15, 1758. John, b. April 8, 1760.

3. SAMUEL KNOWLES, son of Joseph (2), born Oct. 27, 1749; married, March 17, 1772, Sarah Marden. Lived near the "Four Corners" by Alfred Seavey's. Was sergeant in Captain Parsons' company in the Revolutionary War. Children:

Anna Brackett, b. 1773. Samuel, b. 1774. Deliverance, b. 1775. Sarah, b. 1777.

Josiah Knowles and Susannah Godfrey were married April 6, 1820.

JAMES KNOWLES married, first, Oct. 11, 1744, Mary Libby; second, June 30, 1748, Comfort Wallis. Children:
Daniel, bapt. 1746; m. Mary and Comfort, bapt. 1749.

John Knowles married first, Jan. 1, 1741, Sarah Moulton; and second, perhaps, Tryphene Locke. Children:
Sarah, b. 1741. John, b. 1743. Tryphene, b. 1745.

LAMPREY.

1. BENJAMIN LAMPREY, son of Benjamin, and grandson of Henry and Gillyen, who came to Hampton about 1660, was born Oct. 9, 1688; married, Feb. 7, 1711, Sarah, daughter of Simon Dow. Children:

Sarah, b. March 8, 1713; m. Nov. 11, 1736, Israel Dolbear. Hannah, b. April 7, 1717. Jane, b. April 9, 1719. Mary, b. Jan. 7, 1722. Benjamin, b. Jan. 11, 1726; m. first, Abigail Dearborn; second, Comfort Shepard. Deborah, b. Nov. 19, 1727.
2. Simon. Elizabeth, bapt. Aug. 26, 1733; m. Jonathan Godfrey; d. March 30, 1811.

2. SIMON LAMPREY, son of Benjamin (1), married, first, Patience, daughter of James Hobbs; second, widow Martha Dow. Children:

Sarah, b. 1760; m. Francis Marden.
3. Simon, b. 1765. Molly, m. Daniel Moulton. Lucy, m. Asa Tilton. Hannah, m. Samuel Knowles.
4. James, b. Aug. 10, 1770. Betsey, b. Dec., 1774; m. William Norton; d. Oct. 30, 1868. Asa, b. Jan. 12, 1780; m. Nancy Shannon.

3. SIMON LAMPREY, son of Simon (2), born 1765; married Margaret Jones. Children:

Betsey, b. 1790; m. first, Josiah Folsom; second, Richard Jenness. Charlotte, b. Aug. 3, 1793; m. Henry Jenness; d. Sept. 3, 1867. Joseph, m. Edgerly. Mary, b. March 9, 1803; m. Charles Green.

4. JAMES LAMPREY, son of Simon (2), born Aug. 10, 1770; married, first, Sarah Brown; second, Elizabeth Edgerly. Children:

Benning. James. Sarah. Hannah. Lucy. David. Dorothy. Joseph Brown.

LANE.

JOHN LANE, son of John, and grandson of William and Sarah, who came to Hampton about 1686, was born Oct. 12, 1709, and married, first, Sept. 28, 1732, Hannah Lamprey; second, March 10, 1738, Mary, daughter of Ezekiel Knowles. Removed to Chester about 1749. Children by first wife:

John, b. Oct. 11, 1733. Daniel, b. July 8, 1735.

Children by second wife:

Ezekiel, b. July 4, 1739. David, b. Feb. 21, 1740-'41. Mary, b. Feb. 24, 1742-'43. Hannah, b. Dec. 25, 1744. Nathan, b. June 12, 1747. Isaac, b. 1749; d. 1757. Sarah, b. 1758. Isaac, b. 1760. Jonathan, b. 1763.

JOHN LANE, married, Aug. 7, 1854, Hannah O. Locke. He died Aug. 12, 1854, and she married John William Randall. Child:

Belle, b. Oct. 9, 1854; m. Daniel Woodbury Dalton, and was divorced.

LANG.

JOHN LANG, of English origin, was at Portsmouth before 1692. In a later generation a family of Langs lived at Hampton Falls, from which the Sanbornton lines are descended.

The following, probably brothers, lived at Rye:
1. William.
2. John.
3. Benjamin.

1. WILLIAM LANG, probably married, second, Dec. 9, 1751, Elizabeth Rand. Children:
4. Mark, bapt. 1741. Molly, bapt. 1744.

2. JOHN LANG, married Sarah Bickford, who lived at Portsmouth near the mill dam. She died in 1801, aged 96 years. Children:
5. George, b. 1745.
6. Bickford. John, m. Judith Babb; lived at Greenland.

7. Thomas. William, carpenter by trade; m. and had a dau., Dolly. Dorothy, m. Ebenezer Wallis; no child. Sarah, m. Nov. 1, 1750, Job Foss. Hannah, m. John Weeks; lived at Gilmanton. Grace, m. Philip Babb; lived at Epsom.

3. BENJAMIN LANG is said to have married, first, Eleanor Burley. He married, second, Deborah Varrell. A Benjamin Lang married, June 4, 1756, Mary Thompson of Portsmouth. Removed to Ohio. Children:

 Eleanor, b. April 11, 1759; m. Jonathan Pulsifer; lived at Deerfield.
 Hannah, b. Jan. 5, 1761; m. William Burleigh; lived at Candia.
8. Benjamin, b. July 28, 1765. Betsey, b. Aug. 25, 1771; m. Jonathan Lang; removed to Sanbornton, where she d. Jan. 8, 1806.

4. MARK LANG, son of William (1), baptized in 1741; married Salome Goss. He died July 25, 1808; lived on the new road in Portsmouth. Children:

 Elizabeth, bapt. 1761; m. Job Locke. Anna, bapt. 1763; m. April 22, 1784, John Varrell. Hannah, bapt. 1765; m. Nov. 10, 1785, Job. Locke.
9. Mark, b. 1768.
10. Richard.
11. Jonathan, b. 1773.
12. William, b. 1774.

5. GEORGE LANG, son of John (2), born 1745; married, Oct. 23, 1770, Sarah Johnson. Removed to Greenland. He died Oct. 16, 1790, and she married James Whidden. Children:

 George, b. 1773; d. Nov. 15, 1833. Sarah, m. May 4, 1800, Thomas Berry; d. 1869.

6. BICKFORD LANG, son of John (2), married, March 8, 1764, Martha Locke. Removed to Epsom. Blacksmith by trade. Children:

13. John, b. April, 1767. Hannah, b. Sept. 16, 1769; m. Dowrst Rand. Martha, b. Feb. 7, 1772; m. first, Jeremiah Fogg; second, John Batchelder; lived at North Hampton.
14. Bickford, b. Nov., 1774. Sarah, b. Oct., 1776; m. first, Jonathan Crockett; second, Josiah Tuck; lived at Effingham. William, b. 1782; d. aged two months.

7. THOMAS LANG, probably son of John (2), married, Sept. 16, 1757, Mary Goss. Children:

GENEALOGY. 407

Susannah, bapt. 1758. William, b. 1761; went to Ohio. Levi, b. 1763; m.; lived at Deerfield. Anna, b. 1767; d. unm.
15. Richard, b. Aug. 12, 1770. Sarah or Salome, b. 1774; m. Ebenezer Collins; lived at New Gloucester, Me. Betsey, m. Nathaniel Berry. Samuel, went to Ohio.

8. BENJAMIN LANG, son of Benjamin (3), born July 28, 1765, married Deborah Bean. Removed to Candia. Children:

David, m. Sally Sanborn. John, m. Relief Brown. Mary, m. Washington Varrell. Samuel, m. Martha Sanborn. Nathan, m. Robinson.

9. MARK LANG, son of Mark (4), born 1768; married, Oct. 9, 1792, Hannah Marden. He died in 1845. Lived on the new road in Portsmouth. Children:

Elizabeth, b. June 28, 1793; m. June 7, 1813, David S. Marden. Annaniah, b. Oct. 22, 1794; d. April 30, 1803. Polly, b. June 25, 1796; d. Jan. 14, 1797. Daniel, b. Sept. 15, 1797; d. unm. May, 1861. Mark, b. March 5, 1799; d. Feb. 23, 1862. Hannah, b. Sept. 14, 1800; m. Sept. 23, 1821, Benjamin W. Marden; d. Oct. 9, 1827. Aaron, b. March 7, 1802; d. April 11, 1803. Polly, b. Jan. 21, 1804; m. July 7, 1822, Elias Perkins. Sarah A., b. Jan., 1806; d. unm. Jan. 9, 1879. John Langdon, b. June 12, 1809; d. Aug. 27, 1833. Esther, b. Feb. 24, 1811; m. David Moulton of Portsmouth, who d. in California; she d. April 13, 1875. Lucy, b. Nov. 24, 1815; m. William Willey; d. Nov., 1876. Aaron, b. May 5, 1813; d. unm.

10. RICHARD LANG, son of Mark (4), born 1778; married, Dec. 31, 1798, Nancy Walker. Served in the War of 1812 under Capt. Ephraim Philbrick. He died May 6, 1854. Children:

Fanny Goldthwait, b. 1798; m. Thomas Adams. Edward, b. 1799; m. Deborah Marston; lived at North Hampton, and d. April 1, 1866. Polly, b. 1800; m. first, Trefethern; second, Nathaniel B. Abbott. William, b. Nov., 1802; m. first, Eliza A. Brady; second, Elizabeth Hazzard; he d. April 3, 1869.
16. Nancy. Eliza, m. Jacob Holmes; had before m. Mary Ann. Samuel, removed to Georgia. Richard, m. first, Almira Hobbs; second, Winn; third, Matilda Spinney; on the Boston police force; shot himself accidentally Nov. 14, 1862. Sarah, m. Nathan Fellows.

11. JONATHAN LANG, son of Mark (4), born 1773; married ————. Was called "Doctor." Removed to Sanbornton, where he died Jan. 8, 1806. Children:

Hannah, bapt. 1799. Elly, bapt. 1799. David. Jonathan.

12. WILLIAM LANG, son of Mark (4), born 1774; married, Nov. 13, 1794, Betsey Walker. He died May 3, 1831. Children:

Mary Ann, b. Feb. 22, 1795; m. Thomas Marden. Harriett, b. April, 1797; d. young. Elizabeth Beverly, b. April 17, 1799; m. John Sampson. Fanny G., b. Dec., 1801.
17. Leonard, b. Jan., 1804. Hannah, b. Jan., 1806; d. unm. Feb., 1882. Eleanor, b. Sept., 1808. Harriett, b. July 22, 1811; m. Sherburne Somerby. Maria, b. Sept. 25, 1813; had Joseph Button Marden.
18. Thomas Marden, b. Jan. 6, 1817.

13. JOHN LANG, son of Bickford (6), born April, 1767; married Mercy Drake. Lived at Effingham and at Limerick, Me. Children:

Frances, bapt. 1789. Huldah, bapt. 1793. Polly, bapt. 1795. Data, bapt. 1796.

14. BICKFORD LANG, son of Bickford (6), born Nov., 1774; married, Jan. 2, 1797, Abigail Locke. Removed to Epsom, and afterwards to Ohio. Children:

Billy, bapt. 1797. Reuel, bapt. 1799.

15. RICHARD LANG, son of Thomas (7), born Aug. 12, 1770; married, Sept. 28, 1797, Comfort Foss, born May 7, 1772, and died April 4, 1854. He died Jan. 24, 1823. Children:

Fanny, b. April 12, 1799; d. unm. Dec. 27, 1870.
19. Ebenezer Wallis, b. July 30, 1802. Mary Ann, b. Jan. 20, 1808; m. Nov. 25, 1829, Mark R. Webster. Sarah, b. Sept. 21, 1809; m. May 29, 1829, Joseph Whidden Seavey. Almira, b. April 22, 1813; m. Andrew Gardiner.

16. NANCY LANG, daughter of Richard (10), married, May 22, 1832, Jacob Holmes. Before marriage she had:
20. George H. Lang, b. June 6, 1827.

17. LEONARD LANG, son of William (12), born Jan., 1804; married Data Garland. Removed to Stratham. Children:

Emeline, b. Sept. 28, 1829; m. Nathaniel Gilbert Jenness. Elizabeth Ann, b. Feb. 9, 1832. William B., b. Feb. 18, 1835. Augustus. Data.

18. THOMAS MARDEN LANG, son of William (12), born Jan. 6, 1817; married, Oct. 25, 1840, Martha E. Varrell. Lived on the new road in Portsmouth. Children:

Harvey V., b. March 8, 1841. Thomas W., b. June 24, 1844; m. Nov. 29, 1866, Jennie C. Fuller. Charles T., b. Aug. 8, 1846; m. Mrs. Charlotte Johnson. Frances E., b. Oct. 5, 1850. Eliza E., b. Feb. 17, 1853. Martha, b. Oct., 1855; d. Nov. 10, 1855, aged five weeks.

19. EBENEZER WALLIS LANG, son of Richard (15), born July 30, 1802; married Florenza Trefethern. He died Oct. 13, 1891, and she died Oct. 30, 1896. Children:

Richard W., b. 1830.
21. Eben M., b. April, 1833.
22. Alfred M. Clarinda, b. July 6, 1839; d. June 30, 1895. Charles W., b. 1848; m. Oct. 7, 1895, Clara I. Trefethern.

20. GEORGE H. LANG, son of Nancy (16), born June 6, 1827; married Lydia Golden. Was out in the Civil War in the 17th regiment of Massachusetts, Co. D, for three years. Enlisted second time for one year in the first N. H. heavy artillery. He died July 12, 1901. Children:

George William, b. May 17, 1855; m. 1882, widow Lydia Lowell, and had Arkell C., b. Sept. 20, 1883, and Florina A., b. May 20, 1887. Sophronia, b. Jan., 1857; m. Thomas Taylor, and went to England.
23. Hezekiah Perry, b. June 21, 1859.

21. EBEN M. LANG, son of Ebenezer Wallis (19), born April, 1833; married, 1859, Hannah C. Trefethern. He died Sept. 30, 1878. Children:

Willis O., b. July 31, 1860. A son, b. Oct. 14, 1865; d. Oct. 18, 1865.

22. ALFRED M. LANG, son of Ebenezer Wallis (19), married, first, Maria Parker. Was in the 32d Maine regiment in the War of 1861-'65. Child:

——, b. Feb. 27, 1869.

23. HEZEKIAH PERRY LANG, son of George H. (20), born June 21, 1859; married Alice Gray. Children:

Oren, b. Jan. 21, 1880. Lizzie, b. June 5, 1881.

Josiah Lang and Pearn Johnson, both of Greenland, were married Dec. 17, 1771.

LANGDON.

1. TOBIAS LANGDON came from England. He married in 1656, Elizabeth Sherburne. He died July 27, 1664, and his widow married Tobias Lear. Children:

2. Tobias, b. 1660. Elizabeth, m. William Fernald. Oner, m. 1686, John Laighton. Margaret, m. Nichols Moule.

2. CAPT. TOBIAS LANGDON, son of Tobias (1), born 1660; married, Nov. 17, 1686, Mary Hubbard. He died Feb. 20, 1725. Lived at Portsmouth. Children:

Mary, b. Nov. 17, 1687; m. George Pierce. Tobias, b. Oct. 11, 1689; m. 1714, Sarah Winkley. Martha, b. March 7, 1693; m. 1715, Nichols Shapley. Richard, b. April 14, 1694; m. Thankfull; d. at Newtown, L. I.
3. Joseph, b. Feb. 28, 1696.
4. Mark, bapt. Sept. 15, 1698. Samuel, b. Sept. 6, 1700; m. 1725, Hannah Jenness.
5. William, b. Oct. 20, 1702.
6. John, b. May 28, 1707.

3. CAPT. JOSEPH LANGDON, son of Tobias (2), born Feb. 28, 1696; married Dec. 1, 1720, Mary Banfield, who died Aug. 10, 1753. He died Aug. 10, 1767. Children:

7. Samuel, b. 1721. Mary, b. 1725; m. Amos Seavey; d. Feb. 23, 1807. Hannah, m. Jan. 8, 1745, Samuel Whidden of Greenland; d. April 21, 1801. Elizabeth, m. James Seavey; d. July 14, 1804.

4. DEACON MARK LANGDON, son of Tobias (2), born Sept. 15, 1698; married, first, Mehitable ———; she died Oct., 1764, and he married, second, Mary ———. He died in 1776. Child:

Joseph, b. 1724; d. Oct. 30, 1749.

5. WILLIAM LANGDON, probably son of Tobias (2), born Oct. 20, 1702; married Sarah ———. He died in 1770. Children:

William, b. 1748; m. Mary Pickering; she d. Feb. 8, 1802, aged 52 years; he d. Sept. 30, 1820. John, m. Mary Evans; he d. May 21, 1789; she d. March 10, 1825, aged 61 years. Mary, m. Nichols Pickering.

GENEALOGY.

6. JOHN LANGDON, son of Tobias (2), born May 28, 1707; married, Feb. 26, 1780, Mary Hall, who died April 11, 1789, aged 72 years. Children:

Mary, m. first, Storer; second, Hill; third, McCobb. Woodbury, m. Sarah Sherburne. John, m. Elizabeth Sherburne. Elizabeth, m. Barrell. Abigail, m. Goldthwaite. Martha, m. first, Barrell; second, Simpson; third, Gen. James Sullivan.

7. CAPT. SAMUEL LANGDON, son of Joseph (3), born 1721; married, Sept. 29, 1748, Hannah Storer. He died Sept. 8, 1796. Lived at Portsmouth. Children:

Elizabeth, b. Oct. 16, 1749; d. Dec. 3, 1749. Mary, b. April 16, 1751; m. first, Tallent; second, Joseph White; lived at Newcastle; d. 1836.
8. Samuel, b. June 9, 1753. Anna, b. Nov. 3, 1755; m. James Whidden; d. May 24, 1790.
9. Joseph, b. May 12, 1758. Elizabeth, b. March 18, 1761; m. Andrew Sherburne; d. 1831. Hannah, b. June, 1766; m. Edward Gove.

8. MAJOR SAMUEL LANGDON, son of Samuel (7), born June 9, 1753; married Lydia Brewster, who died May 21, 1840. He died July 5, 1834. Children:

Comfort M., b. March, 1807; m. Samuel Drown. Thankfull, b. May, 1809; m. Joseph Marston.
10. Samuel, b. May 13, 1811.
11. William, b. Feb. 10, 1818.

9. REV. JOSEPH LANGDON, son of Samuel (7), born March 12, 1758; married, Dec. 9, 1790, Patience Pickering. He died June 27, 1824. Children:

Mary L., b. Sept. 18, 1791; m. Col. Amos S. Parsons. Elizabeth, b. Aug. 9, 1795; m. March 1, 1827, Samuel Whidden, 3d. Temperance, b. April 29, 1797; m. Joseph Langdon Seavey. Hannah, b. March 16, 1805; m. Samuel Langdon; d. Dec. 15, 1839.

10. CAPT. SAMUEL LANGDON, son of Samuel (8), born May 13, 1811; married, first, June 12, 1832, Hannah Langdon; second, Sarah A. Coleman. Lived in Portsmouth. Children:

John, b. Nov. 28, 1832; d. young. Joseph, b. March 16, 1834; d. March 10, 1838. Harriett, b. June 5, 1836; m. Mark L. Jenkins; d. Feb. 19, 1877. Samuel, b. Aug. 17, 1838; m. Martha Ellen Willey.

11. WILLIAM LANGDON, son of Samuel (8), born Feb. 10, 1818; married Mary Locke. Children:
Mary Ann, m. Alfred Marden. Woodbury. Emeline, m. Burrows. Andrew J., m. Lane. John. Samuel, m. Beal.

LANGMAID.

WILLIAM LANGMAID, married, Dec. 10, 1738, Deborah Berry. Children:
John, b. April 3, 1745. Samuel, bapt. 1740. William, b. 1742. Samuel, b. 1748. Abigail, b. 1750.

LEAR.

1. Alexander Lear. Children:
2. Benjamin (?).
3. Samuel (?). Molly, bapt. April 6, 1777. Mehitable O., b. 1778.

2. BENJAMIN LEAR, son of Alexander (1), married, Nov. 25, 1790, Mary Morrison. Children:
Alexander, enlisted under Lieut. Henderson and died at Sackett's Harbor during the War of 1812. Nathaniel, ran away from Solomon Marden, was a prisoner at Dartmoor during the War of 1812. Benjamin, served under Marshall, and afterwards under Walback, in the War of 1812. Went to New Orleans and it is said died in Mobile bay or up the river. Samuel, drowned at Epsom while rafting logs.
4. John, b. Dec. 9, 1804. Daniel, b. 1807; d. March 22, 1813, aged six years.

3. SAMUEL LEAR, son of Alexander (1), married, Feb. 5, 1792, Sally Salter. Child:
Alexander Salter, bapt. 1793.

4. JOHN LEAR, son of Benjamin (2), born Dec. 9, 1804; married, 1827, Nancy Downes of Gosport. He lived on the Sandy Beach road. Fisherman. Children:
Mary Abby, m. Edward Downes; d. Dec. 27, 1866. Elizabeth Ann, m. Feb. 22, 1864 or '67, Joseph Jackson Seavey. Harriet N., m. John W. Randall. Charles H., b. July 24, 1844; m. Dec. 16, 1880, Mrs. Elizabeth R. (Clough) Rumsey. Christinia, b. 1846 (?); m. July 4, 1870, Frank A. Otis. John W., b. Dec. 7, 1850; m. Jan. 7, 1871, Addie Remick of Eliot; d. Aug. 13, 1899. Sarah P., m. March 4, 1863, John O. Downes. Martha Jane, m. William Neal.

LEAVITT.

1. ELDER EBENEZER LEAVITT, son of ———, married Jewell. Children:

Benning, m. 1812, Olive Jenness. Eben. Sarah Ann, m. Jan. 20, 1824, Richard R. Locke. John, m. first, Nov. 23, 1826, Eliza J.; Perkins; second, Moore.
2. Carr. Joseph, m. May, 1840, Esther R. Marden.
3. William B. Sula, m. Morris Dalton.

2. CARR LEAVITT, son of Ebenezer (1), married, Sept. 5, 1837, Eliza Jane Lane. He died Sept. 8, 1863. Children:

Eben True, b. April 15, 1839. Eliza True, m. Gilman Harrison Jenness. John Edwin, b. March, 1854 or '55; m. Philbrick. Vienna J., b. April 16, 1857; m. David Rand (?).

3. WILLIAM B. LEAVITT, son of Ebenezer (1), married, June 20, 1837, Louisa Dalton. He died in California. Children:

Eliza F., m. first, Hiram Jones; second, Frank Jones; child, m. Sinclair of Littleton. Daniel Eben, m. Nellie Hadley of Portsmouth.

LEWIS.

LANGLEY B. LEWIS, son of ———, married Abigail, daughter of Joseph J. Berry. He died in California. Child:

Abby Frances, b. Sept. 29, 1857; d. July 26, 1871.

LIBBIE — LIBBY.

1. JOHN LIBBIE came from England about 1630 and was in the employ of Trelawny four years, settling at Scarborough. The location on which he settled was laid out to him by Henry Jocelyn, who was probably the first settler at Jocelyn's Neck in Rye, afterwards known as Locke's Neck. John Libbie lost everything save his plantation during King Philip's War. Children:

John, b. 1636; m. Agnes. James, killed in King Phillip's War. Samuel, killed in King Philip's War. Joanna, m. Thomas Bickford. Henry, b. 1647; m. Honor Hinkson.

2. Anthony, b. 1649. Rebecca, m. Joshua Brown. Sarah, b. 1653; m. Robert Tidy. Hannah, m. Daniel Fogg.
3. David, b. 1657. Matthew, b. 1663; m. Elizabeth Brown. Daniel, m. Mary Ashton.

2. ANTHONY LIBBY, son of John (1), born 1649; married Sarah, daughter of Abraham and Jane Drake of Hampton. He lived at Scarborough until some years after King Philip's War. Children:

Sarah, m. June, 18, 1701, Israel Smith of Hampton. Mary, m. March 7, 1709, John Lane of Hampton.
4. Abraham.
5. Isaac, b. 1690. Hannah.
6. Jacob, b. May 25, 1695. Jane, b. Aug. 5, 1700; m. Deacon Abraham Moulton of Hampton.

3. DAVID LIBBY, son of John (1), born 1657; married Eleanor ———. Children:

David, m. Esther Hanscom. Samuel, m. Mary Libby. Solomon, m. Martha Hanscom.
7. John. Elizabeth, m. Edward Cloudman. Ephraim, m. Mary Ambler. Eleanor, m. Zebulon Trickey. Abigail, m. Richard Nason.

4. ABRAHAM LIBBY, son of Anthony (2), married Sabina Philbrick of Hampton. Children:

Betty, b. Oct. 6, 1713; m. E. Holmes.
8. Joseph, b. Aug. 15, 1715. Sarah, b. Nov. 4, 1717; m. P. Chapman. Phebe, b. April 15, 1720; probably d. young. Abraham, b. May 2, 1722; probably d. young. Anthony, b. Dec. 13, 1724; probably d. young. Ephraim, bapt. 1734.

5. ISAAC LIBBY, son of Anthony (2), born 1690; married Mary Farmer. Children:

9. John, b. Aug. 1, 1720. Mary, b. Nov. 4, 1722; m. Oct. 11, 1744, James Knowles. Elizabeth, b. Feb. 28, 1725; m. Oct. 11, 1744, Amos Knowles.
10. Isaac, Jr., b. Feb. 28, 1725.
11. Arthur, b. April 5, 1728. Ruth, b. Sept. 5, 1730; m. Joseph Edmunds (?). Jane, b. Sept. 11, 1733.
12. Reuben, b. Aug. 11, 1734. Joanna, b. Oct. 16, 1737; m. Amos Blazo.

6. JACOB LIBBY, son of Anthony (2), born May 25, 1695; married, Oct. 29, 1719, Sarah Marston. Children:

GENEALOGY. 415

13. Samuel, b. Feb. 9, 1720. Anthony, b. Jan. 7, 1722; d. young. Sarah, b. Feb. 2, 1724-'25; m. Nov. 2, 1743, Samuel Blake. Ruth, b. Jan. 21, 1727; m. Jacob, b. July 25, 1729; d. young. Hannah, b. June, 1731; m. Benjamin Jenness. Job, b. Jan. 15, 1734-'35; d. young.
14. Joseph, b. Feb. 25, 1737.
15. Benjamin, b. Feb. 25, 1737.
16. Abraham, b. Dec. 29, 1739. Hepsibah, bapt. Aug., 1742; d. young.

7. JOHN LIBBY, son of David (3), married, Nov. 14, 1724, Sarah Libby, born in Portsmouth. Children:

Elisha, b. 1725; m. Esther Fogg. Matthew, b. Feb. 25, 1729; m. Sarah Hanscom. Mark, b. June 8, 1731; m. Lydia Skillings.
17. Allison, b. Sept. 12, 1733. Nathaniel, b. Sept. 5, 1735; m. Mary Meserve. Luke, b. Aug. 15, 1738; m. Dorothy McKenney. John, b. Sept. 15, 1744.

8. JOSEPH LIBBY, son of Abraham (4), born Aug. 15, 1715, in that part of Hampton which is now called Rye; married Margaret Abbott. He died in 1764. Children:

18. Reuben, bapt. March 13, 1743. Mary, bapt. Sept. 2, 1744; m. Joseph Glidden. Jane, bapt. Jan. 11, 1747; m. Rowe. Abraham, bapt. 1748; d. young. Abraham, bapt. Aug. 26, 1750; m. Hannah Copp. He fought at Bunker Hill. Joseph, bapt. Nov. 5, 1752; unm.; killed at assault on Quebec. Moses, bapt. Nov. 29, 1754; d. young. Ephraim, bapt. Nov. 30, 1755; m. Judith Page. Olley, bapt. April 30, 1758; unm. Anthony, m. Lydia Ayers. Benjamin, b. June 12, 1761; m. Sarah Mason. Margaret, d. unm.

9. JOHN LIBBY, son of Isaac (5), born Aug. 1, 1720; married, June 26, 1743, Eleanor Berry. He removed to Epsom and probably died there. Children:

Keziah, bapt. May 20, 1744. Meshech, bapt. May 5, 1745. John, bapt. March 29, 1747. Mary, bapt. Sept. 25, 1748. Jonathan, bapt. April 14, 1751. Enoch, bapt. April 13, 1755.

10. ISAAC LIBBY, JR., son of Isaac (5), born Feb. 28, 1725, at Rye; married, first, Feb. 5, 1748, Ann Symmes; second, Margaret Kalderwood. He removed to that part of Epsom which is known as New Rye. Children by first wife:

Mary, bapt. Sept., 1748; m. Abner Evans. Isaac, bapt. April 18, 1750; m. Sept. 20, 1766, Margaret Kalderwood. Elizabeth, bapt.

Jan. 5, 1752; m. Aaron Burbank. Arthur Remick, bapt. Jan. 27, 1754; m. Eleanor Haynes. Susannah, bapt. Sept. 19, 1756; m. T. Cass. Job, b. Feb. 14, 1759; m. Rebecca Pearson. Abigail, m. Jethro Libby.
Children by second wife:
Nathan, b. July 20, 1767; m. Abigail Fowler. Lucy, b. April 17, 1769; m. Capt. John Ham. Abraham, b. Aug. 15, 1773; m. Abigail Pearson.

11. ARTHUR LIBBY, son of Isaac (5), born April 5, 1728, at Rye; married, April 23, 1752, Deborah Smith. He lived at Rye and removed to Candia. Children:
Deborah Smith, b. May 27, 1754; d. unm. 1828. James, b. May 14, 1757; captain in the Revolutionary War; drowned. Jonathan, b. Jan. 29, 1759; unm. Daniel, b. Jan. 12, 1762; Revolutionary soldier. Meribah Smith, b. Nov. 9, 1765; unm. Abraham, b. April 5, 1767; m. Ruth Palmer. Isaac, b. Jan. 9, 1771; m. Ann Seavey. Jacob, b. March 20, 1774; m. Polly King.

12. REUBEN LIBBY, son of Isaac (5), born Aug. 11, 1734, at Rye; married, first, Sarah Goss of Rye; second, Sarah Tucker of Rye. Children:
Olive, bapt. Feb. 2, 1755; m. J. Harris.
19. Samuel, b. July, 1757. Jethro, bapt. Dec. 9, 1759; m. Abigail Libby. Richard, b. 1762; m. Sarah Ross; went to Gorham, Me. Reuben, b. 1763; m. Abigail Irish; went to Gorham, Me. Sarah, bapt. Aug. 30, 1767; m. Bayley. Isaac, bapt. March 3, 1769; d. young.
Children by second wife:
Abigail, m. Isaac Allece. Isaac, b. June 21, 1776; m. Rebecca Crockett. Mary, b. July 30, 1779; m. Wallis Foss.

13. SAMUEL LIBBY, son of Jacob (6), born Feb. 9, 1720; married, first, Dec. 4, 1744, Abigail Symens; second, Penelope Barber. Children:
Sarah, bapt. 1745. Jacob, bapt. 1747. Hannah, bapt. May 19, 1751.

14. JOSEPH LIBBY, son of Jacob (6), born Feb. 25, 1737, at Rye; married Mary ———. In 1763 he bought the Paul Randall inn near West Rye and died a year later. In 1765-'66 his widow married Reuben Dearborn of North Hampton. Child:
Molly, bapt. March, 1763; m. Nathaniel Batchelder of Deerfield.

15. BENJAMIN LIBBY, son of Jacob (6), born Feb. 25, 1737, at Rye; married, first, Jane ———; second, Oct. 3, 1765, Abigail, daughter of Matthias and Abigail Haines of Greenland. Removed to Chester, N. H. Child by first wife:

Sarah, bapt. Aug. 17, 1760; m. Lane of Candia.
Children by second wife:
Jane, b. 1766; m. Samuel Worthen. Abigail. Mary, bapt. Sept. 30, 1770; m. Henry Hill. Josiah, bapt. Sept. 15, 1776; d. young.

16. ABRAHAM LIBBY, son of Jacob (6), born Dec. 29, 1739, at Rye; married, first, Feb. 24, 1763, Abigail Page. She died June 2, 1764. Married, second, 1767, Mary Tarlton of Portsmouth. He was a farmer at Rye until the death of his brother Joseph in 1764. He administered on Joseph's estate and run the tavern (Paul Randall's Inn) until it burned. He removed to Chester. He lived near the West schoolhouse. Was a sergeant in Captain Parsons' company in the Revolutionary War and was on town committee to hire men for the Continental army. Child by first wife:

Abigail, b. Nov. 13, 1763; m. John Morrison.
Children by second wife:
20. Joseph, b. Nov. 10, 1765. Job, b. June 18, 1767. Mary, b. Aug. 28, 1768; m. Benjamin Gross. Jacob, b. Dec. 19, 1770. Elias, b. Nov. 28, 1773. Abraham, b. Feb. 13, 1777. Sarah, b. June 10, 1779. Benjamin, b. June 20, 1782.

17. ALLISON LIBBY, son of John (7), born Sept. 12, 1733; married, first, Sarah Skillings; second, Sept. 12, 1775, Mary Libby. Children by first wife:

21. Simeon, b. Sept. 3, 1755. Allison, b. April 6, 1757; m. Sarah Dow. Edward, b. Feb. 10, 1759; m. Elizabeth Libby. Sarah, b. Jan. 3, 1761; m. Josiah Libby. Joseph, d. young. Solomon, d. young. Mark, b. Feb. 15, 1765; m. Anna Libby. Betsey, b. Feb. 8, 1767; m. Paul Lombard. Hannah, b. Nov. 2, 1769; m. William Jones. Josiah, b. Oct. 21, 1773; m. Sarah Libby. Alexander, d. young.
Children by second wife:
Simon, d. young. Morris, b. Sept. 7, 1780; m. Mary Ann Swain. Charlotte, b. Jan. 18, 1783; m. Joseph Bryant. Solomon, b. March 22, 1785; m. Fanny Sylvester. Demas, b. May 4, 1787; m. Mary Berry. Naomi, b. Sept. 11, 1789.

18. CAPT. REUBEN LIBBY, son of Joseph (8), baptized March 13, 1743, at Rye; married, first, Sarah Fullerton; second, Abigail Smith. At the age of sixteen he enlisted in the English army and, it is said, was at Crown Point when George III was crowned king of England. Removed to Wolfeborough. Children by first wife:

> Sarah, b. March 22, 1768; m. Joseph Cotton. Joseph, d. young. Mary, b. Jan. 22, 1773; m. S. Allard. Nancy, m. Samuel Small. Esther, m. Timothy Young. Reuben. Margaret. Olive. Hannah. Jeremiah.

Children by second wife:

> Smith. Abigail.

19. SAMUEL LIBBY, son of Reuben (12), born July, 1757, at Rye; married, Sept. 21, 1780, Mehitable, daughter of William and Ruth (Moses) Seavey of Rye. He lived where Charles Lear now resides near the Center schoolhouse. Children:

> Aaron, b. Aug. 10, 1781; d. Surinam of yellow fever, aged about 23 years. Samuel, b. March 14, 1783; d. unm. about 1850, at Epsom. Sarah, b. May 15, 1785; m. Dec. 14, 1806, Webster Salter. William Seavey, b. Feb. 26, 1787; m. first, about 1812, Sarah Farrington of Salem; second, Elizabeth Winfield; lived at Salem, Mass. Nancy Griffith, b. July 13, 1789; m. Amos Davis of Epsom. Hetty, bapt. Sept. 3, 1792; d. young. Mehitable, b. Feb. 1, 1795; m. Caleb Patterson of Chichester. Ruth Moses, bapt. Jan. 4, 1797; d. 1804. Daniel Rand, b. Feb. 28, 1800; d. 1804. Richard, b. April, 1802; m. Sarah T. Sanborn. Maria, bapt. April 10, 1804; m. first, Amasa Seavey; second, Jonathan Brown.

20. JOSEPH LIBBY, son of Abraham (16), born Nov. 10, 1765, at Rye; married, Feb. 12, 1789, Deborah, daughter of Joseph and Deborah (Seavey) Rand of Chester. Children:

> Mary, b. Sept. 22, 1789, at Rye; m. first, Abraham Folsom; second, Gilman. Joseph, b. Oct. 19, 1791; m. Mehitable C. Rand. Benjamin, b. July 27, 1796; m. R. Robinson. Elias, b. March 17, 1802; m. Jemima Rand. Sally. Abraham.

21. SIMEON LIBBY, son of Allison (17), born Sept. 3, 1755; married, first, Abigail Smith; second, Mrs. Ann Phinney. He served in the Revolutionary War. Children by first wife:

Simeon, b. Jan. 11, 1784; m. Sally Lombard. Joseph, b. Dec. 4, 1785; m. first, Betsey Phinney; second, Love Phinney. Rebecca, b. Oct. 4, 1787; m. Benjamin Cassely. Olive, b. March 19, 1790; m. Caleb Richardson.
22. Daniel, b. March 18, 1792. Abigail, b. June 28, 1794; m. Enoch Libby. Samuel, b. April 21, 1797. Ai, b. Nov. 21, 1790; m. Martha Skillings.
Child by second wife:
Stephen, b. Aug. 8, 1808; went whaling about 1845 and was never heard from again.

22. DANIEL LIBBY, son of Simeon (21), born March 18, 1792; married, first, Jan. 22, 1818, Martha Morton; second, Alice Morton (sister of Martha). Children:

Albert H., b. Dec. 20, 1819; m. Eliza A. Woodward.
23. Daniel F., b. Aug. 24, 1823. Samuel S., b. Jan. 22, 1825; m. Patience Farr. Martha, m. Alden Reed.

23. DANIEL F. LIBBY, son of Daniel (22), born Aug. 24, 1823; married Roxanna L. Jones of Gorham, Me. Children:

Sarah Francis, b. Oct. 27, 1844; m. Adoniram Soule. Ellen Maria, b. Dec. 29, 1845; d. May 18, 1861. Julia E., b. Nov. 13, 1847; m. Albert Wallace.
24. Albert Francis, b. Dec. 1, 1849. Samuel W., b. June 22, 1852; m. Mary Leland. Edward L., b. July 16, 1854; m. Hattie Crockett. Clara L., b. Aug. 15, 1858; m. Henry L. Merrill. Rosa Belle, b. July 22, 1866. Lillian May, b. May 24, 1867; d. June 1, 1871.

24. ALBERT FRANCIS LIBBY, son of Daniel F. (23), born Dec. 1, 1849; married Martha Jane, daughter of John B. and Mary B. Johnson of Rye. Children:

Lillian Bertha, b. July 15, 1873. Daniel, b. April 29, 1881. Leonie, b. Sept. 6, 1890. Justin, b. Jan. 1, 1893.

LITTLEFIELD.

1. DUDLEY CHASE LITTLEFIELD, son of ———, born March 5, 1844; married Sarah Abigail Drake, Feb. 25, 1862. Lived at Stratham. Children:

Abner, b. March 20, 1863. William Dudly, b. March 29, 1869.

LOCKE.

1. JOHN LOCKE, came from Yorkshire, Eng., about 1644, and settled first at Dover, N. H., where he had a right of

land. He removed to what is known as Fort Point, in Newcastle, and about 1652 married Elizabeth, daughter of John Berry, who was probably the first settler at a place called Sandy Beach, now Rye. A few years later, Mr. Locke moved to Sagamore creek, and from there to a neck of land in Rye called Joscelyn's Neck, Locke's Neck, until 1876, and now known as Straw's Point. John Locke was killed by the Indians, August 26, 1696, while he was reaping grain in his field, but two sons who were with him hid and escaped. It is said Captain Locke, after being shot, struck one of the Indians with his sickle and partly cut off his nose. He was by trade a house carpenter. Children:

2. John, b. 1654. Elizabeth, d. unm. before 1708. Alice (or Elsey ?), m. March 14, 1714, Nehemiah Berry.
3. Nathaniel, b. 1661.
4. Edward. Tryphena, m. Dec. 31, 1713, John Knowles. Rebecca, was living in 1708. Mary, was living in 1708.
5. William, b. April 17, 1677.
6. James.
7. Joseph.

2. JOHN LOCKE, son of John (1), born 1654; married Elizabeth ————. Children:

8. John, b. about 1683; m. Sarah; d. 1774.
9. Jethro. Richard(?).

3. NATHANIEL LOCKE, son of John (1), born 1661; married, Jan. 22, 1688-'89, Dorothy, daughter of Jasper Blake, who was born Sept. 17, 1668, and died at Hampton, N. H., Sept. 28, 1737. He died Nov. 12, 1734, aged 73. Tradition says he had 19 children. Children:

John, b. 1689; nothing further is known of him. Dorothy, b. March 20, 1690-'91; m. Jan. 7, 1720, Jethro Locke. Tryphena, m. Dec. 13, 1713, John Knowles, who was b. May 14, 1686. Elizabeth, b. 1693-'94; m. Nov. 24, 1715, Thomas Leavitt. Rachel, b. Dec. 12, 1695; m. Jan. 6, 1715, William Moulton; she d. Jan. 20, 1774, at Hampton.
10. Nathaniel, b. Oct. 18, 1698.
11. Samuel, b. 1701-'02.
12. Jonathan, b. Dec. 22, 1705. Deborah, m. Oct. 19, 1732, William Buckinan (Bucknan). They removed to Falmouth, Me., and she with her infant and her brother Nathaniel's wife, and a Mrs. Noyes, were all lost in a vessel from Casco bay to Cape Ann or Boston, about 1735. Joseph, b. about 1700. Abijah. Timothy.

GENEALOGY. 421

4. EDWARD LOCKE, son of John (1), married Hannah, daughter of Frances Jenness. She was born March 26, 1673. Lived at Hampton and Rye. Children:

13. Francis, b. July 18, 1694. Samuel, b. Sept. 4, 1698; m. Feb. 11, 1725, Margaret Ward of Northampton; had Margaret, bapt. Nov. 20, 1726, at Hampton Falls.
14. Edward, b. May 28, 1701. Prudence, b. May 30, 1707; m. first, April 3, 1735, Ebenezer Weare; second, Dec. 29, 1742, Andrew Webster.
15. James, b. Oct. 4, 1709. Thomas, b. June 10, 1713.

5. DEACON WILLIAM LOCKE, son of John (1), born April 17, 1677; married Nov. 23, 1699, Hannah Knowles, who was born April 18, 1678, and died Sept. 12, 1769, in her 92d year. He died Jan. 22, 1768 in his 91st year. Children:

16. Jonathan, b. March 15, 1702.
17. William. Abigail, b. 1706; m. Jan. 4, 1726-'27, Joseph Philbrick; lived at Rye; d. Aug. 12, 1783. Hannah, d. young. Patience, b. 1710; m. Nov. 16, 1749, Noah Moulton, son of Daniel. Sarah, m. Francis Jenness (?) Barrington.
18. Elijah.
19. Elisha. Eliphalet, d. young. Jemima, b. Jan. 20, 1720-'21; m. May, 1740, John Blake of Greenland. Hannah, b. July 1, 1724; m. Oct. 3, 1745, Jeremiah Berry; she d. July 1, 1770, aged 46 years; had a son, Levi.

6. JAMES LOCKE, son of John (1), married ————. Child:

20. James, m. Sarah ————.

7. JOSEPH LOCKE, son of John (1), married Salome White (?). He died March, 1768. Lived at Locke's Neck, was a selectman. He bought land of Nathaniel Berry at Sandy Beach, May 25, 1713. Made another purchase, 1728, of four acres near "Dry Point," now Wallace S. Goss'. Children:

Salome, b. Oct. 20, 1710; m. May 22, 1735, Jonathan Goss, "weaver," of Rye.
21. Joseph, b. April 27, 1716. Elizabeth, b. Dec. 1, 1718; m. Jan. 6, 1743, Jude Allen. Mary, b. May 1, 1720; m. June 25, 1745, Solomon White of Newcastle; lived at Epping. Annis, or Ann, b. March 25, 1723; m. March 10, 1748, John Perkins. Abigail, b. Nov. 6, 1725; m. Jan. 25, 1748, Robinson Trefethen.
22. Jeremiah, b. Aug. 4, 1728.

8. JOHN LOCKE, son of John (2), born about 1683; married Sarah ————. Resided at Rye and died 1774 or '75, aged 91 years. Children:

    John, b. 1714.
23. Richard, b. July 28, 1720. Mary, b. Nov. 13, 1722; d. July, 1736.
    Jacob, b. Nov. 12, 1727; d. Aug., 1736. John, d. July 23, 1730.
    Abner, d. Aug. 11, 1736. Tryphena, d. Aug. 13, 1736.

9. JETHRO LOCKE, son of John (2), married, Jan. 7, 1720, his cousin, Dorothy Locke. He resided at Rye and died in 1737. Children:

    Dorothy, bapt. June 28, 1721. Simon, bapt. Dec. 29, 1723; d. young.
24. Jethro, b. June 27, 1727.

10. NATHANIEL LOCKE, son of Nathaniel (3), born Oct. 18, 1698; married, first, Jan. 6, 1726, Abigail Prescott, who was drowned in 1735, going from Casco bay to Cape Ann or Boston; second, Mary Stubbs of Yarmouth. He died at Falmouth, 1780 or '81. Children by first wife:

    John, bapt. Nov. 29, 1727; d. young. Nathaniel, d. at Falmouth, 1756 or '58, aged 28 years.
    Children by second wife:
    Jonathan, shipmaster; m. Sarah Dunbar of Hingham; had a son, Jonathan, b. 1772; m. second, Hannah Tate of Boston, 1797; shipwrecked, 1804, in Mediterranean. John, lived at Falmouth; had a son, Ebenezer. Abijah, was a captain; 1775, helped build Fort Falmouth. Josiah, probably d. April 12, 1841, aged 84 years, at Falmouth; was in expedition to Penobscot, 1779.

11. SAMUEL LOCKE, son of Nathaniel (3), born 1701-'02; married Dec. 11, 1729, Jerusha Shaw. Resided at Hampton and died Dec. 5, 1789, aged about 88. She died Nov. 4, 1780, aged 71. Children:

    Esther, b. 1730-'31; d. April 22, 1736.
25. Jonathan, b. Sept. 29, 1732; m. April 14, 1757, Hannah Fogg, Hampton. Nathaniel, b. 1735; d. May 3, 1736. Deborah, bapt. May 5, 1737; d. same day, aged 3 weeks.
26. Caleb, b. Aug. 12, 1738; m. Betsey Dyer; went to Hollis, Me.
27. Samuel, b. July 28, 1740; said to have had three wives; Brentwood. Merriam, b. June 16, 1743; m. Elisha Moulton. Joseph, bapt. Aug. 18, 1745; d. Dec. 10, 1745, aged four months. Mary, b. Dec. 14, 1746; m. first, Tristram Redmond; second, Joseph Towle.

12. JONATHAN LOCKE, son of Nathaniel (3), born Dec. 22, 1705; married ———, daughter of Samuel Norton. It is said old Jonathan Locke was killed by falling down a bank while on his way home, having been to see Francis Locke's wife, and that Israel Marden, when going home from the same woman, horseback, the horse stumbled, and he was killed. Child:

28. Jonathan, b. about 1726.

13. FRANCIS LOCKE, son of Edward (4), born July 18, 1694; married, first, Deliverance ———; second, March 11, 1733, Sarah Moulton. He resided at Rye and died about 1754. Children by first wife:

Hannah, b. Jan. 8, 1719-'20. Sarah, b. Feb. 17, 1722; d. Dec. 6, 1735.
29. Francis, b. June 27, 1724. Deliverance, b. Aug. 16, 1726. Eleanor, b. March 16, 1728-'29; m. Feb. 15, 1749, William Ham of Dover.
30. Ephraim, b. Feb. 4, 1730-'31. Prudence, b. March 20, 1731-'32; m. Dec. 27, 1753, Israel Marden. Elizabeth, b. May 2, 1735. Frances, b. Oct. 2, 1737.

14. EDWARD LOCKE, son of Edward (4), born May 28, 1701; married, Dec. 17, 1724, Hannah, daughter of Moses Blake. Lived at Kensington. Children:

Lydia, b. Dec. 22, 1725; d. Nov. 17, 1735. Abigail, bapt. April 12, 1730; d. Dec. 18, 1735.
31. Moses, b. July 8, 1733.
32. Timothy Blake, b. Oct. 30, 1735. Lydia, b. April 5, 1738; m. July 7, 1759, Benjamin Eastman; d. about 1816. Abigail, b. July 25, 1741; m. Onesephorus Page. Edward, b. March 6, 1744; d. Jan. 12, 1747. Hannah, b. April 26, 1747; m. Oct. 30, 1765, Jeremiah Dearborn of Kensington.

15. JAMES LOCKE, son of Edward (4), born Oct. 4, 1709; married Mercy. He was a cordwainer at Rochester in 1737.

16. JONATHAN LOCKE, son of William (5), born March 15, 1702; married March 2, 1727, Sarah, daughter of William Haines of Greenland. He resided at Rye, and died Jan. 2, 1774, aged 72. She died Oct., 1753. Tradition says that mother and nine children died of throat distem-

per in Oct., 1753. He lived where Deacon Jonathan Locke resides. Children:

Sarah, b. Jan. 3, 1728; d. Sept. 26, 1742. Patience, b. Feb. 10, 1730.
33. Jonathan, b. Jan. 29, 1732. Mary, b. Sept. 20, 1733.
34. David, b. Aug. 24, 1735. Abigail, b. Sept. 5, 1736; m. Feb. 23, 1758, James Perkins. William, b. July 26, 1738. Margaret, b. July 20, 1740. Abner, b. July 31, 1742; d. Oct., 1753. Sarah, b. Aug. 28, 1744; unm.; d. in Rye, Dec. 31, 1796. Hannah, b. Dec. 18, 1746. John, b. Dec. 9, 1748.

17. WILLIAM LOCKE, son of William (5), married, first, Feb., 1729, Meribah Page; second, Jan. 5, 1735, Betsey Rand. Lived in Rye near Charles and Gilman Garland. A mason by trade. Children by second wife:

Meribah, b. Aug. 5, 1735. Hannah, b. Feb. 18, 1737-'38. Elizabeth, b. March 3, 1739-'40. Abigail, b. March 4, 1743; m. Sept. 18, 1764, Joshua Foss.
35. William, b. Sept. 9, 1745. Samuel, b. Aug. 14, 1748. Mary, b. April 6, 1751.

18. ELIJAH LOCKE, son of William (5), married, March 22, 1739, Huldah Perkins, who was born Sept. 23, 1718. Resided at Rye. Was a deacon. Died about 1782. Lived near Knowles' Corner, where Charles and Gilman Garland reside. Children:

Huldah, b. Oct. 2, 1739; m. Moses Seavey. Martha, bapt. Jan. 3, 1742; m. March 8, 1764, Bickford Lang. Mary, bapt. Nov. 25, 1744; m. July 7, 1765, Robert Saunders. Elijah, bapt. Sept. 29, 1746; d. young. Elizabeth, bapt. Jan. 15, 1749. Levi, bapt. Dec. 9, 1750. William, bapt. April 15, 1753; d. young.
36. Elijah, bapt. Dec. 15, 1754.
37. William, b. June 16, 1758.

19. ELISHA LOCKE, son of William (5), married, Jan. 13, 1743, Tryphena Moulton. Resided at Haverhill, N. H. Children:

Elisha, b. 1743; d. young. Daniel, b. 1745; d. young. Mary, b. 1747; m. Ladd of Haverhill. Hannah, b. 1755; m. Ladd of Haverhill, brother of above. William, a peculiar man; stone-cutter; called "Picker Locke"; d. at Rye April 19, 1828. Elisha, b. 1760; Revolutionary soldier. David, b. 1767; m. first, 1787, Hannah Lellingham; 2d, Nov. 6, 1809, Rachel Brainard. He d. 1832.

20. JAMES LOCKE, son of James (6), married Sarah ———. Lived at Rye. Children:
Sarah, b. July 27, 1825; m. March 28, 1746, John Marden. Ann, b. Oct. 10, 1726; d. Nov. 10, 1735.
38. James, b. June 30, 1729. Elizabeth, b. Oct. 22, 1730. Mary, b. Jan. 21, 1732. Meribah, b. Oct. 13, 1733. Lydia, or Love, b. June 3, 1735. John, b. Oct. 3, 1737; d. in Revolutionary War. Abigail, b. March 25, 1741.

21. JOSEPH LOCKE, son of Joseph (7), born April 27, 1716; married, first, Dec. 4, 1739, Hannah Jenness; second, April 20, 1768, widow Mary Odiorne. He lived at Rye and died 1790 or '91. His second wife died Jan. 28, 1805, aged 81 years. Lived where John Oliver Locke resides. Children by first wife:
Hannah, b. June 3, 1740. Joseph, bapt. April 4, 1742; d. young.
39. Richard, b. Sept. 4, 1744. Joseph, bapt. July 21, 1751; d. young.
40. Joshua, bapt. April 28, 1753 or '54. Mary, bapt. Nov. 21, 1756; m. Levi Towle (?).
Children by second wife:
41. Joseph, b. 1768; m. first, Nov. 16, 1794, Mary Brown; second, 1804, Olive Foss. Benjamin, b. 1770; d. young. Hannah, b. March, 1773; m. Samuel Mow; resided at Rye. Benjamin, b. 1776; d. young.

22. JEREMIAH LOCKE, son of Joseph (7), born Aug. 4, 1728; married, Feb. 5, 1753, Mary Elkins. Farmer. Resided at Rye. The place is now owned by Wallace Goss. He died Jan. 28, 1795. Children:
42. Joseph, b. Oct. 23, 1753-'54. Mary, b. May 25, 1755; m. Samuel Jenness, March 21, 1775; North Hampton.

23. RICHARD LOCKE, son of John (8), born July 28, 1720; married Elizabeth Garland. Lived at Rye. He died May 15, 1804, aged 84 years. Children:
43. John, Jr., bapt. Oct. 19, 1746. Abner, b. March 13, 1748; d. young.
44. Richard, bapt. Jan. 7, 1750. Jacob, bapt. Feb. 23, 1752; d. young. Abner, bapt. May 26, 1754; d. April 15, 1825, aged 71 years.
45. Jacob, bapt. Jan., 1757. Tryphena, b. June, 1759; unm., d. Aug. 3, 1830; had William, m. first, July 31, 1825, Elizabeth Knowles; second, Marston of New Hampton, and had William Harvey, b. Aug. 9, 1830, d. Feb. 19, 1887, m. June 25, 1852, Maria L. Johnson, had Willie E., b. Oct. 7, 1855, d. Sept. 22, 1863; Parmelia Ann, b. Oct. 14, 1827, m. Joseph W. Berry.

46. Job, bapt. Sept. 26, 1762. Sarah, bapt. Sept. 8, 1765; d. Feb. 8, 1813. Elizabeth, bapt. April 10, 1768.
47. Simon, bapt. Sept. 23, 1770.

24. JETHRO LOCKE, son of Jethro (9), born June 27, 1727; married, Feb. 2, 1748, Hannah Rand. Lived at Barrington. She died Feb. 15, 1831. He died Oct. 29, 1807. Children:

    Hannah, b. 1748. Dorothy, b. 1750; m. July 19, 1771, Elijah Otis.
48. Simon, b. 1753. Merribah, b. 1756; m. Babb of Strafford. Elizabeth, b. 1758-'59; m. twice.
49. Jethro, b. March 6, 1764.

25. JONATHAN LOCKE, son of Samuel (11), born Sept. 29, 1732; married, April 14, 1757, Hannah Fogg, who died June 10, 1819, aged 83 years. He resided at Hampton and died Jan. 27, 1800, aged 67 years. Children:

    Hannah, d. Feb. 14, 1789, aged 27 years. Jonathan, m. Deborah Knowles; she d. March 4, 1790, aged 25 years.
50. Nathaniel, b. Aug. 22, 1766. Miriam, m. Dudley Lamprey; she d. June 25, 1796, aged 23 years. Mary, m. Nov. 2, 1791, Stephen Locke of Hollis; d. 1852.

26. CALEB LOCKE, son of Samuel (11), born Aug. 12, 1738; married Betsy Dyer. He resided at Hollis, Me., and died April 10, 1820. She died Dec. 17, 1825, aged 82 years. Children:

    Betsy, b. June 17, 1763; m. Joseph Hooper. Stephen, b. Feb. 2, 1765; m. Nov. 2, 1791, Mary Locke; resided at Hollis, Me.; he d. Dec. 21, 1812. Thomas D., b. June 13, 1768; m. Chadbourn; resided at Hollis, Me. Tristram, b. Oct. 19, 1771; d. June 2, 1832. Caleb, b. Dec. 7, 1773; m. Sarah Clark; resided at Hollis, Me. Joseph, b. Jan. 1, 1779; d. Oct. 26, 1799. Samuel, b. Aug. 16, 1784; schoolmaster; resided at Hallowell, Me. Mary, b. Aug. 12, 1787.

27. SAMUEL LOCKE, son of Samuel (11), born July 28, 1740; married, first, Aug. 15, 1768, Esther Dow; second, Jan. 25, 1771, Hannah Magoon. Children:

    Benjamin. Betsey. Deborah, m. Smith. Weir. Samuel. Miriam. Lucy.

28. JONATHAN LOCKE, son of Jonathan (12), born about 1726; married Abigail Perry. Children:

Samuel. Jacob. Mary. Abigail, living in 1850. Ann.

29. FRANCIS LOCKE, son of Francis (13), born June 27, 1724; married, first, Jan. 24, 1751, Sarah Page; second, Dec. 31, 1767, Elizabeth Bachelder. Farmer. Sold a portion of his farm to Col. Benjamin Garland and went to Epsom. Children by first wife:

Sarah, b. Oct. 13, 1751. Deliverance, bapt. April 11, 1754. Elizabeth, b. May 2, 1755; m. Cass. Francis, b. Oct. 12, 1757; m. Molly Sceren. Abraham, bapt. June 28, 1760; m. April 6, 1779, Mary Sanborn. Hannah, bapt. Jan. 9, 1763; m. Bickford.

30. EPHRAIM LOCKE, son of Francis (13), born Feb. 4, 1730-'31; married, May 14, 1752, Comfort Dowse. Lived at Epsom. Children:

Prudence, b. 1753. Ephraim, b. 1757. Asa, b. 1763; m. widow Mary (Nason) Shaw; removed to Vermont. Samuel, m. Mary Evans of Epsom. Francis.

31. MOSES LOCKE, son of Edward (14), born July 8, 1733; married, March 12, 1755, Mary Organ. Children:

Mehitable, bapt. Dec. 4, 1757. Ann, bapt. Feb. 13, 1760. Jonathan, bapt. April 19, 1762. Hannah, bapt. May 6, 1764. Mary, bapt. Sept. 6, 1766. Elijah, bapt. July 4, 1768.

32. TIMOTHY BLAKE LOCKE, son of Edward (14), born Oct. 30, 1735; married, first, June 1, 1757, Lydia Dow; second, Jan. 22, 1781, Patience Perkins. Resided at Kensington and Seabrook. Children by first wife:

Josiah, b. Nov. 10, 1757; m. Bethia ———; he was drowned Sept. 23, 1816. Simon, b. Aug. 13, 1759. Edward, b. Dec. 15, 1760; m. Nov. 27, 1781, Betty Perkins of Kensington. James, b. Nov. 14, 1762; kept tavern at Andover, Mass. John, b. Feb. 29, 1764. Blake, b. Feb. 20, 1766. Lydia, bapt. April 28, 1771. Joseph, bapt. April 10, 1773. Jeremiah, bapt. May 5, 1776.

33. JONATHAN LOCKE, son of Jonathan (16), born Jan. 29, 1732; married, June 8, 1757, Abigail Towle, who died March 22, 1817, aged 81 years. Resided at Rye, where Deacon Jonathan Locke lived in 1903. He died Sept. 13, 1813, aged 82 years. Children:

51. Jonathan, b. 1759. Abner, b. 1760; d. in Revolutionary army Aug. 16, 1778. Mary, b. July 21, 1763; d. 1763. Abigail, b. July 21, 1764; m. March 18, 1785, Jonathan Jenness of Rye; she d. May 24, 1844.
52. John, b. July 15, 1767.
53. Joseph, b. 1770. Daniel, b. 1772; d. unm. Jan. 1, 1840.
54. Jethro, b. 1775.
55. Hall Jackson, b. 1777; m. Abigail Amazeen of Newcastle. Elvin.

34. DAVID LOCKE, son of Jonathan (16), born Aug. 24, 1735; married, first, Feb. 9, 1758, Hannah Lovering, who died Sept. 23, 1807; second, May 24, 1809, widow Olive Elkins, who died Dec. 4, 1835, aged 89 years. He resided at Rye and died June 7, 1810. His residence was in "Fern Avenue." Children by first wife:

56. Reuben, b. April 26, 1758.
57. Simeon, b. March 21 or 31, 1760. Sarah, b. Nov. 24, 1761; m. Josiah Webster of Rye. Mary, b. May 7, 1763-'64; m. Joseph Sanborn.
58. David, b. Nov. 24, 1765. Jonathan, b. Feb. 9 or 19, 1768; m. Dec. 23, 1790, Lydia Hall; d. June, 1839.
59. Levi, b. Feb. 7, 1770. John, b. May 22, 1772; m. Abigail Dearborn. Annah, b. March 27, 1774; m. Jan. 2, 1794, Timothy Prescott. William, b. April 9, 1776; m. 1824, Esther Knowles; d. March 3, 1841. Abigail, b. Nov. 20, 1778; m. Jan. 2, 1797, Bickford Lang. Benjamin, b. Dec. 28, 1780; m. July 8, 1816, Parmelia Conner. Nancy, b. March 9, 1785; m. 1800, Morris Lamprey of North Hampton.

35. WILLIAM LOCKE, son of William (17), born Sept. 9, 1745; married Betsy Babb. Resided at Barrington. Children:

Samuel, m. Lucy Cate. John, b. Sept. 17, 1769; m. first, Sept. 20, 1792, Abigail Page; second, Mercy Dame; third, Margaret Pierce. William. Elisha, b. Oct. 26, 1780; m. Dec. 18, 1806, Sophia Pinkham. Benjamin, m. Betsey Heard. Hannah, m. Winthrop Reynolds; Mirabah, m. 1792, Amos Main; lived in Rochester. Molly, m. Jesse Woodman. Betsy, m. Moses DeMerritt. Dolly, b. Aug. 11, 1784; m. Sept. 9, 1810, Barzilla Shurtleff; removed to Illinois. Alice, m. Samuel DeMerritt.

36. ELIJAH LOCKE, JR., son of Elijah (18), baptized Dec. 15, 1754; married Nov. 21, 1776, Elizabeth Brown. Served in the Revolutionary War under Capt. Joseph Parsons. Children:

60. Elijah, b. 1781. Mary, b. 1784; m. John Wallis; lived at Epsom. Levi, m. Rachel Towle; lived at Chichester. Several daughters (names not known).

37. WILLIAM LOCKE, son of Elijah (18), born June 16, 1758; married, Oct. 28, 1778, Abigail Saunders, who died Oct. 23, 1828. Removed from Rye to Epsom about 1780, and thence to Alexandria. Blacksmith. He died April 9, 1828. Children:

61. John, b. March 17, 1780. Abigail, b. Sept. 3, 1781; m. Jeremiah Page; lived at Epsom; she d. Nov. 5, 1847. Huldah, b. Aug. 4, 1783; m. John Page; lived at Epsom; she d. May 28, 1829.
62. William, b. Sept. 6, 1785; m. Dec. 25, 1808, Mary Shaw. Elizabeth, b. July 11, 1788; m. John Langley; she d. April 22, 1823.
63. Reuben, b. March 14, 1791; m. Jane McMurphy.

38. JAMES LOCKE, son of James (20), born June 30, 1729; married, June 14, 1750, Sarah Leavitt. Resided at Rye. Children:

Moses, b. 1751. Ruth, b. 1752; unm.
64. James, b. 1753. Hannah, b. 1755. John, b. 1757; was a refugee and went to Nova Scotia. Sarah, b. 1759. Samuel, b. 1761. Elizabeth, b. 1763.

39. RICHARD LOCKE, son of Joseph (21), born Sept. 4, 1744; married Huldah Hobbs, who died Dec. 5, 1824. Resided at Rye. He died Oct. 20, 1823. Children:

Hannah, b. 1767; unm. Hannah Jenness, b. May 22, 1769 or '70; m. John Marston; he d. July 19, 1815; she d. Sept. 6, 1825, at Rye. Sarah, b. Feb. 29, 1771-'72; m. Job Locke; she d. Aug. 29, 1852.
65. James Hobbs, b. June 3, 1773.
66. Asa, b. Aug. 14, 1775. Joshua, b. Aug. 14, 1775; d. an infant.
67. Richard, b. Oct. 5, 1779.

40. JOSHUA LOCKE, son of Joseph (21), baptized April 28, 1753 or '54; married, Jan. 18, 1776, Charity Marden. Resided at Rye. Children:

Nabby, m. Furber. Polly, m. Nov. 5, 1805, Jonathan Brown, Jr., of Rye. Rachel, m. March 15, 1810, Joseph Brown of Deerfield.

41. JOSEPH LOCKE, son of Joseph (21), born 1768; married, first, Nov. 16, 1794, Mary Brown, who died Dec.,

1803; second, July 16, 1804, Olly or Olive Foss, who died March 5, 1825. Children:

68. John, b. 1795. Mary Brown, b. 1809; m. John W. P. Locke, who d. April 25, 1841, aged 38 years.

42. JOSEPH LOCKE, son of Jeremiah (22), born Oct. 23, 1753-'54; married, June 25, 1778, Martha Dow, who was born Oct. 6, 1758, and died Jan. 31, 1792. He resided in Rye and died April 22, 1790. Children:

69. Jeremiah, b. Dec. 9, 1778. Henry, b. Aug. 25, 1780; d. an infant. Mary, b. April 31, 1782; m. Jonathan Perkins (?). Mercy, b. Jan. 11, 1784; m. Samuel Mason, Nov. 12, 1801.
70. Joseph, b. May 4, 1787.

43. JOHN LOCKE, JR., son of Richard (23), baptized Oct. 19, 1746; married, first, Sept. 29, 1769, Sarah Jones; second, Aug. 18, 1796, Thankful Blaisdell. Children:

John, bapt. 1770.
71. Jeremiah, b. 1771. Richard, b. 1773. Molly, b. 1773. George Washington, b. 1777.

44. RICHARD LOCKE, son of Richard (23), baptized Jan. 7, 1750; married, Nov. 2, 1769, Sarah Palmer. Served in the Revolutionary War under Capt. Parsons. Children:

Richard, b. 1773; d. young.
72. Joseph, b. 1775.

45. JACOB LOCKE, son of Richard (23), baptized Jan., 1757; married, June 4, 1778, Mehitable Higgins. Resided at Wakefield. Children:

John, m. (Locke) (Jurnald) Mary Allen. Jacob, unm. Nathaniel, m. Hannah Pitman. Mary, m. Allen. Sarah, m. Cook. Betsey, m. Joseph Pitman.

46. JOB LOCKE, son of Richard (23), baptized Sept. 26, 1762; married, first, Nov. 10, 1785, Hannah Lang; second, Dec. 6, 1806, Abigail Philbrick; third, Nov. 25, 1810, Sally Locke. Lived where Otis Goss lives and built the house. Children by first wife:

Daniel, bapt. April 15, 1787. Sally, bapt. May 29, 1791. Polly W., b. 1793; m. 1815, James Bowley of Stratham. Elizabeth G., b. 1797; m. 1816, John Caswell.

GENEALOGY. 431

73. Job, bapt. May 5, 1799.
74. John W. P., b. April, 1803.
Children by second wife:
Anna or Nancy, b. 1807. Hannah, bapt. July 21, 1813; m. William Randall. Sally, bapt. July 21, 1813.

47. SIMON LOCKE, son of Richard (23), baptized Sept.· 23, 1770; married, first, Abigail Mace; second, Nov. 10, 1803, Elizabeth L. Allen, who died Nov. 29, 1862. Served on the Alarm List under Captain Jonathan Wedgewood during the War of 1812, and died July 31, 1863, aged 92 years, 11 months. Children by first wife:
Mehitable Berry, b. June, 1792; m. Daniel Burley; adopted Sylvester and Daniel Caswell. Richard, b. 1794; m. Oct. 21, 1823, Margaret Welch of Chichester. Sarah Frost, b. 1796; m. June 13, 1819, Edward Caswell. Simon, b. 1797; d. Aug. 1, 1819, aged 22 years. William, b. 1799; m. Nov. 6, 1825, Charlotte Wentworth of Boston. Elizabeth Garland, bapt. April 16, 1801. Rachel Berry, bapt. April 16, 1801.
Children by second wife:
Abner, b. 1804; m. first, Eunice Wallis; second, Mary A. Young. Abigail Mace, b. 1805; m. April 15, 1824, Asa Locke; second, Lemuel Locke (brothers). Thomas D., b. 1808; d.
75. John Langdon, b. Aug. 30, 1811. Elizabeth, b. 1811. Edwin, b. 1819; m. Adeline Sheppard. David, b. 1819. Alfred.

48. REV. SIMON LOCKE, son of Jethro (24), b. 1753; married, March 29, 1774, Lydia Foss; died Sept. 1, 1839. Children:
Ephraim, b. Feb. 8, 1775; d. Aug. 2, 1832, in N. Y.; m. Sally Foss. Jesse, b. Sept. 9, 1777; m. June 9, 1799, Hannah Danielson. Joshua, b. Dec. 11, 1779; d. at sea Aug. 16, 1802. Simon, b. Feb. 3, 1786; m. first, Oct., 1806, Mirian Day; second, 1833, Mary H. Staples. Lydia, b. Jan. 10, 1792; m. Dec. 17, 1807, John Dennett. Hannah, b. May 16, 1797; m. Sept. 3, 1812, Joshua Dennett.

49. JETHRO LOCKE, son of Jethro (24), born March 6, 1764; married Abigail Locke, who died April 5, 1829. Lived at Barrington. Children:
Simon, m. Olive Chadbourne. Hannah, m. Elias Varney. Isaac. Howard. Jethro. Nathaniel. Joshua. Abigail.

50. NATHANIEL LOCKE, son of Jonathan (25), born Aug. 22, 1766; married Lydia Page. Lived at Hampton. Children:

Hannah, b. Aug. 3, 1792; m. John Towle of Saco. Jonathan, b. 1794; m. Mary Elkins of Hampton. Merriam, b. March 13, 1796; m. Joseph Palmer of Hampton. Samuel, m. July 3, 1825, Mary Dearborn of New Hampton. Sherburne, b. 1800; m. Louisa Lamprey of Hampton. Mary Ann, m. Reuben Brown of New Hampton. Nathaniel, b. 1803; m. Mary Lane of Hampton. Sarah, b. 1806; d. unm. Lydia, b. Aug. 3, 1814; m. John Lamprey of Hampton.

51. JONATHAN LOCKE, JR., son of Jonathan (33), born 1759; married, Nov. 23, 1785, Mary Rand. Lived at Newcastle. Children:

76. Jonathan, bapt. Nov. 18, 1787. William, b. Feb. 10, 1788; seafaring man; unm.; d. Feb. 5, 1869. Nabby, b. Dec. 27, 1789; m. Nov. 1, 1807, William Neil of Newcastle.
77. Joseph L., b. March, 1792. Michael, b. 1796 (?); unm.; lived at Newcastle. Sarah Ann, b. 1799. John, b. 1800; m. Dec. 14, 1820, Martha Rand of Newcastle. Polly, b. 1804; m. Asa Watson of Portsmouth.

52. JOHN LOCKE, JR., son of Jonathan (33), born July 15, 1767; married, Sept. 30, 1787, Abigail Jenness, who died July 4, 1812. He died March 27, 1814. Children:

Elizabeth, bapt. Nov. 30, 1788.
78. Samuel Jenness, b. March 1, 1790. Abigail, b. Nov. 21, 1792; m. June 2, 1816, Thomas Goss. Olle Shapley, b. May 11, 1795; m. William Berry of Greenland and Newington.
79. Jethro, b. Nov. 19, 1797. Jonathan, b. April 9, 1800; d. unm. June 14, 1826. Mary, b. Feb. 11, 1803; m. John Clark.
80. Elvin, b. March 29, 1809.

53. JOSEPH LOCKE, son of Jonathan (33), married, Dec. 4, 1794, Abigail Marden. Lived at Rye. Children:

Hannah Wallis, b. Feb. 7, 1795; m. Joseph J. Berry (second wife); she d. June 30, 1893. Abigail Towle, b. Feb. 8, 1797; m. Aug. 31, 1815, Benjamin Berry of Moultonborough. Sarah Ann, b. April 1, 1799; m. Amos S. Jenness; she d. Dec. 17, 1889; lived at Rye. Patty, b. May 14, 1801; m. June 11, 1826; Reuel Garland of Rye. Lucretia, b. June 8, 1803; m. July 18, 1822, Moses L. Garland; she d. Dec. 22, 1869; he d. 1890, at Rye.
81. Joseph, b. Nov. 30, 1806. Mary, b. Sept. 25, 1809; m. John A. Trefethern of Rye. William, b. Aug. 17, 1813; d. Jan. 26, 1816.
82. Jonathan, b. Aug. 17, 1813. James William, b. Oct. 1, 1816; m. Nancy Drown; he d., and she m. Moses L. Garland.

GENEALOGY.

54. JETHRO LOCKE, son of Jonathan (33), born 1775; married, April 26, 1801, Martha Webster. Lived at Rye. Children:

Hiram, bapt. 1802; m. Duncan. Daniel Treadwell, b. 1805. John Webster, b. 1808. David, m. Mary Grant.

55. HALL JACKSON LOCKE, son of Jonathan (33), born 1777; married Abigail Amazeen. Children:

William B., b. Dec. 22, 1801; m. April 10, 1831, Olive C. Fernald. John, unm. Fanny, b. 1808; m. 1829, Jonathan Vennard.

56. REUBEN LOCKE, son of David (34), born April 26, 1758; married Phebe Chapman of Epsom. Resided at Corinth. Children:

David. Mary. Hannah. Sarah. Reuben. John. Hains. Nancy.

57. SIMEON LOCKE, son of David (34), born March 21 or 31, 1760; married Abigail Blake. Lived at Epsom. Children:

Anna, b. Dec. 16, 1784; m. John Saunders. Samuel, b. Oct. 29, 1786; m. July 1, 1813, Betsey Philbrick. David, b. Oct. 19, 1788; m. Oct. 11, 1810, Florinda Locke. Simmion, b. Dec. 14, 1790; m. July 4, 1813, Clarissa Tash. John, b. March 14, 1794; m. Rachel Sanborn. Josiah, b. Sept. 16, 1796; m. Lydia Philbrick. James, b. Sept. 18, 1798; m. first, Nov. 23, 1826, Clarissa Wallace; second, Phebe Ames; lived at Concord.

58. DAVID LOCKE, son of David (34), born Nov. 24, 1765; married Ann Towle. Lived at Epsom. Children:

David, bapt. 1790; m. Polly Carleton of Canaan; lived at Epsom. Abigail, b. April 26, 1796; m. Jonathan Green of Epsom. Nancy, b. Aug. 9, 1801; m. Ebenezer Gove of Pittsfield.

59. LEVI LOCKE, son of David (34), born Feb. 7, 1770; married, Aug. 31, 1796, Hannah Prescott. Resided at Rye. Children:

Simon Prescott, bapt. Jan. 20, 1799; m. Sarah Cass of Epsom. Benjamin Lovering, b. July 28, 1801; m. May 25, 1825, Hannah Moses of Epsom. Lucy M., b. July 11, 1807; m. Oct. 30, 1830, Daniel Tilton of Deerfield. Thomas D., b. Oct. 29, 1808; m. Oct. 4, 1837, Sarah Cochrane of Manchester. Betsey, b. March 5, 1811; m. Feb. 2, 1831, Jacob Tilton. Almira, b. Aug. 1, 1814; m. Sept. 16, 1847, John B. Johnson of Rye. Rev. Joseph, b. Sept. 8, 1816; m. 1841, Sarah Webster.

60. ELIJAH LOCKE, son of Elijah, Jr. (36), born 1781; married Jan. 21, 1802, Hannah Saunders. Children:
Betsey, b. Dec. 11, 1802; m. Aikins. Samuel, b. June 22, 1805; m. Mary Wallis (his cousin); Reuben, b. Jan. 29, 1809; m. 1832, Irene Healey of Alexandria. Nancy, b. Dec. 15, 1811; m. Martin L. Witcher of Boston. Benjamin, b. Aug. 15, 1817; m. Appia Wallis of Concord. George, b. Oct. 18, 1820; m. 1844, Elizabeth Cheney of Alexandria.

61. JOHN LOCKE, son of William (37), born March 17, 1780; married, first, Abigail Locke; second, Mehitable Bickford. Children by first wife:
William, b. Dec. 24, 1799. Patty, b. Nov. 25, 1801. Francis, b. Nov. 25, 1803.

Children by second wife:
Abigail, b. Aug. 28, 1810; d. April 29, 1817. John, b. Jan. 10, 1812; m. Sarah Sanborn. Samuel, b. March 17, 1814; m. Lucia Sanborn. Sally, b. Feb. 12, 1816; m. Peter Seavey. George, b. Feb. 12, 1816; m. June 31, 1845, Sabra Kimball. Benjamin, b. Sept. 15, 1818; m. 1850, Julia M. Currie. Abigail, b. Jan. 3, 1821; m. Reuben Saunders. Martha, b. July 5, 1825; m. Pierce Bickford.

62. WILLIAM LOCKE, son of William (37), born Sept. 6, 1785; married, Dec 25, 1808, Mary Shaw. Children:
Woodbury, b. March 4, 1813; d. 1883. Mary, b. Aug. 4, 1814; m. Nathaniel Ray. Theresa R., b. April 6, 1818; m. Gilman ———. Martha, b. Jan. 22, 1822; m. Sargent.

63. REUBEN LOCKE, son of William (37), born March 14, 1791; married Jane McMurphy. Lived at Alexandria. Children:
James C., b. April 4, 1816; d. aged one and a half years. James C., b. Sept. 3, 1818; d. aged about 25 years. Forrest M., b. Jan. 9, 1821; d. aged about 16 years. Harvey, b. Nov. 11, 1824; m. Ann Tuckesbury of Alexandria. David, b. Aug. 6, 1826; d. aged about 22 years. Warren, b. Feb. 29, 1829. George, b. July 4, 1831; lived in Ohio.

64. JAMES LOCKE, son of James (38), born 1753; married, Sept. 29, 1774, Martha Seavey. Lived at Portsmouth. Children:
Sarah, bapt. 1777; m. Aaron Riggs.
83. James, bapt. 1777. Aaron, unm. John, m. Abigail Goodwin of Portsmouth. Martha, b. July 27, 1792; m. Samuel Rand. Hannah, b. Nov. 18, 1795; m. Samuel Rand.

65. JAMES HOBBS LOCKE, son of Richard (39), born June 3, 1773; married April 17, 1801, Hannah Berry, who died Jan. 10, 1810, aged 36 years. Children:

84. Jonathan Hobbs, b. Nov. 17, 1802. Eleanor Dow, b. 1806; m. May 21, 1826, Joseph Rand, Jr.

66. ASA LOCKE, son of Richard (39), born Aug. 14, 1775; married, Nov. 12, 1799, Elizabeth Hobbs; died May 23, 1857. Served on the Alarm List under Capt. Wedgewood in the War of 1812. Children:

Sally H., b. Feb. 15, 1800; d. Aug. 12, 1825.
85. Asa, b. Oct. 18, 1801.
86. James Hobbs, b. Nov. 24, 1804.
87. Lemuel, b. Nov. 19, 1806. Mary Elizabeth, b. 1809; d. 1809. Perna T., b. 1809; d. 1809.
88. Jonathan Dearborn, b. April 1, 1811. John Oliver, b. 1811. Perna T., b. June 16, 1813; d. Oct. 31, 1829.
89. Gardiner Towle, b. Feb. 8, 1816.

67. RICHARD LOCKE, son of Richard (39), born Oct. 5, 1779; married, first, March 19, 1807, Sarah Woods; second, Feb. 20, 1817, Betsey Tucker. Children:

Worthy Dearborn, b. 1807; unm., drowned in Newburyport river. James, b. 1809. Gordon H., b. 1812. Sheridan, b. 1814. Sarah W., m. Knowles. William.

68. JOHN LOCKE, son of Joseph (41), born 1795; married Mary Ann Rindge of Portsmouth. Children:

John Rindge, b. 1818; d. Feb. 10, 1837.
90. Oliver Luther, b. Feb. 1, 1833. Woodbury, b. 1827; d. up country Feb. 25, 1852.

69. JEREMIAH LOCKE, JR., son of Joseph (42), married, Jan. 14, 1800, Mehitable Rand. Lived at Barrington. Children:

Hannah Dow, b. March 5, 1800; m. Dearborn of Boston. Henry, b. April 23, 1801; unm.; insane; d. May, 1870, at Lebanon, Me. Mary, b. Feb. 16, 1803; m. 1829, Wendell. Apphia, b. March 13, 1806; m. Thomas Shapley of Boston; he afterwards m. Mary ———. Jeremiah, b. April 9, 1811; m. March, 1835, Hannah Young. Martha, b. 1814; m. 1842, John Farmer.

70. JOSEPH LOCKE, son of Joseph (42), born May 4, 1787; married Olive Berry, who was born June 24, 1793.

Lived in the Oliver Luther Locke house; destroyed by fire.
Children:
Mary, b. Oct. 31, 1811; d. Jan. 21, 1812. Martha Dow, b. April 16, 1813; m. Adams Knox. John Newton, b. June 22, 1815; m. Oct. 20, 1839, Harriet Weatherbee. Sarah Goss, b. April 19, 1817; m. James C. Davis. Charles Miller, b. Aug. 9, 1819; d. Aug. 27, 1846. Jeremiah, b. Jan. 26, 1823; d. May 26, 1823 (?). Mary Perkins, b. Jan. 20, 1828; m. George W. Kimball. Hannah Salter, b. March 14, 1830; m. Richard Pigott. Levi, b. Dec. 27, 1831; d. Feb. 27, 1832. Caroline, b. April 2, 1833; m. Albert S. Baker. James Davis, b. Jan. 11, 1838; m. Maria Holmes.

71. JEREMIAH LOCKE, son of John, Jr. (43), born 1771; married, Nov. 26, 1793, Susan Rand. Children:
91. Richard Rand, b. July 16, 1794.
92. John W., b. June 28, 1796. Hamilton C., b. Dec. 28, 1798; m. Jan. 2, 1825, Mary Ann Rand. Ira, b. 1802; d. Oct. 14, 1823, aged 23 years. Jeremiah, b. May 15, 1804; m. Feb. 14, 1828, Mary Wentworth of Dover and Madbury.

72. JOSEPH LOCKE, son of Richard (44), born 1775; married, first, May 13, 1795, Lucy Marden, who died May 9, 1813; second, Sept. 11, 1814, widow Hannah Berry. Children by first wife:
Jane, bapt. Oct. 30, 1796; m. first, March 31, 1817, Benjamin Brown; second, John Randall. Nathaniel, bapt. Oct. 30, 1798; m. Mary Weed (who was a Whitten) of Sandwich. Joseph, bapt. May 4, 1800; unm. Lived at Sandwich. Sarah Palmer, b. Sept. 17, 1801; m. April 4, 1823, Lemuel Caswell of Gosport. Locada, b. 1804; m. Levi B. Trefethern. Hannah. Richard, b. 1805; unm. Elizabeth, b. April 20, 1808; m. 1835, Sebastian J. Trefethern. Jonathan Marden, b. Jan. 19, 1810; m. Nov. 28, 1841, widow Elizabeth Collins.
93. Jesse, b. Feb., 1809.
Children by second wife:
William, b. 1815; went to sea. John Quincy, b. 1826; d. in Mexican War. Hannah, b. 1817; m. first, Nov. 16, 1837, Stephen Ferguson; second, Joseph Holmes.

73. JOB LOCKE, son of Job (46), baptized May 5, 1799; married Hannah Randall. Built G. T. Locke's house and lived there. Children:
Charles F., b. Aug. 25, 1826; m. Aug. 25, 1851, Hannah E. Locke. Ellen, b. May 14, 1830; d. at Boston, 1855. Anna, b. 1838; m. William Young. Granville, b. 1835; d. of smallpox at Boston,

1855. Sarah Ann, b. 1833; m. July 2, 1854, William Dudley Varrell of Portsmouth. John, b. 1837; d. 1839. Thomas B., b. 1837; d. Jan. 11, 1839.

74. JOHN W. P. LOCKE, son of Job (46), born April, 1803; married, Nov. 19, 1826, Mary B. Locke; died April 25, 1841. Lived where Otis Goss lives (1903). Children:

Hannah Olive, m. first, Aug. 7, 1854, John O. Lane of Portsmouth; second, John W. Randall. Ann M., b. 1830; m. Nov. 12, 1852, Otis Goss.

75. JOHN LANGDON LOCKE, son of Simon (47), born Aug. 30, 1811; married, May 16, 1833, Mary Randall. Lived at Boston. Children:

John Henry, b. Aug. 1, 1835; m. June 30, 1859, Emma J. Johnson. Elmer F., b. July 25, 1838; m. Oct. 14, 1863, Mary E. Osborn. Mary Susan, b. Aug. 8, 1841; m. April 24, 1873, Harvey C. Glifford. Malvina A., b. July 5, 1848. Clarence S., b. July 27, 1854; d. Sept. 1, 1855.

76. JONATHAN LOCKE, son of Jonathan, Jr. (51), baptized Nov. 18, 1787; married, Dec. 24, 1812, Mary Vennard. Lived at Newcastle. Children:

George, b. June 14, 1813; m. first, April 9, 1840, Mehitable Lear; second, Hannah White. Dolly, b. Aug. 13, 1814; m. April 7, 1837, Henry Tredick. Mary, b. March 15, 1816; m. William Langdon. John, b. Aug., 1822; m. Oct. 7, 1849, Sarah Trefethen. Woodbury, b. 1822; m. June 16, 1852, Jane Smith. Emerline, b. Aug. 8, 1826; m. John Gardiner. Alvira, b. Aug. 12, 1829; m. March 10, 1849, Alfred Tucker.

77. MAJOR JOSEPH L. LOCKE, son of Jonathan, Jr. (51), born March, 1792; married, Nov. 29, 1816, Sarah W. Wedgewood. He died Sept. 6, 1858, aged 66 years. She died Nov. 30, 1879. Children:

Thaddeus, b. March 31, 1817; lost at sea. Adeline P., b. Nov., 1819; m. Oct. 19, 1839, Hiram Trefethern. Joseph Prentiss, b. 1820; m. Frances Manson of Portsmouth. Olive Rand, b. Feb., 1823; m. Feb. 28, 1847, Thomas H. Philbrick of Rye. Elbridge Gerry, b. 1825; d. March 24, 1839. Andrew Jackson, b. 1829; m. Caroline Hayes. Martin Van Buren, b. 1832; d. Aug. 21, 1871. William, b. 1834; d. July, 1853. Joseph L., b. Sept., 1836; m. June 24, 1859, Helen Woodsum of Portsmouth.

78. CAPT. SAMUEL JENNESS LOCKE, son of John, Jr. (52), born March 1, 1790; married, first, Dec. 21, 1817, Polly W. Waldron; died Aug. 22, 1831; second, April 24, 1834, Betsey Marden; died Sept. 20, 1877. Lived at Rye. Served in Capt. Coleman's company of cavalry in the War of 1812. He died March 29, 1861. Children by first wife:

John W., b. March 25, 1819; d. May 19 ——. Robert W., b. May 7, 1821; d. Aug. 30, 1825. Abigail J., b. Dec. 1823; d. Jan. 19, 1824. Elizabeth Emerett, b. April 1, 1826; m. May 21, 1848, Nathaniel Marden. Mary O., b. May 1, 1828; d. Aug. 5. Olive W., b. July 31, 1830; d. Sept. 14, ——.

79. JETHRO LOCKE, son of John, Jr. (52), born Nov. 19, 1797; married, Sept. 3, 1826, Martha Mason. Lived at Center where Albert M. Walker resides. Children:

John Sewell, b. Nov. 20, 1827; d. Dec. 11, 1854, of smallpox at Portsmouth. Cornelius, b. April 27, 1830. Fidelia, b. May 28, 1832; m. June 4, 1818, Webster Hurd; lives in Boston. Emily, b. June 29, 1834.

80. LIEUT. ELVIN LOCKE, son of John, Jr. (52), born March 29, 1809; married, April 5, 1835, Louisa Berry. Lived at Rye. Farmer. He died June 23, 1882. Children:

94. John Elvin, b. Aug. 25, 1835; m. first, 1862, Sarah Hayes; second, Laura Hayes. Mary E., b. Aug. 25, 1840; unm.
95. Oliver E., b. July 24, 1842. Charles A., b. March 6, 1844; d. Sarah L., b. March 25, 1845; m. Dec. 20, 1872, Clarence V. Marston of Exeter. Samuel Jenness, b. Nov. 19, 1846; went to California. Emily or Emma Amanda, b. Nov. 29, 1848; m. Oliver B. Fogg of North Hampton. Abby A., b. March 12, 1851; d.

81. JOSEPH LOCKE, son of Joseph (53), born Nov. 30, 1806; married, first, Nov. 28, 1833, Hannah Knowles; second, April 3, 1860, widow Esther R. Leavitt. Lived at Rye. Farmer. She died Aug. 17, 1902, aged 86 years. He died May 23, 1886. Children:

Horace W., b. June 2, 1837; d. Jan. 3, 1839. Sarah Abby, b. March 2, 1840; d. March 22, 1858. Elizaette E., b. March 18, 1844; m. Jan. 12, 1868, True W. Jones of Portsmouth; she d. March 10, 1872. Adna Parsons, b. Feb., 1849; d. May 26, 1877.

82. DEACON JONATHAN LOCKE, son of Joseph (53), born Aug. 17, 1813; married, first, Dec. 2, 1838, Almira Brown; second, 1862, Martha J. French. Lives at Rye. Deacon Jonathan (living 1903) is the oldest male resident in town; seldom wears glasses and very active on his farm. Children by first wife:

96. Freeman J., b. Oct. 7, 1843. Emma Ann, m. July, 1870, Cyrus Fogg of North Hampton. Horace, b. March 26, 1854. Abby, b. Oct. 1, 1856; d. Oct. 2, 1877.

83. JAMES LOCKE, JR., son of James (64), baptized 1777; married, Feb. 18, 1808, Eleanor Berry. Children:

Hannah, b. Jan. 12, 1807; m. in England. Adeline, b. June 10, 1813; m. Joel N. Foss; she d. Aug. 13, 1870. Martha Seavey, b. April, 1819; m. Aaron L. Riggs.

97. James John, b. Sept. 12, 1821. Ellen, b. April 22, 1830; m. Aug. 25, 1851, Charles F. Locke. Two d. young.

84. JONATHAN HOBBS LOCKE, son of James Hobbs (65), married, Sept. 17, 1831, Izettee Lewis of Kittery. He died Feb. 16, 1847. Children:

Joseph B., b. Nov. 13, 1837; m. Feb. 13, 1859, Sarah A. Murdoch. Delia Ann, b. April 17, 1843; m. Oliver Hutchings; d. Dec. 25, 1862. John, b. April 9, 1847; d. May 17, 1864.

85. ASA LOCKE, JR., son of Asa (66), born Oct. 18, 1801; married, April 15, 1824, Abigail Macy Locke, who afterward married Lemuel Locke. He died Nov. 1, 1863. Children:

Mary E., b. March 2, 1824; d. Feb. 26, 1825. Sally Hobbs, b. 1825; m. 1848, Joseph Dunbar. Thomas Lemuel, unm.; drowned on schooner *Fishing*.

98. John Oliver, b. June 16, 1829. Margaret, m. first, Daniel Burley; second, Edward Caswell. Abby, b. Oct., 1840; m. first, Sylvester Burley; second, Edward Caswell.

86. JAMES HOBBS LOCKE, son of Asa (66), born Nov. 24, 1804; married, Aug. 19, 1827, Mrs. Sally (Mow) Allen. Children:

Levi Dearborn, b. Jan. 18, 1829; d. May 13, 1902.

99. Hannah Elizabeth, b. Sept., 1832.

100. James Gardiner, b. March 29, 1834. Mary Jane, b. Feb. 1, 1839; d. Feb. 18, 1867.

87. LEMUEL LOCKE, son of Asa (66), born Nov. 19, 1806; married, first, Belinda Bunker; second, May 31, 1832, Esther Y. Remick; third, 1863, Abigail Locke. He died Aug. 26, 1897. Children by second wife:

    Elizabeth Garland, b. Sept. 14, 1832; m. Sept. 17, 1855, Samuel Jackson Jones.
101. Isaac Moses, b. June 18, 1834. Asa Dearborn, b. June 18, 1834; d. June 3, 1900.

88. JONATHAN DEARBORN LOCKE, son of Asa (66), born April, 1811; married, Dec. 23, 1838, Caroline G. Garland. Lived at Rye. She died Sept. 7, 1902, aged 85 years, 11 months. He died Oct. 16, 1885. Was captain of coasting vessels. Children:

    Amos G., b. June 13, 1840; m. Nov. 9, 1875, Nancy Helmer. Caroline, b. April 8, 1849; m. Sept. 25, 1878, A. Willis; d. 1898. Laura G., b. Dec. 22, 1851; m. May 12, 1875, Charles H. Hill. Georgianna, b. Jan. 20, 1854; m. Nov. 25, 1876, Melvin Hutchins of York, Me.

89. CAPT. GARDINER TOWLE LOCKE, son of Asa (66), born Feb. 8, 1816; married, first, Dec. 29, 1844, Julia A. Garland, who died July 14, 1873; second, Jan. 3, 1876, widow Anna D. Garland. Divorced. He died Feb. 13, 1901. Master of several vessels in the coastwise trade. Children by first wife:

    Woodbury Augustus, b. Feb. 26, 1846; m. Feb. 23, 1876, Martha Perkins of Hampton; d. 1893. David Parsons, b. April 28, 1850; m. Feb. 12, 1877, Ann Golding. Frank Buchanan, b. March 28, 1857.

90. OLIVER LUTHER LOCKE, son of John (68), born Feb. 1, 1833; married Olive A. Hodgdon. He died of smallpox in Rye March 17, 1876. Carpenter. Children:

    Frederick, b. July 27, 1859. Arabella Ringe, b. Sept. 27, 1856; m. March 25, 1884, Charles E. Walker of Portsmouth. Emma, b. May, 1864. Marcia, b. July 19, 1866. Clarence Elmer, b. Aug. 22, 1868; insane.

91. CAPT. RICHARD RAND LOCKE, son of Jeremiah (71), born July 16, 1794; married, Jan. 20, 1824, Sarah Ann Leavitt. She died May 14, 1870. Lived at Rye, Locke's Neck. Went privateering in the War of 1812. Captured

in the privateer *Thomas* and put in Dartmoor prison. Was captain of several coasting vessels out of Rye harbor. He died Jan. 20, 1877. Children:

Lula Ann, b. Oct. 11, 1824; m. first, Aug. 10, 1845, Samuel W. Foss; second, Oct. 7, 1855, John S. Goss. Sarah Emeline, b. Oct. 16, 1826; m. Oct. 15, 1848, Woodbury Jenness. Abby Maria, b. June 18, 1829; m. April 28, 1850, DeWitt Clinton Jewell of Stratham.
102. Richard L., b. Oct. 26, 1831. Harriet J., b. Jan. 15, 1835; m. Richard P. Goss of Rye.
103. Albert Carr, b. Jan. 22, 1837.

92. JOHN W. LOCKE, son of Jeremiah (71), born June 28, 1796; married, Oct. 27, 1816, Mary Powers. Lived at Rye (Locke's Neck). Children:

Susan, b. Feb. 22, 1817; m. Timothy Knowlton.
104. Robert P., b. Sept. 30, 1819; m. Sarah Elizabeth, b. Aug., 1822. Laura Augusta, b. Feb. 2, 1825; m. Timothy C. Knowlton; he d. July 9, 1869.
105. Calvin (a twin), b. Jan., 1830; m. Maria Adelaide, b. Feb. 20, 1836; m. Sept. 24, 1863, Woodbury Berry of Rye.

93. JESSE LOCKE, son of Joseph (72), born 1808; married Mary B., widow of J. W. P. Locke. Lived at Rye. Child:

106. John W., b. June 10, 1846.

94. JOHN ELVIN LOCKE, son of Elvin (80), born Aug. 25, 1835; married, Jan. 4, 1862, Sarah Hayes; second, Laura A. Hayes, 1879. Children:

Willie M., b. May 23, 1862. Mary Emma, b. 1863; d. 1863, aged 11 weeks. Ida L., b. May 29, 1865; m. H. F. Ray; d. June 21, 1895. Charles Elvin, b. Aug. 29, 1874; m. widow Stewart, June 30, 1903. Henry H., b. Aug. 13, 1877; d. March 9, 1902.

95. OLIVER E. LOCKE, son of Elvin (80), born July 24, 1842; married, Dec. 20, 1873, Belle Clough. Lived at Portsmouth. Children:

Hellen C., b. Aug. 31, 1878; m. Oct. 17, 1903, Harry LeGrand Hilton. Elizabeth D., b. Dec. 17, 1885.

96. FREEMAN J. LOCKE, son of Jonathan (82), born Oct. 7, 1843; married, April 13, 1864, Mary A. Otis. Lived at Rye. Blacksmith. He died Feb. 10, 1904. Children:

Ethel May, b. April 9, 1866; m. June 16, 1888, George A. Batchelder of North Hampton. Martha Kate, b. Oct. 31, 1867; m. Nov. 9, 1892, Thomas W. Parsons.

97. JAMES JOHN LOCKE, son of James, Jr. (83), married, March 4, 1847, Mrs. Hannah J. Frisbee. Lived at Rye. Children:

107. Aaron, b. Aug. 11, 1847. Clara E., b. Sept. 14, 1849; m. Sept., 1872, James I. Watson of Exeter. John Franklin, b. April 14, 1851; m. Mary E. Ward. Elsie C., b. May 18, 1852; m. Aug. 7, 1870, Christopher Grant from Nova Scotia. Martha J., b. Jan. 25, 1855; m. Jan. 24, 1876, Charles E. Hodgdon of Portsmouth; she d. Dec. 23, 1879. Mary E., b. Feb. 19 or 24, 1857; d. Aug. 19, 1875. Ida G., b. March 24, 1859.

98. JOHN OLIVER LOCKE, son of Asa, Jr. (85), born June 16, 1829; married, first, Feb. 29, 1864, Anna M. Tarlton; second, Feb. 19, 1867, Hannah Josephine Trefethern. Children by second wife:

Charles Dunbar, b. Dec. 8, 1867; carpenter. Anna Tarlton, b. Feb. 18, 1870; m. May 22, 1894, Charles Ellinwood. George E., b. Aug. 4, 1872. John, b. July 21, 1875; d. Sept. 24, 1875.

99. HANNAH ELIZABETH LOCKE, daughter of James Hobbs (86), born Sept., 1832; married, first, Aug. 29, 1864, Benjamin W. Marden; second, Gilman Varrell. Children:

Sarah Isabell, b. Sept., 1855.
108. George Allen, b. 1858.

100. JAMES GARDINER LOCKE, son of James Hobbs (86), born March 29, 1834; married Angelina Dockham. Child:

109. Andrew Gardiner, b. July 2, 1868.

101. ISAAC MOSES LOCKE, son of Lemuel (87), born June 18, 1834; married, March 11, 1865, Jennie E. Williams. Child:

Willie L., b. March 21, 1865; d. Aug. 20, 1870.

102. RICHARD LEAVITT LOCKE, son of Richard Rand (91), born, Oct. 26, 1831; married, Nov. 15, 1859, Sarah P. Jenness. Carpenter and proprietor of a boarding house at Rye Beach. Children:

R. Jenness, b. May 31, 1863; m. Feb. 23, 1898, Bessie L. Batchelder; had Richard Jenness, b. April 3, 1903. Annie, b. Feb. 22, 1865; m. April 11, 1894, Langdon B. Parsons. Arthur, b. Oct. 2, 1868; d. March 11, 1887.

103. ALBERT CARR LOCKE, son of Richard Rand (91), born Jan. 22, 1837; married, July 9, 1865, Eliza E. Varrell. Lived at Rye (Locke's Neck) on the homestead. Carpenter by trade and was selectman for many years. Children:

Everett True, b. Oct. 5, 1868. Olive Ann, b. Jan. 4, 1870. Mabel Jenness, b. Nov. 12, 1872; d. July 30, 1891. Ethel Maud, b. June 24, 1875; m. Feb. 23, 1900, William E. Garland.

104. ROBERT P. LOCKE, son of John (92), born Sept. 30, 1819; married, 1851, Clarinda A. Batchelder. Lived at North Hampton. Mason by trade. Child:

Walter E., b. Dec. 8, 1855; m. May 28, 1879, Elvira G. Marden.

105. CALVIN LOCKE, son of John (92), born Jan., 1830; married Frances Priest. Children:

Ella Frances, b. July, 1859. Mary Augusta, b. 1862.

106. JOHN W. LOCKE, son of Jesse (93), born June 10, 1846; married, 1872, Sarah H. Randall. Lived at Rye. Child:

Willie H., b. June 26, 1873.

107. AARON LOCKE, son of John James (96), born Aug. 11, 1847; married, April 24, 1871, Francesene M. Rand. Child:

Alvah, m. Feb. 4, 1893, Emma Smart; she d. July, 1893.

108. GEORGE ALLEN LOCKE, son of Hannah Elizabeth (99), born 1858; married, Jan. 22, 1892, Margaret E. Gillis. Children:

Sarah, b. Feb. 21, 1893. Margaret, b. April 7, 1894. Annie, b. Sept. 11, 1896. Doris, b. Feb. 26, 1902.

109. ANDREW GARDINER LOCKE, son of James Gardiner (100), born July 2, 1868; married, Oct. 20, 1897, Ella B. Haley. Blacksmith by trade. Child:

Edison G., b. Oct. 2, 1898.

LORD.

CAPT. DANIEL LORD, born 1798; married, Nov. 24, 1725, Sarah Goss. Lived at Rye. He died Dec. 13, 1882. Child:
- Martha Ann, m. Benjamin Batchelder of Rye.

LOUGEE.

GEORGE G. LOUGEE, born July, 1828; married, first, Sophia Leavitt of Hampton Falls; second, Oct., 1859, Semira Brown; third, Josephine Adams. She died Oct. 25, 1885. Proprietor of the Sea View House, Rye Beach. Child by first wife:
- Augustus, b. July 18, 1850.

Children by second wife:
- Bertha, b. Sept. 22, 1860; m. W. H. Hayward. Amory, b. July 9, 1863.

Children by third wife:
- Gilman Marston, b. July 19, 1869; m. Mable Wilkins. Adams. Margaret, b. 1879; m. Sept. 17, 1902, Dr. F. H. Verhoeff.

LOWD.

WILLIAM HENRY LOWD, married Florence W. Rand. Child:
- Henry M., b. June 10, 1869.

MACE.

1. ITHAMAR MACE, son of ———, married, Dec. 6, 1764, Rachel Berry. Came from Isles of Shoals. Tradition says that he enlisted in the French War when eighteen years of age, was taken prisoner, and was away from home nine years. Children:

2. John, b. 17—. Sarah, b. Aug., 1765 (?); unm.; had Sally, b. 1804, who m. first, July 13, 1822, G. Johnson; second, Feb. 8, 1827, Ithamer Mace. Abigail, b. 1776; m. Feb. 14, 1792, Simon Locke.

2. JOHN MACE, son of Ithamar (1), married, June 27, 1793, Rachel Randall. After his death she married, sec-

GENEALOGY. 445

ond, Joseph Hall. She died Feb. 17, 1830, aged 66 years.
Children:
3. Ithamar, b. May 30, 1795.
4. John, b. Jan. 12, 1798. Edward. A daughter.

3. ITHAMAR MACE, son of John (2), born May 30, 1795;. married, first, Nov. 6, 1817, Deborah Varrell; died Nov. 18, 1824; second, Feb. 8, 1827, widow Salley B. Johnson. Children by first wife:
5. John W., b. about 1820.
6. Nathaniel.
Children by second wife:
7. William Randall, b. July 15, 1827. Mary Jane, b. Dec. 2, 1830; d. Oct. 15, 1838.
8. Charles Ithamar, b. June 20, 1833.
9. Woodbury N., b. Feb. 14, 1836. Everett Ann, b. Aug. 12, 1838; d. March 11, 1864. James, b. Nov. 11, 1841; d. July 3, 1864, at navy yard.

4. JOHN MACE, son of John (2), born Jan. 12, 1798; married, Oct. 18, 1821, Mary Berry. He was knocked overboard by the main boom and drowned off Boone Island. His widow married, second, March 4, 1824, Richard Varrell. Child:
10. John A., b. Jan. 28, 1822.

5. JOHN W. MACE, son of Ithamar (3), born about 1820; married, Jan., 1841, Abigail Philbrick. Children:
John Henry. Emma. Hattie. Isabella. Fred. Fannie.

6. NATHANIEL MACE, son of Ithamar (3), married Abby S. Johnson. After his death she married David Remick. Children:
Ambretta Jane, b. Oct. 2, 1842; m. Benj. T. Odiorne.
11. Charles William, b. April 24, 1844 (?).

7. WILLIAM RANDALL MACE, son of Ithamar (3), born July 15, 1827; married Mary O. Downes. Children:
William Henry, b. June 6, 1853; m. Abbie Lord.
12. Horace S., b. Dec. 1, 1857. Wilmot Upham, b. Dec. 30, 1866. Martha A., b. Feb. 24, 1869; m. Dec. 28, 1885, Fred L. Smart.

8. CHARLES ITHAMAR MACE, son of Ithamar (3), born June 20, 1833; married, Feb. 21, 1864, Francis Olive Matthews. She died Jan. 29, 1876. He died May 20, 1903. Children:

    Lillian, b. Aug. 15, 1864; m. Joseph L. Jessome. Fannie, b. Sept. 2, 1865; m. Oct. 2, 1884, John B. Lewis; d. 1890. Carrie, b. April 10, 1868. Gertrude, b. Jan. 24, 1869; m. Nov. 6, 1891, James D. Davidson.

9. WOODBURY N. MACE, son of Ithamar (3), born Feb. 14, 1836; married, first, Mary E. Varrell; second, widow Mary Randall.

10. JOHN A. MACE, son of John (4), born Jan. 28, 1822; married Elizabeth Ann Caswell. He died Feb. 24, 1861. Children:

    Mary F., b. Feb. 29, 1856; had a dau. Oct. 26, 1874; m. first, Jan. 23, 1876, Clarence Goss; second, Albert Johnson. Anna C., b. July 30, 1857; m. Nov. 3, 1876, Albert L. Remick. Addie M., b. Aug. 29, 1859; d. Nov. 18, 1881; m. Horace Mace. John A., b. Oct. 24, 1861.

11. CHARLES WILLIAM MACE, son of Nathaniel (6), born April 24, 1844 (?); married, July 4, 1868, Eliza S. Tucker. Children:

    Leander George, b. May 5, 1869. A daughter, b. Nov. 15, 1871.

12. HORACE S. MACE, son of William Randall (7), born Dec. 1, 1857; married, first, Addie M. Mace, who died Nov. 18, 1881, and he married, second, Melissa Garland. Children:

    Hattie. Addie. Maria.

Ithamar Mace of Gosport and Ruth Seavey married April 16, 1785.

MARDEN.

1. JAMES MARDEN settled at Rye or Newcastle. Children:

2. William.
3. James (?). Nathan (?). Sarah (?).

GENEALOGY. 447

2. WILLIAM MARDEN, son of James (1). Children:
4. William.
5. Jonathan (?). David (?). Samuel (?). Mary. Dorcas, m. March 10, 1738 (?), William Harvey of Bradford, Mass. Sarah.
6. John (?).

3. JAMES MARDEN, probably son of James (1), married, Oct. 23, 1695, Abigail Webster. Lived at Newcastle, where he died prior to 1726. Children:
Stephen, m. Lang (?).
7. Thomas.
8. Ebenezer. Rachel, m. Job Chapman. Hannah, m. Stephen Emerson. Abigail, m. first, George Foss; second, Nathaniel Drake.
9. James, b. Sept. 25, 1697.

4. WILLIAM MARDEN, son of William (2), married Dorcas. Child:
10. Benjamin, b. June 28, 1727.

5. JONATHAN MARDEN, probably son of William (2), married Hepzibah. Children:
Nathan, b. March 11, 1730; d. Dec. 7, 1735. Jonathan, b. Oct. 9, 1732; perhaps m. and had Hepzibah, b. 1756; Elizabeth, b. 1758; William, b. 1760; and perhaps Hannah, bapt. 1764; Jane, bapt. 1765; Hepzibah, bapt. 1767. Hepzibah, b. Nov. 1, 1742. Timothy, b. Aug. 28, 1735.
11. Joseph, b. March 22, 1738. Nathaniel, b. July 25, 1745. Samuel, b. Sept. 11, 1750.

6. JOHN MARDEN, probably son of William (2), married, March 20, 1746, Sarah Locke. Children:
12. John, b. Nov. 30, 1747. Sarah, m. March 17, 1772, Samuel Knowles.

7. THOMAS MARDEN, son of James (3), married, first, March 4, 1729, Mary Smith; second, June 9, 1761, widow Hannah Fogg. Children:
James.
13. Israel. Mary, m. Oct. 31, 1765, David Smith, Jr.

8. EBENEZER MARDEN, son of James (3), married, Jan. 13, 1735, Esther Berry. Children:
Abigail, b. Sept. 18, 1737; d. young. Abigail, b. Aug. 12, 1740; d. unm. March 28, 1820.

14. George, b. June 29, 1741. Elizabeth, b. Dec. 18, 1743; m. Dec. 29, 1763, Timothy Dalton.
15. Nathaniel, b. March 22, 1746. James, b. April 5, 1748; d. Feb. 14, 1749-'50. Mary, b. Feb. 1, 1750; m. Jonathan Philbrick.

9. JAMES MARDEN, son of James (3), born Sept. 25, 1697; married Judith Bates, born June 13, 1703; died July 31, 1796. He died July, 1777. Children:

16. Nathan, b. Nov. 15, 1721. John, b. Feb. 29, 1724; m. Sarah Saunders, and d. July 31, 1756, at Epping. Mary, b. Sept. 25, 1727.
17. James, b. Sept. 6, 1729. Abigail, b. March 21, 1731; d. July 7, 1736. William, b. Oct. 13, 1733; d. July 18, 1736. Hannah, b. May 14, 1736; m. Clark. Abigail, b. Sept. 11, 1738. Judith, b. June 11, 1741; m. 1780, George Foss.
18. William, b. May 30, 1744. Olive, b. Jan. 6, 1747; d. Dec. 3, 1835; m. first, 1773, Samuel Elkins; second, David Locke.

10. BENJAMIN MARDEN, son of William (4), born June 28, 1727; married, May 12, 1746, Rebeckah Whidden. Children:

Samuel, b. April 30, 1748.
19. Benjamin, b. Feb. 4, 1751. William Gould, b. 1752; d. young. Elizabeth, b. June 30, 1754; m. Joseph Hardy or Simon Towle. Molly, b. 1758. William, b. Sept. 19, 1759. John, b. May 6, 1762. Jesse, b. 1766. Mary. Samuel, b. Jan. 25, 1773.

11. JOSEPH MARDEN, probably son of Jonathan (5), born March 22, 1738; married first, ———; second, June 30, 1773 (?), Mary Hunt. Children by first wife:

Abigail, b. 1758. Sarah, b. 1759. Mary, b. 1761. Joseph, b. 1769; d. young.

Children by second wife:

Joseph, b. April 3, 1774. Samuel Hunt, b. Jan. 14, 1777. Jonathan, b. Feb. 22, 1780. Daniel, b. Aug. 14, 1782. Timothy, bapt. March 25, 1787.

12. JOHN MARDEN, son of John (6), born Nov. 30, 1747; married, March 23, 1769, Sarah Saunders. Lived at Epping. Children:

John.
20. Samuel, b. 1775. James, m. Langmaid. Benjamin. Sarah. Olive, m. French. Hannah, m. Catlin.

GENEALOGY. 449

13. ISRAEL MARDEN, son of Thomas (7), married, first, Dec. 27, 1753, Prudence Locke; second ———. Children by first wife:

    Thomas, b. 1756. Sarah, b. 1758; d. young. Sarah, b. 1761; m. Morrill.
21. Francis, b. 1763.
    Children by second wife:
    Israel, b. 1765; m. Dowrst. Prudence, b. 1768; m. Cate. Thomas, b. 1770; m. Wiggin.
22. John.

14. GEORGE MARDEN, son of Ebenezer (8), born June 29, 1741; married, Jan. 19, 1769, Sarah Webster. Lived at Chester. Children:

    James, b. Oct. 23, 1769 (?); m. July 14, 1791, Sarah Burbank. George. Sarah, b. 1771. Mary, b. 1772; m. George Carr. Elizabeth, b. 1775, m. Jonathan Basford. Abigail, b. May 18, 1777; m. Asa Prescott.
23. Josiah, b. Oct. 23, 1778; m. Dec. 24, 1801, Hannah Berry. Ebenezer, b. Jan. 29, 1781 (?); m. Nancy Colby. Nancy, b. 1790; m. June 11, 1807, Joshua Prescott.

15. DEACON NATHANIEL MARDEN, son of Ebenezer (8), born March 22, 1746; married Elizabeth Moulton, who was born Feb. 8, 1752, and died Nov. 1, 1831. He died March 30, 1823. Children:

    Jonathan, b. April 24, 1770; d. unm. April 8, 1853. Hannah, b. Jan. 5, 1772; m. Oct. 9, 1792, Mark Lang. Olive, b. Aug. 27, 1774; m. Joseph Rand. Lucy, b. Sept. 28, 1776; m. May 13, 1795, Joseph Locke, 3d.
24. Ebenezer, b. Jan. 22, 1779.
25. James, b. May 6, 1781.
26. Reuben, b. April 21, 1783. Esther, b. July 20, 1785; m. Joshua Rand. Elizabeth, b. Dec. 17, 1787; d. July 12, 1788. Elizabeth M., b. Nov. 6, 1793; m. Samuel J. Locke.

16. NATHAN MARDEN, son of James (9), born Nov. 15, 1721; married, Oct. 7, 1743, Susannah Berry. Lived at Epsom. Children:

    Sarah, b. 1744. James, b. 1746. Judith, b. 1752. Nathan, b. 1754.

17. JAMES MARDEN, son of James (9), born Sept. 6, 1729; married, Jan. 2, 1751, Priscilla Foss. Lived at Barrington. Children:

Rachel, b. Oct. 16, 1751; m. Oct. 1, 1772, John Blake. Hincks, b. May 25, 1753. James, b. Aug. 17, 1761. Abigail, b. April 8, 1768.

18. WILLIAM MARDEN, son of James (9), born May 30, 1744; married, April 29, 1773, Hannah Wallis. He died Nov. 14, 1816. She died Sept. 21, 1830. Children:
Abigail, b. March 31, 1776; m. Joseph Locke. Sarah, b. Oct. 29, 1778; m. Dec. 17, 1801, Thomas Goss. Hannah, b. April 4, 1781; m. William Whidden.
27. James, b. April 21, 1784.

19. BENJAMIN MARDEN, son of Benjamin (10), born Feb. 4, 1751; married, first, Jan. 26, 1772, Hannah Rand, who died Sept. 1, 1812; second, Jan. 23, 1817, Mrs. Deliverance Johnson. Lived in pasture by Gammon's brook and moved house up by Baptist church. Served in Capt. Parsons' company in the Revolutionary War, and died Feb. 26, 1826. Children by first wife:
Rebekah, b. Jan. 10, 1773; d. unm. Nov. 22, 1845. Benjamin, b. 1775. Nancy Tredwell, b. March 20, 1777; m. March 2, 1800, Samuel Marden. Mary, b. March 24, 1779; m. Lowell Sanborn.

20. SAMUEL MARDEN, son of John (12), born 1775; married, March 2, 1800, Nancy Tredwell Marden. She died July 22, 1832. Children:
28. Benjamin W., b. July 27, 1800. Clarissa A. Davis, b. Feb. 9, 1816; d. Dec. 14, 1878; m. Bartholomew Barry of Portsmouth.
29. Lowell Sanborn, b. Jan. 13, 1819.

21. FRANCIS MARDEN, son of Israel (13), born 1763; married Sarah Lamprey. Lived at Portsmouth. Children:
30. James, b. 1786. Simon, bapt. Nov. 18, 1787.
31. Israel, bapt. Oct. 11, 1789.
32. Thomas. Frances, bapt. Aug. 3, 1794. Joseph, m. Marston. Patience, bapt. Aug. 21, 1796; m. Levi Berry. Prudence, m. Capt. Thomas.

22. JOHN MARDEN, son of Israel (13), married Mary Elizabeth Sherburn. Lived at Portsmouth. Children:
Israel, m. Sally Tilton of Hampton Falls; he was killed by an explosion on Lafayette road, caused by drilling out a charge of powder. Francis, m. Eliza Langmaid of Gilmanton. Jonathan.

33. Thomas, b. July 28, 1805. Henry, d. aged about 20 years. James, b. 1809; m. Varina Currier.
34. John. Hunking, m. Winnifred Lockhart. Robert, m. first, Ann Bartlett; second, Maria ———. Lydia, m. Abner Blaisdell. Mary, m. James Young. Hannah, d. aged about 7 years.

23. JOSIAH MARDEN, son of George (14), born 1778; married, Dec. 24, 1801, Hannah Berry. Children:

35. William, b. Aug. 8, 1802.
36. George, b. Feb. 8, 1804. Jesse, b. March 19, 1806; m. Roxanna Bown. Samuel B., b. May 28, 1808; d. Dec. 28, 1846. David L., b. Jan. 29, 1811; d. unm. March 8, 1864. Sarah W., b. April 11, 1813; m. Abner Kidder. Olivia B., b. Dec. 27, 1815; m. April 6, 1837, Joseph P. Trefethern. Dorothy B., b. Dec. 29, 1817; m. Jan. 7, 1836, Charles F. Trefethern. Hannah J., b. June 9, 1820; m. Oct. 22, 1842, John Gustin. Eliza Ann, b. Sept. 27, 1824; m. 1846, Samuel Trefethern.

24. EBENEZER MARDEN, son of Nathaniel (15), born Jan. 22, 1779; married, June 26, 1806, Love Berry. He died Dec. 5, 1862, and she died July 21, 1876. Children:

Love B., b. Oct. 31, 1807; d. Jan. 31, 1896. Elizabeth M., b. April 26, 1810; d. 1888. Mary B., b. Aug. 10, 1813; d. March 29, 1882. Esther R., b. March 3, 1816; m. first, May, 1840, Joseph Leavitt; second, Joseph Locke, 3d. Eben W., b. June 22, 1824; m. first, Julia (?) Garland; second, Sarah B. Brown. Frances Jane, b. March 22, 1824; d. April 2, 1824.
37. John Salter, b. April 8, 1825.

25. JAMES MARDEN, son of Nathaniel (16), born May 6, 1781; married, Jan. 4, 1803, Sarah Webster. Children:

Rhoda, b. April 2, 1803; had Charles F., m. Alfred S. Trafton. Lovina, b. Jan. 8, 1810.

26. REUBEN MARDEN, son of Nathaniel (16), born April 21, 1783; married, first, April 14, 1810, Hannah Moulton, who died Jan. 26, 1822, aged 40 years; second, widow Charlotte Towle Moulton, born Jan., 1803. She died May 17, 1901, aged 97 years and 11 months. He died Oct. 22, 1851. Children by first wife:

Anna B., b. June 5, 1810; m. June 22, 1828, Richard G. Caswell.
38. Nathaniel, b. Feb. 20, 1817.

Children by second wife:

39. John Towle, b. Feb. 26, 1836. Daniel W., b. Dec. 23, 1837. Mary E., b. Jan. 16, 1840; m. Dec., 1866, Alfred S. Goss. Eliza A., b. May 13, 1842; m. Joseph J. Goss. Charles H., b. May 13, 1842.

27. JAMES MARDEN, son of William (18), born April 21, 1784; married, May 11, 1809, Polly Jenness. She died Oct., 1853. Children:
40. William, b. Dec. 24, 1810. A child, b. Dec. 24, 1810.

28. CAPT. BENJAMIN W. MARDEN, son of Samuel (20), born July 27, 1800; married, first, Sept. 23, 1821, Hannah Lang; second, Dec. 28, 1834, widow Eliza J. Drake, who died Aug. 28, 1861; third, Aug. 29, 1864, Hannah E. Locke. He died Oct. 27, 1882. Shoemaker by trade. Children by first wife:
Gilman D., b. Oct. 7, 1821. Nathaniel D., b. April 15, 1823; d. aged four years. Albert S., b. June 30, 1825; m. Bristow.
Children by second wife:
Benjamin Franklin, b. July, 1836; m. Julia ———; he died Jan. 3, 1901. Sarah Priscilla, b. 1838; m. Charles A. Haskell. Frances Ann, b. 1840; m. Thomas Lefrancis. Henry Hubbard, b. Feb. 1842; m. Kate Butler.
Child by third wife:
Ella Grace, b. June 7, 1865; d. March 24, 1866.

29. LOWELL SANBORN MARDEN, son of Samuel (20), born Jan. 13, 1819; married Mary Jane Page. After his death she married, second, William E. Willacy. Children:
Elbridge. Gilman, b. Dec. 15, 1849; m. June 8, 1871, Abby J. I. Going. Laura Ann, b. 1845; d. Jan. 14, 1849. Ida May, b. Feb. 9, 1861. Mary E. Stewart, b. June 13, 1864.

30. JAMES MARDEN, son of Francis (21), born 1786; married, first, ———; second, Mercy Page. Lived at Portsmouth. Children by first wife:
Francis. James. Elizabeth.
Children by second wife:
Sarah. Alfred. John. Oliver. Adeline. Emily. Mercy. Susan.

31. ISRAEL MARDEN, son of Francis (21), baptized Oct. 11, 1789; married Nudd. He died June 11, 1865. Lived at Portsmouth. Children:

Asa, lived on Winchester farm; m. Abigail Marston. Benjamin. Sarah W., d. March 7, 1882; m. Nov. 28, 1845, William Rand. George, m. Elizabeth Holmes. Israel, m. Hannah Walker.

32. THOMAS MARDEN, son of Francis (21), married Mary Lang. Lived at Portsmouth. Children:

> Joseph P., m. Emily Norton. Simon, m. Hannah Norton.

33. THOMAS MARDEN, son of John (22), born July 28, 1805, married Mercy Holbrook of Brunswick, Me. Children:

> Sarah M. Mary Jane M. Albert B. M. Georgianna M., m. Charles Stevens.

34. JOHN MARDEN, son of John (22), married Elizabeth Ann Haley. Lived at Portsmouth. Children:

> Alfred Henry. John Calvin, m. Arabella Norton. Susan S., m. I. Purrington. Trueman H., m. Coffin. Florence B.

35. WILLIAM MARDEN, son of Josiah (23), born Aug. 8, 1802; married Martha W. Mason. After his death she married, second, March 29, 1851, George Marden, brother of William. Children:

> Jesse, b. Nov. 21, 1828; m. Mary C. Cochrane. Joseph Mason, b. 1830; sailed whaling from New Bedford and never heard from. Daniel Towle, b. March 3, 1833; m. 1858, Clara J. Philbrick.
> 41. Francis Marion, b. Nov., 1836. William Jackson, b. Aug. 12, 1838; m. 1865, Lizzie F. Ewing. Mary Jane, b. July 23, 1848; m. July 9, 1868, Henry L. Varrell.

36. GEORGE MARDEN, son of Josiah (23), born Feb. 8, 1804; married, March 29, 1851, Martha W. (Mason) Marden, widow of his brother William. Children:

> Sarah Ann, b. July 23, 1851; m. Jan., 1871, Gates Wentworth. Samuel Foss, b. Feb. 13, 1855; unm.

37. JOHN SALTER MARDEN, son of Ebenezer (24), born April 8, 1825; married, Aug. 5, 1855, Sophia C. Holmes. He died Sept. 16, 1900. Children:

> Annie B., b. 1861; m. Nov. 23, 1869, Clarance Matthews.

38. NATHANIEL MARDEN, son of Reuben (26), born Feb. 20, 1817; married, May 21, 1848, Elizabeth Emerett Locke. He died March 9, 1891. Children:

Polly A. W., b. July 7, 1848; m. 1869, George White. Clara A., b. Jan. 27, 1850; m. Jan. 15, 1879, Charles Walker. Ervin W., b. Nov. 21, 1851. Samuel A., b. March 3, 1854. Hollis N., b. May 23, 1856; m. Dec. 28, 1883, Carrie K. Foss. Elvira G., b. Nov. 8, 1857; m. May 28, 1879, Walter Locke. Fred H., b. Nov. 20 (?), 1859; d. May 11, 1893. Willie P., b. Dec. 14, 1861; d. 1868. Emerett E., b. Oct. 6, 1863; m. Sept. 26, 1888, Edward Ramsdell. Abby, b. June 10, 1866; unm.

39. JOHN TOWLE MARDEN, son of Reuben (26), born Feb. 26, 1836; married, April 25, 1867, Fannie S. Brown. He died Jan. 2, 1902. Children:

Fred, b. May 15, 1868. Florence, b. July 21, 1869. Newell, b. Jan. 30, 1880.

40. WILLIAM MARDEN, son of James (27), born Dec. 24, 1810; married, 1832, Lucy Ann Garland. She died Aug. 24, 1870. He died Jan. 15, 1883. Children:

James L., b. Dec. 1, 1832; d. July 6, 1837.
42. Jenness, b. July 9, 1837. James, b. Oct. 2, 1839; m. Harriett Jenness, and had Nellie and Fanny.
43. Levi Watson, b. March 27, 1843. Emery B., b. Oct. 14, 1849; d. young.

41. FRANCIS MARION MARDEN, son of William (35), born Nov., 1836; married Anna S. Joice. He was a blacksmith, and died Nov. 25, 1890. Children:

Willie, b. Nov., 1867. John Francis, b. April 10, 1869; d. 1897, at Portsmouth.

42. JENNESS MARDEN, son of William (40), born July 9, 1837; married, 1860, Mary Ann Garland. He died Sept. 11, 1880. Children:

Charles Frost, b. Aug. 4, 1864; m. Aug. 2, 1888, Julia L. Brown. Sarah A., b. Sept. 7, 1870; m. Dec. 14, 1898, Frank Broad. Nettie Jane, b. Sept. 2, 1873; m. Jan. 17, 1900, Geo. G. Reddin. Theresa, b. March 3, 1880.

43. LEVI WATSON MARDEN, son of William (40), born March 27, 1843; married Emma Downes. Children:

Anna Belle, b. July 28, 1866; m. Edward Phillips. Mary E., b. Oct. 29, 1870; m. Dec. 17, 1889, Charles Spear.
44. Wilbur L., b. Aug. 5, 1875.

GENEALOGY. 455

44. WILBUR L. MARDEN, son of Levi Watson (4̃2), born Aug. 5, 1875; married, July 25, 1895, Lizzie Rhodes. Children:

Lucy R., b. Feb. 14, 1896. Florence M., b. July 23, 1898.

1. STEPHEN MARDEN may have been a son of James (3), married Charity ———. Cordwainer. Lived near Chas. B. Odiorne's at Little Harbor, and had a ferry to Great Island (now Newcastle). Children:

 Hannah, b. March 13, 1723.
2. Benjamin, b. Aug. 9, 1729. Ruth, b. Dec. 8, 1731; m. Oct. 11, 1753, Levi Towle. Elizabeth, b. April 12, 1734; Stephen, b. Sept. 27, 1736; m. Aug. 28, 1760, Elizabeth Webster. Abigail, b. July 22, 1739; m. first, Daniel Philbrick; second, William Davidson.

2. BENJAMIN MARDEN, son of Stephen (1), born Aug. 9, 1729, married, Jan. 31, 1754, Rachael Dowrst. She died Dec. 11, 1812, aged 59 years. Lived on the Solomon Dowrst farm, at present (1903) occupied by Samuel Marden and his son-in-law, Adams E. Drake. Children:

 Solomon Dowrst, b. Sept. 25, 1757. Charity, b. March 9, 1760; m. first, Joshua Locke; second, Oct. 19, 1797, Peter Ackerman. Elizabeth, b. Feb. 9, 1762; m. Simon Towle. Rachael, b. Jan. 9, 1766; d. Jan. 28, 1766. Abiel, b. Feb. 27, 1767; m. William Foss. Benjamin, b. June 14, 1769; d. June 24, 1769. Sarah, b. 1771; m. Jonathan Philbrick.
3. Stephen, b. Nov. 3, 1773.
4. Solomon, b. March, 1774.
5. Samuel, b. Sept. 8, 1776. Merribah or Mary, b. 1779.

3. STEPHEN MARDEN, son of Benjamin (2), born Nov. 3, 1773; married, Nov. 12, 1789, Molly Smith. He died Sept. 21, 1844. Children:

6. David Smith, b. July 27, 1790. Stephen, bapt. July 5, 1795.
7. Thomas, b. Aug. 17, 1801.

4. SOLOMON MARDEN, son of Benjamin (2), born March, 1774; married, July 15, 1802, Huldah Remick. She died Jan. 30, 1841. He died Dec. 10, 1843. Lived near the Center schoolhouse, where Charles Lear resides. Children:

456   HISTORY OF RYE.

    Elizabeth, b. Aug. 26, 1802; unm.; had Langdon Marden; d. Oct. 29, 1828. Thomas, d. April 26, 1804. Benjamin, b. Aug. 28, 1807; m. widow Margaret Nason; d. Feb. 11, 1876. Moses, b. March, 1809; d. Nov. 20, 1810. Abigail, b. April, 1810; d. Aug. 7, 1810. Moses R., b. Aug. 14, 1811; d. unm., Jan. 25, 1884; fisherman. Abigail, b. April 6, 1813; m. Nathan Clough of Seabrook. Mary Jane, b. May 26, 1815; m. Henry Day. Almira, b. Feb. 11, 1817; d. unm., March 5, 1881, at Portsmouth.

5. SAMUEL MARDEN, son of Benjamin (2), born Sept. 8, 1776; married, April 3, 1806, Sarah Philbrick, born Aug. 30, 1788, and died March 23, 1860. Served in the War of 1812 under Capt. Samuel Berry. He died May 11, 1853. Children:

    Hannah, b. July 27, 1806; d. Sept. 14, 1835. Sally, b. Jan. 5, 1811; d. June 10, 1839.
8. Daniel, b. June 14, 1812.
9. Samuel, b. Feb. 19, 1821. Charles, b. May 3, 1827; d. March 23, 1828.

6. DAVID SMITH MARDEN, son of Stephen (3), born July 27, 1790; married, June 7, 1813, Elizabeth Lang. Served under Capt. Ephraim Philbrick in the War of 1812. Children:

    May, b. Sept. 27, 1814; m. William C. Garland. Hannah, m. Thomas Lewis. Stephen, b. Feb. 5, 1822; m. Oct. 15, 1843, Mary Holmes of Portsmouth; d. Oct. 9, 1888. Elizabeth. Sarah Ann. Lucy.
10. David.

7. THOMAS MARDEN, son of Stephen (3), born Aug. 17, 1801; married Eliza Garland. After his death she married, June 1, 1853, David Brown. Children:

    Clarissa, b. 1823; d. July 15, 1831. Mary Ann, b. 1824. Daniel, b. Feb. 11, 1827; m. Jane Miller; he removed about 1847 to the South.
11. Charles C., b. Oct. 15, 1830.
12. Thomas Ira, b. Feb. 15, 1833; m. 1864, Eliza J. McDowell. Gilman, b. Sept. 25, 1837; m. Caroline T. Seavey. William, b. April 19, 1841; d. Aug. 7, 1865. Eliza Ann, b. Dec. 13, 1843; m. Robert Griggs.

8. DANIEL MARDEN, son of Samuel (5), born June 14, 1812; married, May 29, 1842, Artimessa R. Brown. He died March 4, 1860. Children:

Sarah Auzolette, b. Nov. 6, 1844; d. March 29, 1864. Louisa M., b. Nov. 22, 1846; m. June 1, 1879, Howard S. Rand. Daniel Otis, b. May 2, 1849; d. Dec. 31, 1874. Samuel Woodbury, b. April 9, 1851. Artimessa, b. Aug. 2, 1854. Charles Everett, b. April 21, 1855; d. May 16, 1867.

9. SAMUEL MARDEN, son of Samuel (5), born Feb. 19, 1821; married, June 7, 1842, Ann Cecilia Foye. She died April 9, 1897. He died Jan 18, 1904. Children:

Sarah Amanda, b. Nov. 8, 1844; m. May 24, 1866, John Oren Foss. Martha Abby, b. May 20, 1846; m. June 11, 1865, J. Jenness Rand. Laura Emma, b. Oct. 19, 1850; m. June 24, 1871, Adams E. Drake.

10. DAVID MARDEN, son of David Smith (6), married Eunice Abby, daughter of James Brown. After his death she married Edward Walcott. Child:

Eva Augusta, b. Aug., 1854; d. March 6, 1872.

11. CHARLES C. MARDEN, son of Thomas (7), born Oct. 15, 1830; married, first, May, 1851, widow Mary A. Garland; second, Dec. 13, 1875, widow Mary O. Burton. Children by first wife:

Elsie Jane, b. April 16, 1854; m. Sam F. Godfrey of Hampton. Ida Florence, b. Feb. 3, 1857; m. Herbert Philbrick. Emma Jennette, b. March 26, 1860; m. Abbott Young of Hampton.

12. THOMAS IRA MARDEN, son of Thomas (7), born Feb. 15, 1833; married, 1864, Eliza J. McDowell. Child:

Horton, b. 1871; m. Oct. 24, 1895, Ardelle G. Page.

NATHANIEL MARDEN, probably son of William, who also had Timothy and Jonathan; married, first, July 22, 1768, Hannah Berry. She died April 11, 1773, aged 25 years, and he married, second, May 29, 1777, Anna Towle. He died Nov. 21, 1804. Lived between Dr. Parsons and George Perry in what was then known as "Marden town." Children by first wife:

Prudence Perry, b. Jan. 1, 1769; m. Eben Seavey. Keziah, b. Feb. 22, 1770; unm.; had John H. Marden, who m. Sarah Seavey.

Children by second wife:

Betty, b. Jan. 6, 1777; d. Dec. 17, 1781. Hannah, b. Jan. 12, 1780; m. Samuel Walker. Nathaniel, b. April 26, 1792; m. Mary Ann Loutz; he removed to Washington, D. C., in 1816, and died Feb. 21, 1876. Jonathan Towle, b. Jan. 29, 1795; killed by falling from a tree, 1803.

SAMUEL MARDEN, possibly son of William (2), married Sarah ―――. Children:

    Sarah, b. June 27, 1727. Hepsibeth, b. April 2, 1729; d. in seventh year. Phebe, b. May 3, 1731; d. in fifth year. Mary, b. Nov. 1, 1733; d. in second year. Dorcas, b. April 14, 1735; m. first, Sept. 8, 1754, Ephraim Mow; second, Oct. 4, 1776, Jude Allen. Hepsibah, b. Sept. 28, 1738.

WILLIAM MARDEN, JR., married Rachael ―――――, and had Mary, bapt. 1737; Elizabeth, b. Jan. 6, 1746.

Daniel Marden and Elizabeth Curtis of Portsmouth married Aug. 28, 1828.

Samuel Marden and Betsey Marden, both of Portsmouth, married Aug. 6, 1799.

Stephen Marden of Candia and Ann Stead of Portsmouth married Dec., 1877.

Deacon Thomas Marden and widow Hannah Fogg married June 9, 1761.

SAMUEL MARDEN married Oct. 22, 1769, Margaret Seavey. Children:

    Mehitable, b. March 5, 1770. Samuel, b. Oct. 1, 1771. Jonathan, b. Oct. 25, 1772; cooper by trade. Hepzibah, b. June 7, 1774.

MARSTON.

JOHN MARSTON, son of John, born 1771; married, Feb. 1, 1796, Hannah J. Locke. She died Sept. 6, 1825, aged 56 years, and he died July 15, 1815. Children:

    Catherine Elkins, b. 1798; m. first, Oct., 1817, William Caswell; second, William S. Randall; she d. May 13, 1850. Willard S., b. July 1, 1802; m. Martha D. Brown, b. Aug. 15, 1801. John, b. May 24, 1804. Mary, b. Dec. 29, 1806; m. Asa Caswell. Huldah, b. Oct. 22, 1811; m. John Hazelton.

1. JACOB MARSTON, son of Nathaniel and Eliza (Miller) of Portsmouth, married, Feb. 25, 1851, Sarah Parsons Drake, who died Jan. 11, 1892. Children:

    2. John Drake, b. Sept. 8, 1851. Anna Parsons, b. May 27, 1856; m. March 30, 1875, Otis S. Jenness, and afterwards was divorced.

2. JOHN DRAKE MARSTON, son of Jacob (1), born Sept. 8, 1851; married Sarah J. Gove. He was a justice of the peace. Children:
  Ella P., b. Nov. 5, 1878; d. ——. Walter, b. July 16, 1880. Ardelle, b. March 21, 1887.

THOMAS W. MARSTON married Clara D. Garland. He left home and was never heard from. Children:
  Ida B., b. Feb. 24, 1861; d. March 21, 1862. Ina Belle, b. Aug. 14, 1862; m. Oct. 6, 1880, Robert Hearn.

Reuben Marston had Reuben, baptized May, 1746, and James, baptized March 26, 1749.

Joseph Marston married Hannah ———, and had Hannah, born Sept. 25, 1726.

Jonathan Marston of Hampton and Sarah Weeks married June 30, 1743.

Paul Smith Marston and Catherine Elkins married Feb. 15, 1762.

David Marston and Clarissa Marston, both of Hampton, married May 19, 1825.

Simon Marston of Portsmouth and Eliza Rand married Dec. 14, 1834.

David Marston, Jr., of North Hampton and Olive D. Stephens of Stratham married July 28, 1839.

MASON.

1. SAMUEL MASON married Hannah Neal, and lived at Stratham. Children:
  2. Daniel. Nicholas; d. in France.

2. DANIEL MASON, son of Samuel (1), married, April 30, 1775, Elizabeth, daughter of William Norton. Children:
  3. Samuel.
  4. Daniel.
  5. Nicholas. Ruhamah, b. 1785; m. Feb. 10, 1805, Aaron Moses. Robert, d. aged six years.

3. SAMUEL MASON, son of Daniel (2), married, Nov. 12, 1801, Mercy Locke. Children:

    Martha, m. Sept. 3, 1826, Jethro Locke. Mary, b. Feb. 8, 1807; m. Daniel Adams. Samuel. Laurinda, b. 1810; m. George Ball. Robert, m. Edwards. Elizabeth, m. Joseph M. Edwards.

4. DANIEL MASON, son of Daniel (2), married, April 7, 1807, Mercy Rand. Children:

    Elizabeth, b. June 5, 1809; m. Joseph Martin. Mary, d. 1837, aged 27 years. Caroline, m. Frank Donnells. Emery, m. Frank Wyman. Maria, m. Samuel Cruch. Sarah Ann, d. unm. Daniel, m. Augusta Manson. Nicholas, m. Sarah Ranson. Woodbury. Clarissa, m. Eben Atwood.

5. NICHOLAS MASON, son of Daniel (2), married, Aug. 25 (?), 1807, Mary M. Rand. Children:

    Elizabeth. Ruhamah, m. Nov. 1, 1840, John I. Trefethern. Charles, m. Mary J. Fletcher. Gilman, m. Sarah Philbrick. Aaron, m. Hanscom. Lucy M., b. 1807; d. Oct. 28, 1873; m. Samuel Odiorne. Martha L., m. Lil—— Boyce.

Joseph Mason married, Jan. 25, 1809, Patty W. Foss. After his death she married Robinson Foss. By the first marriage was born Martha, Nov. 30, 1809 or 1810, who married, first, William Marden; second, George Marden, brother of William.

Joseph Mason had a daughter, Betsey, baptized June 27, 1790.

MATTHEWS.

1. ABRAHAM MATTHEWS married, June 26, 1774, Mary (Saunders), widow of William Thomas. She died April 19, 1816, aged 72 years. Children:

    Mary, bapt. May 21, 1775; m. Robinson. Sally, bapt. Nov. 23, 1777; d. unm. Abraham, bapt. July 9, 1780; ran away from home.
2. Robert, b. 1783. Elizabeth, bapt. March 20, 1785; m. Robinson.
3. William Thomas, bapt. Nov. 15, 1790.

2. ROBERT MATTHEWS, son of Abraham (1), born 1783; married, Feb. 12, 1807, Betsey M. Randall. After his death she married John Downs. Children:

Edward, d. Aug. 28, 1814.
4. Abraham, b. Jan. 7, 1810. Robert. William, b. 1814; m. Hannah Foye.

3. WILLIAM THOMAS MATTHEWS (sometimes spelled Mathes), son of Abraham (1), born Nov. 15, 1790; married, Feb. 17, 1812, Elizabeth Foss. Children:

Harriett, b. June 7, 1812; m. Oct. 6, 1833, Samuel P. Mow. Mary E., b. Nov. 6, 1815; m. Jan., 1839, Jonathan W. Verrill. John F., b. Feb. 12, 1817; m. Mary E. Rodgers of Kittery. William T., b. Aug. 23, 1819; killed June, 1864, in the Civil War.
5. Asa Robinson, b. April 15, 1822. Sally Ann, b. Aug. 5, 1824; d. Aug. 27, 1874. Ira, b. Aug. 27, 1827; drowned May 12, 1848. Oscar, b. Feb. 28, 1830; d. Sept. 9, 1862. Frances O., b. July 24, 1832; d. 1876; m. Feb. 2, 1864, Charles I. Mace. Hannah, b. Nov. 21, 1838; m. Henry Rider.

4. ABRAHAM MATTHEWS, son of Robert (2), born Jan. 7, 1810; married, Oct. 23, 1829, Betsey M. Berry. Children:

Ann E., b. Jan. 28, 1830; m. July 4, 1853, James M. Hall. Mary Esther, b. 1832. Joseph William, b. 1835. Clara A., b. March, 1840; m. Henry D. Foss.
6. Bezaleel Smith, b. July, 1841. Mary, b. May, 1844; m. July 10, 1864, John Caswell, and lived at Portsmouth.

5. ASA ROBINSON MATHEWS, son of William Thomas (3), born April 15, 1822; married Eliza Carter and lived at Kittery. He died Jan. 25, 1855. Child:

7. Clarence, b. 1852.

6. BEZALEEL SMITH MATTHEWS, son of Abraham (4), born July, 1841; married Caroline T. (Seavey), widow of Gilman M. Marden. Child:

William, b. Dec. 8, 1867.

7. CLARENCE MATTHEWS, son of Asa Robinson (5), born 1852; married, Nov. 25, 1889, Annie B. Marden. Child:

Emma, b. April 20, 1894.

MOORE.

WILLIAM MOORE and wife, Anna, had Anna, born May 22, 1750.

MORRILL.

Rev. Nathaniel Morrill, born July 20, 1701; married Sarah Odiorne, daughter of Jotham, about 1724. He was the first minister in Rye, ordained Sept. 14, 1726; dismissed, 1733. Children:
Sarah, b. Feb. 8, 1724-'25. Nathaniel, b. April 26, 1727. Levi, b. Feb. 28, 1728-'29. Amelia, b. May 6, 1736.

Joseph Morrill married Tabitha ———. Children:
Benjamin, b. Feb. 17, 1728; d. Feb. 20, 1728. Theophilus, b. Dec. 20, 1730.

MORRISON.

Alexander Morrison married, first, Sarah Coats; second, July 6, 1773, Rebecca Rand. Children by first wife:
Mary, b. May 22, 1770.
Children by second wife:
Anna, b. 1774. Beckey, b. 1778; m. Lieut. Dennett (?). Alexander, b. 1780. Rachael, bapt. 1789. Samuel Rand, b. 1790. John (?).

Samuel Morrison married, Dec. 2, 1775, Mary Billings of Kittery. Lived at the Jedediah Rand place and afterwards removed to Gilmanton. Children:
Rachael, bapt. 1779; m. Simon Garland. Robert, bapt. 1779; lived at the Beach. Benjamin. Samuel, bapt. 1788. Betsey, b. 1780; m. Isaac Twombly.

William Morrison married, Nov. 14, 1779, Abigail Trefferin. Child:
William Rogers, b. 1781.

MOSES.

1. Aaron Moses, son of John and Ann, of Sagamore Creek, Portsmouth, married Mary, who after his death married Sherburn. Children:
2. James. Josiah. Joseph. Mark. Martha. Hannah. Abigail Sarah, m. Sylvanus Scott.

2. James Moses, probably son of Aaron (1), married Martha Jackson. Children:

Mary. John.
3. Aaron. Sarah, bapt. Sept. 10, 1721; m. Samuel Wallis. Martha, m. Bartholomew Stavers. Ruth, m. Jan. 23, 1752, William Seavey.

3. AARON MOSES, probably son of James (2), married Mary ————. Child:
4. Nadab.

4. NADAB MOSES, son of Aaron (4), married, June 13, 1776, Abigail Wallis. Children:
5. James. Elizabeth, b. May 12, 1785; d. May 6, 1876; m. Michael W. Tucker. Aaron, m. R. Mason. Levi, m. Elizabeth Ross. Martha, m. Billy Rand. Abigail, d. aged 12 years.

5. JAMES MOSES, son of Nadab (4), married Mary Odiorne. Children:
Dorothy, m. Samuel M. Rand. Eliza, m. Simon Odiorne.
6. William. Samuel Wallis. James. Mary B., m. Henry F. Wendell. Martha J.

6. WILLIAM MOSES, son of James (5), married Abigail A. Seavey. Children:
Julia A., m. Alfred D. Moses. Augusta O., m. William Seavey. Joshua S.

MOSHER.

ELDER SAMUEL MOSHER married ————, and had Hannah, born April 13, 1826, who married, Nov. 7, 1850, Rufus W. Philbrick.

MOULTON.

1. DANIEL MOULTON, son of Daniel and Mary of Hampton, married, Dec. 27, 1721, Phebe, daughter of Joseph Philbrick of Hampton. Children:
2. Daniel, b. Oct. 3, 1722, at Hampton. Esther, b. Oct. 25, 1723, at Hampton; d. young. Joseph, b. Jan. 24, 1726, at Hampton. Tryphena, b. Jan. 24, 1726, at Hampton.
3. Noah, b. Nov. 14, 1726, at Hampton. Mary, b. May 13, 1729. Esther, bapt. Aug. 25, 1734. Phebe, b. Aug. 3, 1735. Nathan, b. March 2, 1738. Lydia, b. Aug. 18, 1740.
4. Nehemiah (?).

2. DANIEL MOULTON, son of Daniel (1), born Oct. 3, 1722; married, Nov. 21, 1744, Ruth Watson. Children:
John, bapt. Sept. 17, 1745. Hannah, bapt. Aug. 18, 1751. John, bapt. April 15, 1753. Daniel, bapt. April, 1755. Michael, bapt. May 29, 1757. Samuel, b. 1759. Noah, b. 1761. Sarah, b. 1767.

3. NOAH MOULTON, son of Daniel (1), born Nov. 14, 1726; married, Nov. 16, 1749, Patience Locke. Children:
Sarah, bapt. April 14, 1751. Job. b. 1752. Mary, b. 1754. Noah, b. 1759. Daniel, b. 1761.

4. NEHEMIAH MOULTON, probably son of Daniel (1), married Sarah ———. Lived in West Rye. Children:
Anna, b. June 14, 1762; d. unm. Molly, b. 1765; d. Dec. 31, 1858. Sally, b. 1769; m. June 16, 1796, William Jones. Bethia, b. 1776.

1. JONATHAN MOULTON, son of Robert and Lucy, born June 5, 1702, at Hampton; married, Dec. 21, 1727, Elizabeth, daughter of Benjamin Lamprey. Children:
2. Reuben, b. Jan. 4, 1729. Jonathan, b. April 1, 1730; m. Sarah Dow. Daniel, b. May 29, 1731; d. Aug. 26, 1809; m. Grace Runnells. Robert, b. May 20, 1733; m. first, Elizabeth Philbrick; second, Sarah ———. Lucy, b. March 12, 1735.

2. REUBEN MOULTON, son of Jonathan (1), born Jan. 4, 1729; married, first, Nov. 24, 1748, Hannah, daughter of Joses Philbrick; second, Margaret Jones. Children:
Jonathan, b. Oct. 27, 1749; d. March 24, 1767. Elizabeth, b. Feb. 8, 1751; m. Nathaniel Marden. Lucy, b. Aug. 4, 1757; m. Page Philbrick.

Joseph Moulton married Bethia Swaine and had Bethia, born Nov. 26, 1683.

Thomas Moulton and Hannah Drown of North Hampton were married Aug. 1, 1750.

Simon Moulton and Olive Garland were married June 23, 1825. He died March 3, 1875. Children: Oliver; George; Eliza.

JACOB MOULTON married Emma Philbrick. He died Jan. 10, 1901. Children:

Edith, b. Dec. 3, 1870; m. Sept. 29, 1896, Byron J. Jenness. Albert, b. June 22, 1872; d. June 19, 1873. Harry, b. July 25, 1873; m. Oct., 1899, Mabel F. Abbott. Percy, b. July 23, 1886.

MILLETTE.

JOHN MILLETTE of Canada, born 1863; married Augusteen Erickson. Children:

Theodore, b. Jan. 6, 1891. Delia, b. Aug. 16, 1893. Bertha, b. May 7, 1896. Stella, b. March 1, 1899. Elida, b. March 11, 1902.

MOW.

1. EPHRAIM MOW married, Sept. 8, 1754, Dorcas Marden. After his death she married, Oct. 4, 1776, Jude Allen. Children:

Sarah, b. Dec. 6, 1755; m. Jonathan Dockum of Greenland. Mary, b. Dec. 16, 1757; m. Richard Green, an Englishman, and a Revolutionary soldier. Hannah, b. —— 10, 1760; m. Remick of Eliot.
2. Samuel, b. 1772.

2. SAMUEL MOW, son of Ephraim (1), born 1772; married, Oct. 2, 1803, Hannah Locke. Children:

3. Ephraim L. Sally, m. first, April 8, 1824, Samuel Allen; second, Aug. 19, 1827, James H. Locke.
4. Samuel Plummer.

3. EPHRAIM L. MOW, son of Samuel (2), married Olive Coombs. After his death she married, Dec. 12, 1840, Benjamin Mason. Children:

Mary Ann, b. April 24, 1824; d. April 8, 1884; m. Calvin Garland. Elizabeth, b. 1826; d. April 30, 1850, at the town farm. Ephraim, b. 1828. Jacob, soldier in the Civil War. Frances.

4. SAMUEL PLUMMER MOW, son of Samuel (2), married, Oct. 6, 1833, Harriett Mathes. Children:

Harriett, b. Feb. 8, 1834; m. Oct., 1853, Wesley Jenness. Mary, b. 1837; m. Gilman Johnson.
5. John, b. Dec. 19, 1843.

5. JOHN MOW, son of Samuel Plummer (4), born Dec. 19, 1843; married, Jan., 1867, Flora A. Caswell. Children:

Harry P., b. Jan. 4, 1867. A son, b. July 18, 1868.

MURRAY.

SAMUEL MURRAY married, first, Elizabeth ———; second, May 4, 1769, Hannah Dalton. Children:

Samuel, b. Jan. 19, 1757. Susannah, b. April 6, 1759. Elizabeth, b. July 29, 1770. William, b. 1772. Joseph, b. 1775. John, b. 1776.

NORTON.

1. BONUS NORTON settled near Hampton causeway (turnpike). It is said that he brought from England, packed in boxes, his apple trees, which were of choice quality. He married Mary ———, and died April 30, 1718, aged 61 years. Children:

2. Joseph, b. Nov. 17, 1695. William. Samuel, b. Sept. 12, 1699. Elizabeth, b. March 31, 1703; m. first, Thomas Jenness; second, Benjamin Swett. Lucy, b. Sept. 10, 1706; m. John Jenness. Anna, b. March 20, 1708; m. Jonathan Towle.

2. JOSEPH NORTON, son of Bonus (1), born Nov. 17, 1695; married, Jan. 6, 1721, Abigail, daughter of John Gove. Children:

3. John. Jonathan, m. Mary Piper. Sarah, m. William Cate of Greenland. Samuel, d. unm. Nathan, m. Elizabeth Hill of Chester. Daniel, d. at sea. Joseph, m. Hannah Hill. Abigail, m. Nathan Goss of Hampton.
4. William (?); and five other children.

3. JOHN NORTON, son of Joseph (2), married Hannah Burleigh of Stratham, and lived at Portsmouth. Children:

5. William.Betsey, m. Simon Garland or John Cate. Eleanor, m. May 8, 1808, John Verrill. Abigail, m. Simon Garland (?).

4. WILLIAM NORTON, probably son of Joseph (2), married Ruhamah Neils. Children:

Lucy, d. unm. Elizabeth, m. Daniel Mason of Greenland. Ruhamah, m. Levi Ayers of Portsmouth. Maria, m. William Varrell.
6. Dudley.

5. WILLIAM NORTON, son of John (3), married Betsey Lamprey, born Dec., 1774, and died Oct. 30, 1866. Children:

Eliza, b. June 13, 1798 or 1800; m. Dec. 17, 1818, Joseph Odiorne. William B., m. Maria Pickermail. Hannah, m. Simon Marden. Jefferson, b. Dec. 4, 1807; d. unm. Sarah, m. Samuel C. Berry. Mary, m. Charles Maine of Portsmouth. Patience B., m. Odiorne. Emily, m. Joseph P. Marden.

6. DUDLEY NORTON, son of William (4), married, first, March 6, 1785, Hannah Varrell; second, widow Merribah Ayers. Children:

Hannah Bartlett, bapt. April 30, 1786. William, bapt. Nov. 9, 1788. Polly, bapt. Dec. 19, 1790. Sally, bapt. Dec. 19, 1790. Lucy, bapt. July 21, 1793. Abigail, bapt. July 16, 1797.

BENJAMIN NORTON married Merribah Johnson. Children:

Simon, m. Sarah Haines of Greenland. Benjamin, m. Abigail Weeks of Greenland. James. Thomas, m. Hannah Cotton of Portsmouth. Levi. Sally. Polly, m. Bennett.

Benjamin Norton and Mary S. Webster married May 10, 1840.

NUDD.

SAMUEL NUDD married Nancy, daughter of John Perkins, and removed to Wolfeborough. Children:

Ira. James. Ruth, m. Nathaniel Huggins. Mary.

ODIORNE.

1. JOHN ODIORNE appears as an inhabitant as early as 1657. A grant of 42 acres on Great Island, lying at the entrance to the harbor, was made to him Jan. 13, 1660. In 1686 he was a member of the grand jury. The family name was originally written "Hodierne, Odiurne, Odierene." John Odiorne was born about 1627 and died in 1705 at Newcastle. He married Mary Johnson when about at middle age, as none of his children were born until he was past 45 years of age. He had a brother Philip, who lived at the Isles of Shoals. Children:

Jotham, b. about 1675; d. Aug. 16, 1748; m. Sarah Bassum.
2. John.

2. DEACON JOHN ODIORNE, son of John (1), married Catherine ———. Lived at Odiorne's Point on the property received from his father. Children:

    Ebenezer, b. about 1704; d. 1745-'46; m. Catherine Sherburne. Samuel. Nathaniel, b. 1712; m. Mary Yeaton (?).
3. John.

3. JOHN ODIORNE, son of Deacon John (2), married ———. He died in 1780. Children:

    Lydia, b. about 1737; d. unm. Catharine, m. Tarlton. John, b 1740; d. 1779, in a British prison ship.
4. Benjamin, b. 1747. Abigail. Joseph, d. 1777.
5. Samuel, b. about 1748; Deborah, b. about 1752. Elizabeth.

4. BENJAMIN ODIORNE, son of John (3), born 1747; married Mary Beck, born 1745, and died Dec., 1822. He died July, 1804. Children:

6. Ebenezer, b. Sept. 27, 1772. Elizabeth, b. 1774; m. John Beck. Mary, b. 1776; d. 1856; m. James Moses of Portsmouth. Benjamin, b. 1777; d. Nov., 1823; m. Dorothy Yeaton of Newcastle. George Beck, b. 1782; d. in a snow storm in 1833; m. 1805, widow Ruth Kinneas. John, b. 1783; d. of sunstroke July, 1825; m. Olive W. Cook.
7. Joseph, b. 1788.

5. SAMUEL ODIORNE, son of John (3), born about 1748; married ———. He was a mariner and fought in the Revolution, dying in a British prison ship in 1779. Child:

8. Samuel, b. 1776.

6. EBENEZER ODIORNE, son of Benjamin (4), born Sept. 27, 1772; married, first, Mary Seavey; second, Feb. 3, 1822, Martha Webster. He died Jan. 19, 1826. Children:

9. William Seavey, b. Sept. 26, 1797. Mary, b. Sept. 26, 1797; d. young.
10. Ebenezer Lewis, b. April 16, 1800. Abigail, b. Sept. 2, 1801; d. May 8, 1805.
11. Benjamin, b. Sept. 10, 1804. John Seavey, b. Jan. 10, 1808; d. Nov. 2, 1847, of cancer; m. Charlotte Savage. James, b. Nov. 20, 1809; m. Dorothy Gardiner.

7. JOSEPH ODIORNE, son of Benjamin (4), born 1788; married, Dec. 19, 1818, Eliza Norton. He died Feb. 20, 1863. Children:

GENEALOGY. 469

Mary Elizabeth, b. about 1831; unm.
12. John Emery, b. 1833. Hannah Walton, b. Feb. 8, 1834; m. Dec., 1855, John Foss, Jr.
13. Joseph William, b. Oct. 6, 1836.

8. SAMUEL ODIORNE, son of Samuel (5), born 1776; married, June, 1801, Olive Thomas. He died June 2, 1840. Children:

14. Samuel, b. about 1802. Joseph, d. aged about 20 years.
15. Charles Blunt, b. 1804 (?). Sarah Holbrook, b. 1805; m. first, May, 1834, Ezra H. Williard; second, 1847, William L. Neal. Hannah Smith, b. 1809; d. 1830. Ellen Thomas, b. 1811; m. Woodbury Gerrish.

9. WILLIAM SEAVEY ODIORNE, son of Ebenezer (6), born Sept. 26, 1797; married Mary T. Amazeen, born Jan. 16, 1801; died April 7, 1867. He died Nov. 4, 1869. A member of Captain Ephraim Philbrick's company in the War of 1812. Children:

16. Truman Seavey. Mary Hannah, b. April 6, 1827; m. Nov. 4, 1868, Lewis Stark.
17. Ebenezer Lewis.
18. Benjamin Tarlton. William Sylvester, b. May 15, 1833. Sarah Abby, b. July 7, 1835; m. Feb. 3, 1858, Thomas A. Sterling. Georgianna, b. Oct. 18, 1838; d. Jan. 27, 1869.
19. John James, b. Jan. 22, 1841; m. April 19, 1871, M. Louisa Miller.

10. EBENEZER LEWIS ODIORNE, son of Ebenezer (6), born April 16, 1800; married, Nov. 27, 1825, Mary Brown, born March 6, 1806; died Dec. 17, 1859. He died Nov. 11, 1865. Children:

Jonathan, b. March 26, 1826; d. May 24, 1859, aged 33 years. Moses H., b. May 22, 1830. Ebenezer J., b. Feb. 11, 1834; d. Oct. 28, 1864, aged 30 years. Abigail, d. young. Charles A., b. March 31, 1836; m. March 26, 1864, Anzolette A. Bell, and had a son, Ralph, b. July 9, 1875; m. Winifred S. Barter. Clara E., b. Aug. 24, 1841; m. Nov. 7, 1862, Howard Rand. Cynthia Ann, b. May 17, 1847; m. Jan. 9, 1872, Daniel Webster Philbrick. Mary Abby, d. Oct. 5, 1857; unm.

11. BENJAMIN ODIORNE, son of Ebenezer (6), born Sept. 10, 1804; married, April 7, 1825, Olive Seavey. Children:

Mary A., m. April 30, 1848, Oren Drake. Eben L., m. Clara E. Seavey. Elvira W., m. J. Sullivan Rand. Charlotte E., m. William Benson.

12. JOHN EMERY ODIORNE, son of Joseph (7), born 1833; married, June 23, 1859, Lucy Foss. Children:

Edgar Bailey, b. Aug. 3, 1866. Elzada Arabella, b. May 1, 1868.

13. JOSEPH WILLIAM ODIORNE, son of Joseph (7), born Oct. 6, 1836; married, Dec. 15, 1863, Martha A. Varrell. Children:

Mary Ellen, b. June 28, 1864; m. Frank Foss. Anne Louisa, b. Aug. 11, 1867; m. Herman Trefethern.

14. SAMUEL ODIORNE, son of Samuel (8), born about 1802; married, June 23, 1830, Hannah Rand. Children:

Olive Ann, b. 1833; d. March 26, 1835. Joseph T. West, b. 1836; drowned, Sept. 5, 1854, at Pembroke.

15. CHARLES BLUNT ODIORNE, son of Samuel (8), born about 1804; married, Sept. 27, 1840, Mary Sheaf Yeaton, born, July 26, 1823. He died Feb. 13, 1894. She died in Portsmouth, Feb. 13, 1904. Lived at Little Harbor. Children:

Olive Ann, b. 1842; m. Andrew Jackson Preble of East Boston. Sarah Williard, b. 1844; m. Nov. 22, 1864, George Foss. Charles Woodbury, b. 1847. Almon, d. aged nine months. Frank Pierce, b. 1850; m. Nov. 23, 1879, Lavinia T. Murray. Marietta, b. 1854. Maria Adelade, b. 1856; drowned at Little Harbor. Samuel, b. July, 1858; m. Annie O. Trefethen.

16. TRUMAN SEAVEY ODIORNE, son of William Seavey (9), married, April 23, 1864, Mary Olive Moulton. He died Dec. 3, 1881. Children:

William Wallace, b. Sept. 11, 1864.
20. Jonathan Everett, b. July 18, 1866. Lydia Ann, b. Aug. 13, 1869. Charlotte Seavey, b. Aug. 3, 1872; m. Feb., 1894, Herbert Foss. Mary Amazeen, b. Dec. 12, 1873.

17. EBENEZER LEWIS ODIORNE, son of William Seavey (9), married, June 5, 1858, Augusta A. Stoddard. Children:

Emma Grace, b. July 4, 1861; d. April 16, 1889; m. July, 1881, Thomas Gothrope. Cora Isabella, b. April 16, 1864; m. Maria Louisa, b. Dec. 14, 1865. Alfred Alonzo, b. March 3, 1869.

18. BENJAMIN TARLTON ODIORNE, son of William Seavey (9), married, first, Dec. 22, 1858, Ambrinetta J. Mace; second, Mary McCanon. Children:

> William Peavey, b. July 3, 1859. George, b. July 10, 1864. Georgianna, b. July 25, 1870. Almond.

19. JOHN JAMES ODIORNE, son of William Seavey (9), married, April 19, 1871, M. Louisa Miller of Milford, Mass. Child:

> Georgia Ella.

20. JONATHAN EVERETT ODIORNE, son of Truman Seavey (16), born July 18, 1866; married, April 7, 1888, Ella Holmes. She died 1903. Children:

> Edith, b. Oct. 27, 1888. Harry, b. 1891 (?).

John Odiorne and Eunice Seavey were married July 25, 1753.

OTIS.

REV. ISRAEL TAINTOR OTIS, born July 3, 1805; married, Sept. 12, 1838, Olive Morgan Osgood at Lebanon, Conn. He died May 30, 1889. He was pastor of the church at Lebanon, Conn., ten years and from 1847 to 1866 was pastor of the Congregational church in Rye. He then removed to Exeter. As a man he was much beloved, his general influence was salutary, and his example such as might be safely imitated. Children:

> Martha, m. Pennell. Charles, d. 1888. John T., d. May 3, 1848. Caroline T. Edward O., a physician. Nellie, d. Dec., 1879. Henry S., d.

PAGE.

STEPHEN PAGE, son of Samuel and Anne, born (bapt.) Jan. 22, 1716; married, first, Nov. 11, 1740, Ann, daughter of James Perkins; second, Mary Burnham, who died Jan. 30, 1828, aged 97 years. He died March 21, 1804. Children by first wife:

> Anna, bapt. Sept. 6, 1741; m. George Saunders. Samuel, bapt. Oct. 2, 1743; m. Theodate Drake. Susan, bapt. Oct. 4, 1747; m. Samuel Shaw. Huldah, bapt. Aug. 6, 1749; m. Dec. 31, 1778, Job Brown of Rye.

Children by second wife:
> Mary, d. Feb. 24, 1836; m. Richard Jenness. Sarah, bapt. 1761; d. April 15, 1852; m. Thomas J. Rand. Stephen, b. about 1764; drowned Aug. 9, 1798. Hannah, went to Canaan.

DANIEL PAGE married, Dec. 24, 1812, Jane Foss. Children:
> Martha M., b. 1813; m. Manley W. McClure. Mary G., b. 1813; m. Gilman Merrill. Rhoda F., m. Samuel Wilson. Nathaniel F., m. Olive R. Pease. Daniel C., m. Margaret B———. Abby G., m. Calvin Ewings. John W. C. Jane E.

PAIN.

JOHN PAIN married Sarah ———. Children:
> Mary, b. July 1, 1736. Christianna, b. May 3, 1740; m. William Locke. John, b. 1742.

WILLIAM PAIN married Susannah ———. He was a weaver by trade. Children:
> Moses, b. April 16, 1736. Joseph, b. May 8, 1740. William, b. Sept. 18, 1744.

AMOS PAIN married Lydia ———. Children:
> John, b. 1754. Sarah, b. 1755. Richard, b. 1757. Lydia, bapt. April 8, 1759. Joanna, b. 1760. Dorothy, b. 1762. Deborah, b. 1763.

PALMER.

1. CHRISTOPHER PALMER, son of Samuel and Ann of Hampton, born Feb. 12, 1687; married, July 24, 1705, Elizabeth Locke. Children:
> Jonathan, b. May 16, 1707; d. young.
> 2. Jonathan, b. April 28, 1710.
> 3. William, b. May 3, 1712.

2. JONATHAN PALMER, son of Christopher (1), born April 28, 1710; married, May 20, 1746, Abigail Rowe of Hampton.

3. WILLIAM PALMER, son of Christopher (1), born May 3, 1712; married, June 27, 1736, Jane Foss. William and wife and son Joseph deeded land July 12, 1764, to Richard Jenness, lying partly in Rye and partly in North Hampton. Children:

Joseph, b. May 8, 1740. Sarah, b. 1742. Jeremy, b. 1745. William, b. 1748.

Joseph Palmer and Sarah Willey were married March 9, 1767.

Benjamin Palmer of North Hampton and Lydia Knowles were married Oct. 10, 1768.

PARSONS.

It does not appear that there has ever been any attempt to collect even the materials for a history of the English family of Parsons, notwithstanding there have been many individuals among them of great distinction, as knights, baronets and noblemen. Prior to 1672, Andrew Parsons, gentleman, was of Somersetshire, and Philip Parsons, gentleman, of Worcestershire, but the earliest record we have noticed is in 1290. Walter was then a resident of Mulso in Ireland. How long before this he or his ancestors went there we know not. Over 100 years ago Bishop Gibson remarked: "The honorable family of Parsons have been advanced to the dignity of viscounts, and more lately, Earls of Ross." In 1481 Sir John was mayor of Hereford. In 1546 Robert, afterwards the noted Jesuit, was born, and died April 18, 1610, aged 64 years. He published several works, and established an English college at Rome. In 1556 Francis was vicar of Rothwell in Nottinghamshire. In 1618 Bartholomew appears as the author of three sermons. In 1634 Thomas Parsons was knighted by Charles I. His coat of arms is still retained in the family in the United States and by his descendants in London, among whom were Sir John and Sir Humphrey; the former lord mayor of that city in 1704; the latter, in 1731 and 1740. Sir Thomas Parsons of Great Milton in Oxfordshire (before mentioned), married, in 1614, Catharine, a daughter of Edward Radcliff of London, son of Alderman Radcliff, by whom he had Robert, Thomas, Richard, Anthony and six daughters. His second wife was Sarah, daughter of Edmund Waller, by whom he had three sons, John, Edmund, Francis, and two daughters, Elizabeth and Ann. The grandfather of Sir Thomas was Thomas of Great Milton, who married Catharine, daughter of Hester Sydenham, by whom he had Thomas, Hugh and Richard. Richard married Miss —— Pierpont, and had a son, John, of London, who married, first, a daughter of Joshua Whistler, by whom he had a daughter Catharine; second, Mary Gualter of London. Some of this family were among the early emigrants to America. The first name we find in New England is:

1. JOSEPH PARSONS (known as Cornet Joseph), came from England, and in 1635 settled in Springfield, Mass. He was a witness to the Indian deed, July 15, 1636, whereby the land in and around Springfield is held. In 1645 he founded Northampton, Mass., and returned to Springfield in 1679 and died there Oct. 9, 1683. He was an extensive landowner and trader in furs. He married at Hartford, Conn., Nov. 26, 1646, Mary, daughter of Thomas and Margaret Bliss. His wife died Jan. 29, 1711-'12, aged 92. "Joseph Parsons did, at a court in Northampton, holden March, 1662, testifie that he was a witness to a deed of the lands at Springfield, and a bargain between the Indians and Mr. Pynchon, dated July 15, 1636, for 18 fathoms of Wampon, 18 coates, 18 hatchets, 18 hoes, 18 knives." Children:

2. Joseph, b. Nov. 1, 1647. Benjamin, b. Jan. 22, 1649; d. June 22, 1649. John, b. Aug., 1650; m. Sarah Clark; d. April 19, 1728. Samuel, b. Nov. 23, 1652; m. first, about 1677, Elizabeth Cook; second, Rhoda Taylor; third, Mary Wheeler. Ebenezer, b. May 1, 1655; d. Sept. 8, 1675. Jonathan, b. June 7, 1657; m. Mary Clark; d. Dec. 19, 1694; lived at Northampton, N. Y. David, b. April 30, 1659; d. young. Mary, b. June 27, 1661; m. first, Oct. 1685, Joseph Ashley; second, Joseph Williston; d. Aug. 23, 1711. Hannah, b. Aug. 1, 1663; m. Jan. 7, 1685-'86, Peletiah Glover, Jr.; d. April 1, 1739. Abigail, b. Sept. 3, 1666; m. Feb. 19, 1684, John Colton; d. 1689. Esther, b. Dec. 29, 1672; m. Sept. 15, 1698, Rev. Joseph Smith; d. May 30, 1760.

2. JOSEPH PARSONS, son of Joseph (1), born Nov. 1, 1647; married, first, March 17, 1669, Elizabeth Strong;

second, Elizabeth, daughter of Dr. Benjamin and Susanna Thompson of Roxbury, Mass. She was born Jan. 14, 1685, and died June 16, 1774, at Kensington, N. H. Child by first wife:

   3. Joseph, b. Jan. 28, 1671-'72.

   Children by second wife:

     John (Lieut.), b. Jan. 11, 1674; m. first, Dec. 23, 1696, Sarah Atherton; second, June 12, 1729, Hannah Clapp, widow of Abraham Miller; he d. Sept. 4, 1746. Ebenezer (Capt.), b. Dec. 31, 1675; m. Dec. 15, 1703, Mercy Stebbins, b. Feb. 12, 1683-'84, d. Nov. 1, 175—. Resided at Northampton, Mass. He died July 1, 1744. Elizabeth, b. Feb. 3, 1678; m. Sept. 18, 1706, Ebenezer Strong (who m. second Mary Halton). She died April 17, 1763. David (Rev.), b. Feb. 1, 1679-'80; m. Oct. 22, 1707, Sarah Stebbins. He was minister at Leicester, Mass., and d. Oct. 12, 1743. He had six children, one of whom was Rev. David of Amherst, Mass. Josiah, b. Jan. 2, 1682; m. first, June 22, 1710, Sarah, dau. of Isaac, Jr., and Sarah Warner Sheldon, b. July 16, 1688; second, Elizabeth Bartlett. ————, twin infants; d. 1683. Lewis, b. Aug. 18, 1685; m. June 2, 1709, Abigail Cooley; he d. Jan. 27, 1774; innkeeper, Springfield. Moses, b. Jan. 15, 1687; m. Jan. 20, 1709-'10, Abigail Ball; she d. 1760; he settled in Durham, Conn., 1709, and d. Dec. 26, 1754. Abigail, b. Jan. 1, 1690; m. Dec. 10, 1712, Ebenezer Clark; he d. Aug. 17, 1763. Noah, b. Aug. 15, 1692; m. Jan. 17, 1712-'13, Mindwell Edwards; he d. Oct. 27, 1779.

3. REV. JOSEPH PARSONS, son of Joseph (2), born June 28, 1671-'72, at Northampton, Mass. He was graduated from Harvard in 1697, and ordained at Lebanon, Conn., Nov. 27, 1700, and was dismissed in 1708. He married, 1701, Elizabeth, daughter of Dr. Benjamin Thompson of Roxbury. He died in Salisbury, March 13, 1739, in the 69th year of his age and the 21st year of his ministry. Children:

     Joseph (Rev.), b. Oct. 29, 1702, at Lebanon, Conn.; m. first, Frances, dau. of Lieut. Gov. John and Elizabeth Allen Usher of New Hampshire; she d. Sept. 18, 1747, aged 42 years; second, Elizabeth Scott. He was graduated from Harvard, 1720, was ordained at Bradford, Mass., June 8, 1726, and died there May 4, 1765, aged 63 years, after a ministry of 39 years.

   4. Samuel, b. Sept. 13, 1707. William (Rev.), b. April 21, 1716; m. Sarah Burham of Durham. He was graduated from Harvard,

1735, settled in South Hampton, 1743, dismissed in 1762, went to Gilmanton, N. H., Aug., 1763, preached there 10 years and d. in 1796. Elizabeth, b. 1718, at Salisbury; m. July 17, 1739, Rev. Jeremiah Fogg, who was b. May 6, 1712, at Hampton, Mass., d. Dec. 1, 1789; she d. March 5, 1779, at Kensington, N. H. John, b. Oct. 15, 1725; d. Oct. 28, 1740, while a sophomore at Harvard.

4. REV. SAMUEL PARSONS, son of Joseph (3), born Sept. 13, 1707, at Salisbury, Mass.; married, Oct. 9, 1739, in Boston, Mary, daughter of Samuel and Mary (Adams) Jones. Her grandfather, John Adams, was an uncle of Samuel Adams, the Revolutionary patriot. She died Oct. 15, 1796. He was graduated from Harvard, 1730, settled in Rye, N. H., Nov. 3, 1739, and died there Jan. 4, 1789, aged 82 years, in the 53d year of his ministry. He was the second ordained minister in Rye; one of the original grantees of the township of Croydon, and received, in 1771, from Timothy Brown, clerk of Harpswell, Province of Massachusetts, three thousand and three hundred acres of land in Hopkinton and vicinity for £43. Children:

Mary, b. July 15, 1740; m. March 4, 1762, Rev. John Tuck of Epsom, N. H. He was graduated from Harvard in 1758, settled in Epsom, 1761, dismissed 1774, and d. (probably with smallpox) while on his way to join the Revolutionary army as chaplain. Samuel, b. Aug. 1, 1742.

5. Joseph, b. Dec. 14, 1746. John, bapt. Sept. 25, 1748; d. probably in the great sickness of 1752 or '53. William, bapt. June 10, 1750; d. probably in the great sickness of 1752 or '53. Hannah, bapt. Oct. 22, 1752; d. probably in the great sickness of 1752 or '53. Elizabeth, bapt. July 14, 1754; m. Nov. 16, 1773, Lieut. Samuel Wallis; d. June 9, 1827. Abigail, bapt. Aug. 22, 1756. Hannah, bapt. Dec. 10, 1758; d. unm. June 25, 1840.

5. DR. JOSEPH PARSONS, son of Samuel (4), born Dec. 14, 1746; married, Jan. 31, 1768, Mary, daughter of Amos and Mary Langdon Seavey, who died Sept. 28, 1836. Resided at Rye, N. H. He died Feb. 8, 1832. He served five or six terms as captain in the Revolution at Newcastle, Peekskill, N. Y., Onion River and Rhode Island (and No. 4, Charlestown). He also went one cruise privateering. He was a representative to the General Court for twenty years (being the first representative under the new consti-

tution), was a justice of the peace and quorum. He studied medicine with Dr. Dearborn of North Hampton, 1770. He was appointed with two others to stand by the Sons of Liberty to enlist minute men. While dangerously sick with his company in Rhode Island, Richard Webster being his waiter, the company having orders to march, the first lieutenant went to Webster and told him to wait while he (Parsons) died and see him buried, and then hasten to join his company, but his slight speech caused Webster to be more assiduous in his attentions and very desirous that Capt. Parsons might recover and join his company, which he soon did. There was persistence and patience and long-sustained endurance in the make-up of this man of action. Children:

6. Amos Seavey, b. Oct. 9, 1768. Mary, b. 1770; m. Jan. 19, 1790, James Dow; she d. Dec. 7, 1842. Samuel, b. 1772; d. aged about 8 years; well sweep broke and injured him.
7. Joseph, b. 1774. Betsey or Elizabeth, b. 1776; m. Aug. 15, 1799, John Garland.
8. John Wilkes, b. Dec. 12, 1778.

6. COL. AMOS SEAVEY PARSONS, son of Joseph (5), born Oct. 9, 1768; married, first, Aug. 3, 1796, Patty Dow; died July 7, 1819; second, March 3, 1828, Mary Langdon. Resided at Rye, N. H. He died Nov. 7, 1850. Promoted to lieutenant-colonel Sept. 28, 1813, and took an active part in the War of 1812. Children by first wife:

Polly Dow, b. Jan. 29, 1797; m. Jan. 9, 1825, Joseph Dalton.
9. Isaac Dow, b. May 7, 1799. Eliza, b. Dec. 27, 1800; m. April 4, 1822, Lyman Seavey; she d. Dec. 23, 1853. Martha, b. Nov. 24, 1802; m. July 14, 1822, Cotton W. Drake; lived at Rye.
10. Samuel, b. Feb. 27, 1804. Anna Seavey, b. Dec. 24, 1806; m. Nov. 22, 1822, John Drake; lived at Rye. Almira, b. Jan. 20, 1809; m. Jan. 3, 1832, Jonathan Brown; she d. April 15, 1841; lived at Rye. Joseph, b. Feb. 11, 1811; d. unm. Dec. 20, 1891. Lovina, b. June 11, 1813; m. May 11, 1839, Lewis L. Perkins. James Monroe, b. Aug. 7, 1816; m. Nov. 15, 1844, widow Minerva Cox; went to California.

7. JOSEPH PARSONS, son of Joseph (5), born 1774; married, first, 1798, Hannah Perkins; second, 1822, Elizabeth Monroe of Washington. Children by second wife:

Mary Ann Wallis, b. Aug. 1, 1804; m. 1818, Abraham Connor of Maryland. Eliza, d. aged about 18 months. William, d. an infant. Samuel, b. Jan. 26, 1807; d. 1828; midshipman in U. S. navy. Eliza, b. Jan. 13, 1812; m. Jacob Cragin of Va. William, b. April 23, 1813; d. Dec. 25, 1833; printer and book-binder.

8. DR. JOHN WILKES PARSONS, son of Joseph (5), born Dec. 12, 1778; married, Aug. 11, 1803, Abigail Garland, who died Sept. 22, 1857. He was a physician in Rye about

DR. JOHN WILKES PARSONS.

50 years; a justice of the peace and quorum. He went privateering one cruise in the War of 1812, and was a member of the senate and state legislature for several years. He died Sept. 18, 1849. Resided at Rye. Children:

11. Thomas Jefferson, b. Jan. 4, 1804. Emily, b. May 2, 1806; m. March 24, 1829, Joseph, son of Jonathan and Hannah Brown; lived at Rye. Charles G., b. Feb. 29, 1808; d. unm. Sept. 9, 1844; grad. of Dartmouth. Abigail, b. Jan. 4, 1811; d. March 21, 1816.
12. William Harrison, b. July 21, 1813.
13. John, b. Jan. 4, 1816.
14. Warren, b. May 28, 1818. Abby Semira, b. March 3, 1820; unm.· Semira, b. Feb. 27, 1822; d. Sept. 15, 1829.

9. CAPT. ISAAC DOW PARSONS, son of Amos Seavey (6), born May 7, 1799; married, Sept. 30, 1824, Elizabeth Rice, who died Dec. 12, 1860. Resided at Portsmouth. He died Aug. 9, 1850. Children:

William Rice, b. Oct. 28, 1828; m. ———; she d. Louis Phillipe, b. Sept. 31, 1831; m. Mary R. Pierce; she d. Sept. 10, 1858. Walter, b. 1841; d. May 7, 1862.

10. SAMUEL PARSONS, son of Amos Seavey (6), born Feb. 27, 1804; married, first, Sept. 8, 1824, Abigail Philbrick; died Jan. 27, 1848; second, Oct. 26, 1853, widow Mary J. Marston. Resided at Portsmouth. Children:

Mary, b. March 2, 1825; d. Feb. 8, 1826.
15. John Henry, b. April 2, 1826. Martha Ann, b. Nov. 28, 1827; m. Albert Fernald; lived at Portsmouth. David Smith, b. April 5, 1830; d. April 28, 1844, at Mobile. Albert Wilson, b. Nov. 20, 1831; m. Mary Trefethern; she d. Nov. 11, 1882. Sarah Abby, b. Aug. 12, 1833; d. March 2, 1836. Leonidas Appleton, b. April 2, 1836; d. Aug. 13, 1837.
16. William Dexter, b. March 23, 1838. Joseph Monroe, b. April 2, 1840. Elizabeth Abby, b. March 20, 1845; d. Dec. 14, 1848. Abigail Philbrick, b. Jan. 27, 1848; d. Oct. 1, 1848.

11. COL. THOMAS JEFFERSON PARSONS, son of John Wilkes (8), born Jan. 4, 1804; attended school at Hampton and Exeter, 1818-'20; taught school in Rye in 1821; clerk in a store at Portsmouth with Isaac D. Parsons in 1823-'24; sailed for Jeremie, Hayti, in 1827; was justice of the peace and quorum; in 1829, adjutant of the 35th regiment of militia in New Hampshire, with the rank of captain; in 1830 was appointed by Gov. Harvey major of the 35th regiment; in 1833-'34 he was a member of the N. H. legislature and was appointed by Gov. Dinsmore major of the 1st regiment of militia in N.

H.; in 1835-'36, a member of the N. H. senate; in 1836 was appointed by Governor Hill lieutenant-colonel of the 1st regiment, and the same year he was appointed aide-de-camp to his excellency with the rank of colonel. He married, April 21, 1824, Eliza, daughter of Lieut. Simon and Esther Brown. He died March 4, 1890. She died Dec. 20, 1888. Children:

Thomas Henry, b. , ; d. April 1, 1857, at Bay Port, Fla.
17. Albion Dalton, b. Feb. 17, 1829. Charles William, b. Jan. 4, 1831; d. Feb. 1, 1834, of dropsy on the brain. Daniel Dearborn, b. May 5, 1833; lost at sea. Charles Henry, b. Dec. 23, 1835; d. Sept. 13, 1867. Was in Fla. several years. Eliza Esther, b. June 10, 1838; d. Sept. 29, 1839, of dysentery. John William (M. D.), b. Aug. 1, 1841; m. Feb. 12, 1873, M. Augusta Adams; lives at Portsmouth; assistant surgeon in the 24th Mass. Vol. Regt. infantry in the war 1861-'65, and at present the oldest resident practising physician in Portsmouth.
18. Langdon Brown, b. Dec. 24, 1844; m. April 11, 1894, Annie Locke.

12. CAPT. WILLIAM HARRISON PARSONS, son of John Wilkes (8), born July 21, 1813; married, April 11, 1854, Anna Pine Decatur, who was born Sept. 2, 1812, at Newark, N. J., and died May 3, 1896. He died Sept. 3, 1867, at Homburg, Germany. He was interested in commercial and shipping interests with Governor Goodwin of Portsmouth, and was captain of some of the famous "Clipper ships" built in that city. Children:

William Decatur, b. May 29, 1855; m. March 14, 1899, widow Christine Ulrich of Detroit; resided at N. Y. John Pine, b. June 19, 1857; d. Feb. 11, 1858.

13. MAJOR JOHN PARSONS, son of John Wilkes (8), born Jan. 4, 1816; married, Aug. 8, 1855, Susan Decatur. Resided at Bay Port, Fla. She died March 20, 1873, at New York City, aged 52 years. He died May 28, 1888, at Bay Port, Fla., aged 72 years. At the age of 20 years he served under General Harney in the Seminole War in Florida, and was on the staff of General Reed when he received his title. He was associated with Senator Yulee of Florida in the inception and construction of the first railroad in that state. He was a man of fine presence and great personal

dignity, with a refined and cultivated taste. At one time he was a large landowner in Florida, possessing a greater number of acres than there are in this town. Children:

John Decatur, b. June 5, 1862; d. Sept. 29, 1884, at New York City.
Susan, b. Sept. 3, 1864; d. at Plainfield, N. J.

14. DR. WARREN PARSONS, son of John Wilkes (8), born May 28, 1818; married, first, Jan. 1, 1845, Sarah A. Dow, who died Nov. 2, 1850; second, Feb. 23, 1854, Julia A. Gove,

WARREN PARSONS, M. D.

who was born April 13, 1829. Resided at Rye. He died May 20, 1902. Graduated from Columbian University of Washington, where he received his degree of M. D. Appointed May 9, 1843, surgeon First Regiment, N. H. militia.

He practised for nearly sixty years. Children by first wife:

William Irving, b. June 27, 1848; d. March 30, 1851. Joseph Warren, b. June 1, 1850; m. Annie Emerson; he d. June 4, 1895; lived at Brooksville, Fla.

Children by second wife:
19. Frederick Dupeytien, b. April 13, 1858. Ella Maria, b. June 20, 1860; m. Sept. 29, 1880, John Fraser. Anna Decatur, b. June 22, 1864.

15. JOHN HENRY PARSONS, son of Samuel (10), born April 2, 1826; married Caroline Francis Stanley. Children:

Elizabeth Stanley. Carrie.

16. WILLIAM DEXTER PARSONS, son of Samuel (10), born March 23, 1838; married, Dec., 1857, Elizabeth Newhall. Children:

Emma Alice. Willie.

17. ALBION DALTON PARSONS, son of Thomas Jefferson (11), born Feb. 17, 1829; married, Feb. 23, 1851, Martha S. Jenness. He died Sept. 15, 1890. Children:

Frank Edward, b. June 17, 1851; m. Nov. 18, 1880, Sara Hubbard of Holden, Mass., and divorced. Eva, b. Nov. 4, 1856; d. Nov. 5, 1856.
20. Daniel Jenness, b. Oct. 26, 1857.
21. Thomas Wentworth, b. Nov. 6, 1861. Eliza Anna, b. Feb. 11, 1864; m. Oct. 23, 1890, Ralph Marden. Clara Ellen, b. Sept. 24, 1868.

18. LANGDON BROWN PARSONS, son of Thomas Jefferson (11), born Dec. 24, 1844; married, April 11, 1894, Annie Locke. For several years a commission merchant in New York city and for the past thirty years in the mercantile business in Florida. Children:

John Langdon, b. June 3, 1895. Corinne Brown, b. May 13, 1896.

19. FREDERICK DUPEYTIEN PARSONS, son of Warren (14), born April 13, 1858; married, Dec. 4, 1889, Abby Parsons Brown. Resided at Rye. Children:

Charles Warren, b. June 5, 1897. George Fred, b. June 16, 1900. Arthur Carleton, b. Sept. 25, 1902.

20. DANIEL JENNESS PARSONS, son of Albion Dalton (17), born Oct. 26, 1857; married, Oct. 30, 1889, Annie M. Leavitt of Stratham. Child:

Norman, b. July 19, 1892.

21. THOMAS WENTWORTH PARSONS, son of Albion Dalton (17), born Nov. 6, 1861; married, Nov. 9, 1892, Martha Kate Locke. Lives in Portsmouth. Child:

Dorothy, b. June 19, 1896.

PERKINS.

1. ABRAHAM PERKINS, born about 1613, came from England with his wife, Mary, on account of their religion, and settled in Hampton about 1638. The Perkins Bible, now in the possession of James H. Perkins of Rye, was printed in London, 1599. Children:

2. Abraham, b. Sept. 2, 1639. Luke. Humphrey, b. Jan. 23, 1641-'42; d. young. James, b. April 11, 1644; d. young. Timothy, b. July, 1646; d. young.
3. James, b. Oct. 5, 1647.
4. Jonathan, b. May 30, 1650. David, b. Feb. 28, 1654. Abigail, b. April 12, 1655. Timothy, b. June 24, 1657. Sarah, b. July 26, 1659.
5. Humphrey, b. May 17, 1661.

2. ABRAHAM PERKINS, son of Abraham (1), born Sept. 2, 1639; married, June 27, 1668, Elizabeth Sleeper. He is said to have been the first male white child born in Hampton. He was killed on his own doorstep, June 13, 1677, by the Indians. Children:

Mary, b. Sept. 20, 1673; m. Aug. 6, 1692, John Moulton. Mercy, b. May 3, 1671; m. May 12, 1694, Samuel Chandler. Elizabeth, b. Feb. 9, 1676; m. Feb. 5, 1697, Jeremiah Dow.

3 JAMES PERKINS, son of Abraham (1), born Oct. 5, 1647; married, first, Mary ———; second, Dec. 13, 1681, Leah Cox, who was born July 25, 1661. Children by first wife:

James, b. July 1, 1671. Jonathan, b. March 6, 1675.

Children by second wife:
> Sarah, b. Oct. 30, 1682; d. young. Mary, b. Dec. 2, 1686; m. Jonathan Taylor. Lydia, b. 1689; m. Clifford. Hannah, b. Aug. 18, 1691; m. March 2, 1722, Simon Moulton. Elizabeth, m. Joseph Philbrick. James, b. March 17, 1696; m. Feb. 22, 1728, Shua Mason.
> 6. Moses, b. July 30, 1698. David, b. Nov. 30, 1701.

4. JONATHAN PERKINS, son of Abraham (1), born May 30, 1650; married Sarah ———. Children:
> Abraham. Abigail, b. April 30, 1687.

5. HUMPHREY PERKINS, son of Abraham (1), born May 17, 1661; married Martha Moulton. Children:
> 7. James, b. Nov. 9, 1695. John. Jonathan, d. young. Joseph. Abraham. Abigail, m. Leonard of Bridgewater. Martha, m. Tilton. Sarah, m. Flanders of Exeter.

6. MOSES PERKINS, son of James (3), born July 30, 1698; married ———. Children:
> 8. James, b. Feb. 23, 1731. Samuel, b. Jan. 9, 1733. Leah. Betsey, m. Josiah Lane; lived at Hampton. Mary. David, b. Jan. 15, 1739. Moses, b. Nov. 1, 1742. Jonathan, b. June 15, 1745. Reuben, b. Dec. 5, 1747. Mary, b. 1750. John, b. Feb. 24, 1753.

7. JAMES PERKINS, son of Humphrey (5), born Nov. 9, 1695; married Huldah Roby. He moved from Hampton to Rye in 1730, at which time there was only a footpath from his house in Rye to the meeting-house. He exchanged farms with Thomas Jenness. During the Revolution he dug iron ore on his farm in Rye and hauled it to Amesbury Mills. Before the war he loaded shallops with it and with the money thus obtained bought a clock which is still in the family. He died April 18, 1774. She died May 7, 1774, aged 81 years. Children:
> Huldah, b. July 23, 1718; m. deacon Elijah Locke. Anna, m. Stephen Page of Hampton.
> 9. John.
> 10. Abraham. Martha, b. April 23, 1732; m. first, Henry Dow; second, Simon Lamprey.
> 11. James, bapt. Jan. 5, 1735.

8. JAMES PERKINS, son of Moses (6), born Feb. 23, 1731; married, first ——— Knowles; second, Jane Moulton. Re-

sided at Hampton. He was a lieutenant in the Revolution. Children by first wife:

Moses, m. Mary Palmer. Abigail Knowles.
Children by second wife:
John, m. Joanna Elkins. Mary, m. Lieut. James Perkins of Rye. Hannah.

9. JOHN PERKINS, son of James (7), married, first, 1748, Ann Locke; second, ——— Hoit of Exeter. Resided at Epping. Children by first wife:

Jonathan, bapt. 1749; m. Folsom. Anna, m. Philbrick. John, b. 1750; m. Prescott. Joseph. Benjamin.
Children by second wife:
James. Mary.

10. ABRAHAM PERKINS, son of James (7), married Hitty Towle. Children:

Huldah, m. Stephen Huse of Greenland. Hitty, m. Robert Pike of Newmarket. Polly, m. Dr. Nat. Batchelder of Epping. Nancy, m. Martin. Abraham, m. Trask.

11. JAMES PERKINS, son of James (7), bapt. Jan. 5, 1735; married, Feb. 23, 1758, Abigail Locke. He died Nov. 2, 1805, aged 72 or 73 years. Resided at Rye. Children:

Mary, b. June 28, 1759; m. April 1, 1777, Nathaniel Emery of Hampton. Abigail, b. Oct. 10, 1760; m. Oct. 18, 1778, John Garland. Sarah, b. Sept. 7, 1762; m. William Emery of Hampton.
12. John, b. Nov. 7, 1764. Nancy or Anna, b. May 12, 1767; m. March 4, 1787, Jonathan Sherburne of Portsmouth.
13. James, b. April 20, 1769.
14. Jonathan, b. Jan. 30, 1772.
15. Josiah, b. July 13, 1774. Huldah, b. April 7, 1777; m. Sept. 8, 1799, Nathaniel Thurston of Bradford, Mass. Hannah, b. May 9, 1780; m. 1798, Joseph Parsons.

12. JOHN PERKINS, son of James (11), born Nov. 7, 1764; married, Feb. 26, 1789, Ruth Nudd. Children:

James, b. 1790; m. Huldah Seavey of Wolfeborough.
16. Jonathan, b. 1792. Nancy, b. 1795; m. Samuel Nudd.
17. Elias, b. March 13, 1797.

13. LIEUT. JAMES PERKINS, son of James (11), born April 20, 1769; married, first, Mary Perkins, who died Jan. 7, 1810; second, June 14, 1812, widow Mehitable Garland.

Resided at Rye. He died May 2, 1852. Children by first wife:

    Abigail, b. Sept. 3, 1791; m. March 1, 1810, Samuel W. Jenness; lived at Rye. Polly, b. Sept. 26, 1793; m. Nov. 21, 1811, Levi Garland, Jr. Hannah, b. May 26, 1796; m. April 6, 1820, Daniel Goss. Jane Moulton, b. Aug. 29, 1798; m. Ira Brown. James, b. March 23, 1801; d. Sept. 26, 1806. Huldah, b. Feb. 12, 1804; m. Jan. 7, 1822, Josiah Jenness. Eliza J., b. March 2, 1807; m. Nov. 23, 1826, John Leavitt. John, b. May 1, 1809; d. Feb. 3, 1816.

  Children by second wife:

    James, b. 1814; d. Nov. 3, 1816.
18. Abraham, b. Jan. 13, 1818.

14. JONATHAN PERKINS, son of James (11), born Jan. 30, 1772; married Mary Locke (his cousin). He died Aug. 13, 1809. Children:

    Edward, m. Knox; he left four sons, and one dau. who m. Gilman. James. Jeremiah.

15. JOSIAH PERKINS, son of James (11), born July 13, 1774; married, 1807, Betsey Batchelder, who was born 1786. Children:

    Nancy, b. Nov. 1, 1807; m. Aug. 2, 1828, David P. Brown of North Hampton. James, b. Dec. 6, 1809; d. June 20, 1838.
19. Lewis L., b. Dec. 28, 1814.

16. JONATHAN PERKINS, son of John (12), born 1792; married Phebe Robinson. Children:

    John, m. Eliza J. Smith. James. George, m. Mary Knowles. Phebe, m. July 2, 1853, Joshua J. Norton.

17. ELIAS PERKINS, son of John (12), born March 13, 1797; married, July 7, 1822, Polly Langdon, who was born Jan. 21, 1804. Resided at Wolfeborough and Portsmouth. Children:

    Martha Jane, b. Aug. 6, 1823; m. John S. Wendell; she d. Jan. 12, 1864. John Emery, b. April 20, 1825; d. Feb. 21, 1863. Mary Ann, b. May 19, 1827; d. Jan. 1, 1859. Elizabeth Whidden, b. Feb. 26, 1829; m. Tucker; she d. April 13, 1877. Charles Elias, b. Nov. 21, 1831; d. Sept. 14, 1865. Mark Langdon, b. April 23, 1834; m. Lucy Parker; lived at Portsmouth. Esther, b. Nov. 15, 1836; d. July 12, 1838. James, b. Aug. 3, 1838; d. March 15, 1848. Caroline E., b. Aug. 1, 1840; d. April 15, 1865. George Aaron, b. Aug. 3, 1842; m. Eliza Rothwell; lived at Portsmouth.

18. ABRAHAM PERKINS, son of James (13), born Jan. 13, 1818; married, Dec., 1838, Christianna Philbrick. She died July 23, 1886. Resided at Rye. He died Dec. 23, 1899. Children:

Sarah Emeline, b. July 2, 1839; m. May 10, 1860, Job Rienza Jenness; he afterward m. Emerett Brown. Abbie G. and Mary (twins), b. May. 5, 1842; Abbie m. May 15, 1862, David H. Montgomery; he d. Nov. 14, 1885; Mary d. 1845.

20. James Henry, b. June 22, 1851.

19. LEWIS LAMPREY PERKINS, son of Josiah (15), married, June 11, 1839, Lovina Parsons, who was born Jan. 11, 1815. He died June 1, 1880, aged 66 years. She died May 7, 1880. Children:

Sarah Jane, b. June 17, 1840; m. Levi Thomas Sanborn of Hampton Falls, who was born March 21, 1836. Harriet Adeline, b. April 27, 1846; m. Mary Izette, b. Dec. 30, 1847; d. Nov. 19, 1885. Morris Emery, b. March 30, 1852; m. Dec. 26, 1887, Margaret Norman.

20. JAMES HENRY PERKINS, son of Abraham (18), born June 22, 1851; married Mary Goodwin. Resided at Rye. Children:

Ada, b. April 20, 1875; d. March 20, 1888. Jas. Goodwin, b. Sept., 1876. Christianna, b. Jan. 1, 1879. Lizzie and Josephine (twins), b. Aug. 6, 1881; Josephine m. June 5, 1901, Parker Straw of Manchester.

PEEK.

WALTER PEEK, born in London, England, May 9, 1859; married, October 5, 1882, Mary B. Schiele of St. Louis, who was born June 9, 1863. Children:

Gertrude Clara, b. Sept. 19, 1883. Walter Jesse, b. Jan. 14, 1885. Alice May, b. Jan. 3, 1888. Edwin Henry, b. Oct. 21, 1890. Benjamin Franklin, b. May 21, 1895.

PHILBRICK—FILBRICK—PHILBROOK— PHILBRUCKE.

1. THOMAS PHILBRICK, it is said, came from Lincolnshire, Eng. He and his family sailed from Yarmouth, April 8, 1630, and arrived at Salem, June 14. He settled in Charlestown, but soon removed to Watertown, and in

1645-'46 moved to Hampton. He married Elizabeth ———. He died in 1667. Children:
2. James.
3. John.
4. Thomas, b. about 1630. Elizabeth, m. first, 1642, Thomas Chase; second, John Garland; third, Henry Roby. Hannah, m. Stephen Sanborn. Mary, m. first, Edward Tuck; second, James Wall. Martha, b. 1633; m. first, John Cass; second, William Lyon.

2. JAMES PHILBRICK, son of Thomas (1), married Ann Roberts. He was a mariner and was drowned Nov. 16, 1674, in Hampton river. Children:
5. James, b. July 13, 1651. Apphia, b. March 19, 1655; m. Timothy Hilliard. Esther, b. March 1, 1657; m. Sylvanus Nock of Dover. Thomas, b. March 14, 1659; m. April 14, 1681, Mehitable Dalton; cordwainer. Sarah, b. Feb. 14, 1661.
6. Joseph, b. Oct. 1, 1663. Elizabeth, b. July 24, 1666. Mehitable, b. July 19, 1668; m. Timothy Hilliard (second wife).

3. JOHN PHILBRICK, son of Thomas (1), married Ann Palmer. On Aug. 20, 1659, he and his wife and daughter, Sarah, were drowned as they were going out from Hampton river on their way to Boston. Children:
John, b. Sept. 26, 1650; m. Dec. 26, 1667, Prudence Swain; lived with his grandfather. Hannah, b. Sept. 26, 1651; m. first, Joseph Walker of Portsmouth; second, 1686, John Seavey. Martha, b. Sept. 26, 1651; m. John Brackett. Sarah, drowned Aug. 20, 1659. Abigail, b. Nov. 8, 1654. Ephraim, b. April 24, 1656; m. Elizabeth Barron; lived at Groton, Mass.

4. THOMAS PHILBRICK, son of Thomas (1), born about 1630; married, first, Ann Knapp; second, widow Hannah White. Settled in Seabrook. Children by first wife:
Mary, b. Sept. 11, 1651; m. Jacob Perkins. Bethia, b. Dec. 15, 1654; m. Caleb Perkins. Jonathan, b. June 4, 1657; m. widow Shaw.
7. Samuel. Elizabeth, b. Nov. 1, 1603; d. May 21, 1667. Elizabeth, b. May 3, 1667.

Children by second wife:
William, b. June 27, 1670; m. Oct. 10, 1689, Mary Neal of Greenland. Jane, b. Aug. 17, ,1700; m. Joseph Cram. Hannah, bapt. Oct. 31, 1697.

5. JAMES PHILBRICK, son of James (2), born July 13, 1651; married, Dec. 1, 1674, Hannah Perkins. He was a mariner and resided at Hampton. Children:

Hannah, b. April 30, 1676; m. July 26, 1693, Stephen Sanborn. James, m. Sarah ———; weaver in Newcastle, 1703. Daniel, b. Feb. 19, 1679. Jonathan, b. Dec. 9, 1680; m. Mary ———. Sarah, b. June 11, 1682; m. first, Aug. 8, 1701, John Sanborn; second, Thomas Rawlins.

8. Ebenezer, b. Oct. 29, 1683; m. Apphia, b. April 8, 1686; d. unm. 1759. Isaac, b. Aug. 5, 1688; m. Oct. 20, 1719, Mary Palmer. Abigail, b. 1692; m. Thomas Haines. Joseph, b. Feb. 3, 1694; m. first, Dec. 5, 1717, Ann Dearborn; second, Elizabeth Perkins; third, Sarah Nay. Nathan, b. Aug. 19, 1697; m. Oct. 30, 1721, Dorcas Johnson; blacksmith. Mary, bapt. Dec. 7, 1701.

6. JOSEPH PHILBRICK, son of James (2), born Oct. 1, 1663; married, 1685-'86, Triphena, daughter of William and Rebecca Marston of Hampton. He was the first of the name to come to Rye and settled about 1702 near Daniel Dalton's, near the house of Frances Jenness. He was ordered to court for building a house on the town's land. It is said that his wife was a daughter of one of the first three settlers of Hampton. She died Nov. 15, 1729, aged 66 years. He died Nov. 17, 1755. Children:

Joseph, b. Dec. 22, 1686; d. young. Joseph, b. Feb. 19, 1688. Zachariah, b. March 11, 1690; m. Mary ———. Sabina, b. 1691; m. Abraham Libby. Ann, b. Jan. 13, 1694; m. Stephen Berry of Rochester (?). Ephraim, b. Aug. 12, 1696; m. Martha Wadleigh; lived at Exeter. Hester, b. May 2, 1699. Phebe, b. June 9, 1701; m. Daniel Moulton.

9. Joses, b. Nov. 5, 1703. Elizabeth, b. Dec. 8, 1706.

7. SAMUEL PHILBRICK, son of Thomas (4), married Jane ———. Children:

Thomas, b. March 3, 1688. John, b. Oct. 13, 1689. Mary, b. Feb. 1, 1694.

8. EBENEZER PHILBRICK, son of James (5), born Oct. 29, 1683; married Bethiah Marston. Children:

10. James, b. June 21, 1714. Ruth, b. May 15, 1711; m. Rand; d. before 1755. Bethia, b. June 8, 1718. Ebenezer, Jr., b. May 27, 1721; m. March 12, 1747, Hannah Moulton; was a cordwainer in Rye about 1750.

9. JOSES PHILBRICK, son of Joseph (6), born Nov. 5, 1703; married Abigail Locke. Children:

Hannah, b. April 24, 1729; m. Reuben Moulton. Tryphena, b. April 24, 1729; m. first, Jan. 29, 1760, John Sanders; second, April 16, 1780, Jonathan Berry. Abigail, b. Nov. 11, 1730; m. Nov. 24, 1748, Mark Randall; lived at Moultonborough. Sarah, b. Nov. 9, 1732; m. Robert Moulton; lived at Gilmanton, N. H.
11. Joseph, b. Aug. 10, 1735.
12. Reuben, b. Sept. 27, 1737.
13. Daniel, b. Feb. 2, 1740.
14. Jonathan, b. Nov. 26, 1745. Mary, b. Feb. 12, 1749; d. Nov. 15, 1834.

10. JAMES PHILBRICK, son of Ebenezer (8), born June 21, 1714; married, Nov. 14, 1736, Elizabeth Rand. Resided at Rye. Children:

James, b. Aug. 30, 1737. Elizabeth, b. May 22, 1739. Jonathan, b. April 6, 1741. Titus, b. April 4, 1743; lived at Rye near Joseph Brown and Ben Dalton. Sarah, b. 1745. Nathaniel, b. 1747. Ruth, b. 1751. Mary, b. 1753. Anna, b. 1755. Joses, b. 1758. Stephen, b. 1763. Benjamin, b. 1770.

11. JOSEPH PHILBRICK, son of Joses (9), born Aug. 10, 1735; married, Dec. 2, 1760, Anna Towle. Children:

15. Joses, b. Sept. 12, 1761. Abigail, b. Sept. 28, 1768; m. Job Locke. Anna, b. Jan. 23, 1769; m. Josiah Weeks of Greenland. Hannah, b. Dec. 12, 1770; d. unm. 1831.
16. Jonathan, b. Sept. 17, 1773. Daniel, b. Jan. 19, 1776; m. 1800, Dolly Grover. Levi, b. May 6, 1778; m. Mary Nudd.
17. James, b. July 8, 1780. Joseph, b. June 14, 1783; d. in Demerara, W. I. Sally, b. Aug. 30, 1788; m. Samuel Marden.

12. DEACON REUBEN PHILBRICK, son of Joses (9), born Sept. 27, 1737; married, first, Hannah Locke; second, widow Mary Wedgewood, who died Dec. 25, 1805; third, widow of Richard Jenness; fourth, Sept. 9, 1806, Molly Beck. He died June 26, 1819. Child by first wife:

18. Reuben, b. Sept. 9, 1773.
Children by second wife:
Hannah, b. Jan. 7, 1776; m. Amos Towle. Sally, b. April 13, 1778; m. Lieut. Joseph Jenness.
Child by third wife (?):
19. Joses, b. May 19, 1781.

13. DANIEL PHILBRICK, son of Joses (9), born Feb. 2, 1740; married Abigail Marden. Children:

Mercy, b. Jan. 8, 1763; m. Michael Dalton. Sarah, b. July 30, 1764; m. Amos Brown (called old "Dragon").
20. Joses, b. July, 1776.

GENEALOGY.

14. JONATHAN PHILBRICK, son of Joses (9), born Nov. 26, 1745; married, Dec. 8, 1768, Mary Marden. Lived at Rye and died April 1, 1822. He was a blacksmith. Children:

Jonathan, b. 1772; m. June 1, 1797, Sarah Wells; lived at Epsom.
Abigail, b. 1777; m. James Chapman.
21. Ephraim, b. Sept. 9, 1779-'80.
22. Joseph, b. May, 1788. Daniel, m. Betsey Wells. Betsey, m. Dec. 8, 1809, Lieut. Joseph Jenness.

15. JOSES PHILBRICK, son of Joseph (11), born Sept. 12, 1761; married, July 7, 1782, Susannah Pitman. He was a blacksmith; lived where Fred D. Parsons resides. Children:

Polly, b. Dec. 5, 1782; m. Samuel H. Rand.
23. Benjamin P., b. Sept. 27, 1785.
24. Joseph, b. Sept. 19, 1788. Nancy, b. April 8, 1792; m. George Ormsbury. Hannah, b. April 7, 1795; m. Hezekiah Kimball. Reuben, b. Sept. 1, 1798. Charles P., b. Oct. 7, 1799. Lyman, b. Oct. 3, 1802; m. Lydia Watkins.
25. G. Clinton, b. May 29, 1805. John Walbach, b. Aug. 28, 1808; d. Feb. 2, 1861.

16. JONATHAN PHILBRICK, son of Joseph (11), born Sept. 17, 1773; married, Oct. 22, 1795, Sarah Marden. Children:

Betsey Brown, b. Feb. 7, 1796; m. Feb. 17, 1825, John Y. Remick; lived at Rye.
26. Joseph, b. Nov. 12, 1797. Sally, b. April 7, 1800; m. March 5, 1821, Benjamin Ackerman.
27. Jonathan, b. May 5, 1802.
28. Daniel, b. June 10, 1805. Ira, b. Sept. 24, 1807.
29. Newell, b. Jan. 28, 1810. Sheridan, b. May 20, 1813; d. June 30, 1824; struck by lightning in the schoolhouse.

17. JAMES PHILBRICK, son of Joseph (11), born July 8, 1780; married, May 21, 1801, Abigail Perviere. She died Feb., 1862. Children:

Oliver, m. Mary Staples. James, m. Margaret Godsoe. Jesse A., m. Oct. 26, 1836, Irena Philbrick, dau. of Benj. Harriet, b. 1802; d. Aug. 16, 1821. Langdon, b. 1805; d. June 30, 1824; struck by lightning in schoolhouse. Adeline, b. 1811; d. March 18, 1816. Emerson, b. 1813; d. March 21, 1816.

30. Thomas H., b. 1822.
31. Rufus W., b. Feb. 1, 1824. Abigail, m. Sept., 1835, Josiah H. Sanborn. Sarah A., m. May 6, 1838, Peter Lord. Mary Ann, m. Dec. 26, 1842, John Batchelder.

18. REUBEN PHILBRICK, JR., son of Reuben (12), born Sept. 9, 1773; married, Sept. 14, 1794, Betsey Jenness. Children:

Reuben, bapt. June 25, 1795; d. in West Indies. Sarah, b. Sept., 1804; m. Joseph Batchelder of North Hampton.

19. JOSES PHILBRICK, son of Reuben (12), born May 19, 1781; married, first, Polly Page; second, Nancy Woodman. Children:

Reuben, bapt. Sept. 11, 1798. Mary, b. 1804; m. Leavitt Batchelder of North Hampton. Joseph, d. March 25, 1826, at Port au Prince.

20. JOSES PHILBRICK, JR., son of Daniel (13), born July, 1776; married, Jan. 12, 1790, Sarah Smith. He died Dec. 21, 1842. Children:

32. Daniel, b. April 13, 1790. Mary, b. Feb. 5, 1792; m. Richard Webster; lived at Epsom. Sally or Polly, b. Oct. 24, 1794; m. Benjamin Garland, son of John G. and Abigail Perkins.
33. David, b. Oct. 3, 1796.
34. Thomas, b. July 29, 1799.
35. John, b. Jan. 5, 1804. Abigail, b. Sept. 1, 1805; m. Sept. 8, 1824, Samuel Parsons, son Amos S. Parsons; lived at Portsmouth. William, b. June 20, 1812; m. Abigail Williams.

21. CAPT. EPHRAIM PHILBRICK, son of Jonathan (14), born Sept. 9, 1779-'80; married Sarah Webster. Lived at Rye. Commissioned May 17, 1811, captain of the militia. He died Jan. 25, 1860. Children:

36. Josiah W., b. Oct. 2, 1807. Sarah Ann, b. Nov. 7, 1811; m. July 7, 1835, Daniel Philbrick, son Jonathan P.; lived at Rye. Moses C., b. April 6, 1813; m. Sarah A. Garland, dau. of Levi G.; she d. Sept. 28, 1898; he d. April 8, 1875; lived at Rye.
37. John C., b. April 9, 1818. Christianna, b. Aug. 27, 1822; m. Dec., 1838, Abraham Perkins, son of James P.; lived at Rye.

22. JOSEPH PHILBRICK, son of Jonathan (14), born May, 1788; married, May 10, 1810, Betsey Page. He died April 12, 1879. Children:

Silas, m. Maria Goodwin of Portsmouth. Mary, m. Newell Philbrick. Olive, m. Dec. 9, 1834, Edmon Mason of Hampton. Abigail, m. John W. Mace. Elizabeth, m. Nov. 9, 1839, Levi Mason. Martha Ann, m. George Nay.
38. Samuel Bickford, b. 1821. Daniel.

23. BENJAMIN P. PHILBRICK, son of Joses (15), born Sept. 27, 1785; married, first, Feb. 8, 1807, Polly, widow of Richard T. Varrell; second, ———, daughter of Hannah Randall. Children:

Emeline, b. June 30, 1807; m. Greenleaf. Julia Ann, b. Sept. 6, 1809; d. Dec. 17, 1831. Mary S., b. May 8, 1811; m. Daniel Sanborn.
39. Oliver B., b. Feb. 28, 1813. Irena, b. Oct. 28, 1815; m. Jesse Philbrick.
40. Benjamin Pitman, b. Dec. 13, 1819.

24. JOSEPH PHILBRICK, son of Joses (15), born Sept. 19, 1788; married, March 9, 1813, Sally Emery. Lived at Bartlett. Children:

41. Hiram, m. M. Woods.

25. GEORGE CLINTON PHILBRICK, son of Joses (15), born May 29, 1805; married Mary A. Nutting. Lived at Boston. Children:

Charles C., b. 1829. George F. Adeline E., b. 1837. Joseph P. Lizzie T., b. May 12, 1840. Katie A. Samuel N. Mary Ann.

26. JOSEPH PHILBRICK, son of Jonathan (16), born Nov. 12, 1797; married, Dec. 27, 1818, Patty Knowles. Lived at Rye. He died Dec. 9, 1873. Children:

Martha Ann, b. Oct. 18, 1820; m. Jan., 1839, Woodbury Seavey. Sarah E., b. Feb. 18, 1823; m. Gilman Mason. Adeline, b. Dec. 23, 1825; m. William S. Rand.
42. Joseph Newell, b. March 2, 1830. Clarissa, m. Hiram Chase; lived at Stratham. John Ira, b. April 4, 1835; d. Feb. 26, 1838.

27. JONATHAN PHILBRICK, son of Jonathan (16), born May 5, 1802; married, Feb. 26, 1834, Abigail Brown. Lived at Rye. Children:

Mary Abby, m. 1861, Joseph William Seavey. John Tyler, b. 1842; d. Feb. 28, 1866.
43. Jonathan Curtis.

28. DANIEL PHILBRICK, son of Jonathan (16), born June 10, 1805; married, July 7, 1835, Sarah Ann, daughter of Elder Ephraim Philbrick. She died March 22, 1901. He died March 11, 1882. Lived at Rye. Children:

Emily, b. 1837; d. 1858. Harrison, b. 1840. Lemira, b. April, 1842; m. Dec., 1882, Thomas Knowles of North Hampton.
44. Daniel Webster, b. May 29, 1844. Ira P., b. April, 1847; d.

29. NEWELL PHILBRICK, son of Jonathan (16), born Jan. 28, 1810; married Mary Philbrick. Children:

Sarah. Sheridan. Newell. Joseph. Spaulding.

30. THOMAS H. PHILBRICK, son of James (17), born 1822; married, Feb. 28, 1847, Olive R. Locke. Lived at Rye near Jenness Beach. Died, Oct. 13, 1879. Children:

Charlotte, b. 1849; d. Aug. 10, 1863. Emma, m. Jan. 3, 1869, Jacob Moulton. Willie J., b. Nov. 13, 1855; m. first, Oct. 22, 1874, Arvilla F. Jenkins of Kittery, Me.; second, Lizzie N. Breed. Herbert, b. June 28, 1858; m. Ida Florence Marden. Ida, b. Oct. 30, 1863; m. Breed of Lynn.

31. RUFUS W. PHILBRICK, son of James (17), born Feb. 1, 1824; married, Nov. 7, 1850, Hannah E. Mosher. Carpenter by trade, and for several years captain of the Rye Beach life saving station. Children:

Samuel E., b. Aug. 31, 1851. Frank M., b. Oct. 30, 1852; m. Melissa Jenness; he d. April 27, 1898.
45. Walter, b. April 18, 1855.
46. Fred, b. June 25, 1856. Edward P., b. Dec. 15, 1858; m. Estelle Goss. Flora Belle, b. Jan. 25, 1863; m. Jan. 6, 1886, Albert W. Seavey; he d.

32. DANIEL PHILBRICK, son of Joses, Jr. (20), born April 13, 1790; married Pamelia Gunnison. Lived at Portsmouth. Children:

Ann E. Daniel, m. Trundy. Louisa. Olivia. Pamelia. George.

33. DAVID PHILBRICK, son of Joses, Jr. (20), born Oct. 3, 1796, married Sarah Lamos. Lived at Portsmouth. Children:

Sarah. Harriet.

GENEALOGY. 495

34. THOMAS PHILBRICK, son of Joses, Jr. (20), born July 29, 1799; married Clarissa Shaw. Lived on the hill in the house now occupied by Mrs. A. D. Parsons. Children:

John Dearborn, b. March 20, 1824; m. and separated; he d. June 20, 1880. David Smith, b. April 29, 1825; d. Oct. 23, 1827. Sarah A., b. Nov. 17, 1828; m. Abel Horton. Moses W., b. Sept. 17, 1830; m. Esther Dority; he d. Oct. 10, 1886; Ann E., b. May 19, 1832; m. Christopher Harriold. David S., b. Jan. 29, 1834; m. Caroline A. Young. Clarissa Jane, b. Dec. 15, 1836; m. Daniel T. Marden. Daniel Dalton, b. June 26, 1840; d. Martha F., b. Feb. 8, 1844; m. Richard B. Tindall.

35. JOHN PHILBRICK, son of Joses, Jr. (20), born Jan. 5, 1804; married, Dec. 25, 1831, Sarah Brown. Lived at Rye. He died Sept. 12, 1877. Children:

Ann Matilda, b. Feb. 9, 1833; d. Aug. 3, 1851. Caroline, b. Nov. 3, 1837; d. Nov. 15, 1855. Louisa, b. Nov. 26, 1840; d. Feb. 25, 1842. Mary Abby, b. Nov. 24, 1843; m. James Alby Rand; she d. Feb. 7, 1866. John William, b. April 11, 1847; d. Aug. 9, 1866.

36. JOSIAH W. PHILBRICK, son of Ephraim (21), born Oct. 2, 1807; married, June 25, 1833, Sarah Ann Brown. Lived at Rye. She died Sept. 22, 1870. He died Oct. 17, 1870. Children:

47. Emmos B., b. Nov. 14, 1833. Horace, b. July 23, 1838; d. May 19, 1852. Ellen, b. Jan. 9, 1853; m. April 3, 1879, Sylvanus W. Foss; lived at Rye.

37. JOHN COLBY PHILBRICK, son of Ephraim (21), born April 9, 1818; married, May 25, 1845, Eliza Jenness, who died Sept. 18, 1893. He died Jan. 15, 1869. He was proprietor of the Atlantic House, the first hotel built at Rye Beach. Children:

Frank A., b. Jan. 7, 1850; m. Dec. 21, 1881, Lizzie Hill of North Hampton; for many years proprietor of the Farragut House; he d. Jan. 27, 1901. Fannie, b. Aug. 24, 1852; m. first, Albert Salter; second, William Carter. Carrie, b. Dec. 10, 1856; m. Frank Sweet; she d. May 17, 1897.

38. SAMUEL BICKFORD PHILBRICK, son of Joseph (22), born 1821; married Lydia Moulton. Lived at Rye. Children:

Rebecca, m. George Jenness. Louisa. Lydia, m. Herman Jenness. Mary, b. March 5, 1859. Martha, b. March 5, 1859; d. March 7, 1864. Eliza, b. Nov. 15, 1861; d. March 15, 1864. Joseph, b. Nov. 30, 1863; m. John, b. 1855. Moses, m. Oct. 26, 1892, Lucretia Catlin. David, deranged. Daniel.

39. OLIVER B. PHILBRICK, son of Benjamin P. (23), born Feb. 28, 1813; married, Nov. 1, 1844, widow Alice Sanderson, who died in 1898. Lived at Rye. He died April 21, 1883. Children by adoption:

Cornelius, m. May Powers of Hampton.
48. Ezra B.

40. BENJAMIN PITMAN PHILBRICK, son of Benjamin P. (23), born Dec. 13, 1819; married Angelina Batchelder. Children:

Albion Reuben, b. April 2, 1846; m. Oct. 10, 1872, Georgianna Pressey; he d. Jan. 24, 1898. Emeline, b. Oct. 30, 1852; m. Abraham Drake.

41. HIRAM PHILBRICK, son of Joseph (24), married Margaret Woods. Lived at Bartlett. Children:

John, b. May 1, 1844. Catherin, b. March 4, 1846. Mary Frances, b. July 13, 1848. Roxanna, b. Aug. 15, 1850. Elvina, b. Feb. 20, 1853. A boy, D. April 19, 1855.

42. JOSEPH NEWELL PHILBRICK, son of Joseph (26), born, March 2, 1830; married Ann Gwinn. Children:

Joseph Woodbury, b. Dec. 5, 1855; m. March 12, 1874, widow Eliza J. Fogg. Adeline M., b. Jan. 28, 1857; m. Oct. 29, 1873, Henry Laskey. James A., b. May, 1858; m. Aug. 21, 1880, Mary E. Cumming. Henry R., b. Feb., 1860. Charles Newell, b. June 4, 1862. Emma Chase, b. June 30, 1865. Horace, b. Sept. 12, 1868. Lizzie, b. Sept. 21, 1871.

43. JONATHAN CURTIS PHILBRICK, son of Jonathan (27), married, Oct., 1869, Nellie Hodgdon. Lived at Rye. Children:

Bertha Louise, b. Nov. 16, 1870; d. March 7, 1883. Lester W., b. Oct. 21, 1875; m. June 17, 1896, Frances S. Barrett. Charles B., b. Jan. 12, 1877; m. May 29, 1891, Phebe W. Greening; had a dau. b. Dec. 4, 1902.
49. William C., b. Jan. 28, 1879; m. Oct. 8, 1899, Nellie T. Rand, dau. of Charles Henry. Harry, b. Nov. 21, 1881. Manning, b. March 29, 1884.

44. DANIEL WEBSTER PHILBRICK, son of Daniel (28), born May 29, 1844; married, Jan. 9, 1872 ,Cynthia A. Odiorne. Lived at Rye. Children:

Emily May, b. Aug. 8, 1873. Alfred Cheney, b. June 2, 1875; m. Oct. 31, 1900, Ethel L. Stone. Irving Chever, b. June 18, 1877. Carrie, b. Oct. 9, 1883.

45. WALTER PHILBRICK, son of Rufus W. (31), born April 18, 1855; married Emma L. Brown. Children:

Son, b. March 15, 1886; d. an infant. Son, b. March 2, 1888; d. May 5, 1888.

46. FRED PHILBRICK, son of Rufus W. (31), born June 25, 1856; married Clara H. Perkins. Children:

Harold, b. Jan. 7, 1883. Byron, b. Dec. 31, 1890.

47. EMMONS B. PHILBRICK, son of Josiah W. (36), born Nov. 14, 1833; married, first, April 17, 1859, Vienna Dalton; second, Oct. 14, 1875, Mary Charlotte Seavey. Lived at Rye. He died Oct. 16, 1902. He spent a number of winters teaching school, in which he was successful. In 1878 he was a member of the state senate and again in 1879 and 1880. Children by first wife:

Wilmar, b. June 28, 1864. Freddy, b. May 8, 1869; d. March 16, 1875.

Children by second wife:

Shirley, b. Aug. 16, 1876. Annie, b. May 4, 1879.

48. EZRA B. PHILBRICK, adopted son of Oliver B. (39), married, Oct. 6, 1893, Nellie M. Dow. Children:

Jennie May, b. July 26, 1896. George Oliver, b. Oct. 10, 1897. Benning, b. June 18, 1899; d. Sept. 9, 1899. Josephine Marjorie, b. July 22, 1900. John Ezra, b. Feb. 26, 1902.

49. WILLIAM C. PHILBRICK, son of Jonathan Curtis (43), married, Oct. 8, 1899, Nellie T. Rand. Child:

Ellen R., b. March 20, 1900.

PICKERING.

1. THOMAS PICKERING, married Mary Janveins, who died July 20, 1772, aged 57 years. He died Dec. 9, 1786. Children:

Elizabeth, b. March 24, 1744; m. Timothy Dame. William, b. July 27, 1745; m. Abigail Fayben. Mary, b. Feb. 7, 1749; m. Oct. 15, 1778, William Langdon, tanner. Benjamin, b. May 13, 1751; m. Martha Pickering. Sarah, b. Jan. 5, 1754; m. May 2, 1782, George Gaines. Alice, b. Feb. 6, 1757; m. Nov. 22, 1781, Joshua Brackett. Patience, b. Aug. 21, 1758; m. Joseph Langdon. Temperance, m. John Knight. Nichols.

2. John Gee. James, m. Fabyan. Richard, b. April 15; m. Mary Thompson.

2. JOHN GEE PICKERING, son of Thomas (1), married, June 10, 1773, widow (Furber) Mills. Children:

Polly, b. June 16, 1774. Temperance, b. Dec. 7, 1775. Gee, b. Sept. 19, 1777. Thomas, b. Aug. 6, 1779.

POOL.

JOHN POOL married, June 25, 1860, Angelina E. Caswell. Children:

Carrie E., b. Feb. 18, 1861. Richard E., b. Feb. 5, 1863. Lizea, b. April 5, 1865. Nellie, b. June 3, 1867. Lillie B., b. Jan. 19, 1870. Minnie E., b. June 23, 1872. Nellie G., b. April 23, 1875. Ida M., b. April 21, 1877. Ethel V., b. July 21, 1879.

POOR, OR POWERS.

ROBERT POOR came from England, served under Paul Jones in the Revolution, and married, July 4, 1788, Betsey Shapley. Children:

Robert, b. 1787; d. at sea, 1810. Judith, bapt. Nov. 22, 1789; m. Abner Blaisdell of Portsmouth. Sally, bapt. Nov. 27, 1791; d. unm., May 21, 1867. Eliza, bapt. Nov. 9, 1794; d. unm. Dec. 26, 1871. Mary, bapt. April, 1796; m. John Locke. George, bapt. April 22, 1798; d. Abigail Daniels, bapt. May 3, 1801; m. Calvin Knowlton; lived at Boston. Daniel Sheafe, bapt. Nov. 4, 1804. Nancy, bapt. 1806.

PORTER.

REV. HUNTINGTON PORTER, born 1755; married, first, June 28, 1786, Susannah Sargent; second, March 30, 1797, Sarah Moulton; died Jan. 2, 1835. He had a salary of $300 a year. His sermons were always the fruit of close application, and finished with a degree of accuracy that few attempt and fewer attain. He died at Lynn, Mass., March 7, 1844. Children by first wife:

GENEALOGY. 499

Samuel H., bapt. July 11, 1787; d. Nathaniel Sargent, bapt. May 29, 1789; m. Elizabeth Comstock; he d. Sept. 27, 1827. John, b. Sept. 6, 1791; d. March 29, 1825. Caroline, b. Oct. 23, 1793; d. Dec. 8, 1869.

Children by second wife:

Maria, b. Feb. 12, 1798; m. Dec. 18, 1821, Asa Robinson; lived at Brentwood. Eliphalet, b. May 4, 1800; lost at sea about 1824. Oliver, b. March 3, 1802; m. Louisa, b. May 18, 1803; m. May 26, 1835, William Weeks; lived at Greenland. Martha R., b. June 11, 1805; m. C. K. Dilloway; lived at Boston. Sarah E., b. June 2, 1809; m. July 31, 1833, Rev. Charles Adams; lived at Stratham. Olivia, b. Feb. 15, 1811; m. Aug. 16, 1837, Luther Hall; lived at Boston. Huntington, b. Dec. 4, 1812; d. June 7, 1836. Emery Moulton, b. Sept. 24, 1815; m. Wentworth. Charles, b. Aug. 7, 1816; d. Sept. 1, 1816. Charles H., b. Sept. 19, 1817; d. William H., b. Sept. 19, 1817; d.

RAMSDELL.

EDWARD E. RAMSDELL, married, Sept. 25, 1888, Emerett E. Marden. Lived at Rye. Children:

Blake, b. March 17, 1889. Fred, b. Feb. 6, 1891. Edna G., d. Aug. 20, 1893. Ralph, b. Feb. 3, 1898. Dexter, b. Aug. 18, 1900.

RAND.

1. FRANCIS RAND, married Christina ———. He was killed by the Indians at Sandy Beach Sept. 29, 1691. His will was dated 1689, and proved Feb. 19, 1691-'92. He came over here with Mason's men. Children:

2. Thomas. Samuel. John, b. 1645; m. Remembrance Ault, dau. of John of Oyster River (Durham).
3. Nathaniel. Sarah, m. Herrick. Mary, m. Barnes.

2. THOMAS RAND, son of Francis (1), married ———. His will was dated Feb. 25, 1731-'32. Children:

4. Thomas, m. Hannah Pray. William.
5. Joshua, m. Mary Moses.
6. Samuel. Hannah. Christina, m. Shute. Mary, m. William Chamberlain. Elizabeth. Lydia, m. Foss.

3. NATHANIEL RAND, son of Thomas (2), married Elizabeth ———. Children:

7. Joshua, b. Dec. 25, 1703. Elizabeth, b. Aug. 2, 1716.

4. THOMAS RAND, son of Thomas (2), married, first, May 24, 1722, Hannah Pray; second, July 5, 1748, E. Moulton. Children by first wife:

> Mary, b. 1726. Hannah, b. 1728. Elizabeth, b. 1730. Thomas, b. 1732; m. Dec. 9, 1756, Hannah Jenness. Merribah, b. 1735; m. Sept. 18, 1760, Thomas Foss.
> 8. Ephraim, b. 1737. Reuben, b. 1739; m. Elizabeth Philbrick; lived on Garland road. Samuel, b. 1741.

5. JOSHUA RAND, son of Thomas (2), married Mary Moses of Portsmouth. He died about 1787. Children:

> 9. John, b. 1742. Mary, b. 1744; m. first, Samuel Hunt; second, Joseph Marden.
> 10. Joseph. Sarah, b. 1749; m. Aug. 18, 1767, Levi Goss; she d. Sept. 17, 1808. Hannah, b. 1752; m. July 26, 1772, Benjamin Marden. Rebecca, m. July 6, 1773, Alexander Morrison.
> 11. Joshua, b. 1758.
> 12. Samuel, b. 1762.

6. SAMUEL RAND, son of Thomas (2), married Sarah Dowrst. Children:

> Thomas, b. March 27, 1749. Sarah, b. Nov. 16, 1751. Samuel, b. Dec. 10, 1753. Elizabeth, b. Jan. 8, 1757. Abigail, b. Oct. 16, 1758; engaged to marry Tobias Trundy, who was lost at sea.
> 13. Thomas, b. June 6, 1760 (?). Rachel, b. April 20, 1762; m. Daniel Seavey.
> 14. Dowrst, b. June 24, 1764.
> 15. Billey, b. Oct. 30, 1766.

7. JOSHUA RAND, son of Nathaniel (3), born Dec. 25, 1703; married Mary Moses. She died Dec. 13, 1752. Children:

> Philemon, b. Jan. 18, 1732. Ruth, b. July 2, 1733; m. Joseph Bickford. Temperance, b. June 13, 1735. Joshua, b. Aug. 23. Joseph, b. 1739. Sarah, b. March 30, 1740. Bethia, b. 1742.
> 16. George, b. April 4, 1744. John. Mical, b. Nov. 28, 1748. Elizabeth, b. Feb. 16, 1751.

8. EPHRAIM RAND, son of Thomas (4), born 1737; married, Sept. 22, 1757, Mary Smith. Lived beyond William Cutter Garland. He died in the Revolutionary army of smallpox. Children:

GENEALOGY.   501

Samuel, b. Nov. 18, 1757; d. March 2, 1825; a cripple. Israel, b.
   July 12, 1761; m. Danforth; lived in Warner; d. at Plattsburg.
   Sarah, b. Nov. 2, 1764; m. Edward Hall. Jonathan, b. Sept. 5,
   1767; m. Davis or Norris; lived at Warner. Ephraim, b. Nov.
   2, 1769.
17. David, b. Oct. 17, 1772.
18. Simon, b. 1775.

9. JOHN RAND, son of Joshua (5), born 1742; married, June 4, 1772, Hannah Seavey. He died May 13, 1812. Children:

Elizabeth, b. May 20, 1773; m. Joshua Rand. Mary, b. 1776; d. unm.
   1825.
19. John, b. May 23, 1778. Hannah, b. 1781; m. first, 1804, William
   Foye; second, John Y. Randall. Joshua, b. March 17, 1784; unm.;
   supported at town farm, Rye; d. Jan. 22, 1867. Sally, b. 1786;
   bapt. Sept. 2, 1787; m. April 12, 1812, Jonathan Woodman. Olive,
   b. 1788; bapt. July 11, 1789; d. unm. 1825. Nancy, bapt. April
   14, 1794; m. Ephraim Rand Hall.

10. JOSEPH RAND, son of Joshua (5), married, May 24, 1764, Susannah Goss. Children:
20. Joseph, b. 1769; d. Aug. 18, 1855.
21. Samuel Hunt, b. 1777.
22. Joshua, b. Aug. 23, 1779. Zebedee, d. Polly, d. young. Levi, went
   to sea with Aaron Libby and both lost. Sally, bapt. Oct. 2, 1785;
   d. Aug. 9, 1825, *non compos mentis.*

11. JOSHUA RAND, JR., son of Joshua (5), born 1758; married Ruth, daughter of William Seavey, who died July 2, 1829. He died March 13, 1791. Children:

Joshua, b. 1780; m. Betsey Houston of Concord; lived at Portsmouth. William S., b. 1781; m. Aug. 12, 1804, Dolly Rollins; he
   d. June 22, 1854. Samuel, b. 1783; m. first, Martha Locke; second, Hannah Locke; lived at Portsmouth. Theodore, bapt. April
   15, 1787; unm.; d. at sea. Hitty, bapt. 1788; m. James Elkins.
   Moses, bapt. Aug. 30, 1789; d. June 1, 1811, at Portsmouth, of
   smallpox. James, d. Nov. 23, 1807; knocked overboard at sea.
   Mary, m. Nicholas Mason.
23. Daniel, bapt. Dec. 25, 1777.

12. SAMUEL RAND, son of Joshua (5), born 1762; married, Jan. 5, 1784, Hannah Dolbear, who afterward married Joseph Foye. Children:

Stephen Dolbear, bapt. June 25, 1785. Ellie Morrison, bapt. Sept. 6, 1789. Aaron, bapt. Sept. 9, 1794.
24. Reed Vennard, b. Nov. 10, 1797. John, b. 1800 (?). Mary.

13. THOMAS RAND, son of Samuel (6), born June 6, 1760 (?); married, April 4, 1790, Mary Tuck, who was born March 24, 1763. Lived at Rye. He died Feb. 27, 1839. Children:

25. John Tuck, b. July 7, 1791. Mary Jones Wallis, b .March 11, 1793; d. unm.
26. Samuel, b. Feb. 16, 1796. Thomas, bapt. June 23, 1799; d. Florinda, b. April 4, 1801; d. unm. Aug. 25, 1866.
27. Thomas, b. July 22, 1802.
28. Edward, b. Dec. 22, 1806.
29. Jedediah, b. Dec. 2, 1808.

14. DOWRST RAND, son of Samuel (6), born June 24, 1764; married Hannah Lang. He died Jan. 12, 1847; she died May 16, 1860, aged 90 years. He was a member of Captain Wedgewood's company in the War of 1812. Lived near the West schoolhouse. Children:

30. Billey, bapt. Jan. 11, 1789. Patty Lang, b. Oct., 1791; m. first, Nov. 11, 1813, Simon Dow; second, George Bragg. Samuel, b. 1793; m. Sarah Foss. Bickford Lang, b. 1795; m. first, Carter; second, Martha Batchelder. Sarah, b. 1797; m. James Perkins of Hampton.
31. Trundy, bapt. June, 1800. Oliver, b. 1802; d. 1802. Hannah, b. 1805; m. Samuel Odiorne, Jr. Oliver Porter, b. Nov. 9, 1807; m. June, 1828, Polly Bean.

15. BILLEY RAND, son of Samuel (6), born Oct. 30, 1766; married, May 29, 1800, Patty Moses. Lived at East Rye. Children:

Sarah, b. April 12, 1801; m. July 10, 1824, William Hall.
32. Samuel M., b. July 20, 1803. Levi Moses, b. Oct. 24, 1810; d. unm. March 11, 1874.

16. GEORGE RAND, son of Joshua (7), born April 4, 1744; married, May 19, 1768, Naomie Sherburne. Children:

Martha, b. Jan. 20, 1769. John, b. March 5, 1772. Betsey, b. Feb. 14, 1774. George, b. April 9, 1777. Richard, b. Oct. 29, 1778. Enoch, b. Sept. 20, 1780. Ebenezer, b. Feb. 15, 1784.

GENEALOGY. 503

17. DAVID RAND, son of Ephraim (8), born Oct. 17, 1772; married, July 22, 1798, Polly Salter of the Isles of Shoals. Lived at Rye. Was a member of the Alarm List in the War of 1812, under Captain Jonathan Wedgewood. Children:

33. Reuben, b. Oct., 1798. David, b. Aug. 15, 1800; d. Jan. 16, 1820, in schooner *Cadmus*, at sea. Sarah, b. Jan., 1813; m. first, James Rand; second, Robert Lyons. Mary Ann, b. Aug., 1804; m. Hamilton C. Locke.
34. William Watson, b. April 7, 1809.

18. SIMON RAND, son of Ephraim (8), born 1775; married Hannah Johnson of Northwood. Children:

Mary, m. Reuben Rand. Olive, m. first, James McCannon; second, Thomas Marden. Gilman J., b. 1809; m. Sarah Marden.

19. JOHN RAND, son of John (9), born May 23, 1778; married, first, Sidney Lang, who died July 31, 1850; second, Nancy Haley, who died Aug. 13, 1852; third, Deborah Burleigh. He died Aug. 5, 1861. Children by first wife:

Harriett J., b. Sept. 4, 1809; m. William Keene. Eliza, b. May 25, 1812; m. Dec. 14, 1834, Simon Marston, Jr.; lived at Portsmouth.
35. Thomas Jefferson, b. June 11, 1813.
36. David L., b. Feb. 27, 1815.
37. John Oris, b. March 13, 1820.

20. JOSEPH RAND, son of Joseph (10), born 1769; married, Oct. 18, 1795, Olive Marden. She died Dec. 15, 1859. Children:

38. Joseph, b. Jan. 21, 1796.
39. Samuel Hunt, b. April 28, 1803. Eliza, b. Nov. 14, 1804; m. Jeremy Webster.
40. Nathaniel Marden, b. Sept. 16, 1806. Mary, b. Jan. 29, 1808; m. William Holmes. Susan, b. July 28, 1809; d. Feb. 1, 1859; deranged, hung herself.
41. Levi, b. April 23, 1811.
42. Ira, b. Sept. 28, 1814. Polly Zebudu, d. young, 1803, of throat distemper. Olive, d. young, 1803, of throat distemper.

21. SAMUEL HUNT RAND, son of Joseph (10), born 1777; married, May 12, 1808, Polly Philbrick. Lived at Rye. He died June 25, 1846. Children:

Mary, b. 1808; d. May 22, 1858.
43. Samuel, b. June, 1810; d. Jan. 24, 1880. Olive, b. Dec. 28, 1818; m. Jonathan Moulton; lived at Reading, Mass.
44. Charles Clinton, b. 1820. Emily, b. 1822; unm. Joshua, b. 1824; d. Dec. 24, 1836, aged 12 years.

22. JOSHUA RAND, son of Joseph (10), born Aug. 23, 1779; married, first, Nov. 4, 1802, Esther Marden; second, March 29, 1810, Elizabeth Rand. He died Sept. 20, 1852. Children by first wife:
45. Harry, b. June 10, 1803.
46. Obed, b. Aug. 18, 1804.
Children by second wife:
Ezra, b. Oct. 2, 1810; d. Aug. 29, 1827.
47. Nahum, b. Nov. 29, 1813.
48. Aaron, b. March 19, 1816.

23. CAPTAIN DANIEL RAND, son of Joshua, Jr. (11), baptized Dec. 25, 1777; married, Feb. 24, 1801, Dorothy Seavey. He died Oct. 10, 1851. She died Oct. 8, 1865. Served in the War of 1812 under Capt. E. Philbrick. Children:
Martha, b. May 28, 1801; m. Dec. 14, 1820, John Locke; she d. July 13, 1847. Moses, b. April 7, 1804; m. first, Adeline Vennard; second, Hannah Seavey. Louisa, b. March 2, 1806; m. Henry Amazeen; she d. Sept. 12, 1863. James, b. June 10, 1808; m. Harriet Mussey. Daniel, b. May 17, 1810; m. Esther Locke. Anna Trefethern, b. July 2, 1812; m. Aug. 1838, Allen Porter of North Carolina.
49. Elvin, b. Aug. 12, 1814. Adeline, b. Jan. 27, 1817; m. Thomas J. Rand. William, b. April 17, 1819; m. first, Adeline Philbrick; second Caty M. Trickey. Amos Seavey, b. May 8, 1821; d. Nov. 26, 1821.

24. REED VENNARD RAND, son of Samuel (12), born Nov. 10, 1797; married, May 7, 1824, Hannah Parsons Garland. He died Dec. 28, 1879. Lived at Portsmouth. Children:
Mary Abbie, b. Aug. 16, 1826; unm.; d. Marianne, b. Feb. 2, 1830; d. Sept. 14, 1831. Edwin Reed, b. April 6, 1833; m. Jan. 6, 1864, Lydia Storey. Louis Henry, b. April 2, 1836.

25. JOHN TUCK RAND, son of Thomas (13), born July 7, 1791; married Betsey Dow. Lived at Rye. He died May 29, 1867. She died March 18, 1834. Children:

Elizabeth Martha, b. Jan. 26, 1821; d. unm. April 26, 1896; lived at Rye. Isaac Dow, b. Dec. 14, 1828; unm.; lived at Rye. Mary Tuck, b. Jan. 31, 1831; unm.; lived at Rye.

26. SAMUEL RAND, son of Thomas (13), born Feb. 16, 1796; married widow Sarah Currier, who died Feb. 23, 1878, aged 79 years. Lived at Newcastle. Children:
Veranus. Thomas. Mary. Edward A.

27. MAJOR THOMAS RAND, son of Thomas (13), born July 22, 1802; married, Nov. 24, 1831, Sarah Ann Brown. Lived at Rye, Portsmouth, and Boston. He died Jan. 22, 1866. She died in New York, June 5, 1891. Children:
Charles Edward, b. March 24, 1833, at Rye; d. May 2, 1863; shot in Civil War; was captain Co. I, First Mass. Vol. Inf. S. Anzolette, b. Oct. 21, 1835, at Rye; d. Jan. 6, 1838.
50. Thomas Brown, b. May 1, 1839, at Portsmouth.
51. John Howard, b. June 24, 1841, at Portsmouth. George Wallis, b. Dec. 21, 1846, at Portsmouth; unm.; captain Seventh Regt., N. G. N. Y.; enlisted, 1869; discharged, 1898; and senior major 201st Regt. N. Y. Vol. Inf. in the Spanish-American War. He died in New York City Jan. 19, 1904.

28. EDWARD RAND, son of Thomas (13), born Dec. 22, 1806; married Caroline Paul. Lived at Portsmouth. He died Nov. 18, 1868. Children:
Edward. William, lived at Seabrook. Caroline, d. 1877. Manning.

29. JEDEDIAH RAND, son of Thomas (13), born Dec. 2, 1808; married Eliza J. Yeaton. He was a storekeeper and farmer at Rye, and died Jan. 23, 1892. She died June 2, 1865. Children:
52. Thomas William, b. 1831. Eliza Jane, b. Aug. 23, 1835; m. Oct. 19, 1862, Orlando Garland. Augustus Yeaton, b. Nov., 1839; m. June 26, 1870, Amanda Downs; lived at Rye. Leroy Odell, b. Jan. 24, 1852; m. Oct. 12, 1876, Emma Shaw of Braintree, Mass.

30. BILLEY RAND, son of Dowrst (14), baptized Jan. 11, 1789; married, Feb. 28, 1811, Charlotte Batchelder, who was born Feb., 1793, and died Sept. 15, 1873. He died Dec. 26, 1846. Served in Captain Samuel Berry's company in the War of 1812. Children:

James B., b. Sept. 5, 1811; d. March 28, 1880; m. Nov., 1838, Abigail Berry; lived at Greenland Depot.
53. William J., b. March 2, 1815. Mary Abby, b. June 23, 1818.
54. John Ira, b. May 20, 1823.

31. TRUNDY RAND, son of Dowrst (14), baptized June, 1800; married Elizabeth Stevens of Brentwood, N. H. Children:
Hannah, m. first, Broughton; second, Joel Leighton. Edward. Abby. Almeria.

32. SAMUEL M. RAND, son of Billey (15), born July 20, 1803; married Dorothy Moses. Lived at East Rye. He died Oct. 17, 1864. Children:
Albert, b. 1831; m. Hattie Patten.
55. James Moses. William E., m. Emily Bell. Amos, m. Clara Frisbee. Mary Abby, m. Dec. 14, 1864, Albert Brackett Trefethern; lived at Portsmouth. Charles Wallis, m. Ella M. Parker. Martha S., m. Brackett B. Green.
56. Henry S.

33. REUBEN RAND, son of David (17), born Oct., 1798; married Mary Rand. Lived at Portsmouth. Children:
Reuben, b. June 30, 1823. J. Sullivan, b. Feb. 11, 1827; m. May 3, 1859, Elvira Odiorne. Alonzo, b. Jan. 11, 1831. Mary C., b. Jan., 1833. Franklin, b. Nov. 30, 1835. Warren L., b. Dec., 1837. Irving W., b. Jan., 1839.

34. WILLIAM WATSON RAND, son of David (17), born April 7, 1809; married Sarah W. Marden. Lived at Portsmouth. Children:
Josephine W., m. Mosher. Charles F. Cyrus H. Frank P., m. Letitia Caswell of Rye. Anna L.

35. THOMAS JEFFERSON RAND, son of John (19), born June 11, 1813; married, Oct. 27, 1839, Adeline Rand. Lived at Rye. She died May 8, 1902. He died April 30, 1875. Children:
Abby A., b. Dec. 28, 1840; m. Dec. 22, 1872, Reuel G. Shapley; lived at Rye. Christina, b. April 30, 1843; m. Evans. Allen Porter, b. Sept. 8, 1845. Daniel W., b. March 8, 1847; m. Nov. 19, 1879, Vienna J. Leavitt. David L., b. Nov. 2, 1849; m. Dec. 31, 1880, Florence Remlele. Martha Ann, b. Jan. 19, 1853; m. July 2, 1892, Joseph H. Garland; lived at Dover; he d. May 19, 1899. Charles M., b. June 27, 1855; m. Nov. 19, 1879, Augusta E. Drake; lived at Rye. James B., b. Sept. 20, 1857; m. Minnie Doane.

36. DAVID LANG RAND, son of John (19), born Feb. 27, 1815; married, Oct., 1839, Mary S. Yeaton. He died Aug. 20, 1854, after lying in bed eleven years without speaking. Children:

Francis W., d. Jan. 20, 1864, at Chatauqua, of dysentery. John Alonzo. Edwin B.

37. JOHN ORIS RAND, son of John (19), born March 13, 1820; married Sally J. Thomas. She died Sept. 22, 1873. They did not live together. Child:

Manning C.

38. JOSEPH RAND, JR., son of Joseph (20), born Jan. 21, 1796; married, May 21, 1826, Eleanor D. Locke. Lived at Rye. Children:

Olive W., b. Oct. 14, 1826. Hannah B., b. April 13, 1829; m. Sept. 5, 1852, George Merriam; lived at Rye. Sylvia, b. April 11, 1831; d. Sept. 23, 1831. Julia Ann P., b. Feb. 10, 1833; m. May 24, 1868, Henry B. Bickford of Deerfield. Sarah G., b. Feb. 6, 1835; m. Samuel Rand. Mary Emerett, b. Jan. 4, 1838; m. Francis Burgess; she d. March 18, 18—; lived at Waltham, N. Y. Susan E., b. Aug. 22, 1841; m. May 16, 1882, Francis Burgess. Cyrus James, b. May 19, 1845. Serena M., b. June 25, 1847; d. Sept. 15, 1877. Florence, b. Oct. 27, 1850; m. Nov., 1868, W. H. Lowd.

39. SAMUEL HUNT RAND, JR., son of Joseph (20), born April 28, 1803; married, Nov. 29, 1835, Emily Jenness. Lived at Rye. He died Jan. 5, 1876. She died Aug. 5, 1866. Child:

57. Jonathan Jenness, b. Dec. 14, 1838; m. June 11, 1865, Martha A. Marden; lived at Rye.

40. NATHANIEL MARDEN RAND, son of Joseph (20), born Sept. 16, 1806; married, first, Nancy W. Shorey, who died Jan. 20, 1862; second, widow Norton. Lived at Robinstown, Mass., and Portsmouth. Children:

Adeline, b. 1835; m. first, Charles Foye; second, William Shapley.
66. Charles Henry, b. Jan. 2, 1836. John, b. Feb., 1837; d. Aldana, d. Isabel, m. Joseph Fernald. Cyrus, m. Sarah Mead. Thomas, m. Pottle. Nathan. Caddie. Mary, d.

41. LEVI RAND, son of Joseph (20), born April 23, 1811; married Hannah T. Warren. Lived at Rye. He died Sept. 7, 1885. Children:

Abby M., b. April, 1835; d. Amanda, b. June, 1837; d. William Bramwell, b. Aug., 1840; m. first, Jane Dently, divorced; second, April, 22, 1877, Sarah Trefethern. Clara, b. Aug., 1843. Abby A., b. 1849.

42. IRA RAND, son of Joseph (20), born Sept. 28, 1814; married, April 28, 1839, Sarah Ann Goss, who died Aug. 18, 1892. Lived at Rye. He died Jan. 17, 1880. Children:

Sylvanus, b. May 31, 1843; d. Aug. 1, 1862. Gilman, b. April 27, 1847. Horace, d. May 14, 1870. Albert.

43. SAMUEL RAND, son of Samuel (21), born June, 1810; married Sarah Jane Rand. Children:

Ada Philbrick. Emma, d. Oct. 3, 1862. Bertha, b. June 30, 1856. Mina, b. Dec. 16, 1858. Mary, b. 1865. Alice. Edith P., b. July, 1872.

44. CHARLES CLINTON RAND, son of Samuel Hunt (21), born 1820; married, first, Sarah Smith of Holderness; second, Feb. 20, 1848, Sophia Brown. Lived at Rye. Sophia died May 30, 1850. Child by first wife:

Sarah Olive, b. Oct. 19, 1845; m. Albert Warner.

45. HARRY RAND, son of Joshua (22), born June 10, 1803; married Persis Merriam. He died Feb. 5, 1868. Children:

Albert. Ellen.

46. OBED RAND, son of Joshua (22), born Aug. 18, 1804; married Anna Jenness. Children:

Esther, m. Jerome Fessenden; lived at Arlington, Mass. Charles Obed, m. Sarah Ann Stewart.
58. Joseph Jenness.

47. NAHUM RAND, son of Joshua (22), born Nov. 29, 1813; married, Feb. 15, 1841, Dorothy Bristol of Rumford, Me. Children:

W. Alonzo, b. July 28, 1843; m. July, 1866, Minerva L. Cutting. Sarah Elizabeth, b. Aug. 25, 1844; m. Sept. 10, 1865, Edward Rhodes. Ezra D., b. Sept. 10, 1848; m. first, Mary C. Horman; second, Oct., 1896, Mrs. Augusta Buker. Asenath, b. May 20, 1851. Kate M., b. April 19, 1855; m. Nov. 29, 1877, Marchant Hodgsdon. Samuel, b. June 21, 1857. Anna, b. July 19, 1861; m. Oct. 15, 1891, F. Roberts.

48. AARON RAND, son of Joshua (22), born March 19, 1816; married, Nov. 11, 1840, Elizabeth Yeaton. Lived at Rye. He died Nov. 3, 1890. She died Dec. 1, 1896. Children:

> Wesley Adams, b. March 24, 1841; m. first, June 8, 1865, Carrie J. Fuller; second, 1892, Henritta Tower. Atwell Yeaton, b. Dec. 17, 1842; d. April 7, 1865. Francina M., b. Sept. 20, 1848; m. April 25, 1871, Aaron R. Locke.
> 59. Martin H., b. March 2, 1852. Addie S., b. May 3, 1856; m. Jan. 10, 1878, Jeremiah Shaw, who was b. Nov. 20, 1854; she d. Sept. 17, 1900.

49. CAPT. ELVIN RAND, son of Captain Daniel (23), born Aug. 12, 1814; married, Nov., 1839, Martha A. Willey. He died March 23, 1888. Lived at Rye. She died March 1, 1901. Children:

> 60. Howard S., b. Sept. 25, 1840. Charles E., b. Aug. 23, 1852; d. April 3, 1875. Clara.

50. CAPT. THOMAS BROWN RAND, son of Major Thomas (27), born May 1, 1839, at Portsmouth; married widow Josie B. Bartlett. He died in New York March 31, 1901. He was captain of Co. C, 33d regiment, Mass. Vol. Inf., in the War 1861-'65, and lieutenant-colonel, Ninth regiment, N. Y. N. G., in the Spanish-American War, 1898-'99. Child:

> Edward Stern, b. May 24, 1877.

51. JOHN HOWARD RAND, son of Major Thomas (27), born June 24, 1841; married, April 19, 1866, Julia Dodd Spinney of Lynn, born May 19, 1839, who died March 23, 1888. Lived at New York. Was graduated from Harvard college. Children:

> Mabel H., b. Jan. 7, 1867. Lotta S., b. Aug. 26, 1868. Charles Edward, b. Sept. 13, 1875.

52. THOMAS WILLIAM RAND, son of Jedediah (29), born 1831; married, May, 1858, Louise Hodgdon, who died Oct. 6, 1900. Lived at Rye. Farmer, and kept a general store. Children:

> Blake H., b. Dec. 21, 1863; m. June 19, 1889, Leonie Drake.
> 61. Jedediah, b. July 16, 1870.

53. WILLIAM J. RAND, son of Billey (30), born March 2, 1815; married, March 4, 1844, Elizabeth Jenness. Lived at West Rye. She died March 15, 1902. He died Nov. 11, 1903. Blacksmith and farmer. Children:

Ellen, b. Feb. 10, 1845; m. Dec. 3, 1871, Emery Curtis Jenness; lived at Rye. Maryette, b. March 19, 1852; d. April 8, 1852.
62. Joseph William, b. Oct. 6, 1855.

54. JOHN IRA RAND, son of Billey (30), born May 20, 1823; married Mary Jane Garland. Lived at Rye on Sandy Beach road. Farmer. Children:

Eben Watson, b. May 11, 1851; m. June 14, 1882, Annie Hodgdon. Emma J., b. April 26, 1860; d. May 1, 1861.

55. JAMES MOSES RAND, son of Samuel M. (32), married, first, Rosilla Green; second, Sept., 1902, widow Grogan. Lived at East Rye. Blacksmith. Children:

Lizzie, b. Aug. 18, 1868; m. Dec. 6, 1888, Harry O. Rand; she d. March 13, 1896. Joseph P., b. May 8, 1871. Samuel M., b. Aug. 28, 1873; d. Sept. 11, 1874.

56. HENRY S. RAND, son of Samuel M. (32), married, Dec. 6, 1863, Mary O. Trefethern. Lived at Rye. Children:

Arthur, b. June 23, 1864; m. Oct. 30, 1890, Elzader A. Odiorne. Lizzie, b. April 2, 1868; m. Jan. 18, 1895, Herman O. Rand.
63. Harry Osmond. Joseph P., b. 1871; d. 1874. Kate, b. 1874; m. Dec. 20, 1892, Orville F. Varrell.

57. JONATHAN JENNESS RAND, son of Samuel Hunt, Jr. (39), born Dec. 14, 1838; married Martha A. Marden, daughter of Samuel Marden. Lived at Rye. Farmer. Children:

Herman Otis, b. March 28, 1870; m. Jan. 17, 1895, Lizzie A. Rand. Edgar Jenness, b. July 22, 1879.

58. JOSEPH JENNESS RAND, son of Obed (46), married, May 28, 1874, Helen A. Fife of Pembroke, where he resides. Child:

Mary, b. 1875.

59. MARTIN HICKMAN RAND, son of Aaron (48), born March 2, 1852; married, Nov. 25, 1875, Florence L. Berry. Divorced. Child:
64. Irvin, b. 1876.

60. HOWARD S. RAND, son of Captain Elvin (49), born Sept. 25, 1840; married, first, Nov. 7, 1862, Clara E. Odiorne; died Oct. 7, 1875; second, June 1, 1879, Louisa Marden. Lived at Rye. Children by first wife:
Mary Emma, b. March, 1865; m. 1883, George Brown.
65. Frank H., b. Dec., 1867.

61. JEDEDIAH RAND, son of Thomas William (52), born July 16, 1870; married, April 9, 1896, Edith Foss. Mason by trade. Children:
Wallace, b. June 24, 1897. Louise, b. Oct. 24, 1900.

62. JOSEPH WILLIAM RAND, son of William J. (53), born Oct. 6, 1855; married, April 19, 1884, Emily J., daughter of Robert Foss. Lived at Rye. Children:
Annie Emery, b. Jan. 20, 1885. Mary Lizzie, b. Nov. 15, 1886. William, b. July 18, 1888.

63. HARRY OSMOND RAND, son of Henry S. (56), married, first, Dec. 13, 1888, Lizzie W. Rand, who died March 13, 1896; second, Nov. 28, 1898, widow Carrie A. Foster. Children by first wife:
Ada, b. Dec. 6, 1888. James O., b. Feb. 7, 1891. Horace V., b. Jan. 27, 1894. Esther May, b. March 3, 1896.

Children by first husband:
Walter W. Foster, b. Jan. 25, 1890. Arthur W. Foster, b. Jan. 17, 1892.

64. IRVIN RAND, son of Martin Hickman (59), born 1876; married, June 12, 1894, Edith Trefethern. Children:
Bessie, b. Nov. 27, 1894. Son, b. Sept. 14, 1898.

65. FRANK H. RAND, son of Howard S. (60), born Dec., 1867; married, Aug. 4, 1889, Nora Varrell. Lived at Rye. Child:
Mildred, b. Dec. 3, 1889.

66. CHARLES HENRY RAND, son of Nathaniel Marden Rand (40), born Jan. 2, 1836; married, Jan., 1862, Rosamond Jenness, who died June 13, 1883. Children: Walter H., b. March 2, 1862. Etta J., b. Feb. 8, 1864. Fanny, b. May 5, 1869; d. Aug. 20, 1899. Nellie T., b. Nov. 27, 1876; m. Oct. 8, 1899, William C. Philbrick.

1. RICHARD RAND, married Abiel ———. He died April, 1769. Children:
   Mary, b. Feb. 8, 1726.
2. Nathaniel, b. March 12, 1737. Olive, b. July 9, 1739.

2. NATHANIEL RAND, son of Richard (1), born March 12, 1737; married, Dec. 8, 1757, Mary Leavitt. Lived at Rye and Northwood. Children:
Richard, b. March 18, 1758; lost privateering in Revolutionary War. Samuel, b. Jan. 28, 1760; lost privateering in Revolutionary War. Olly, b. April 5, 1762; m. Jonathan Locke. Mary, b. March 21, 1764; m. Richard Cate. Nathaniel, b. Sept. 8, 1766; m. Abigail Trefethern; she afterwards m. George Bell of North Carolina. Susannah, b. Aug. 31, 1768; m. Jeremiah, son of John Locke. Mehitable, b. Dec. 10, 1770; m. Jeremiah Locke. Sally, b. Dec. 25, 1772; d. young. Sarah, b. July 31, 1774; m. March 2, 1797, Benjamin Mason of Stratham. Ruth, b. Aug. 1, 1776; m. Samuel Cate. Tabitha, bapt. 1777. Samuel, b. Jan. 11, 1780; m. Mary Hanson. Molly, b. 1782. Aphia, b. Feb. 5, 1784; d. while a young woman.

AMOS RAND, married Esther Philbrick. Cordwainer. Lived opposite Charles D. Garland's store. Children:
Anna, b. Aug. 13, 1727. Philbrick, b. Dec. 11, 1729. Esther, b. May 13, 1732. Joseph, b. March 1, 1734. Elizabeth, b. April 12, 1736. Sarah, b. Feb. 12, 1738. Nathaniel, b. May 21, 1740. One of the daughters married and lived up country; she was killed by lightning.

REUBEN RAND married ———. Children:
Thomas, b. Dec. 31, 1750. Reuben, b. Aug. 22, 1753.

BENJAMIN RAND married ———. Children:
Abigail, b. 1755. Lucy, b. 1757. Benjamin, b. 1765.

1. STEPHEN RAND, married, July 3, 1759, Mercy Palmer of Hampton. He died in 1759 on his way home from the French War. Child:
2. Stephen, b. Sept. 12, 1759.

GENEALOGY.

2. STEPHEN RAND, son of Stephen (1), born Sept. 12, 1759; married, first, Sarah Fogg, who was born Sept. 10, 1764, and died June 18, 1803; second, Sept. 17, 1807, Ruth Tarlton. He died March 31, 1826. Children:

Stephen, b. May 12, 1782; d. Jan. 4, 1871; m. June 8, 1806, Betsy Tarlton, who d. Sept. 3, 1869; no child.
3. Polly, b. Aug. 15, 1785. Mercy, b. March 26, 1788-'89; m. April 7, 1807, Daniel Mason. Daniel Fogg, b. Jan. 7, 1792; m. Mary Richardson; he d. Oct. 1, 1859. Caroline, b. Nov. 6, 1796; m. Richard Jenness. Sarah, b. July 25, 1799; d. Sept. 9, 1802; aged three years.

3. POLLY RAND, daughter of Stephen (2), born Aug. 15, 1785, married, Nov., 1839, John Brown. Children:

4. Eldred Rand, b. Aug. 2, 1808; b. before marriage. Sarah, m. Shackford, b. Aug., 1805.

4. ELDRED RAND, son of Polly (3), born Aug. 2, 1808; married Susan Otis. Lived at Boston. Children:

Harriet. Charles. Fannie.

JOHN RAND married ———. Children:

Rachel, b. 1745; m. Jacob Berry (?). Lucy, b. 1747. John, b. 1749; m. Hannah Seavey. Samuel, b. 1751. Nathaniel, b. 1753. William, b. 1755. Samuel, b. 1758. Anna. Jeremiah, b. 1761.

NATHANIEL RAND, 3D, married, Jan. 22, 1761, Bethia Rand. Children:

Molly, b. 1764. Amos, b. Jan. 29, 1767. Joshua, b. April 22, 1769.

SAMUEL RAND, JR., married Abigail Marden. Child:

Sarah, b. 1774.

NATHANIEL RAND married Mary Odiorne. Child:

Sally, bapt. 1779; m. Joshua Rand.

OLIVER PORTER RAND married, June, 1828, Mary Bean. Children:

Sarah Abigail, b. 1829; m. William B. Fessenden; he d. Feb. 12, 1864; she d. Dec. 2, 1861. John Trueman, b. 1830; d. Dec. 25, 1830. Frances Adelaide, b. Nov. 20, 1839.

JOHN GILMAN RAND married ———. Children:

John G. Clinton. Ernest. Daughter, m. Marston. Daughter, m. Butler. ———, m. Kingsbury. ———, m. Marshall. Ida.

BICKFORD RAND married, first, Eunice Carter; second, Martha Batchelder. He died Dec. 20, 1860. Was in Captain Berry's company in the War of 1812. Children:

Sarah, m. Stone. David, m. Rachel Farnum. Bickford, m. Elizabeth Cilley. Edward. Charles. Adelaide, d. unm. Ezekiel, m. Elizabeth Chesley.

WILLIAM RAND (Deaf Billey), married Betsey ———. Children:

William, m. Sanders. Richard. Mercy, m. first, Nat. Colman; second, Josiah Weeks. Nabby, m. Stephens. Nathaniel. Stephen. Patty, m. Howard.

CHARLES WALLIS RAND, son of Samuel M. (32), married Ella M. Parker. He died May 21, 1902. Children:

Helen, d. Nov. 17, 1893. Susan P., b. Jan. 24, 1879; m. April 27, 1898, William E. Chesley; he d. Jan. 7, 1903. Byron W., b. 1880; m. July 28, 1901, Mable M. Greggs.

RANDALL.

1. EDWARD RANDALL, married Hannah ———. Lived at Little Harbor and at Portsmouth, 1670. Children:

George, b. Sept. 13, 1733. George, b. March 7, 1746.
2. John.
3. William. } Brothers (?).
4. Mark, b. Oct. 25, 1726.

2. JOHN RANDALL, son of Edward (1), married Hannah ———. Children:

John, bapt. April 14, 1746. Abigail, b. 1749.

3. WILLIAM RANDALL, son of Edward (1), married, April 24, 1745, Hannah Marston, a schoolmistress. Children:

James Marston, b. March 7, 1746. William, b. May, 1748; m. ———; had Thomas, b. Sept. 4, 1770. Mary, b. Sept. 20, 1750; m. Joseph Morse. Stephen, b. July 23, 1753. Joseph, b. April 17, 1756; m. Phebe Drew; lived at Nottingham. Jonathan, b. March 27, 1759; m. Eleanor Osgood. Samuel, b. May 2, 1762; m. Carr. Lucy, b. Dec. 29, 1767; lived to be 100 years old; lived at Epsom.

4. MARK RANDALL, son of Edward (1), born Oct. 25, 1726; married, Nov. 24, 1748, Abigail Philbrick, who was born Nov. 11, 1730, and died 1816. Children:

GENEALOGY. 515

Abigail, bapt. Dec. 5, 1749; m. Gideon Marshall; lived at Hampton Falls. Joses, b. April 11, 1751; m. Elizabeth Galloway; he d. a prisoner in a Jersey prison ship; she m. second, Noah Jenness; third, Thomas Goss. Sally, b. Oct. 28, 1752; m. John Jenness. Elizabeth, b. April 10, 1755; m. Richard Webster.
5. Mark, b. June 18, 1757.
6. Reuben, b. Feb. 9, 1760. John, b. June 18, 1762; d. Oct. 19, 1781, in Revolutionary prison. Deborah, b. June 11, 1764; m. Abner Downs; she d. June 1, 1803. Samuel, b. July 3, 1767; m. Tibbets; lived in Maine. Daniel, b. Oct. 26, 1769; m. Elizabeth Quimby, or Becky (?); lived at Sandwich. Olly, b. Oct. 21, 1772; d. unm. at Moultonborough. Hannah, b. Aug. 30, 1778; d. Sept. 6, 1778.

5. MARK RANDALL, son of Mark (4), born June 18, 1757; married ———. Child:

Mark, m. Augusta Berry.

6. REUBEN RANDALL, son of Mark (4), born Feb. 9, 1760; married Sarah Young. Children:

Sarah, m. Eben Berry. Joses, m. Dorothy Randall.
7. Levi D.

7. LEVI D. RANDALL, son of Reuben (6), married, April, 1809, Abigail Webster. Lived at Kittery. Children:

Elizabeth W., b. Aug. 15, 1809; m. Mary, b. Dec. 18, 1810; m. Elder Abner Hall. Reuben, b. Dec. 7, 1812.

1. GEORGE RANDALL, son of ———, married, July 18, 1751, Sarah, daughter of Jotham Berry. He was drowned at Sandy beach. Came from the Isles of Shoals. Children:

Sarah, bapt. 1752. Sarah, b. 1754; m. Jan. 3, 1788, John Nelson; lived where the poorhouse was. Edward, b. 1758; went to sea in Revolutionary War and d. Amelia B., b. 1760; m. first, Nov. 29, 1792, Samuel Sanders; second, John Bragg.
2. George, b. 1762. Rachel, b. 1765; m. June 27, 1793, John Mace. Abigail, b. 1769; m. John Nelson.
3. William Bates, b. 1771.

2. GEORGE RANDALL, son of George (1), born 1762; married, first, Mary Foss; second, Nov. 14, 1782, Elizabeth Berry. He died Dec. 24, 1820. Children:

Mary, b. 1782; m. Joseph Hall; had a son who d. of consumption. Edward, b. 1785; d. at sea. Abigail, d. aged seven or eight years, of throat distemper. Betsey, b. 1787; m. first, Robert Mather; second, John Downs.

4. Samuel B., b. Jan. 11, 1789. William B., b. Nov., 1791; m. April 8, 1821, Sally Johnson Goss, who afterwards m. his brother. Lovey Brackett, b. 1793; m. first Samuel Haley; second, Samuel Robinson.
5. George, b. 1800.

3. WILLIAM BATES RANDALL, son of George (1), born 1771; married, Feb. 26, 1793, Deborah Yeaton. She died Dec. 21, 1807. He died at sea, June 10, 1811. Children:

John Yeaton, b. April 28, 1792; m. widow Hannah (Rand) Foye. Nancy, bapt. Nov. 8, 1795; m. Richard Sleeper of Kensington, N. H. William, b. 1800. Susanna Lang, bapt. Sept. 17, 1797; unm. George.

4. SAMUEL BERRY RANDALL, son of George (2), born Jan. 11, 1789; married Betsey Smith. Children:

Joseph Smith, b. Jan. 22, 1817; d. June 30, 1824; killed by lightning. Mary Ann, b. Aug. 25, 1819; m. Sylvester Gilbert; lived at Portsmouth. Prudence N., b. July 13, 1821; m. George Badger; lived at Portsmouth.

5. GEORGE RANDALL, son of George (2), born 1800; married Sally (Johnson Goss) Randall, the widow of his brother. Children:

William, m. Clara Adams. Sarah Olive, d. 1852.

1. DANIEL RANDALL, married ———. Children:
2. Benjamin. Richard. Betsy. Daniel. Mary.

2. BENJAMIN RANDALL, son of Daniel (1), married Betsey Shapley. Children:

3. Benjamin, b. Oct. 2, 1769. Reuben, m. Dolly Wendell. Mercy, m. James Shapley. Mary, m. Reuben Shapley. Hannah, m. Elijah Locke.

3. BENJAMIN RANDALL, son of Benjamin (2), born Oct. 2, 1769; married, first, Polly Rugg; second, Aug. 27, 1793, Sarah Saunders, who was born Aug. 21, 1773. Child by first wife:

Benjamin, m. Pierce; lost in ship *Capt. Beck* on Salisbury beach.

Children by second wife:

Reuben S., b. March 16, 1794; m. Elizabeth Berry. Samuel Saunders, bapt. Dec. 4, 1796. George Saunders, b. Nov. 6, 1799; m. Nov. 15, 1832, Betsey Downs; he d. April 23, 1872. Hannah, b. March 6, 1801; m. Job Locke, Jr. Dorothy, b. Oct. 15, 1803; m. Oct. 19, 1820, James Shapley.

4. William S., b. Nov. 15, 1805. May S., b. Feb. 21, 1812; m. John L. Locke. Sarah, b. Jan. 14, 1815; m. Richard H. Waldron. Benjamin, b. July 21, 1817; d. 1845; lost at sea. Samuel.

4. WILLIAM S. RANDALL, son of Benjamin (3), born Nov. 15, 1805; married, first, Dec. 11, 1827, widow Eliza G. Caswell; second, widow Catherine Caswell; third, widow Hannah Randall. Children by ——— wife:

5. John William. Ira Gilbert, m. Mary, dau. of William Varrell. Jane G., m. John Caswell; had a child, Eva, who was drowned. Frank Waldron, b. Sept. 16, 1835; m. Sarah J. Baston; he d. Jan. 3, 1876, and she m. second, Oct. 21, 1884, James W. Smith.

5. JOHN WILLIAM RANDALL, son of William S. (4), married, first, April 17, 1853, Ann M. Verrill; second, widow Hannah O. Lane; third, 1858, Harriet Lear. Child by third wife:

6. William O., b. July 26, 1861.

6. WILLIAM O. RANDALL, son of John William (5), born July 26, 1861; married, Oct. 16, 1899, Jessie M. Lear. Child:

Gladys May, b. Oct. 29, 1900.

1. WILLIAM BUNKER RANDALL, married, first, Hannah Locke; second, Mary Downs. Lived at Isles of Shoals. Children by first wife:

William, m. Hannah Pitman; she afterwards m. William S. Randall. Job Locke, d. at Great Falls (?).

Children by second wife:

James Abner, m. Abby Anna Caswell, dau. of Joseph; he was drowned at the Isles of Shoals. Judson (John), m. Haley. Josiah, m. Eliza Esther Caswell. Mary, m. Woodbury Mace of Rye. Sarah Hannah, m. John Wilkes Locke. William Monroe, m. McDonald.

PAUL RANDALL, son of Edward (1), married, first, Feb., 1752, Hannah Adams; second, Margaret Tuckerman; third, 1763, Abigail ———. Innkeeper, about 1760. Children by first wife:

John. Paul, bapt. 1755; unm.

Children by second wife:

Mercy Sewell, m. Sept. 13, 1802, John Redding. Hannah, b. 1737; m. Dec. 18, 1778, James Towle Berry. Abigail, b. 1762; m. Sellers. Permelia, m. Sellers. Deborah, m. Trefethern. Betsey, m. Trefethern. Margaret, m. Paddleford.

JAMES RANDALL, son of Edward (1), married, Nov. 24, 1748 ———; died in the Revolutionary army, July 22, 1778. Child:
> Hannah, unm., had dau., Polly, who m. Benj. Philbrick.

GEORGE RANDALL (called Jack), married, March 1, 1824, widow Abigail Whidden. Lived at Isles of Shoals. (The widow had two children, Hannah and Abigail Whidden, the latter of whom married George Randall). Children:
> Mary Ann, m. William Robinson. Sarah Jane, m. a Frenchman. John Porter, ran away to sea. Ruth Maria.

JOHN COOK RANDALL married, first, Feb. 19, 1850, Mary H. Caswell. She died, and he married, second, Baker. Children by first wife:
> Horace, d. at the Shoals. Flora Ann, b. Aug. 22, 1849; m. Jan. 13, 1867, John S. Mow; lived at Rye and Portsmouth. May Louilla, b. Aug. 18, 1855.

GILBERT IRA RANDALL married Mary E. Varrell. Child:
> Arthur, d. June 10, 1879.

RAWDING.

ROBERT J. RAWDING married, April 29, 1899, widow Fannie (Jones) Mitchie of Rye. Child:
> Joseph William, b. Nov. 6, 1899.

REMICK.

1. ISAAC REMICK (whose father was an Englishman, and mother a Scotch woman), married Meribah Smith. Children:
> Sarah, bapt. 1756. Meribah, b. 1760; m. Cotton Palmer. Mary, b. 1765; d. unm. Feb. 23, 1829. Thomas, b. 1767; went to sea and never returned. David, b. 1769; went to sea and never returned.
2. Joseph, b. 1769.
3. Isaac, b. 1769. Betsey, b. 1771; m. Jonathan Hobbs of North Hampton; lived at Effingham. Hannah, b. 1774; m. Andrew Clark. Huldah, b. 1776; m. Solomon Marden. Jane, b. 1778; m. Solomon Foss. Moses, b. 1781; m. Mary Lang of Lee; had one child; both soon d.

2. JOSEPH REMICK, son of Isaac (1), born 1769; married, March 5, 1801, Sally Paul. Children:

Moses. Nancy, b. June 6, 1803; d. Jan. 27, 1869; *non compos mentis.* Eliza A., b. Oct. 3, 1812; d. May 29, 1871; insane.
4. David, b. Jan. 18, 1814. Amos, d. Nov. 15, 1821, aged six years.

3. ISAAC REMICK, son of Isaac (1), born 1769; married, first, Jane Foss; second, Esther Yeaton, who died Jan. 18, 1808; third, Nov. 24, 1808, Lydia Varrell; fourth, Hannah Varrell, who died July 31, 1831. He died Feb. 3, 1834. Children by second wife:

5. John Y., b. March 3, 1795. Isaac, b. 1796.

Children by third wife:

Moses, b. 1809; m. Mary Floyd. Esther Y., b. Feb., 1811; m. Lemuel Locke.
6. William, b. Oct. 27, 1813. Thomas, b. 1816. Sally, b. 1819. David, b. 1821.

Children by fourth wife:

Joseph, b. 1829; d. March 12, 1832. Amos, b. 1831.

4. DAVID REMICK, son of Joseph (2), born Jan. 18, 1814; married, first, widow Abby S. Mace; second, May 18, 1873, Merinda P. Porter. He died March 7, 1892. Children by first wife:

George O., b. June 20, 1850; m. Oct. 29, 1877, Clara E. Verrill. Amos, b. 1850; d. April 5, 1851. A dau., b. March 28, 1852; d. Oct. 24, 1853.
7. Albert D., b. Dec. 25, 1854.

5. JOHN Y. REMICK, son of Isaac (3), born March 3, 1795; married, Feb. 17, 1825, Betsey Philbrick. Lived at Rye. She died Aug. 27, 1878. He died April 13, 1860. Children:

8. John S., b. Sept. 26, 1826. Charles M., b. April, 1830; d. Nov. 14, 1851.

6. WILLIAM REMICK, son of Isaac (3), born Oct. 27, 1813; married, Sept. 27, 1832, Caroline Fox. Lived at Rye on Sandy Beach road. He died May 15, 1875. Children:

George William, b. Aug. 1, 1834; d. Sept. 23, 1854, at Calcutta. Joseph, b. Oct. 4, 1836; d. Oct. 19, 1852. Mary Pauline, b. March 11, 1839; m. Henry W. Morin of Portsmouth. James F., b. Nov. 10, 1840; d. Nov. 12, 1841. Lydia Esther, b. July 16, 1842. Sarah Eliza, b. Oct. 7, 1844. Moses M., b. Oct. 15, 1846. ———, b. Sept. 8, 1850; d. Daniel L., b. Nov. 17, 1852; d.

7. ALBERT D. REMICK, son of David (4), born Dec. 25, 1854; married, Nov. 3, 1875, Anna C. Mace. Lived at Rye. For many years captain of the life-saving station. Children:

> Mabel, b. March 4, 1877. Walter, b. Feb. 29, 1880. Albert M., b. Jan. 11, 1885.

8. DEACON JOHN S. REMICK, son of John Y. (5), born Sept. 26, 1826; married, June 22, 1851, Mary T. Seavey. Lived at Rye. He died Sept. 5, 1885. Children:

> Lizzie S., b. Sept. 12, 1852; m. June 13, 1879, Charles W. Spear; she d. Nov. 10, 1886; lived at Rye. Esther Y., b. Oct. 2, 1854; unm.
> 9. Charles M., b. Sept. 10, 1857. John A., b. Jan. 11, 1860; m.; he d.

9. CHARLES M. REMICK, son of John S. (8), born Sept. 10, 1857; married, Dec. 24, 1884, Emily B. Brown. Lived at Rye. Children:

> May Blanche, b. March 27, 1886. Harold John, b. Aug. 2, 1888. Bernice, b. Feb. 6, 1891. Francis, b. Oct. 12, 1898.

RIEB.

PATRICK RIEB married Anna Smith. Electrician. Children:

> Ernest. Florence. Fred, b. Sept. 11, 1885. Ethel C., b. May 19, 1888; d. Aug. 18, 1898. George, b. Jan. 14, 1891.

ROBINSON.

1. JOHN ROBINSON, married ———. Children:
2. Robert.
3. James.
4. John. Nabby, m. Benjamin Downs.

2. ROBERT ROBINSON, son of John (1), married Sally Downs. Children:

> Lovina, b. March, 1806; m. Reuben Shapley. Margaret, m. first, Samuel Grant; second, Serg. Lewis; third, Leonard Dale. Mehitable, unm.

3. JAMES ROBINSON, son of John (1), married, Feb. 27, 1821, Sally Downs, widow of Abner. Lived at Rye. Children:

Sarah Elizabeth, b. 1827; m. Sept. 16, 1863, Charles Reuben Caswell. James Monroe.

4. JOHN ROBINSON, son of John (1), married Mary Shapley. Lived at Gosport. Children:

5. Samuel, b. 1803. Sally, b. 1806; m. June 6, 1824, Cleveland B. Holt. William, b. March 20, 1812; m. Mary Ann Randall.

5. SAMUEL ROBINSON, son of John (4), born 1803; married Olive or Lovey Haley. He died May 26, 1869. Lived at Gosport. Children:

Abigail, m. first, Brown; second, William Shields. Samuel, m. Elizabeth Newton.

ROLLINS.

HENRY ROLLINS married Anna ———. Child:

Martha, bapt. July 9, 1775.

RUGG.

——— RUGG married ———. Lived at the Isles of Shoals. Child:

Judah Mace, bapt. Nov. 6, 1793.

RYDER.

HENRY RYDER married Hannah Mathes. Child:

A son, b. Dec. 9, 1866.

SALTER.

1. JOHN SALTER married Amy ———. Children:

2. Alexander, b. April 2, 1718. Molly, b. March 27, 1721. John, b. June 12, 1722.

2. ALEXANDER SALTER, son of John (1), born April 2, 1718; married Elizabeth, daughter of Enoch and Elizabeth Sanborn, born March 16, 1715. Came to Rye Jan. 28, 1742; died Nov. 1, 1801. Children:

Mary, b. March 27, 1741. John, b. June 12, 1742-'43. Alexander, b. Oct. 3, 1744. Elizabeth, b. May 22, 1746.

3. John, b. Sept. 19, 1748.

3. JOHN SALTER, son of Alexander (2), born Sept. 19, 1748; married Abiah Webster, who died May 10, 1811. He died May 22, 1804. Lived at Rye. Children:
 Lucy, b. July 16, 1769; m. Levi Garland; lived at Rye. Sarah, b. Aug. 25, 1771; m. Samuel Lear. John, b. Dec. 10, 1776; d. 1804, aged 28 years; bled to death at Carroll's store.
4. Alexander, b. June 4, 1778. Webster, b. Jan. 5, 1782; m. Dec. 14, 1806, Sarah Libby; no child. Mary, had a dau. by Mackey; m. David Rand.

4. ALEXANDER SALTER, son of John (3), born June 4, 1778; married, first, March 18, 1803, Mary Berry, who died May 13, 1810; second, Anna Webster, who died 1850. Children:
 Louise, b. April, 1804; m. John Langley. John, b. Aug. 8, 1806; m. Sarah Brown. Sally, b. Aug. 8, 1808; m. first, Reuel L. Buzzell; second, Jere Page. Joseph, b. Nov. 19, 1811; m. Hannah Dana. Mary Ann, b. June 15, 1818; m. Ephraim Davis.
5. Jeremiah Webster, b. Nov. 9, 1822.

5. JEREMIAH WEBSTER SALTER, son of Alexander (4), born Nov. 9, 1822; married Fanny Davis. Child:
 Webster, m. Dec. 30, 1880, Florence L. Berry; lived at Rye.

ALBERT E. SALTER married Fannie Philbrick June 21, 1872; divorced; and she married, second, W. E. Carter of Vermont. Child:
 Huldah Salter, b. Aug., 1879.

SANBORN.

BENNING SANBORN married Polly Jenness. Lived at Deerfield. Children:
 Benning W., lived at Concord. Peter, lived at Concord. Mary Jane, m. Harris. Jenness. Josiah.

SAMUEL SANBORN married Mary Barnes. Children:
 Nathan, b. 1768. Sarah, b. 1770.

LEVI THOMAS SANBORN came from Hampton Falls; married, Sept. 29, 1864, Sarah Jane Perkins. Lived at Rye. Children:
 Charles Richmond, b. Aug. 2, 1865. Mary Carrie, b. Oct. 14, 1866.

SAUNDERS.

1. ——— SAUNDERS. Children (all of whom were probably brothers):
2. John.
3. Samuel.
4. George, b. April 18, 1732.
5. Robert.

2. JOHN SAUNDERS, born 1720, perhaps son of ——— (1), came from Torbay, Eng., and settled at the Isles of Shoals; married, first, April 7, 1740, Mary Berry; second, 1760, Tryphena Philbrick, who afterwards married Jonathan Berry. He was lost in the big October gale, 1770. Children by first wife:

> Esther, bapt. Sept. 17, 1741; m. first, John Yeaton, who was lost in the big gale, 1770; m. second, 1783, Simon Knowles; lived at Rye.
> 6. Robert, bapt. July 3, 1743. Mary, bapt. Oct. 20, 1744; m. first, 1763, William Thomas; second, William Mathes of Gosport; lived at Rye.
> 7. John, bapt. Nov. 9, 1746. George Berry, bapt. Sept. 11, 1748; m. Anna Page. He was killed by falling from his horse; lived at Epsom.

Children by second wife:

> Abigail, b. Oct. 7, 1760; m. William Locke (second wife). William, bapt. June 19, 1763. Sarah, bapt. July 28, 1763; m. first, March 6, 1783, William Saunders; second, Joseph Verrill. Olly, b. 1766; m. William Tucker.

3. SAMUEL SAUNDERS, perhaps son of ——— (1), came from Torbay, Eng., and settled at the Isles of Shoals; married, 1746, Hannah Foss. He was lost in the gale. Children:

> Mary, bapt. Jan. 8, 1744; d. Samuel, b. July 14, 1745. Sarah, b. Oct. 4, 1747; m. Foss. Hannah, b. Aug. 28, 1749; m. Blake. Elizabeth, b. Oct. 21, 1753. Robert, b. Dec. 7, 1755. George, b. Aug. 3, 1760. Levi Dearborn, b. March 9, 1766.

4. GEORGE SAUNDERS, perhaps son of ——— (1), born April 18, 1732; came fom Torbay, Eng., and settled at the Isles of Shoals; married, 1756 or '57, Sarah Kive, who was born Jan. 13, 1736. A member of Captain Parsons' company in the Revolutionary War. He died in 1786. Children:

Elizabeth, b. June 29, 1755. Sarah, bapt. Sept. 18, 1757; d.
8. William, b. Oct. 19, 1759. Martha, b. May 29, 1766; m. Elijah Wadleigh. Mercy Haines, b. Aug. 24, 1767; m. James Shapley.
9. George, b. June 3, 1769.
10. Samuel, b. Nov. 21, 1771. Sarah, b. Aug. 20, 1773; m. Benjamin Randall. Mary, b. Aug. 13, 1776; m. Reuben Shapley. Hannah, b. June 4, 1779; m. Elijah Locke.

5. ROBERT SAUNDERS, perhaps son of ———— (1), came from Torbay, Eng., and settled at the Isles of Shoals; married Elizabeth Berry. He died March 7, 1807, aged 92 years. Child:

Robert, bapt. March 30, 1742; d.

6. ROBERT SAUNDERS, son of John (2), baptized July 3, 1743; married, July 7, 1765, Mary Locke, who lived 96 years. Lived at Epsom, and was buried at Effingham. Children:

11. Robert, bapt. Oct. 12, 1766. Mary, bapt. Aug. 16, 1767; m. Joseph Chapman.
12. Elijah Robert, Jr., b. Aug. 20, 1769. John, b. April 10, 1774; m Chatham. Nathaniel, b. Nov. 29, 1778; m. Goss. William, m. Hall.

7. JOHN SAUNDERS, JR., son of John (2), baptized Nov. 9, 1746; married Dorcas Pitman. He was lost at sea. Children:

Mary, bapt. May 14, 1769; m. first, George Saunders; second, Levi Goss. John, m. Eliza Ann; he d. Feb., 1846, at Boston.

8. WILLIAM SAUNDERS, son of George (4), born Oct. 19, 1759; married Sarah Saunders. She afterwards married, Aug. 25, 1794, Joseph Verrill. Children:

William, b. Nov. 7, 1783; d. aged 26 years in Demerara, W. I. Betsey, b. Sept. 15, 1785; m. Feb. 6, 1810, Daniel Page of Epsom. John, b. March 2, 1789; unm.; sailor; d. Feb. 26, 1868, in Rye almshouse.

9. GEORGE SAUNDERS, son of George (4), born June 3, 1769; married Mary Saunders, who afterwards married Levi Goss. Children:

Henry Shapley, bapt. March 26, 1791; lost at sea (?) George, bapt. Dec. 23, 1792. Mary Mead, bapt. July 16, 1794.

10. SAMUEL SAUNDERS, son of George (4), born Nov. 21, 1771; married, Nov. 29, 1792, Amelia Randall. He died before Oct. 5, 1794. Children:
Sarah, bapt. Oct. 5, 1794. Molly, bapt. Oct. 5, 1794.

11. ROBERT SAUNDERS, son of Robert (6), baptized Oct. 12, 1766; married Molly Foss. Children:
John, m. Buzzell. Betsey. Robert, m. Huldah Philbrick.
13. Job, b. Nov. 24, 1792. Elijah, m. Olly Philbrick. Frederick, m. Manson. William, m. Wallace.

12. ELIJAH ROBERT (?) SAUNDERS, JR., son of Robert (6), born Aug. 20, 1769; married, Nov. 29, 1792, Mercy Rand. Child:
Patience Locke, bapt. June 29, 1794.

13. JOB SAUNDERS, son of Robert (11), born Nov. 24, 1792; married ———. Lived at Derry. Children:
O. H., lived at Boston. W. H., lived at Chicago.

SAWYER.

HORACE SAWYER, from Haverhill, Mass., married, Nov. 5, 1868, Susan M. Jenness. Lived at Rye. Children:
Anna Knox, b. Oct. 1, 1869; m. April 24, 1902, Joseph Watt. Edward, b. Jan. 11, 1872. Horace Russell, b. April 12, 1876; m. Oct. 10, 1900, Mary W. Whidden. Mildred, b. Jan. 19, 1889.

SCADGEL.

BENJAMIN SCADGEL married ———. Children:
Mary, b. 1748. Sarah, b. 1750. Hannah, b. 1752. Abigail, b. 1754. Benjamin, b. 1757. Abigail, b. 1761.

The Scadgel place was where Mr. Joseph Langdon Seavey lives. They kept a tavern and the sign hung on the large elm tree which stands southerly from the house.

SCHEDEL—SCHEGEL.

CHRISTOPHER SCHEDEL married Deborah ———. Children:
Mary, b. May 1, 1720. Benjamin, b. Nov. 27, 1727; m. Dorcas; lived in Rye in 1763. Jacob, b. Oct. 25, 1736.

SCOTT.

DANIEL P. SCOTT married ———. Lived on Lafayette road. Children:
Walter P. Haven. Daniel O.

SEAVEY.

1. WILLIAM SEAVEY, sent from England in 1631 to the Piscataquqa settlement by Captain John Mason. He was a selectman and otherwise of some consequence in the settlement. In 1660, he was William the elder. He died about 1688. Children:
2. William, b. 1640.
3. John, b. 1650. Stephen. Elizabeth, m. Odiorne.

2. WILLIAM SEAVEY, son of William (1), born 1640; married Hannah ———, who was born about 1663, and died Jan. 31, 1748. He was on the grand jury in 1682, and was a surveyor in 1683. In 1728, he desired at a "proprietors' meeting" to be excused by reason of "age and infirmity" from any further service in laying out lands. His will was dated March 25, 1728-'29, and proved, June, 1733. Her will was made Sept. 10, 1741, proved, Feb. 28, 1748. She gave to her son Stephen, ten shillings; James, ten shillings; Ebenezer, a bed; to the children of son Thomas, £10; to her negro woman Anna, one cow. Children:
4. William, 3d.
5. James. Hannah, m. Samuel Wells, who d. before Sept., 1741. Hepzibah, m. Thomas Wright, mariner, who died before 1741. Mary, b. 1704; m. Capt. Samuel Banfield, who d. 1743; she d. 1753. Thomas (twin), went down East, d. before Sept. 1741. Ebenezer (Capt.), (twin), went down East; d. at Newcastle, 1744. Stephen, m. widow Mary True.

3. JOHN SEAVEY, son of William (1), born 1650; married, July 29, 1680, Hannah Walker, daughter of John Philbrook of Hampton and widow of Joseph Walker. Children:
6. Thomas. Nathaniel. They united in 1690 in petitioning for the jurisdiction of Massachusetts.

GENEALOGY. 527

4. WILLIAM SEAVEY, 3D, son of William (2), married, first, Mary Hincks, who died 1744; second, Sept. 25, 1748, Hannah Seavey, who died 1781 or 1786. Proprietors' clerk for some years, and probably ensign in Captain Jotham Odiorne's company, 1716. Children:

7. Amos. William, b. 1714; d. Sept. 24, 1744; a clothier; perhaps had a child, Mark, bapt. July 4, 1742. Ephraim, b. 1723; d. 1735-'36. Elizabeth, m. Nov. 30, 1732, John Jenness; d. Feb. 14, 1744-'45. John, b. Oct. 5, 1716; d. July 24, 1741. James, m. Elizabeth Langdon, sister of Amos' wife.

5. JAMES SEAVEY, son of William (2), married, June, 1718, Hannah Pickering; in 1755 had wife, Abigail. Children:

Hannah, b. May 4, 1719; m. July 24, 1740, Jacob Sheafe.
8. James.
9. Paul.

6. THOMAS SEAVEY, son of John (3), married Thomasine. He died Feb. 1707-'08. Lived at Newcastle. Children:

Benjamin. Samuel. Damaris. Oslow. Rebecca, m. John Shute.

7. AMOS SEAVEY, carpenter, son of William, 3d (4), born 1718; married, 1744, Mary Langdon, who died Feb. 23, 1807, aged 82 years. He died Feb. 19, 1807, and they were buried in one grave. Lived in the old Seavey house at East Rye. Children:

10. William, 5th, b. 1745. Mary, b. Dec., 1746; m. Jan. 31, 1768, Dr. Joseph Parsons; lived at Rye. Hannah, b. 1749; m. Feb. 22, 1774, Richard Jenness of Deerfield.
11. Joseph Langdon, b. Jan. 7, 1751. Elizabeth, b. June 19, 1753; m. Aug. 21, 1777, Isaac Dow, son of Henry. Anna, b. 1755; m. Nov. 20, 1791, John Seavey; she d. Jan. 26, 1827. Martha, b. 1758; m. March 11, 1787, Benjamin Jenness; she d. May 27, 1830. Dolly, b. 1761; d. unm. Jan. 27, 1827. Abigail, b. 1764; m. Jan. 28, 1790, John Garland, Jr., son of Simon; she d. March 14, 1851.

8. JAMES SEAVEY, son of James (5), married Elizabeth Langdon, who died July 14, 1804. He died Oct. 19, 1801. Children:

James, b. 1757; d. unm. July 15, 1811. John, b. 1761; m. Nov. 20, 1791, Anna Seavey.
12. Joseph, b. Dec. 20, 1767.

9. PAUL SEAVEY, son of James (5), married, May 10, 1764, Sarah Wallis. Lived on the Samuel M. Rand place in East Rye. Children:

13. Ebenezer, b. 1765. Deborah, b. 1767; d. probably before 1790. Hannah, b. 1769; m. Jonathan Wedgewood. Sarah, b. 1772; m. March 6, 1791, Joseph Goss. Mehitable, b. Feb. 19, 1775; m. first, Peter Garland; second, James Perkins; she d. May, 1850.
14. Samuel Wallis, b. 1779.
15. Joshua, b. 1777. William, b. 1782; d. in Demerara, W. I. Fanny, b. Oct., 1787; m. May 15, 1803, Benjamin Garland, aged 32 years. Gideon; old Uncle Eben Wallis undertook to keep him but he ran away.

10. LIEUT. WILLIAM SEAVEY, son of Amos (7), born 1745; married Anna Trefethern. He died March 15, 1829. First lieutenant under Captain Joseph Parsons at Newcastle in the Revolutionary War. Children:

Elizabeth, m. Lieut. John Foye; lived at Rye. Mary, b. Dec., 1769; m. Ebenezer Odiorne; lived at Rye. Anna, b. April, 1772; m. Levi Dearborn of North Hampton; lived in Illinois.
16. William, b. May 19, 1774. Hannah, b. 1776; m. William Foye; she d. Nov. 14, 1803. Martha, b. 1780; m. Samuel Willey; she d. July, 1855. Dorothy, b. June 7, 1782; m. Feb. 17, 1801, Daniel Rand.
17. Amos, b. 1787. Abigail, b. July 3, 1791; m. Joseph Whidden.
18. John Langdon, b. Sept. 8, or May 24, 1793.

11. JOSEPH LANGDON SEAVEY, son of Amos (7), born Jan. 7, 1751; married, first, Nov. 19, 1786, Elizabeth, daughter of Col. Benjamin Garland; second, Martha Patten. He died March 4, 1803. Children by first wife:

Sarah, b. Oct. 26, 1777; d. about 1797. Polly, b. Jan. 5, 1780; m. March 16, 1806, Lieut. Simon Brown; lived at Rye. Elizabeth, b. March 23, 1783; m. first, April 26, 1804, Joseph Brown; second, Dec. 18, 1809, Richard Jenness, Jr.
19. Theodore J., bapt. July 3, 1785.

Children by second wife:
20. Ephraim, bapt. Feb. 19, 1792. Matty, or Martha, b. July 21, 1793; m. Nov. 28, 1816, Amos S. Garland, son of John. Sidney S., b. July 19, 1795; m. Dec. 22, 1813, John L. Seavey, son of William.
21. Joseph Langdon, b. Oct. 30, 1798.

12. JOSEPH SEAVEY, son of James (8), born Dec. 20, 1767; married Mary Whidden, who was born June 18, 1776-'77, and died Aug. 7, 1853. He died Nov. 7, 1849. Children:

    Eliza Mary Langdon, b. March 1, 1804; m. Joseph Foss. Alfred, b. March 7, 1806; d. Oct. 29, 1821.
22. Joseph Whidden, b. Dec. 9, 1807.
23. Edward, b. July 20, 1810.
24. James, b. Sept. 21, 1812. Hannah W., b. July 19, 1814; m. Oct. 13, 1851, Moses Rand. Sarah Lang, b. Nov. 10, 1816; d.
25. Eben Leavitt, b. Jan. 28, 1819.

13. EBENEZER SEAVEY, son of Paul (9), born 1765; married, first, Prudence P. Marden; second ———, daughter of Nathaniel and Hannah Berry. Lived at Rochester. Children:

    Hannah, bapt. May 13, 1792; m. William Jenness. Sarah, bapt. May 13, 1792; m. Leighton. Betsey, b. Dec. 28, 1794; m. Solomon Jenness. Ebenezer Wallis, b. June 30, 1796. Anna Towle, b. July 1, 1798; m. Jenness. William, b. Dec. 15, 1800; m. Jenness. Mary, unm. Gideon, d. young.

14. SAMUEL WALLIS SEAVEY, son of Paul (9), born 1779; married widow Dorothy or Dolly (Parsons) Follett of Kittery, Me. Children:

    William, m. Ackerman. Henry. Samuel. Calvin. Paul. Sarah.

15. JOSHUA SEAVEY, son of Paul (9), born 1777; married, April 16, 1797, Betsey Webster. Lived in Illinois. Children:

    Betsey, b. July 31, 1797; m. Thompson; lived at Sandwich. Sally, b. Nov. 2, 1798; m. Marden; lived at Sandwich. Olive, b. May 15, 1800; m. Benjamin Odiorne. Winthrop, b. Jan. 26, 1802. Mary Moses, b. Sept. 24, 1803. Abigail, b. Jan. 29, 1805; m. William Moses. Jesse, b. Aug. 11, 1810. Hannah, b. May 16, 1812; m. Taylor. Asa.

16. WILLIAM SEAVEY, son of Lieut. William (10), born May 19, 1774; married Elizabeth Ayers of Greenland, who was born June 13, 1781. He died Sept. 20, 1854. Commissioned lieutenant under Captain E. Philbrick, May 17, 1811. Children:

William L., b. July 8, 1801; d. Sept. 26, 1802.
26. Lyman, b. Aug. 31, 1802. Emeline, b. Sept. 26, 1804; m. Dec. 29, 1824, John N. Frost; she d. July 2, 1853. Eliza Ann, b. July 12, 1806; d. unm. March 28, 1877.
27. William Warren, b. Nov. 8, 1807. Susan H., b. April 27, 1811; m. Jan. 22, 1832, John A. Brown of Gloucester. Hannah J., b. May 31, 1813; m. James N. Tarlton of Newcastle. Caroline L., b. Jan. 17, 1816; d. Oct. 10, 1840, aged 23 years. Mary A., b. May 13, 1819; m. Enoch Love; she d. Feb. 19, 1902.
28. Harrison, b. March 17, 1822.

17. LIEUT. AMOS SEAVEY, son of Lieut. William (10), born 1787; married, June 16, 1807, Sarah Drake. She died April 3, 1874. Lived at Rye and Greenland. A member of Captain James Coleman's company of cavalry in the War of 1812. He died in Greenland, Sept. 5, 1852. Children:

Lettis, b. Sept. 12, 1809; m. April 16, 1828, Thomas J. Berry; she d. April 12, 1844; he d. Jan. 23, 1880. Mary, m. Jan. 4, 1837, Simon Brown; she d. Aug. 10, 1885; lived at Rye and Lynn, Mass. Amos, b. 1818; m. Eliza J.; he d. Aug. 20, 1879. Charles W., b. 1820; m. Sarah A. Hatch; he d. Dec., 1863. Sarah D., m. Thomas J. Berry. Anna T., m. Nathaniel Drake of North Hampton. Clara B., m. J. Harry Philbrick of Candia. Andrew P., m. Gerrish; she afterwards m. Langdon Whidden; lived at Portsmouth.

18. JOHN LANGDON SEAVEY, son of Lieut. William (10), born Sept. 8, 1793; married, Dec. 22, 1813, Sidney, daughter of Joseph L. Seavey. She died March 8, 1858. Children:

29. Woodbury, b. June 10, 1815. William, b. June 5, 1817; d. March 13, 1824. Sidney Langdon, b. June 17-20, 1823; m. Dec. 22, 1842, Oliver Jenness, son of Richard; lived at Rye. Ann Elizabeth, b. Dec. 20, 1825-'26; m. Nov. 21, 1847, Albert Dow. John William, b. Oct. 16, 1828; m. Emily Seavey, who d. Dec. 28, 1855; he d. Dec. 23, 1855. Caroline Theresa, b. Oct. 18, 1840; m. first, Jan. 17, 1860, Gilman Marden; second, Nov. 3, 1866, Bezaleel Mathes.

19. THEODORE J. SEAVEY, son of Joseph Langdon (11), baptized July 3, 1785; married, Dec. 21, 1820, Betsey Stevens, who died June 12, 1835. Children:

William, b. April 24, 1821; m. Abby Pottle; lived at Dorchester. Sophronia, b. Jan. 6, 1823; d. Charles, d. Oliver, went to sea. Samuel, d. Jan. 10, 1855, at Newport, R. I. Eliza Jane, d.

GENEALOGY.   531

20. EPHRAIM SEAVEY, son of Joseph Langdon (11), baptized Feb. 19, 1792; married, Nov. 28, 1816, Betsey, daughter of John Garland, Jr. Lived at Rye. Children:

> Frederick, b. April 13, 1826; d. May 28, 1897. Mary Abigail, b. Feb. 1, 1828; d. *non compos mentis.* Martha Elizabeth, b. May 4, 1829; m. Albert M. Walker; lived at Rye. Hannah P., b. June 24, 1831; m. May 20, 1852, Jeremiah H. Robie; lived at North Hampton. Joseph William, b. Nov. 26, 1835; m. 1861, Mary Abby Philbrick, dau. of Jonathan Philbrick.

21. JOSEPH LANGDON SEAVEY, son of Joseph Langdon (11), born Oct. 30, 1798; married, Nov. 15, 1832, Temperance Langdon. Lived at Rye. He died March 2, 1860. Children:

> Martha Adeline, b. 1836; unm. Mary Jane, b. 183*; m. March, 1871, J. Wesley Foye. Joseph Langdon, b. 1840; unm.

22. JOSEPH WHIDDEN SEAVEY, son of Joseph (12), born Dec. 9, 1807; married, May 29, 1829, Sarah Lang. Children:

> Mary F., b. Jan. 18, 1830; m. June 24, 1851, John S. Remick; she d. March 1, 1861. Emily C., m. Joseph William Seavey; both d. Aug. 28, 1858. Charles E., b. June 10, 1834; m. first, Jan. 31, 1861, Fidelia Garland; second, —— Garland.
> 30. Alfred V., b. July 31, 1836. Sarah H., b. Feb. 14, 1839; d. Aug. 6, 1860. Frank H., b. Dec. 16, 1843; m. Leavitt. Charlotte, b. Sept. 14, 1844; m. Joseph R. Holmes; lived at Portsmouth. Alina A., b. June 17, 1847; m. Dec. 25, 1867, John W. Hobbs of North Hampton.
> 31. Irving J., b. 1852.

23. EDWARD SEAVEY, son of Joseph (12), born July 20, 1810; married Mary Willey. Children:

> 32. James E. Martha Ann.
> 34. George Henry, m. Dec. 24, 1871, Sarah Adeline Moulton.

24. JAMES SEAVEY, son of Joseph (12), born Sept. 21, 1812; married, first, Mary Trefethern; second, Eliza Whidden. Lived at Portsmouth. He died Jan. 19, 1891. Children:

> Clara E., m. Ebenezer Odiorne. M. Eva, *non compos mentis.* Hanson W., m. March 7, 1886, Lizzie, dau. of John Hunt Foss.

25. EBEN LEAVITT SEAVEY, son of Joseph (12), born Jan. 28, 1819; married, Dec. 25, 1849, Julia A. Holmes, who was born Jan., 1827. Lived at Rye. He died March 20, 1886. Children:

Everett Charles, b. Nov. 1, 1850; d. Jan. 2, 1862. Mary Charlotte, b. Jan. 4, 1854; m. Oct. 14, 1875, Emmons B. Philbrick; lived at Rye. Albert Storer, b. Jan. 11, 1863; d. July 11, 1864.

26. LYMAN SEAVEY, son of William (16), born Aug. 31, 1802; married, April 4, 1822, Eliza S. Parsons. He died Nov. 8, 1862. Lived at Spinney, Me. Children:

Isaac, b. July, 1822; m. Elizabeth Weeks of Portsmouth; he d. Dec. 3, 1862; lived at Newburyport. Martha, m. first, R. W. Trask; second, James Copeland. Susan, m. Wilson; she killed her child, aged seven years, during a fit of insanity, at Boston. Adeline, d. Otis, lived in California. Amos, d.

27. WILLIAM WARREN SEAVEY, son of William (16), born Nov. 8, 1807; married, March 17, 1835, Hannah M. Jewell of Stratham, who was born March 22, 1809. He died Jan. 3, 1861. Children:

Calivena E., b. Aug. 4, 1836; m. Jan. 27, 1867, Amos P. Brown. Elizabeth S., b. Dec. 13, 1837. William Harrison, b. May 22, 1842; m. Jan., 1875, Annie E. Smith of New Hampton; she d. Feb. 10, 1904. Lived at Rye.

28. HARRISON SEAVEY, son of William (16), born March 17, 1822; married, May 21, 1854, Martha J. Webster. He died Oct. 8, 1858. Children:

William J., b. Jan. 31, 1856. Lizzie A., b. Oct. 25, 1858.

29. WOODBURY SEAVEY, son of John Langdon (18), born June 10, 1815; married, Feb. 1, 1839, Martha, daughter of Joseph Philbrick, Jr. Lived at Rye and Portsmouth. Children:

Angenette, b. June 23, 1840; m. Joseph Barnard. John Langdon, b. Sept. 21, 1841; m. 1875, Frances Goodall; lived at Greenland. Sarah Elizabeth, b. Jan. 10, 1844; m. Sept. 12, 1871, James N. Tarlton, Jr.

30. ALFRED V. SEAVEY, son of Joseph Whidden (22), born July 31, 1836; married, first, Jan. 31, 1861, Charlotte

A. Garland; second, Feb. 17, 1870, Mary A. Drake; third, May, 1877, Clara Drake. She died Jan. 26, 1903. Children:

Albert W., b. July 10, 1862; m. Jan. 6, 1886, Flora Philbrick; he d. Aug. 9, 1891. Charlotte Ann, b. Feb. 22, 1869; unm.

31. IRVING J. SEAVEY, son of Joseph Whidden (22), born 1852; married, Nov. 24, 1872, Sarah O. Drake. He died Jan. 4, 1896. Children:

33. Everett H., b. Sept. 6, 1875; m. April 21, 1897, Lizzie H. Bebee. Joseph Oren, b. June 6, 1871.

32. JAMES E. SEAVEY, son of Edward (23), married, June 13, 1869, Charlotte Foss. He died Aug. 12, 1873. Child:

Ella May, b. May, 1873; m. 1902, Fred L. Pancoast, and had Winnifred, b. May, 1903.

33. EVERETT H. SEAVEY, son of Irving J. (31), born Sept. 6, 1875; married, April 21, 1897, Lizzie Bebee. Child:

Irvin G., b. Jan. 5, 1898.

34. GEORGE H. SEAVEY, son of Edward (23), married, Dec. 24, 1871, Sarah A. Moulton. He died. Child:

Edward E., b. Feb. 24, 1874; m. April 30, 1898, Maud E. Wiggin, and had a dau. born July 11, 1903.

1. SAMUEL SEAVEY, son of ———; married Abigail ———. Children:

2. Ithamar, b. Jan. 27, 1712.
3. Samuel, b. May 18, 1714. Sarah, b. Nov. 20, 1716.
4. Henry, b. April 23, 1719. Mary, b. April 25, 1721. Abigail, b. Feb. 25, 1723. Mehitable, b. Oct. 21, 1729; m. Jan. 6, 1745, Joshua Atwood of Bradford, or Jan. 4, 1753, Edward Blue.
5. Jonathan, b. Feb. 2, 1732. Moses, b. Jan. 30, 1735; d. Sept. 4, 1830.

2. ITHAMAR SEAVEY, son of Samuel (1), born Jan. 27, 1712; married Mary ———. Children:

Mary, b. Dec. 25, 1734. Elizabeth, b. June 10, 1737.

3. SAMUEL SEAVEY, JR., son of Samuel (1), born May 18, 1714; married ———. Children:

534 HISTORY OF RYE.

Deborah, bapt. Jan. 1, 1738. Hannah, b. 1747. Isaac, b. 1749. Margaret, b. 1750. Isaac, b. 1752. William, b. Jan. 9, 1754. Sarah, b. 1756. Ruth, b. 1766. Henry Dow, b. 1773. Benjamin, b. 1778.

4. HENRY SEAVEY, son of Samuel (1), born April 23, 1719; married, Sept. 15, 1740, Mary Kingman. Children:
John, bapt. 1741. Elijah, b. 1742. Ruth, b. 1742. Hannah, b. 1750.

5. JONATHAN SEAVEY, perhaps son of Samuel (1), born Feb. 2, 1732; married Stevens. Lived in Greenland; moved to Bartlett. Children:
Comfort, b. 1756; m. Ellen Tasker.
6. Jonathan, b. 1758. Levi, b. 1760. Joseph. Simon, m. Polly Randall of Conway.

6. JONATHAN SEAVEY, son of Jonathan (5), born 1758; married Priscilla Philbrick of Greenland. Children:
Ellen, m. David Blake of Hampton. Deborah, d.
7. Jonathan, m. Sally Seavey (his cousin). George. Simon, m. Betsey Handly; lived at Conway.

7. JONATHAN SEAVEY, son of Jonathan (6), married Sally Seavey (his cousin). Children:
Jonathan. Mary. Caroline. Elizabeth. Carlton. Edwin. Charles. Ithamar.

1. HENRY J. SEAVEY, son of ———, married Smith. He lived between David Remick's and Wallis' Four Corners, East Rye. Was under Captain Joseph Parsons at Newcastle; afterwards went privateeering. Went to Epsom; removed to Rye; died in 1803. Children:
2. Joseph, bapt. Oct. 7, 1744. Ruth, b. 1744. Hannah, bapt. May 20, 1750; m. John Rand, son of Joshua. James, b. 1754; m. Patience Berry; he d. April 1, 1829.

2. JOSEPH SEAVEY, son of Henry J. (1), baptized Oct. 7, 1744; married Frances Locke of Epsom. Children:
Abraham. Frances. Ebenezar. Jeremiah. Hannah.

1. WILLIAM SEAVEY, son of ———, married, July 23, 1752, Ruth Moses. Lived at Rye, near the Captain Elvin Rand farm. Children:

Hannah, b. May 20, 1753; m. June 4, 1772, John Rand. Martha, b. Dec. 15, 1754; m. Sept. 29, 1774, James Locke. Ruth, b. May 30, 1756; m. Joshua Rand. Mehitable, b. Feb. 12, 1758; m. Samuel Libby. Aaron, b. Aug., 1759. William, b. June 14, 1761.
2. Daniel, b. May 1, 1763. Moses, b. March 31, 1765; lived at Chichesester. Mark, b. Dec. 7, 1766; lived at Chichester. Shadrach, b. Dec. 24, 1769; lived at Chichester. Simon, b. May 17, 1772; lived at Chichester.

2. DANIEL SEAVEY, son of William (1), born May 1, 1763; married, Dec. 5, 1783, Rachel Rand. Children:

Aaron, bapt. May 22, 1785. Sally, b. July 8, 1787. William, b. Oct. 10, 1790. Lucy Wainwright, b. Jan. 4, 1797. Mehitable, b. Feb. 14, 1802.

1. SAMUEL SEAVEY, son of ———, married ———. Lived on Samuel P. Garland's farm, now owned by Clarence Goss. Children:

2. Isaac. Sarah.

2. ISAAC SEAVEY, son of Samuel (1), married, April 6, 1785, Abigail Gardiner of Portsmouth. Child:

Joseph Mason, b. Aug. 14, 1785.

JOSEPH SEAVEY, son of ———, married Hannah ———. Children:

Joanna, b. Aug. 21, 1712. Hannah, b. June 5, 1713. Joseph. Henry. Sarah.

HENRY SEAVEY, son of ———, married, first, Mary ———; second, Abigail ———. Children:

Elijah, b. Aug. 15, 1716. Ruth, b. Oct. 11, 1735. Caroline, b. Oct. 21, 1741. James, b. March 1, 1743; m. Abigail ———.

SAMUEL SEAVEY, son of ———; married Mary ———. Child:

Mary, b. Dec. 23, 1734.

HENRY SEAVEY, JR., son of ———; married Elizabeth Fuller. Children:

Joseph, bapt. 1744; d. Joseph, b. 1746. Catherine. Olive, b. 1748.

JAMES SEAVEY, son of ———, married Abigail Pickering. Child:

James, b. March 1, 1743.

JOSEPH SEAVEY, son of ———, married, Nov. 22, 1744, Sarah Scott. Child:
   Sarah, b. 1745.

SOLOMON SEAVEY, son of ———, married, March 30, 1758, Fallen. Children:
   Joseph, bapt. 1759. Daughter, b. 1762.

JOSEPH SEAVEY, son of ———, married, first, Dec. 24, 1769, Sarah Locke; second, Oct. 2, 1771, Susannah Kennison. Children:
   Joseph, bapt. 1770. Mary, b. 1776. Samuel, b. 1779. Abigail, b. 1782. Sally, b. Aug. 13, 1786. Joseph, b. July 6, 1788. William, b. Oct. 19, 1791.

NOAH SEAVEY, son of ———, married, May 6, 1763, Temperance Rand. Lived on Gomorrah road, Portsmouth. Children:
   John, b. 1764. Ruth, b. 1766; m. first, Mace; second, John Nelson. Temperance, b. 1768; unm., had child, Nancy, who lived at Greenland. Sarah, b. 1771. Thomas, b. 1778. Noah. Molly, m. Levi Mace of the Isles of Shoals.

ELIJAH SEAVEY, son of ———, married, Sept. 4, 1764, Sarah Berry. Lived at Barrington. Children:
   Phudesy (Fredrick), b. June 1, 1765. Olly (Olive), b. Aug. 28, 1768.

WILLIAM SEAVEY, son of Henry, born Aug. 3, 1761; married, May 17, 1780, Dolly Foss, daughter of Ichabod Foss. Lived at Barrington. Children:
   Isaac, b. Dec. 10, 1780. John, b. Oct. 26, 1782. Samuel, b. Oct. 15, 1784. Elijah, b. March 1, 1787. William, b. Jan. 25, 1790. Lucy, b. Jan. 1, 1792; d. April 22, 1807. Henry, b. Aug. 3, 1794. Ichabod, b. Nov. 29, 1796. Sally, b. Nov. 28, 1799.

JOSEPH SEAVEY, son of ———, married ———. Children:
   Sally, bapt. Aug. 13, 1786. Joseph, b. July 6, 1788. William, b. Oct. 9, 1791.

BENJAMIN SEAVEY, son of ———, married ———. Children:
   Sarah, m. Samuel Marden. Moses, m. Huldah Locke. Hepzibah, m. Charles Fay or Foye. Hannah, m. Dixon; lived at Kittery. Mary.

WINTHROP SEAVEY married ———. Lived in Illinois. Child:
  Gideon W., attorney, Fort Wayne, Ind.

MOSES SEAVEY, son of Benjamin, married Huldah Locke. Removed to Deerfield. Lived at the foot of the hill on Washington avenue, where John Philbrick resided. He conveyed to Amos Seavey, in 1762, all his share of his late father's right in the common land. Children:
  Samuel, b. 1762. Huldah, b. 1763. Levi, b. 1766; m. Tilton. Moses, b. 1767; m. Ruth Tarlton of Newcastle. Abigail, b. 1770. Elijah, b. 1774.

SHANNON.

THOMAS SHANNON married, May 31, 1753, Ann Rand. Lived at Chester. Children:
  Bettie, b. Sept. 18, 1753. William, b. Aug. 25, 1755. John, b. Aug. 16, 1757. Thomas, b. 1759. Samuel, b. 1762.

SHAPLEY.

1. HENRY SHAPLEY, married Elizabeth Saunders. Lived at Gosport. Children:
2. Henry Carter, b. 1743 (?). Reuben, m. first, Blaisdell; second, Ann Clark; lived at Portsmouth. John, m. Leighton.
3. James. Robert, lost at sea. Sarah, m. first, Sept. 22, 1776, John Mace; second, Daniel Goss. Betsy, m. first, Benjamin Randall; second, William Pierce. Mary, m. John Robinson; lived at the the Isles of Shoals. Benjamin, m. Nancy Blaisdell.
4. Edward.

2. HENRY CARTER SHAPLEY, son of Henry (1), born 1743 (?); married, first, Judith Randall; second, Dorcas Saunders; third, Sally Caswell. He died March 17, 1830. Served as corporal under Captain J. Parsons in the Revolutionary War. Children by first wife:
  Betsey, b. (before m.) 1766; m. July 4, 1788, Robert Poor of Portsmouth; lived at Rye.
5. Henry J., b. 1767.
  Children by second wife:
  Reuben, b. 1774; m. Feb. 19, 1796, Mary Saunders. Judith. Sally.

Children by third wife:
George W. (b. before m.); m. Ann Gray.
6. Robert, b. Feb., 1812.

3. JAMES SHAPLEY, son of Henry (1), married Mercy Saunders. Lived at Gosport and Rye. Children:
Sally, b. Oct. 12, 1791; d. unm. Dec. 4, 1875; lived down Beach road. Henry, lost in privateer *Portsmouth.*
7. Judith, b. 1796. Betsey, b. 1803; d. Sept. 20, 1882, at county house.
8. James, b. 1807. Betsey, bapt. Jan. 19, 1790. Benjamin, bapt. Jan. 19, 1790.

4. EDWARD SHAPLEY, son of Henry (1), married Hepzibah Rand. Children:
Sally, d. unm. at the Isles of Shoals, aged 18 years. James, cast away in a whaling vessel. Robert, enlisted in the navy as a marine; ordered to the Lakes and never heard from.

5. HENRY J. SHAPLEY, son of Henry Carter (2), born 1767; married Mary Berry. Lived at Rye. Children:
9. Samuel, b. Jan. 16, 1791. Dorcas Pitman, b. Nov. 17, 1792; m. Benjamin Foss. Jotham Berry, b. 1794; m. Chalcedonia ———.
10. Henry, b. 1797. Eliza, b. June 1, 1799; m. Richard Foss.
11. Reuben, b. Aug., 1806.

6. ROBERT SHAPLEY, son of Henry Carter (2), born Feb., 1812; married, Nov. 1, 1854, Ann Knowland. Children:
Frances Ann, b. May 14, 1853 (b. before m.). William Henry, b. Feb. 3, 1856. James Albert, b. June 1, 1858. John Palmer, b. June 12, 1860. Olive Jane, b. Nov. 11, 1862. A girl, b. 1864. Sarah Caroline, b. 1865. George Washington, b. Jan. 18, 1867.

7. JUDITH SHAPLEY, daughter of James (3), born 1796. Children:
Sarah Ann, b. Nov., 1822. James Henry Locke, b. May 29, 1830; m. Anna Trefethern of Kittery.

8. JAMES SHAPLEY, son of James (3), born 1807; married, Oct. 19, 1820, Dorothy Randall. Children:
Reuben, b. Nov. 12, 1824; d. May 11, 1846. George, b. Sept. 6, 1822; drowned Oct. 4, 1851, in a gale while fishing in the bay.

9. SAMUEL SHAPLEY, son of Henry J. (5), born Jan. 16, 1791; married, April 17, 1817, Rachel Foss. He died Feb.

17, 1862. Served in the War of 1812 under Captain E. Philbrick. Children:

Joshua, b. Aug. 2, 1817; d. Aug. 6, 1817. Samuel B., b. Oct. 24, 1821; m. Harriet T. Gilman; lived at Plaistow. Sarah A., b. Nov. 23, 1824; m. first, John Berry; second, John Grogan, who d. Sept., 1893, at Stoneham, Mass.

12. William H., b. June 3, 1831.

10. HENRY SHAPLEY, son of Henry J. (5), born 1797; married Abigail Parker. Children:

Henry, m. Emeline Jones. David, m. Sarah F. Coleman. Harriet E., m. John Keyes. Jotham. Mary Jane, m. John Clark.

11. DEACON REUBEN SHAPLEY, son of Henry J. (5), born Aug., 1806; married, April 21, 1825, Lovina Robinson. Lived at Rye. He died June 10, 1868. She died June 27, 1880. Children:

13. Reuel G., b. Oct. 23, 1825. Jotham, b. Dec., 1830; d. Sept. 1, 1850, at Rye. Emily, b. Oct. 10, 1833; m. Daniel Dalton; lived at Rye. Robert P., b. May 10, 1836; d. June 2, 1865, in War 1861-'65, at Darnstown, Md. John, b. June, 1838; d. Sept., 1864; shot at Wainsborough, Va., in Civil War. Semira, b. Dec., 1842; d. June 9, 1869; thrown from a wagon and killed.

12. WILLIAM H. SHAPLEY, son of Samuel (9), born June 3, 1831; married, first, Sarah J. Hill; second, Margaret Thompson. Children by first wife:

James Hill. Abby Jane, b. May 27, 1854.

Children by second wife:

Mary R., b. April 4, 1858. Harriet E., b. June 8, 1861.

13. REUEL G. SHAPLEY, son of Reuben (11), born Oct. 23, 1825; married, first, Dec. 22, 1872, Abby A. Rand, who died Oct. 2, 1881; second, Maria Haines of Greenland. Children by first wife:

Nora S., b. March 26, 1874. Abby Ruth, b. Oct. 1, 1881.

SHEAFE.

SAMUEL SHEAFE of Canebrook, England.

THOMAS SHEAFE married Marion ———, who died, 1383, in England.

EDMUND SHEAFE, born 1605; married Elizabeth Cotton. Children:
Rebecca. Elizabeth. Sampson, b. 1650.

JACOB SHEAFE married, 1625, Margaret Webb, who died in 1698. Children:
Jacob, d. Dec. 26, 1760. Two children, burned in their house at Boston.

JACOB SHEAFE married ———. Children:
Elizabeth, b. 1644; m. Robert Gibbs. Mehitable, b. 1656; m. 1677, Sampson Sheafe, son of Edmund (?).

1. SAMPSON SHEAFE, came from Boston to Newcastle in 1675 and died in Boston, aged 76 years. Children:
2. Jacob, b. 1677; m. Mary ———. Sampson, b. 1681.

2. JACOB SHEAFE, son of Sampson (1), born 1677; married Mary ———. Children:
Abigail. Mary, b. 1718; m. Sampson Sheafe in Boston. Elizabeth. Margaret.

1. SAMPSON SHEAFE, born 1611; married Sarah Walton of Newcastle. Children:
Sampson, b. 1712.
2. Jacob, b. Oct. 21, 1715. Henry. Samuel. Sarah. Mehitable. Elizabeth.

2. JACOB SHEAFE, son of Sampson (1), born Oct. 21, 1715; married, July 21, 1740, Hannah Seavey, who died in 1773, aged 54 years. Children:
Matthew, b. Aug. 13, 1741; a shipmaster. Abigail, b. April 26, 1744; m. Judge John Pickering; she d. Dec. 10, 1805. Jacob, b. Sept. 6, 1745. Sarah, b. Aug. 1, 1748; m. John Marsh; he d. 1777; she d. June 8, 1839. Hannah, b. April 24, 1750; m. first, Hugh Emerson; second, Hart; she d. Sept. 1, 1845. Thomas, b. April 16, 1752; d. Sept. 4, 1831. Mary, b. Nov. 22, 1753; m. 1774, Joseph Williard; she d. March 6, 1826. James, b. Nov. 16, 1755; d. Dec. 25, 1829. William, b. Sept. 11, 1758; d. March, 1839. Mehitable, b. April 12, 1760; m. Eben Smith of Durham; she d. Sept. 4, 1843. John, b. July 13, 1762; d. Jan. 24, 1812.

SHERBURNE.

HENRY SHERBURNE married Rebecah Gibbon; died 1681. Child:

Elizabeth, m. Capt. Samuel Banfield.

ANDREW SHERBURNE, born May 22, 1738; married Susannah Knight, who was born March 6, 1741. Lived at Portsmouth. Children:

Thomas, b. June 15, 1761. Martha, b. July 7, 1762; d. March 14, 1763. Martha, b. March 7, 1764. Andrew, b. Sept. 30, 1765. Samuel, b. May 16, 1767. Elizabeth, b. Nov. 20, 1768.

1. HENRY SHERBURNE married Sarah Warner. Children:

Samuel, m. Warner.
2. Jonathan. Henry, unm. Nathaniel, m. Polly Cotton. Edward. John.

2. JONATHAN SHERBURNE, son of Henry (1), married, March 4, 1787, Nancy Perkins, who was born 1767, and died April 4, 1811. Lived at Portsmouth. Children:

Anna. Jonathan, b. March, 1790. Adeline, b. Feb. 23, 1792; d. Oct. 26, 1872, at the insane asylum, Concord, aged 75 years. Edward, b. 1796; drowned on Lisbon bar, aged 18 years. James Henry, b. 1803; d. March 7, 1810.

SHORTRIDGE.

RICHARD SHORTRIDGE married, 1662, Esther, daughter of Godfrey Dearborn of Hampton. Children:

Richard. Robert. Ann, m. Nov. 18, 1686, George Wallis of Sandy Beach.

SHUTE.

JAMES SHUTE married ———. He owned a field opposite Gilman Berry's. Child:

Sarah, bapt. 1737.

SLEEPER.

1. AARON SLEEPER, married ———. Lived at Kingston. Children:

2. Benjamin. Thomas. John. Aaron. Moses. Joseph.

2. BENJAMIN SLEEPER, son of Aaron (1), married Abigail Coffin. He died (?), and she married, second, Richard Jenness. Children:

    Tristram Coffin, b. 1744; m. Dec. 18, 1766, Ruth Tarlton. Thomas, b. Sept., 1767; m. Sally Brown.
3. Eliphalet, b. Nov. 19, 1769. Mary, b. Dec. 13, 1771; m. David Wedgewood.
4. William, b. April 28, 1775. Benjamin, b. April 28, 1778; m. Marion Clough.

3. ELIPHALET SLEEPER, son of Benjamin (2), born Nov. 19, 1769; married, March 31, 1800, Molly Jenness. Lived at Rye. Cordwainer. He died March 17, 1843. Children:

    Nancy, b. 1790; m. Simon Jenness, an adopted child.
5. Richard Jenness, b. July 17, 1801. Sally J., b. July 21, 1808; m. Dec. 24, 1826, Zachariah Chickering.

4. WILLIAM SLEEPER, son of Eliphalet (3), born April 28, 1775; married Sally Smith of Exeter, who was born June, 1775, at Exeter. Lived at Rye. Children:

    Sarah Ann, b. Oct., 1804; m. Abraham Nudd. Theophilus William, b. 1807; m. Sarah Boardman. Oliver, b. 1810.
6. Charles Benjamin.

5. RICHARD JENNESS SLEEPER, son of Eliphalet (3), born July 17, 1801; married, June 6, 1829, Emily Garland, who was born Sept. 4, 1808. Lived at Rye. Children:

    Edward D., b. Oct. 7, 1829; d. Feb. 16, 1832.
7. Martin V., b. June 22, 1835.

6. CHARLES BENJAMIN SLEEPER, son of William (4), married Mary Marston, who died Oct. 19, 1898. He died Sept. 23, 1893. Lived at Rye. Children:

    Charles Everett, b. May 23, 1845. Amanda, b. April 1, 1848; d. Jan. 30, 1893. Hattie F., b. March 12, 1855.

7. MARTIN V. SLEEPER, son of Richard Jenness (5), born June 22, 1835; married Martha J. Jenness. Children:

    Jane. Frank, m. Alice Moulton; had Walter, b. Dec. 29, 1882. Elizabeth. Annie L., b. Sept. 23, 1871.

THOMAS SLEEPER married, first, 1798, Sally Berry; second, 1815, Mehitable Crockett. Lived at Rye in the lane near Alfred Seavey's, and at Newington. Mariner. Children:

Ruth Tarlton, bapt. Nov. 2, 1800; unm. Nabby, b. 1803; d. April, 1871, at North Hampton. Mary, b. 1807; m. Jonathan Cotton of North Hampton; she d. April, 1880. Daniel, b. March, 1816; m. Bean.

SMART.

1. SAMUEL G. SMART, married, April 9, 1866, Mary Watson Garland, daughter of Edward L. Children:

2. Fred L., b. Nov. 27, 1866. Sophia J., b. May 20, 1871; m. Elmer Caswell. Emma L., m. Alva Locke; she d. July 5, 1893.

2. FRED L. SMART, son of Samuel G. (1), born Nov. 27, 1866; married, Dec. 28, 1885, Martha A. Mace. Children:

Wilmot Manning, b. June 23, 1888. Maurice H., b. Oct. 12, 1891. Emma L., b. Sept. 20, 1894.

SMITH.

1. DAVID SMITH, perhaps son of Israel and Sarah of Hampton, married Sarah ———. Lived near David Marden's at Rye. His sister Mary married Thomas Marden of "Long Lane." Children:

Israel, b. Oct. 1, 1728. Deborah, b. June 18, 1730. Hannah, b. 1736. Mary, b. Sept. 25, 1738; m. Sept. 22, 1757, Ephraim Rand; he d. of smallpox in the Revolution and she m., second, Joseph Hall.
2. David, b. Jan. 18, 1741. Sarah, b. 1742. Jonathan, b. 1745. Joanna. Israel.
3. Samuel (?).

2. DAVID SMITH, son of David (1), born Jan. 18, 1741; married Mary Marden. Children:

Molly, b. 1769; m. Stephen Marden. Sally, b. 1771; m. Joses Philbrick.

3. SAMUEL SMITH, perhaps son of David (1), married, March, 1786, Elizabeth Hall, who died Sept. 11, 1847, aged 87 years. He died Jan. 4, 1824, aged 72 years. Children:

William, b. Oct. 4, 1788; m. Margaret Felear. Esther, b. Dec., 1789; m. Jeremiah Sanborn. John, b. March 2, 1791; m. Nancy Sanborn; lived at Hampton Falls and Seabrook. Betsey, b. May 23, 1795; m. Jan. 22, 1817, Samuel B. Randall. Joseph, b. July 28, 1797; d. Jan. 20, 1816, aged 17 years.

SPEAR.

1. SAMUEL B. SPEAR, born Nov. 7, 1823; married Adeline Cook, who died Jan. 12, 1892. He died April 27, 1900. Painter by trade. Children:

  2. Charles W., b. June 17, 1856. Addie E., b. May 25, 1857; m. Dec. 21, 1876, James W. Barton.

2. CHARLES W. SPEAR, son of Samuel B. (1), born June 17, 1856; married, first, June 13, 1879, Lizzie Remick, who died Nov. 10, 1886; second, Dec. 17, 1889, Mary L. Marden. Children:

  Elva, b. June 12, 1880. Mary Frances, b. Jan., 1884; d. March 20, 1886.

SQUIRE.

JOHN SQUIRE married Eliza Burnell. Electrician. Children:

  Alice, b. May 13, 1887. Frances, b. April 10, 1889.

SWENSON.

ANDERS SWENSON married Louise Swenson of Sweden. Children:

  Carl A., b. Sept. 31, 1872; m. Aug. 19, 1900, Carrie W. Lewis. Emilie, b. May 31, 1877. Agnes, b. April 10, 1883. Inez, b. April 23, 1890.

TARLTON.

Two brothers Tarlton came from Liverpool, Eng. One landed in the Carolinas, the other, Elias, settled at or near Little Harbor, or Newcastle. He had a son Elias.

1. ELIAS TARLTON served his time at Strawberry Bank (Portsmouth), and at that time knew every person in the place. He married Rendall. Children:

  Richard.
2. Elias.

GENEALOGY. 545

2. ELIAS TARLTON, son of Elias (1), married Hannah Ackerman. Children:
    Elias. Benjamin. John, m. Yeaton.
3. Joseph. Stedman. William. James.

3. JOSEPH TARLTON, son of Elias Tarlton, married, Dec. 30, 1784, Comfort Cotton. Children:
    Nathaniel. Elias, b. 1803; d. unm. 1852. Stephen, m. Sarah A. Hartshorn. Betsey, m. Stephen Rand. Samuel, b. 1795; m. Abigail Brown; d. 1877. Comfort, m. first, Dorr; second, Chamberlain. Hannah, m. Asa Reynolds.

JOSEPH TARLTON married, Jan. 10, 1762, Mary Goss. She married, second, Nat Jenness. He was lost privateering. Child:
    A girl, m. Stephen Rand.

THOMAS.

WILLIAM THOMAS (probably son of James and Alice of Nottingham, baptized May 24, 1741), married, Nov. 24, 1768, Mary Saunders. She married, second, Abraham Mathes. Children:
    James, b. 1764. William, b. 1766; lost privateering in Revolutionary War; captured by British. John Saunders, b. 1768. Thomas, d. young.

JAMES THOMAS married, 1809, Lois Clarke. Children:
    Ann L., b. June 28, 1811; m. Sept. 13, 1860, John K. Walker; lived at Portsmouth; had a child, Elbridge Thomas. Sally J., b. Aug., 1813; m. John O. Rand; had a child, Manning C.; she d. Sept. 22, 1873. Mary Elizabeth, b. Sept., 1825; m. Sept. 24, 1845, George E. Marden of Portsmouth.

ELBRIDGE A. THOMAS married, Dec. 25, 1865, Ellen M. Picot. Children:
    Ann Louise, b. Jan. 15, 1866. George Augustus, b. May, 1869.

TIBBETTS.

JACOB TIBBETTS married Judith Berry. Lived at Ragged Neck. Children:
    Mary, b. 1767. Samuel, b. 1771. Mary, b. 1773. Thomas, b. 1776. Edward Rendall, b. 1778.

TOWLE.

It is said the Towles came from Ireland.

1. JONATHAN TOWLE, son of Joseph and Mehetable (Hobbs) Towle of Hampton, married Anna Norton. Children:
   2. Jonathan, b. July 4, 1729.
   3. Levi, b. Sept. 22, 1731. Joseph, b. March 21, 1733.
   4. Samuel, b. Nov. 5, 1735.
   5. James, b. Oct. 28, 1737. Anna, b. March 28, 1741; m. Dec. 2, 1760, Joseph Philbrick.
   6. Nathan, b. May 19, 1745.

2. JONATHAN TOWLE, son of Jonathan (1), born July 4, 1729; married Elizabeth Jenness. Lived where Lemuel Bunker resided. Children:
   7. Simon, b. 1753. Mary, b. 1755; m. Jan. 6, 1774, James Hobbs.
   8. Levi, b. 1757. Anna, b. 1759; m. May 29, 1777, Nathaniel Marden. Hannah, b. 1762; m. Sept. 17, 1780, William Yeaton. Elizabeth, b. 1764; d. unm. 1835.
   9. Joseph, b. 1766.
   10. Benjamin, b. 1769. Sally, b. 1776; m. Lemuel Bunker.

3. LEVI TOWLE, son of Jonathan (1), born Sept. 22, 1731; married, Oct. 11, 1853, Ruth Marden. Children:
   Jonathan, b. 1754 (?). Sarah, b. 1756. Jeremiah, b. 1758. Joseph, b. 1761. Betty, b. 1763. Anna, b. 1766.

4. SAMUEL TOWLE, son of Jonathan (1), born Nov. 5, 1735; married, first, Aug. 4, 1760, Rachel Elkins; second, Nov. 18, 1762, Esther Johnson. Children by second wife:
   Olly, b. 1763; m. Ham. Sarah, b. 1765. Molly, b. 1767. Job, b. 1770. Esther, b. 1772. Dolly, b. 1774. Nabby, b. 1778.

5. JAMES TOWLE, son of Jonathan (1), born Oct. 28, 1737; married ———. Children:
   James. John.

6. NATHAN TOWLE, son of Jonathan (1), born May 19, 1745; married ———. Children:
   Lucy, b. 1767. Nathan, b. 1771. Jonathan, b. 1774.

7. SIMON TOWLE, son of Jonathan (2), born 1753; married Elizabeth Marden. Children:

Benjamin Marden, b. 1782; m. Betsey Sanborn. Simon, m. Hannah Yeaton. Perna, unm.

8. LEVI TOWLE, son of Jonathan (2), born 1757; married, first, Feb. 7, 1782, Mary Locke; second, Lucy Hobbs; third, Perna Judkins. Children by first wife:

Dearborn, b. 1783; m. Rhoda Harvey.

Children by second wife:

L. Gordon, b. 1786; m. Mary French. Perna, b. 1788; m. John Wilson. Joseph, b. 1790; m. Nancy Rundlett. Gardiner G., b. March 1791; m. first, Elizabeth Fogg; second, Hannah Ely.

Child by third wife:

Sally, b. 1798; m. first, James Rundlett; second, Abraham Blake.

9. JOSEPH TOWLE, son of Jonathan (2), born 1766; married, Dec. 25, 1781, Sally Wallis. Children:

Hannah, m. Jonathan Yeaton. Susan, m. Samuel Goss. Sally, m. Hersey.

10. BENJAMIN TOWLE, son of Jonathan (2), born 1769; married Betsey Woods. Lived at Epsom. Children:

James, m. Sally Lake. Jonathan, m. Emery. Lemuel, m. Ann Prescott. Maria, m. Langley. Elizabeth. Sally, unm. Rhoda, unm. Nancy, m. James Sanborn.

MATTHIAS TOWLE married ———. Children:

Matthias. Samuel.

TREFETHERN, OR TREFERRIN.

The Trefetherns came from Scotland to Newcastle.

1. HENRY TREFETHERN married Mary ———. Child:
2. Robinson, b. 1721.

2. ROBINSON TREFETHERN, son of Henry (1), born 1721; married, Jan. 25, 1748, Abigail Locke "of the Neck." He came from Newcastle, and lived on the Col. Benjamin Garland place at Rye Center, and sold it to him and others in 1756. Children:

Mary, b. April 12, 1748; m. Miller.
3. William, b. June 5, 1751. Robinson, b. March 3, 1753; d. at sea. Abigail, b. April 6, 1755; m. William Morrison. Joseph, b. Aug. 14, 1757; d. Joseph, b. March 5, 1759. Lucretia, b. May 24, 1763. Salome, b. May 1, 1765; m. Samuel, son of Nath. Foss. Margaret, b. May 28, 1767. Henry, b. Aug. 16, 1769; m. Patridge.

3. WILLIAM TREFETHERN, son of Robinson (2), born June 5, 1751; married, Jan. 27, 1774, Elizabeth Tucker. She died Feb. 12, 1837, aged 87 years. He died June 17, 1820. Was a member of Captain Parsons' company in the Revolutionary War. Children:
4. William, b. April 24, 1775. Nathaniel, b. Oct. 27, 1777; d. June 11, 1784. Nabby, b. Dec. 28, 1779; d. June 20, 1784. Betsey, b. Dec. 2, 1782; d. unm., at Barnstead.
5. Nathaniel, b. Feb. 22, 1785.
6. Joseph, b. Aug. 20, 1787. Nancy, b. 1790; m. Samuel Ayers; lived at Barnstead. Polly, b. Aug. 27, 1792; m. George Ramstead. Henry, b. Oct. 5, 1794; m. Mary Brown; he d. Sept. 8, 1828.
7. John Adams, b. July 27, 1799.
8. Sebastian, b. Jan. 27, 1801.

4. CAPT. WILLIAM TREFETHERN, son of William (3), born April 24, 1775; married, first, Jan. 20, 1801, Lydia Berry, who died June 9, 1820, aged 43 years; second, Susannah Piper. He died Oct. 8, 1853. Lived where George Perry resides. Children by first wife:
9. Levi Berry, b. Oct. 21, 1801.
10. Benjamin Bailey, b. Sept. 22, 1805.
11. William, b. March 7, 1810. Sabrina, b. March 6, 1813; m. Daniel Trefethern; she d. Jan. 6, 1842.

Child by second wife:
Hanson Hoit, b. June, 1822; d. Oct. 12, 1853; he lived on the old Trefethern place, where George Perry lived in 1900.

5. NATHANIEL TREFETHERN, son of William (3), born Feb. 22, 1785; married, July 6, 1807, Charlotte Jewell, who was born Sept., 1784. Lived at Rye. He died March 18, 1856. Children:
12. Charles F., b. 1807.
Florence, b. March 17, 1809; m. Ebenezer W. Lang; lived at Rye. Daniel J., b. 1812; m. April 7, 1861, Sabrina Trefethern; he d. June 8, 1841; lived at Rye. Louvia, m. Simon G. Trefethern; lived at Rye.

6. JOSEPH TREFETHERN, son of William (3), born Aug. 20, 1787; married, Jan. 29, 1810, Hannah Berry. Lived at Rye. He died Feb. 10, 1859. Children:
13. Simon Goss, b. March 10, 1810. Mary, b. 1812; m. James Seavey.
14. Joseph Parsons, b. June 12, 1814.

15. John Ichabod, b. June 11, 1816. Levi, b. 1818; m. Martha Moulton, who d. July 15, 1848.
16. Samuel A., b. April 3, 1822.
17. Oliver, b. March 4, 1826. William Henry Jackman, b. 1831; d. May 7, 1838. Emily, m. first, Charles W. Hall; second, Alfred S. Trafton.
18. Supply Foss, b. July 12, 1833. Albert B., b. April 13, 1835, m. Mary Abby Rand; lived at Portsmouth. Sarah E., b. March 24, 1838; m. William I. Holmes.

7. JOHN ADAMS TREFETHERN, son of William (3), born July 27, 1799; married, Nov. 30, 1834, Mary Locke, who died Sept. 30, 1888. Lived at Rye. He died Oct. 4, 1870. Children:

Izette Morris, b. May 31, 1835; m. Feb. 1, 1880, Oren Drake.
19. Dennis Hill, b. Oct. 21, 1837. Martha Semira, b. July 6, 1841; m. first, Woodbury Green; second, Story Gates. John Edwin, b. Dec. 16, 1843; unm.

8. SEBASTIAN J. TREFETHERN, son of William (3), born Jan. 27, 1801; married, Nov., 1835, Eliza Locke, who died Dec. 29, 1854. He died Aug. 18, 1875. Lived at Rye and Kansas. Children:

Alfred M., b. May 7, 1837. Ellen, b. Nov. 20, 1840; m. April 20, 1862, George Perkins. Octavia, b. Nov. 17, 1846; m. May 11, 1864, Dalrymple. Hanson, b. Jan. 17, 1843; d. 1884. David.

9. LEVI BERRY TREFETHERN, son of Capt. William (4), born Oct. 21, 1801; married, first, Locada Locke; second, Harriet Keen. He died Oct. 5, 1858. Children:

Mary J. James Oren. Emily A. Frances L. Lewis W. Charles.

10. BENJAMIN BAILEY TREFETHERN, son of Capt. William (4), born Sept. 22, 1805; married Patience Riggs. Lived at Lynn. He died March 8, 1872. Children:

Anna. Frederick A. Elvina Porter.

11. WILLIAM TREFETHERN, son of Capt. William (4), born March 7, 1810; married, Aug. 24, 1837, Hannah L. Garland. She died Feb. 25, 1899. He died Aug. 11, 1890. Carpenter by trade. Children:

Lydia M., b. Jan. 10, 1839; m. Aug. 24, 1858, John W. Adams. Hannah Josephine, b. Nov. 29, 1844; m. Feb. 19, 1867, John Oliver Locke. She d. June 6, 1875.

12. CHARLES F. TREFETHERN, son of Nathaniel (5), born 1807; married, Jan. 7, 1836, Dorothy Marden. He died Feb. 14, 1896, aged 89 years. Lived at Rye. Children:

Hannah, b. April 7, 1838; m. Eben M. Lang. Jane, b. Aug. 9, 1840; m. April 26, 1862, Levi Hall. Anna, b. Feb. 1, 1843; m. Horace Pickering. Julia, b. Dec. 20, 1846; m. Gilman D. Trefethern.
20. Charles Elvin, b. Oct. 18, 1849. Flora Ida, b. March 2, 1852; m. first, Dec. 25, 1870, Shadrach Dunbrach; second, Jenness. Nellie G., b. Nov. 28, 1855; m. July 19, 1879, George F. Haynes of Exeter. Clara, b. Dec. 23, 1858.

13. SIMON GOSS TREFETHERN, son of Joseph (6), born March 10, 1810; married, April 1, 1833, Louisa Trefethern. She died March 5, 1865. He died Sept. 8, 1861. Lived at Rye. Children:

21. Horace L., b. Sept. 4, 1834. Walter A., b. May 5, 1836; d. March 2, 1850, of fits. Henry H., b. Jan. 6, 1838; d. June 11, 1853. Daniel J., b. Jan. 3, 1840, *non compos mentis*. Sabrina E., b. April 7, 1843, m. April 7, 1861, Daniel C. Webster. Adeline, b. April 9, 1845; m. 1867, Ellsworth E. Clemens. Thaddeus R., b. June 26, 1846; d. March 20, 1895, *non compos mentis;* had fits. Charlotte H., b. April 8, 1849; m. Oliver Clark. Laura F., b. March 13, 1855; m. Morris Drake.

14. JOSEPH PARSONS TREFETHERN, son of Joseph (6), born June 12, 1814; married, April 6, 1837, Olivia B. Marden. She died April 14, 1889. He died Dec. 24, 1889. Children:

22. George Leroy, b. Oct. 13, 1841. Mary Salter, b. March 3, 1843; m. Dec. 6, 1863, Henry S. Rand.
23. Gilman D., b. Sept. 10, 1845.

15. JOHN ICHABOD TREFETHERN, son of Joseph (6), born June 11, 1816; married, first, Nov. 1, 1840, Elizabeth Mason; second, 1864, Adna Nutter. Children:

Frank, b. Nov. 1, 1842; d. in the army. Mary O., b. Feb., 1845; m. Dec. 6, 1863, Henry S. Rand. Josephine and Abby Grace (twins), Josephine m. Benjamin Hart; Abby Grace m. C. H. Lefavor. Hope G., b. 1853. Maud.

16. SAMUEL A. TREFETHERN, son of Joseph (6), born April 3, 1822; married, July, 1846, Eliza Ann Marden. She died May 19, 1903, aged 78 years. Children:

Oliver Winslow, b. Jan. 6, 1847; m. Oct. 27, 1874, Alvedea H. Clough. Frank Pierce, b. June 12, 1850; d. Aug., 1853. Samuel H., b. June 29, 1853; d. Dec. 22, 1873; killed by falling from a building in Boston. Joseph, b. June 11, 1849; d. Aug. 4, 1855. Martin Percy, b. Dec. 25, 1857. Jennie, b. June 26, 1868.

17. OLIVER TREFETHERN, son of Joseph (6), born March 4, 1826; married Sarah Moulton. She died Sept. 13, 1875. Children:

24. Albert B. Grace. Gertrude.

18. SUPPLY FOSS TREFETHERN, son of Joseph (6), married, June 18, 1862, Mary Emily Clark. Lived at Rye. She died June 16, 1902. Children:

Lizzie Wallis, b. Jan. 13, 1863. Edith Mabel, b. July 8, 1872; m. June 12, 1894, Irvin Rand.

19. DENNIS HILL TREFETHERN, son of John Adams (7), born Oct. 21, 1837; married, Dec. 17, 1868, widow Ella M. Maxwell. Lived at Portsmouth. Children:

Austin, b. Jan. 28, 1872; m. April 7, 1894, Mary L. Gilbert. Nellie, b. Oct. 6, 1877; m. Nov. 28, 1900, George R. Newick.

20. CHARLES ELVIN TREFETHERN, son of Charles F. (12), born Oct. 18, 1849; married, Sept. 24, 1877, Martha Ellen Balch. Children:

Susie E., b. July 1, 1878; d. Jan. 6, 1880. Austin Wallace, b. Sept. 5, 1880. George Chester, b. Feb. 15, 1882. Arthur Elwyn, b. April 24, 1883. Elmer Balch, b. July 10, 1885. Willie Marshal, b. Dec. 23, 1886. Julia Alice, b. Feb. 5, 1888. Raymond Hall, b. Aug. 9, 1889. Marcie Elizabeth, b. April 19, 1891. Ruth Mable, b. May 11, 1893.

21. HORACE L. TREFETHERN, son of Simon Goss (13), born Sept. 4, 1834; married, Oct. 1, 1856, Ann M. Clark. Lived at Rye. Children:

25. Hermon O., b. Jan. 6, 1862. Annie, b. Jan. 24, 1864; m. Samuel Odiorne. Frank J., b. 1873; m. July 5, 1899, Maggie A. Burchell.

22. GEORGE LEROY TREFETHERN, son of Joseph Parsons (14), born Oct. 13, 1841; married, Oct. 16, 1860, Rozette Webster. Children:

Freddy Irving, b. March 18, 1862. Mary Elvira, b. Nov. 29, 1863;
d. Aug. 20, 1865. Mary Gilman, b. April 16, 1866; m. Jan. 29,
1883, William Tucker. Emma B., b. Jan. 12, 1868; m. May 9,
1889, Joseph Freeman. Hattie O., b. July 9, 1871. Sarah P., b.
June 9, 1875.

23. GILMAN D. TREFETHERN, son of Joseph Parsons
(14), born Sept. 10, 1845; married Julia Trefethern. Lived
at Rye. Children:
Grace E., b. Sept. 10, 1868. Willard A., b. June 30, 1876; m. June
3, 1900, Bertha W. Abbott. Oliver B., b. Feb. 9, 1878. Louisa R.,
b. Oct. 12, 1880.

24. ALBERT BRACKETT TREFETHERN, son of Oliver (17),
married, first, Emily Seavey; second, Dec. 14, 1864, Mary
Abby Rand. Lived at Portsmouth. Children:
Everett, m. Jan. 2, 1897, Carrie L. Furlough. Frank. Wallis.
Ralph.

25. HERMAN O. TREFETHERN, son of Horace L. (21),
born Jan. 6, 1862; married, Dec. 10, 1891, Annie L. Odiorne. She died May 9, 1900. Children:
A boy, b. April 8, 1897. A girl, b. Oct. 18, 1898.

TUCK, OR TUCKE.

1. REV. JOHN TUCK, son of Deacon John and Bethia
(Hobbs) of Hampton, married Mary Dole. He declined
a call to settle in Chester and devoted himself to labor
among the Isles of Shoals. He was pastor of the church
in Gosport forty-one years, and died in office there. Children:
Love, m. Muchmore; lived in Maine.
2. John.

2. REV. JOHN TUCK, son of Rev. John (1), married,
March 4, 1762, Mary, daughter of Rev. Samuel Parsons.
Children:
Mary, b. March 24, 1763; m. Thomas Rand. John, b. Dec. 27, 1765.
Samuel, b. May 4, 1768; m. Judith Gardiner. Love Muchmore, b.
Sept. 23; m. Simon Drake; "Simon Drake wanted a mate, And
for a duck took Lovey Tuck;" this was a common saying when

they were married, and has been handed down to the present time. Joseph, b. July 27, 1770; went to sea and never heard from. Richard, b. March 22, 1772; went to sea and never heard from. Abigail, b. April 5, 1774; m. Bishop. Thomas.

TUCKER.

1. WILLIAM TUCKER married, April 5, 1721, Mary Archer. Children:

> Mary, b. Feb. 11, 1725. William, b. June 19, 1727. Susannah, b. Aug. 25, 1730.
> 2. Nathaniel, b. Sept. 18, 1732-'33. Elizabeth Esther, b. Dec. 28, 1734. Sarah, b. May 18, 1737. Mary, b. Oct. 25, 1740.

2. NATHANIEL TUCKER, son of William (1), born Sept. 18, 1732-'33; married, Feb. 8, 1753, Elizabeth Hall. He was in the French and Indian war. Children:

> Elizabeth, b. Nov. 19, 1753; m. William Trefethern. Sarah, b. May 31, 1756; m. March 6, 1783, John Foss. Nathaniel, b. Sept. 23, 1758; d. 1807, at sea.
> 3. William, b. Jan. 31, 1761. Richard, b. Nov. 27, 1764; lost or died at sea.
> 4. Joseph, b. Sept. 19, 1773.

3. WILLIAM TUCKER, son of Nathaniel (2), born Jan. 31, 1761; married, March 13, 1787, Olive Saunders. He died Nov. 4, 1816. Children:

> Sally, m. Levi Jenness. Trefenna. William, m. Betsey Saunders. Richard, bapt. March 21, 1790; d. Betsey, m. Feb. 20, 1817, Richard Locke, 3d. Nathaniel. John, bapt. Nov. 23, 1788. Olive, b. Nov. 2, 1794; m. Daniel Weeks.

4. JOSEPH TUCKER, son of Nathaniel (2), born Sept. 19, 1773; married, first, July 23, 1795, Elizabeth Lear; second, Jan. 29, 1806, Betsey Rand. Children by first wife:

> Nathaniel, bapt. Sept. 4, 1796. Joseph Parsons, b. Sept. 30, 1797; d. Sept. 8, 1834. John, b. Jan. 11, 1799; d. Elizabeth H., b. Nov. 13, 1802.

> Children by second wife:
> John W., *alias* Joy Wilmot Upham, b. June 11, 1808; m. Mary Fogg of Eliot; he d. May 14, 1880.
> 5. James, b. Aug. 17, 1810.

5. JAMES TUCKER, son of Joseph (4), born Aug. 17, 1810; married, Feb. 7, 1850, Betsey H. Hayes. Lived at Eaton, N. H., and Parsonfield, Me. Children: Mary Elizabeth, b. Nov. 17, 1850. Nancy, b. March 1, 1852.

1. WILLIAM TUCKER, married ———. Children:
2. Joseph. William, b. at Bay of Honduras, and d. there. Elijah. Richard. A girl. A girl.

2. JOSEPH TUCKER, son of William (1), married, first, Jan. 21, 1756, Sarah Slooper; second, Dec. 25, 1781, Mary Wallis. Children:
Samuel. Woodbury, m. Elizabeth Fernald. Joseph. Abigail. Sarah, m. James Marden.
3. Michael Wallis. Daniel, d. aged four years. William, m. Mary Mason.

3. MICHAEL WALLIS TUCKER, son of Joseph (2), married, Feb. 18, 1808, Elizabeth Moses. Lived at Portsmouth on Elwyn road. Children:
Elizabeth M., m. Nathaniel Balch. Charles W., unm. Edward W., d. March, 1885. Adeline J., b. June 28, 1810; m. John Clark; she d. March 10, 1899. Joseph. James. Susan A., b. April 28, 1829; m. Moses Clark. Mary, unm.

WILLIAM W. TUCKER married, Jan. 29, 1883, Mary G. Trefethern. Painter by trade. Children:
Ernest Albert, b. July 27, 1883. Florence Emma, b. July 28, 1885. Madge Levia, b. March 9, 1889. Edna Maud, b. May 24, 1890. Joseph Wallis, b. Dec. 23, 1892. Phillip Willard, b. Sept. 10, 1894. Mildred Francis, b. Jan. 30, 1899. Norman Delbert, b. Jan. 30, 1899; d. George Lester, b. March 31, 1902.

RICHARD TUCKER married ———. Child:
William, b. Dec. 4, 1791.

TURNER.

JOHN TURNER came from France about the time of the Revolution, married, first, Seward of Barnstead; second, Hannah Perkins of Kittery, Me. She died in 1854. He died in 1833. Children by first wife:
John. William. Sarah. Lucy.

Children by second wife:

    Joseph, m. Rebecca Shillaber. Mary, d. Charles, d. Harry, b. Oct. 11, 1811; came to Rye when 16 years of age and lived with John Foye five years.

VARRELL.

1. SOLOMON VARRELL, probably came from Kittery, Me., married Deborah Bartlett. Children:

    Elizabeth, m. Lear. Rebecca, m. first, Lang; second, John Clay of Candia. Hannah, m. Dudley Norton; lived at Portsmouth.
2. John, bapt. 1759. William, b. 1763; m. Maria Norton; he d. March 20, 1813; lived at Rye. Mary, b. 1765; m. Jacob Morrison. Sarah, b. 1768; m. Andrew Beck.

2. JOHN VARRELL, son of Solomon (1), baptized 1759; married, first, April 22, 1784, Anna Lang; second, May 8, 1808, Eleanor Norton. He died Sept. 10, 1811, aged 52 years. Children:

3. Nathaniel, bapt. April 30, 1786. Sally, b. June 21, 1789; burned to death. Betsey, b. 1792; d. Jan. 26, 1811. John, b. Aug. 1, 1795; a soldier at the fort in War of 1812; he ran away.
4. Washington, bapt. Dec. 21, 1800.

3. NATHANIEL VARRELL, son of John (2), baptized April 30, 1786; married, 1811, Hannah Lewis. Child:

    Lydia, b. 1811; d. June 28, 1845.

4. WASHINGTON VARRELL, son of John (2), baptized Dec. 21, 1800; married Mary Lang. Children:

5. John.
6. Benjamin. Sarah, m. first, Nov. 3, 1851, Nathaniel Palmer; second, Samuel Caswell. Mary O., m. Charles R. Caswell; he m. second, Sarah E. Robinson.
7. James T., b. Feb. 4, 1840.

5. JOHN VARRELL, son of Washington (4), married, first, Aug. 11, 1844, Mary H. Lord; second, 1868, Margaret Muchmore. Children:

    John J., b. Aug. 28, 1867. Mary. Henry J., b. May 7, 1870; m. May 26, 1897, Collista Dotie.
8. Charles William. Fannie E., m. Nov. 7, 1898, Charles E. Burrell.

6. BENJAMIN VARRELL, son of Washington (4), married, Jan., 1850, Mary Caswell. Children:
John C., b. 1841. Granville, b. 1845. John Milkfield, b. 1848. Nathan, b. 1852. A girl, b. April 18, 1854. Luther, b. Oct. 14, 1857.

7. JAMES T. VARRELL, son of Washington (4), born Feb. 4, 1840; married, July 21, 1861, Henrietta F. Chickering, who was born Sept. 18, 1838. Lived at Candia. Children:
Clara Susan, b. April 26, 1862. Mary Eliza, b. Dec. 24, 1863; d. Jan. 30, 1864. Charles Edward, b. Jan. 8, 1867; d. Jan. 14, 1867. A girl, b. May 26, 1868.

8. CHARLES WILLIAM VARRELL, son of John (5), married, July 16, 1893, Annie M. Burrell. Children:
Inez W., b. Oct. 28, 1893; d. Jan. 19, 1897. Ida M., b. Sept. 10, 1899. Elsie Victoria, b. May 24, 1901. Kenneth Eugene, b. Dec. 12, 1902.

1. JOHN VARRELL, married ———. Lived at Greenland. Children:
2. William. Deborah, m. Clay; lived at Candia. A girl, m.

2. WILLIAM VARRELL, son of John (1), married Maria Norton, who died July 13, 1836, aged 77 years. He came from Greenland to Rye and died in 1803. Children:
Nancy, bapt. Nov., 1796. Lydia, m. Nov. 24, 1808, Isaac Remick. Anna, d. young. Hannah, m. Jan. 28, 1827, Isaac Remick. Mary, m. Oct. 31, 1824, Frederick Rowe.
3. Nathaniel, b. 1789. Solomon, d. 1813.
4. William, b. May, 1801. Deborah, m. Ithamar Mace. Sally, m. Edward Caswell. Tryphena Philbrick.

3. NATHANIEL VARRELL, son of William (2), born 1789; married, 1816, Mary Hanson. Children:
John. Frank. William. Jacob. Lorina. Clarissa. Martha.

4. CAPT. WILLIAM VARRELL, son of William (2), born May, 1801; married, May 22, 1825, Nancy J. Berry, who died Feb. 19, 1880. He died Dec. 2, 1884. Lived at Rye. Mariner. Children:
Sarah Olive, m. Levi Brown; lived at Rye. Anna Maria, m. April 17, 1853, John W. Randall.

5. William Dudley. Mary Elizabeth, m. Ira Gilbert Randall; lived at Rye. Hannah Jane, b. March 8, 1834; m. Daniel Moulton; she d. Feb., 1889; lived at North Hampton.
6. Henry L. Eliza E., m. Albert Carr Locke; lived at Rye. Lydia Christina, drowned Sept. 10, 1864, at the Isles of Shoals.

5. WILLIAM DUDLEY VARRELL, son of Capt. William. (4), married Sarah O. Locke. Lived at Portsmouth. Children:

Anna, b. July 22, 1855. Ida, b. June 20, 1859.

6. HENRY L. VARRELL, son of Capt. William (4), married, July 9, 1868, Mary Jane Marden. Lived at Little Neck, Rye. He died July 28, 1901. Children:

Lydia Nora, b. Sept. 7, 1868; m. Aug. 4, 1889, Frank Rand. Emma Eliza, b. Jan. 7, 1878; m. 1903, John T. Ward; had dau., b. Sept. 14, 1903. Bessie, b. Feb. 16, 1883.

1. EDWARD VARRELL (said to be a cousin of Solomon), came to Rye from York; married, first, Nov. 4, 1773, Elizabeth Saunders; second, Nov. 19, 1784, Mary Berry. He died Oct. 13, 1819, aged about 75 years. Children by first wife:

Rachel, bapt. Nov. 13, 1774; m. Perkins. Betty, bapt. June 9, 1776; unm.; had child, Samuel Clark, by Andrew Clark; she d. Feb. 15, 1869, at Portsmouth, aged 93 years. William, bapt. July 12, 1778; m. widow Lydia Kien of Portsmouth. Richard Tucker, bapt. April 3, 1785; m. Oct. 31, 1803, Polly Randall; he was lost at sea; she m. second, Benjamin Philbrick. Betsey. Edward, bapt. April 3, 1785; m. Aug. 3, 1809, Mary Dearborn of Greenland.

Children by second wife:
2. Samuel, bapt. June 10, 1787. Mary, bapt. April 10, 1791; m. Eben Gore.
3. John, bapt. March 9, 1794. Sarah, bapt. Aug. 11, 1799; m. first, Judkins; second, Grove. Abigail, b. Jan., 1799; m. Jonathan Batchelder.
4. Joseph, bapt. April 19, 1801. Nancy, d. young.
5. Richard, bapt. 1805.

2. SAMUEL VARRELL, son of Edward (1), baptized June 10, 1787; married, Nov. 26, 1812, Elizabeth Waldron. Children:

Elizabeth Mary, b. Aug. 31, 1813; m. Joseph T. Jenness.
6. Jonathan W., b. Oct. 30, 1814.

7. Robert Waldron. Martha Lang, b. April 12, 1822; m. Thomas M. Lang of Portsmouth; she d. Feb. 12, 1875. Harvey, d. in Boston.

3. JOHN VARRELL, son of Edward (1), baptized March 9, 1794; married Betsey Brown of Seabrook. He was in the War of 1812 under Marshall. Child:
   Eliza Jane, b. Feb., 1811; m. William Rowe; she d. Nov., 1862; had John, William and Caroline.

4. JOSEPH VARRELL, son of Edward (1), baptized April 19, 1801, married Eunice Brown. Lived at Meredith. Children:
   Edna. Hiram. John Wesley. Joseph. Jefferson B. Mary Jane. Elbridge Gerry. Eunice. Samuel.

5. RICHARD VARRELL, son of Edward (1), baptized 1805; married, March 4, 1824, Molly, widow of John Mace, and daughter of Nat Berry. Children:
   Gilman, d. March 29, 1831. Clementina, b. 1830; m. first, William Heath; second, William Young.
8. Gilman N., b. Jan. 16, 1837. Cordelia, b. 1824; d. Aug. 18, 1837.

6. JONATHAN W. VARRELL, son of Samuel (2), born Oct. 30, 1814; married, Jan., 1839, Mary Elizabeth Mathes. She died Nov. 7, 1889. He died Jan. 24, 1873. Children:
   Mary, b. Feb. 1841; m. Woodbury N. Mace. Martha, b. 1843; m. Dec. 15, 1863, Joseph W. Odiorne. Richard Harvey, b. March 1, 1844; d. 1855. William S., b. June 6, 1846; d. Sept. 16, 1862. Thomas Ira, b. May 1, 1848; m. June 5, 1899, widow Martha Hanscom. John Albert, b. 1852; d. May 5, 1855. Lulu M., b. Aug. 6, 1857; m. George Boss; lived at Portsmouth.

7. ROBERT WALDRON VARRELL, son of Samuel (2), married Eliza Foss. Children:
   Laura E., b. 1848; m. Orin Webster.
9. Richard F., b. May 6, 1850. Ellen A., b. 1854; m. Richard Long. George A., b. Nov. 18, 1856; m. Sadie Campbell. Fanny E., b. 1858. Lizzie A., b. Feb. 6, 1862; m. Feb. 28, 1890, Herbert Locke. Robert Walter, b. June, 1866.

8. GILMAN NATHANIEL VARRELL, son of Richard (5), born Jan. 16, 1837; married, first, Dec. 4, 1856, Sarah A. Caswell; second, the widow of Benjamin W. Marden. Children:

John C. F., b. Sept. 1856; d. Jan., 1857. William, b. Dec. 19, 1857. Carrie Etta, b. Jan. 28, 1858. Clara Emma, b. Jan. 27, 1860; m. Oct. 29, 1877, George O. Remick.

10. Charles F., b. March 25, 1862. Gilman Henry, b. Dec. 25, 1863. Herman, b. Feb., 1867; d. Oct. 12, 1868. Carrie Etta, d. April 3, 1859, aged four months. Alma G., b. May 2, 1869. Eddie H., b. Nov. 15, 1872; d. Dec. 23, 1890.

11. Orville F., b. Feb. 26, 1874. Edith M., b. 1875; m. Jan., 1893, Alfred W. Torrey; he d., and she m. second, George Clough. Ann Anzolette, b. May 24, 1877; d. Sept. 18, 1877.

9. RICHARD F. VARRELL, son of Robert Waldron (7), married Amy J. Caswell. Lived in Rye. Carpenter. Child

Forrest C., b. April 27, 1873; m. June 17, 1903, Mary E. Waldron. Ernest,-b. Feb. 10, 1886.

10. CHARLES F. VARRELL, son of Gilman Nathaniel (8), born March 25, 1862; married Lilla L. Pethick. Children:

Son. Daughter, b. June 10, 1889.

11. ORVILLE F. VARRELL, son of Gilman Nathaniel (8), born Feb. 26, 1874; married, Dec. 20, 1892, Kate M. Rand. Child:

Daughter, b. March 21, 1893.

JOSEPH VARRELL married, Aug. 25, 1794, Sarah Saunders, widow of William S. Saunders. Removed to Alexandria. Children:

Joseph, b. Dec. 8, 1794. Joses, b. Dec. 8, 1794. Joseph, b. June 21, 1796. Sally, b. April 18, 1799. Phebe Philbrick, b. March 23, 1801. Abigail Locke, b. Aug. 25, 1803. Betsey.

WALDRON.

1. JONATHAN B. WALDRON, came from Portsmouth Plains, married, Sept. 24, 1789, Elizabeth, daughter of Joshua Foss, who died Jan. 5, 1835, aged 72 years. He died Oct. 25, 1813, aged 52 years. Children:

Elizabeth Saunders W., b. Dec. 16, 1790; m. Samuel Varrell. Polly Westbrook, b. Aug. 19, 1792; m. Samuel J. Locke; lived at Rye.
2. Robert Saunders, b. June 9, 1794.
3. Joshua Foss, b. Dec. 11, 1796.
4. Richard Harvey, b. Sept. 30, 1798. George, b. 1801; m. Huldah Ladd of Brentwood.

2. ROBERT SAUNDERS WALDRON, son of Jonathan B. (1), born June 9, 1794; married, first, Martha Lang, who died Nov. 25, 1831, aged 42 years; second, Hannah Drown. He died July 25, 1835, aged 42 years. Children by second wife:

Robert, m. Anna ———. Martha, m. Samuel K. Choate.

3. JOSHUA FOSS WALDRON, son of Jonathan B. (1), born Dec. 11, 1796; married Sophia Towle. Children:

Mary E. Shaw. Richard. John, drowned.

4. RICHARD HARVEY WALDRON, son of Jonathan B. (1), born Sept. 30, 1798; married, first, Sarah Randall; second, Lydia Todd. Lived at Rye where Lewis Foss resides. Children:

Sarah Elizabeth, b. 1842; m. William Stickney; had one child; he died, and she m. second, May 30, 1871, William Hunton. Mary C., b. 1846; d. July 20, 1846.
5. Benjamin Franklin (adopted), son of Ben Randall of Gosport.

5. BENJAMIN FRANKLIN WALDRON, adopted son of Richard H. (4), married Sarah Jane Baston, who died Nov. 5, 1884. Lived at Rye. Children:

Eva Jane, b. 1867. Mina L., b. Sept. 15, 1869. Lois, b. Nov. 25, 1872. Grace. Daisy.

ISAAC WALDRON of Barrington married, May 8, 1796, Mary Jane Wallis. Children:

Samuel Wallis, m. Martha Melcher. Elizabeth Parsons, m. Hall J. Howe. Isaac, m. Eliza ———. Henry, m. Mary F. ———. Alfred A., m. Elizabeth P.

JACOB WALDRON of Portsmouth married, June 3, 1811, Margaret Tarlton of Newcastle.

WALKER.

1. SAMUEL WALKER, born Jan. 5, 1776, came from Portsmouth; married, July 26, 1799, Hannah Marden. He died April 2, 1862. Served in Captain Samuel Berry's company of light infantry in the War of 1812. Children:

GENEALOGY.

2. Jesse Merrill, b. 1799.
3. Jonathan Towle, b. Sept. 27, 1804.
4. Levi Towle, b. June, 1809. William, b. 1806; d. May 3, 1831, aged 24 years; drowned. Eliza Ann, b. 1812; d. unm., Feb. 18, 1893. Nathaniel Marden, b. 1817 (?); d. Feb. 24, 1854, at Georgetown, D. C., aged 36 years.

2. JESSE MERRILL WALKER, son of Samuel (1), born 1799; married, March 2, 1825, Jane B. Sleeper, who was born April 1, 1808, and died March 24, 1894. He died Oct. 8, 1867. Children:

Benjamin Franklin, b. July 4, 1825; m. April 5, 1849, Harriet Stevens of Newport R. I.
5. Albert M., b. Aug. 3, 1827.
6. William J., b. Dec. 30, 1830. Samuel, m. first, Charlotte King; second, Katie Hamilton; he d. May 16, 1901, at Portsmouth.
7. Charles A., b. June, 1838. Annie, m. April 22, 1863, Daniel H. Trefethern; lived at Kittery. George Storer, b. 1844; d. March 11, 1848.
8. George S., b. June, 1848.

3. JONATHAN TOWLE WALKER, son of Samuel (1), born Sept. 27, 1804; married, July 12, 1831, Mary E. Brown, who died April 11, 1858. He died Dec. 29, 1884. Lived at Rye. Was a carpenter by trade and held the office of postmaster for more than thirty years. Children:

William Chauncy, b. Feb. 15, 1833; m. June 3, 1867, Ellen A. McLawlin; lived at Rye. Levi Henry, b. Feb. 9, 1840; d. Oct. 30, 1845.
9. Lewis Everett, b. Aug. 8, 1842.

4. LEVI TOWLE WALKER, son of Samuel (1), born June, 1809; married, Sept. 5, 1855, Harriet A. Dow, who died Sept. 1, 1858. Lived at Rye. He died Aug. 12, 1874. Lived in the Trefethern House, now occupied by George Perry. Child:

Helen S., b. March 30, 1857; d. Nov. 28, 1858.

5. ALBERT M. WALKER, son of Jesse Merrill (2), born Aug. 3, 1827; married, 1850, Martha Elizabeth Seavey. Lived at Rye. By trade a blacksmith. Children:

Alice J., b. Jan. 25, 1852; m. Dec. 29, 1871, William H. Berry.
10. Edwin, b. Jan. 31, 1854. Cora. Jenness, b. 1863; d. Aug. 24, 1865.

6. WILLIAM J. WALKER, son of Jesse Merrill (2), born Dec. 30, 1830; married, Oct. 22, 1861, Mary Ann Robinson, born Sept. 5, 1842; died Oct. 9, 1899. Lived at Rye. Blacksmith by trade. Children:
> Ralph, b. April 29, 1863; m. Jan. 5, 1895, Nellie Hobbs. Isabella, b. Nov. 19, 1864; m. Oct. 25, 1898, Roscoe Berry. Gilman, b. Jan. 12, 1870; m. Sept. 12, 1892, Susie E. Garland. Lila, b. April 26, 1872.

7. CHARLES A. WALKER, son of Jesse Merrill (2), born June, 1838; married, first, Margaret Neil, who died Jan., 1874; second, Jan. 15, 1879, Clara Marden. Lived at Rye. Child by first wife:
> Hermon E., b. Dec. 14, 1864; m. May 3, 1889, Sarah Wright of Wilton, N. H.

8. GEORGE S. WALKER, son of Jesse Merrill (2), born June, 1848; married, first, Sept. 9, 1871, Augusta M. Page, who died March 7, 1886; second, Feb. 14, 1889, Christie Foss. Children by first wife:
> Archie, b. Dec. 8, 1872; d. Dec. 12, 1872. Arthur, b. Nov. 17, 1873; m. Nov. 5, 1897, Adelaide Banks. Maud, b. March 7, 1876; m. Nov. 18, 1895, Fred Hankin. Eliza Ann, b. Jan. 16, 1882; m. Nov. 17, 1901, Charles Grant.

Children by second wife:
> Chalcedona, b. Dec. 23, 1891. Raymond, b. Oct. 6, 1893.

9. LEWIS EVERETT WALKER, son of Jonathan Towle (3), born Aug. 8, 1842; married, May 13, 1873, Annie Julia Foss. Lived at Rye. Child:
> 11 Ezra Howard, b. Oct. 21, 1875; m. Dec. 4, 1901, E. Annie Manson.

10. EDWIN WALKER, son of Albert M. (5), born Jan. 31, 1854; married, Dec. 23, 1886, Cora Belle Jenness. Divorced. Children:
> Fannie Grace, b. May 31, 1888. Jesse M., b. Dec. 30, 1889.

11. EZRA HOWARD WALKER, son of Lewis E. (9), born Oct. 21, 1875; married, Dec. 4, 1901, E. Annie Manson. Child:
> Harlan Manson, b. March 4, 1903.

GENEALOGY.   563

NATHANIEL WALKER married Catharine Beck. Lived at Portsmouth. Children:

> John K., b. Dec. 4, 1810; m. Ann Thomas; lived at Portsmouth. Almira, b. Dec. 25, 1813; m. Robert Shillaber. Mary W., b. Dec. 19; m. John Moran (?). Gideon, b. April, 1826 (?); m. first, Mary Anderson; second, Margaret Anderson; lived at Manchester. Hannah Beck, m. Israel Marden.

WILLIAM WALKER married, first, April 21, 1804, Anna Cater; second, Betsey Peverly.

WALLIS.

1. RALPH WALLIS, son of George Wallis, who came to Portsmouth from London, in 1635, in the *Abigail*, bringing his son Ralph with him. George was then about 40 years old. Ralph married, Nov. 18, 1686, Ann Shortridge. Lived at Sandy Beach. Children:

> 2. Samuel. William. Jane, m. Stephen Lang. Mary. Sarah, m. Joshua Foss. Ebenezar.
> 3. George. Mary, m. Peter Ball.

2. SAMUEL WALLIS, son of Ralph (1), married, first, Sarah Moses, daughter of James Moses of Sagamore; second, Deborah, widow of James Reeder. He died about 1793. Was lieutenant in Captain Richard Jenness' company, 1729. They owned two slaves, Phillis and Caesar, who were given their freedom and went to Salem, Mass., but afterwards came back to the old homestead in Rye and were buried on the Wallis farm. Children:

> Sarah, m. May 10, 1764, Paul Seavey. Hannah, b. Aug. 2, 1745; m. April 29, 1773, William Marden. Abigail, m. June 13, 1776, Nadab Moses; lived at Portsmouth; she d. about 1833. Mary, m. Dec. 25, 1781, Joseph Tucker.
> 4. Samuel (Lieut.), b. 1747. Martha L., b. 1752; m. March 1, 1796, John Langmaid; lived at Chichester, N. H.

3. GEORGE WALLIS, son of Samuel (2), married Margaret McCleary and removed to Epsom. Children:

> Hannah, bapt. 1740. Martha, bapt. 1742. Margaret, bapt. 1744.

4. LIEUT. SAMUEL WALLIS, son of Samuel (2), born 1747; married, Nov. 16, 1773, Elizabeth Parsons, who died

June 9, 1827, aged 73 years. He died Feb. 25, 1832, aged 85 years. Was ensign in Captain Parsons' company in the Revolutionary War. Inherited the Wallis farm. It is from the early Wallis settlement at Rye that "Wallis Sands" derived its name. Children:

> Sarah, bapt. March 20, 1777; d. Mary Jones, b. June 1, 1778; m. May 8, 1796, Isaac Waldron of Portsmouth; she d. Dec. 1, 1839.

WILLIAM WALLIS married Molly Brown and removed to Northwood. Children:

> William, m. first, ———; second, Comstock. Moses, m. Susan Lucas. John, m. Phebe Rand. Mary, m. William Knowlton. Comfort, m. Atwood. Sally, m. Sanborn. Nancy, m. Silas Burnham. Betsey, m. Edward Sanborn. A dau., m. Morrill.

WATSON.

THOMAS WATSON married ———. He lived on Captain Elvin Rand's place at East Rye. Children:

> Samuel, b. 1739. John, b. 1741; m. Oct. 25, 1767, Alice Clark.

WEBSTER.

1. JOHN WEBSTER, son of Thomas Webster and Sarah of Hampton, born Feb. 16, 1674; married, Sept. 21, 1703, Abiah Shaw. Lived at Rye. Children:

> Jeremiah, b. Dec. 21, 1703; m. Ladd. Charity, b. April 2, 1706.
> 2. Josiah, b. April 2, 1706. John, b. Feb. 10, 1712. Thomas, b. July 1, 1715. Caleb, b. March 19, 1719; d. July 17, 1735. Abiah, b. Jan. 20, 1722; d. July 2, 1736. Elizabeth, b. Sept. 27, 1724; m. William Kingman. Charity, bapt. Aug. 6, 1727; m. Zachariah Berry.

2. JOSIAH WEBSTER, son of John (1), born April 2, 1706; married, Sept. 21, 1738, Patty Goss, who was born in 1714, and died Nov. 18, 1798. Children:

> John, b. 1739; d. Elizabeth, b. Feb. 19, 1740; m. Aug. 28, 1760, Stephen Marden, Jr., probably. Abiah, b. Sept. 8, 1742; m. Alexander Salter. Sarah, b. April 19, 1745; m. George Marden; lived at Chester. Josiah, b. July 9, 1748; d.
> 3. John, b. Jan. 18, 1751.
> 4. Richard, b. Jan. 1, 1754. Martha, b. Feb. 11, 1755; m. Ozem Dowrst.
> 5. Josiah, b. May 14, 1757.

GENEALOGY.

3. JOHN WEBSTER, son of Josiah (2), born Jan. 18, 1751; married Dorothy Chapman of North Hampton, who died Aug. 9, 1837. He died Sept. 22, 1823. Children:

    Abiah, m. John Salter. Abigail, b. 1777; m. Samuel B. Berry. Mary, b. 1779; m. Alex Salter (?); lived where Sam Hunt and Rand did; house burned. Martha, b. 1781; m. Jethro Locke; lived at Rye. Dolly, b. 1784; m. July 20, 1806, Stephen Green. Anne, b. 1787.
  6. Jeremy, b. April 12, 1792.
  7. John Hobbs, b. May, 1795. Mary, b. April, 1798; m. 1815, Noah Wiggin; lived at Stratham.

4. RICHARD WEBSTER, son of Josiah (2), born Jan. 1, 1754; married, Oct. 29, 1778, Elizabeth Randall. He died Jan. 16, 1836. She died March 14, 1826, aged 71 years. He was a patriot in the Revolutionary War, serving under Captain Parker at Fort Sullivan and Captain Parsons in Rhode Island. He also went several cruises privateering. Children:

    Betsey, b. March 3, 1779; m. Joshua Seavey. Abigail, b. Aug. 24, 1780; m. April, 1809, Levi Randall. Martha, b. Nov. 25, 1781; m. first, Feb. 3, 1822, Ebenezer Odiorne; second, John Foye. Sarah, b. July 12, 1783; m. James Marden. Hannah, b. Dec. 16, 1784; m. John Jenness. Olive, b. Nov. 19, 1786; d. Aug. 15, 1802.
  8. Richard, b. Oct. 6, 1788.
  9. Mark Randall, b. April 20, 1791.

5. JOSIAH WEBSTER, son of Josiah (2), born May 14, 1757; married Sarah Locke, who was born in the house where Joseph J. Drake lived. He lived where Oren Drake did. Children:

    Mary, b. April 17, 1781; m. 1806, Henry Elkins. Josiah, b. Jan. 6, 1783; m. Hannah Grant; d. 1841.
  10. David, b. Sept. 23, 1784. Sally, b. March 16, 1786; m. Ephraim Philbrick. Fanny, b. March 26, 1790; d. 1808, at Boston. Nathaniel, b. March 4, 1793; d. at New Orleans. Martha, b. April 10, 1795; m. Dec. 9, 1819, James Brown. Levi Locke, b. March 24, 1797; m. E. Macy.

6. JEREMY WEBSTER, son of John (3), born April 12, 1792; married, March 24, 1837, Eliza Rand. Lived at Rye. Served in Captain Coleman's company of cavalry in the War of 1812. Children:

Mary Chatman, b. March, 1840; d. June 8, 1842. Rozette, b. Aug. 18, 1841; m. Oct. 16, 1860, George Leroy Trefethern.

7. JOHN HOBBS WEBSTER, son of John (3), born May, 1793; married, Sept. 20, 1827, Elizabeth H. Clark. Lived at Rye. A member of Captain Samuel Berry's company of light infantry in the War of 1812. He died Aug. 2, 1866. Children:

> John, b. Oct. 4, 1827-'28; unm.; lived at Rye. Emily C., b. Oct. 12, 1829-'30; d. unm. Daniel C., b. July 2, 1832-'33; m. April 7, 1861, Sabrina Trefethern; lived at Rye; both died.

8. RICHARD WEBSTER, son of Richard (4), born Oct. 6, 1788; married Polly Philbrick. Lived at Epsom and Rye. Children:

> Daniel, b. July 1, 1814; d. Nov. 21, 1865. Roswell, m. Susan Johnson. Mary, m. Benjamin Norton. Benjamin Franklin, m. Sarah Senter. David, m. Arvill Johnson. Richard. John, m. Sarah Dunn. Emily, m. Parker. Ursula, d. in Epsom, aged about one year.

9. MARK RANDALL WEBSTER, son of Richard (4), born April 20, 1791; married, Nov. 26, 1829, Mary Ann Lang. Lived on Sandy Beach road, Rye. He died July 17, 1865. Children:

> Martha J., b. June 11, 1830; m. May 21, 1855, Harrison Seavey. Richard, b. June 1, 1833; m. Nov., 1854-'55, Fanny Conner. Mary E., b. Jan. 22, 1836; m. April 24, 1862, Charles P. Abbott. Daniel, b. Nov. 13, 1838; m. Brackett; lived at Portsmouth. Abby, b. July 28, 1841; d. Sept. 19, 1862. Sarah L., b. Jan. 5, 1845; m. Jan. 7, 1864, John H. Locke. William Wallis, b. Dec. 26, 1847. Warren P., b. Feb. 14 or 15, 1852; m. July 5, 1882, Francis M. White.

10. DAVID WEBSTER, son of Josiah (5), born Sept. 23, 1784; married Nowell. Children:
> John Gerrish; lived at Boston.
11. David Locke. Andrew Jackson; lived at Providence. Charles Edward; lived at Boston.

11. DAVID LOCKE WEBSTER, son of David (10), married Johanna Rich. Lived at Boston. Children:

> Andrew Gerrish; m. Lizzie F. Briggs; lived at Boston. Augustus Floyd, m. Lizzie Josselyn. Elizabeth, m Arthur Reid; d. in Paris, 1870.

ORIN WEBSTER married Laura E. Verrill. Lived at Boston. Children:

Hattie, b. 1874. Archie, b. 1877.

WEDGEWOOD.

1. DAVID WEDGEWOOD, son of Jonathan and Mary of North Hampton, born April 11, 1740; married, Nov. 21, 1762, Mary, daughter of Jonathan Marston. Children:
2. Jonathan.
3. David. Mary, m. Nathaniel Jenness.

2. JONATHAN WEDGEWOOD, son of David (1), married, March 23, 1790, Hannah Seavey. Lived at Rye. He died Aug. 10, 1841. Children:
4. David, b. May 17, 1792. Betsey, bapt. July 12, 1795; m. Joseph J. Berry; she d. April 1, 1817; lived at Rye. Sally Wallis, bapt. Sept. 24, 1797; m. Nov. 29, 1816, Joseph L. Locke; she d. Nov. 30, 1879; lived at Rye. Hannah, bapt. April, 1800; m. Eliphalet S. Wedgewood; lived at Rye.

3. DAVID WEDGEWOOD, son of David (1), married, March 2, 1794, Mary Sleeper. Lived at Rye. Children:
Hannah, b. 1794; m. John Jenness.
5. Eliphalet Sleeper, b. 1798.

4. CAPTAIN DAVID WEDGEWOOD, son of Jonathan (2), born May 17, 1792; married, 1816, Polly Jenness. Lived at Rye. Served in the light infantry under Captain Samuel Berry in the War of 1812. He died Aug. 31, 1878. Children:

Charles, b. 1819; d. Dec. 27, 1862. Abby, b. Oct. 7, 1821; d. unm. Nov. 29, 1882; deranged. David William, b. 1831; d. June 23, 1837, aged 6 years. Sarah, d. Jan. 22, 1838, aged seven years.

5. ELIPHALET SLEEPER WEDGEWOOD, son of David (3), born 1798; married, first, Hannah Wedgewood; second, April 15, 1861, Hannah Brown. Lived at Rye. He died Aug. 28, 1865. Children:

Gilman, d. Nov. 19, 1855, at Chicago, Ill. Emily, m. Miller.

WEED.

GEORGE WEED, it is said, lived in Rye and removed to Amesbury, Mass., prior to 1700.

WEEKS.

JOSHUA WEEKS married, Sept. 4, 1760, Sarah Marston. Lived in Rye, 1761. He died about 1776. Children:

Sarah, bapt. June 21, 1761. John, bapt. June 10, 1764. Molly, bapt. June 14, 1767. Betty, bapt. March 19, 1769. Abigail, bapt. March 24, 1771. Abigail, bapt. Nov. 3, 1776.

CHARLES WENDELL married, first, Mamie Dow; second, ———. Children:

Auburn. Olive.

WELLS.

1. SAMUEL WELLS married Priscilla Brock (?). He lived on the hill where George Lang lives, east side of A. D. Parsons' house. Children:

2. Samuel, b. Dec. 2, 1735. Simon, b. May 11, 1738. Deborah, b. Oct. 5, 1740. Isaiah, b. April 29, 1743. John, b. Oct. 4, 1745; probably m. Nov. 9, 1769, Elizabeth Rollins. Anna, b. Oct. 19, 1747. Sarah, b. Aug. 12, 1750. Jeremiah, b. 1757.

2. SAMUEL WELLS, son of Samuel (1), born Dec. 2, 1735; married, April 28, 1763, Elizabeth Thompson. Lived at Rye. Children:

Sarah, b. Nov. 21, 1765. Simeon, b. 1768; m. first, Sally Batchelder; second, Shaw. Olly, b. 1770; m. Josiah Batchelder. Elizabeth, b. 1773. Samuel, b. 1776; m. Hannah Brown. Molly, b. 1778; m. Nov. 16, 1796, Jethro Goss. Deborah, b. 1780.

WENTWORTH.

CHARLES E. WENTWORTH married Minerva S. Jenness of Rye. Child:

Charles Sumner, b. April 7, 1873.

WEYMOUTH.

SHADRACH WEYMOUTH married ———. Children:

George, b. Sept., 1749. Eunice, bapt. 1756. Thomas Cotton, b. 1758. James, b. 1759; d. 1852, at Belmont, Me., aged 93 years; was in Revolution. Samuel, b. 1761.

WHIDDEN.

1. SAMUEL WHIDDEN, born Feb. 2, 1769; married Goodman Brown. Children:
   Hannah, b. June 11, 1770. Thomas, b. Aug. 19, 1772. Sarah, b. Aug. 2, 1774. Mary, b. Jan. 18, 1776. Elizabeth Anna, b. Oct. 18, 1778.
2. Joseph, b. Oct. 26, 1780. Richard, b. Feb. 5, 1783. Mark, b. Oct. 15, 1785. Fanny, b. March 31, 1788. Daniel, b. March 23, 1791. Peggy Sherburn, b. March 28, 1793.
3. William, b. Feb. 29, 1772 (?).

2. JOSEPH WHIDDEN, probably son of Samuel (1), born Oct. 26, 1780; married Abigail ———. Lived on Lafayette road, Portsmouth. Children:
   Mary Ann, m. Daniel Colman. Sarah L., m. Reuel G. Bean. Frances A., m. Richard L. Palmer. Joseph W., m. Elizabeth Berry. John H. Andrew J., m. Gerrish of Portsmouth. Hannah L. Harnett A. Ellen A.

3. LIEUT. WILLIAM WHIDDEN, probably son of Samuel (1), born Feb. 29, 1772; married, first, Hannah Whidden; second, Dec. 1, 1811, Hannah Marden. Child by first wife:
4. Samuel, b. Jan. 18, 1801.

4. CAPT. SAMUEL WHIDDEN, son of William, married, March 1, 1827, Elizabeth Langdon. Lived on Lafayette road, Portsmouth. Children:
   William, d. Langdon, m. widow Anna P. Seavey. William, d. Elizabeth, b. 1843; unm. Samuel Storer, unm.

SAMUEL H. WHIDDEN, son of ———, married, Dec. 22, 1842, Data Brown, who died 1878. He died Jan. 26, 1886. Lived at Portsmouth. Children:
   Nettie, b. Oct. 6, 1848, m. Dec. 27, 1869, Horace Garland. Charles, b. April 27, 1852; m. Oct. 2, 1876, Alice Jenness, dau. of Samuel Jenness of Rye. Horace, b. April 27, 1852, m. Mary Heheir. Anna, b. Jan. 1, 1856; m. Dec. 19, 1877, Irvin Garland of Rye.

HORACE WHIDDEN married Mary Heheir. Both died. Children:
   Samuel S., b. April 9, 1889. Charles H., b. June 10, 1892.

WHITE.

GEORGE WHITE married, Sept. 29, 1869, Polly W. Marden. Lived in Rye. Children:

Nellie, b. March 16, 1870. Willie, b. Nov. 25, 1871. Rolla G., b. Aug. 2, 1874. Isabella, b. Aug. 29, 1876; m. Oct. 15, 1894, Thomas Whenal (?). Abbott, b. Oct. 10, 1878. Irving, d. June 29, 1886. Ada Emerett, b. Sept. 22, 1888.

WILLEY.

1. SAMUEL WILLEY married, April 5, 1798, Martha Seavey. Children:

Clarissa, m. Nov. 28, 1822, Thomas Foye. Mary, b. 1809; m. Edward Seavey.
2. William S., b. 1814 (?). Martha A., b. 1816 (?); m. Elvin Rand.

2. WILLIAM S. WILLEY, son of Samuel (1), born 1814; married Lucy Lang. Children:

Ellen, b. 1837; d. Feb. 9, 1840. Charles.

WILSON.

ISAAC WILSON married, May 14, 1879, Hannah Cragg of Sweden. Children:

Helena, b. Dec. 5, 1890. Bertha H. and Albert H. (twins), b. June 5, 1895. Herbert C., b. Nov. 2, 1896.

WOODMAN.

1. JONATHAN WOODMAN, came to Rye when 14 years old and lived with John Foye; married, April 12, 1812, Sally Rand (who had before marriage Emily Rand, married Nathan Waldron of Portsmouth). Children:

Nancy Ann, b. Aug., 1812; m. Moses Norris. John, b. April, 1815; m. Sarah French. William, b. May 5, 1820; m. Harriet Briard.
2. Emery, b. Jan. 20, 1825. Mary Elizabeth, b. July 7, 1829; m. Andrew Davis.

2. EMERY WOODMAN, son of Jonathan (1), born Jan. 20, 1825; married, 1860, Mary Ann Bickford. Lived at Rye. She died Jan. 20, 1886. Child:

Chauncy, b. May 11, 1863; m. Sept. 10, 1893, Carrie S. Russell; lived at Rye.

JONATHAN WOODMAN married, Dec. 12, 1769, widow Hannah (Jenness) Rand. Children:
Mary, b. 1771. Betsey, b. Sept. 28, 1773; m. Jonathan Garland. Nancy, m. Joses Philbrick; no children.

YEATON.

Three persons by the name of Yeaton came over and established themselves, it is said, in fishing at Newcastle. But they did not agree, and one went to Fryeburg, Me., one to Somersworth, and one remained at Goat Island, since called Newcastle.

1. JOSEPH YEATON, married, first, ———; second, July 17, 1751, Susannah Lang. Children by first wife:
Mary, m. Peter Johnson. Sarah, b. 1746.
Children by second wife:
2. Joseph, b. 1752. Anna, b. 1753.
3. William, b. 1756. Elizabeth, b. 1758; m. Samuel Shapley; lived at Kittery or Eliot. John, b. 1761. Hannah, b. 1763; m. Stephen Tucker of Eliot. Susannah, b. 1765. Philip, b. 1768; m. 1797, Huldah Saunders. Susan, m. Jacob Remick of Eliot. Deborah, m. William Bates Randall.

2. JOSEPH YEATON, JR., son of Joseph (1), born 1752; married, Feb. 5, 1776, Elizabeth Rand. Child:
Samuel, b. 1776.

3. WILLIAM YEATON, son of Joseph (1), born 1756; married, Sept. 17, 1780, Hannah Towle. Lived on Sandy Beach road. Children:
Sally, m. Jonathan Goss. John, b. 1781; m. first, his brother's widow; second, Rebecca Bickford; third, Betsey Towle. Hannah, m. Simon Towle. Billy, or William, b. 1783; m. Elizabeth Ham. Jonathan, m. Hannah Towle, his cousin. Joseph, m. Betsey Brown. Towle, m. Sarah Coochman. Hopley, m. Salome Lear. Levi, m. Mary Mathews.

JOHN YEATON, perhaps brother of Joseph (1), married, Aug. 24, 1759, Esther Saunders. He was lost in a gale, and she married, second, Simon Knowles. Children:
John, b. 1762; m. Hayes. Mary, b. 1764. Elizabeth, b. 1766; m. John Staunton. Esther, b. 1769; m. Isaac Remick; she had Betsey Drew before m. Merribah, m. Palmer. Polly.

JOHN YEATON married Ruth Grant. Lived at Newcastle. Children:

Richard, m. Abigail Gaudy. Dolly, m. Benjamin Odiorne. Tamah, m. Simon Smith. Isaac, m. Jane Mitchell. John, m. Abigail Bell; he was lost at sea. William, d. aged about 17 years while at sea. Peggy, m. John Mullin. Hitty, m. David Gardiner. Ruth, m. first, John Connor; second, George Odiorne; lived at Portsmouth.

2. Hopley, b. Jan. 20, 1792. Eben, m. Hepsibah Bell; he was lost at sea.

1. HOPLEY YEATON, son of Ebenezer of Newcastle, born Jan. 20, 1792; married, Jan. 7, 1813, Lydia Foye. Lived at Wallis farm, Rye, and Newcastle. Children:

2. William Foye, b. March 16, 1814. Mary L., b. 1816; m. Oct. 4, 1839, David L. Rand. Elizabeth H., b. Dec. 27, 1818; m. Nov. 1, 1840, Aaron Rand; lived at Rye. Lydia Ann, m. Richard Cushing; lived in North Carolina. Adeline, m. Byron Strout. Madelaide M., m. Henry Stoddard. Sarah, m. John E. Yeaton. Lucina, m. Alexis Torrey. L. Jane, m. John Stoddard.

2. WILLIAM FOYE YEATON, son of Hopley (2), born March 16, 1814; married Lovina Berry. Lived at Moultonborough. He died Aug. 8, 1880. Children:

Lucie Adelaide, b. June 17, 1843; m. Sylvester Yeaton. Arvilla Augusta, b. April 15, 1845; m. and had Abby, b. July, 1864. Sarah Elizabeth, b. Sept. 6, 1847; m. Charles F. Garland. Charles William, b. Oct. 19, 1860.

Marriages, Not Included in Foregoing Records.

Marriages by Rev. Nathaniel Morrill commence in 1726; Rev. Samuel Parsons in 1736; Rev. Huntington Porter in 1785; Rev. B. Smith in 1829; Rev. James McEwen in 1841; Rev. I. T. Otis, in 1847.

John Allen of Stratham and Elizabeth Cate of Greenland, Nov. 21, 1738.

Samuel Abbot and Ruth Ayers of Greenland, Dec. 3, 1764.

William Atwood and Sarah Marden of Bradford, Mass., Dec. 29, 1743.

Joshua Atwood of Bradford and Mehitable Seavey, Jan. 6, 1745.

Christopher Amazeen and Mehitable Rand, Sept. 1, 1783.

Henry Amazeen of Newcastle and Louisa Rand of Rye, Sept., 1826.

John Ayers and Polly Patterson, both of Greenland, March 12, 1793.

John Ayers and Mercy Tarlton of Portsmouth, March 18, 1796.

John Ayers of Greenland and Anna Drake of Hampton, Jan. 7, 1812.

Levi Ayers and Ruhannah Norton, Dec. 10, 1778.

Nathaniel Ayers of Portsmouth and Ruth Shapley of the Isles of Shoals, Nov. 23, 1750.

Peter Barnes and Abigail Lang, June 21, 1759.

Nathaniel Batchelder of Deerfield and Molly Libbee of Hampton, June 10, 1781.

Samuel Batchelder of Greenland and Abigail Norton of Portsmouth, Aug. 3, 1815.

Jeremiah Batchelder of North Hampton and Caroline M. P. Chesley of Rye, Sept. 10, 1823.

Edmund C. Batchelder and Nancy Philbrick, both of North Hampton, 1810.

John Batchelder and Betsey Burleigh of Newmarket, April 8, 1825.

Charles E. Batchelder and Martha M. Brown, both of North Hampton, Jan. 1, 1863.

John Batchelder and Martha Fogg, both of North Hampton, April 30, 1815.

Jacob Brown of Hampton Falls and Abigail Berry of Greenland, Aug. 29, 1792.

Nathan Brown and Molly Jenness, both of North Hampton, April 11, 1801.

Caleb Brown and Phila Fellows of Kensington, April 9, 1822.

Simon Brown, Jr., of Hampton and Lucinda Batchelder of North Hampton, April 29, 1824.

Stacy W. Brown of Hampton and Nancy M. Batchelder of North Hampton, Feb. 28, 1841.

John E. Brown and Abba L. Yeaton, both of Portsmouth, Aug. 14, 1863.
Dearborn Blake of Epping and Eliza Shaw of Hampton, Oct. 23, 1777.
William Blake of Hampton and Ruth L. Batchelder of North Hampton, Aug. 10, 1838.
Joseph Blake of Hampton and Susan L. Batchelder of North Hampton, Nov. 28, 1837.
Moses B. Blake of Hampton and Sarah A. Goss of Rye, 1836.
Ivory Blazo and Adeline E. Brown, both of Stratham, Nov. 7, 1862.
John Butterfield and Sarah Dolbee of Chester, Sept. 28, 1767.
Thomas Beck of Portsmouth and Hannah Elkins, May 28, 1761.
Henry Beck and Eliza Thompson of Greenland, Jan. 20, 1763.
John Beck and Betsey Odiorne, both of Portsmouth, Sept. 16, 1798.
Caleb Brewster and Elizabeth Lear of Portsmouth, Dec. 28, 1766.
John G. Brewster and Deborah Muchmore of Portsmouth, Aug. 7, 1808.
John Bond and Esther Rand, Aug. 17, 1752.
Richard Billings and Hannah Newmarch of Portsmouth, Aug. 22, 1777.
Joseph T. Burgin and Charity Grover, both of Portsmouth, April 4, 1811.
Phillip Bowers and Mary Gove of Portsmouth, Aug. 15, 1828.
Solomon Berry and Martha Kate, both of Greenland, Oct. 5, 1794.
Peter Briar and Rachel Briar, Oct. 23, 1758.
Edward Butler and Elizabeth Langdon, Oct. 5, 1759.
Benjamin, a negro man, and Martha, a negro woman, of Newcastle, June 26, 1777.
Edward Call of Portsmouth and Eleanor Marston of Greenland, Oct. 9, 1809.
Benjamin Carr of Salisbury, Mass., and Sarah Shaw of Kensington, 1816.
Isaac C. Carleton of Pelham, Me., and Lydia H. Lord of Berwick, Me., March 26, 1856.
Job Chapman of Hampton and Rachel Goss of Rye, June 6, 1737.
James Chapman and Abigail Philbrick, both of North Hampton, Dec. 10, 1801.
Moses Chase, Stratham, and Lucia Moulton, Dec. 22, 1755.
Elisha Chase and Betsey L. Merrill, both of Stratham, Sept. 13, 1809.
Daniel Connor and Sarah E. Adams, both of Exeter, Sept. 1, 1805.
John R. Cronk and Dorothy Brown of Portsmouth, Nov. 29, 1827.
Peter Clifford and Hannah Dolbee, July 25, 1738.
Pelahah Crockett and Mary Marden of Stratham, Dec., 1760.
William Currier of Epping and Eliza Robey of Hampton, May 31, 1770.
Thomas Currier and Mary Ring of Portsmouth, Dec. 3, 1772.
John Crosby and Elizabeth Woodman of Greenland, Oct. 15, 1778.
Levi Clark of Stratham and Lovina Wiggin of Greenland, June 6, 1790.
Joseph Cornelius and Emily Francis Howe, both of Portsmouth, 1859.

MARRIAGES. 575

Phinneas W. Coleman of Greenland and Minerva A. Brown of Hampton, March 4, 1867.

Rev. George Walker Christie of Kittery, Me., and Sarah Pauline Aldrich of Rye, April 29, 1875.

Jonathan Dolbee and Hannah Marden, Dec. 25, 1744.

Jonathan Dearborn of Hampton and Sarah Wait of Amesbury, April 24, 1746.

Joseph Dearborn and Mary Dearborn of North Hampton, Jan. 29, 1776.

Samuel Dearborn, Jr., and Sarah Meserve of Greenland, Jan. 7, 1807.

John Dearborn of Hampton and Mrs. Deborah Cate of Stratham, Jan. 6, 1827.

William Dennett, Jr., and Olive Paul of Portsmouth, June 16, 1816.

Abner Down and Sarah Down of Gosport, Oct. 13, 1810.

John L. Downs and Susan M. Marten of Portsmouth, April 25, 1858.

John T. Dow and Mrs. Betsey Newman of North Hampton, June 16, 1822.

Benjamin W. Dow of Exeter and Sarah A. Locke of North Hampton, April 8, 1857.

Thomas Downing and Martha Norris of Greenland, Aug. 14, 1796.

Eben H. Dalton and Celia A. Hainer of North Hampton, Nov. 6, 1864.

Benjamin Woodbridge Dean of Exeter and Eunice Libby, Sept. 26, 1765.

Thomas Disco and Mary Damrell, Dec. 6, 1753.

William Emery of New Britain and Joanna Elkins, Oct., 1766.

John Emery and Sarah A. Wiggin of Stratham, June 30, 1861.

Chester W. Eaton and Emma Giles Leach, May 14, 1868.

Jeremiah Fuller and Mary Scadgel, July 26, 1745.

David Tenny Foss of Barrington and Betsey Sargent of Haverhill, Mass., Jan. 7, 1793.

Andrew French of Dover and Eliza W. Ayers of Greenland, Oct. 25, 1813.

Bradbury C. French and Mary Batchelder, Jan. 7, 1827.

David J. French and Irena Jewell of Stratham, Feb. 13, 1861.

John Fellows of Deerfield and Lois Fellows of Kensington, Nov. 21, 1811.

Ebenezer C. Fogg and Jemima Philbrick of North Hampton, May 17, 1824.

Ebenezer Fogg and Mrs. Lydia Brown of North Hampton, Dec. 22, 1846.

Harold M. Foye and Lizzie Odiorne of Portsmouth, Jan. 20, 1859.

Jonathan Godfred of Hampton and Elizabeth Lamprey, Oct. 3, 1749.

David Haines and Lydia Cater of Greenland, Feb. 17, 1743.

Thomas Haines and Deborah Lamprey of Hampton, Aug. 8, 1745.

Richard Haines and Prudence Brackett of Greenland, May 25, 1774.

Nathan Haines of Greenland and Hannah Johnson of Portsmouth, March 16, 1780.

Andrew Herrick of Cape Ann and Sarah Goodwin, Oct. 20, 1763.

Benjamin Holmes and Margaret Holmes of Portsmouth, July 6, 1780.
John Holmes and Sarah Ann Hall of Portsmouth, Dec. 2, 1844.
James M. Haley of Gosport and Hattie A. Clark of Kittery, Me., July 3, 1866.
Hartwell Hall of Lee and Abigail Elkins of Portsmouth, 1823.
Jeremiah Hart and Mary Kimball of Portsmouth, July 20, 1799.
Elisha Hart and Phebe Caverly of Portsmouth, May 4, 1794.
Charles Hardy and Mary Cochrane of Portsmouth, Aug. 14, 1802.
William Ham and Mary L. Holbrook of Portsmouth, Jan. 28, 1809.
Francis Harney and Mehitable Tarlton of Newcastle, May 24, 1814.
Moses Head and Catherine Osborne of Portsmouth, May 19, 1816.
Daniel Henderson of Dover and Betsey Hatch of Newington, Aug. 10, 1788.
James Hoig and Sally Palmer of Kensington, July 20, 1818.
Edward Johnson and Sarah Allard, Feb. 25, 1743.
Ebenezer Johnson and Margaret Barnes of Portsmouth, Feb. 19, 1748.
Jacob Johnson and Phebe Ayers of Greenland, June 4, 1789.
Samuel Johnson and Ann Morrison Boyd of Londonderry, Aug. 5, 1805.
Samuel Johnson and Sally Johnson of Northwood, July 5, 1828.
Mendum Janvram and Elizabeth Leach Hyde of Portsmouth, Sept. 21, 1815.
John L. Jewell and Sophie E. Marston of Stratham, Nov. 23, 1837.
Henry Jenness of North Hampton and Charlotte Lamprey, Aug. 5, 1813.
Peter Jenness of Meredith and Betsey Leavitt of North Hampton, Feb. 20, 1819.
H. A. Jenness and Sarah E. Foster of Newmarket, Oct. 12, 1860.
Seth Jenness of New Durham and Sophronia Smiley of Portsmouth, May 27, 1858.
Jonathan L. Kennison and Maria Aspinwall of Portsmouth, April 19, 1807.
John T. Kerseys and Olive Dearborn of Greenland, July 19, 1812.
Joshua W. Kenney of Newcastle and Isabella T. Neal of Portsmouth, Sept. 1, 1816.
John Kinsman, Jr., of Portsmouth, and Elizabeth F. Brown of North Hampton, 1828.
Eleazer Knowles of Candia and Hannah Knowles of Rye, Oct. 21, 1810.
Josiah Knowles and Susannah Godfrey, April 6, 1820.
Amos Knowles and Sally Perkins of Hampton, March 8, 1827.
Samuel M. Knowles of North Hampton and Elizabeth M. Jewell of Stratham, March 24, 1840.
Samuel Knowles and Abby A. Tarlton of North Hampton, May 19, 1848.
John Lane and Hannah Lamprey, Sept. 28, 1732.
Joel Lane and Mahala Brown of Kensington, Jan. 2, 1814.
John D. Lane and Margaret Dow of North Hampton, Nov. 30, 1843.

MARRIAGES.

John Lang of Portsmouth and Catherine Pope of Kittery, Dec. 31, 1747.

Jeffrey Lang and Esther Morril of Salem, Dec. 5, 1751.

Benjamin Lang and Mary Thompson of Portsmouth, June 4, 1756.

Josiah Lang and Pearn Johnson of Greenland, Dec. 17, 1771.

Moses Lufkins of Ipswich, Mass., and Sarah Brown, June 30, 1756.

Isaac Libbee, Jr., and Margaret Kalderwood, Sept. 20, 1766.

Nathan Longfellow and Tryphene Huntley, Aug. 24, 1756.

Edmund Rand Leavitt of Hampton and Mehitable Edmonds, Oct. 19, 1709.

John Lovering of North Hampton and Lydia Towle of Hampton, June 20, 1776.

Caesar Liberty and Phebe Ozel (probably colored), Aug. 2, 1783.

Curtis Law of Fort Constitution and Olive Mullen of Newcastle, Sept. 16, 1811.

Jonathan Locke and Mary Vennard of Newcastle, Dec. 24, 1812.

Sherburne Locke and Louisa Lamprey of Hampton, Aug. 15, 1824.

Eli Lamprey and Hannah Sanborn of Hampton, Oct. 12, 1823.

Tappan Leavitt and Elizabeth Page of North Hampton, Oct. 2, 1814.

Amos T. Leavitt of Hampton and Abigail L. Brown of North Hampton, June 14, 1829.

Edson L. Littlefield and Lydia S. Davis of North Hampton, Nov. 30, 1837.

George P. Ladd and Sarah J. Hanson of Great Falls, June 20, 1870.

John Lear and Eliza Varrell, March 21, 1775.

Joseph Melown and Deliverance Walker of Greenland, Dec. 31, 1741.

Jonathan Marston of Hampton and Sarah Weeks of Rye, June 30, 1743.

David Marston and Clarissa Marston of North Hampton, May 19, 1825.

Thomas Moulton and Hannah Down of North Hampton, Aug. 1, 1750.

Daniel Moulton of Gilmanton and Molly Lampre of North Hampton, Feb. 12, 1789.

Nathan Moulton of Hampton Falls and Charlotte A. Prescott of Kensington, 1816.

Daniel N. Moulton and Molly Brown of North Hampton, Aug. 9, 1818.

John Moulton and Charlotte Towle of Hampton, March 7, 1827.

Morris H. Moulton and Harriett Fogg of North Hampton, Sept. 17, 1860.

David Marston, Jr., of North Hampton and Olive D. Stevens of Stratham, July 28, 1839.

Joseph Mace and Elizabeth Rugg of Gosport, March 11, 1787.

Joseph Mace of Hampton and Abigail Fogg of North Hampton, Nov. 15, 1796.

Stephen Marden of Candia and Anne Stead of Portsmouth, Dec. 18, 1777.

James Marden of Portsmouth and Mercy Page of North Hampton, Dec. 22, 1822.

Samuel Marden and Betsey Marden of Portsmouth, Aug. 6, 1799.
Daniel Marden and Elizabeth Curtis of Portsmouth, Aug. 28, 1828.
Henry Maloon and Susannah Symes of Greenland, Aug. 16, 1750.
Samuel Moses of Epsom and Bridget Weeks of Greenland, April 9, 1760.
Nathaniel Morgan and Mary Bickford of Epsom, March 9, 1777.
Aaron Moses of Portsmouth and Ruhanna Mason, Feb. 10, 1805.
William Miller and Eliza Ann Dean, Feb. 18, 1813.
John B. Mead and Sarah H. Smith of North Hampton, 1817.
Benjamin Moore, Jr., and Eleanor Jewell of Stratham, March 11, 1822.
Thomas C. Marsh of Hampton Falls and Elizabeth Turner of Hampton, March 30, 1823.
Thomas Moses and Margaret Huntress of Portsmouth, April 4, 1811.
Alva Herman Morrill of Rye and Elizabeth Lake Hubbard of Wells, Me., Dec. 3, 1872.
Henry W. Moran and Mary P. Remick of Portsmouth, March 1, 1858.
B. N. Marden of Lewiston, Me., and Louise Chamberlain of Auburn, Me., Jan. 1, 1866.
David Nelson and Mary Atwood of Ipswich, Mass., Sept. 26, 1740.
John Nelson of Portsmouth and Ruth Mace of Rye, 1803.
William Nelson and Anne Whitten, June 24, 1763.
John Nelson and Mrs. Sarah Randall, Jan. 3, 1788.
William Nelson and Hannah Sliggins of Portsmouth, Sept. 25, 1803.
Christopher Noble and Martha Rowe of Portsmouth, Dec. 26, 1744.
Robert Neal and Alice Clark of Newcastle, April 19, 1750.
Samuel Norris and Elizabeth Holmes of Portsmouth, Oct. 30, 1766.
Samuel Norris and Sally Holmes of Portsmouth, Oct. 6, 1808.
Moses Norton and Elizabeth Goddard, Nov. 23, 1775.
Isaac Newton and Mrs. Mary Newton of the Isles of Shoals, July 23, 1804.
Mark Newton and Mary Caswell of the Isles of Shoals, March 31, 1817.
John Newton and Mary Haley of the Isles of Shoals, July 23, 1804.
Samuel Nudd and Hannah Tarlton of Greenland, June 17, 1779.
John Nowell and Sarah Randall of Gosport, Sept. 8, 1782.
Lemuel Ordway and Anna Dearborn of Loudon, Nov. 14, 1802.
George Odell of North Hampton and Sally B. Towle of Hampton, Oct. 15, 1818.
William Pierce and widow Randall of Gosport, Nov. 11, 1780.
Joseph Plaisted and Mary Fitzgerald, Nov. 13, 1780.
Benjamin Page and Mary Fogg of North Hampton, May 30, 1781.
Jeremiah Palmer and Lucy Yeaton of Portsmouth, June 26, 1819.
Sewell Pike of Hampton Falls and Polly Prescott of Kensington, Nov 11, 1813.
Noah Piper of Stratham and Mary Crimble of North Hampton, April 12, 1820.
Daniel Perrier of Exeter and Abigail P. Moulton of Stratham, Dec. 30, 1821.

MARRIAGES.

Noah Piper and Hannah Crimble of Stratham, March 12, 1837.
Nathaniel F. Page and Olive K. Pierce of Portsmouth, Dec. 31, 1845.
Thomas W. Philbrick and Jane C. Benson of Portsmouth, July 4, 1852.
Ivory T. Purrington of Exeter and Susan T. Marden of Portsmouth, March 28, 1863.
Josiah D. Prescott and Lucy A. Batchelder, June 3, 1865.
Arvillion Vincy Palmer of Rye and Elizabeth Anna Smith of Newmarket, Sept. 25, 1875.
John Ruswick and Mary Barker of Hampton, Dec., 1739.
John Rawlin and Esther Abbott of Greenland, July 29, 1754.
Job L. Randall and Lizzie Randall of Gosport, Aug. 18, 1838.
John Randall and Hannah Bragg, 1816.
Samuel Rowe and Merribah Rowe of Portsmouth, July 10, 1761.
Benjamin Randall and Mary Bragg of Gosport, Jan. 14, 1791.
Jeremiah Robinson of Exeter and Mary Page of North Hampton, Oct., 1784.
John Robinson and Mary Shapley of Gosport, April 27, 1789.
Peter Robinson and Hannah Randall of Gosport, July 16, 1811.
Asa Robinson of Brentwood and Maria Porter, Dec. 18, 1821.
Asa C. Robinson of Stratham and Mary B. Downs, Feb. 12, 1824.
Samuel Robinson of Gosport and Nancy Knowles of Seabrook, Aug. 29, 1824.
Robert Robinson and Tammy Caswell of Gosport, May 18, 1826.
Nathan Robie and Lucy Kenniston of Hampton Falls, May 2, 1821.
William Rugg and Judith Mace of Gosport, Dec. 8, 1792.
Christopher Rhymes and Sarah Hale of Exeter, May 21, 1767.
Ebenezer Sanborn of Hampton and Martha Salter of Newcastle, May, 1740.
John Simpson and Sarah Sheafe of Newcastle, Sept. 4, 1748.
Enoch Sanborn and Hannah Walker of Newbury, Dec. 16, 1773.
Jeremiah Sanborn of Sanbornton and Sally Page of North Hampton, Nov. 29, 1800.
Henry Saymore and Ann Cutt of Portsmouth, Sept. 13, 1750.
Esekiel Stanton and Mary Yeaton of Barrington, Sept. 11, 1782.
Kitteridge Sheldon and Eliza Holmes of Portsmouth, July 12, 1826.
Dearborn T. Shaw and Clarissa Blake of Hampton, May 4, 1828.
Andrew Shaw and Clarissa L. Marston, Jan., 1843.
Josiah Shaw, Jr., and Rhoda Dow of Hampton, Dec. 23, 1816.
Elijah Shaw of Kensington and Mrs. Sarah Wells of North Hampton, March 26, 1809.
William Stackpole and Elizabeth W. Jenness of Portsmouth, May 26, 1844.
Robert Stockels and Elizabeth Tucker of Portsmouth, Aug. 30, 1810.
John Shaw and Betsey Folsom of Exeter, June 19, 1785.
John Snell of Portsmouth and Olive Cate of Greenland, March 2, 1797.
Andrew Sherburne of Portsmouth and Susannah Knight of Rye, Dec. 4, 1760.

Lieut. John Smith of Fort Constitution and Caroline G. Willard of Newcastle, June 3, 1813.
Samuel A. Spinney and Mary E. Waldron of Portsmouth, Nov. 7, 1852.
Joseph E. Stoddard and Elizabeth Lightford of Portsmouth, Aug. 28, 1864.
Josiah Searcy and Lucinda, widow of James M. Goss.
Josiah Seavey and widow Alton.
James Seavey, Jr., and Patience Berry, May 23, 1780.
John Seavey and Ann Seavey, Nov. 20, 1791.
Isaac Towle and Elizabeth Philbrick of Hampton, Feb. 17, 1754.
Amos Towle and Hannah Philbrick of Rye, Aug. 1, 1792.
Darius Towle and Sally Downs of Hampton, 1836.
James Tarlton of Portsmouth and Katherine Odiorne of Newcastle Jan. 16, 1755.
James Tarlton and Harriett Atkins of Portsmouth, Dec. 20, 1806.
Joseph Taylor and Mary Lovering of North Hampton, June 20, 1776
Edward Tredick and Jane Trundy of Newcastle, Oct. 13, 1776.
Samuel Todd and Sally Grover of Portsmouth, Sept. 1, 1804.
Benjamin Thomas and Hannah Cushing of Portsmouth, 1812.
Lyford Thing of Brentwood and Lydia Pickering of North Hampton, Jan. 18, 1826.
John Varrell and Eleanor Norton of Portsmouth, May 8, 1808.
Edward Varrell of Salem and Mary Dearborn of Greenland, Aug. 3, 1809.
William Wallis and Comfort Cotton of Portsmouth, Aug. 15, 1738; lived at Epsom.
Weymouth Wallis and Martha Wallis of Greenland, July 8, 1772.
Benjamin Wallis and Deborah Fuller, March 18, 1780, both of Greenland.
Joseph Wallis and Margaret Fuller of Greenland, Nov. 23, 1769.
Reuben Wallis of Greenland and Elizabeth Rand of Rye, Jan., 1785.
Comfort Wallis and James Knowles, June 30, 1748.
Joshua Weeks and Sarah Jenness, Oct. 24, 1834.
Moses Wells, Jr., and Polly Merrill of Hampton Falls, May 31, 1804.
Hiram Wells of Sandown and Lydia V. Green of Rye, 1860.
Solomon White and Mary Locke, June 25, 1745.
Thomas Whidden, Jr., and Frances P. Foss of Rye, Jan. 3, 1830.
Samuel Whidden of Greenland and Hannah Langdon of Portsmouth, Jan. 8, 1745.
Samuel Whidden and Hannah Jones, July 5, 1874.
Simon Ward and Abigail Fullerton of North Hampton, March 2, 1784.
Daniel Welch and Elizabeth Abbot of Greenland, Feb. 29, 1744.
William Wormwood and Love Fuller, Oct. 26, 1747.
John F. Williams and Peggy Appleton, July 4, 1790.
Hunkin Wheeler and Betsey Tarlton of Portsmouth, July 6, 1808.
David Webster and Eunice Nowell of Portsmouth, Feb. 1, 1809.
Stephen Wiggin and Hannah Wiggin, Oct. 5, 1809.

MARRIAGES. 581

John Wiggin and Sally H. Marsh of Greenland, Aug. 19, 1827.
Abraham Wendell and Sukey Gardiner of Portsmouth, Oct. 24, 1809.
Jacob Waldron and Margaret Tarlton of Newcastle, June 3, 1811.
Samuel S. Warner and Abigail Leavitt of North Hampton, Aug. 20, 1833.
James Young of Wakefield and Ruth Smith of North Hampton, 1816.
David Young and Mary Durgin of Portsmouth, June, 1834.

Deaths, Not Included in Foregoing Records.

Ayers, Ruhannah, Aug. 24, 1831, aged 74 years.
Allen, Dorcas, Oct. 31, 1817, aged 83 years.
Berry, William, son of Jeremiah, Dec. 16, 1827, aged 75 years.
Berry, Levi, son of Jeremiah, April 1, 1833, aged 74 years.
Brown, Polly, widow of Jonathan, Dec. 6, 1853, aged 65 years.
Brown, Martha, widow of Joseph, May 19, 1842, aged 85 years.
Bunker, Izette, March 8, 1850, aged 26 years.
Caswell, Joseph, Aug. 20, 1896.
Coleman, Nathaniel, 1803.
Davidson, Abigail, Jan. 20, 1817, aged 77 years.
Davidson, William, March 21, 1807.
Downs, widow Betsey, April 27, 1863, aged 75 years.
Downs, Abner, April 7, 1818.
Edmonds, Jonathan, June 26, 1829.
Elkins, Henry, Nov. 16, 1834, aged 95 years.
Fisher, John, 1803.
Foye, Eunice, wife of William, May 26, 1830, aged 29 years.
Foss, Job, son of John, April 15, 1827, aged 42 years.
Foss, widow Rachael, wife of Joshua, March 15, 1818, aged about 75 years.
Foss, William, son of Joshua, Dec. 7, 1814, aged 46 years.
Garland, widow Mary L., May 12, 1826, aged 90 years.
Garland, Jonathan, Oct. 23, 1826, aged 62 years.
Goss, Levi (at Portsmouth), July 23, 1836, aged 88 years.
Goss, Sally, Oct. 29, 1845, aged 80 years.
Goss, Joseph, April 27, 1795.
Goss, Sally, wife of Daniel, Nov. 27, 1819, aged 68 years.
Goss, Sarah Berry, wife of Simon, May 16, 1822, aged 35 years.
Goss, Esther, daughter of Jethro, Dec. 14, 1822, aged 82 years.
Goss, Thomas, son of Thomas, Feb. 17, 1823, aged 76 years.
Goss, Elizabeth, July 7, 1824, aged 70 years.
Godfrey, Nabby, wife of John, Dec. 9, 1818.
Gould, widow, supported by town, 1805.
Gerry, William F., Feb. 15, 1898, aged 56 years.
Grove, Nathaniel, Feb. 15, 1810.
Green, Richard, March 4, 1832, aged 94 years.
Hall, Edward, drowned June 6, 1827, aged 62 years.
Haines, Reuben, March 24, 1806.
Hobbs, Perney, daughter of James, March 26, 1809.
Holmes, Nancy, wife of Jacob, March 25, 1834, aged 30 years.

DEATHS. 583

Johnson, Polly, wife of Jacob, Feb. 25, 1830, aged 62 years.
Johnson, Mary, widow of Peter, Aug. 20, 1831, aged 84 years.
Johnson, Giles (captain), 1801.
Johnson, Sally, May 2, 1794.
Jenness, Anna, daughter of Job, Feb. 26, 1825, aged 75 years.
Jenness, Jonathan, son of Joseph, Dec. 29, 1836, aged 76 years.
Knox, Margaret, Aug. 2, 1832, aged 80 years.
Knox, Drisco, Sept. 5, 1835, aged 87 years.
Lang, Sarah, 1801, aged 96 years.
Lang, George, Oct. 6, 1789, aged 44 years.
Lang, Stephen, died in Revolutionary army, July 6, 1778.
Langdon, Ann, daughter of Samuel, Jan. 20, 1725.
Lear, Mary, wife of Benjamin, June 13, 1834, aged 60 years.
Locke, Richard, Oct. 23, 1823, aged 79 years, at Northwood.
Locke, Joseph, April 22. 1790.
Lear, William, Revolutionary army, July 4, 1778.
Mason, Daniel, Oct. 30, 1834, aged 92 years.
Mason, Betsey, Nov. 20, 1820.
Murry, Elizabeth, wife of Samuel, Dec. 17, 1750.
McGregory, William, Jan. 13, 1812, aged about 38 years.
Mosher, Samuel, Nov. 9, 1878.
Moulton, Nehemiah, Aug. 15, 1816, aged about 75 years.
Nelson, Sarah, 1803.
Philbrick, Polly, widow of Benjamin, Jan. 18, 1842, aged 56 years.
Philbrick, Reuben, son of Reuben, June 12, 1831, aged 59 years.
Philbrick, Anna, wife of Joseph, Jan. 5, 1824, aged 78 years.
Poursel, Phebe, Nov. 26, 1820, aged 90 years.
Powers, Elizabeth, June 10, 1850, aged 84 years.
Poor, Robert, April 29, 1807.
Randall, William, son of George, Sept. 17, 1827.
Randall, Hannah, wife of William, Oct. 15, 1833, aged 40 years.
Randall, Sarah, Feb. 27, 1812, aged 80 years.
Rand, Esther, wife of Joshua, Oct. 2, 1809.
Rand, Hannah, relict of John, May 13, 1812, aged 62 years.
Rand, Ruth, relict of Stephen, Nov. 1, 1837, aged 75 years.
Rand, Dowrst, Jan. 12, 1847, aged 82 years.
Robinson, Mary, Aug. 21, 1814, aged 82 years.
Robinson, Sally, wife of Robert, Dec. 21, 1825.
Robinson, James, Sept. 1, 1840, aged 53 years.
Remick, Nancy, wife of Moses, Jan. 29, 1808.
Remick, Joseph, Oct. 5, 1808.
Saunders, widow Sarah, May 5, 1813, aged 78 years.
Seavey, Ann, wife of John, Jan. 26, 1827, aged 72 years.
Seavey, Cato (colored), April 4, 1829, aged 98 to 108 years.
Seavey, widow Mary, Aug. 7, 1853, aged 77 years.
Shapley, James, Aug. 4, 1821, aged 62 years.
Shapley, Benjamin, May 8, 1828, aged 35 years.

Shapley, Betsey, wife of Henry, Feb. 3, 1808.
Sleeper, Ruth, Feb. 23, 1832, aged 85 years.
Sleeper, Tristam, Jan. 26, 1811, aged 67 years.
Smith, David, June 1, 1804, aged 70 years.
Wedgewood, David, Aug. 23, 1814, aged 44 years.
Whidden, Hannah, 1801, aged 91 years.
Wallis, Phillis (colored), March 17, 1821, aged 80 years.
Wallis, Caesar Seavey (colored), Nov. 18, 1821, aged 81 years.
Total number of deaths during the nineteenth century—1,931.

"An account of ye number of people have died with ye late fattel distemper in several towns in ye province of New Hampshire Between ye Month of June, 1735, and Month of July, 1736.

In Rye have died under ten years	34
Between 10 and 15	6
Above 15	4
Total	44

Two families lost 3. one lost all. one lost 4 one lost 5."

Nicholas Hodge is said to have lived to the great age of 112 years. A Mrs. Tucker died in 1803, aged 100 years. Sarah Norris died in 1853, aged 102 years.

General Index.

	Page.
Abenaqui Golf Club	216
Agricultural Fairs	134
Ambassador	183
Ancient Names	70
Anecdotes	251
of Inhabitants	225
Assembly, first member of	21
Atlantic Cable	185, 186
House	117
Road	80
Baptist Church	174
Bells	219
Boulevard	94
Boundaries of Rye	38
Boutwell	133
Brackett Lane (see Brackett Road).	
Road	80
Brackett's Lane Massacre	245
Breakback Hill (see Meeting House Hill).	
Breakfast Hill Massacre	247
Bridge Road	80
Bridges	72
Cable Road	80
Station	185
Carriage, first in town	210
Causeway Road	80
Cemetery	194
Census	53, 55
Central Cemetery	194
Road	80
Christian Church	174
pastors of	174
Church Bells	219
Churches	149, 160
Baptist	174
Christian	174
Congregational	160
Episcopal	175
Methodist Episcopal	173
Second Advent	175
Civil War	279
men enrolled	280
Clark Road	80
Columbus Road	80
Common	132
Lands	126

586 GENERAL INDEX.

Concord Point	121
Congregational Church	160
Society, parsonage of	167
vestry of	165
Council of Plymouth	6, 8
Dacia	185
Dark Day of 1780	207
Destructive Storm of 1754	191
Discover	3
Discovery of Rye	2
Dow Road	80
Dover Neck, settlement of	14, 15
Drake's Lane (see Fern Avenue).	
Early Houses	57
Earthquakes	206
Ecclesiastical Affairs	149
Elections, earliest record of	32
Electric Railway	179
Elwyn Road	80
Episcopal Church	175
Explorers	2
Fair Hill Road	80
Fairs	134
Faraday	185
Farragut House	117
Road	80
Fern Avenue	80
Ferries	73
Fires	207
First Carriage	210
First Settlers	149
French War	253
men enrolled	254
Garland Road	80
Garrison Houses	250
Glebe	159
Golf Club	216
Gosport (see Isles of Shoals).	
Grove Road	80
Gun House	132
Hampton, map of	43
and North Hampton, separation of	49
Rye, boundaries of	41
Harbor Road	80
Hearse	199
High School	106
Hilton's Point (see Dover Neck).	
Hotels	109, 117
(summer)	
Atlantic House	117
Farragut House	117
Ocean House	117
Ocean Wave House	121
Prospect House	119
Sagamore House	121
Sea View House	119
Surf House	119
Washington House	119

GENERAL INDEX. 587

Houses in Early Days	57
Indian Depredations	244
Industries	176
Inhabitants (see Residents).	
Inn Holders	111
Inns	109
Isles of Shoals	6, 228
churches and ministers	236
discovery of	3
first hotel	235
Jenness Beach Road (see Cable Road).	
Jennesstown	133
Jonathan	7
Juan	277
Jurors	133
Laconia Company	7
Lafayette Road	80
Land Apportionment	127
Liberty Pole	133
Life Saving Station	187
Light and Power Co	216
Little Harbor Bridge	76
settlement of	9
Locke Road	80
Locke's Neck (see Straw's Point).	
London Bridge	77
Love Lane	80
Mail Service	213
Mardentown	66
Marsh Road	80
Mason Road (see Wentworth House Road).	
Mason's Hall	10
Massacres by Indians	244
Meeting House Hill	67
Houses	160
Merrimack River, discovery of	3
Methodist Episcopal Church	173
pastors of	173
Mills	217
Moderators	283
Names of Residents in 1696	71
1726	77
Negro Slaves	212
Newcastle, boundaries of	40
and Rye, political separation	33
petition for separation of Rye from	21, 29
Toll Bridge	83
New Hampshire, name fixed	19
province of, established	17
North Hampton and Hampton, separation of	49
boundaries of	40
and Rye, boundaries of	51
North Tree	39
Ocean Front Boulevard	94
House	117
Road	80
Wave House	121
Odiorne's Point, settlement of	8

GENERAL INDEX.

Old Residents	57
Orlando	279
Pannaway	9
House	12
Parish of Rye	20
Schools	97
Perkins Road	80
Petition to General Court in 1785, Relative to Military Grievances	272
Phillips-Exeter Academy, students from Rye attending	108
Physicians	215
Pine Tree Bridge	78
Pioneer Road	80
Piscataqua, exploration of	3
House	10
Play Grounds	105
Plymouth Council	6
Population	53
Postmasters	213
Portsmouth	271, 279
Portsmouth Road	80
Pound	131
Powder and Guns, inventory of	54
Privateers, men sailing on	279
Prospect House	119
Public Library	222
Lotteries	199
Worship, first established	150
Purchas His Pilgrimes	3
Receiving Vault	199
Record of Town Officers	283-289
Rendez-vous Point	10
Representatives to General Court	286
Residents	57, 71, 139, 160
removed to other towns	72
Revolutionary War, list of men lost	153
men enrolled	255
Roads	73, 84-94
Atlantic Road	80
Brackett Road	80
Bridge Road	80
Cable Road	80
Causeway Road	80
Central Road	80
Clark Road	80
Columbus Road	80
Dow Road	80
Elwyn Road	80
Fair Hill Road	80
Farragut Road	80
Fern Avenue	80
Harbor Road	80
Garland Road	80
Grove Road	80
Lafayette Road	80
Locke Road	80
Love Lane	80
Marsh Road	80
Ocean Road	80

GENERAL INDEX. 589

Roads, Perkins Road	80
Pioneer Road	80
Portsmouth Road	80
Sagamore Road	80
South Road	80
Wallis Road	80
Washington Road	80
Wentworth Road	80
West Road	80
Wood Road	80
Rockingham County Light and Power Co	216
Rye and Newcastle, political separation of	33
North Hampton, boundaries of	51
boundaries of	38
discovery of	2
first settlers	17
Glebe	159
Harbor	176
battle of	277
History	17
Men in Privateers	279
Parish of, incorporated	20
Sagamore Creek Bridge	75
House	121
Road	80
St. Andrews By-the-Sea (see Episcopal Church).	
Sandy Beach (see Parish of Rye).	
Sawmills	217
Scholars Attending First High School	106
in 1848	107
Schoolhouse playgrounds	105
Schoolhouses	104
Schools	96-108
appropriations for	105
establishment of	96
School teachers	100
Sea Road (see Ocean Road).	
Seavey's Creek Bridge	77
Sea View House	113
Second Advent Church	175
Select School or High School	106
Selectmen	21, 288
Senators	286
Sermon of Rev. Mr. Porter, extract from	149
Settlement of Rye	2
Settlers, first	149
Sheep	132
Shoals (see Isles of Shoals).	
Slaves	55, 212
Sleeper Legacy	222
Smith's Isles (see Isles of Shoals).	
South Road	80
Speedwell	3
State Senators	286
Stores	209
Stories of local interest	225
Storms	192
Straw's Point	38

GENERAL INDEX.

Students at Phillips-Exeter Academy ... 108
Submerged Forest ... 183
Summer Hotels ... 117
    Residents ... 123-125
    Resort ... 113
Surf House ... 119
Tavern Keepers ... 110
Taverns ... 109
Taxes, 1777 ... 142
Tax List ... 134
Teachers ... 100
    record of ... 105
Tenedos ... 277
Thomas ... 279
Toleration Act Passed by Legislature ... 162
Town Accounts ... 134
    Affairs ... 126
    Clerks ... 285
    Hall ... 221
    Meeting, votes in ... 129
    Officers, record of ... 283-289
    Pound ... 131
    Treasurers ... 286
Traditions ... 251
United States Life Saving Station ... 187
Vessels Owned in Rye ... 177
    Wrecked ... 17
Wallis Road ... 80
War of 1812 ... 274
    men enrolled ... 274-276
War Periods ... 253
Warwick ... 17
Washington House ... 119
    Road ... 80
Wentworth Road ... 80
    House Road (see Wentworth Road).
West Road ... 80
Wood Road ... 80
Wreck of Vessels ... 178

Index of Names.

	Page.
ABBA, Joanna	309
ABBOT, Elizabeth	580
Ruth (Ayers)	573
Samuel	573
ABBOTT, Bertha W	552
Charles A	280
Charles P	566
Esther	579
Mabel F	465
Margaret	415
Mary E. Webster	566
Nathaniel B	407
Polly (Lang-Trefethen)	407
Sarah	356
ACKERMAN-AKERMAN.	
Bartlett	293
Benjamin	491
Benjamin M	293
Charity (Locke)	293
Charity (Marden-Locke)	455
Clara M	342
Hannah	545
Henry C	293
Ira	293
John	293
Joseph	293
Peter	143, 145, 264, 273, 293, 346, 455
Phineas	293
Rachel (Foss)	293, 346
Sally (Philbrick)	293, 491
ADAMS, Charles	499
Charles W	293
Clara	516
Daniel	460
Fanny Goldthwaite (Lang)	487
Freddie O	293
Hannah	517
J. F	173
James T	173
John	476
John F	173
John W	173, 293, 549
Josephine	444
Lorenzo	293
Lydia M. (Trefethen)	293, 549
Lydia Viola	293, 351
M. Augusta	480
Mary	303, 476
Mary Jane (Foss)	293, 349
Mary (Mason)	460
Nathaniel	7, 247
Olive	370
Oliver	293, 349
Sadie Elvira	293
Samuel	476
Sarah E	574
Sarah E. (Porter)	499
Thomas	407
William Fisk	293
AIKINS, Betsey (Locke)	434

	Page.
ALARD, James	134
ALDRICH, J. K	159
Jeremiah K	159
Sarah Pauline	575
ALLARD, Mary (Libby)	418
S	418
Sarah	339, 576
ALLECE, Abigail (Libby)	416
Isaac	416
ALLEN	173
Abigail	336
Dorcas	582
Dorcas (Marden-Mow)	68, 293, 438, 465
Elizabeth (Cate)	573
Elizabeth L	431
Elizabeth (Locke)	293, 421
Elizabeth Locke	293
George L	125
Joseph	143
Joshua	293
John	16, 573
Jude	293, 421, 438, 465
Maria	344
Mary	430
Mary (Locke)	430
Nathaniel	293
Sally (Mow)	294, 439, 465
Salome	293, 313
Samuel	294, 465
Samuel Osborn	294
Sarah	312
Sarah (Hall-Sinclair)	377
AMAZEEN	209
—— (Berry)	298
Abigail	428, 433
Caroline	349
Christopher	57, 573
Hannah (Brown)	310
Henry	504, 573
John	71
Joseph	349
Joshua	310
Louisa (Rand)	504, 573
Mary (Foss)	349
Mary T	469
Mehitable (Rand)	573
William	298
AMBLER, Mary	414
AMES, Phebe	432
AMY, Elizabeth (Dowst)	294, 339
Joel	262, 294, 339
ANDERSON, Augusta	319
Margaret	563
Mary	563
Sarah Ann	301
APPLETON, Mary (Foss)	352
Peggy	580
ARCHER, Mary	553
ARNOLD, Thomas	263, 265
ARNUP, William	71

INDEX OF NAMES.

ASHLEY, Joseph............ 474
  Mary (Parsons) 474
ASHTON, Mary............. 414
ASPINWALL, Maria.......... 576
ATHERTON, Sarah........... 475
ATKINS, Harriett........... 580
ATKINSON, Theodore.......71, 127, 192
ATWELL, Joseph............ 71
ATWOOD, Clarissa (Mason)........ 460
  Comfort (Wallis)......... 564
  Eben 460
  Elizabeth (Godfrey)....... 367
  Joshua................533, 573
  Mary 578
  Mehitable (Seavey)....... 573
  Sarah (Marden).......... 573
  William 573
AULT, John................ 499
  Remembrance 497
AVERY, Jeremiah..........267, 268
AYERS, Anna Day........... 294
  Anna (Drake) 573
  Caroline Matilda......... 294
  Caroline P. (Garland).......294, 362
  Eliza W................. 575
  Elizabeth 529
  Elizabeth Garland....... 294
  Henry 294
  John 573
  Levi 466, 573
  Lizzie A................ 374
  Lydia 415
  Mercy (Tarlton)......... 573
  Merribah 467
  Nancy (Trefethen)....... 548
  Nathaniel 573
  Oliver 294, 362
  Ph..be 576
  Polly (Patterson)......... 573
  Ruhamah 582
  Rubamah (Norton).......466, 573, 582
  Rukannah, see Ruhamah.
  Ruth 573
  Ruth (Shapley).......... 573
  Samuel 548
  Sarah (Shields)......... 294
  Thomas...............267, 268
BABB, Betsey.............. 428
  Grace (Lang)........... 406
  Judith 405
  Merribah (Locke)....... 426
  Philip 406
BABBITT, Cora D........... 394
  George H............... 397
BACHELDER, Elizabeth..... 427
BACHELER, ———......... 328
BADSON, John...........71, 217
BADGER, George 516
  Prudence N. Randall..... 516
BAILEY, N. M.............. 173
BAKER, Albert S........... 436
  Anna 303
  Caroline (Locke)........ 436
  Ida V. (Jenness)........ 395
BALCH, Edward H 294, 321
  Elizabeth M. (Tucker).......294, 554
  Grace 395
  Gracia 294
  Julia (Bunker)......294, 321
  Martha C............... 294
  Martha Ellen........... 551
  Nathaniel..............294, 554
BALDWIN, Abel C.......... 353
  Hannah J. (Foye)....... 353
BALL, ——— (Brown)....... 294
  Abigail 475
  George 460

BALL, Hannah............. 294
  John 294
  Laurinda (Mason)....... 460
  Mary...............294, 313
  Mary (Wallis)........294, 563
  Peter...........136, 294, 563
  Susan 294
BANFIELD 225
  Elizabeth (Sherburne)..... 541
  Mary 294, 410
  Mary (Seavey).......294, 526
  Samuel............234, 526, 541
BANKS, Adelaide........... 562
BARBER 243
  D. W................... 173
  Penelope 416
BARBOUR, Daniel........... 107
BAREFOOT, Walter......... 225
BARKER, Mary............. 579
BARNARD, Angenette (Seavey)........ 532
  Calvin..............294, 395
  Charles 294
  James 294
  Joseph 532
  Sarah E. (Jenness).........294, 395
BARNES, Abigail (Lang)..... 573
  Margaret 576
  Mary 522
  Mary (Rand)............ 499
  Peter 573
  Thomas, Jr............. 127
BARRELL, Elizabeth (Langdon)....... 411
  Martha (Langdon)....... 411
BARRETT, Frances S....... 496
BARRON, Elizabeth......... 488
BARRY, Bartholomew....... 456
  Clarissa A. Davis (Marden)....... 450
  Jeremiah...............31, 260
  John 254
  Nathaniel...............26, 260
  Nehemiah 26
  Samuel 260
  Thomas F.............. 174
  William............26, 31, 254
BARTER, Winifred S....... 469
BARTLETT, Ann........... 451
  Deborah 555
  Elizabeth 475
  Elizabeth (Dalton)....... 330
  John...............259, 330
  Josiah Hall............. 259
  Josie B. (———)........ 509
BARTON, Addie E. (Spear)........ 544
  Eliza P. (Jenness Fogg-Philbrick) 390
  James 390
  James W............... 544
  Stephen 261
BARY, see Barry.
BASBRIDGE, John.......... 266
BASFORD, Elizabeth (Marden)........ 449
  Jonathan 449
BASSUM, Sarah............ 467
BASTON, Sarah J........... 517
  Sarah Jane............. 560
BATCHELDER, Abigail..... 295
  Abigail (Cotton)......... 295
  Abigail D............... 398
  Abigail (Jenness)....... 386
  Abigail (Norton)....295, 557
  Albert 295
  Almira...............295, 393
  Amanda 295
  Ambrose 295
  Angelina 295, 496
  Annie 295
  Benjamin 444

INDEX OF NAMES. 593

BATCHELDER, Benjamin D..........291, 295
Bessie L............................... 443
Betsey 295, 486
Betsey (Burleigh)..................... 573
Caroline M. P. (Chesley)............ 573
Charles E............................. 573
Charlotte 505
Clara A............................... 295
Clarinda 295
Clarinda A............................ 443
Comfort 295
Deborah 378
Dearborn 386
Edmund C............................. 573
Eliza (Brown-Ward)................. 314
Elizabeth....................295, 310, 378
Elizabeth (Batchelder)............... 295
Emily 295
Ethel May (Locke)................... 442
George A.............................. 442
George W............................. 281
Helen W.............................. 295
Izette (Green)....................... 374
James..............................295, 329
Jane 295
Jeremiah........................48, 50, 573
John............263, 295, 398, 406, 492, 573
John E................................ 295
Jonathan..........................172, 557
Jonathan Cotton...................... 295
Joseph...........................295, 492
Josiah...............263, 276, 295, 311, 568
Josiah M............................. 146
Leavitt 492
Lucinda 573
Lucy A............................... 579
Mandana 295
Mark 268
Martha...........................502, 514
Martha Ann 295
Martha Ann (Lord).................. 444
Martha (Fogg)....................... 573
Martha (Lang-Fogg)................. 406
Martha M. (Brown).................. 573
Martha M. (Lord).................... 295
Mary........................295, 355, 575
Mary Ann (Philbrick)...........295, 492
Mary (Philbrick).................... 492
May A................................ 295
Mehitable (Dalton) 329
Molly (Brown)....................... 311
Molly (Libbee)...................... 573
Molly (Libby)....................... 416
Nancy M............................. 573
Nancy (Philbrick)................... 573
Nathaniel..............295, 314, 416, 485, 573
Olive (Wells) 295
Olly (Wells)......................... 568
Phineas 268
Polly (Jenness)..................... 386
Polly (Perkins)..................... 485
Ruth L............................... 574
Sally 568
Samuel.............................263, 573
Sarah...........................295, 360
Sarah A.............................. 295
Sarah (Philbrick)..............295, 492
Stephen 42, 137
Susan 295
Susan L.............................. 574
Theodate 378
Warren 295
BATES, Judith...................295, 448
Mary...........................295, 298
William 295
BAYLEY, Sarah (Libby)............. 416
BEALE, John.......................... 71

BEAN, Deborah........................ 407
Eliza 332
Hulda (Berry)....................... 303
John W............................... 303
Mary 513
Polly 502
Reuel G.............................. 569
Sarah L. (Whidden)................. 569
BEARY, Jacob......................... 31
Nathaniel 22
Nemiah 22
Samuel 22
Stephen..........................22, 26
Timothy 31
William 22
BEBEE, Abigail (Foss).............. 352
Lizzie 533
Lizzie H............................. 533
BECK, Andrew........................ 555
Betsey (Odiorne)..............295, 574
Catharine 563
Deborah (Lear)...................... 295
Elizabeth (Odiorne)................. 468
Eliza (Thompson).................... 574
Hannah (Elkins)..................... 574
Henry 574
James 295
John..........................295, 468, 574
Mary 468
Molly 490
Samuel.........................136, 265, 266
Sarah (Varrell)..................... 555
Thomas...........................136, 574
BEEBE, George....................... 243
J. A................................. 175
BEEL, ——............................ 264
BELCHER, Jonathan 44
Samuel 239
BELECHER, see Belcher.
BELKNAP, Jeremy.........7, 15, 192, 207, 233
                            246, 247, 249
BELL, Abigail........................ 572
Abigail (Trefethen-Rand).......... 512
Anzolette A......................... 469
Dorothy (——)....................... 296
Elizabeth (——)..................... 296
Emily 506
Frederick Morgan.................... 296
George 512
Grace (Tucker)...................... 296
Hepsebah 572
Margaret 296
Mary (——).......................... 296
Matthew 296
Sampson 296
Shadrach........................71, 127, 296
Theodore 32
Thomas 296
BENNETT, John....................... 203
Polly (Norton)...................... 467
Stephen 203
Charlotte E. (Odiorne)............ 469
BENSON, Jane C...................... 579
William 469
BERERLAND, David.................... 296
Margaret 296
BERRY............................53, 72, 253
(Brasbridge) 299
—— (Carter)........................ 300
—— (Drake)......................... 305
—— (Tarlton)....................... 298
—— (Ward).......................... 305
Abby Ann 306
Abigail.......296, 297, 298, 300, 301, 302
                            304, 305, 399, 413, 506, 573
Abigail (——)....................... 297
Abigail (Brown)...............305, 315

INDEX OF NAMES.

BERRY, Abigail (Lane)............... 304
  Abigail (Rand)................... 304
  Abigail Towle (Locke)............ 432
  Abigail (Webster)............300, 565
  Adelaide (French)................ 302
  Alexander 304
  Alfred 301
  Alice J.......................... 302
  Alice J. (Walker)............302, 561
  Alice (Locke)................306, 420
  Alice Pearl...................... 303
  Alice (Willet)................... 302
  Alonzo 303
  Ann 303
  Ann (Philbrick) 489
  Anna B........................... 301
  Anna (Baker)..................... 303
  Anna M. (Gove)................... 303
  Anna (Philbrick)................. 297
  Augusta...............304, 306, 399, 515
  Bathsheba (Shaw)................. 305
  Beatrice 303
  Belinda 299
  Benjamin.........278, 297, 299, 303, 432
  Betsey....299, 300, 303, 305, 306, 371, 387
  Betsey (Berry)..............299, 303
  Betsey (Lang)...............301, 407
  Betsey M....................302, 461
  Betsey (Wedgewood)..........301, 567
  Betsey (Yeaton).................. 297
  Blanche.....................303, 350
  Blanche M........................ 351
  Brackett 300
  Brackett M....................... 301
  Caleb.......................253, 304
  Carrie 302
  Charity 297
  Charity (Webster)...........304, 564
  Charles.....................300, 301
  Charles Edward................... 306
  Charles F........................ 302
  Charlotte...................300, 322
  Clarissa L....................... 302
  Cora B. (Caswell)................ 303
  Cora (Caswell)................... 324
  Cordelia F....................... 303
  Daniel 305
  Deborah.....................297, 412
  Deborah (Hanscom)...........304, 306
  Dennis J......................... 302
  Dolly 299
  Dorothy (Emerson)................ 297
  Drucilla 303
  Eben......................24, 213, 515
  Ebenezer......22, 26, 27, 35, 57, 58, 65, 88
                135, 137, 142, 205, 273
                297, 288, 289, 298, 299
                300, 303, 304, 306, 359
  Edwin 303
  Eleanor...........297, 299, 358, 415, 437
  Eleanor (Brackett)............... 298
  Eleanor (——— Brackett)........ 297
  Eleanor Dow (Brackett).......308, 335
  Elinor (Jenness)................. 381
  Eliza 299
  Eliza (Marden)................... 306
  Elizabeth..........299, 300, 304, 305, 306
                420, 515, 516, 524, 569
  Elizabeth (Dalton).........301, 302, 331
  Elizabeth (Hobbs)................ 304
  Elizabeth (Hatch)................ 305
  Elizabeth J. (Caswell).......302, 322
  Elizabeth Lang................... 305
  Elizabeth (Marden)............... 300
  Elizabeth (Wendell).............. 299
  Elsey (Locke).................... 420
  Esther......................304, 348, 447

BERRY, Esther (———)............... 304
  Esther (Hall)................301, 376
  Ephraim 297
  Fanny (Hayes) 298
  Flora M.......................... 302
  Florence L..................302, 511, 522
  Francis Albert.............305, 306, 314
  Frederica A 304
  Frederick 296
  Geneva 320
  George......................304, 305
  George W......................... 302
  George William................... 302
  Gilman 541
  Gilman C....................301, 302, 322
  Gilman Woodbury.............302, 303
  Hannah...297, 298, 299, 303, 353, 368, 369
          435, 436, 449, 451, 457, 529, 548
  Hannah L......................... 299
  Hannah (Locke)............297, 298, 421
  Hannah (Randall)..........298, 303, 517
  Hannah (Vittam)............303, 306
  Hannah Wallis (Locke)......301, 432
  Harriet (Hodgdon)................ 301
  Harrison 303
  Hazel 303
  Hilda 303
  Horace A 302
  Horace B....................303, 324
  Huldah......................298, 303, 306
  Huldah (Towle)................... 298
  Ira 301
  Isaac 298
  Isabella (Walker)...........303, 562
  Isaiah 305
  Ithamar 296
  Jacob..............139, 143, 160, 204, 262
                273, 297, 298, 513
  James.............26, 71, 134, 139, 143
                296, 297, 303, 306, 381
  James Towle............35, 273, 298, 303
                304, 306, 517
  Jane 296
  Jane (———)..................... 296
  Jennie (Cole).................... 305
  Jeremiah............33, 35, 66, 75, 141
            143, 160, 176, 177, 203, 205
            256, 261, 262, 273, 285, 286
            289, 296, 297, 298, 299, 301
            308, 335, 421, 539, 582
  Jessie (Hanson).................. 303
  Joanna (Jenness)................. 306
  John.................70, 71, 127, 134, 149
            253, 296, 297, 301, 302
            303, 304, 305, 345, 420
            539, 574
  John Francis..................... 306
  John Gilman...................... 306
  John A........................... 302
  John W........................... 303
  John W. P........................ 302
  Jonathan..............262, 296, 490, 523
  Joseph................71, 127, 279, 297, 299
                300, 303, 304, 306
  Joseph Hall 302
  Joseph J...................413, 432, 567
  Joseph Jenness..............299, 301
  Joseph W....................374, 425
  Joseph Whidden................... 301
  Joseph William.........280, 302, 303
  Joses 298
  Joshua 305
  Jotham................70, 141, 143, 273, 297
                298, 300, 306, 515
  Jotham S......................... 302
  Judith.............70, 297, 299, 303, 545
  Judith (Locke)................... 296

INDEX OF NAMES.

BERRY, Julia A. (Butler).............. 303
Keziah....................297, 299
Keziah (Merryfield)................ 297
Laura (Wilson).................... 303
Lavinia 306
Lettis (Seavey)................305, 530
Levi..................66, 75, 141, 143, 205
265, 266, 273, 276, 298
299, 305, 385, 450, 582
Linda 302
Linden O.......................... 303
Lorenzo D......................... 303
Louisa..........................301, 438
Love............................299, 451
Love (Brackett)................299, 308
Lovina..........................304, 572
Lovina (Weeks).................... 302
Lydia......................298, 299, 548
Malvina (Hanscom)............304, 306
Maria Adelaide (Locke)........302, 441
Martha Adeline (Brown)..305, 306, 314
Martha Ann....................... 302
Martha (Kate).................... 574
Martha M......................... 302
Martha Olivia.................... 306
Mary............297, 298, 299, 300, 304
305, 306, 347, 378, 417
445, 522, 523, 538, 557
Mary (———)....................... 296
Mary A. (Gorham)..............304, 306
Mary Abby........................ 302
Mary (Adams)..................... 303
Mary Adelaide (Green)........303, 374
Mary Ann......................... 301
Mary Ann (Berry)................. 301
Mary (Bates)..................... 298
Mary (Caswell)................... 382
Mary E........................... 323
Mary Esther...................... 302
Mary (Foss)..............300, 306, 345
Mary (Garland)................... 359
Mary H. (Odiorne)................ 302
Mary (Kingman)................... 297
Mary Louise...................... 306
Mary Louise (Berry).............. 306
Mary (Randall)................... 304
Mary (Tucker).................... 300
Mehitable 299, 300, 304, 305
Mehitable (Berry)................ 305
Merrifield........57, 58, 139, 142, 143, 160
205, 212, 262, 273, 297, 298
Merrill 302
Merilla 302
Millage 306
Millard F........................ 303
Molly...................300, 301, 378, 558
Moses Granville.................. 302
Nabby 305
Nabby F. (Locke)................. 303
Nancy J.......................299, 556
Nathan 305
Nathaniel......24, 27, 102, 134, 136, 137
141, 143, 160, 169, 203
205, 278, 288, 296, 297
300, 301, 303, 304, 321
376, 407, 421, 529, 558
Nathaniel Foss...............302, 303
Nehemiah..........24, 27, 87, 88, 134, 136
137, 296, 297, 306, 420
Olive......................299, 396, 435
Olive Ann (Goss)................. 372
Olive (Holmes)................... 298
Olive Shapley (Locke).......305, 432
Oliver..............301, 302, 305, 315, 331
Olly 298
Pamelia Ann (Locke)..........301, 425
Patience...............298, 534, 580

BERRY, Patience (Marden)........305, 450
Patty 299, 348
Patty (Kate)..................... 299
Phebe, see Tryphena
Phebe (Moulton).................. 306
Polly (Garland)........57, 65, 299, 359
Polly (Keen)..................... 306
Polly (Randall)..............304, 306
Rachel...........297, 299, 351, 377, 444
Rachel (Rand)................298, 513
Ralph 303
Rebecca (Caswell).............303, 321
Richard....................204, 277, 298
Robinson F....................... 301
Roscoe........................303, 562
Rosella 326
Ruth.........................297, 303
S 148
Sally.............299, 301, 304, 306, 321, 543
Sally A. (Caswell)............... 303
Sally (Foss)..................... 301
Sally J. (Chapman)............... 305
Samuel....24, 27, 35, 88, 129, 135, 136, 138
141, 143, 147, 161, 169, 288
297, 299, 300, 301, 304, 306
345, 348, 376, 390, 456, 505
Samuel B......................... 391
Samuel Brackett........69, 275, 276, 278
289, 290, 299, 300, 324, 370
374, 514, 560, 565, 566, 567
Samuel C...................300, 302, 467
Samuel Foss..................301, 302
Samuel Symes..................... 304
Sarah.............297, 298, 299, 300, 304
369, 370, 383, 515, 536
Sarah A. (Shapley)...........301, 539
Sarah Ann........................ 301
Sarah D. (Seavey)................ 530
Sarah (Jenness)..............299, 385
Sarah (Lane)..................... 297
Sarah (Lang)..................305, 406
Sarah M. (Norton)................ 302
Sarah (Norton)................... 467
Sarah (Randall)........303, 304, 306, 515
Sarah Sargent.................... 299
Sarah (Seavey)................... 305
Sarah W.......................... 301
Sarah Wentworth.................. 299
Simon........................297, 306
Solomon............205, 273, 298, 299, 574
Stephen.....24, 27, 136, 296, 297, 304, 489
Susanna 297
Susannah................297, 300, 305, 449
Susannah (———)................... 296
Thomas.........27, 137, 299, 304, 305, 406
Thomas Garland....57, 65, 163, 164, 171
172, 173, 299, 300, 359
Thomas J......................... 530
Timothy..............35, 141, 143, 203
256, 261, 273, 299, 300
Tryphena 297
Tryphena (Philbrick-Sanders)..490, 523
Tryphena (Sanders)..........298, 306
William.........24, 27, 32, 38, 66, 70, 75
88, 126, 127, 129, 133, 134
135, 137, 141, 143, 160, 273
288, 296, 297, 298, 299, 300
304, 305, 306, 308, 432, 582
William C........................ 303
William H....................302, 561
Winfield S....................... 303
Woodbury..............107, 301, 302, 441
Zachariah.........27, 68, 136, 304, 564
BETTON, James.................... 268
BICKFORD, Clarence F............. 396
Ethel 307
Etta (Jenness)................... 396

INDEX OF NAMES.

BICKFORD, Hannah (Locke) 427
  Henry B 306, 507
  Joanna (Libbie) 413
  John 71
  Joseph 306, 500
  Joshua 306
  Julia Ann P. (Rand) 306, 507
  Martha (Locke) 434
  Mary 578
  Mary Ann 570
  Mehitable 434
  Pierce 434
  Rebecca 571
  Ruth (Rand) 306, 500
  Sarah 405
  Thomas 413
BILLINGS, Hannah (Newmarch) 574
  Mary 462
  Richard 574
BIRD, Almira (Caswell) 322
  Charles 322
BISHOP, Abigail (Tuck) 553
BLACK, E 399
  Elisha 307
  Hannah 307, 368
  John 334
  Mary 307
  Mary (Sanders) 307
BLAISDELL, Abner 307, 451, 498
  Adelaide 307
  George 364
  John 395
  John C 307
  Judith (Poor) 498
  Judith (Powers) 307
  Lovina 307
  Lydia (Marden) 451
  Mary (Garland) 364
  Nancy 537
  Nettie (Jenness) 395
  Thankful 430
BLAKE, — 70
  Abigail 433
  Abraham 547
  Annie G 325
  Clarissa 579
  David 534
  Dearborn 574
  Dorothy 520
  Elisha 307
  Eliza (Shaw) 574
  Ellen (Seavey) 534
  Hannah 423
  Hannah (Saunders) 523
  Hepzibah 307
  James 307
  Jasper 420
  Jemima (Locke) 307, 421
  John 265, 307, 421, 450
  Jonathan 311
  Joseph 574
  Josiah 265
  L 265
  Levi 265
  Mary 307
  Mary (Garland) 358
  Molly (Brown) 311
  Moses 315, 423
  Moses B 574
  Paul 263
  Rachel (Marden) 450
  Ruth L (Batchelder) 574
  Sally 332
  Sally (Towle-Rundlett) 547
  Samuel 307, 358, 415
  Sarah 307
  Sarah A. (Goss) 574

BLAKE, Sarah Ann (Brown) 315
  Sarah (Libby) 307, 415
  Susan L. (Batchelder) 574
  William 574
BLANCHARD, Joseph 160
  Adeline E. (Brown) 574
BLAZO, Amos 414
  Benjamin 280
  Ivory 574
  Joanna (Libby) 414
  John T 280
BLISS, Margaret 474
  Mary 474
  Thomas 474
BLODGETT, — 173
BLUE, Edward 307, 533
  Jonathan 267, 268, 307
  Mehitable (Seavey) 307
BLUNT, — 70
  George F 307
  Hannah (Frost) 307
  John 212, 259, 261, 262, 307
  Jonathan 47
BOARDMAN, Sarah 542
BOICE or BOYCE.
  A. Mandana (Foye) 307, 354
  Alice F 307
  Frank F 307, 320
  Gladys 307
  Hester 307
  Jeremiah 307, 354
  L 460
  Martha A. (Brown) 307
  Martha L. (Mason) 460
  Mattie (Brown) 320
BOND, Esther (Rand) 308, 574
  John 308, 574
  Mary 308
BOSS, George 558
  Lulu M. (Varrell) 558
BOWDITCH, S. B 174
BOWERS, Mary (Gove) 574
  Phillip 574
BOWLEY, James 430
  Polly W. (Locke) 430
BOWN, Roxanna 451
BOYD, Ann Morrison 576
BOYNTON, F. H 159
BRACKETT 53, 68, 135, 149, 246
  Alice (Pickering) 498
  Anna 308
  Anthony 70, 126, 127, 245, 308
  Eleanor 298, 308
  Eleanor (Dow) 308, 335
  Frances (Dow) 335
  Isaac 335
  Jane 308
  John 22, 71, 134, 160, 308, 488
  Joshua 75, 498
  Keziah 308
  Love 299, 308, 403
  Lydia Ann 331
  Martha (Philbrick) 488
  Mary 308
  Nabby (Berry) 305
  Phebe 308
  Prudence 575
  Samuel 21, 22. 24, 26, 27, 127, 134
    137, 138, 283, 289, 308, 335
  William 70, 305
BRADBURY, Mary 310
BRADY, Eliza A 407
BRAGG, Abigail 337
  Amelia B. (Randall-Sanders) 515
  Amelia (Sanders) 308
  Edward 308
  George 308, 502

INDEX OF NAMES. 597

BRAGG, Hannah.................... 579
 Henry 308
 John....................275, 308, 515
 Mary 579
 Molly 308
Patty Lang (Rand-Dow)......308, 502
 Polly 308
BRAINARD, Rachel.................. 424
BRASBEE, John..................... 265
BREED, Bernice.................... 321
 Edith 321
 Ethel 321
 Frederick 321
 Ida F (Philbrick).............. 321
 Ida (Philbrick)............... 494
 Lizzie N...................... 494
BREWSTER, Caleb................... 574
 Charles W.................247, 248, 249
 Deborah (Muchmore)............ 574
 Elizabeth (Lear).............. 574
 John G........................ 574
 Lydia 411
 Margaret 400
BRIAR, Peter...................... 574
 Rachel 574
 Rachel (Briar)................ 574
BRIARD, Harriet................... 570
BRICKETT, Joseph W................ 281
BRIDGES, Bethia................... 329
BRIGGS, Lizzie F.................. 566
BRISTOL, Dorothy.................. 508
BROAD, Clara...................... 367
 Frank 454
 Sarah A. (Marden)............. 454
BROCK, John...................238, 239
 Priscilla 568
BROCKETT, see Brackett.
BROOKLIN, Sarah................... 309
BROOKS, Samuel.................... 261
BROUGHTON, Hannah (Rand)......... 506
BROWN, ———........60, 91, 146, 218, 253
 ——— (Moulton)................. 309
 Abaitha (Coffin).............. 320
 Abba L. (Yeaton).............. 574
 Abby Ann...................... 316
 Abby (Doleby)................. 311
 Abby P........................ 316
 Abby Parsons..............318, 482
 Abial (Shaw).................. 309
 Abigail........106, 305, 309, 310, 311, 312
       313, 315, 331, 332, 493, 545
 Abigail (Berry)............... 573
 Abigail (Berry-White)......... 300
 Abigail (Dolbee).............. 334
 Abigail (Goss).............311, 368
 Abigail (Johnson)............. 309
 Abigail L..................... 577
 Abigail (Lamprey)............. 312
 Abigail (Philbrick)........... 312
 Abigail (Robinson) 521
 Abraham 309
 Ada 322
 Adeline 314
 Adeline E..................... 574
 Adna 393
 Agnes 318
 Alan Francis.................. 318
 Aleck Forbes.................. 318
 Alexander..................320, 330
 Alfred....................315, 317
 Alfred G. (Jenness)........... 319
 Alice Eliza................... 318
 Alice S....................... 320
 Almira.....................315, 439
 Almira A...................... 319
 Almira (Parsons)..........316, 477
 Amos...................310, 311, 490

BROWN, Amos Parsons..281, 317, 318, 393, 532
 Amos Simon.................316, 317
 Angelina...................315, 336
 Ann 311
 Ann (Brown).................. 311
 Ann (Cilley).................. 311
 Ann Eliza..................316, 396
 Ann (Heath)................... 309
 Ann (Lapish).................. 310
 Ann (Leavitt)................. 310
 Anna.......................311, 313
 Anna (Jenness)................ 387
 Anna Leavitt.................. 312
 Anna Leavitt (Brown).......... 312
 Anna Maria.................... 319
 Anna Sanborn.................. 311
 Annie M....................... 395
 Annie Mary.................... 316
 Artemissa R................315, 456
 Artimessa R., see Artemissa R.
 Argentine (Cram).............. 309
 Arthur L...................318, 372
 Augusta (Anderson)............ 319
 Augusta (Marston)............. 316
 Belinda S..................... 312
 Benjamin........309, 310, 313, 315, 436
 Bessie Marion................. 318
 Betsey....................311, 397, 558, 571
 Betsey (Berry)................ 305
 Caleb...................265, 266, 573
 Calvena E. (Seavey), see Calvinia E. (Seavey).
 Calvin 315
 Calvinnia E. (Seavey).......318, 532
 Carrie G...................... 318
 Carroll W..................... 318
 Charles Jonathan......64, 108, 285, 286
                   292, 316, 318, 341
 Charles O..................... 318
 Charles Rand.................. 318
 Charles W..................... 317
 Charles Woodbury.............. 319
 Clara Belle................... 317
 Clara E. A. Augusta........... 316
 Clara Emma.................... 319
 Clara N....................... 319
 Clarissa 315
 Clarissa (Brown).............. 315
 Clement 310
 Comfort (Jenness).........311, 313, 383
 Cora J. (Moulton)............. 318
 Daniel....................311, 319, 361
 Daniel W...................... 320
 Data.......................314, 569
 David..................311, 312, 360, 456
 David P....................... 486
 Deborah (Lucy)................ 310
 Dolly 311
 Dorcas (Fanning).............. 309
 Doris Julyn................... 318
 Dorothy...................330, 392, 574
 S. S. (Wedgewood)............. 319
 Ebenezer 309
 Edna Olive.................... 318
 Eli 312
 Elihua.....................315, 317
 Eliza......................314, 480
 Eliza Ann..................... 315
 Eliza G. (Wedgewood).......... 314
 Eliza (Garland-Marden)......360, 456
 Elizabeth..........309, 310, 311, 312, 313
            358, 369, 414, 428
 Elizabeth Ann (Garland-Frost)... 366
 Elizabeth (Batchelder)........ 310
 Elizabeth (Brown)............. 309
 Elizabeth (Dow)............316, 336
 Elizabeth F................... 576

598 INDEX OF NAMES.

BROWN, Elizabeth (Fellows).......... 310
Elizabeth (Jenness)................ 392
Elizabeth (Johnson).............. 311
Elizabeth (Mace)................. 312
Elizabeth (Maloon).............. 310
Elizabeth (Moody)................ 310
Elizabeth (Moulton).............. 310
Elizabeth (Sanborn).............. 314
Elizabeth (Seavey)........313, 320, 528
Elizabeth (Tilton)................ 311
Emeline....................315, 319, 395
Emeline (Downing)................ 336
Emerett.........................317, 487
Emerett A......................... 396
Emily 315
Emily Blanche................318, 520
Emily (Drake).................... 314
Emily (Parsons)..............316, 479
Elmira M.......................... 396
Emma Adeline...................... 317
Emma L............................ 497
Emma (Locke)..................... 320
Ernest Lamper.................... 317
Esther 480
Esther (Dalton)..............313, 329
Etta...........................317, 320
Eunice 558
Eunice Abby....................... 457
Fannie S.......................... 454
Fannie (Jenness-Dow)............. 317
Fannie Wesley (Jenness-Dow).... 393
Florence Mudge.................... 317
Frances A......................... 317
Franklin 319
Frank G.......................317, 318
Fred 342
Fred A............................ 403
Genevra (Berry)................... 320
George.....................281, 336, 511
George A.......................... 317
George Henry..............288, 316, 318
George W..................281, 317, 318
Goodman 569
Gracie (Drake).................... 342
Hannah.......310, 311, 314, 319, 331
                        395, 479, 567, 568
Hannah (Drake)..........314, 320, 340
Hannah (Garland).............319, 361
Hannah (Jenness)................. 319
Hannah (Lamprey)................. 312
Hannah (Smith)................... 311
Harriet Annetta..............317, 337
Harriet Annette, see Harriet Annetta.
Harriet W. (Dow)................. 318
Helen Vercilda.................... 318
Henrietta (Downs)............317, 338
Henrietta (Garland)..........319, 366
Henry..........................314, 393
Henry J........................... 317
Herbert W......................... 317
Horace S.......................... 364
Howard 59
Huldah (Page)................311, 471
Ira........58, 148, 164, 166, 169, 170, 172
             173, 290, 314, 315, 319, 361, 486
Ira Arvin......................... 316
Ivory..172, 177, 285, 287, 315, 317, 337, 398
J 61
J. Arthur....................291, 292
Jacob..........305, 309, 310, 311, 312, 573
James............31, 35, 273, 274, 300, 311
                    313, 315, 317, 374, 457, 565
James Franklin...............319, 320
James Webster.................... 318
Jane Lamprey..................... 310
Jane (Locke).................315, 436

BROWN, Jane M. (Perkins).......... 315
Jane Moulton (Perkins)........... 486
Jenness 314
Jennie E. (Fraser)................ 320
Jeremiah...........31, 205, 2:5, 309, 310
                         312, 313, 314, 330
Jessie N.......................... 317
Joanna (———— Brown).......... 309
Joanna (Abba).................... 309
Joanna (Jones)................... 309
Job..............33, 256, 262, 311, 313, 471
John....31, 140, 170, 173, 205, 207, 208, 273
             276, 293, 308, 309, 311, 312
             313, 314, 315, 319, 320, 373
             383, 387, 388, 392, 399, 513
John A......................315, 530
John E............................ 574
John H............................. 59
John Henry..................59, 314, 316
John Howard...................... 316
John Lucy........................ 310
John Sam Jenness................. 313
John Shirley..................... 316
Jonathan.......64, 140, 143, 160, 169, 170
             203, 205, 262, 279, 283, 284
             285, 287, 289, 290, 309, 310
             311, 312, 313, 314, 315, 316
                        320, 340, 358, 418
                             429, 479, 582
Jonathan Alva.................... 315
Joseph ..22, 33, 44, 45, 87, 135, 137, 138, 142
             160, 164, 172, 177, 208
             255, 257, 288, 289, 309
             310, 311, 312, 313, 319
             320, 334, 347, 358, 368
                 429, 479, 490, 528, 582
Joseph A......................286, 291
Joseph Arthur.................... 318
Joseph I......................... 281
Joseph Ira....................... 319
Joseph Ward..................314, 316
Joshua.................265, 266, 309, 414
Josiah........................310, 313
Julia L.......................... 454
Langdon.............59, 172, 314, 316, 336
Laura 317
Laura E. (Garland)............... 362
Leonard 314
Levi 556
Levi Webster.................315, 317
Lizzie Abby (Knowles)............ 403
Lucetta (Gray)................... 313
Lucetta S........................ 314
Lucinda (Batchelder)............. 573
Lucy Ann (Hallett)............... 314
Luella M......................... 318
Lydia 312, 575
Lydia Brown...................... 312
Lydia D.......................... 320
Lydia (Dalton)...............320, 330
Lydia (Ward)..................... 314
Mahala 576
Margaret Ann (Jenness).......318, 393
Margaret Medesta................. 318
Margaret Vercilda (Green)........ 317
Maria 317
Maria (Groom).................... 317
Maria (Libby-Seavey)............. 418
Martha................106, 312, 313, 314
                         320, 331, 332, 582
Martha A......................... 307
Martha Adeline..............305, 306, 314
Martha (Coffin).................. 313
Martha D......................... 458
Martha (Davidson)................ 312
Martha E. (Mudge)................ 317
Martha Hannah................317, 392

INDEX OF NAMES.

BROWN, Martha (Haskell)............ 311
  Martha M........................... 573
  Martha (Webster)..............315, 565
  Mary......172, 309, 310, 311, 312, 313, 314
    315, 333, 425, 429, 469, 548
  Mary A. (Clark).................315, 317
  Mary Abby (Davis)................. 316
  Mary Abby (Garland)............... 363
  Mary Ann (Jenness).............319, 392
  Mary Ann (Locke).................. 432
  Mary (Ball)....................... 313
  Mary (Bradbury)................... 310
  Mary (Brown)...................... 311
  Mary C. (Johnson)..............317, 398
  Mary D. (Foss).................319, 347
  Mary (Dalton)..................... 330
  Mary E..........................319, 561
  Mary Emma (Rand)........317, 318, 511
  Mary Esther.....................314, 316
  Mary (Flanders)................... 310
  Mary (Fogg)....................... 319
  Mary (Garland).................312, 358
  Mary (Godfrey).................... 310
  Mary (Gould)...................... 319
  Mary (Green)...................... 309
  Mary (Heath)...................... 309
  Mary (Jenness).................... 388
  Mary (Johnson).................337, 399
  Mary L. (Drake)................... 318
  Mary (Leavitt).................312, 333
  Mary Letitia (Drake).............. 341
  Mary (Locke)...................... 315
  Mary (Morrell).................... 311
  Mary (Page)....................... 310
  Mary (Philbrick).................. 311
  Mary (Seavey)..................316, 530
  Mary (Smith)...................311, 315
  Mary (Weare)...................... 309
  Mattie............................ 320
  Mehitable......................... 310
  Mehitable (Locke)................. 317
  Mehitable (Towle)................. 309
  Mercy............................. 313
  Minerva A......................... 575
  Minnie..........................317, 351
  Moody............................. 310
  Molly..........................311, 564, 577
  Molly (Jenness)................... 573
  Moses..................311, 312, 319, 366
  Nabby............................. 312
  Nabby Berry....................... 305
  Nabby (Elkins-Hall)............... 344
  Nancy............................. 312
  Nancy H. (Downing)................ 312
  Nancy (Jenness)................315, 387
  Nancy M. (Batchelder)............. 573
  Nancy (Perkins)................... 486
  Nathan..................310, 311, 315
    388, 392, 573
  Norman Howard..................... 318
  Norris E.......................... 317
  Olive............................. 311
  Olive A. (Goss)................... 318
  Oliver.......................319, 320, 330
  Oliver B. Fogg.................... 320
  Olly.............................. 311
  Otis Simon........................ 316
  Patty, see Martha.
  Perley William.................... 318
  Phila (Fellows)................... 573
  Polly..................163, 169, 319, 582
  Polly (Dalton).................... 320
  Polly (Gould)..................... 373
  Polly (Jenness)................314, 388
  Polly (Locke)..................... 429
  Polly (Rand)...................319, 513
  Polly (Seavey).................314, 528
  Rachel (Locke).................313, 429

BROWN, Rachel (Marston)............ 311
  Rachel (Sanborn).................. 309
  Rebecca (Libbey).................. 414
  Relief............................ 407
  Reuben............................ 432
  Rhoda............................. 315
  Richard........31, 32, 35, 139, 143, 267
    268, 284, 289, 313, 384
  Richard B......................... 311
  Robert William.................... 319
  Rosilla........................... 315
  Ruth Beatrice..................... 318
  Ruth (Kelly)...................... 309
  Ruth (Lamprey).................... 312
  Sally..........................315, 542
  Sally Leavitt..................... 312
  Salome (Allen).................293, 313
  Samuel.........................309, 310, 311
  Sarah..........309, 310, 311, 312, 313, 315
    333, 404, 495, 522, 577
  Sarah (———)....................... 309
  Sarah (Allen)..................... 312
  Sarah Ann..............314, 315, 495, 505
  Sarah Ann (Garland)............319, 361
  Sarah (Anzolette)................. 316
  Sarah B........................... 451
  Sarah (Brooklin).................. 309
  Sarah (Brown)..................... 309
  Sarah (Foss)...................... 315
  Sarah Frances..................... 317
  Sarah (Giles)..................... 311
  Sarah (Gove)...................... 309
  Sarah Hook.....................313, 320, 402
  Sarah (Jenness)................313, 384
  Sarah (Leavitt)................... 309
  Sarah Olive (Varrell)..........317, 556
  Sarah (Philbrick)..............311, 490
  Semira............................ 444
  Semira J.......................... 316
  Shirley........................... 318
  Simon......59, 68, 164, 170, 172, 173, 208
    311, 312, 313, 314, 316, 329
    333, 344, 480, 528, 530, 573
  Sophia.........................315, 317, 508
  Stacy W........................... 573
  Stephen........................303, 310
  Susan H. (Seavey)................. 530
  Susan Minnie...................... 318
  Susannah.......................... 311
  Susannah (Knowles)................ 311
  Theodore.......................... 311
  Thomas.........................309, 310
  Timothy........................... 476
  Vercilda (Green).................. 374
  Viennah F. (Garland).............. 364
  Warren............................ 363
  William......2, 309, 312, 313, 315, 317, 338
  William Goss...................... 318
  William M......................... 317
  William S......................... 362
  Woodbury.......................... 366
  Zaccheus.......................311, 312
  Zacchariah.....................310, 311
BRYANT, Allen G.................... 302
  Charlotte (Libbey)................ 417
  Flora M. (Berry).................. 302
  Joseph............................ 417
BUTLER, Edward..................... 574
  Hannah (Jenness).................. 387
BUCHANAN, Abigail M. (Foss)........ 348
  William........................... 348
BUCKINAN, Deborah (Locke).......... 420
  William........................... 420
BUCKLEY, Richard................... 71
BUCKNAN, see Buchanan.
BUKER, Augusta..................... 500
BUNKER............................. 60
  Addie P........................... 321

INDEX OF NAMES.

BUNKER, Anna R. (Towle) 320
  Belinda 320, 440
  Christy Ann 321
  Christy (Laws) 321
  Cora E. (Palmer) 321
  Frank 321
  Gardner Towle 320
  Izette 321, 582
  Izette (Garland) 363
  Izette S. (Garland) 320
  James 320, 379
  Julia 294, 321
  Lemuel 320, 363, 546
  Lemuel James 320
  Mary Ann 320
  Nancy (Hobbs) 320, 379
  Oliver Dearborn 320, 321
  Rosabella 321
  Sally (Towle) 320, 546
  Sophronie Lillian 321
  Willie 321
BUNTON, Charles 323
  Mary (Caswell-Varrell-Clay) 323
BURBANK, Aaron 416
  Elizabeth (Jenness) 384
  Elizabeth (Libbey) 415
  Enoch 384
  Sarah 449
BURCHELL, Maggie A. 551
BURGES, James 71
BURGESS, Francis 507
  Mary Emerett (Rand) 507
  Susan E. (Rand) 507
BURGIN, Charity (Grover) 574
  Joseph T. 574
  Walter S. 281
BURHAM, Sarah 475
BURLEIGH or BURLEY.
  Abby (Locke) 322, 439
  Betsey 573
  Daniel 322, 431, 439
  Deborah 503
  Eleanor 406
  Hannah 466
  Hannah (Lang) 406
  Margaret (Locke) 322, 439
  Mehitable Berry (Locke) 431
  Susan E. 354
  Sylvester 322, 431, 439
  William 259, 406
BURNELL, Eliza 544
BURNET, William 41
BURNHAM, Elizabeth 367
  Mary 471
  Nancy (Wallis) 564
  Noah 105
  Sarah (Brown) 313
  Silas 564
BURRELL, Annie M. 556
  Charles E. 555
  Fannie E. (Varrell) 555
BURROWS, Emeline (Langdon) 412
BURTON, Mary O. 457
BUTLER, —— (Rand) 513
  Elizabeth (Langdon) 574
  Enoch 267, 268
  Jerome 208
  Joseph 347
  Josiah 387
  Julia A. 303
  Kate 452
  Patience (Foss-Newton) 347
BUTTERFIELD, John 574
  Sarah (Dolbee) 574
BUZZELL, Reuel L. 522
  Sally (Salter) 522
CALFE, James 270

CALL, Edward 574
  Eleanor (Marston) 574
CAMPBELL, Archibald 264
  Sadie 558
CANNEY, Annie (Odiorne) 324
  Herbert S. 324
  J. Newman 324
CARD, John 127
CARLETON, Isaac C. 574
  Lydia H. (Lord) 574
  Polly 433
CARLTON, Abigail (Dalton) 329
  Benjamin 329
CARPENTER, A. A. 125
CARR, Benjamin 574
  George 449
  Mary (Marden) 449
  Rowland 265, 266
  Sarah (Shaw) 574
CARROLL, (——) 100, 522
  Arnold 321
  John 66, 75, 105, 111, 209, 321, 369
  Polly 321
  Richard 321
  Sally (Goss) 321, 369
CARTER, Charlotte 343
  Eliza 461
  Eunice 514
  Fannie (Philbrick-Salter) 495, 522
  Margaret E. 349
  W. E. 522
  William 495
CARY, Edward 71
CASS, Elizabeth (Locke) 427
  John 488
  Martha (Philbrick) 488
  Sarah 433
  Susannah (Libby) 416
  T. 416
CASSELY, Benjamin 419
  Rebecca (Libby) 419
CASWELL 72
  —— (Raynes) 322
  Abby Anna 517
  Abby (Locke-Burley) 439
  Ada (Brown) 322
  Albert 280
  Albert M. 322
  Alfred 323
  Alfred S. 322
  Almira 322
  Alvah L. 324
  Amy J. 323, 559
  Angelina E. 498
  Angeline 322
  Anna B. (Marden) 322, 451
  Arthur 323
  Asa 321, 322, 458
  Augustus 61, 324, 397
  Catherine (——) 517
  Catherine Elkins (Marston) ... 321, 458
  Charles 323
  Charles G. 322
  Charles Law 322
  Charles Reuben 280, 281, 322
                  323, 521, 555
  Charlotte (Berry) 300, 322
  Clarence Kimball 322
  Cora 324
  Cora B. 303
  Cynthia 323
  Daniel, see Burleigh Daniel.
  Dorcas (Green) 322
  Dorcas Marden (Green) 373
  E. Gay 324
  Edward 321, 322, 431, 439, 556
  Edwin 322

INDEX OF NAMES. 601

CASWELL, Eliza Esther............. 517
  Eliza G. (————)............. 517
  Elizabeth A..................... 322
  Elizabeth Ann................... 446
  Elizabeth G. (Locke).........321, 430
  Elizabeth J..................302, 322
  Elizabeth (Randall)............. 321
  Ella............................ 323
  Elmer........................... 543
  Elmer W......................... 324
  Emily........................... 322
  Emma Albertina.................. 323
  Ethelyn......................... 324
  Eva............................. 517
  Fannie (Hildreth)............... 322
  Flora A......................... 465
  Flora (Frye).................... 324
  Frank O......................322, 323
  G. E............................ 280
  George.......................... 323
  George Brewster................. 322
  Gracie.......................... 323
  James W......................... 323
  Jane G. (Randall)............... 517
  John.........280, 321, 322, 430, 461, 517
  John William.................... 323
  Joseph...........148, 300, 322, 517, 582
  Joseph M....................147, 301, 321
  Ida............................. 324
  Harry........................... 324
  Hattie.......................... 324
  Hattie M. (Matthews)............ 323
  Henry M......................... 323
  Henry N......................... 322
  Horace Washington............... 323
  Leila A. (Jenness).............. 324
  Lemuel.......................321, 436
  Leonora......................... 375
  Letitia......................323, 506
  Lizzie.......................... 323
  Lucy (Hart)..................... 322
  Lula A. (Jenness)............... 397
  Lula Ann........................ 322
  Lydia C. (Randall).............. 323
  Lynden.......................... 323
  Manasseh (Dutton).............. 321
  Margaret (Locke-Burley)......... 439
  Maria Salter.................... 322
  Marion.......................... 323
  Martha Jane (Randall)........... 323
  Mary........302, 321, 322, 323, 556, 578
  Mary Augusta.................... 323
  Mary E. (Berry)................. 323
  Mary Elizabeth.................. 322
  Mary Esther (Berry)............. 302
  Mary (Green).................322, 373
  Mary (Green-Caswell).........322, 373
  Mary H.......................322, 518
  Mary (McGuire).................. 322
  Mary (Marston)...............321, 458
  Mary (Matthews)................. 461
  Mary O. (Varrell)............323, 555
  Mary (Page)..................... 322
  Maud Arabella................... 323
  Maud I. (Gilbert)............... 323
  Michael.....................321, 322, 373
  Myrtle V........................ 324
  Nabby........................... 321
  Ova............................. 324
  Polly (Green)................... 321
  Polly (Green-Caswell)........... 321
  Rebecca......................303, 321
  Rebekah, see Rebecca.
  Richard Green...........169, 322, 451
  Rosa............................ 323
  Sally........................... 537
  Sally A......................... 303

CASWELL, Sally (Berry)..........301, 321
  Sally (Varrell)..............322, 556
  Samuel......279, 321, 322, 323, 373, 555
  Sarah........................323, 372
  Sarah A......................322, 558
  Sarah E. (Varrell-Palmer)....323, 555
  Sarah Elizabeth (Knowles)....323, 403
  Sarah Elizabeth (Robinson)...... 323
                                  521, 555
  Sarah Frost (Locke)..........322, 431
  Sarah Palmer (Locke)............ 436
  Sherman......................... 323
  Sophia G. (Smart)............... 324
  Sophia J. (Smart)............324, 543
  Sylvester, see Burleigh Sylvester.
  Tamah........................... 321
  Tammy........................... 579
  Thomas Green.................... 322
  Warren........107, 287, 302, 322, 323, 403
  William............280, 321, 322, 373, 458
CATE, Deborah..................... 575
  Elizabeth....................386, 573
  John............................ 466
  Lucy............................ 428
  Mary (Rand)..................... 512
  Olive........................386, 579
  Prudence (Marden)............... 449
  Richard......................... 512
  Ruth (Rand)..................... 512
  Samuel.......................... 512
  Samuel White.................... 267
  Sarah (Norton).................. 466
  William......................... 466
CATER, Anna....................... 563
  Lydia........................... 575
CATES, Samuel..................... 268
CATLIN, Hannah (Marden).......... 448
  Lucretia........................ 496
CAVERLEY, Hanson.................. 352
  Lucinda (Foss).................. 352
  Phebe........................... 576
CHADBORN, Ann (Berry)............303
  John............................ 303
CHADBOURNE, Olive................. 431
CHAMBERLAIN, Comfort (Ta:lton-
    Dorr)......................... 545
  John............................ 324
  Louise..........................578
  Lydia........................... 324
  Mary............................ 324
  Mary (Rand)..................... 499
  Mary (Randall).................. 324
  Samuel.......................... 324
  William...................254, 324, 499
CHAMBERLIN, see Chamberlain.
CHAMPLAIN, Samuel De...2, 3, 4, 5, 6, 228
CHANDLER, Alice F. (Boice)....... 307
  Mercy (Perkins)................. 483
  Samuel.......................... 483
  William P....................... 307
CHAPMAN, Abigail (Philbrick)....491, 574
  Dorothy......................... 565
  Electa Jane (Clough)............ 327
  Elizabeth....................... 356
  Hannah (Foss)................... 345
  James........................491, 574
  Job......................324, 368, 447, 574
  Jonathan........................ 324
  Joseph.......................327, 524
  Martha Wallis (Jenness).........388
  Mary (————).................... 324
  Mary (Saunders)................. 524
  P............................... 414
  Phebe........................324, 433
  Rachel (———— Goss)..........368, 574
  Rachel (Marden).............324, 447
  Sally J......................... 305

INDEX OF NAMES.

CHAPMAN, Samuel... 388
  Sarah (Libby)... 414
  Simon... 345
  Smith... 259
CHARLES I... 6, 238, 473
  II... 10
CHASE... 173
  Betsey L. (Merrill)... 574
  Clarissa (Philbrick)... 493
  Elisha... 574
  Elizabeth... 356
  Elizabeth (Philbrick)... 356, 488
  Hiram... 493
  Joseph... 253
  Lucia (Moulton)... 574
  Moses... 574
  Oliver... 290
  Thomas... 488
CHAUNCY, Julia... 375
CHENEY, Elizabeth... 434
CHESLEY, Caroline M. P... 573
  Eliza B... 325
  Elizabeth... 514
  Ella (Moulton)... 325
  Frank E... 325
  Hannah P... 325
  Hannah P. (Locke)... 325
  Jackson... 325
  John... 325
  Olive (Elkins)... 324, 344
  Samuel... 325
  Simon... 278, 324, 344
  Simon L... 61, 209, 280
  Simon Locke... 325
  Susan M. (Green)... 325
  Susan P. (Rand)... 325, 514
  William... 209
  William E... 61, 325, 514
  William Elkins... 325
CHICK, Anna G. (Blake)... 325
  Ernest... 325
  Ethel... 325
  Everett E... 325
  Ralph E... 325
  Susie... 325
CHICKERING, Henrietta F... 556
  Sally J. (Sleeper)... 542
  Zachariah... 542
CHOATE, Martha Waldron... 560
  Samuel K... 560
CHRISTIE, George Walker... 575
  Sarah Pauline (Aldrich)... 575
CHURCHILL, John... 71
CILLEY, Ann... 311
  Bradbury... 391
  Clara E. A. Augusta (Brown)... 316
  Deborah (Jenness)... 391
  Elizabeth... 514
  Elizabeth (Jenness)... 391
  Gate... 387
  Horatio... 391
  Joseph... 260
  Sally (Jenness)... 387
  William W... 316
CLAPP, Catherine... 386
  Elizabeth Garland (Ayers)... 294
  Hannah... 475
  Warden B... 294
CLARK... 129
  Abby S... 326
  Abigail (Parsons)... 475
  Adeline J. (Tucker)... 326, 554
  Albert... 326
  Alice... 564, 578
  Amos... 326
  Andrew... 276, 325, 518, 557
  Ann... 537

CLARK, Anna (Kerns)... 326
  Anna M... 326, 551
  Anna (Merrill)... 326
  Betsey... 325, 326
  Charles... 326
  Charles II... 326
  Charlotte H. (Trefethen)... 326, 550
  Clara A... 326
  Daniel... 267, 303, 325, 326
  Deborah... 325
  Drucilla (Berry)... 303
  Ebenezer... 475
  Edward... 325
  Eliza Jane... 326
  Elizabeth II... 566
  Emily... 325
  Emmons... 326
  Hannah... 325, 326
  Hannah (Marden)... 448
  Hannah (Remick)... 325, 518
  Harriett Augusta... 326, 376
  Hattie A... 576
  Jacob... 71, 129
  Jane... 326
  Jenny... 326
  John... 131, 267, 268, 290, 325
    326, 350, 432, 539, 554
  Joseph... 325
  Josephine (———)... 326
  Josiah... 325
  Judith... 327
  Levi... 326, 574
  Louisa (Gordon)... 326
  Lovina (Wiggin)... 574
  Lucy Ann... 326, 350
  Lyman... 326
  Marcia B... 326, 342
  Maria (Greenough)... 325
  Marietta... 326
  Mary... 474
  Mary A... 315, 317, 325
  Mary Emily... 326, 551
  Mary Frances... 326
  Mary (Hutchins)... 326
  Mary Jane (Shapley)... 539
  Mary (Locke)... 326, 432
  Mary (Mace)... 325
  Molly... 325
  Moses... 287, 290, 291, 326, 554
  Oliver... 326, 550
  Polly... 325, 326
  Rosella (Berry)... 326
  Samuel... 557
  Sarah... 426, 474
  Susan A. (Tucker)... 326, 554
  Susannah... 326
  Thomas... 203, 326
  Thomas Remick... 123, 325, 355
  William... 325, 326
  Lois... 545
CLARKSON, James... 137
CLAY, Deborah (Varrell)... 556
  John... 555
  Mary (Caswell-Varrell)... 323
  Rebecca (Varrell-Lang)... 555
CLEMENS, Ellsworth E... 550
  Adeline (Trefethen)... 550
CLEMENT, Joseph... 328
  Mary (Dalton)... 328
CLEMMENS, Abigail (Jenness)... 385
  Abraham... 385
  Sarah (Jenness)... 385
CLERK, Hannah (Marden)... 326
  John... 326
  Judith... 326
  Olly... 326
  Samuel... 326

INDEX OF NAMES. 603

CLIFFORD, Abigail (Seavey).......... 326
  Abraham..153, 255, 256, 257, 264, 268, 326
  Betsey 402
  Catherine 343
  Elizabeth......................333, 356
  Hannah 402
  Hannah (Dolbee)..........326, 333, 574
  Israel 356
  Louisa (Jenness)................... 389
  Lydia (Perkins).................... 484
  Mary (Garland).................... 356
  Newell 389
  Peter.......................326, 333, 574
CLLARK, John........................ 71
CLOUDMAN, Edward.................. 414
  Elizabeth (Libby)................. 414
CLOUGH, Alvedea H., see Alvida.
  Alvida..........................327, 551
  Abigail (Marden)..............327, 456
  Arabella 327
  Belle 441
  Edith M. (Varrell-Torrey).....327, 559
  Electa Jane....................... 327
  Elizabeth Rosamond...........327, 412
  George 559
  George A.......................... 327
  Jane Ann.......................327, 333
  Mahlon L......................... 327
  Marion 542
  Martha Mosher................... 327
  Nathan.................68, 327, 333, 456
  Nellie 354
  Selina 327
  Willis S........................... 327
COATS, Sarah........................ 462
COCHRAN, (———).................. 258
COCHRANE, Mary.................... 576
  Mary C............................ 453
  Sarah 433
COFFIN, Abartha.................... 320
  Abigail........................384, 542
  Abigail (Brown).................. 312
  Caroline T. (Foss)................ 352
  Hannah (Knowles)................ 402
  Martha 313
  Martha Olive (Green).........327, 374
  Mary 388
  Nabby 388
  Nathaniel......................327, 374
  Ovid G............................ 327
  Stephen 352
  Theodore......................312, 402
COFFRAN, Elizabeth (Dearborn)...... 333
COGSWELL, John C.................. 315
  Mary (Brown).................... 315
COLBY, Nancy....................... 449
  Patty (Jenness)................... 387
  Phineous 387
COLCORD, Eliza..................... 392
  Elizabeth (Jenness)............... 392
  Frederick 392
COLE, ———........................ 175
  Eli 348
  Jennie 305
  Olly (Foss)....................... 348
COLEMAN, ——— (Philbrick)........ 327
  Daniel 569
  Eliza B. (Chesley)................ 325
  James.............279, 314, 327, 340, 360
                  402, 438, 530, 565
  Lydia 327
  Mary Ann (Whidden)............. 569
  Mercy (Rand).................... 514
  Mercy (Sanders).................. 327
  Minerva A. (Brown).............. 575
  Nathaniel.............68, 327, 514, 582
  Phineas W........................ 575

COLEMAN, Robert Hodgkins.......... 327
  Samuel 325
  Sarah A.......................... 411
  Sarah F.......................... 539
COLLCUTT, David................... 259
  Joseph 259
  Josiah 260
COLLIER, Thomas.................... 205
COLLINS, Ebenezer................... 407
  Elizabeth 436
  Salome (Lang)................... 407
  Sarah (Lang).................... 407
COLMER, Abraham................... 8
COLTON, Abigail (Parsons)........... 474
  John 474
COPELAND, James.................... 532
COMFORT, Samuel................... 71
COMSTOCK, Elizabeth................ 499
CONES, ———....................... 105
CONEY, John........................ 302
  Martha M. Berry................. 302
CONNER, Parmelia................... 428
CONNOR, Abraham................... 478
  Benjamin 327
  Daniel 574
  Fanny 566
  John 572
  Joseph 327
  Mary Ann Wallis (Parsons)....... 478
  Mary (Seavey)................... 327
  Ruth (Yeaton).................... 572
  Samuel 327
  Sarah 327
  Sarah E. (Adams)................ 574
COOCHMAN, Sarah................... 571
COOCT, John........................ 71
COOK, Adeline...................... 544
  Elizabeth 474
  Olive W.......................... 468
  Sarah (Locke).................... 430
COOLEY, Abigail..................... 475
COOMBS, Olive...................... 465
COOPER, William.................... 270
COPELAND, Martha (Seavey-Trask)... 532
COPP, Hannah...................... 415
  Rebecca 343
CORBETT, Thomas................... 71
CORNELIUS, Emily Frances (Howe).. 574
  Joseph 574
COSSON, Thomas.................... 263
COTTON, Abigail...................295, 327
  Adam 327
  Addie P. (Bunker)................ 321
  Comfort........................545, 580
  Elizabeth 540
  Elvira 331
  Fred L........................... 363
  George D......................... 321
  Hannah........................327, 467
  Hannah (———).................. 327
  Huldah (Webber)................. 330
  Jonathan 543
  Joseph 418
  Judith (Clark)................... 327
  Leonard 65
  Mary (Sleeper).................. 543
  Morris 330
  Nathaniel......................203, 327
  Polly 541
  Sarah 390
  Sarah Abby 354
  Sarah (Libby).................... 418
  Theodata (Garland).............. 363
  Thomas......................202, 203, 327
COUSINS, Frank..................... 394
  Gertrude (Jenness)............... 394
COX, Leah.......................... 483

INDEX OF NAMES.

Cox, Minerva.................... 477
Cracy, Barnabas................. 127
Cragg, Hannah................... 570
Cragin, Eliza (Parsons)......... 478
   Jacob 478
Craig, Almira (Foye)............ 353
   William F..................... 353
Cram, Argentine................. 309
   Jane (Philbrick).............. 488
   Joseph 488
   Mary (Brown)................. 309
   Thomas 309
Cranch, Andrew.................. 71
Crane, Harriet.................. 372
Cranfield, ——................ 231
Crimble, Hannah................. 579
   Mary 578
Crockett, Hattie................ 419
   Jonathan 406
   Mary (Marden)................. 574
   Mehitable 543
   Pelahah 574
   Rebecca 416
   Sarah (Lang) 406
Croombs, Joseph................. 145
Crosby, Elizabeth (Woodman)..... 574
   John 574
Cronk, Dorothy (Brown).......... 574
   John R........................ 574
Crouse, Mary Butler............. 393
Cruch, Maria (Mason)............ 460
   Samuel 460
Cumming, Mary E................. 496
Cunningham, Hattie E............ 398
Currie, Julia M................. 434
Currier, Eliza (Robey).......... 574
   Emma C. (Jenness)............. 395
   Jefferson 71
   Joseph 307
   Lovina (Blaisdell)............ 307
   Mary (Ring)................... 574
   Sarah 505
   Thomas 574
   Varina 451
   William 574
Curtis, Elizabeth..........458, 578
Cushing 173
   Hannah 580
   Lydia Ann (Yeaton)............ 572
   Richard 572
Cushman, Mary................... 353
Cutt, Ann....................... 579
   John 231
Cutting, Minerva L.............. 508
Cutts, Edward................... 210
Daker, Elizabeth................ 354
Dale, Leonard................... 520
   Margaret (Robinson-Grant-Lewis) 520
Dalton, ——.................68, 72
   —— (Whidden)................ 329
   Abby 331
   Abiah 328
   Abigail.................328, 329, 330
   Abigail (Brown)............... 331
   Abigail (Gove) 328
   Anna 329
   Anna Leavitt.............331, 362
   Belle (Lane).................. 405
   Belle O. (Lane)............... 332
   Benjamin....61, 278, 329, 330, 359, 490
   Benjamin B................330, 331
   Bethia (Bridges).............. 329
   Betsey (Norton)............... 329
   Betsey (Rand)................. 330
   Caleb 328
   Celia A. (Hainer)............. 575
   Charles 330

Dalton, Clara 331
   Curtis E...................... 331
   Daniel............314, 331, 332, 489, 539
   Daniel Curtis................. 331
   Daniel P..................313, 320
   Daniel Philbrick..........330, 331
   Daniel Woodbury........208, 332, 405
   Dorothy 328
   Dorothy (Brown)............... 330
   Dorothy (Swan)................ 328
   Eben H........................ 575
   Ebenezer Leavitt.............. 331
   Ebenezer Marden............... 329
   Eliza A....................... 332
   Eliza (Bean-Parsons).......... 332
   Elizabeth......201, 3C2, 328, 329, 330, 331
   Elizabeth (Marden)........329, 448
   Elizabeth W. (Scammon)........ 331
   Elvina (Cotton)............... 331
   Elvira....................331, 365
   Emily 390
   Emily B....................... 331
   Emily (Shapley)...........332, 539
   Emma Perkins (Jenness)....331, 396
   Esther....................313, 329
   George E..................331, 396
   Hannah................328, 329, 330, 466
   Hannah (Brown)............314, 331
   Huldah (Webber-Cotton)........ 330
   James 330
   Jennie 331
   Jeremiah 329
   John......................328, 329
   Joseph.............105, 328, 330, 477
   Joseph Brown 314, 331
   Joseph M...................... 330
   Josiah 329
   Louisa....................331, 413
   Love (Hobbs).................. 329
   Lucetta 330
   Lydia.....................320, 330
   Lydia Ann (Brackett).......... 331
   Lydia (Glimper)............... 330
   Maria 329
   Maria (Prestwick)............. 330
   Martha (Brown)......313, 314, 320, 332
   Martha D...................... 330
   Martha (Wiggin)............... 330
   Mary......328, 329, 330, 331, 3C3, 382
   Mary Dow (Parsons)............ 330
   Mary (Smith).................. 329
   Mary (May).................... 330
   Mary (Palmer) 330
   Mary W........................ 331
   Mehitable.................328, 329, 488
   Mehitable (Palmer)............ 328
   Mercy 331
   Mercy (Philbrick).........330, 490
   Michael.......140, 144, 169, 172, 205, 256
      259, 320, 329, 330, 331, 490
   Morris 413
   Morris Benjamin............... 331
   Morris Cotton.............330, 331
   Moses.....................60, 329, 331
   Nancy (Nudd).................. 329
   Patty (Brown)................. 331
   Philemon..................328, 329
   Polly.....................320, 330
   Polly Dow (Parsons)........... 477
   Ruth 328
   Sally W....................... 331
   Samuel....................328, 329
   Sarah.....................329, 330
   Sarah (Garland)...........331, 359
   Sarah (Mason)................. 329
   Sarah (Scott)................. 329
   Sula (Leavitt)................ 413

INDEX OF NAMES. 605

DALTON, Timothy............328, 329, 448
   Tristram........................329, 330
   Tristram S......................... 331
   Ursula (Leavitt).................. 331
   Vienna M......................331, 497
DALRYMPLE, Octavia (Trefethen).... 549
DAME, Benjamin.....................267, 268
   Caturah 385
   Elizabeth (Pickering).............. 498
   John............................265, 266
   Joseph 105
   Mercy 428
   Timothy 498
DAMRELL, Mary.....................342, 575
DANA, Hannah......................... 522
DANIELSON, Hannah................... 431
DARTMOUTH, Earl of................... 257
DAVERSON, see Davidson.
DAVIDSON, ——— (Roberts)......... 332
   Abigail 582
   Abigail (Marden-Philbrick)....332, 435
   Abigail (Shaw).................... 332
   Abigail Taylor..................... 332
   Elias 332
   Gertrude (Mace)................... 446
   James D............................ 446
   John 332
   Josiah......................205, 276, 332
   Josiah Marsters.................... 332
   Martha 312
   Nancy 332
   Newhall 332
   Patty..........................332, 370
   Sally (Blake)....................... 332
   William..140, 144, 205, 262, 332, 455, 582
DAVES, see Davis.
DAVIS, Abigail (Brown)...........311, 332
   Almira (Dearborn)..............332, 333
   Amos 418
   Andrew 570
   Betsey 332
   Billy 332
   Charles A.......................... 332
   David 332
   Elizabeth W........................ 348
   Edwin P........................... 281
   Ephraim........................332, 522
   Eunice (Seavey)................... 332
   Fanny 522
   James 39
   James C............................ 436
   John 332
   John M............................. 295
   Lucinda 386
   Lydia S............................ 577
   Mary 336
   Mary Abby......................... 316
   Mary Ann (Salter)................. 522
   Mary Elizabeth (Woodman)........ 570
   Nancy (Griffith)................... 418
   Robert 332, 333
   Samuel...................31, 144, 311, 332
   Sarah Goss (Locke)................ 436
   Susan (Batchelder)................. 295
   William 332
DAY, Henry........................... 456
   Mary Jane (Marden).............. 456
   Miriam 431
DEAN, Benjamin Woodbridge......... 575
   Eliza Ann.......................... 578
DEARBORN, ———..............215, 477
   Abigail...................333, 340, 404, 428
   Almira..........................332, 333
   Ann 489
   Anna..........................333, 578
   Anna (Seavey).................... 528

DEARBORN, Caroline.................. 333
   Carrie 342
   Daniel 333
   Deborah (Cate).................... 575
   Dorothy (Dalton) 328
   Elizabeth.......................333, 358
   Esther 541
   Esther (Hobbs).................... 378
   Eunice (Libby).................... 575
   Gilman 299
   Godfrey ....328,·541
   Hannah Dow (Locke)............. 435
   Hannah (Locke)................... 423
   Henry 46
   Henry Washington................ 333
   James..........................263, 266
   James C............................ 265
   Jeremiah 423
   John.............267, 268, 333, 358, 575
   Jonathan 575
   Joseph 575
   Josiah..........................263, 333
   Levi..........................68, 333, 528
   Lucinda 333
   Lucy F............................. 364
   Mary.....................432, 557, 575, 580
   Mary Ann Adeline................. 333
   Mary (Brown)..................... 333
   Mary Brown....................312, 333
   Mary (Dearborn).................. 575
   Mary (Garland)................... 357
   Olive 576
   Reuben......................333, 378, 416
   Sally (Jenness).................... 391
   Samuel 575
   Sarah 388
   Sarah Ann......................... 333
   Sarah (Brown).................312, 333
   Sarah (Meserve)................... 575
   Sarah Sargent (Berry)............ 299
   Sarah (Wait)...................... 575
   Sarah (Ward)..................... 333
   Simon..........................312, 333
   Thomas 357
   Trueworthy.................274, 312, 333
DECATUR, Anna Pine................. 480
   Susan 480
DELANEY, Anna...................... 333
   Charles........................327, 333
   Estelle 333
   Fred 333
   Jane Ann (Clough).............333, 327
DEMONS, ———..................3, 4
DEMERITT, Sally (Jenness).......... 386
   Thomas 386
   Alice (Locke)...................... 428
DEMERRITT, Betsey (Locke)......... 428
   Moses 428
   Samuel 428
   Beckey (Morrison)................ 462
   Hannah Locke..................... 431
DENTLEY, Jane....................... 508
DENNETT, John...................... 431
   Joshua 431
   Lydia (Locke)..................... 431
   Olive (Paul)....................... 575
   William 575
DERBORN, see Dearborn.
DEXTER, Adelaide (Blaisdell)........ 307
   George 307
DIBLEE, Henry....................... 125
DILLOWAY, C. K.................... 499
   Martha R. (Porter)............... 499
DINSMOOR, Samuel.................. 479
DINSMORE, see Dinsmoor.
DISCO, Mary (Damrell)............... 575
   Thomas 575

INDEX OF NAMES.

Dixon, ———............ 175
  Hannah (Seavey)............ 536
Doane, Minnie............ 506
Dockham, Angelina............ 442
Dockum, Jonathan............ 465
  Sarah (Mow)............ 465
Dodd, Sarah............ 389
Doe, Mary Jane............ 367
  Nancy............ 367
  Susannah (Berry)............ 297
Doleby, Abby............ 311
Dolbear, see Dolbee.
Dolbee or Dolbeer.
  ———............ 72
  Abigail............ 334
  Aston............ 334
  Billy............ 334
  Daniel............333, 334
  Eli............ 334
  Elizabeth (Clifford)............ 333
  Hannah............129, 142, 326
    331, 333, 334, 501, 574
  Hannah (Marden)............ 575
  Isabella............ 334
  Israel............333, 334, 404
  Jesse............ 334
  John............ 288, 333, 334
  Jonathan............58, 88, 333, 334, 575
  Judith............ 334
  Margaret (Haines)............ 334
  Mary............ 333
  Mary (Randall)............ 334
  Molly............ 334
  Nicholas......31, 32, 35, 59, 135, 137, 139
    143, 204, 262, 273, 289, 333, 334
  Nichols............ 334
  Patty............ 334
  Ruth............ 334
  Sally (Sherburne)............ 334
  Sarah............334, 574
  Sarah (Lamprey)............334, 404
  Sarah (Smith)............ 333
  Sarah (White)............ 334
  Stephen............33, 334
Dolbeer, see Dolbee.
Dole, Mary............ 552
Dolbey, see Dolbee.
Donnells, Caroline (Mason)............ 460
  Frank............ 460
Dority, Esther............ 495
Dorr, Comfort (Tarlton)............ 545
Dotie, Collista............ 555
Douse, see Dowrst.
Doust, see Dowrst.
Dovost, see Dowrst.
Dovst, see Dowrst.
Dow............ 60
  Albert............93, 336, 530
  Amos............ 335
  Angelina (Brown)............315, 336
  Ann Elizabeth (Seavey)......336, 530
  Benjamin............ 265
  Benjamin W............ 575
  Betsey............335, 504
  Betsey (Newman)............ 575
  Cazendana............ 336
  Charity............ 87
  Charity (Philbrick)............ 334
  Charles H............ 336
  Clara Maria............ 336
  Daniel............ 336
  Data (Drake)............335, 340
  Eleanor............308, 335
  Eli............ 93
  Eli Sawtell............ 336
  Eliza Ann............ 335
  Elizabeth............316, 335, 336

Dow, Elizabeth (Fabens)............ 335
  Elizabeth (Perkins)............ 483
  Elizabeth (Seavey)............335, 527
  Ella F............ 336
  Emery............ 280
  Emiline............ 335
  Esther............ 426
  Ezra............ 267
  Fanny Wesley (Jenness)......317, 393
  Flora............ 336
  Flora B............ 51
  Frances............ 335
  George E............ 393
  Hannah............335, 383, 388
  Harriet A............107, 336, 561
  Hattie W............ 318
  Henry...142, 160, 246, 289, 335, 484, 527
  Isaac........26, 31, 33, 135, 137, 139, 144
    161, 167, 204, 262, 272
    273, 289, 334, 335, 527
  Jabez............ 378
  James..........91, 163, 166, 170, 172, 273
    275, 289, 335, 340, 477
  James Henry............291, 315, 336
  Jefferson............ 335
  Jeremiah............ 483
  John H............ 336
  John T............ 575
  Jonathan............262, 336
  Jonathan D............172, 336
  Joseph............89, 217, 245, 265, 300
  Langdon............ 335
  Lucy............ 378
  Lydia............335, 427
  Lydia (Fabens)............ 335
  Lydia P............ 335
  Lydia (Pickering)............ 335
  Mamie............336, 568
  Margaret............ 576
  Margaret (Downs)............ 337
  Martha............335, 404, 430
  Martha Ann............ 336
  Martha Leavitt............ 335
  Martha Locke............ 353
  Martha (Perkins)............335, 484
  Mary............63, 335, 339, 382, 385
  Mary (Parsons)............335, 477
  Molly (Clark)............ 325
  Moses............ 337
  Nathan............57, 336
  Nellie M............ 497
  Noah............57, 142, 336
  Patty............335, 477
  Patty Lang (Rand)............308, 502
  Phebe............ 385
  Phebe (Palmer)............ 336
  Priscilla............ 335
  Rachel............ 357
  Reuben............ 325
  Rhoda............ 579
  Samuel............ 357
  Sarah......106, 398, 403, 404, 417, 464
  Sarah A............ 481
  Sarah A. (Locke)............ 575
  Sarah Ann............ 336
  Sarah (Berry)............ 300
  Simon.....308, 336, 382, 383, 398, 404, 502
  Valentine............ 335
  Wallis............ 335
  Washington............ 335
Dowes, John............ 134
Down............ 72
  Abner............ 575
  Hannah............ 577
  Sarah............ 575
  Sarah (Down)............ 575
Downes, Charles H............ 401

INDEX OF NAMES. 607

DOWNES, Edward	412
Emma	454
Georgianna (Keen)	401
John O	412
Mary Abby (Lear)	412
Mary O	445
Nancy	412
Sarah P. (Lear)	412
DOWNING, Ebenezer	336
Eliza	336
Emeline	336
Abigail (Allen)	336
Abraham	336
Hannah (———)	336
Hannah C. (Knowles)	336, 337
John	336
Lydia (Ellsworth)	336
Mary (Davis)	336
Martha (Norris)	337, 575
Nancy H.	312
Samuel	336
Sarah	336
Thomas	337, 575
William C.	336
DUTTON, Manasseh	321
DYER, Betsey	422, 426
William C.	337
DOWNS, ———	226
——— (Holmes)	338
Abigail	337, 339, 378
Abigail (Bragg)	337
Abigail (Randall)	338
Abner	337, 338, 347, 515, 520, 582
Adeline (Hodgdon)	338
Amanda	505
Amanda A.	338
Ann	339
Ann Thomas	338
Appia	338
Benjamin	338, 339, 520
Betsey	338, 339, 516, 582
Betsey (——— Tucker)	337
Betsey M. (Randall-Matthews)	460
Betsey (Matthews)	337
Betsey (Randall-Mather)	515
Billy	337
Caroline	338
Charles H.	338
Deborah (Randall)	515
Dorothy Emma	338
Edward	337
Edward M.	337, 338
Edward N.	338
Eliza	337
Eliza A.	338
Eliza (Parson)	338
Elizabeth P. (Foss)	337, 338, 347
Elizabeth P. (Foss-Downs)	338, 347
Emma R.	338
Ephraim P.	337
Frederick	338
George E.	338
Georgie Ann (Kean)	338
Hannah Jane (Foss)	337, 347
Harriet	337
Harry	338
Henrietta	317, 338
Henry	337, 338, 347
Huldah (Randall)	338
James K.	338
Jane (Locke)	339
John	278, 337, 460, 515
John B.	235, 236
John Bragg	337, 348
John H.	280, 337, 347
John L.	338, 575
John Matthews	338
DOWNS, John Randall	339
Joseph W.	146
Julia M. (True)	338
Levi W.	236
Lillian	338
Love	337
Margaret	337
Margaret (———)	337
Mark	337
Mary	337, 517
Mary Abby (Lear)	338
Mary B.	579
Mary (Grant)	337, 338
Mary Olive	338
Nabby (Robinson)	520
Nancy	337
Olive (Foss)	337
Olly (Foss-Cole)	348
Ralph W.	338
Robert	337, 338
Sally	337, 339, 520, 580
Sally (———)	520
Sally (Downs)	337
Samuel	337
Samuel Washington	338
Sarah J.	338
Solomon F.	338
Susan M. (Marston)	338
Susan M. (Marten)	575
True J.	338
Wallace	338
William	337, 338, 339
Willis A.	338
DOWRST	135
Abial	339
Abigail	339
Abigail (Brown)	309
Anna	339
Betsey	339
Comfort	339, 427
Elizabeth	291, 339
Elizabeth (———)	339
Elizabeth (Brown)	309
Elizabeth (Jenness)	339
Elizabeth (Seavey)	339
Elizabeth (Shannon)	339
Henry	339
Isaac	339
John	31, 273, 309, 335, 339
Jonathan	273, 339
Lydia	339
Martha	339
Martha (Webster)	339, 564
Mary	227, 339, 346
Mary (Dow)	335, 339
Molly	339
Oreno	26
Ozem	27, 31, 32, 58, 87, 135, 137, 139, 142, 160, 177, 254, 339
Ozem J.	266, 339, 564
Rachel	339, 455
Rachel (———)	339
Samuel	22, 24, 27, 70, 71, 88, 134, 135, 136, 137, 339, 346
Samuel Morrill	339
Sarah	339, 391, 500
Simon	339
Solomon	24, 26, 27, 70, 135, 136, 137, 309, 339, 455
Thomas	339
DOWST, see Dowrst.	
DRAKE, ———	67
A. J.	80
Abbott B.	341
Abigail	388
Abigail (Dearborn)	340
Abigail (Marden-Foss)	447

INDEX OF NAMES.

DRAKE, Abraham......46, 92, 101, 208, 279
    314, 340, 357, 389, 390, 496
Abraham J........................ 341
Adams Elisha......70, 341, 342, 455, 457
Adeline 399
Adeline (Brown).................. 314
Albert Herman.........58, 253, 291, 298
    341, 342, 380
Alice G. (Wilson)................. 342
Amos G........................... 340
Anna.......................106, 340, 573
Anna D........................... 367
Anna Seavey (Parsons)........341, 477
Anna T. (Seavey)................. 530
Annie D.......................... 341
Annie L.......................... 342
Augusta Emma...............341, 506
Carrie 342
Carrie (Dearborn)................ 342
Charles 107
Charles A.........60, 281, 288, 291, 292
Charles Abraham................. 341
Chester 342
Clara 533
Clara Josephine.................. 341
Clara M. (Ackerman)............. 342
Clarissa (Knowles)...........341, 403
Cora 342
Cora W.......................... 350
Cotton Ward......60, 163, 166, 169, 170
    172, 173, 340, 358, 477
Data 335, 340
David T.......................... 342
E. Maria (Upham)................ 341
Edwin Howard.............326, 341, 342
Eliza Ann........................ 340
Eliza J. (Garland)........340, 361, 452
Elizabeth (Dow)..............340, 394
Elizabeth (Jenness).............. 385
Elizabeth Martha................. 341
Emeline 340
Emeline A. (Philbrick)........341, 496
Emily 314
Emma (Holmes).............342, 380
Emma (Marden).................. 342
Evelyn 342
Francis E........................ 125
George Weston................... 342
Gilman J......................... 340
Gracie 342
Hannah....................314, 320, 340
Helen 342
Helen A. (Weeks)................ 341
Izette Morris (Trefethen).....341, 549
James Buchanan.................. 341
James McEwen................... 341
Jane (—— Berry).............. 296
Jennie 342
John............60, 67, 163, 164, 170, 172
    209, 290, 340, 341, 477
John Harvey..................... 341
John Oren......65, 286, 291, 292, 341, 342
Jonathan..........60, 209, 286, 340, 361
Joseph Holmes................... 342
Joseph J.......65, 287, 290, 291, 403, 565
Joseph Jenness..............340, 341
Kate Augusta.................... 341
Laura Emma (Marden)........... 457
Laura F. (Trefethen).........342, 550
Leonie S.....................341, 509
Linden A........................ 342
Love Muchmore (Tuck)........... 552
Marcia 342
Marcia B. (Clark).............326, 342
Martha Maria................107, 340
Martha (Parsons)...........340, 477
Mary 342

DRAKE, Mary A.................... 533
Mary A. (Odiorne)............341, 469
Mary J.......................... 341
Mary (Jenness)..........340, 385, 389
Mary Letitia................318, 341
Mercy 408
Merton 342
Minnie E. (Wood)................ 341
Morris 550
Morris A....................341, 342
Nathan D........................ 341
Nathaniel..79, 127, 296, 314, 385, 447, 530
Oliver 340
Oren......132, 227, 280, 285, 287, 290, 291
    340, 341, 342, 371, 469, 549, 565
Orin, see Oren.
Percy 341
Ruth 342
Sarah......................340, 357, 530
Sarah Abigail...............341, 419
Sarah Olive.................341, 533
Sarah Parsons...............341, 458
Sarah (Ward).................... 340
Sarah Ward..................340, 394
Simon 552
Theodate 471
Willard 342
William 340
DREW, Henry..................... 173
Phebe 514
DRISCO, John..................... 342
Mary (Damrell).................. 342
Robert 342
Thomas 342
DROWN, Comfort M. (Langdon)....... 411
Hannah......................464, 560
Mary 352
Nancy 432
Samuel 411
DUDLEY, Elizabeth (Jenness-Colcord) 392
Jeremiah 392
DUNBAR, Annie May (Jenness)........ 395
Fred B.......................... 395
Joseph 439
Sally Hobbs (Locke)............. 439
Sarah 422
DUNBRACH, Flora Ida (Trefethen)... 550
Shadrack 550
DUNBRACK, Ida.................... 395
DUNN, Sarah...................... 566
DURGIN, Lydia.................... 348
Mary 581
Richard.....................265, 266
EASTMAN, Benjamin................ 423
Charles F....................... 125
Emily (Caswell)................. 322
Lydia (Locke)................... 423
Rufus 322
EATON, Amos..................265, 266
Chester W....................... 575
Emma Giles (Leach).............. 575
Reuben 268
Samuel 268
EDGERLY, Elizabeth............... 404
EDMONDS, Edward.................. 343
Elsie 343
Erie 343
Hannah 343
John 203
Jonathan....................343, 582
Mary 343
Mehitable...................343, 577
Nathaniel 343
Polly J.....................343, 391
Samuel 343
Sarah Rand...................... 343
Susanna (Tucker)................ 343

INDEX OF NAMES. 609

EDMONDS, Susannah............ 343
  Thomas 343
  William 343
EDMUNDS, Benjamin..........203, 343
  Catherine (Clifford)........... 343
  Charlotte (Carter)............ 343
  Fanny 343
  Hannah 343
  Hannah (Fullington).......... 343
  Hannah (Merrill)............. 343
  Jane 343
  John 343
  Jonathan 343
  Joseph..................203, 342, 414
  Polly 343
  Rebecca (Copp) 343
  Ruth (Libby)..............342, 414
  Thomas 24
EDWARDS, Elizabeth (Mason)........ 460
  Joseph M.................... 460
  Mindwell 475
EISINER, Allen F.................. 365
  Fanny E. (Garland)........... 365
ELDREDGE, Nellie P................ 343
  Roy K...................... 343
  William F................... 343
  Willie S.................... 343
ELKINS 61
  Abigail 576
  Catharine (Marston).......... 343
  Catherine..................343, 344, 459
  David 344
  Elizabeth 343
  George 344
  Hannah.....................343, 574
  Henry...........31, 32, 35, 138, 140, 144
          160, 343, 344, 565, 582
  Hitty (Rand)................ 501
  James......................344, 501
  James Seavey................ 344
  Jeremiah 376
  Joanna...................343, 485, 575
  Joanna (Roby).............. 343
  Jonathan 343
  Levi 344
  Lydia (Jenness)............. 396
  Maria (Allen)............... 344
  Mary...................343, 344, 425, 432
  Mary (Lord)................ 344
  Mary (Webster).............344, 565
  Mehitable (Rand)............ 344
  Mercy 343
  Moses 344
  Nabby 344
  Olive......................324, 344, 428
  Olive (Marden).............343, 448
  Rachel 546
  Samuel....32, 35, 140, 144, 160, 205, 209
          226, 263, 273, 343, 344, 448
  William 344
ELLINWOOD, Anna Tarlton (Locke).. 442
  Charles 442
ELLSWORTH, Lydia.................. 336
ELWYN 274
ELY, Hannah..................... 547
EMERSON, Annie................... 482
  Hannah 387
  Hannah (Marden)............. 447
  Hannah (Sheafe)............. 540
  Hugh 540
  Jacob 243
  Stephen 447
EMERY, Joanna (Elkins)..........343, 575
  Mary (Perkins).............. 485
  N 89
  Nancy 105
  Nathaniel 485

EMERY, Sally.................... 493
  Sarah A. (Wiggin)............ 575
  Sarah (Perkins).............. 485
  William.................343, 485, 575
ENDERSON, William................. 71
ERICKSON, Augusteen.............. 485
ESTWICK, Steven................... 71
EVANS, Abner..................... 415
  Almira (Dearborn-Davis)........ 333
  Asper 333
  Christina (Rand)............. 506
  Elizabeth M................. 366
  Mary......................410, 427
  Mary (Libby)............... 415
EVERINGHAM, J. E................. 175
EWING, Lizzie F.................. 453
EWINGS, Abby G. (Page).......... 472
  Calvin 472
FABENS, Elizabeth................ 335
  Lydia 335
FABINS, Mehitable (Berry)......... 304
FALLS, Lizzie................... 374
FANNING, Dorcas.................. 309
FARMER, John.................... 435
  Martha (Locke)............. 435
  Mary 414
FARNUM, Rachel.................. 514
FARR, Patience.................. 419
FARRAGUT, David G................ 117
FARRELL, Florence W.............. 398
FARRINGTON, Sarah................ 418
FAY, Charles.................... 536
FAYBEN, Abigail................. 498
FELEAR, Margaret................ 544
FELKER, Augusta................. 349
  Eliza 349
FELLOWS, Elizabeth.............. 310
  John 575
  Lois 575
  Nathan 407
  Phila 573
  Sarah (Lang)................ 407
  William 25
FERGURSON, Hannah (Locke)........ 436
  John Q. A.................. 338
  Sarah J. (Downs)............ 338
  Stephen 436
FERNALD, Albert................. 479
  Eliza (Downing)............. 336
  Elizabeth 554
  Elizabeth (Langdon).......... 410
  Hannah 352
  Isabel (Rand).............. 507
  Joseph 507
  Martha Ann (Parsons)......... 479
  Olive C.................... 433
  William....................336, 410
FESSENDEN, Esther (Rand)......... 508
  Jerome 508
  Sarah Abigail (Rand)......... 513
  William B.................. 513
FIELDS, Hannah (Ball)............ 294
FIFE, Helen A................... 510
  Mary 375
FIFIELD, Jonathan................ 291
FINLAYSON, Archibald............. 344
  Donnel 344
  Elizabeth (Lord)............ 344
  Mary 344
FISHER, John.................... 582
FITCH, Jabez.................... 240
FITZGERALD, Daniel..........205, 273, 344
  Mary 578
  Molly 344
  Nancy 344
  Richard 300
  Susannah (Berry)........... 300

INDEX OF NAMES.

FITZGERELL, Daniel, see Fitzgerald, Daniel.
FLAGG, Josiah.......................... 267
FLANDERS, Mary....................... 310
  Sarah (Perkins).................... 484
FLETCHER, Mary J..................... 460
FLOOD, Humphrey............263, 265, 266
FLOYD, Mary............................ 519
FOGG, Abigail........................... 577
  Alvin 344
  Bertha Emma......................... 344
  Cyrus 439
  Daniel........................46, 49, 414
  Ebenezer.........................320, 575
  Ebenezer C.......................330, 575
  Eliza J. (———).................... 496
  Eliza P. (Jenness)................. 390
  Elizabeth........................378, 547
  Elizabeth (Parsons)................ 476
  Emily (Locke)....................... 438
  Emma Amanda (Locke)................ 438
  Emma Ann (Locke)..............344, 439
  Esther 415
  Hannah.............422, 426, 447, 458
  Hannah (Libby)..................... 414
  Harriett 577
  Jemima (Philbrick)................. 575
  Jeremiah.....................150, 406, 476
  Lydia (Brown)...................... 575
  Lydia Dalton....................... 344
  Lydia (Dalton-Brown)..........320, 330
  Martha 573
  Martha (Lang)...................... 406
  Mary.......................319, 553, 578
  Oliver B............................ 438
  Oliver Brown....................... 344
  Richard 390
  Sarah 513
FOLLETT, Dorothy (Parsons)........... 529
FOLSOM, Abraham...................... 418
  Abram 173
  Ann 381
  Ann L............................... 397
  Betsey 579
  Betsey B............................ 397
  Betsey (Lamprey)................... 404
  Jeremiah........................265, 266
  Jonathan 259
  Josiah 404
  Martha A............................ 395
  Mary 399
  Mary (Libby)........................ 418
FOOLER, see Fuller.
FOOS, see Foss.
FOSS........................53, 72, 246
  ———— (Berry).................... 345
  ———— Marden..................... 352
  ———— Merrill.................... 350
  ———— Tilton..................... 351
  Abiel (Marden).................347, 455
  Abigail.......................346, 351, 352
  Abigail (————).................... 351
  Abigail (Locke).................352, 424
  Abigail M........................... 348
  Abigail Marden..................... 447
  Abigail (Reid)..................... 347
  Adeline (Locke)............349, 351, 439
  Alba H......................317, 349, 351
  Alexander 348
  Alice...........................349, 394
  Alice Adams........................ 351
  Almira P............................ 349
  Almira Pitman...................... 351
  Alonzo H............................ 348
  Amanda (Marden).................... 350
  Amy (Thompson)..................... 346
  Analesa 351

FOSS, Ann E. (Moulton)............... 350
  Anna Louise........................ 350
  Anna Partridge..................... 347
  Annie Julia....................349, 562
  Arthur M....................303, 350, 351
  Augusta (Felker)................... 349
  Benjamin 538
  Benjamin Marden................347, 349
  Bertha 351
  Betsey 347
  Betsey (Hunt)...................... 345
  Betsey (Sargent)................... 575
  Blanche M. (Berry)........303, 350, 351
  Caroline.......................347, 366
  Caroline (Amazeen)................. 349
  Caroline M......................... 348
  Caroline T......................... 352
  Carrie K............................ 454
  Carrie M............................ 350
  Catharine 347
  Chalcedony......................348, 350
  Chalcedony (Foss).............348, 350
  Charles.........................349, 371
  Charles B........................... 348
  Charles Edward..................... 350
  Charles Henry...................... 350
  Charles Osmond..................... 350
  Charlotta (Holmes)................. 348
  Charlotte 533
  Charlotte Drown.................... 348
  Charlotte M........................ 349
  Charlotte Seavey (Odiorne)....351, 470
  Christie.......................350, 562
  Clara A. (Matthews)...........349, 461
  Comfort.......................345, 408
  Cora W. (Drake)................342, 350
  Daniel Morrison......208, 280, 348, 350
  David 352
  David Tenney....................... 575
  Dolly 536
  Dorcas Pitman (Shapley)......349, 538
  Dorothy 345
  Dowrst 227
  Ebenezer..........176, 177, 345, 346, 347
  Edith 511
  Edith C............................. 350
  Edward Sargent..................... 348
  Eliza 558
  Eliza Ann........................... 349
  Eliza Esther....................... 348
  Eliza (Felker)..................... 349
  Eliza (Haywood).................... 352
  Eliza Mary Langdon (Seavey)...... 529
  Eliza (Shapley)................348, 538
  Elizabeth......346, 348, 352, 374, 461, 559
  Elizabeth (Locke).................. 352
  Elizabeth P...................337, 338, 347
  Elizabeth (Titcomb)................ 352
  Elizabeth W. (Davis)............... 348
  Ella Mary.......................... 350
  Ellen (Philbrick).............351, 495
  Elvira (Holmes).................... 349
  Emily Jones....................350, 511
  Emma (Hoyt)........................ 351
  Emma L.............................. 351
  Ernest..........................342, 350
  Esther (Berry)..................... 348
  Esther J............................ 347
  Esther Y............................ 400
  Ezra Drown......................... 349
  Ezra H.............................. 349
  Frances P........................... 580
  Frank 470
  Frank M............................. 350
  George.........260, 345, 346, 447, 448, 470
  George E............................ 349
  H 208

INDEX OF NAMES. 611

Foss, Hannah........345, 347, 351, 382, 523
  Hannah (———)................... 352
  Hannah Jane..........337, 347
  Hannah (Jones)................. 348
  Hannah Walton (Odiorne)........ 469
  Hardison...................290, 348, 349
  Harriet F......................... 349
  Harriett N........................ 348
  Harriett (Spear).................. 352
  Henry 351
  Henry D..........107, 281, 348, 349, 461
  Henry Herman.................... 349
  Herbert E...................350, 351, 470
  Hickerson 297
  Hinkson 351
  Ichabod 536
  Isaac Dallas...................... 349
  Isaac W.......................... 349
  James 346
  James N.......................... 348
  James Seavey..................347, 348
  Jane..............146, 345, 346, 472, 519
  Jane (Remick)..................347, 518
  Jeremiah 348
  Jeremiah B....................... 348
  Jeremiah Berry................... 347
  Joanna (———).................. 351
  Joanna (Seward)................. 349
  Job.................31, 67, 70, 141, 144
            153, 160, 203, 255, 262
            267, 273, 299, 345, 346
            347, 348, 352, 406, 582
  Joel N........................351, 439
  Joel U........................... 349
  John...........31, 33, 70, 71, 79, 127, 129
       134, 137, 141, 144, 176, 177, 257
       259, 260, 273, 275, 326, 344, 345
       346, 347, 351, 352, 469, 553, 582
  John H......................208, 281, 291
  John Henry...................... 348
  John Hunt..................348, 349, 531
  John Oren......80, 107, 348, 350, 374, 457
  Joseph 529
  Joseph Remick.................347, 349
  Joseph S.................281, 326, 349, 350
  Joshua.........21, 22, 24, 26, 27, 129, 135
       136, 137, 193, 288, 297, 345, 346
       347, 351, 352, 424, 559, 563, 582
  Joshua Marden....208, 285, 348, 349, 350
  Judith B.......................... 348
  Judith (Marden).................. 448
  Lena Forbes...................... 351
  Lewis 560
  Lewis Henry...............293, 350, 351
  Lizzie.........................349, 531
  Lizzie Haven..................... 350
  Lottie (Odiorne)................. 350
  Lucinda 352
  Lucy 470
  Lucy Ann (Clark)..............326, 350
  Lucy Ann (Locke)................ 441
  Lydia 431
  Lydia (Durgin)................... 348
  Lydia (Rand)..................... 499
  Lydia (Troop).................... 352
  Lydia Viola (Adams)...........293, 351
  Mabel Jane...................... 350
  Mabel Josephine................. 351
  Margaret 347
  Margaret E. (Carter)............. 349
  Mark......................259, 345, 346
  Martha A........................ 348
  Martha W....................... 347
  Mary................300, 306, 345, 346, 347
          349, 350, 352, 377, 515
  Mary (Berry).................... 347
  Mary D......................319, 347

Foss, Mary (Dowrst)........227, 339, 346
  Mary (Drown).................... 352
  Mary Ellen (Odiorne)............. 470
  Mary Esther (Goss)............... 371
  Mary (Foss)..............345, 346, 347
  Mary J.......................... 348
  Mary Jane...................293, 349
  Mary Jane (Green).............350, 374
  Mary Jenness.................... 384
  Mary (Libby).................347, 416
  Mary (Marden)................... 346
  Mary (Townsend)................ 338
  Mary (Tucker)................... 345
  Mehitable..............146, 346, 348, 350
  Mehitable (Foss)..............348, 350
  Merribah 351
  Merribah (Rand).............351, 500
  Minnie (Brown)..............317, 351
  Molly.....................300, 377, 525
  Moses 338
  Myron 350
  Nathaniel........35, 70, 141, 144, 254, 267
         273, 276, 345, 346, 384, 547
  Olive..........337, 345, 347, 348, 425, 430
  Oliver 348
  Olly, see Olive.
  Oran 348
  Patience 347
  Patty (Berry)................299, 348
  Patty (Mason)................... 348
  Patty W......................346, 460
  Patty W. (Foss-Mason)........346, 460
  Phineas 346
  Polly......................346, 347, 370
  Priscilla 449
  R 208
  Rachael, see Rachel.
  Rachel...........293, 346, 347, 538, 582
  Rachel (Berry)..............297, 351
  Rachel (Marden)................ 346
  Reginald 351
  Reinza 350
  Richard........107, 163, 166, 169, 170, 172
       173, 177, 278, 347, 348, 538
  Richard H....................... 348
  Robert.....................349, 352, 511
  Robert S.....................348, 350
  Robinson.......208, 276, 346, 347, 348, 460
  Robinson T...................... 348
  S. F............................. 280
  Sally.....................301, 348, 431
  Sally (Hodgdon).................. 348
  Salome (Trefethen)...........346, 547
  Samuel.........71, 137, 208, 274, 278, 279
       300, 345, 346, 347, 352, 547
  Samuel Dowrst.........35, 89, 141, 144
            262, 298, 346, 347
  Samuel F........................ 346
  Samuel W...................347, 372, 441
  Sarah.............315, 345, 346, 347, 502
  Sarah Amanda (Marden)......... 457
  Sarah (Dalton).................. 330
  Sarah (Foss).................345, 346
  Sarah G......................... 349
  Sarah (Lang).................345, 406
  Sarah (Saunders)................ 523
  Sarah (Tucker)..............347, 553
  Sarah (Wallis)...............345, 563
  Sarah Williard (Odiorne)........ 470
  Solomon...........278, 346, 347, 518
  Sula A. (Locke).................. 372
  Supply C......................... 346
  Susan H......................... 348
  Susan Minette................... 349
  Sylvanus 70
  Sylvanus W........286, 291, 349, 351, 495
  Theodora R..................... 349

INDEX OF NAMES.

Foss, Thomas............345, 351, 500
  Ursula Ann (Locke)............... 347
Wallace 254
Wallis..........31, 141, 144, 160, 202, 203
        227, 339, 345, 346, 347, 416
William..........71, 153, 176, 255, 263, 275
        345, 346, 347, 349, 352, 455, 582
William Ham...................... 352
Willey John....................... 350
Zachariah 351
Foster, Arthur W.................. 511
  Carrie A. (——)................. 511
  Carrie (Drake).................... 342
  George 342
  Sarah E........................... 576
  Sarah J........................... 395
  Walter W......................... 511
Fowl, Jonathan.................... 203
Fowler, Abigail................... 416
  James 22
Fox, Caroline..................... 519
  Miralda 386
Foye, ——— (Hill)................ 354
  A. Mandana...................307, 354
  Adeline 353
  Adeline (Rand)................... 507
  Almira 353
  Amos Dolbee 354
  Ann Cecilia...................353, 457
  Ann Mary......................... 354
  Apphia 353
  Betsey 352
  Charles..................353, 354, 507, 536
  Clarissa (Willey)...............353, 570
  Edward 354
  Eliza 353
  Eliza Ann......................... 353
  Eliza Josephine................... 354
  Elizabeth (Daker)................. 354
  Elizabeth (Seavey).............352, 528
  Ellen Ruthdian.................... 353
  Eunice...................352, 353, 582
  Eunice A.......................... 354
  Eunice (Weeks).................... 354
  Fidelea E......................... 353
  Frank Harrison.................... 354
  Hannah........................353, 461
  Hannah (Berry)................303, 353
  Hannah (Dolbear-Rand)............. 501
  Hannah Elizabeth.................. 354
  Hannah (Fernald).................. 352
  Hannah G. (Williams).............. 354
  Hannah J.......................... 353
  Hannah N. (Mason)................. 353
  Hannah (Seavey)................353, 528
  Hannah (Rand).........352, 353, 501, 516
  Harold M.......................... 575
  Helen 389
  Isaac 354
  James Nathaniel...............353, 354
  John..........33, 69, 75, 92, 121, 129, 141
      144, 163, 166, 169, 170, 172 173
      205, 259, 268, 273, 275, 276 303
      307, 352, 353, 528, 555, 565, 570
  John Harrison 353
  John Oren......................... 353
  John W........................281, 354
  John Wesley...................354, 531
  Joseph....................352, 353, 501
  Josiah W.......................... 354
  Lizzie (Odiorne).................. 575
  Luther P.......................... 354
  Lydia 572
  Lydia (Stevens)................... 352
  Lydia Stevens..................... 352
  Martha 170
  Martha Abby....................... 353

Foye, Martha Leavitt (Dow)........ 335
  Martha Locke (Dow)............... 353
  Martha (Odiorne)................. 565
  Martha T......................... 353
  Martha (Webster-Odiorne)......... 565
  Mary ((Cushman).................. 353
  Mary Elizabeth................353, 389
  Mary H........................... 354
  Mary Hannah...................... 354
  Mary Jane (Seavey)...........354, 531
  Mattie 354
  Morris Cotton.................... 354
  Nathaniel Graves..........93, 169, 172
                  276, 335, 353
  Nellie (Clough).................. 354
  Orion Leavitt..80, 166, 179, 180, 353, 354
  Richard 172
  Samuel D......................... 354
  Sarah Abby (Cotton-Jenness)..... 354
  Sarah Ann........................ 353
  Sophia Jenness................... 353
  Stephen..................121, 352, 353, 355
  Stephen J........................ 354
  Susan 352
  Thomas..............153, 255, 276, 570
  Thomas F......................... 354
  Thomas Fernald................... 353
  William...69, 276, 352, 353, 501, 528, 582
  William L.....................353, 354
Fraser, Ella Maria (Parsons)...354, 482
  Frederick John................... 354
  Jennie E......................... 320
  John..........................354, 482
  Julius Warren.................... 354
  Phillip 354
  Susan Parsons.................... 354
Frazer, Frederick J............... 108
Frazier, Frances.................. 365
Freeman, Emma B. (Trefethen)..... 552
  Joseph 552
French, Adelaide.................. 302
  Alvin C. M....................... 355
  Andrew 575
  ——— (Martin).................... 355
  Betsey (Jenness)................. 387
  Bradbury C.................295, 355, 575
  Clara Etta....................... 355
  Clara P.......................... 355
  Clara W. (Wiggin)................ 354
  Daniel 267
  Daniel James..................... 355
  David.........................354, 387
  David Alfred..................... 355
  David J.......................355, 575
  Eliza W. (Ayers)................. 575
  Emma 367
  George B......................... 355
  Irena (Jewell)................... 575
  John 105
  John Otis........................ 355
  Jonathan 111
  Josiah B......................... 355
  Martha 355
  Martha Bell...................... 355
  Martha J......................... 439
  Mary 547
  Mary Amanda...................... 355
  Mary (Batchelder)..........295, 355, 575
  Mary (Marston)................... 355
  Olive (Marden)................... 448
  Otis 355
  Rachel Emma...................... 355
  Samuel 106
  Sarah 570
  Susan E. (Burley)................ 354
  William 267
Friendy, Tobias................... 256

INDEX OF NAMES. 613

FRISBEE, Clara............................ 506
 H 280
 Hannah J................................ 442
FROST 121
 Aaron 355
 Elizabeth Ann (Garland).......... 366
 Elliot 326
 Emeline (Seavey).................... 530
 George............................47, 160, 212
 Hannah 307
 Henry 278
 J. C....................................... 366
 Jane (Clark)........................... 326
 John N.................................. 530
 Lizzie 319
 Lizzie (Garland)..................... 319
 Samuel 160
 William 32
FRY, Leonard.............................. 301
 Sarah W. (Berry).................... 301
FRYE, Flora................................ 324
FULLER, ——— (Gale)................. 356
 ——— (Hartshorn)................... 356
 Anna (Drake)......................... 340
 Carrie J................................. 509
 Christopher 355
 David 355
 Deborah............................355, 580
 Elizabeth..........................355, 535
 George 355
 Hannah 355
 Hannah (Jenness)..............356, 384
 Hiram 340
 James.....24, 26, 27, 44, 45, 135, 137, 355
 Jane 355
 Jennie C................................. 409
 Jeremiah...........................355, 575
 Jeremiah S............................. 355
 Joanna 355
 Joanna (Seavey)..................... 355
 John 355
 Joseph.............................355, 356
 Love 580
 Lovey 355
 Margaret..........................355, 580
 Mary 355
 Mary (———)....................... 355
 Mary (Scadgel)..................355, 575
 Nancy 356
 Olly 355
 Rachel 355
 Richard 355
 Sarah 355
 Sarah (Abbott)...................... 356
 Theodore 384
 Theodore Atkinson..............355, 356
FULLERTON, Abigail..................... 580
 Sarah 418
FULLINGTON, Hannah................... 343
FUMUEL, John............................ 203
FURBER, Lucy............................. 364
 Lydia (Dow).......................... 335
 Nabby (Locke)....................... 429
 Pierce P................................ 278
 John 335
FURLOUGH, Carrie L.................... 552
GAINES, George.......................... 498
GALLOWAY, Elizabeth.................. 515
GAMBLING 29
GAMMON, Ann Thomas (Downs).... 338
 Thomas 338
 William..............24, 26, 27, 135, 136
GANDY, Abigail.......................... 572
GARDINER, Abigail..................... 535
 Almira (Lang)....................... 408
 Andrew 408
 David 572

GARDINER, Dorothy.................... 468
 Emeline (Locke).................... 437
 Hitty (Yeaton)...................... 572
 John 437
 Judith 552
 Sukey 581
GARDNER, Christopher................ 263
GARLAND, ———........................ 251
 ——— (Leavitt).................... 366
 ——— Roberts..................... 363
 ——— (Yeaton)..................... 366
 Abby A................................. 364
 Abby Annah......................... 366
 Abby P................................. 107
 Abegonia 358
 Abigail....357, 358, 359, 361, 384, 387, 478
 Abigail (Norton)...............360, 466
 Abigail P.............................. 364
 Abigail (Perkins)..........361, 485, 492
 Abigail (Seavey)...............360, 527
 Abijah 358
 Adeline S. (Jenness)..........363, 391
 Albert Sumner....................... 366
 Albert W.............................. 363
 Alfred B............................... 362
 Alfred Curtis........................ 362
 Alfred Kimball..................... 365
 Amos..170, 171, 205, 273, 359, 361, 365, 387
 Amos R................................ 363
 Amos S................164, 169, 172, 276
 Amos Seavey...............360, 362, 528
 Ann M................................. 364
 Anna A................................ 403
 Anna A. (Whidden)...........363, 569
 Anna D................................ 440
 Anna D. (Drake).................. 367
 Anna Leavitt (Dalton).........331, 362
 Anna (Streeter).................... 366
 Anne..............................358, 359
 Annette 365
 Annie D. (Drake)................. 341
 Angenette 366
 Benjamin.......31, 35, 57, 65, 108, 141
  143, 160, 203, 205, 212, 253, 256
  262, 263, 267, 273, 300, 358, 359
  361, 364, 383, 427, 492, 528, 547
 Bethia (Taylor).................... 358
 Betsey 531
 Betsey Brown....................... 360
 Betsey Godfrey..................... 360
 Betsey (Parsons).................. 477
 Betsey (Woodman)............360, 571
 C. E..................................... 280
 Calvin....................61, 319, 347, 465
 Calvin Thompson.................. 366
 Caroline...........................294, 361
 Caroline (Foss).................347, 366
 Caroline G........................... 440
 Caroline Harwood................. 365
 Caroline P............................ 362
 Charles......281, 363, 364, 365, 391, 424
 Charles Barrows................... 364
 Charles David....58, 59, 60, 79, 80, 195
  210, 214, 285, 286, 291, 292, 363, 365, 512
 Charles F............................. 572
 Charles Frost....................... 365
 Charles William................... 366
 Charlotte........................361, 362
 Charlotte Ann..................363, 533
 Charlotte (Garland)..........361, 362
 Cilden 362
 Clara (Broad)...................... 367
 Clara D............................362, 459
 Clara J............................363, 365
 Daniel 367
 Data...............................361, 408
 David 364, 366, 367

INDEX OF NAMES.

GARLAND, David Howe.................. 362
Edna C..................................... 362
Edna May................................. 367
Edward 363
Edward L.....................331, 365, 543
Eliza............................360, 456
Eliza D. (Marston)................... 365
Eliza Ella.....................365, 373
Eliza J.....................340, 361, 365
Eliza J. (Garland)................... 365
Eliza Jane (Rand)................... 505
Elizabeth..........356, 357, 358, 359, 360
                      365, 366, 425, 528
Elizabeth (————).................. 357
Elizabeth Ann.......................... 366
Elizabeth (Brown).............310, 358
Elizabeth (Burnham)................. 367
Elizabeth (Chapman)................ 356
Elizabeth (Clifford)................ 356
Elizabeth (Dearborn)................ 358
Elizabeth Fidelia..................... 363
Elizabeth H................362, 367, 378
Elizabeth H. (Garland).......362, 367
Elizabeth (Howe)..................... 361
Elizabeth J. (Rand)................. 362
Elizabeth M. (Evans)................ 366
Elizabeth (Parsons)...........364, 477
Elizabeth (Philbrick-Chase)...356, 488
Elizabeth (Philbrook).............. 357
Elizabeth (Riley).................... 366
Elizabeth (Robinson)................ 356
Elizabeth (Spead).................... 366
Elmira 362
Elvira...................106, 331, 364, 394
Elvira (Dalton)....................... 365
Elvira Jenness........................ 367
Elvira (McDaniels).................. 363
Emeline A................................ 362
Emily...............................360, 542
Emma (French)......................... 367
Emma L.................................... 365
Emma (Manson)......................... 366
Emmons Cutter......................... 363
Estelle 366
Esther 356
Ethel Maud (Locke)...........367, 443
Eunice (Kenney)....................... 366
Fanny E................................... 365
Fanny (Seavey)..................361, 528
Fidelia 531
Florence W.............................. 362
Frances (Frazier).................... 365
Franklin 366
George W................................. 366
Gertrude 365
Gideon 363
Gilman..........64, 360, 363, 365, 392, 424
Hannah......................319, 357, 361
Hannah (————)....................... 357
Hannah Jane............................ 366
Hannah L................................. 549
Hannah (Marston)............358, 366
Hannah Parsons................364, 504
Hannah (Sanborn).................... 357
Harold B................................. 366
Harriett 360
Harriett (Kimball).................. 364
Helen (McKee)......................... 366
Henrietta........................319, 366
Horace 569
Horace Woodbury..................... 362
Ida (Mayo).............................. 365
Irvin 569
Irving W................................. 363
Izette S............................320, 363
Jacob....................................356, 357
James......................357, 358, 361, 366

GARLAND, James Filmore.............. 365
James Weston........................... 367
Jane (Garland)........................ 365
Jane (Stickney)....................... 357
Jerome 366
John..............21, 22, 26, 27, 35, 41, 59
    60, 87, 136, 137, 138, 139, 144
    170, 176, 204, 205, 210, 263, 273
    276, 283, 288, 289, 310, 312, 356
    357, 358, 359, 360, 361, 364, 367
    384, 477, 485, 488, 527, 528, 531
John Calvin......................364, 366
John G.................................... 492
John Langdon.......................... 360
John Wesley............................ 366
Jonathan..............205, 273, 357, 358
                       359, 360, 571, 582
Joseph..........35, 205, 263, 273, 276, 357
                358, 359, 360, 362, 367
Joseph H................................. 506
Joseph Oris............................ 367
Joseph Parsons.................364, 366
Joseph W..108, 280, 285, 286, 291, 341, 355
Joseph William..............58, 364, 367
Julia 451
Julia Ann......................... 364, 440
Julia H................................... 363
Laura E.................................. 362
Leander 366
Lepine Hall............................. 365
Levi..........59, 60, 205, 276, 279, 359, 360
                     363, 486, 522
Levi G.................................... 492
Lizzie Junkins........................ 365
Lucinda 390
Lucinda R............................... 362
Lucretia Emeline..................... 363
Lucretia (Locke)...............363, 432
Lucy Ann..........................363, 454
Lucy F. (Dearborn).................. 364
Lucy (Furber)......................... 364
Lucy (Salter)...................360, 522
Lydia (Moulton)....................... 358
Malvina 363
Mariah A................................. 363
Marshall W.............................. 366
Martha 362
Martha A................................. 390
Martha Ann (Rand).................. 506
Martha H................................ 365
Martha J. (Jenness)...........365, 392
Martha (Seavey)................362, 528
Mary..312, 313, 356, 357, 358, 359, 360, 364
Mary A.................................... 457
Mary Abby........................363, 366
Mary Ann......................362, 364, 454
Mary Ann (Garland)...........362, 364
Mary Ann (Mow)...................... 465
Mary Caroline......................... 367
Mary (Dalton)......................... 363
Mary Jane.........................363, 510
Mary Jane (Doe)...................... 367
Mary L.............................362, 582
Mary (Leavitt)....................... 359
Mary (Lowe)............................ 362
Mary (Marden)........................ 363
Mary Patten.....................362, 365
Mary (Philbrook)..................... 356
Mary (Rand)............................ 358
Mary (Tarleton)...................... 366
Mary (Trickey)........................ 366
Mary W.................................... 365
Mary W. (Dalton).................... 331
Mary (Watson)........................ 363
Mary Watson........................... 543
Mary (Williams)..................... 364
May (Marden).......................... 456

INDEX OF NAMES. 615

GARLAND, Mehitable............... 485
   Mehitable G................... 360
   Mehitable (Seavey)...........360, 528
   Melissa....................365, 446
   Morris Jenness..............364, 366
   Moses....................361, 363, 391
   Moses I....................166, 432
   Moses Leavitt................... 363
   Nabby (Knowles).................. 360
   Nancy............................ 359
   Nancy (Doe)...................... 367
   Nancy (Drown-Marden)........... 432
   Nancy (Leavitt).................. 360
   Nancy (Locke).................... 363
   Nathan W......................... 362
   Nathaniel 358
   Nettie R. (Whidden)...........362, 569
   Olive.........................361, 464
   Olive (Jenness)...............361, 387
   Oliver....................51, 364, 366
   Oliver P.......................... 281
   Oliver Perry..................362, 365
   Olly 358
   Oris 355
   Orlando.......................362, 505
   Parsons 366
   Patience (Marston)............... 360
   Patty (Locke).................364, 432
   Peter.......31, 108, 139, 144, 160, 204, 205
      267, 273, 356, 357, 358, 359, 360, 528
   Polly...............57, 65, 299, 359, 392
   Polly Jane........................ 363
   Polly Leavitt..................... 360
   Polly (Perkins)...............363, 486
   Polly (Philbrick).............364, 492
   Rachel 358
   Rachel (Dow)..................... 357
   Rachel Emma (French)........... 355
   Rachel (Morrison).......358, 367, 462
   Rebecca 357
   Rebecca (Sears).................. 356
   Reuel.............57, 58, 164, 166, 172
      213, 276, 287, 290, 297
      298, 359, 361, 364, 432
   Richard 358
   Rufus I.....................361, 364, 391
   Sally......................169, 359, 360
   Sally (Knowles).................. 362
   Sally Philbrick.................. 492
   Samuel...............59, 357, 358, 367
   Samuel Austin.................... 365
   Samuel P......................58, 535
   Samuel Parsons...............364, 366
   Samuel Patten................362, 365
   Sarah................65, 331, 356, 357
      358, 359, 384, 390, 392
   Sarah A.......................... 492
   Sarah Adeline.................... 363
   Sarah Ann.....................319, 361
   Sarah (Batchelder)............... 360
   Sarah (Drake).................... 357
   Sarah Elizabeth.................. 366
   Sarah Elizabeth (Yeaton)......... 572
   Sarah (Jenness)..............359, 383
   Sarah L.......................... 365
   Sarah L. (Knowles).............. 402
   Sarah (Pickering)................ 498
   Sarah (Taylor)................... 357
   Semira 362
   Semira P. (Jenness)...........364, 391
   Simon.....108, 139, 160, 205, 254, 258, 261
      263, 273, 276, 289, 310, 357, 359
      360, 364, 367, 402, 462, 466, 527
   Simon Elridge.................... 362
   Simon G.......................360, 362
   Sophia (Jenness).............365, 391
   Susannah 358

GARLAND, Susie Emma..............365, 562
   Tabitha 357
   Theodata 363
   Thomas....................357, 359, 361, 364
   Thomas Berry.................362, 364
   Thomas Leavitt................... 360
   Thomas Reuel..................... 364
   Viennah F........................ 364
   Walter 365
   William........108, 171, 300, 359, 360, 361
   William A.....................362; 365
   William Alfred................... 365
   William C.................59, 210, 456
   William Cutler, see William Cutter.
   William Cutter..59, 60, 207, 360, 363, 500
   William E..................365, 367, 443
   William Harvey................331, 363
   William S..............61, 170, 209, 285
      287, 290, 331, 361
   William Seavey...............360, 362
GATES, Charles....................... 367
   Martha Semira (Trefethen-Green)
      367, 549
   Story 549
   Stover 367
GAUS, see Goss.
GENNINS, see Jenness.
GENNINGS, see Jenness.
GEORGE II............................ 218
GERRISH, Ellen Thomas (Odiorne)... 469
   Paul 42
   Woodbury 469
GERRY, William F.................... 582
GIBBEE, A............................ 265
GIBBON, Rebeccah..................... 541
GIBBONS 19
GIBBS, Elizabeth (Sheafe)............ 540
   Robert 540
   William 262
GIBES, see Gibbs.
GIBSON 473
   Richard......................237, 238
GILBERT, Mary Ann (Randall)........516
   Mary L........................... 551
   Maud L........................... 323
   Sylvester 516
GILES, Sarah.........................311
GILLIS, Margaret E................... 443
GILLMAN, see Gilman.
GILMAN 370
   ——— (Perkins).................. 486
   David.........................263, 270
   Harriet T........................ 539
   Jonathan 40
   Mary (Libby-Folsom)............. 418
   Nathaniel 259
   Nicholas......................39, 40, 42
GILSON, Adeline (Foye)............... 353
GLAS, Richard........................ 71
GLIDDEN, Joseph...................... 415
   Mary (Libby)..................... 415
GLIFFORD, Harvey C................... 437
   Mary Susan (Locke).............. 437
GLIMPER, Lydia....................... 330
GLOVER, Hannah (Parsons)............ 474
   Peletiah 474
GODDARD, Elizabeth................... 578
GODFRED, Jonathan.................... 575
GODFREY, ——— (Seavey)............ 61
   Abigail 367
   Abigail (Seavey)................. 367
   Anna Brown....................... 367
   Elizabeth 367
   Elizabeth (Lamprey)...........404, 575
   Elsie Jane (Marden)............. 457
   Harriet Annetta (Brown)....317, 337

INDEX OF NAMES.

GODFREY, Harriette Annette (Brown), see Harriet Annetta (Brown).
Jacob T........................... 337
John.....................61, 367, 582
Jonathan 404
Mary 310
Nabby 582
Nancy 367
Sam F............................ 457
Susan 367
Susannah....................403, 576
GODSOE, Margaret................... 491
GOING, Abby J. I................... 452
John 265
GOLD, Christopher, see Gould.
GOLDEN, Lydia...................... 409
GOLDING, Ann....................... 440
GOLDTHWAITE, Abigail (Langdon).....411
GOMERSAWL, Lizzie.................. 373
GOODALL, Frances................... 532
GOODWIN, ————.............60, 392, 480
Abigail 434
Maria 493
Mary 487
Sarah 575
GOOKIN, Nathaniel.................. 150
GOOSS, see Goss.
GORDON, Louisa..................... 326
Lydia A. (Jenness)............... 389
William 389
GORE, Eben......................... 557
Mary (Varrell).................. 557
GORGES, Ferdinando............7, 8, 13, 18
230, 231, 236
Robert 13
GORHAM, Mary A................304, 306
GORS, see Goss.
GOSNOLD 228
Goss, Abby Francette............... 371
Abigail......................311, 368
Abigail (Locke)..............370, 432
Abigail (Norton)................. 466
Abigail (Randall)................ 371
Alfred Seavey..............371, 372, 452
Amanda M......................... 372
Ann M. (Locke)...............372, 437
Annie 373
Annie Marie...................... 372
Arthur L.....................291, 372
Betsey.......................369, 371
Betsey (Berry)...............306, 371
Betsey (Seavey).................. 368
Carrie S......................... 372
Charles Carroll.................. 372
Clarence.................58, 446, 535
Clarence A...............365, 372, 373
Daniel....174, 227, 370, 371, 486, 537, 582
Daniel James..................... 371
Data (Mason)..................... 370
Eliza 371
Eliza A. (Marden)............372, 452
Eliza Ella (Garland)...........365, 373
Eliza (Seavey)................... 371
Elizabeth......57, 172, 368, 369, 370, 582
Elizabeth Amy.................... 372
Elizabeth (Brown)............311, 369
Elizabeth (Galloway-Jenness)..... 515
Elizabeth (Randall-Jenness)...... 368
Elzada 372
Erastus 372
Estelle......................372, 494
Esther..............68, 143, 368, 369, 582
Esther (Rand).................... 368
Fannie B. (Knowles).............. 372
Gilman P......................... 372
Hannah 368
Hannah (Berry)...........368, 369, 371

Goss, Hannah (Black).............. 368
Hannah (Leavitt)................. 371
Hannah (Perkins).............371, 486
Harriet (Crane).................. 372
Harriett 373
Harriett J. (Locke)..........372, 441
Helen 370
Isabella 372
J. Greenville.................... 371
James.........35, 139, 143, 205, 220, 226
262, 273, 280, 368, 369
James G.......................... 107
James Madison.....57, 286, 369, 371, 580
James W.......................... 372
Jethro.............27, 71, 135, 136, 137
138, 368, 370, 568, 582
John.........................205, 370, 371
John S.......................347, 441
John Sheridan...............65, 370, 372
John Sterling.................... 372
John W 368
Jonathan....33, 58, 72, 136, 142, 153, 160
205, 255, 262, 265, 278, 279
311, 368, 369, 370, 421, 571
Joseph..........58, 69, 205, 276, 346, 368
369, 370, 371, 528, 582
Joseph Jackson.............371, 372, 452
Joshua.......................370, 371
Josiah Snow...................... 371
Leon Wallace..................... 372
Levi...........31, 33, 68, 141, 143, 176
205, 262, 273, 368, 369
370, 371, 500, 524, 582
Lucinda 580
Lucinda (Snow)................... 371
Lula Ann (Locke-Foss)............ 441
Margaret 368
Martha (————).................... 367
Mary......................143, 368, 406, 545
Mary Ann......................... 371
Mary C........................... 372
Mary Eliza (Marden).........372, 452
Mary Esther...................... 371
Mary F. (Mace)...............373, 446
Mary Jane........................ 371
Mary (Hall)...................... 368
Mary (Saunders).................. 371
Mary (Saunders-Saunders)........ 524
Melville Jewell.................. 372
Michael D.............57, 101, 286, 369
Michael Dalton................... 130
Molly 369
Molly (Wells).................... 568
Nancy 371
Nathan.............32, 33, 35, 54, 72, 90
142, 143, 160, 176, 203, 205
219, 256, 261, 262, 264, 266
267, 268, 269, 273, 284, 286
289, 292, 369, 371, 398, 466
Nathan R......................... 372
Nellie A......................... 370
Olive (Adams).................... 370
Olive Ann....................318, 372
Otis.........................372, 430, 437
Patty........................368, 564
Patty (Davidson)................. 370
Patty (Wells).................... 370
Philip Nathan.................... 372
Polly 170
Polly (Foss).................346, 370
Rachel.......................368, 574
Rachel (————).................... 368
Richard......21, 22, 24, 27, 41, 57, 71, 127
129, 135, 137, 153, 160, 255
288, 346, 367, 368, 369, 370
Richard P................291, 369, 441
Richard Pickering................ 372
Robert 367

INDEX OF NAMES. 617

Goss, Sally..............170, 321, 369, 582
  Sally (Berry)...............299, 304, 306
  Sally Johnson........................ 516
  Sally (Seavey)...................... 370
  Sally (Trundy)..................... 369
  Sally (Yeaton).................... 571
  Salome 368, 406
  Salome (Locke)................368, 421
  Samuel 368, 547
  Sarah......................368, 416, 444
  Sarah A............................. 574
  Sarah Abbie........................ 372
  Sarah Ann......................370, 508
  Sarah Ann, see Brown, Sarah Ann.
  Sarah (Berry)..................369, 370
  Sarah Berry........................ 582
  Sarah Blake........................ 370
  Sarah (Caswell)...............323, 372
  Sarah Jane......................... 371
  Sarah (Johnson) 369, 398
  Sarah Mace........................ 371
  Sarah (Marden)...............370, 450
  Sarah (Rand).................369, 500
  Sarah (Seavey)..................... 528
  Sarah (Shapley-Mace)............. 537
  Seavey....................304, 306, 370
  Sheridan 370
  Simon..................66, 67, 203, 286
                299, 321, 369, 582
  Sula A. (Locke-Foss).............. 372
  Susan (Towle)..................... 547
  Susannah........................368, 501
  Susie (Knowlton)................. 372
  Thomas...............57, 58, 65, 72, 88
      101, 170, 172, 205, 274, 275
      276, 278, 284, 286, 289, 368
      369, 370, 432, 450, 515, 582
  Tobias T........................... 369
  Ursula Ann (Locke-Foss)......... 347
  Wallace 323, 425
  Wallace S......65, 79, 274, 291, 372, 421
  Walter W.......................... 372
  William...........178, 287, 306, 370, 371
  William Davidson.................. 370
Gosse, see Goss.
Gothorpe, Emma Grace (Odiorne)... 470
  Esther Agatha...................... 373
  Hilda Gwendoline.................. 373
  Lizzie (Gomersawl)................ 373
  Sarah Gertrude.................... 373
  Thomas........................373, 470
Gould, ———........................... 582
  ——— (Waters)................... 373
  Christopher...105, 153, 160, 203, 255, 373
  Ephraim 61, 373
  Hannah 373
  Mary, see Gould, Polly.
  Molly (Towle)..................... 373
  Polly 319, 373
  Ruth 373
Gove, Abigail....................328, 466
  Anna M............................. 303
  Ebenezer 433
  Edward 328, 411
  Hannah (Langdon)................. 411
  John 466
  Julia A............................. 481
  Mary 574
  Nancy (Locke)..................... 433
  Samuel 26
  Sarah 309
  Sarah J............................. 459
Gowen, John........................... 266
Grace, Benjamin....................... 352
  Eunice (Foye)..................... 352
Grant, Charles........................ 562
  Charles Emery..................... 373
  Christopher 442

Grant, Christopher G................. 373
  Ella Jane.......................... 373
  Elsie C. (Locke)...............373, 442
  Eliza Ann (Walker)............... 562
  Hannah 565
  Margaret (Robinson).............. 520
  Mary.......................337, 338, 433
  Peter 262
  Ruth 572
  Samuel 520
Graves, Alice S. (Brown)............ 320
  Frank L............................ 320
Gray, Alice........................... 409
  Ann 538
  Lucetta 313
Green, ——— (Waldron)............ 374
  Abigail 373
  Abigail (Locke)................... 433
  Abigail (Nutter).................. 373
  Alonzo 374
  Alpheas 106
  Ann Treadwell..................... 374
  Benjamin 309
  Brackett 374
  Brackett B.....................281, 506
  Charles......58, 148, 164, 166, 170, 172
         278, 290, 317, 373, 374, 404
  Charles Alpheus................... 374
  Charles Oren...................... 374
  Clara A. (Haven).................. 374
  Cyrus Fayette..................... 374
  Dolly (Webster)................374, 565
  Dorcas 322
  Dorcas Marden.................... 373
  Elizabeth 374
  Elizabeth (Brown)................ 309
  Elizabeth (Foss)...............348, 374
  Ephraim 373
  Frank 373
  Fred Charles 374
  Harry 374
  Izette 374
  John 373
  Jonathan 433
  Joseph 373
  Kate H............................. 374
  Lizzie A. (Ayers)................. 374
  Lizzie (Falls)..................... 374
  Lydia V............................ 580
  Margaret Vercilda................. 317
  Maria Elizabeth................... 374
  Marion E........................... 374
  Martha Olive...................327, 374
  Martha S. (Rand)..............374, 506
  Martha Semira (Trefethen)....... 367
                      374, 549
  Mary.........................309, 322, 373
  Mary A............................. 303
  Mary Adelaide..................... 374
  Mary J.........................107, 350
  Mary Jane......................... 374
  Mary (Lamprey)................... 404
  Mary (Mow)....................373, 465
  Mary Smith (Lamprey)............ 374
  Mary (White)...................... 373
  Oren S........................58, 286, 291
  Oren Smith........................ 374
  Polly 321
  Richard............268, 273, 373, 465, 582
  Rosella........................374, 510
  Samuel Marden.................... 373
  Sarah W........................... 374
  Silas 374
  Stephen........68, 170, 278, 290, 374, 565
  Susan M............................ 325
  Thomas...............279, 285, 287, 348, 373
  Thomas L.......................... 374
  Thomas Otis....................... 374

INDEX OF NAMES.

GREEN, Vercilda............... 374
  Woodbury............107, 367, 549
  Woodbury C........280, 286, 374
GREENING, Phebe W.............. 496
GREENLEAF, Charles W........... 281
  Emeline (Philbrick)............. 493
  Nathan 263
  Daniel 240
GREENOUGH, Daniel............... 127
  Maria 325
GREGGS, Mabel M................. 514
GREGORY, William................ 268
GRIFFIN, Philip.................. 309
  Sarah (Brown)................... 309
GRIGGS, Eliza Ann (Marden)...... 456
  Robert 456
GRINDIFF 178
GROGAN, Addie.................... 375
  Elizabeth 375
  Frank 375
  Harriett 375
  John....................301, 375, 539
  Samuel 375
  Sarah A. (Shapley-Berry)........ 301
                              375, 539
  Walter 375
GROOM, Maria..................... 317
GROSS, Benjamin.................. 417
  Mary (Libby).................... 417
GROVE, Nathaniel................. 582
  Sarah (Varrell-Judkins)......... 557
GROVER, Anna..................... 375
  Annie Mary (Brown).............. 316
  Charity 574
  Charles C....................... 375
  Dolly 490
  Ella 375
  Emma 375
  James J......................... 316
  John.......................375, 395
  John Henry...................... 375
  Malvina B. (Jenness)........375, 395
  Mary 401
  Sally 580
GUALTER, Mary.................... 474
GUNNISON, Pamelia................ 494
GUSTIN, Hannah J. (Marden)...... 451
  John 451
GWINN, Ann....................... 496
HACKETT, Frank Warren..........7, 10
HADLEY, Nellie................... 413
  Willis A........................ 159
HAINES, Abigail.................. 417
  Abigail Philbrick............... 489
  Celia A......................... 575
  David 575
  Deborah (Lamprey)............... 575
  Elisha......................267, 268
  Hannah (Johnson)................ 575
  Jane (Brackett)................. 308
  Lydia (Cater)................... 575
  Margaret 334
  Maria 539
  Mary (Fifield).................. 375
  Mary (Lewis).................... 375
  Matthias....................381, 417
  Mehitable (Jenness)............. 381
  Mercy 386
  Nathan......................265, 575
  Noah 267
  Prudence (Brackett)............. 575
  Reuben 582
  Richard 575
  Samuel 375
  Sarah 375, 423, 467
  Thomas 489, 575
  William 375, 423
HALE, Benjamin................... 375

HALE, Edward..................71, 267
  Nathan 264
  Richard 71
  Sarah 579
HALEY, Daniel.................... 375
  Elizabeth Ann................... 453
  Elizabeth M..................... 375
  Ella B.......................... 443
  Harriett Augusta (Clark)....326, 376
  Hattie A. (Clark)............... 576
  Hattie L........................ 376
  James I......................... 376
  James M.................326, 375, 376, 576
  Joseph B........................ 375
  Julia (Chauncy)................. 375
  Leonora Caswell................. 375
  Love (Randall).................. 375
  Lovey 521
  Lovey Brackett (Randall)........ 516
  Lucy J. (Randall)............... 375
  Mary 578
  Nancy 503
  Olive 521
  Otis F.......................... 375
  Richard G....................... 375
  Samuel......................243, 375, 516
  Susanna 243
HALL....................175, 239, 299
  Abigail (Dalton)................ 328
  Abigail (Elkins)................ 576
  Abner........................174, 515
  Alice M......................... 377
  Ann E. (Matthes)............377, 461
  Betsey 377
  Charles W....................... 549
  Charles William................. 377
  Charlotte (Jenness)............. 387
  Deborah (Pickering)............. 377
  Edward..........31, 176, 267, 273, 275
              278, 376, 377, 501, 582
  Edward William.................. 377
  Elizabeth...................376, 543, 553
  Emily (Trefethen)...........377, 549
  Emma 377
  Ephraim 153, 255
  Ephraim Rand..............279, 376, 501
  Erie (Edmonds).................. 343
  Esther......................301, 376
  Esther (Tucker).............376, 377
  Frank 377
  Frank A......................... 117
  George 377
  George H........................ 377
  Grace (Harrington).............. 377
  Hannah......................146, 376
  Hartwell....................344, 576
  Herbert C....................... 377
  Ida 377
  James M......................... 461
  James Moses..................... 377
  Jane (Trefethen)................ 550
  John 377
  John F.......................... 281
  Joseph.........31, 141, 143, 153, 255, 259
      262, 273, 376, 377, 445, 515, 543
  L. W............................ 280
  Levi 550
  Levi Wallace.................... 377
  Lucenna Jane (Trefethen)........ 377
  Lydia 428
  Martha Ann...................... 377
  Mary........................368, 411
  Mary O.......................... 376
  Mary T.......................... 376
  Mary (Merrifield)............... 377
  Mary (Randall)..............376, 515
  Mary (Smith-Rand).......376, 377, 543
  Moses 377

INDEX OF NAMES. 619

HALL, Nably (Elkins)............... 344
  Nancy (Rand)..................376, 501
  Olivia (Porter)..................... 499
  Luther 499
  Rachel (Berry-Mace)..........376, 377
  Rachel (Randall-Mace)............ 444
  Richard 328
HALLETT, Lucy Ann.................. 314
HALTON, Mary....................... 475
HALL, Sarah....................376, 377
  Sarah Ann.....................376, 576
  Sarah (Rand)..............376, 501, 502
  William.........68, 153, 255, 376, 377, 502
  William Tucker.................... 376
HAM, Eleanor (Locke)............... 423
  Elizabeth 571
  Isaac L............................ 170
  J. L............................... 68
  John 416
  John H........................347, 377
  Lucy (Libby)...................... 416
  Mary Foss.....................347, 377
  Mary L. (Holbrook)............... 576
  Molly (Foss)...................... 377
  Olly (Towle)...................... 546
  William...............267, 268, 423, 576
HAMILTON, Katie..................... 561
HANDLY, Betsey...................... 534
HANKIN, Clyde....................... 377
  Frances 377
  Fred 562
  Fred W............................ 377
  Grace 377
  Marshall 377
  Maud G. (Walker).............377, 562
  Russell 377
HANSCOM, Deborah................304, 306
  Esther 414
  Malvina 304, 306
  Martha 414
  Martha (———)..................... 558
  Nathaniel 371
  Sarah 415
  Sarah Jane (Goss)................. 371
  Betsey (Jenness).................. 386
HANSON, Jessie...................... 303
  Mary 556
  Paul 386
  Sarah J............................ 577
HARDING, Clara N. Brown............ 319
  William G......................... 319
HARDY, Anna (Jenness).............. 383
  Charles 576
  Enoch 383
  Hannah (Jenness)................. 383
  Joseph 448
  Mary (Cochrane).................. 576
HARNEY 480
  Mehitable (Tarlton)............... 576
HARRINGTON, Grace.................. 377
  John 264
HARROLD, Ann E. (Philbrick)....... 495
  Christopher 495
HARRIS 274
  George 71
  J..............................66, 416
  Mary Jane (Sanborn)............. 522
  Nathaniel 261
  Olive (Libby)..................66, 416
  Thaddeus William................3, 6
HARST, John........................ 71
HART, Benjamin..................... 550
  Elisha 576
  Hannah (Sheafe-Emerson)........ 540
  Jeremiah 576
  Josephine (Trefethen)............ 550
  Lucy 322
  Lydia 392

HART, Mary (Kimball).............. 576
  Phebe (Caverly).................. 576
HARTSHORN, Sarah A................ 545
HARVEY 479
  Clara A........................... 374
  Dorcas (Marden).................. 447
  Francis 576
  Rhoda 547
  William 447
HASKELL 65
  Charles A......................... 452
HASKELL, Job..................263, 265
  Martha 311
  Sarah Priscilla (Marden..)....... 452
  William 265, 266
HASLEY, Daniel..................... 26
HASTEY, Daniel.................136, 137
HATCH, Betsey...................... 576
  David 352
  Elizabeth 305
  Elizabeth (Foss).................. 352
  Sarah A........................... 530
HAVEN 227
HAW, Josiah........................ 264
HAYES, Betsey H................... 554
  Caroline 437
  Fanny 298
  Laura 438
  Laura A........................... 441
  Sarah 438, 441
HAYNES, Eleanor................... 416
  George F.......................... 550
  Nellie G. (Trefethen)............ 550
  N 265
HAYWARD, Bertha (Lougee)......316, 444
  W. H...........................316, 444
HAYWOOD, Eliza..................... 352
HAZELTON, Huldah (Marston)...... 458
  John 458
HAZZARD, Elizabeth................. 407
HEAD, Arthur,...................... 71
  Catherine (Osborne).............. 576
  Moses 576
HEALD, Franklin.................... 401
  Susan (Kimball).................. 401
HEALEY, Irene...................... 434
HEARD, Betsey...................... 428
HEARN, Ina Belle (Marston)....... 459
  Robert 459
HEATH 173
  Ann 309
  Clementina (Varrell)............. 558
  Mary 309
  William 558
HEHIER, Mary...................... 569
HELMER, Nancy..................... 440
HENDERSON 412
  Abigail (Berry)................... 305
  Betsey (Hatch)................... 576
  Daniel 576
  Robert 305
HERRICK, Andrew................... 575
HERSEY, Sally (Towle)............. 547
  Sarah (Goodwin).................. 575
  Sarah (Rand)..................... 499
HICKERMAN, Eunice (Foye)......... 353
  J. L............................... 353
HIGGINS, Emeline (Drake)......... 340
  Mehitable 430
  Richard R.............65, 110, 340, 359
HILDRETH, Anna.................... 379
  Fannie 322
HILL 480
  Annie (Batchelder)............... 295
  Charles H......................... 440
  Charles P......................... 362
  Elizabeth 466
  Elizabeth H. (Garland).......... 362

INDEX OF NAMES.

HILL, George............................ 295
  Hannah 466
  Henry 417
  James 48, 50
  Laura G. (Locke).................. 440
  Lizzie 495
  Mary (Langdon-Storer)............ 411
  Mary (Libby)....................... 417
  Sarah J............................... 539
HILLIARD, Apphia (Philbrick)........ 488
  Mehitable (Philbrick)............. 488
  Timothy 488
HILLS, Charles P..................... 378
  Elizabeth G......................... 378
  Elizabeth H. (Garland)........... 378
HILTON, Dudley........................ 260
  Edward..........................14, 15, 16
  Harry Le Grand 441
  Hellen C. (Locke)................. 441
  Maria Elizabeth (Green)......... 374
  Richard 374
  William 14, 15
HINCKS, Mary......................... 527
HINKS, John............................. 71
HINKSON, Honor...................... 413
HOBBS, Abigail (Dow)............... 378
  Alma A. (Seavey)................. 531
  Almira 407
HOBBS 72
  Benjamin 378
  Bethia 552
  Betsey (Remick).................. 518
  Comfort 378
  Deborah (Batchelder)............ 378
  Elizabeth.......................304, 435
  Elizabeth (Batchelder).......... 378
  Elizabeth (Fogg).................. 378
  Elizabeth Jenness................. 379
  Ellen F.(Jenness)................. 395
  Elmira A. (Seavey).............. 379
  Esther 378
  Hervey 379
  Horatio 363
  Huldah 378, 429
  James..........33, 35, 139, 143, 204, 262
              273, 278, 404, 546, 582
  John...........................333, 378, 395
  John W.........................379, 531
  Jonathan....35, 66, 75, 141, 143, 176, 177
        205, 273, 276, 297, 378, 379, 518
  Joseph 378
  Love 329
  Lucinda (Dearborn)............... 333
  Lucretia Emeline (Garland)...... 363
  Lucy............................378, 379, 547
  Lucy (Dow)....................... 378
  Mary 378, 388
  Mary (Berry)..................297, 378
  Mary (Marston).................. 378
  Mary (Towle).................378, 546
  Mehitable 546
  Molly 379
  Molly (Berry).................... 378
  Molly (Dowrst).................. 339
  Morris 378
  Nancy.........................105, 320, 379
  Nathaniel 379
  Nellie..........................379, 562
  Patience 378, 404
  Perna Junkins.................... 379
  Perney 582
  Polly 379
  Sally 379
  Sarah 378
  Sarah (Swett).................... 378
  Simon L........................... 107
  Theodate (Batchelder).......... 378
  Theodate (Page)................. 378

HODGDON, Adeline................... 338
  Alexander II..................379, 394
  Anna Drake (Jenness).......379, 394
  Annie 510
  Annie D........................... 214
  Charles E......................... 442
  Eliza Ann (Foye)................ 353
  Harriet 301
  John 353
  Louise 509
  Mabel H.......................... 379
  Martha J. (Locke).............. 442
  Nellie 496
  Olive A........................... 440
  Sally 348
  Timothy E........................ 281
  Kate M. (Rand)................. 508
HODGSDON, Marchant............... 508
HODGE 129
  Nicholas.............22, 71, 134, 584
HODIERNE, see Odiorne.
HOIG, James........................... 576
  Sally (Palmer).................. 576
HOLAND, Paul......................... 71
HOLBROOK, Apphia (Foye)......... 353
  John 265
  Mary L........................... 576
  Mercy 453
  Robert 353
HOLLAND, Thomas.................... 71
HOLMES, ——— (Cook)............ 379
  ——— (Lowd).................. 379
  Ann 379
  Anna (Hildreth)................ 379
  Benjamin 379, 576
  Betty (Libby)................... 414
  Charlotta 348
  Charlotte (Seavey)...........380, 531
  Charles 280
  Charles Edward................. 379
  David 379
  Deborah (Libby)................ 379
  E 414
  Eliza 579
  Eliza (Lang)..................... 407
  Elizabeth..................379, 453, 578
  Elizabeth (Lang)................ 379
  Elizabeth (Slooper)............. 379
  Ella 380, 471
  Elvira 349
  Emma 342, 380
  Ernest 380
  H. M.............................. 159
  Hannah (Locke-Ferguson)...... 436
  Isaac 379
  Jacob.............170, 379, 407, 408, 582
  James 379
  John 376, 379, 576
  Joseph 436
  Joseph Rand..................380, 531
  Jotham 379
  Julia A........................... 532
  Margaret 379, 576
  Margaret (Holmes)..........379, 576
  Maria 436
  Mary......................298, 379, 456
  Mary (Rand).................380, 503
  Mesach 379
  Molly (Rand)................... 379
  Nancy 582
  Nancy (Lang).................379, 408
  Olive 298
  Oliver 379
  Polly 379
  Polly (Hobbs).................. 379
  Sally 379, 576
  Sarah Ann (Hall)...........376, 576
  Sarah E. (Trefethen)........380, 549

INDEX OF NAMES. 621

HOLMES, Sarah Eliza............... 379
  Shadrach 379
  Sophia C......................380, 453
  William....68, 287, 290, 298, 379, 380, 503
  William I......................68, 281
  William Ira....................380, 549
  William J......................... 208
HOLT, Cleveland B................. 521
  Sally Robinson.................... 521
HANSON, Mary..................... 512
HOOPER, Betsey (Locke)............ 426
  Joseph 426
HOPPINGS 66
HORL, see Hall.
HORMAN, Mary C................... 508
HORN, Benjamin................... 343
  Hannah (Edmunds)............... 343
  Tobias 71
HORTON, Abel..................... 495
  Sarah A. (Philbrick).............. 495
HOUSTON, Betsey................... 501
HOWARD, Patty (Rand)............. 514
HOWE, Elizabeth................... 361
  Elizabeth Parsons (Waldron)..... 560
  Emily Frances.................... 574
  Hall J........................... 560
HOYT, Emma...................... 351
HUBBARD, Elizabeth Lake............ 578
  John 331
  Mary 410
  Nathaniel..........7, 10, 14, 15, 16, 17, 18
  Sally W. (Dalton)................ 331
  Sara 482
HUFF, Andy....................... 134
HUGGINS, Nathaniel................ 467
  Ruth (Nudd)..................... 467
HUGHES 243
HULL, Joseph..................237, 238
HUMPHRIES, Robert................ 159
HUMVILLE, Robert................. 264
HUNKING.......................134, 136, 137
  Mark...........................39, 40
HUNT, Betsey...................... 345
  Elizabeth 380
  Mary 448
  Mary (Rand)..................... 500
HUTCHINS, Melvin................. 440
HUNT, Samuel.............262, 380, 500, 565
  Zebedee 160, 380
HUNTLEY, Tryphene................ 577
HUNTON, Sarah Elizabeth (Waldron-
  Stickney) 560
  William 560
HUNTRESS, Margaret................ 578
HUNTRISS, Samuel.................. 33
HURD, Fidelia (Locke).............. 438
  Benjamin 383
  Mary (Jenness).................. 383
  Webster 438
HURDY, George..................... 280
HUSE, Huldah (Perkins)............ 485
  Stephen 485
HUTCHING, Samuel................. 262
HUTCHINGS 59
  Delia Ann (Locke)................ 439
  Eliza Ann (Foss)................ 349
  Enoch 349
  James 260
  Joseph 263
  Oliver 439
  P. C............................. 281
HUTCHINS, Georgianna (Locke)...380, 440
  Hannah (Seavey)................. 380
  John 380
  Mary 326
  Melvin 380
  Samuel 380
HYDE, Elizabeth Leach.............. 576

IRELAND, William II................ 175
IRISH, Abigail..................... 416
JACKSON, Eben.................... 346
  Ephraim 136
  Hall 260, 264
  John 136
  Joseph..........................70, 71
  Martha 462
  Mehitable (Foss)................. 346
  Thomas 136
JAFFRAY, see Jaffrey.
JAFFREY, George.................28, 189
JAMES I.........................6, 12
JANNES, see Jenness.
JANVEINS, Mary................... 497
JANVRAM, Elizabeth Leach (Hyde)....576
  Mendum 576
JARVICE, Olive.................... 146
JARVIS, Benjamin.................. 340
  Eliza Ann (Drake)................ 340
JEFFERY, see Jeffrey.
JEFFREY, James...........26, 28, 41, 42, 46
  Thomas 26
JEFFRY, see Jeffrey.
JENES, see Jenness.
JENKINS, Arvilla F................. 494
  Harriett (Langdon)............... 411
  Mark L.......................... 411
JENNES, see Jenness.
JENNESS.....................72, 135, 149
  ——— (Batchelder)............385, 387
  ——— (Clark..................... 391
  ——— (Drake).................... 388
  ——— (French)...............387, 396
  ——— (Hall).................... 387
  ——— (Johnson).................. 387
  ——— (McNeil).................. 383
  ——— (Marden).................. 394
  ——— (Moore).................... 387
  ——— (Page)................385, 395
  ——— (Pillsbury)................. 387
  ——— (Stearns).................. 391
  ——— (Wilson).................. 391
Aaron..........................298, 383
Abbott Brown..................... 395
Abbott C.......................... 390
Abby Coffin....................... 391
Abigail..................384, 385, 386, 387
                      388, 392, 396, 432
Abigail (Coffin-Sleeper).........384, 542
Abigail (Drake)................... 388
Abigail (Garland)....358, 359, 384, 387
Abigail (Jenness).............388, 392
Abigail (Knowles).............397, 403
Abigail L......................... 389
Abigail (Locke)...............388, 428
Abigail (Moulton)................. 382
Abigail (Palmer).................. 382
Abigail (Perkins).............391, 486
Abigail (Rand).................... 382
Abraham 354
Abram 390
Adeline S.....................363, 391
Adna (Brown).................... 393
Albert 389
Albert Dana...........280, 319, 393, 395
Albert Jewell..................... 397
Albrion Jewell.................... 397
Alexander Shapley................ 387
Alfred G........52, 80, 319, 361, 362, 390
Alice.......................386, 393, 569
Alice (Foss)..................349, 394
Alice J........................... 392
Almira A. (Brown)................ 319
Almira (Batchelder)............295, 393
Alvado 319
Alvato........................395, 396
Amos 387

INDEX OF NAMES.

JENNESS, Amos J. 386, 390
  Amos Seavey 60, 92, 169, 287
                        290, 388, 391, 432
  Andrew Jackson.................... 386
  Ann 381
  Ann Eliza (Brown) 316, 396
  Ann (Folsom) 381, 397
  Anna 383, 384, 387, 391, 508, 583
  Anna Drake 379, 394
  Anna (Knox) 389
  Anna Maria (Brown) 319
  Anna (Parker) 385
  Anna Parsons (Marston) 396, 458
  Anna Towle (Seavey) 529
  Anna (Yeaton) 389
  Anna Yeaton 389
  Annie M. (Brown) 395
  Annie May 395
  Archie Linden 393
  Arthur A 396
  Benjamin 31, 72, 88, 142, 143, 161, 169
               170, 173, 204, 273, 275
               278, 384, 387, 388, 389
               391, 392, 398, 415, 527
  Benjamin Garland 387
  Benjamin Leavitt 392
  Benning W 391
  Betsey 383, 385, 386, 387, 391, 492
  Betsey B. Folsom 397
  Betsey (Berry) 387
  Betsey (Brown) 397
  Betsey (Dalton-Norton) 329
  Betsey (Jenness) 385
  Betsey (Lamprey-Folsom) 404
  Betsey (Leavitt) 576
  Betsey (Philbrick) 389, 491
  Betsey (Seavey) 529
  Betsey (True) 387
  Betty 384
  Byron J 465
  Caroline (McClintock) 391
  Caroline (Rand) 386, 513
  Carrie 395
  Carrie M 390
  Catherine (Clapp) 386
  Caturah (Dame) 385
  Charles Austin ... 218, 280, 316, 394, 396
  Charles Leavitt 394
  Charles Moore 397
  Charles W 393
  Charlotte 387
  Charlotte (Lamprey) 392, 404, 576
  Clara Ann 394
  Clara Emma 395
  Clara J. (Garland) 363, 395
  Clarence Albert 397
  Clarissa 386, 390, 391, 392
  Clarissa (Jenness) 386, 390, 391, 392
  Comfort 311, 313, 383
  Cora Belle 390, 562
  Cora D. (Babbitt-Willson) 394
  Corasanda 395
  Cornelius 382
  Cotton Ward Drake 349, 394
  Dana 363
  Data 387
  David 286, 287, 291, 331, 383, 385, 390
  David A 291, 340, 379, 391, 394
  David W 279, 340, 388, 389, 393, 403
  David Wedgewood 386, 390, 397
  Deborah 391
  Deborah (Sanborn) 390
  Deliverance 383
  Dorothy (Brown) 392
  Dowrst 391
  Edgar 396
  Edith Maud 396
  Edith (Moulton) 465

JENNESS, Edwin 392
  Edwin Jewell 394
  Elinor 381
  Eliza 106, 392, 495
  Eliza Ann 390
  Eliza (Colcord) 392
  Eliza P 390
  Eliza True (Leavitt) 393, 413
  Elizabeth 339, 383, 384, 385, 387
               389, 391, 392, 510, 546
  Elizabeth (Berry) 304
  Elizabeth f(Cate) 386
  Elizabeth Dow (Drake) 340, 394
  Elizabeth (Galloway) 515
  Elizabeth Howe 397
  Elizabeth (Jenness) 392
  Elizabeth (Locke) 390
  Elizabeth Mary (Varrell) 557
  Elizabeth (Norton) 381, 466
  Elizabeth (Randall) 368, 385
  Elizabeth (Seavey) 382, 527
  Elizabeth (Seavey-Brown) .313, 320, 528
  Elizabeth (Shapley) 384
  Elizabeth (Varrell) 386
  Elizabeth W 579
  Elizabeth (Wallis) 388
  Ellen A. (Rand) 394, 510
  Ellen F 395
  Ellen Ruthdian (Foye) 353
  Elmer B 396
  Elmira (Newell) 394
  Elvira (Garland) 364, 394
  Elvira (Moulton) 397
  Emeline 391, 539
  Emeline (Brown) 319, 395
  Emeline (Lang) 395, 408
  Emeline S. (Locke) 394
  Emerett A. (Brown) 317, 396, 487
  Emery C 64, 181, 208, 210
                    281, 286, 287, 291
  Emery Curtis 394, 510
  Emily 389, 507
  Emily A 395
  Emily B. (Dalton) 331, 390
  Emily (Wharton) 396
  Emira M. (Brown) 396
  Emma C 395
  Emma E 395
  Emma Perkins 331, 396
  Erwin 398
  Esther (Jones) 386
  Ethel 396
  Etta 396
  Fannie Weeks 396
  Fanny 317, 386
  Fanny Wesley 393
  Fidelia 392
  Flora Ida (Trefethen-Dunbrach) . 550
  Flora May 394
  Florence A 397
  Florence W (Farrell) 398
  Francis 31, 32, 54, 63, 72
            87, 139, 142, 143, 160, 177
           204, 217, 218, 261, 262, 283
           284, 288, 289, 358, 380, 381
           382, 384, 386, 387, 396, 421, 489
  Frank A 393
  Frank Benning 394
  Frank P 390
  Frank Towle 395
  George 496
  George M 394
  George W 280
  George Washington 397
  Gertrude 394
  Gilbert 106
  Gilman H 214, 281, 285
  Gilman Harrison 390, 393, 413

INDEX OF NAMES. 623

JENNESS, Grace (Balch), see Gracia (Balch).
Gracia (Balch) 294, 395
Hall Jackson 387
Hannah 65, 356, 381, 382, 383, 384, 385
  387, 388, 410, 421, 425, 500, 571
Hannah (————) 398
Hannah (Brown) 395
Hannah (Dow) 335, 383, 388
Hannah (Emerson) 387
Hannah (Foss) 382
Hannah (Garland-Brown-Wedgewood) 361
Hannah (Langhorn) 383
Hannah (Libby) 415
Hannah (Seavey) 387, 527, 529
Hannah (Swaine) 63, 381
Hannah (Webster) 389, 565
Hannah (Wedgewood) 390, 397, 567
Harriett 454
Harriett (Mow) 393, 465
Harriett O. 394
Harrison N. 394
Harry B. 393
Hattie B. (Weeks) 396
Hattie E. (Cunningham) 398
Helen (Foye) 389
Henry......61, 319, 388, 392, 395, 404, 576
Herbert Leon 396
Herman 395, 496
Hezekiah...22, 24, 26, 27, 71, 136, 381, 383
Hezekiah A. 395, 576
Horace 391
Howard L. 396
Huldah (Perkins) 392, 486
Ida (Dunbrack) 395
Ida M. 396
Ida V. 395
Isaac 160, 205, 319, 335, 384
  385, 386, 388, 392, 395
Ivan Douglass 397
Jacob 385
James 384, 386
James Perkins 390, 392
Jennie 393
Jeremiah 383, 388
Joanna 306, 398
Job 31, 33, 71, 117, 119, 131, 140
  143, 160, 203, 205, 208, 213, 218
  273, 382, 383, 385, 389, 393, 583
Job Rienza 317, 393, 396, 487
John........22, 26, 27, 31, 33, 45, 46, 50
  71, 72, 80, 87, 88, 101, 131
  136, 139, 140, 143, 144, 204
  207, 208, 218, 226, 253, 256
  262, 273, 274, 276, 288, 289
  298, 359, 381, 382, 383, 384
  385, 386, 387, 389, 395, 397
  398, 466, 515, 527, 565, 567
John B. 205, 275
John Bean 396
John H. 294
John Leroy 397, 398
John S. 391
John Scribner 8, 9, 12, 14, 234
John W. 397, 398
Jonathan 24, 31, 33, 143, 144
  153, 169, 172, 205, 255, 262
  273, 276, 278, 289, 290, 359
  360, 382, 384, 385, 386, 387
  388, 389, 390, 392, 428, 583
Jonathan Rollins 117, 389, 393
Joseph 31, 32, 53, 91, 140, 143
  144, 160, 163, 164, 170, 172
  176, 203, 205, 256, 266, 267
  269, 273, 276, 283, 289, 335
  360, 382, 385, 386, 387, 388
  389, 392, 396, 490, 491, 583
Joseph B. 393

JENNESS, Joseph Disco.....63, 80, 353, 389
Joseph G. 52, 60, 287, 364
  384, 391, 394
Joseph Jerome 392, 395
Joseph Tarleton. 384, 386, 557
Josephine G. 394
Joses 386
Joshua.....72, 87, 136, 137, 138, 143, 160
  382, 383
Josiah..........60, 290, 388, 391, 392, 486
Judith (Sanborn) 385
Keziah (Wilson) 393
Langdon 391
Langdon Seavey 397
Leila A. 324
Levi........31, 33, 140, 143, 204, 273, 289
  383, 384, 385, 388, 389, 392, 553
Levi M. 392
Levi Woodbury 391, 394
Louis Wentworth 394
Louisa 389
Lowell 397
Linden 393
Lizzie B. (Shaw) 393
Lucinda (Davis) 383
Lucinda R. (Garland) 362, 390
Lucy 383
Lucy Jane 389
Lucy (Norton) 383, 466
Lulu A. 397
Lydia 396
Lydia A. 389
Lydia (Hart) 392
Lydia (Philbrick) 395, 496
Lydia (Rollins) 389
Lyndon Y. 393
Malvina B. 375, 395
Margaret Ann 318, 393
Mark 382
Martha A. (Folsom) 395
Martha A. (Garland) 362, 390
Martha Hannah (Brown) 317, 392
Martha J. 365, 392
Martha Jane 395, 542
Martha (Philbrick) 386
Martha (Seavey) 388, 527, 391, 482
Martha Wallis 388
Mary 163, 169, 170, 172, 340
  382, 383, 384, 385, 388, 389
Mary (———— Drake) 390
Mary Abby 391, 393, 394
Mary Abby (Jenness) 391, 394
Mary Ann 319, 390, 392
Mary Anna 395
Mary Butler (Crouse) 393
Mary (Coffin) 388
Mary (Dalton) 382
Mary Davis (Poole) 394
Mary (Dow) 63, 335, 382, 385
Mary E. (———— Tarlton) 395
Mary Elizabeth (Foye) 353, 389
Mary (Goss-Tarlton) 368, 545
Mary (Hobbs) 388
Mary J. (Saunders) 387
Mary Jane (Locke) 390
Mary (Jenness) 382, 383
Mary (Jenness-Drake) 340, 389
Mary (Knowles) 393, 403
Mary (Locke) 314, 388, 425
Mary (Mason) 382, 396
Mary (Page) 385, 395, 472
Mary (Richardson) 392
Mary (Tarlton) 383
Mary Wedgewood 383, 386, 567
Mary (Witcher) 385
Matilda 391
Mehitabel 381
Melissa 395, 494
Mercy (Haines) 386

INDEX OF NAMES.

JENNESS, Mercy (Wentworth)........ 385
  Minerva S...................... 397, 568
  Miralda (Fox).................... 386
  Molly..........384, 386, 388, 390, 542, 573
  Molly (Jenness)..................388, 390
  Morris 398
  Moses 383
  Moses Leavitt..................... 360
  Nabby 389
  Nabby Coffin...................... 388
  Nancy..................315, 386, 387, 388, 391
  Nancy Jenness..............386, 388, 391
  Nancy (Sleeper)..................390, 542
  Nathan Brown...................... 392
  Nathaniel........31, 35, 140, 144, 160, 203
    205, 265, 266, 276, 368, 382
    383, 384, 386, 390, 545, 567
  Nathaniel Gilbert..181, 280, 391, 395, 408
  Nellie M.......................... 398
  Nettie 395
  Noah..................205, 384, 385, 515
  Olive...............361, 386, 387, 397, 413
  Olive C........................... 389
  Olive (Berry)..................298, 396
  Olive (Cate)...................... 386
  Olive (Johnson)................... 387
  Olive (Shapley)................... 387
  Olivian Mildred................... 396
  Oliver........................57, 397, 530
  Mrs. Oliver....................... 99
  Oliver P..................287, 290, 340
  Oliver Peter.............391, 392, 394
  Olly, see Polly.
  Otis Simpson...............395, 396, 458
  Patty.........................384, 387
  Paul..........................383, 385
  Peter............31, 35, 91, 101, 140, 144
    205, 225, 226, 256, 273 278
    284, 384, 387, 388, 391, 576
  Peter Mitchell.................... 385
  Phebe (Dow)....................... 385
  Polly...............70, 314, 385, 386, 387
    388, 389, 452, 522, 567
  Polly J. (Edmonds)...........343, 391
  Polly Leavitt (Garland).......360, 392
  Polly (True)...................... 391
  Rebecca J. (Rowe)................. 395
  Rebecca (Philbrick)............... 496
  Reuben P..............164, 170, 172, 173
    285, 287, 290, 403
  Reuben Philbrick..............389, 393
  Richard...21, 22, 24, 26, 27, 29, 31, 32, 33
    35, 46, 52, 60, 61, 63, 64, 71
    72, 87, 137, 139, 140, 142
    144, 160, 167, 204, 205, 208
    218, 220, 256, 261, 263, 273
    277, 279, 283, 286, 288, 289
    291, 304, 313, 320, 334, 381
    382, 383, 384, 385, 386, 387
    388, 391, 396, 397, 404, 472
    490, 513, 527, 528
    530, 542, 563
  Rosamond......................391, 512
  Rozanna (Sweeney)................. 390
  Rufus Kittredge................... 397
  Rufus O........................... 397
  Sally..........................386, 387, 391
  Sally (Garland)................... 360
  Sally (Nye)....................... 387
  Sally (Philbrick)................. 490
  Sally (Randall)................... 515
  Sally (True)...................... 391
  Sally (Tucker).................... 553
  Salome (White).................... 381
  Salome (Wilson)................... 393
  Samuel..31, 33, 35, 54, 60, 72, 131, 140, 143
    144, 148, 160, 162, 163, 166

JENNESS, Samuel...169, 170, 173, 176, 203, 205
    207, 255, 256, 262, 265, 269
    273, 278, 279, 283, 284, 286
    289, 290, 291, 314, 382, 383
    384, 386, 388, 391, 425, 569
  Samuel Alba....................... 391
  Samuel C.......................... 358
  Samuel W..........60, 280, 343, 392, 486
  Samuel Wallis..............60, 388, 391
  Sarah.........299, 313, 359, 382, 383, 384
    385, 388, 395, 396, 580
  Sarah A........................... 392
  Sarah A. (Jenness)................ 392
  Sarah Abby (Cotton)............... 354
  Sarah Ann.....................386, 389
  Sarah Ann (Locke).............391, 432
  Sarah B. (Page)................... 397
  Sarah (Berry)..................... 298
  Sarah (Cotton).................... 390
  Sarah (Dearborn).................. 388
  Sarah Dearborn................388, 392
  Sarah Dearborn (Jenness).....388, 392
  Sarah (Dodd)...................... 389
  Sarah (Dowrst).................... 391
  Sarah E.......................294, 395
  Sarah E. (Foster)................. 576
  Sarah E. (Marston)................ 393
  Sarah Emeline (Locke)............. 441
  Sarah Emeline (Perkins)......396, 487
  Sarah (Garland)......358, 384, 390, 392
  Sarah J. (Foster)................. 395
  Sarah (Locke).........381, 383, 396, 421
  Sarah M........................... 393
  Sarah P.......................393, 442
  Sarah (Page)...................... 386
  Sarah (Philbrick)................. 389
  Sarah (Randall)................... 385
  Sarah S. (Randall)................ 395
  Sarah Taylor..................389, 390
  Sarah Taylor (Jenness).......389, 390
  Sarah Ward (Drake)...........340, 394
  Sarah (Yeaton).................... 387
  Semira P......................364, 391
  Seth 576
  Sheridan.....106, 280, 295, 382, 389, 393
  Sydney Langdon (Seavey).....530, 397
  Simon...............31, 33, 35, 64, 140, 143
    148, 161, 164, 166, 172, 176
    204, 210, 266, 273, 278, 284
    285, 290, 291, 292, 382, 384
    386, 387, 388, 390, 391, 542
  Simon Lamprey................392, 395
  Solomon 529
  Sophia 365, 391
  Sophronia (Smiley)................ 576
  Stephen 385
  Susan M.......................393, 525
  Theo 24
  Thomas....22, 26, 27, 61, 71, 136, 204, 217
    277, 288, 329, 381, 382, 384
    386, 387, 390, 391, 466, 484
  Thorton W......................... 396
  Uri Harvey................280, 317, 392
  Warren........................392, 393
  Wesley........208, 210, 317, 389, 393, 465
  Willard M......................... 396
  William...............26, 72, 136, 137, 382
    383, 385, 387, 529
  William B.....................172, 391
  William Benjamin..............391, 394
  Willis 395
  Woodbury......................387, 441
  Woodbury L........................ 394
  Yeaton 392
  Zipporah J. (Shaw)................ 395
JENNINGS, see Jenness.
JESSOM, Joseph L..................... 446

INDEX OF NAMES. 625

JESSOM, Lillian (Mace).............. 446
JEWELL, Abby Maria (Locke)......... 441
   Charlotte 548
   DeWitt Clinton 441
   Eleanor 578
   Elizabeth M...................... 576
   Hannah M........................ 532
   Irena 575
   John L.......................... 576
   Sophie E. (Marston)............. 576
JOANES, Daniel....................... 71
   Thomas 71
JOCELYN, Henry..................20, 413
   Thomas 20
JOHNSON 99
   Abby S......................399, 445
   Abigail 309
   Abigail (Berry)..............298, 399
   Abigail D........................ 398
   Abigail D. (Batchelder).......... 398
   Ada May.......................... 399
   Adeline (Drake).................. 399
   Albert 446
   Albert M......................... 399
   Almira (Locke)................... 433
   Ann Morrison (Boyd).............. 576
   Annie (———)..................... 399
   Annie (Swenson)?................. 399
   Arvill 566
   Augusta (Berry)........304, 306, 399
   Benjamin 358
   Burleigh Albert.................. 399
   Charlotte....................399, 409
   Charles 399
   Charles Clinton 399
   Charles DeWitt Clinton........... 399
   Deliverance 450
   Deliverance (Knowles).......398, 403
   Dorcas 489
   E. (Black)....................... 399
   Ebenezer.....................136, 576
   Edmund..............61, 132, 205, 298
               304, 306, 398, 399
   Edward......................399, 576
   Edward L......................... 282
   Edward S......................... 400
   Eleanor (Brackett)............... 308
   Eliza (Stearns).................. 399
   Elizabeth 311
   Emma J........................... 437
   Esther.......................398, 546
   Esther (Hobbs)................... 378
   Fred 400
   G 444
   G. W............................. 280
   Giles 583
   Gilman W.....................399, 465
   Greenleaf 399
   Hannah.......................503, 575
   Henry 400
   Jacob......................68, 576, 583
   James 127
   John.........................329, 399
   John B....................399, 419, 433
   John Batchelder..............398, 399
   John Edward...................... 399
   John Greenleaf................... 399
   Lizzie (———).................... 399
   Margaret (Barnes)................ 576
   Maria L......................398, 425
   Martha Jane.................399, 419
   Mary.................337, 399, 467, 583
   Mary B........................... 419
   Mary C.......................317, 398
   Mary (Dalton).................... 329
   Mary F. (Mace)................... 399
   Mary F. (Mace-Goss).............. 446
   Mary (Folsom).................... 399

JOHNSON, Mary (Mow)............399, 465
   Mary (Yeaton)................398, 571
   May 398
   Meribah 467
   Minnie Addie..................... 399
   Nathaniel 144
   Olive 387
   Pearn........................409, 577
   Peter....................31, 35, 71, 142
         143, 144, 160, 203, 205, 218
         256, 262, 378, 398, 571, 583
   Phebe (Ayers).................... 576
   Polly 583
   Rachel (Garland)................. 358
   Richard Mentor................... 399
   Rosa 308
   Ruth 398
   Sally....................398, 399, 576, 583
   Sally B.......................... 445
   Sally B. (Mace)..............399, 444
   Sally (Johnson).................. 576
   Samuel 576
   Sarah....................369, 398, 399, 406
   Sarah (Allard)...............399, 576
   Sarah (Dow)...................... 398
   Simon..........35, 142, 144, 205, 259, 262
           270, 278, 398, 399, 403
   Susan 566
JOICE, Alma S........................ 454
   Richard 334
JONES, Abbie (Towle)................ 400
   Abiah 400
   Anna 400
   Anna (Webster)................... 400
   Caroline (Warren)................ 401
   Catherine 400
   Charles W....................280, 400
   Cyrus 61
   Cyrus S.......................... 281
   Cyrus 400
   Eliza F. (Leavitt)............... 413
   Eliza F. (Leavitt-Jones)......... 413
   Elizabeth Garland (Locke)....400, 440
   Elizaette E. (Locke)............. 438
   Emma I........................... 400
   Esther 386
   Esther J. (Foss)................. 347
   Esther Y. (Foss)................. 400
   Fannie E.....................400, 518
   Frank 400, 413
   Hannah 348, 580
   Hannah (Libby)................... 417
   Hiram........................400, 413
   Ira S............................ 174
   Joanna 309
   John.........................347, 400
   John William..................... 400
   Jonathan 401
   Joseph 400
   Margaret................400, 404, 464
   Margaret (Brewster).............. 400
   Martha M......................... 123
   Martha S. (Leavitt).............. 400
   Martha S. (Leavitt-Jones)........ 400
   Mary.........................400, 476
   Mary (Adams)..................... 476
   Mary (Towle)..................... 400
   Montrose 400
   Olly 400
   Paul 498
   Roxanna L........................ 419
   Sally (Moulton).................. 464
   Samuel...................72, 160, 476
   Samuel Jackson...............400, 440
   Sarah........................400, 430
   Sarah (Moulton).................. 400
   Susannah 400
   True W........................... 438

INDEX OF NAMES.

Jones, William.................400, 417, 4C4
Jonson, Simon......................... 31
Jordan, Jeremiah...................23, 24
  Nathaniel 262
  Robert........................71, 129, 237
Jording, see Jordan.
Jose, Richard......................... 334
Joscelyn, Lizzie...................... 566
Joyce, James.......................... 71
Judkins, Betsey (Knowles).......... 402
  Perna 547
  Sarah (Varrell)..................... 557
Julyn, Charles........................ 317
  Jessie M. (Brown)................... 317
Kalderwood, Margaret............415, 577
Kate, Daniel.......................... 401
  Frances 401
  Joseph 401
  Martha 574
  Patty 299
  Polly (Rand)........................ 401
  Prudence (Marden).................. 401
  Richard 401
Kean, Georgie Ann, see Keen, Georgianna.
Keen, Addie P......................... 401
  Carrie M............................ 401
  Emogene 401
  Georgianna......................338, 401
  Harriet 549
  Harriett Elizabeth.................. 401
  Harriett Elizabeth (Keen).......... 401
  Harriett J. (Rand)..............401, 503
  Hattie G............................ 401
  Henry H............................. 401
  Nellie W............................ 401
  Polly 306
  Warren W............................ 401
  William.........................401, 503
Keene, see Keen.
Kelley, John.......................... 267
  Ruth 309
  William 127
Kenney, Eunice........................ 366
  Isabella T. (Neal).................. 576
  Joshua W............................ 576
Kennison, James....................... 263
  Jonathan L.......................... 576
  Maria (Aspinwall)................... 576
  Susannah 536
Kenniston, Lucy....................... 579
Kerns, Anna........................... 326
Kerseys, John T....................... 576
  Olive (Dearborn).................... 576
Keyes, Harriett E. (Shapley)........ 539
  John 539
Keys 105
Kidder, Abner......................... 451
  Sarah W. (Marden).................. 451
Kien, Lydia (————)................... 557
Kimball, Charles...................... 401
  Emma Adeline (Brown).............. 317
  Fabins 401
  Frederick 317
  George W............................ 436
  Hannah (Philbrick)..............401, 491
  Harriett 364
  Hezekiah........................401, 491
  Lafayette 401
  Mary 576
  Mary (Grover)....................... 401
  Mary Perkins (Locke)............... 436
  Sabra 434
  Scott 401
  Susan 401
King, Charlotte....................... 561
  Polly 416
  William 137

Kingman, Dolly (Waterhouse)........ 402
  Elijah 402
  Elizabeth (Webster)............401, 564
  Jeremiah 402
  John 402
  Mary............................297, 401, 534
  Mary (————)......................... 401
  Olive 402
  Ruth 402
  William.........................401, 564
Kingsbury, J. W....................... 159
Kinneas, Ruth (————)................ 468
  Elizabeth F. (Brown)............... 576
Kinsman, John......................... 576
Kive, Sarah........................... 523
Knapp, Ann............................ 488
Knight, John.......................... 498
  Richard 71
  Susannah........................541, 579
  Temperance (Pickering)............ 498
  William 201
Knowland, Ann......................... 538
Knowles 144
  ———— (Emerson)................... 402
  ———— (Libby)..................... 402
  ———— (Locke)..................... 402
  Abby A. (Tarlton).................. 576
  Abby Annah (Garland)............. 366
  Abigail..........................337, 403
  Abigail (Brown-Dowrst)........... 309
  Amos......87, 143, 160, 309, 402, 414, 576
  Anna A. (Garland).................. 403
  Anna Brackett....................... 403
  Annie 403
  Betsey 402
  Betsey (Clifford).................. 402
  Betsey (Palmer).................... 402
  Charles N........................... 64
  Charles Nathan...................... 403
  Clinta Cleveland................... 403
  Clarissa.........................341, 403
  Comfort 404
  Comfort (Wallis)...............404, 580
  Daniel 404
  David 402
  Deborah 426
  Deborah (Palmer)................... 402
  Deliverance 398, 403
  Deliverance (————)................ 403
  Dolly (Quimby)..................... 402
  Eleazer 576
  Elizabeth.......................402, 425
  Elizabeth (Libby).................. 414
  Elizabeth M. (Jewell).............. 576
  Esther 428
  Esther (Saunders-Yeaton)......... 403
                                  523, 571
  Ezekiel......24, 26, 27, 136, 137, 265, 267
                               268, 402, 405
  Fannie B............................ 372
  Hannah.......................402, 421, 438, 576
  Hannah C........................336, 337
  Hannah (Clifford).................. 402
  Hannah (Knowles).................. 576
  Hannah (Lamprey).................. 404
  Isaac 402
  James........................404, 414, 580
  John......22, 26, 27, 41, 87, 136, 138, 205
                   273, 288, 402, 403, 404, 420
  John Clifford....................... 402
  John Langdon....................... 402
  Jonathan 24
  Joseph.................254, 308, 311, 403
  Josiah..........................367, 403, 576
  Lemira (Philbrick)................. 494
  Lizzie Abby......................... 403
  Love 403
  Love (Brackett)................308, 403

INDEX OF NAMES. 627

KNOWLES, Lydia............402, 473
Mary.........393, 402, 403, 404, 405, 486
Mary (Libby).............404, 414
Mary (Wedgewood)............... 402
Nabby 360
Nancy 579
Nancy (Lane).................... 403
Nathan..........31, 35, 99, 142, 144, 147
148, 160, 174, 205, 218, 273
275, 279, 313, 320, 366, 402
Patty 493
Patty B.......................... 402
Rachel 403
Sally 362
Sally (Perkins).................. 576
Samuel....35, 61, 140, 144, 153, 160, 205
254, 255, 256, 261, 262, 265
268, 289, 403, 404, 447, 576
Samuel M........................ 576
Sarah.......................403, 404
Sarah (Brown)................... 311
Sarah Elizabeth..............323, 403
Sarah Hook (Brown).....313, 320, 402
Sarah L.......................... 402
Sarah (Marden).............403, 447
Sarah (Moulton)................. 404
Sarah W. (Locke)................ 435
Seth 402
Simon..............26, 67, 135, 136, 138
268, 273, 403, 523, 571
Susan (Godfrey)................. 367
Susannah....................311, 402
Susannah (Godfrey)..........403, 576
Thomas 494
Tryphena (Locke), see Tryphene (Locke).
Tryphene 404
Tryphene (Locke).............404, 420
KNOWLS, see Knowles.
KNOWLTON, Abigail Daniels (Poor)... 498
Calvin 498
Laura Augusta (Locke)........... 4'1
Mary (Wallis)................... 564
Susan (Locke)................... 441
Susie 372
Timothy 441
Timothy C....................... 441
William 564
KNOX, Adams...................... 436
Anna 389
Drisco 583
Margaret 583
Henry.........................79, 121
Martha Dow (Locke).............. 436
LADD, George P................... 577
Hannah (Locke).................. 424
Huldah 559
Mary (Locke).................... 424
Sarah J. (Hanson)............... 577
LAFAYETTE 203
LAIGHTON, John................... 410
Oner (Langdon).................. 410
LAKE, Eunice (Seavey-Davis)...... 332
James 300
Mehitable (Berry)............... 300
Sally 547
Sarah (Berry-Dow)............... 300
Thomas.......................16, 332
LAMBERT, Joseph.................. 175
LAMOS, Sarah..................... 484
LAMPER, ——— Brown............... 319
Charles 319
John 319
Margaret (Jones)................ 403
Mary E. (Brown)................. 319
Simon 400
LAMPERE, Simon............33, 144, 205
LAMPIER, Simon................... 140
LAMPRE, see Lamprey.

LAMPREE, see Lamprey.
LAMPREY, Abigail................. 312
Abigail (Dearborn).............. 404
Asa 404
——— (Edgerly).................. 404
Beneamen 26
Benjamin..............42, 45, 46, 136
378, 404, 464
Benning 404
Betsey.......................404, 466
Charlotte...........332, 404, 576
Comfort (Batchelder)............ 295
Comfort (Hobbs-Shepard)......... 378
Comfort (Shepard)............... 404
David 404
Deborah......................404, 575
Dorothy 404
Dudley 426
Eli 577
Elizabeth...................404, 464, 575
Elizabeth (Edgerly)............. 404
Gillyen 404
Hannah..............312, 404, 405, 576
Hannah (Sanborn)................ 577
Hezekiah 390
Henry 404
James 404
Jane........................310, 404
John 295, 432
Joseph 404
Joseph Brown.................... 404
Louisa.......................432, 577
Lucy 404
Lydia (Locke)................... 432
Margaret (Jones)................ 404
Martha (Dow).................... 404
Martha (Perkins-Dow)............ 484
Mary 404
Mary Ann (Jenness).............. 390
Mary Smith...................... 374
Miriam Locke.................... 426
Molly........................404, 577
Morris 428
Nabby (Caswell)................. 321
Nancy (Locke)................... 428
Nancy (Shannon)................. 404
Patience (Hobbs).............378, 404
Ruth 312
Sarah.......................334, 404, 450
Sarah (Brown)................... 404
Sarah (Dow)..................... 404
Simon..........50, 321, 378, 404, 484
LANE, Abigail.................... 304
Abigail (Garland)............... 359
Belle O.......................... 332
Belle 405
Betsey (Perkins)................ 484
Daniel.......................312, 405
David........................312, 405
Eliza Jane...................... 413
Elizabeth (Berry)............... 305
Ezekiel 405
Hannah 405
Hannah (Lamprey)............405, 576
Hannah O. (Locke)............... 517
Hannah Olive (Locke).......405, 437
Isaac........................359, 405
James 105
Joel 576
John 71, 136, 137, 402, 403
405, 414, 576
John D.......................... 576
John O.......................... 437
Jonathan 405
Josiah 484
Mahala (Brown).................. 576
Margaret (Dow).................. 576
Martha (Brown).................. 312
Mary........................405, 432

INDEX OF NAMES.

LANE, Mary (Knowles)............402, 405
  Mary (Libby)..................... 414
  Nancy 403
  Nancy (Brown)................... 312
  Nathan 405
  Sally Leavitt (Brown)........... 312
  Sarah 297, 405
  Sarah (Dow)..................... 403
  Sarah (Libby)................... 417
  Thomas 312
  William 405
LANG, ——— (Robinson)............ 407
  ——— (Winn).................... 407
  Aaron 407
  Abigail 573
  Abigail (Locke)..............408, 428
  Alfred 280
  Alfred M..................280, 281, 409
  Alice (Gray)..................... 409
  Almira 408
  Almira (Hobbs))................. 407
  Anna.......................406, 407, 555
  Annaniah 407
  Arkell C......................... 409
  Augustus 408
  Bickford............31, 59, 139, 144, 160
                 161, 203, 204, 262, 273
                 405, 406, 408, 424, 428
  Billy 408
  Benjamin......160, 259, 405, 406, 407, 577
  Betsey......................301, 406, 407
  Betsey (Lang)................... 406
  Betsey (Walker)................. 408
  Catherine (Pope)................ 577
  Charles 399
  Charles T........................ 409
  Charles W....................68, 409
  Charlotte (Johnson)..........399, 409
  Clara I. (Trefethen)............ 409
  Clarinda 409
  Comfort (Foss)...............345, 408
  Daniel 170, 407
  David 407, 408
  Data 408
  Data (Garland)...............361, 408
  Deborah (Bean).................. 407
  Deborah (Marston).............. 407
  Deborah (Varrell).............. 406
  Dolly 406
  Dorothy 406
  Eben M......................409, 550
  Ebenezer Wallis...68, 290, 408, 409, 548
  Edward 407
  Eleanor.....................406, 408
  Eleanor (Burley)................ 406
  Eliza 407
  Eliza A. (Brady)................ 407
  Eliza E.......................... 409
  Elizabeth.............379, 406, 407, 456
  Elizabeth Ann................... 408
  Elizabeth Beverly............... 408
  Elizabeth (Hazzard)............ 407
  Elizabeth (Rand)............... 405
  Ellen A. (Varrell).............. 558
  Elly 408
  Emeline.......................395, 408
  Esther 407
  Esther (Morrill)................ 577
  Fanny 408
  Fanny G......................... 408
  Fanny Goldthwaite.............. 407
  Florence (Trefethen).........409, 548
  Florenza (Trefethen), see Florence (Trefethen).
  Florina A....................... 409
  Frances 408
  Frances E....................... 409
  George.............58, 405, 406, 568, 583

LANG, George II.............280, 408, 409
  George N........................ 280
  George William.................. 409
  Grace 406
  Hannah........406, 407, 408, 430, 452, 502
  Hannah C. (Trefethen).......... 409
  Hannah (Marden).............407, 449
  Hannah (Trefethen)............. 550
  Harriett 408
  Harvey V........................ 409
  Hezekiah Perry................. 409
  Huldah 408
  Jane (Wallis)................... 563
  Jeffrey 577
  Jennie C. (Fuller).............. 409
  John................59, 90, 204, 273, 289
              405, 406, 407, 408, 577
  John Langdon................... 407
  Jonathan 406, 407, 408
  Josiah......................409, 577
  Judith (Babb).................. 405
  Leonard......................361, 408
  Levi 407
  Lizzie 409
  Lucy.........................407, 570
  Lydia (Golden).................. 409
  Lydia (Lowell).................. 409
  Maria 408
  Maria (Parker).................. 409
  Mark.......89, 205, 360, 405, 406, 407, 449
  Martha....................406, 409, 560
  Martha E. (Varrell)............ 409
  Martha Lang (Varrell).......... 558
  Martha (Locke).............406, 424
  Martha (Sanborn).............. 407
  Mary.................407, 453, 518, 555
  Mary Ann................407, 408, 566
  Mary (Goss).................368, 406
  Mary (Thompson)...........406, 577
  Matilda (Spinney)............... 407
  Mercy (Drake).................. 408
  Molly 405
  Nancy....................379, 407, 408
  Nancy (Walker)................. 407
  Nathan 407
  Nathaniel 72
  Oren 409
  Pearn (Johnson)............409, 577
  Polly.......................407, 408
  Rebecca (Varrell).............. 555
  Relief (Brown).................. 407
  Reuel 408
  Richard............68, 226, 246, 275, 276
              289, 345, 406, 407, 408
  Richard W....................... 409
  Sally (Sanborn)................. 407
  Salome 407
  Salome (Goss)...............368, 406
  Samuel 407
  Sarah....305, 345, 406, 407, 408, 531, 583
  Sarah A......................... 407
  Sarah (Bickford)................ 405
  Sarah (Johnson)................. 406
  Sidney 503
  Sophronia 409
  Stephen 137, 563, 583
  Susannah....................407, 571
  Thomas..........31, 35, 68, 141, 144, 256
               261, 273, 368, 406
  Thomas M....................... 558
  Thomas Marden..............408, 409
  Thomas W....................... 409
  William...............405, 406, 407, 408
  William B...................108, 408
  Willis O........................ 409
LANGDON.........................23, 136
  ——— (Beal)................... 412
  ——— (Lane)................... 412

INDEX OF NAMES.

LANGDON, Abigail................ 411
Andrew J...................... 412
Ann 583
Anna 411
Comfort M..................... 411
Elizabeth..........410, 411, 527, 569, 574
Elizabeth (Sherburne).........410, 411
Emeline 412
Hannah...............410, 411, 580
Hannah (Jenness)...........381, 410
Hannah (Storer).............. 411
Harriett 411
John..............257, 370, 410, 411, 412
Joseph....................137, 203, 225
                        294, 410, 411, 498
Lydia (Brewster).............. 411
Margaret 410
Mark 410
Martha 410, 411
Martha Ellen (Willey)......... 411
Mary..................410, 411, 477, 527
Mary (———)................... 410
Mary Ann...................... 412
Mary (Banfield).............294, 410
Mary (Evans).................. 410
Mary (Hall)................... 411
Mary Hubbard.................. 410
Mary L........................ 411
Mary (Locke)..............412, 437
Mary (Pickering)...........410, 498
Mehitable (———)............... 410
Oner 410
Patience 170
Patience (Pickering)........411, 498
Polly 486
Richard 410
Samuel........71, 381, 410, 411, 412, 583
Sarah (———).................. 410
Sarah A. (Coleman)............ 411
Sarah (Sherburne)............. 411
Sarah (Winkley)............... 410
Temperance.................411, 531
Thankful 411
Thankfull (———)............... 410
Tobey 127
Tobias......................381, 410
William.........410, 411, 412, 437, 498
Woodbury...................411, 412
LANGHORN, Hannah............... 383
LANGLEY, Elizabeth (Locke)........ 429
John......................429, 522
Louise (Salter)............... 522
Maria (Towle)................. 547
Sarah (Brown)................. 522
LANGMAID, Abigail................. 412
Deborah (Berry)............... 412
Eliza 450
Henry 264
John......................412, 563
Martha L. (Wallis)............ 563
Samuel.....................71, 412
William 412
LAPISH, Ann....................... 310
LASBURY, Charles J................ 396
Edith-Maud (Jenness).......... 396
LASKEY, Adeline M. (Philbrick)..... 496
Henry 496
LATHAM, Thomas E.................. 280
LAWRY, Stephen.................... 262
LAWS, Christy..................... 321
LEACH, Alexander.................. 266
Benjamin..................265, 266
Emma Giles.................... 575
Giles 159
James......................38, 71
John.......................71, 127
LEAR, Addie (Remick).............. 412

LEAR, Alexander.........139, 141, 144, 205
                        262, 265, 273, 412
Alexander Salter.............. 412
Benjamin...............75, 146, 205, 273
                        276, 278, 412, 583
C. H.......................... 180
Charles................327, 349, 418, 455
Charles H..................67, 412
Christinia 412
Daniel 412
Deborah ....· 295
Eleck..................35, 261, 262, 311
Eliza Jane (Clark)............ 326
Eliza (Varrell)............... 577
Elizabeth 553, 574
Elizabeth Ann................. 412
Elizabeth (Brown-Goss)........ 311
Elizabeth Rosamond (Clough-Rumery)..........................327, 412
Elizabeth Rosamond (Clough Rumsey), see Elizabeth Rosamond (Clough-Rumery).
Elizabeth (Sherburne-Langdon)... 410
Elizabeth (Varrell)........... 555
Ezekiel....................153, 255
Harriet 517
Harriet N..................... 412
Jessie M...................... 517
John..........153, 255, 261, 337, 412, 577
John H........................ 281
John W........................ 412
Martha Jane................... 412
Mary 583
Mary Abby 338, 412
Mary (Morrison)............... 412
Mehitable 437
Mehitable O................... 412
Molly 412
Nancy (Downs)................. 337
Nancy (Downes)................ 412
Nathaniel.............259, 262, 326, 412
Sally (Salter)................ 412
Salome 571
Samuel....................273, 412, 522
Sarah P....................... 412
Sarah (Salter)................ 522
Tobias..............27, 71, 134, 135, 410
William 583
William Alexander............. 68
LEAVITT 218
——— (Jewell).................. 413
——— (Moore)................... 413
——— (Philbrick)............... 413
Abigail 581
Abigail L. (Brown)............ 577
Amos T........................ 577
Ann 310
Annie M....................... 483
Benjamin 264
Benning 397, 413
Betsey 576
Carr................119, 174, 208, 413
Daniel Eben................... 413
Eben.......................331, 413
Eben True..................... 413
Ebenezer..................147, 174, 413
Edmund Rand................... 577
Eliza F....................... 413
Eliza J. (Perkins)..........413, 486
Eliza Jane (Lane)............. 413
Eliza True.................393, 413
Elizabeth (Locke)............. 420
Elizabeth (Page).............. 577
Esther R...................... 438
Esther R. (Marden)..........413, 451
James 263
James P....................... 106
John.....................312, 413, 486

INDEX OF NAMES.

LEAVITT, John E............119, 291
  John Edwin...................... 413
  Jonathan..............263, 265, 359
  Joseph....................413, 451
  Louisa (Dalton)...........331, 413
  Martha S....................... 400
  Mary............312, 329, 333, 359, 512
  Mehitable (Edmonds)............ 577
  Nancy.......................... 360
  Nellie (Hadley)................ 413
  Olive (Jenness)............397, 413
  Samuel............72, 111, 283, 289
  Sarah......................309, 429
  Sarah Ann.................413, 440
  Sophia......................... 444
  Sula........................... 413
  Tappan......................... 577
  Thomas......................... 420
  Ursula......................... 331
  Vienna J..................413, 506
  William B.................331, 413
LEBBEE, see Libbey.
LEBBEY, see Libbey.
LEEAR, see Lear.
LEFAVOR, Abby Grace (Trefethen).... 550
  C. H........................... 550
LEFRANCIS, Frances Ann (Marden)... 452
  Thomas......................... 452
LEGRO, Elihu...................... 173
LEIGHTON, Hannah(Rand-Broughton) 506
  Joel.......................265, 506
  Sarah (Seavey)................. 529
LELAND, Mary...................... 419
LELLINGHAM, Hannah................ 424
LEONARD, Abigail (Perkins)........ 484
LEPINLE, Mary (Merrifield-Hall).... 377
LEVETT, Christopher......13, 14, 16, 229
LEWIS, Abby Frances............... 413
  Abigail (Berry)...........301, 413
  Carrie W....................... 544
  Fannie (Mace).................. 446
  Hannah......................... 555
  Hannah (Marden)................ 456
  Izettee........................ 439
  John B......................... 446
  Langley B.................301, 413
  Margaret (Robinson-Grant)...... 520
  Mary........................... 375
  Thomas......................... 456
LIBBE, see Libby.
LIBBEY, or LIBBIE, or LIBBY.
LIBBEY............................ 61
  Aaron.....................418, 501
  Abigail.........414, 416, 417, 418, 419
  Abigail (Foss)................. 346
  Abigail (Fowler)............... 416
  Abigail (Haines)............... 417
  Abigail (Irish)................ 416
  Abigail (Libby)............416, 419
  Abigail (Page)................. 417
  Abigail (Pearson).............. 416
  Abigail (Smith)................ 418
  Abigail (Symens)............... 416
  Abraham......................23, 24
  Abraham............31, 33, 35, 50, 59
      111, 139, 144, 160, 207, 256
      259, 261, 263, 265, 267, 273
      414, 415, 416, 417, 418, 489
  Agnes (———).................. 413
  Ai............................. 419
  Albert Francis................. 419
  Albert Frank................... 399
  Albert H....................... 419
  Alexander...................... 417
  Alice (Morton)................. 419
  Allison...................415, 417
  Ann (Phinney).................. 418
  Ann (Seavey)................... 416

LIBBEY, Ann (Symnes).............. 415
  Anna........................... 417
  Anna (Libby)................... 417
  Anthony...........40, 71, 414, 415
  Arter.......................... 32
  Arthur...........160, 262, 414, 416
  Arthur Remick.................. 416
  Benjamin.......33, 72. 160, 415, 417, 418
  Betsey......................... 417
  Betsey (Phinney)............... 419
  Betty.......................... 414
  Charlotte...................... 417
  Clara L........................ 419
  Daniel..................414, 416, 419
  Daniel F....................... 419
  Daniel Rand.................... 418
  David.......................... 414
  Deborah........................ 379
  Deborah (Rand)................. 418
  Deborah (Smith)................ 416
  Deborah Smith.................. 416
  Demas.......................... 417
  Dorothy (McKenney)............. 415
  Edward......................... 417
  Edward L....................... 419
  Elias.......................... 417
  Elisha......................... 415
  Elias.......................... 418
  Eliza A. (Woodward)............ 419
  Elizabeth................414, 415, 417
  Elizabeth (Brown).............. 414
  Elizabeth (Libby).............. 417
  Elizabeth (Winfield)........... 418
  Eleanor........................ 414
  Eleanor (———)................ 414
  Eleanor (Berry)................ 415
  Eleanor (Haynes)............... 416
  Ellen Maria.................... 419
  Enoch......................415, 419
  Ephraim...................414, 415
  Esther......................... 418
  Esther (Fogg).................. 415
  Esther (Hanscom)............... 414
  Eunice......................... 575
  Fanny (Sylvester).............. 417
  Hannah..........414, 415, 416, 417, 418
  Hannah (Copp).................. 415
  Hattie (Crockett).............. 419
  Henry.......................... 413
  Hepsibah....................... 415
  Hetty.......................... 418
  Honor (Hinkson)................ 413
  Isaac.............22, 24. 26, 71, 87, 136
      137. 254. 288. 414, 415. 416. 577
  Jacob........22, 24, 26, 71, 87, 136, 137
      288, 414, 415, 416, 417
  James.............259, 263, 413, 416
  Jane.....................414, 415, 417
  Jane (———).................. 417
  Jemima (Rand).................. 418
  Jeremiah....................... 418
  Jethro......................... 416
  Joanna.....................413, 414
  Job...................253, 415, 416, 417
  John..................254, 413, 414, 415
  Jonathan...................415, 416
  Joseph........72, 111, 160, 212, 273, 414
      415, 416, 417, 418, 419
  Josiah......................... 417
  Judith (Page).................. 415
  Julia E........................ 419
  Justin......................... 419
  Keziah......................... 415
  Leonie......................... 419
  Lillian Bertha................. 419
  Lillian May.................... 419
  Love (Phinney)................. 419
  Lucy........................... 416

INDEX OF NAMES. 631

LIBBEY, Luke.......................... 415
Lydia (Ayers).................... 415
Lydia (Skillings)................ 415
Margaret 415, 418
Margaret (Abbott)............... 415
Margaret (Kalderwood).......415, 577
Maria 418
Mark 415, 417
Martha 419
Martha (Hanscom)............... 414
Martha Jane (Johnson)......399, 419
Martha (Morton)................. 419
Martha (Skillings)............... 419
Mary......347, 404, 414, 415, 416, 417, 418
Mary (————)................... 416
Mary (Ambler)................... 414
Mary Ann (Swain)............... 417
Mary (Ashton)................... 414
Mary (Berry)..................... 417
Mary (Farmer)................... 414
Mary (Leland)................... 419
Mary (Libby)................414, 417
Mary (Meserve).................. 415
Mary (Tarlton).................. 417
Matthew 414, 415
Mehitable 418
Mehitable C. (Rand)............. 418
Mehitable (Seavey)..........418, 535
Meribah Smith................... 416
Meshech 415
Molly 416, 573
Morris 417
Moses 415
Naomi 417
Nancy 418
Nancy Griffith................... 418
Nathan 416
Nathaniel 415
Olive.....................66, 416, 418, 419
Olley 415
Patience (Farr).................. 419
Penelope (Barber)............... 416
Phebe 414
Polly (King)..................... 416
R. (Robinson)................... 418
Rebecca 414, 419
Rebecca (Crockett).............. 416
Rebecca (Pearson)............... 416
Reuben..........66, 72, 346, 414, 415, 418
Richard 416, 418
Rosa Belle....................... 419
Roxanna L. (Jones)............. 419
Ruth.......................342, 414, 415
Ruth Moses...................... 418
Ruth (Palmer)................... 416
Sabrina (Philbrick)...........414, 489
Sally 418
Sally (Lombard)................. 419
Samuel..35, 67, 141, 144, 176, 273, 413, 414
                     415, 416, 418, 419, 535
Samuel S......................... 419
Samuel W......................... 419
Sarah......307, 414, 415, 416, 417, 418, 522
Sarah (Dow)..................... 417
Sarah (Farrington).............. 418
Sarah Francis................... 419
Sarah (Fullerton)............... 418
Sarah (Goss).................... 416
Sarah (Hanscom)................ 415
Sarah (Libby)................415, 417
Sarah (Marston)................. 414
Sarah (Mason)................... 415
Sarah (Ross).................... 416
Sarah (Skillings)............... 417
Sarah T. (Sanborn)............. 418
Sarah Tucker.................... 416
Simeon....................417, 418, 419
Simon 417

LIBBEY, Smith................... 418
Solomon.....................414, 417
Stephen 419
Susannah 416
William Seavey................ 418
LIBE, see Libbey.
LIBERTY, Caeser.................. 577
Phebe (Ozel).................. 577
LIGHTFORD, Elizabeth............ 580
LITTLEFIELD, Abby Ann (Berry)..... 306
Abner ....' 419
Dudley Chase...............341, 419
Edson L....................... 577
LITTLEFIELD, Lydia S. (Davis)..... 577
Sarah Abigail (Drake).......341, 419
Walter S...................... 306
William Dudley................ 419
LOCK, see Locke.
LOCKE..... 60, 72, 134, 135, 144, 146, 149
——— (Chadbourne)............. 426
——— (Duncan)................. 433
——— (Marston)................ 425
——— (Norton)................. 423
——— (Stewart)................ 441
A 280
A. G............................. 280
Aaron......................434, 442, 443
Aaron R.......................... 509
Abby 322, 439
Abby A........................... 488
Abby Maria....................... 441
Abigail...170, 172, 352, 370, 388, 408, 421
      423, 424, 425, 427, 428, 429, 431
      432, 433, 434, 440, 485, 489, 547
Abigail (Amazeen)............428, 433
Abigail (Blake)................. 433
Abigail (Dearborn).............. 428
Abigail (Goodwin)............... 434
Abigail J........................ 438
Abigail (Jenness).............385, 432
Abigail (Locke)...........431, 434, 440
Abigail (Mace)...............431, 444
Abigail Mace..................... 431
Abigail Mace (Locke)............ 431
Abigail Mace (Locke-Locke)...... 431
Abigail Macy.................... 439
Abigail Macy (Locke)............ 439
Abigail Macy (Locke-Locke)...... 439
Abigail (Marden).............432, 450
Abigail (Page)................... 428
Abigail (Perry).................. 427
Abigail (Philbrick)..........430, 490
Abigail (Prescott).............. 422
Abigail (Saunders)...........429, 523
Abigail (Towle).................. 427
Abigail Towle.................... 432
Abijah 420, 422
Abner................153, 255, 265, 422
             424, 425, 428, 431
Abraham 427
Adeline 349, 351, 439
Adeline P........................ 437
Adeline (Sheppard).............. 431
Adna Parsons 438
Albert Carr...........291, 441, 443, 557
Alfred 431
Alice.......................306, 420, 428
Almira 433
Almira (Brown)...............315, 439
Alvah 443, 543
Alvira 437
Amanda (Batchelder)............. 295
Amos G........................... 440
Andrew G......................... 57
Andrew Gardiner.............442, 443
Andrew Jackson.................. 437
Angelina (Dockham).............. 442
Ann...................421, 425, 427, 485

INDEX OF NAMES.

LOCKE, Ann (Golding).............. 440
  Ann M...........................372, 437
  Ann (Towle)...................... 433
  Ann (Tuckesbury)................. 434
  Anna 431, 433, 436
  Anna D. (Garland)................ 440
  Anna Leavitt (Dalton-Garland).. 331
  Anna M. (Tarlton)................ 442
  Anna Tarlton..................... 442
  Anna (Trefethen)................. 538
  Annah 428
  Annie.......................443, 480, 482
  Annis 421
  Apphia 435
  Appia (Wallis)................... 434
  Arabella (Clough)................ 327
  Arabella Ringe................... 440
  Arthur 443
  Asa..........170, 172, 275, 379, 427, 429
                                 431, 435, 439
  Asa Dearborn..................... 440
  Belinda (Bunker).............320, 440
  Belle (Clough)................... 441
  Benjamin............425, 426, 428, 434
  Benjamin Lovering................ 433
  Bessie L. (Batchelder)........... 443
  Bethia (———)..................... 427
  Betsey...........426, 428, 430, 433, 434
  Betsey (Babb).................... 428
  Betsey (Dyer)................422, 426
  Betsey (Heard)................... 428
  Betsey (Marden).................. 438
  Betsey (Philbrick)............... 433
  Betsey (Rand).................... 424
  Betsey (Tucker)..............435, 553
  Betty (Perkins).................. 427
  Blake 427
  Brentwood 422
  Caleb........................422, 426
  Calvin.......................441, 443
  Caroline 436, 440
  Caroline G. (Garland)........361, 440
  Caroline (Hayes)................. 437
  Charles A........................ 438
  Charles Dunbar................... 442
  Charles Elvin.................... 441
  Charles F....................436, 439
  Charles Miller................... 436
  Charlotte (Wentworth)............ 431
  Charity 293
  Charity (Marden).............429, 455
  Christianna (Pain)............... 472
  Clara E.......................... 442
  Clarence Elmer 440
  Clarence S....................... 437
  Clarissa (Tash).................. 433
  Clarissa (Wallace)............... 433
  Clarinda A. (Batchelder)......... 443
  Comfort (Dowse).................. 427
  Cornelius 438
  Daniel..................424, 428, 430
  Daniel D......................... 280
  Daniel Treadwell................. 433
  David........31, 35, 65, 89, 142, 144, 205
                 267, 268, 269, 272, 284, 289
                 424, 428, 431, 433, 434, 448
  David Parsons.................... 440
  Dearborn 177
  Deborah......................420, 422, 426
  Deborah (Knowles)................ 426
  Delia Ann........................ 439
  Deliverance...................... 433
  Deliverance (———)............423, 427
  Dolly........................428, 437
  Doris 443
  Dorothy.................420, 422, 426
  Dorothy (Blake).................. 420
  Dorothy (Locke).................. 422

LOCKE, Ebenezer.................... 422
  Edison G......................... 443
  Edward........22, 24, 26, 27, 71, 135, 137
                 381, 420, 421, 423, 427
  Edwin 431
  Elbridge Gerry................... 437
  Eleanor 423
  Eleanor (Berry)..............299, 439
  Eleanor Dow..................435, 507
  Elijah....31, 35, 64, 72, 140, 143, 144, 203
             205, 256, 260, 265, 273, 283
             288, 289, 312, 421, 424, 427
             428, 429, 434, 484, 516, 524
  Eliphalet 421
  Elisha..............254, 421, 424, 428
  Eliza 549
  Eliza E. (Varrell)...........443, 557
  Elizabeth..........293, 352, 330, 420, 421
                 423, 424, 425, 426, 427
                 429, 431, 432, 433, 472
  Elizabeth (Batchelder)........... 427
  Elizabeth (Berry).............296, 420
  Elizabeth (Brown)............312, 428
  Elizabeth (Cheney)............... 434
  Elizabeth (Collins).............. 436
  Elizabeth D...................... 441
  Elizabeth Emerett............438, 453
  Elizabeth G..................300, 430
  Elizabeth (Garland)..........358, 425
  Elizabeth Garland............431, 440
  Elizabeth (Hobbs)................ 435
  Elizabeth Jenness (Hobbs)........ 379
  Elizabeth (Knowles).............. 425
  Elizabeth (Lang)................. 406
  Elizabeth Locke (Allen)......263, 431
  Elizabeth M. (Marden)............ 449
  Elizaette E...................... 438
  Ella B. (Haley).................. 443
  Ella Frances..................... 443
  Ellen 436, 439
  Ellen (Locke).................... 439
  Elmer F.......................... 437
  Elsey 420
  Elsie C......................373, 442
  Elvin......57, 170, 301, 320, 428, 432, 438
  Elvira G. (Marden)...........443, 454
  Emeline 437
  Emeline S........................ 394
  Emily 438
  Emma 320, 440
  Emma A........................... 344
  Emma Amanda...................... 438
  Emma Ann......................... 439
  Emma J. (Johnson)................ 437
  Emma L. (Smart)..............443, 543
  Ephraim..............60, 423, 427, 431
  Esther.......................422, 504
  Esther (Dow)..................... 426
  Esther (Knowles)................. 428
  Esther R. (Marden-Leavitt)...438, 451
  Esther Y. (Remick)...........440, 519
  Ethel M.......................... 367
  Ethel Maud....................... 443
  Ethel May........................ 442
  Eunice (Wallis).................. 431
  Everett True..................... 443
  F. J............................. 195
  Fanny 433
  Fidelia 438
  Florinda 433
  Florinda (Locke)................. 433
  Forrest M........................ 434
  Frances......................423, 534
  Frances (Manson)................. 437
  Frances (Priest)................. 443
  Francesene M. (Rand)............. 443
  Francina M. (Rand)............... 509

INDEX OF NAMES. 633

LOCKE, Francis.....22, 24, 26, 27, 44, 45, 60
    71, 87, 135, 137, 138, 142, 160
    254, 288, 289, 421, 423, 427, 434
  Frank Buchanan.................. 440
  Frederick 440
  Freeman J...........58, 207, 439, 441
  Gardiner Towle...........178, 331, 364
    435, 436, 440
  Gardner T., see Gardiner Towle.
  George............................434, 437
  George Allen..................442, 443
  George E.......................... 442
  George Washington............... 430
  Georgiana 380, 440
  Gordon H......................... 435
  Granville 436
  H. A.............................. 195
  Hall Jackson..............108, 428, 433
  Hamilton 209
  Hamilton C...................436, 503
  Hannah...297, 298, 421, 423, 424, 425, 426
    427, 428, 429, 431, 432, 433
    436, 439, 465, 490, 501, 517
  Hannah (Berry)..........258, 435, 436
  Hannah (Blake)................... 423
  Hannah (Danielson).............. 431
  Hannah Dow...................... 435
  Hannah E.....................436, 452
  Hannah Elizabeth...433, 442, 558
  Hannah E. (Locke)............... 436
  Hannah (Fogg)................422, 426
  Hannah J......................... 458
  Hannah J. (Frisbee)............. 442
  Hannah (Jenness)..65, 381, 382, 421, 425
  Hannah Jenness.................. 429
  Hannah Josephine (Trefethen)...
    442, 549
  Hannah (Knowles).........402, 421, 438
  Hannah (Lang)................403, 430
  Hannah (Lillingham)............. 424
  Hannah (Lovering)...........65, 428
  Hannah (Magoon)................. 426
  Hannah (Moses).................. 433
  Hannah O........................ 405
  Hannah Olive.................... 437
  Hannah (Pitman)................. 430
  Hannah (Prescott).............. 433
  Hannah (Rand)................... 426
  Hannah (Randall)............436, 516
  Hannah Salter................... 436
  Hannah (Saunders)..........434, 524
  Hannah (Tate)................... 422
  Hannah (Vittam-Berry)......303, 306
  Hannah W........................ 301
  Hannah Wallis................... 432
  Hannah (White).................. 437
  Hannah (Young).................. 435
  Harriet J...................372, 441
  Harriet (Weatherbee)............ 436
  Harris 433
  Harvey...................218, 317, 434
  Helen (Woodsum)................. 437
  Hellen C........................ 441
  Henry 430, 435
  Henry H......................... 441
  Herbert 558
  Hiram 433
  Horace 195, 439
  Horace W........................ 438
  Howard 431
  Huldah...............424, 429, 536, 537
  Huldah (Hobbs)..............378, 429
  Huldah (Perkins)............424, 484
  Ida G............................ 442
  Ida L............................ 441
  Ira 436

LOCKE, Irene (Healey)............. 434
  Isaac 431
  Isaac Moses..................440, 442
  Izette (Lewis)................... 439
  J. H............................. 280
  Jacob..................422, 425, 427, 430
  James...22, 24, 26, 27, 33, 64, 71, 87, 136
    138, 143, 261, 262, 298, 299
    325, 420, 421, 423, 425, 427
    429, 433, 434, 435, 433, 535
  James C.......................... 434
  James Davis..................... 436
  James Gardiner..............439, 442
  James H.....................294, 465
  James Henry..................... 538
  James Hobbs...........429, 435, 439
  James John..................439, 442
  James W......................... 363
  James William................... 432
  Jane.....................315, 339, 436
  Jane (McMurphy)...........429, 434
  Jane (Smith).................... 437
  Jemima 307, 421
  Jennie E. (Williams)............ 442
  Jeremiah......65, 72, 90, 139, 143, 144, 160
    177, 256, 262, 268, 276, 284, 292
    421, 425, 427, 430, 435, 436, 512
  Jerusha (Shaw).................. 422
  Jesse......................431, 436, 441
  Jethro.........22, 26, 27, 65, 68, 72, 135
    137, 169, 420, 422, 426, 428
    431, 432, 433, 438, 460, 565
  Job....................169, 406, 426, 429
    430, 431, 436, 490, 516
  John..............22, 26, 27, 58, 71, 136
    139, 143, 144, 152, 153, 205
    251, 252, 253, 255, 256, 260
    262, 273, 275, 278, 296, 385
    419, 420, 422, 424, 425, 427
    428, 429, 430, 432, 433, 434
    435, 437, 430, 442, 504, 512
  John Elvin..................438, 441
  John Franklin................... 442
  John H.......................... 566
  John Henry...................... 437
  John L.......................... 517
  John Langdon................431, 437
  John Newton..................... 436
  John O......................195, 196
  John Oliver...65, 425, 435, 439, 442, 549
  John Quincy..................... 436
  John Rindge..................... 435
  John Sewell..................... 438
  John W.................436, 438, 441, 443
  John W. P...........430, 431, 437, 441
  John Webster.................... 433
  John Wilkes..................... 517
  Jona D.......................... 172
  Jonathan....24, 26, 27, 31, 35, 57, 58, 68
    71, 72, 133, 135, 137, 139
    142, 144, 161, 164, 172, 177
    199, 203, 205, 246, 252, 262
    263, 264, 265, 273, 283, 288
    289, 315, 332, 355, 375, 420
    421, 422, 423, 424, 426, 427
    428, 432, 437, 439, 512, 577
  Jonathan Dearborn.......361, 435, 440
  Jonathan Hobbs................. 439
  Jonathan M...................... 169
  Jonathan Marden................. 436
  Joseph.........21, 22, 24, 26, 27, 28, 33
    35, 39, 40, 58, 65, 71, 75, 92
    129, 137, 139, 143, 144, 161
    169, 172, 203, 262, 264, 273
    274, 275, 276, 283, 284, 285
    286, 288, 290, 299, 303, 306

INDEX OF NAMES.

LOCKE, Joseph......312, 335, 345, 382, 402
  420, 421, 422, 425, 426, 427
  428, 429, 430, 432, 433, 435
  436, 438, 449, 450, 451, 583
Joseph B............................. 439
Joseph L............66, 147, 162, 166, 170
  209, 214, 285, 432, 437, 567
Joseph P............................. 106
Joseph Prentiss 437
Joshua............256, 262, 268, 315, 425
  429, 431, 455
Josiah.................265, 422, 427, 433
Judith 296
Julia Ann (Garland)............364, 440
Julia M. (Currie).................. 434
Laura A. (Hayes)..............438, 441
Laura Augusta...................... 441
Laura G............................ 440
Lemuel................172, 320, 431, 435
  439, 440, 519
Levi..........421, 424, 428, 429, 433, 436
Levi Dearborn...................... 439
Lizzie A. (Varrell)................ 558
Locada 436, 549
Louisa (Berry)................391, 438
Louisa (Lamprey)..............432, 577
Love 425
Lucia (Sanborn)................... 434
Lucretia 3 3, 432
Lucy 426
Lucy (Cate)........................ 428
Lucy M............................. 433
Lucy (Marden)..................436, 449
Lula Ann........................... 441
Lydia...............423, 425, 427, 431, 432
Lydia (Dow)........................ 427
Lydia (Foss)....................... 431
Lydia (Hall)....................... 428
Lydia (Page)....................... 431
Lydia (Philbrick).................. 433
Mabel Jenness...................... 443
Malvina A.......................... 437
Marcia 440
Margaret..........322, 421, 424, 439, 443
Margaret E. (Gillis)............... 443
Margaret (Pierce).................. 428
Margaret (Ward).................... 421
Margaret (Welch)................... 431
Maria Adelaide.................302, 441
Maria (Brown)...................... 317
Maria (Holmes)..................... 436
Maria L. (Johnson)................. 425
Martha.............406, 424, 434, 435, 501
Martha (Dow)...................335, 430
Martha Dow......................... 436
Martha (French).................... 355
Martha J........................... 442
Martha J. (French)................. 439
Martha Kate.....................442, 483
Martha (Mason).................438, 460
Martha (Perkins)................... 440
Martha (Rand)..................432, 504
Martha (Seavey)................434, 535
Martha Seavey...................... 439
Martha (Webster)...............433, 565
Martin Van Buren................... 437
Mary...................170, 227, 314, 315
  326, 388, 412, 420, 421, 422
  424, 425, 426, 427, 428, 429
  430, 432, 433, 434, 435, 436
  437, 486, 524, 547, 549, 580
Mary (———)..................... 435
Mary A. (Otis)..................... 441
Mary A. (Young).................... 431
Mary (Allen)....................... 430
Mary Ann........................... 432
Mary Ann (Rand)................436, 503
LOCKE, Mary Ann (Rindge).......... 435
Mary Augusta...................... 443
Mary B..........................437, 441
Mary B. (Locke)...............437, 441
Mary (Brown)...............312, 425, 429
Mary Brown........................ 430
Mary Brown (Dearborn)............ 333
Mary Brown (Locke)............... 430
Mary (Dearborn).................. 432
Mary E..........................438, 439, 442
Mary E. (Osborn)................. 437
Mary E. (Ward)................... 442
Mary Elizabeth................... 435
Mary (Elkins)................425, 432
Mary Emma........................ 441
Mary (Evans)..................... 427
Mary (Grant)..................... 433
Mary H. (Staples)................ 431
Mary Jane......................390, 439
Mary (Lane)...................... 432
Mary (Locke)..................... 426
Mary (Nason-Shaw)................ 427
Mary O........................... 438
Mary (Odiorne)................... 425
Mary (Organ)..................... 427
Mary Perkins..................... 436
Mary (Poor)...................... 498
Mary (Powers).................... 441
Mary (Rand)...................... 432
Mary (Randall)................... 437
Mary (Sanborn)................... 427
Mary (Shaw)...................429, 434
Mary (Stubbs).................... 422
Mary Susan....................... 437
Mary (Vennard)................437, 577
Mary (Wallis).................... 434
Mary (Wentworth)................. 436
Mary (Whitten-Weed).............. 436
May S. (Randall)................. 517
Mehitable 317, 427
Mehitable Berry.................. 431
Mehitable (Bickford)............. 434
Mehitable (Higgins).............. 430
Mehitable (Lear)................. 437
Mehitable (Rand)..............435, 512
Mercy 430, 460
Mercy (———)..................... 423
Mercy (Dame)..................... 428
Meribah 424, 425
Meribah (Page)................... 424
Merriam 422, 432
Merribah 426
Michael 432
Mirabah 428
Miriam 426
Miriam (Day)..................... 431
Molly 428, 430
Molly (Sceren)................... 427
Moses......................423, 427, 429
Nabby 429, 432
Nabby F.......................... 303
Nancy............363, 428, 431, 433, 434
Nancy (Drown).................... 432
Nancy (Helmer)................... 440
Nathaniel........420, 422, 426, 430, 431
  432, 436
Nimshi...................255, 256, 259
Olive A. (Hodgdon)............... 440
Olive Ann........................ 443
Olive (Berry).................299, 435
Olive C. (Fernald)............... 433
Olive (Chadbourne)............... 431
Olive (Elkins)................... 428
Olive (Foss)...............345, 425, 430
Olive (Marden-Elkins)............ 448
Olive Rand....................437, 494
Olive Shapley.................305, 432

INDEX OF NAMES. 635

LOCKE, Olive W.......................... 438
Oliver 280
Oliver E.....................327, 438, 441
Oliver Luther..............435, 436, 440
Olly (Rand)........................... 512
Pamelia Ann.....................301, 425
Parmelia Ann, see Pamelia Ann.
Parmelia (Conner)................. 428
Patience.....................421, 424, 464
Patience (Perkins)................ 427
Patty.......................364, 432, 434
Patty (Davidson).................... 332
Perna T............................... 435
Phebe (Ames)........................ 433
Phebe (Chapman)................... 433
Picker, see Locke, William.
Polly..............................429, 432
Polly (Carleton).................... 433
Polly W............................... 430
Polly Westbrook (Waldron)...438, 559
Prudence..................421, 423, 427, 449
R. Jenness.......................210, 443
Rachel......................313, 420, 429
Rachel Berry........................ 431
Rachel (Brainard)................. 424
Rachel (Sanborn)................... 433
Rachel (Towle)...................... 429
Rebecca 420
Reuben..................428, 429, 433, 434
Richard..35, 72, 90, 139, 143, 144, 160, 203
        226, 254, 259, 262, 273, 275
        358, 378, 420, 422, 425, 429
        430, 431, 435, 436, 553, 583
Richard Jenness..................... 443
Richard L..................288, 291, 393, 441
Richard Leavitt..................... 442
Richard R................163, 164, 166, 177
        274, 285, 286, 372, 413
Richard Rand..............279, 436, 440
Robert P..................295, 441, 443
Robert W............................. 438
Ruth 429
Sabra (Kimball)..................... 434
Sally.......................430, 431, 434
Sally (Foss)......................... 431
Sally H.............................. 435
Sally Hobbs.......................... 439
Sally (Locke)....................... 430
Sally (Mow-Allen)........294, 439, 465
Sally Wallis (Wedgewood)........ 567
Salome 368, 421
Salome (White)...................... 421
Samuel............22, 24, 26, 27, 333, 420
        421, 422, 424, 426, 427
        428, 429, 432, 433, 434
Samuel J............58, 147, 164, 166, 170
        172, 173, 279, 287, 449, 559
Samuel Jenness................432, 438
Sarah......381, 383, 396, 421, 423, 424, 425
        426, 427, 428, 429, 430, 432
        433, 434, 443, 447, 536, 565
Sarah (————).......420, 421, 422, 425
Sarah A.............................. 575
Sarah A. (Murdock)................ 440
Sarah Abby.......................... 438
Sarah Ann..................391, 432, 437
Sarah Ann (Leavitt)............... 413
Sarah (Cass)........................ 433
Sarah (Clark)....................... 426
Sarah (Cochrane).................. 433
Sarah (Dunbar)..................... 422
Sarah Elizabeth.................... 441
Sarah Emeline...................... 441
Sarah Frost....................322, 431
Sarah Goss.......................... 436
Sarah (Haines)............375, 423
Sarah Hannah (Randall).....443, 517

LOCKE, Sarah (Hayes).............438, 441
Sarah Isabell....................... 442
Sarah (Jones)....................... 430
Sarah L.............................. 438
Sarah L. (Webster)................ 566
Sarah (Leavitt).................... 429
Sarah (Locke)...................... 429
Sarah (Moulton)................... 423
Sarah O.............................. 557
Sarah P. (Jenness)............393, 442
Sarah (Page)........................ 427
Sarah (Palmer).................... 430
Sarah Palmer....................... 436
Sarah (Sanborn)................... 434
Sarah (Trefethen)................. 437
Sarah W.............................. 435
Sarah (Webster)................... 433
Sarah W. (Wedgewood).......... 437
Sarah (Woods)..................... 435
Sherburne......................432, 577
Sheridan 435
Simeon 428, 433
Simmion 433
Simon..........61, 170, 265, 266, 275, 276
        293, 352, 422, 426, 427, 431, 444
Simon Prescott.................... 433
Sophia (Pinkham)................. 428
Stephen 426
Sula A............................... 372
Susan 441
Susan (Rand)....................... 436
Susannah (Rand).................. 512
Thaddeus 437
Thankful (Blaisdell)............. 430
Theresa R........................... 434
Thomas 72, 421
Thomas B........................... 437
Thomas D.................426, 431, 433
Thomas Lemuel.................... 439
Timothy 427
Timothy Blake...............423, 427
Tristram 426
Tryphena 420, 422, 425
Tryphena (Moulton).............. 424
Tryphene 404
Ursula Ann...................106, 347
Walter 454
Walter E............................ 443
Warren 434
Weir 426
William..............21, 22, 24, 26, 27
        31, 35, 58, 64, 71, 87, 136
        137, 138, 140, 144, 161, 273
        283, 288, 290, 291, 420, 421
        424, 425, 429, 431, 432
        434, 435, 436, 437, 472, 523
William B........................... 433
William H........................... 108
William Harvey.................... 425
Willie E............................. 425
Willie H............................. 443
Willie L............................. 442
Willie M............................. 441
Woodbury..................434, 435, 437
Woodbury Augustus............... 440
Worthy Dearborn.................. 435
LOCKHART, Winnifred.............. 451
LOMBARD, Betsey (Libby)......... 417
Paul 417
Sally 419
LONG 274
George 263
Henry 261
Paul 263
Peter 212
Richard 558
LONGFELLOW, Nathan............... 577

INDEX OF NAMES.

LONGFELLOW, Tryphene (Huntley)... 577
LORD, Abbie............................. 445
  Daniel......................177, 370, 444
  Elizabeth 344
  Lydia II............................. 574
  Martha Ann.......................... 444
  Martha M............................ 295
  Mary 344
  Mary II.............................. 555
  Peter 492
  Sarah A. (Philbrick).............. 492
  Sarah Blake (Goss)............370, 444
LOUGEE, Adams......................... 444
  Amory 444
  Augustus 444
  Bertha 316, 444
  George G...............119, 223. 316, 444
  Gilman M............................. 121
  Gilman Marston..................... 444
  Josephine (Adams)................. 444
  Mabel (Wilkins).................... 444
  Margaret 444
  Semira J. (Brown)............316, 444
  Sophia (Leavitt)................... 414
LOUMBEY, Gashiem..................... 261
LOVE, Enoch........................... 530
  Mary A. (Seavey)................. 530
LOVERIN, John......................... 111
LOVERING, Hannah.................65, 428
  John 577
  Lydia (Towle)...................... 577
  Mary 580
LOW, Curtis........................... 577
  Olive (Mullen)..................... 577
LOWD, Florence W. (Rand).......444, 507
  Henry M............................. 444
  William Henry.................444, 507
LOWE, Mary............................ 362
  Moses 385
  Polly (Jenness).................... 385
LOWELL, Lydia......................... 409
  Olem 262
LUCAS, Susan.......................... 564
LUCY, Deborah......................... 310
LUFKINS, Moses........................ 577
  Sarah (Brown)..................... 577
LYBE, see Libbey.
LYON, Martha (Philbrick-Cass)....... 488
  William 488
LYONS, Robert......................... 503
  Sarah (Rand-Rand)................ 503
MCCANNON, James...................... 503
  Olive (Rand)....................... 503
MCCANON, Mary......................... 471
MCCLEARY, Margaret................... 563
MCCLINTOCK, Caroline................. 391
MCCLURE, Manley W.................... 472
  Martha M. (Page).................. 472
  Samuel 348
  Susan H. Foss...................... 348
MCCOBB, Mary (Langdon-Storer-Hill) 411
MCDANIELS, Elvira..................... 373
MCDOWELL, Eliza J................456, 457
MCEWEN, James......................... 573
  James F.............................. 158
MCGREGORY, William................... 583
MCGUIRE. Mary......................... 322
MCKEE, Helen.......................... 366
MCKENNEY, Dorothy.................... 415
MCKIM, W. D............................ 123
MCLAUGHLIN, Ellen A.................. 561
MCMURPHY, Jane...................429, 434
MACP, Archie.......................... 29
MACE 225
  Abbie (Lord)....................... 445
  Abby S. (Johnson)........399, 445, 519
  Abigail..........................431, 444

MACE, Abigail (Fogg)................. 577
  Abigail (Philbrick)...........445, 493
  Addie 446
  Addie M............................. 446
  Addie M. (Mace)................... 446
  Ambretta Jane.................445, 471
  Ambrinetta Jane, see Ambretta Jane.
  Andrew 312
  Anna C..........................446, 520
  Carrie 446
  Charles A........................... 280
  Charles Ithamar.......291, 445, 446, 461
  Charles William...............445, 446
  Deborah (Varrell).............445, 556
  Edward 445
  Eliza S. (Tucker).................. 446
  Elizabeth 312
  Elizabeth Ann (Caswell)......322, 446
  Elizabeth (Rugg)................... 577
  Emma 445
  Everett Ann......................... 445
  Fannie..........................445, 446
  Frances Olive (Matthews).....446, 461
  Fred 445
  Gertrude 446
  Hattie 445, 446
  Horace 365
  Horace S........................445, 446
  Isabella 445
  Ithamar................276, 299, 399, 444
                    445, 446, 556
  James 445
  John........135, 145. 208. 275, 278, 301
         322, 444, 445. 515, 537, 558
  John A..........................445, 446
  John Henry......................... 445
  John W..........................445, 493
  Joseph 577
  Judith 579
  Leander George.................... 446
  Levi 144, 536
  Lillian 446
  Maria 446
  Martha A........................445, 543
  Mary 325, 373
  Mary (Berry)....................... 445
  Mary E. (Varrell).............446, 558
  Mary F..........................399, 446
  Mary Jane.......................... 445
  Mary Olive (Downs)...........338, 445
  Mary (Randall)................517, 446
  Melissa (Garland)............3 5, 446
  Molly (Berry)..................301, 536
  Molly (Seavey).................... 536
  Nathaniel 339, 445
  Rachel 376
  Rachel (Berry)................377, 444
  Rachel (Randall)..............444, 515
  Ruth 578
  Ruth (Seavey).................446, 536
  Sally B........................399, 444
  Sally B. (Mace-Johnson)..399, 444, 445
  Sarah 371, 444
  Sarah (Shapley).................... 537
  William Henry..................... 445
  William R......................195, 338
  William Randall................... 445
  Wilmot Upham...................... 445
  Woodbury 517
  Woodbury N.................445, 446, 558
  Woodbury W......................... 280
MACK, Elizabeth (Garland).......... 360
  John 360
MACKENDS, David...................... 173
MACY, E............................... 565
MAGOON, Hannah....................... 426

INDEX OF NAMES. 637

MAGRAW, Clara A. (Clark) 326
   Michael Henry 326
MAGRIDGE, William .... 2(5
MAIN, Amos 428
   Mirabah (Locke) 428
MAINE, Charles 467
   Mary (Norton) 467
MALOON, Elizabeth 310
   Henry 578
   Mark 264
   Susannah (Symes) 578
MAN, see Mann.
MANN, Joseph 35
MANSON, Augusta 460
   E. Annie 562
   Emma 366
   Frances 437
   Martha Olivia (Berry) 306
   Robert 306
MARCH, George 255
MARDEN, ——— 53, 72
   ——— (Coffin) 453
   ——— (Dowrst) 70, 449
   ——— (Lang) 447
   ——— (Langmaid) 448
   ——— (Marston) 450
   ——— (Nudd) 452
   ——— (Wiggin) 449
Abby 454
Abby J. I. (Going) 452
Abiel 347, 455
Abigail 327, 432. 447, 448, 449
                450, 455, 456, 490, 513
Abigail (Brown) 315
Abigail (Marston) 453
Abigail (Webster) 447
Adeline 452
Albert B. M 453
Albert S 452
Alfred 412, 452
Alfred Henry 453
Almira 456
Amanda 350
Ann (Bartlett) 451
Ann Cecilia (Foye) 353, 457
Ann (Stead) 458
Anna B 322, 451
Anna Belle 454
Anna S. (Joice) 454
Anna (Towle) 457, 546
Anne (Stead) 577
Annie B 453, 461
Arabella (Norton) 453
Ardelle G. (Page) 457
Artimessa 457
Artimessa R. (Brown) 315, 456
Asa 453
Augusta 316
B. N 578
Benjamin ...31, 35, 66, (7. 70. 80, 141, 144
            177, 203, 205, 254, 257, 260
            262, 273, 339, 347, 403, 447
            448, 450, 453, 455, 456, 500
Benjamin Franklin 452
Benjamin W 169, 200, 214, 340
            361, 407, 442, 450, 452, 558
Betsey 438, 458, 578
Betsey (Marden) 458, 578
Betty 457
Caroline Theresa (Seavey) 456
                      461, 530
Carrie K. (Foss) 454
Carrie M. (Foss) 350
Charity 429, 455
(———) 455
Charles 456
Charles C 306, 456, 457

MARDEN, Charles Everett 457
   Charles F 451
   Charles Frost 454
   Charles H 452
   Charlotte Towle (Moulton) 451
   Clara 562
   Clara A 454
   Clara J. (Philbrick) 453
   Clarissa 456
   Clarissa A. Davis 450
   Clarissa Jane (Philbrick) 495
   D. W 280
   Daniel 64, 172, 276, 315, 448
                      456, 458, 578
   Daniel Otis 457
   Daniel T 495
   Daniel Towle 453
   Daniel W 452
   David 315, 447, 456, 457, 543
   David L 451
   David S 276, 407
   David Smith 455, 456
   Deliverance (Knowles-Johnson)
                        403, 450
   Dorcas 68, 293, 447, 458, 465
   Dorcas (———) 447
   Dorothy 550
   Dorothy B 451
   Eben 363
   Eben W 451
   Ebenezer 1 0, 203, 276, 299
                   304, 447, 449, 451
   Ebenezer W .... 10 }
   Elbridge 452
   Eliza 306
   Eliza A 372, 452
   Eliza Ann 451, 456, 550
   Eliza Anna (Parsons) 482
   Eliza (Garland) 360, 456
   Eliza J. (Garland-Drake) 340
                        361, 452
   Eliza J. (McDowell) 456, 457
   Eliza (Langmaid) 450
   Elizabeth 300, 301, 329, 447, 448, 449
               452, 455, 456, 458, 546
   Elizabeth Ann (Haley) 453
   Elizabeth (Curtis) 458, 578
   Elizabeth Emerett (Locke) 438, 453
   Elizabeth (Holmes) 453
   Elizabeth (Lang) 407, 456
   Elizabeth M 170, 449, 451
   Elizabeth (Moulton) 449, 464
   Elizabeth (Webster) 455, 564
   Ella Grace 452
   Elsie Jane 454
   Elvira G 443, 454
   Emerett E 454, 499
   Emery B 454
   Emily 452
   Emily (Norton) 453, 467
   Emma 342
   Emma Jennette 457
   Emma R. (Downs) 338, 454
   Ervin W 286, 454
   Esther 449, 504
   Esther (Berry) 304, 447
   Esther R 413, 451
   Eunice Abby (Brown) 457
   Eva Augusta 457
   F 280
   Fannie S. (Brown) 454
   Fanny 454
   Florence 450
   Florence B 453
   Florence M 455
   Frances 450
   Frances Ann 452

638 INDEX OF NAMES.

MARDEN, Frances Jane................ 451
Francis................404, 449, 450, 452
Francis Marion.................453, 454
Fred 454
Fred H............................... 454
George 448, 449, 451, 453, 4C0, 564
George E............................ 545
Georgianna M....................... 453
Gilman....................452, 456, 530
Gilman D........................... 452
Gilman M........................... 461
Hannah.......326, 407, 447, 448, 449, 450
    451, 455, 456, 457, 5:0, 569, 575
Hannah (Beck-Walker)............. 563
Hannah (Berry)..298, 299, 449, 451, 457
Hannah Elizabeth (Locke)........ 442
    452, 558
Hannah (Fogg).................447, 458
Hannah J........................... 451
Hannah (Lang)................407, 452
Hannah (Moulton)................ 451
Hannah (Norton).............453, 467
Hannah (Rand).............68, 450, 500
Hannah (Walker)................. 453
Hannah (Wallis)..............450, 563
Harriett O. (Jenness)........304, 454
Henry 451
Henry Hubbard.................... 452
Hepsibah 447, 458
Hepsibeth 458
Hepzibah (———)................ 447
Hincks 450
Hollis N......................350, 454
Horton 457
Huldah (Remick)..............455, 518
Hunking 451
Ida Florence....................457, 494
Ida May............................. 452
Irving 58
Israel.........142, 203, 339, 423, 447, 449
    450, 452, 453, 563
J. W................................. 280
James.............22, 24, 26, 27, 68
    70, 72, 88, 134, 135, 136
    138, 160, 163, 166, 168, 169
    170, 172, 191, 192, 203, 208
    278, 283, 288, 289, 290, 295
    389, 446, 447, 448, 449, 450
    451, 452, 454, 554, 565, 577
James L............................. 454
James W.......................C6, 394
Jane 447
Jane (Miller)...................... 456
Jenness....................177, 382, 454
Jesse.........................448, 451, 453
John...........70, 204, 275, 425, 447, 448
    449, 450, 451, 452, 453
John Calvin....................... 453
John Francis...................... 454
John H............................. 457
John S.............................. 108
John Salter........94, 208, 380, 451, 453
John T............................. 291
John Towle.................317, 452, 454
Jonathan.........101, 131, 160, 447, 448
    449, 450, 457, 458
Jonathan Towle.................... 457
Joseph........141, 144, 160, 259, 262, 288
    447, 448, 450, 500
Joseph Button..................... 408
Joseph Mason...................... 453
Joseph P......................453, 467
Joseph W........................... 337
Joshua 68
Josiah...........68, 276, 299, 449, 451
Judith 448, 449

MARDEN, Judith (Bates)..........235, 448
Julia (———)....................... 452
Julia H. (Garland)............363, 451
Julia L. (Brown)................. 454
Kate (Butler)..................... 452
Keziah 457
Langdon 456
Laura Ann......................... 452
Laura Emma....................... 457
Levi W....................70, 132, 338
Levi Watson....................... 454
Lizzie F. (Ewing)................. 453
Lizzie (Rhodes)................... 455
Louisa 511
Louisa M.......................... 457
Louise 208
Louise (Chamberlain)............ 578
Love B............................. 451
Love (Berry).................293, 451
Lovina 451
Lowell S........................... 66
Lowell Sanborn...............450, 452
Lucy......................436, 449, 456
Lucy Ann (Garland)........363, 454
Lucy R............................ 455
Lydia 451
Maria (———)..................... 451
Maria (Lang)..................... 408
Margaret (Foss-Nason)......347, 456
Margaret (Seavey)................ 458
Martha A....................507, 510
Martha Abby..................... 457
Martha (Mason)................. 460
Martha W. (Mason).............. 453
Martha (Mason-Marden)......... 460
Martha W. (Mason-Marden)..... 453
Mary........346, 363, 447, 448, 449, 450
    451, 455, 458, 491, 513, 574
Mary A. (Garland)............... 457
Mary Ann......................... 456
Mary Ann (Garland)........3:2, 454
Mary Ann (Lang)................ 408
Mary Ann (Langdon)............ 412
Mary Ann (Loutz)................ 457
Mary B............................ 451
Mary C. (Cochrane)............. 453
Mary E.......................452, 454
Mary E. Stewart.................. 452
Mary Eliza........................ 372
Mary Elizabeth (Sherburn)..... 450
Mary Elizabeth (Thomas)....... 545
Mary (Holmes)................... 456
Mary (Hunt)...................... 456
Mary Jane.................453, 456, 557
Mary Jane M..................... 453
Mary Jane (Page)................ 452
Mary L............................ 544
Mary (Lang)...................... 453
Mary O. (Burton)................ 457
Mary (Rand-Hunt)................ 500
Mary (Smith)................447, 543
Mary (Trickey-Garland)......... 366
May 456
Mehitable 458
Mercy 452
Mercy (Holbrook)................. 451
Mercy (Page).................452, 577
Merribah 455
Molly 448
Molly (Smith)................455, 543
Moses 456
Moses R........................67, 456
Nancy 449
Nancy (Colby).................... 449
Nancy Tredwell.................. 450
Nancy Tredwell (Marden)....... 450
Nathan..........237, 446, 447, 448, 449

INDEX OF NAMES. 639

MARDEN, Nathaniel......35, 58, 66, 75, 133
141, 145, 205, 259, 260, 262, 273
286, 287, 290, 291, 298, 438, 447
448, 449, 451, 453, 457, 464, 546
Nathaniel D....................... 452
Nellie 454
Nettie Jane....................... 454
Newell 454
Olive..................343, 448, 449, 503
Olive (Rand-McCarmon)......... 503
Oliver 452
Olivia B......................451, 550
Otis D......................64, 210, 291
Patience........................305, 450
Phebe 458
Polly A. W..................454, 570
Polly (Jenness)............70, 389, 452
Priscilla (Foss).................... 449
Prudence..................401, 449, 450
Prudence (Locke)............423, 449
Prudence Perry...............457, 529
Rachael, see Rachel.
Rachel............324, 346, 447, 450, 455
Rachel (———)................... 458
Rachel (Dowrst)..............339, 455
Ralph 482
Rebecca 170
Rebeckah (Whidden)............. 448
Rebekah 450
Reuben...........103, 169, 172, 449. 451
Rhoda 451
Robert 451
Roxanna (Brown)................ 451
Ruth..........................455, 546
S. A.............................. 195
Sally 456
Sally (Philbrick).................. 490
Sally (Seavey).................... 529
Sally (Tilton)..................... 450
Samuel............66, 135, 137, 163, 169
170, 172, 260, 262, 276, 279
353, 447, 448, 450, 455, 456
457, 458, 490, 510, 536, 578
Samuel A....................58, 291, 454
Samuel B......................... 451
Samuel Foss...................... 453
Samuel Hunt...................... 448
Samuel Woodbury................. 457
Sarah..............370, 403, 446, 447, 448
449, 450, 452, 455, 458, 491, 503, 573
Sarah (———).................... 458
Sarah A........................... 454
Sarah Amanda 457
Sarah Ann....................453, 456
Sarah Anzolette................... 457
Sarah B. (Brown)................. 451
Sarah (Burbank).................. 449
Sarah (Dowrst)................... 339
Sarah Frances (Brown).......... 317
Sarah (Lamprey)............404, 450
Sarah (Locke)................425, 447
Sarah M.......................... 453
Sarah (Philbrick)................. 456
Sarah Priscilla.................... 452
Sarah (Saunders)................. 448
Sarah (Seavey)...............457, 536
Sarah (Tucker)................... 554
Sarah W...................451, 453, 506
Sarah (Webster).......449, 451, 564, 565
Simon..................450, 453, 467
Solomon........67, 177, 279, 412, 455, 518
Solomon Dowrst.................. 455
Sophia C. (Holmes)...........380, 453
Stephen...24, 59, 60, 88, 142, 160, 169, 203
205, 273, 285, 288, 289, 447
455, 456, 458, 543, 564, 577
Steven, see Stephen.

MARDEN, Susan..................... 452
Susan S........................... 453
Susan T........................... 579
Susanna (Berry)..............297, 449
Thomas........50, 142, 203, 360, 403, 447
449, 450, 451, 453, 454
455, 456, 458, 503, 543
Thomas Ira...................456, 457
Timothy...................447, 448, 457
Trueman II....................... 453
Varina (Currier)................: 451
Wilbur L...................70, 454, 455
William............22, 24, 26, 27, 35, 70
75, 134, 135, 137, 138, 141
144, 153, 176, 177, 255, 262
263, 267, 268, 273, 289, 363
446, 447, 448, 450, 451, 452
453, 454, 456, 458, 460, 563
William Gould.................... 448
William Jackson.................. 453
Willie 454
Willie P.......................... 454
Winnifred (Lockhart)............ 451
MARSH, Elizabeth (Turner)........ 578
John 540
Sally H........................... 581
Sarah (Sheafe)................... 540
Thomas C......................... 578
MARSHALL, ———.............412, 558
Abigail (Randall)................ 515
Gideon 515
Robert 265, 266
William 278
MARSTON, ——— (Rand)........... 513
Abigail 453
Abigail (Garland)................ 358
Anna Parsons.................396, 458
Ardelle 459
Bethiah 480
Catharine 343
Catharine 343
Catherine (Elkins)............... 459
Catherine Elkins.............321, 458
Clara A. (Garland)............... 459
Clara D. (Garland)............... 362
Clarence V....................... 438
Clarissa.....................459, 577
Clarissa L........................ 579
Clarissa (Marston)...........459, 577
David.....................358, 459, 577
Deborah 407
Eleanor 574
Eliza D........................... 365
Eliza (Rand).................459, 503
Elizabeth 319
Elizabeth (Brown)............309, 311
Ella P............................ 459
Hannah................358, 366, 459, 514
Hannah (———).................. 459
Hannah Jenness (Locke)......429, 458
Huldah 458
Ida B............................. 459
Ina Belle......................... 459
Isaac 309
Jacob...................(0, 311, 341, 458
James........................311, 459
Jeremiah.......................46, 255
John......................205, 263, 429, 458
John D........................60, 292
John Drake...............108, 458, 459
Jonathan...................459, 567, 577
Joseph.............44, 45, 135, 137, 411, 459
Martha D. (Brown)............... 458
Mary.........321, 355, 378, 458, 542, 567
Mary J........................... 479
Olive D. (Stephens), see Olive D.
(Stevens).

INDEX OF NAMES.

MARSTON, Olive D. Stevens......459, 577
 Patience........................358, 360
 Paul Smith.....................343, 459
 Rachel............................ 311
 Rebecca 489
 Reuben 459
 Samuel 343
 Sarah 414, 568
 Sarah E........................... 393
 Sarah J. (Go:e)................... 459
 Sarah (Jenness).................. 382
 Sarah L. (Locke)................. 438
 Sarah Parsons (Drake)........341, 458
 Sarah (Weeks)................459, 577
 Simon..........................459, 503
 Sophie E.......................... 576
 Susan M........................... 338
 Susannah (Brown-Nudd).......... 311
 Thankfull (Langdon)............. 411
 Theodore......................267, 268
 Thomas 362
 Thomas W......................... 459
 Triphena 489
 Walter 459
 Willard S.....................290, 458
 William 489
MARTEN, Susan M..................... 575
MARTIN, Elizabeth (Mason).......... 460
 Joseph 460
 Nancy (Perkins).................. 485
MASSON, Daniel...................... 33
MASON, ———......................... 127
 ——— (Edwards)................... 460
 ——— (Hanscom)................... 460
 Aaron 460
 Augusta (Manson)................ 460
 Benjamin......................465, 512
 Betsey 460, 583
 Caroline 460
 Charles 460
 Clara Ann (Jenness) 334
 Clarence B........................ 394
 Clarissa 460
 Daniel........31, 68, 75, 141, 145, 146, 205
   273, 276, 459, 460, 466, 513, 583
 Data 370
 Edmon 493
 Elizabeth 460, 550
 Elizabeth (Norton)............459, 466
 Elizabeth (Philbrick)............ 493
 Emery 460
 Gilman 460, 493
 Hannah N......................... 353
 Hannah (Neal).................... 459
 J 243
 John........7, 8, 10, 17, 18, 19, 20, 70, 76
   230, 231, 236, 296, 499, 526
 Jonathan 260
 Joseph 346, 460
 Laurinda 460
 Levi 493
 Lucy 146
 Lucy M............................ 460
 Maria 460
 Martha 438, 460
 Martha L.......................... 460
 Martha W.......................... 453
 Mary..................382, 396, 460, 554
 Mary (Rand)...................... 501
 Mary J. (Fletcher)............... 460
 Mary M. (Rand)................... 460
 Mercy (Locke).................430, 460
 Mercy (Rand)..................460, 513
 Nicholas.......146, 276, 290, 459, 560, 501
 Olive (Coombs-Mow)............... 465
 Olive (Philbrick)................ 493
 Patty 348

MASON, Patty W. (Foss).........346, 460
 Robert................19, 329, 459, 460
 Ruhamah...................459, 460, 578
 Ruhama, see Ruhamah.
 Samuel................277, 430, 459, 460
 Sarah 329, 415
 Sarah Ann........................ 460
 Sarah E. (Philbrick)..........460, 493
 Sarah (Rand)..................... 512
 Sarah (Ranson)................... 460
 Shua 484
 Treadwell N....................... 68
 Woodbury 460
MATHER, Betsey (Randall).......... 515
 Cotton 238, 247
 Robert 515
MATHES-MATHEWS-MATTHEWS.
 Abraham......31, 141, 145, 170, 256, 259
   273, 302, 460, 461, 545
 Ann E..........................377, 461
 Annie B. (Marden).............453, 461
 Asa Robinson..................... 461
 Betsey 337
 Betsey (Foss).................... 347
 Betsey M. (Berry).............302, 461
 Betsey M. (Randall).............. 460
 Bezaleel 530
 Bezaled Smith.................... 461
 Caroline Theresa (Seavey-Marden)..........................461, 530
 Clara A.......................349, 461
 Clarence 453, 461
 Edward 461
 Eliza (Carter)................... 461
 Elizabeth 460
 Elizabeth (Foss)................. 461
 Emma 461
 Frances Olive.................446, 461
 Hannah 461, 521
 Hannah (Foye).................... 461
 Harriett 461, 465
 Hattie M......................... 323
 Ira 461
 John F............................ 461
 Joseph William 461
 Mary......................460, 461, 571
 Mary E............................ 461
 Mary E. (Rodgers)................ 461
 Mary Elizabeth................... 558
 Mary Esther 461
 Mary (Saunders-Thomas).460, 523, 545
 Oscar 461
 Robert 460, 461
 Sally 460
 Sally Ann......................... 461
 William...............275, 347, 461, 523
 William T......................... 461
 William Thomas................460, 461
MAVERICK, Samuel..................10, 11
MAY, Mary.......................... 330
 Mimowell 330
MAXFIELD, Robert................265, 266
MAXWELL, Ella M.................... 551
MAYO, Ida.......................... 365
MEAD, John B....................... 578
 Sarah 507
 Sarah H. (Smith)................. 578
MEAL, see Neal.
MELCHER, Edward.................... 135
 Martha 560
MELOWN, Deliverance (Walker)...... 577
 Joseph 577
MELOY, Arthur...................... 265
MERRIAM, George.................... 507
 Hannah B. (Rand)................. 507
 Persis 508
MERRIFIELD, Keziah................. 297

INDEX OF NAMES. 641

MERRIFIELD, Mary................... 377
MERRILL, ———..................... 90
  Anna 326
  Betsey L............................ 574
  Clara L. (Libby)................... 419
  Gilman 472
  Hannah 343
  Henry L............................ 419
  Levi 106
  Mary G. (Page).................... 472
  Phineas 206
  Polly 580
MESERVE, Mary...................... 415
  Sarah 575
MESERVY, Samuel.................... 203
MICHIE, Fannie E. (Jones).......... 400
  Harold A.......................... 400
MILLER, ———...................... 280
  Abraham 475
  David 265, 266
  Eliza Ann (Dean).................. 578
  Emily (Wedgewood)................. 567
  Hannah (Clapp).................... 475
  Jane 456
  M. Louisa......................469, 471
  Mary (Trefethern)................. 547
  William 578
MILLETTE, Augusteen (Erickson)..... 465
  Bertha 465
  Delia 465
  Elida 465
  John 465
  Stella 465
  Theodore 465
MILLS, ——— (Furber)............. 498
  A. W............................... 159
  Charles 313
  John 267
  Mary (Brown)...................... 313
MITCHELL, Jane..................... 572
  Peter 105, 205
  Richard 352
  Robert 259
  Susan (Foye)...................... 352
MITCHIE, Fannie (Jones)............ 518
MOLTON, see Moulton.
MONROE, Elizabeth.................. 477
MONTGOMERY, Abbie (Perkins)........ 487
  David H............................ 487
MOODY, Elizabeth................... 310
  Reuben 243
  Samuel 240
MOOR, Abby Coffin (Jenness-Odiorne) 391
  Christopher 391
  Jonathan 24
MOORE, Abigail (Brown)............. 312
  Anna 461
  Anna (———)...................... 461
  Benjamin 578
  Eleanor (Jewell).................. 578
  Enoch 312
  Isaac 267, 268
  William 42, 461
MOORESON, Samuel................... 31
MORAN, Henry W..................... 578
  John 563
  Mary P. (Remick).................. 578
  Mary W. (Walker).................. 563
MORGAN, Abraham.................... 39
  David 268
  Mary (Bickford)................... 578
  Nathaniel 578
MORIN, Henry W..................... 519
  Mary Pauline (Remick)............. 519
MORRELL, Mary...................... 311
MORRILL, ———..................70, 225
MORRILL, ——— (Wallis)........... 564
  Alva Herman....................174, 578
  Amelia 462
  B. P.....82, 84, 90, 91, 119, 121, 206, 219
  Benjamin 462
  Elizabeth Lake (Hubbard).......... 578
  Esther 577
  Joseph 136, 462
  Levi 462
  Mary (Jenness).................... 383
  Nathaniel......................150, 462, 573
  Sarah 462
  Sarah (Marden).................... 449
  Sarah Odiorne..................... 462
  Tabitha (———)................... 462
  Theophilus 462
MORRIS, James...................... 336
  Sarah (Downing)................... 336
MORRISON, Abigail (Libby).......... 417
  Abigail (Trefethern)..........462, 547
  Alexander..................262, 462, 500
  Alma 462
  Beckey 462
  Benjamin 462
  Betsey 462
  Jacob 555
  John 417, 462
  Luba 163
  Mary 412, 462
  Mary (Billings)................... 462
  May (Varrell)..................... 555
  Rachel......................358, 367, 462
  Rebecca (Rand)................462, 500
  Robert.............153, 255, 256, 260, 462
  Samuel......31, 35, 66, 141, 145, 261, 273
  Samuel Rand....................... 462
  Sarah (Coats)..................... 462
  William........................462, 547
  William Rogers.................... 462
MORSE, Jedediah...............241, 242, 243
  Joseph.........................402, 514
  Lydia (Knowles)................... 402
  Mary (Randall).................... 514
  Nason H........................106, 107
MORTON, Alice...................... 419
  Martha 419
MOSES, Aaron..............459, 462, 463, 578
  Abigail 463
  Abigail A. (Seavey)............463, 529
  Abigail Sarah..................... 462
  Abigail (Wallis)...............463, 563
  Alfred D........................... 463
  Augusta O.......................... 463
  Bridget (Weeks)................... 578
  Dorothy........................463, 506
  Eliza 463
  Elizabeth 463, 554
  Hannah 433, 462
  James................462, 463, 468, 563
  John 463
  Joseph 462
  Joshua S........................... 463
  Josiah 462
  Julia A............................ 463
  Julia A. (Moses).................. 463
  Levi 463
  Margaret (Huntress)............... 578
  Mark 462
  Martha 462, 463
  Martha J........................... 463
  Martha (Jackson).................. 463
  Mary........................463, 499, 500
  Mary (———)..................462, 463
  Mary B............................. 463
  Mary (Odiorne)................463, 468
  Nadab 463, 468

INDEX OF NAMES.

MOSES, Patty 502
  R. (Mason) 463
  Ruhamah (Mason) 459, 578
  Ruhanna, see Ruhamah.
  Ruth 418, 463, 534
  Sarah 463, 503
  Samuel 578
  Samuel Wallis 463
  Thomas 578
  William 463, 529
MOSHER, ———— 175
  Hannah 463
  Hannah E 494
  Josephine W. (Rand) 506
  Samuel 463, 583
MOULE, Margaret (Langdon) 410
  Nichols 410
MOULTON, ————. 64, 272
  Abigail 382
  Abigail (Garland) 357
  Abigail P 578
  Abner 367
  Abraham 414
  Albert 465
  Alice 542
  Ann E 350
  Anna 464
  Anna (Brown) 311
  Bethia 464
  Bethia (Swaine) 464
  Charlotte A. (Prescott) 571
  Charlotte (Towle) 451, 577
  Cora J 318
  Daniel 136, 260, 262, 288, 404
    421, 463, 464, 489, 557, 577
  Daniel N 577
  David 87, 407
  E 500
  Edith 465
  Elisha 422
  Eliza 464
  Elizabeth 310, 449, 464
  Elizabeth (Lamprey) 464
  Elizabeth (Philbrick) 464
  Ella 325
  Elvira 397
  Emma (Philbrick) 464, 494
  Enemiah 31
  Esther 463
  Esther (Long) 407
  George 464
  Gilman 318
  Grace (Runnells) 464
  Hannah 451, 464, 489
  Hannah (Down) 577
  Hannah (Drown) 464
  Hannah Jane (Varrell) 557
  Hannah (Perkins) 484
  Hannah (Philbrick) 464, 490
  Harriett (Fogg) 577
  Harry 465
  Henry 357
  Hervey C 396
  Hezekiah 87
  Ida M. Jenness 396
  Jacob 464, 494
  Jane 484
  Jane (Libby) 414
  Job 464
  John 382, 464, 483, 577
  John Mobbs 311
  Jonathan 288, 464, 504
  Joseph 463, 464
  Josiah 46, 263
  Lucia 574
  Lucy 464

MOULTON, Luella M. (Brown) 318
  Lydia 358, 463, 495
  Mabel F. (Abbott) 465
  Margaret (Brewster-Jones) ... 400, 464
  Martha 484, 549
  Mary 463, 464
  Mary (Garland) 357
  Mary Olive 470
  Mary (Perkins) 483
  Merriam (Locke) 422
  Michael 153, 255, 259, 464
  Molly 464
  Molly (Brown) 577
  Molly (Lamprey) 404, 577
  Morris H 577
  Nancy (Godfrey) 367
  Nathan 463, 577
  Nehemiah 32, 50, 54, 140, 144, 160
    273, 289, 463, 464, 583
  Noah 254, 421, 463, 464
  Olive (Garland) 361, 464
  Olive (Rand) 504
  Oliver 464
  Patience (Locke) 421, 464
  Percy 465
  Phebe 306, 463
  Phebe (Philbrick) 463, 489
  Rachel (Locke) 420
  Reuben 31, 33, 35, 140, 144, 160, 203
    204, 289, 400, 464, 490
  Robert 61, 464, 490
  Ruth (Watson) 464
  Sally 464
  Samuel 153, 255, 262, 464
  Sarah 400, 404, 423, 464, 498, 551
  Sarah (————) 464
  Sarah A 533
  Sarah Adeline 531
  Sarah (Dow) 464
  Sarah (Philbrick) 490
  Simon 361, 464, 484
  Susan (Godfrey-Knowles) 367
  Thomas 464, 577
  Tryphena 424, 463
  William 420
  Worthington 357
MOW, Betsey 145
  Dorcas (Marden) 68, 293, 458, 465
  E 145
  Elizabeth 465
  Ephraim 458, 465
  Ephraim L 465
  Flora A. (Caswell) 465
  Flora Ann (Randall) 518
  Frances 465
  Hannah 465
  Hannah (Locke) 425, 465
  Harriett 393, 465
  Harriett (Matthews) 461, 465
  Harry P 465
  J 280
  Jacob 465
  John 465
  John S 518
  Mary 373, 399, 465
  Mary Ann 465
  Olive 147
  Olive (Coombs) 465
  Sally 294, 439, 465
  Samuel 68, 275, 425, 465
  Samuel P 461
  Samuel Plummer 465
  Sarah 465
MOWE, ———— 277
  Sally, see Sally Mow.
MUCHMORE, Deborah 574

INDEX OF NAMES. 643

MUCHMORE, Love (Tuck)............ 552
  Margaret 555
MUDGE, Martha E.................... 317
MUGRIDGE, William.................. 265
MULLEN, Olive...................... 577
MULLIN, John....................... 572
  Peggy (Yeaton)..................... 572
MURDOCH, Sarah A................... 439
MURRAY, Elizabeth..............466, 583
  Elizabeth (———)................. 466
  Hannah 329
  Hannah (Dalton)................... 466
  John 466
  Joseph 466
  Lavinia T.......................... 470
  Samuel................70, 141, 160, 259
                262, 466, 583
  Susannah 466
  William 329, 466
MURRY, see Murray.................. 259
MUSSEY, Harriet.................... 504
NASON, Abigail (Libby)............. 414
  David 347
  Margaret 456
  Margaret (Foss)................... 347
  Mary 427
  Richard 414
  William H......................... 175
NATTER, Eben, see Nutter, Ebenezer.
NAY, George........................ 493
  Martha Ann (Philbrick).......... 493
  Sarah 489
NEAL, Alice (Clark)................ 578
  Hannah 459
  Isabella T......................... 576
  James..........................264, 265
  John 267
  Martha Jane (Lear)............... 412
  Mary 488
  Robert 274, 578
  Sarah Holbrook (Odiorne-Willard) 469
  Walter..................17, 18, 20, 259
  William 412
  William L.......................... 469
NEALE, see Neal.
NEIL, James........................ 265
  Margaret 562
  Nabby (Locke)..................... 432
  William 432
NEILS, Ruhamah..................... 466
NELSON, Abigail (Randall).......... 515
  Anne (Whitten).................... 578
  David 578
  Hannah (Sliggins)................. 578
  Mary (Atwood)..................... 578
  John..................160, 515, 536, 578
  Ruth (Mace)....................... 578
  Ruth (Seavey-Mace)................ 536
  Sarah 583
  Sarah (Randall)................... 578
  William 578
NEWELL, Elmira..................... 394
NEWHALL, Elizabeth................. 482
NEWICK, George R................... 551
  Nellie (Trefethen)................ 551
NEWMAN, Betsey..................... 575
NEWMARCH, Hannah................... 574
  Joseph 212
NEWTON, Elizabeth.................. 521
  Isaac 321, 578
  James 347
  John 578
  Mark 578
  Mary 578
  Mary (Caswell).................321, 578

NEWTON, Mary (Haley)............... 578
  Mary (Newton)..................... 578
  Patience (Foss)................... 347
NOBLE, Christopher................. 578
  Martha (Rowe)..................... 578
NOCK, Esther (Philbrick)........... 488
  Sylvanus 488
NOLES, see Knowles.
NOLLS, see Knowles.
NORMAN, Margaret................... 487
NORRIS, Elizabeth (Holmes)......... 578
  Martha 337, 575
  Moses 570
  Nancy Ann (Woodman).............. 570
  Sally (Holmes).................... 578
  Samuel 578
  Sarah 584
  Sarah (Jenness)................... 396
NORTON, Abigail..........360, 467, 573, 466
  Abigail (Gove).................... 466
  Abigail (Weeks)................... 467
  Anna 466, 546
  Arabella 453
  Benjamin 467, 566
  Betsey 329, 466
  Betsey (Lamprey)...............404, 466
  Bonus 383, 466
  Daniel 466
  Dudley................273, 466, 467, 555
  Eleanor....................466, 555, 580
  Eliza 467, 468
  Elizabeth.................381, 459, 466
  Elizabeth (Goddard).............. 578
  Elizabeth (Hill).................. 466
  Emily 453, 467
  Hannah 453, 467
  Hannah Bartlett................... 467
  Hannah (Burleigh)................. 466
  Hannah (Cotton)................... 467
  Hannah (Hill)..................... 466
  Hannah (Yarrell)...............467, 555
  James 467
  Jefferson 467
  John..................203, 264, 268, 466
  Jonathan 466
  Joseph 466
  Joshua J........................... 486
  Levi 467
  Lucy..........................383, 466, 467
  Maria 466, 555, 556
  Maria (Pickermail)................ 467
  Mary 467
  Mary (———)...................... 466
  Mary (Piper)...................... 467
  Mary S. (Webster).............467, 566
  Meribah (Ayers)................... 467
  Meribah (Johnson)................. 467
  Moses 578
  Nathan 203, 466
  Patience B........................ 467
  Phebe (Perkins)................... 486
  Polly 467
  Ruhamah 466, 573
  Ruhamah (Neils)................... 466
  Sally 467
  Samuel.....................203, 423, 466
  Sarah 466, 467
  Sarah (Haines).................... 467
  Sarah M........................... 302
  Simon 467
  Thomas 467
  William............144, 205, 404, 459, 466, 467
  William B......................... 467
NOWELL, ———........................ 108
  Eunice 580
  John 578

INDEX OF NAMES.

NOWELL, Sarah (Randall) 578
NOYES, ——. 420
NUDD, Abraham 209, 542
  Hannah (Tarlton) 578
  Ira 467
  James 467
  Mary 467, 490
  Nancy 329
  Nancy (Perkins) 467, 485
  Ruth 467, 485
  Samuel 357, 467, 485, 578
  Sarah Ann (Sleeper) 542
  Susannah (Brown) 311
  Thomas 311
NUTTER, Abigail 373
  Adna 550
  Ebenezer 266, 267, 268
  John 265
NUTTING, Mary A 493
NYE, Sally 387
ODELL, George 578
  Sally B. (Towle) 578
ODIERNE, see Odiorne.
ODIORNE 53, 78, 121, 123, 129, 135
               208, 213, 219, 288
  Abby Coffin (Jenness) 391
  Abigail 468, 469
  Alfred Alonzo 470
  Alma 470
  Almond 471
  Ambretta Jane (Mace) 445, 471
  Ambrinetta J. (Mace), see Ambretta Jane (Mace).
  Anne Louisa 470
  Annie 324
  Annie L 552
  Annie O. (Trefethen) 470, 551
  Anzolette A. (Bell) 469
  Augusta A. (Stoddard) 470
  Benjamin 47, 468, 469, 529, 572
  Benjamin T 445
  Benjamin Tarlton 469, 471
  Betsey 295, 574
  Catherine 468, 576
  Catherine (——) 468
  Catherine (Sherburne) 468
  Charles A 469
  Charles B 455
  Charles Blunt 469, 470
  Charles Woodbury 470
  Charlotte 351
  Charlotte E 469
  Charlotte (Savage) 468
  Charlotte Seavey 470
  Clara E 469, 511
  Clara E. (Seavey) 469, 531
  Cora Isabella 470
  Cynthia Ann 469, 497
  Deborah 468
  Dorothy (Gardiner) 468
  Dorothy (Yeaton) 468, 572
  Eben 208
  Eben L 469
  Ebenezer 276, 468, 528, 531, 565
  Ebenezer J 469
  Ebenezer L 92, 315
  Ebenezer Lewis 468, 469, 470
  Edgar Bailey 470
  Edith 471
  Eliza (Norton) 467, 468
  Elizabeth 468
  Elizabeth (Seavey) 526
  Ella (Holmes) 380, 471
  Ellen Thomas 469
  Elvira 506

ODIORNE, Elvira W 469
  Elzada Arabella 470
  Elzader A 510
  Eunice Grace 470
  Everett 68, 209, 280
  Eunice (Seavey) 471
  Frank Pierce 470
  George 471, 572
  George Beck 468
  Georgia Ella 471
  Georgianna 469, 471
  Hannah (Rand) 470, 502
  Hannah Smith 469
  Hannah Walton 469
  Harry 471
  James 468
  John 70, 127, 134, 137, 153, 255, 259
              263, 467, 468, 471
  John Emery 469, 470
  John James 469, 471
  John S 355
  John Seavey 468
  Jonathan 27, 135, 469
  Jonathan Everett 470, 471
  Joseph 467, 468, 469
  Joseph T. West 470
  Joseph W 558
  Joseph William 469, 470
  Jotham 24, 127, 283, 462, 467, 527
  Katherine 580
  Lavinia T. (Murray) 470
  Lewis 108
  Lizzie 575
  Lottie 350
  Lucy (Foss) 470
  Lucy M. (Mason) 460
  Lydia 468
  Lydia Ann 470
  M. Louisa (Miller) 469, 471
  Maria Adelaide 470
  Maria Louisa 470
  Marietta 470
  Martha 352
  Martha A. (Varrell) 470, 558
  Martha (Webster) 468, 565
  Mary 425, 463, 468, 513
  Mary A 341, 469
  Mary Abby 469
  Mary Amazeen 470
  Mary (Beck) 468
  Mary (Brown) 469
  Mary E 437
  Mary Elizabeth 469
  Mary Ellen 470
  Mary H 302
  Mary Hannah 469
  Mary (Johnson) 467
  Mary (McCanon) 471
  Mary Olive (Moulton) 470
  Mary (Seavey) 468, 528
  Mary Sheaf (Yeaton) 470
  Mary (Smith) 315
  Mary T. (Amazeen) 469
  Mary (Yeaton) 468
  Moses H 469
  Nathaniel 468
  Olive Ann 470
  Olive (Thomas) 469
  Olive (Thompson) 355
  Olive (Seavey) 469, 529
  Olive W. (Cook) 468
  Philip 467
  Patience B. (Norton) 467
  Ralph 469
  Ruth (—— Kinneas) 468
  Ruth (Yeaton-Connor) 572

INDEX OF NAMES. 645

ODIORNE, Samuel.....164, 173, 255, 460, 468
  469, 470, 502, 551
  Sarah 462
  Sarah Abby......................... 469
  Sarah (Bassum).................... 467
  Sarah Holbrook.................... 469
  Sarah Williard 470
  Simon.............................391, 463
  Sylvester 68
  Truman Seavey.................469, 470
  William S...............68, 107, 208, 276
  William Seavey................468, 469
  William Sylvester................. 469
  William Peavey..................... 471
  William Wallace.................... 470
  Winifred S. (Barter).............. 463
ODIURNE, see Odiorne.
OLIVER, Ann (Downs)................ 339
  Francis 339
ORDWAY, Anna (Dearborn)........... 578
  John 261
  Lemuel 578
ORGAN, Mary......................... 427
ORMSBURY, George................... 491
  Nancy (Philbrick)................. 491
  Abigail (Brown-Moore)............ 312
OSGOOD, Eleanor..................... 514
  Olive Morgan....................... 471
  Reuben 312
OSPAW 127
OTIS, Caroline T.................... 471
  Charles 108, 471
  Christinia (Lear)................. 412
  Dorothy (Locke)................... 426
  Edward O........................... 471
  Elijah 426
  Frank A............................. 412
  Henry S............................. 471
  Israel Taintor............158, 471, 573
  John T.............................. 471
  Martha 471
  Mary A.............................. 441
  Nellie 471
  Olive Morgan (Osgood)............ 471
  Susan 513
OWNES, Keziah (Berry).............. 299
  Patrick 299
OXFORD, Eliza Josephine (Foye).... 354
  Herman W........................... 354
OZEL, Phebe..........................105, 577
PADDLEFORD, Margaret (Randall).... 517
PAGE, Abby G........................ 472
  Abigail 417, 428
  Abigail (Locke)................423, 429
  Anna 471, 523
  Anna (Perkins).................471, 484
  Ardella G.......................... 457
  Augusta M.......................... 562
  Benjamin 267, 578
  Betsey 492
  Betsey (Saunders)................. 524
  Charles 268
  Daniel..........................346, 472, 524
  Daniel C............................ 472
  David 326
  Elizabeth 577
  George 395
  Hannah 472
  Hannah (Clark).................... 326
  Huldah 311, 471
  Huldah (Berry).................... 306
  Huldah (Locke).................... 429
  Jane E.............................. 472
  Jane (Foss)....................346, 472
  Jeremiah..................347, 429, 522
  John 142, 429

PAGE, John W. C..................... 472
  Judith 415
  Lydia 431
  Margaret (B———).................. 472
  Martha M........................... 472
  Mary.........310, 322, 385, 395, 472, 579
  Mary Anna (Jenness).............. 395
  Mary (Burnham).................... 471
  Mary (Fogg)........................ 578
  Mary G.............................. 472
  Mary Jane.......................... 452
  Mercy 452, 577
  Meribah 424
  Nathaniel F....................472, 579
  Olive K. (Pierce)................. 579
  Olive R. (Pease).................. 472
  Onesephorus 423
  Polly 492
  Rhoda F............................. 472
  Sally 579
  Sally (Salter-Buzzell)............ 522
  Samuel 471
  Sarah.........................386, 427, 472
  Sarah B............................. 397
  Sarah (Foss)....................... 347
  Solomon 150
  Stacy 306
  Stephen........................471, 472, 484
  Susan 471
  Theodate 378
  Theodate (Drake).................. 471
PAIN 68, 175
  Amos 472
  Christianna 472
  Deborah 472
  Dorothy 472
  Henry 127
  Joanna 472
  John............26, 27, 72, 135, 138, 472
  Joseph 472
  Lydia 472
  Lydia (———)....................... 472
  Mary 472
  Moses 472
  Phillip..........22, 26, 27, 135, 137, 160
  Richard 472
  Sarah 472
  Sarah (———)....................... 472
  Susannah (———)................... 472
  William 472
PAINE, Thomas....................... 127
PALMER, Abigail.................... 382
  Abigail L. (Jenness).............. 389
  Abigail (Rowe).................... 472
  Ann 488
  Arvillion Vincy.................... 579
  Benjamin.......................402, 473
  Betsey 402
  Christopher.....22, 24, 26, 27, 42, 288
    296, 472
  Cora E.............................. 321
  Cotton 518
  Deborah 402
  Elizabeth Anna (Smith)............ 579
  Elizabeth (Berry)................. 296
  Elizabeth (Knowles)............... 402
  Elizabeth (Locke)................. 472
  Frances A. (Whidden).............. 569
  Henry 328
  Hopper 136
  James 267
  Jane (Foss)....................345, 472
  Jeremiah 578
  Jeremy 473
  Jonathan.......................49, 389, 472
  Joseph...........265, 330, 432, 472, 473

INDEX OF NAMES.

PALMER, Lucy (Yeaton)............ 578
  Lydia (Knowles)................. 473
  Mary........................330, 485, 489
  Mehitable 328
  Mercy 512
  Meribah (Remick)................ 518
  Meribah (Yeaton)................ 571
  Merriam (Locke) 432
  Nathaniel 555
  Phebe 336
  Richard L........................ 569
  Ruth 416
  Samuel 382
  Sally 576
  Sarah 430, 473
  Sarah E., see Varrell, Sarah E.
  Sarah (Varrell).................. 555
  Sarah (Willey)................... 473
  Stephen 253
  William............160, 265, 345, 472, 473
PANCOAST, Ella May (Seavey)...... 533
  Fred L........................... 533
  Winnifred 533
PARKER, Abigail................... 539
  Ann (Jenness)................... 381
  Anna 385
  Benjamin F...................... 281
  Ella M........................506, 514
  Emily (Webster)................. 566
  Lucy 486
  Maria 409
  Mary (Brown).................... 309
  Nathan 309
  Robert......................270, 271, 565
  William 212
PARSONS 138, 226, 274, 298, 330
          369, 385, 398, 403, 417, 430
          450, 457, 523, 548, 564, 565
  ——— (Pierpont)................. 474
  ——— (Whistler)................. 474
  Abby Parsons (Brown).......318, 482
  Abby Semira................106, 151, 479
  Abigail................474, 475, 476, 479
  Abigail (Ball)................... 475
  Abigail (Cooley)................. 475
  Abigail (Garland)..............361, 478
  Abigail (Philbrick).............479, 492
  Abigail Philbrick................ 479
  Abram 173
  Albert Wilson................... 479
  Albion Dalton..........66, 208, 214, 391
                       480, 482, 568
  Mrs. Albion Dalton..............58, 495
  Almira 316, 477
  Amos 205
  Amos Seavey....66, 67, 75, 163, 164, 166
          169, 170, 172, 176, 208, 209
          275, 278, 286, 290, 335, 411
                         477, 492
  Andrew 473
  Ann 474
  Anna Decatur.................... 482
  Anna Pine (Decatur)............ 480
  Anna Seavey.................341, 477
  Annie (Emerson)................. 482
  Annie (Locke).............443, 480, 482
  Annie M. (Leavitt).............. 483
  Anthony 473
  Arthur Carleton................. 482
  Bartholomew 473
  Benjamin 474
  Betsey 477
  Caroline Francis (Stanley)...... 482
  Carrie 482
  Catharine 474
  Catharine (Radcliff)............. 473

PARSONS, Catherine (Sydenham)..... 474
  Charles G....................108, 479
  Charles H........................ 107
  Charles Henry................... 480
  Charles Warren.................. 482
  Charles William.................. 480
  Christine (Ulrich)............... 480
  Clara Ellen...................... 482
  Corinne Brown................... 482
  Daniel Dearborn............107, 108, 480
  Daniel Jenness.....57, 291, 348, 482, 483
  David 474, 475
  David Smith...................... 479
  Dorothy 483, 529
  Ebenezer 474, 475
  Edmund 474
  Eliza......................338, 477, 478
  Eliza Anna....................... 482
  Eliza (Bean)..................... 332
  Eliza (Brown)................314, 480
  Eliza Esther..................... 480
  Eliza S.......................... 532
  Elizabeth.....364, 474, 475, 476, 477, 563
  Elizabeth Abby.................. 479
  Elizabeth (Bartlett)............. 475
  Elizabeth (Cook)................ 474
  Elizabeth (Monroe).............. 477
  Elizabeth (Newhall)............. 482
  Elizabeth (Rice)................. 479
  Elizabeth (Scott)................ 475
  Elizabeth Stanley................ 482
  Elizabeth (Strong).............. 474
  Elizabeth (Thompson)........... 475
  Ella Maria....................354, 482
  Emily 316, 479
  Emma Alice...................... 482
  Esther 474
  Eva 482
  Frances (Usher)................. 475
  Francis 473, 474
  Frank Edward................... 482
  Fred D..............67, 209, 286, 318, 491
  Frederick Dupeytien............. 482
  George Fred..................... 482
  Hannah 474, 476
  Hannah (Clapp-Miller).......... 475
  Hannah (Perkins)............477, 485
  Hugh 474
  Humphrey 473
  Isaac Dow.............108, 277, 477, 479
  J 537
  James................80, 95, 104, 121, 269
  James M.......................... 67
  James Monroe................... 477
  John..........473, 474, 475, 476, 479, 480
  John Decatur.................... 481
  John Henry...................479, 482
  John Langdon................... 482
  John Pine........................ 480
  John W......101, 105, 106, 108, 163, 169
          170, 172, 173, 277, 279, 286
  John Wilkes..........3, 108, 210, 215, 284
             286, 291, 361, 477, 478
  John William...............107, 108, 480
  Jonathan 474
  Joseph........29, 35, 67, 89, 100, 101, 105
        108, 141, 144, 209, 215, 219
        226, 255, 256, 257, 259, 260
        262, 263, 264, 265, 266, 267
        268, 269, 270, 272, 273, 275
        283, 284, 285, 289, 291, 300
        347, 359, 361, 428, 474, 475
        476, 477, 485, 527, 528, 534
  Joseph Monroe.................. 479
  Joseph Warren.................. 482
  Josiah 475

INDEX OF NAMES. 647

Parsons, Julia A. (Gove).......... 481
Langdon Brown....67, 195, 286, 291, 368
                          369, 443, 480, 482
Leonidas Appleton................. 479
Lewis 475
Louis Phillipe.................... 479
Lovina 477, 487
M. Augusta (Adams)............... 480
Martha 340, 477
Martha Ann........................ 479
Martha Kate (Locke)..........442, 483
Martha Seavey (Jenness).....391, 482
Mary.................240, 335, 474, 476
                                477, 479, 552
Mary Ann Wallis.................. 478
Mary (Bliss)...................... 474
Mary (Clark)...................... 474
Mary Dow.......................... 330
Mary (Gualter).................... 474
Mary J. (Marston)................. 479
Mary (Jones)...................... 476
Mary L. (Langdon)............411, 477
Mary R. (Pierce).................. 479
Mary (Seavey)................476, 527
Mary (Trefethen).................. 479
Mary (Wheeler).................... 474
Mercy (Stebbins).................. 475
Mindwell (Edwards)............... 475
Minerva (Cox)..................... 477
Moses 475
Noah 475
Norman 483
Patty (Dow)...................335, 477
Philip 473
Polly Dow......................... 477
Rhoda (Taylor).................... 474
Richard................131, 253, 473, 474
Robert 473
Samuel..........150, 151, 152, 157, 160
              167, 170, 240, 474, 475, 476
              477, 478, 479, 492, 552, 573
Sara (Hubbard).................... 482
Sarah Abby........................ 479
Sarah Ann (Dow)...............336, 481
Sarah (Atherton).................. 475
Sarah (Burnham)................... 475
Sarah (Clark)..................... 474
Sarah (Sheldon)................... 475
Sarah (Stebbins).................. 475
Sarah (Waller).................... 473
Semira 479
Susan 481
Susan (Decatur)................... 480
Thomas........................473, 474
Thomas Henry..................106, 480
Thomas Jefferson.....3, 57, 67, 106, 107
            108, 147, 148, 164, 165, 166
            169, 172, 173, 206, 209, 214
           223, 246, 275, 276, 277, 279, 284
          285, 286, 287, 291, 314, 340, 479
Thomas Wentworth.........442, 482, 483
Walter 473, 479
Warren......66, 67, 215, 292, 336, 479, 481
William 475, 476, 478
William Decatur................... 480
William Dexter................479, 482
William Harrison..........108, 479, 480
William Irving.................... 482
William Rice...................... 479
Willie 482
Patten, Hattie.................... 506
Martha 528
Patterson, ————-...................195, 345
Caleb 418
Charles F.....................216, 341
Kate Augusta (Drake)............. 341
Mehitable (Libby)................. 418

Patterson, Polly.................. 573
Paul, Caroline.................... 505
Olive 575
Sally 518
Payne, Phillip.................... 24
Pearson, Abigail.................. 416
Rebecca 416
Pease, Olive R.................... 472
Peek, Alice May................... 487
Benjamin Franklin................. 487
Edwin Henry....................... 487
Gertrude Clara.................... 487
Mary B. (Schiele)................. 487
Walter 58, 487
Walter Jesse...................... 487
Peirce, George W.................. 123
James S........................... 123
Joshua W.......................... 277
Penhallow, Samuel................. 28
Pennell, Martha (Otis)............ 471
Perkins 72, 127
——— (Folsom)................... 485
——— (Hoit).................... 485
——— (Knowles)................. 484
——— (Knox).................... 486
——— (Prescott)................ 485
——— (Trask)................... 485
Abbie 487
Abbie G........................... 487
Abigail........361, 391, 483, 484, 485, 486, 492
Abigail Knowles................... 485
Abigail (Locke)................424, 485
Abraham..........72, 139, 181, 208, 483
                484, 485, 486, 487, 492
Ada 487
Ann 471
Ann (Locke)...................421, 485
Anna 484, 485
Annis (Locke)..................... 421
Benjamin 485
Bertha (Philbrick)................ 488
Betsey 484
Betsey (Batchelder)...........295, 486
Betty 427
Caleb 488
Caroline E........................ 486
Charles Elias..................... 486
Christianna 487
Christianna (Philbrick).......487, 492
Clara H........................... 497
David 483, 484
Edward 486
Elias...................278, 407, 485, 486
Eliza J.......................413, 486
Eliza J. (Smith).................. 486
Eliza (Rothwell).................. 486
Elizabeth.................483, 484, 489
Elizabeth (Sleeper)............... 483
Elizabeth Whidden................. 486
Ellen (Trefethen)................. 549
Esther 486
George 486, 549
George Aaron...................... 486
Hannah...371, 477, 484, 485, 486, 488, 554
Harriet Adeline................... 487
Herbert 66, 379
Hitty (Towle)..................... 485
Huldah...............392, 424, 484, 485, 486
Huldah (Roby)..................... 484
Huldah (Seavey)................... 485
Humphrey 483, 484
Jacob 487
James.................35, 61, 71, 138
           140, 143, 144, 174, 205, 262
           288, 289, 290, 381, 424, 471
           483, 484, 485, 486, 502, 528
James Goodwin.................... 487

648 INDEX OF NAMES.

PERKINS, James H. 288, 291, 483
  James Henry........................ 487
  James P. 492
  Jane (Moulton).................... 484
  Jane Moulton.................315, 486
  Jeremiah 486
  Joanna (Elkins).................. 485
  John...........205, 421, 467, 484, 485, 486
  John Emery........................ 486
  Jonathan......398, 430, 483, 484, 485, 486
  Joseph.........................205, 484, 485
  Josephine 487
  Josiah........276, 279, 295, 381, 485, 486
  Leah 484
  Leah (Cox)........................ 483
  Lewis L.................285, 287, 290, 291
                                              381, 477, 486
  Lewis Lamprey.................... 487
  Lizzie 487
  Lovina (Parsons).............477, 487
  Lucy (Parker).................... 486
  Luke 483
  Lydia 484
  Mabel H. (Hodgdon).............. 379
  Margaret (Norman).............. 487
  Mark Langdon.................... 486
  Martha.......................335, 440, 484
  Martha Jane....................... 486
  Martha (Moulton)................ 484
  Mary................483, 484, 485, 487
  Mary (———)................... 483
  Mary Ann.......................... 486
  Mary (Goodwin).................. 487
  Mary Izette........................ 487
  Mary (Knowles).................. 486
  Mary (Locke).................430, 486
  Mary (Palmer).................... 485
  Mary (Perkins).................... 485
  Mary (Philbrick).................. 488
  Mehitable (Seavey-Garland)..485, 528
  Mercy 483
  Morris Emery..................... 487
  Moses 484, 485
  Nancy...............467, 485, 486, 541
  Patience 427
  Phebe 486
  Phebe (Robinson)................ 486
  Polly............................363, 485, 486
  Polly (Lang)....................... 407
  Polly (Langdon).................. 486
  Rachel (Varrell).................. 557
  Reuben 484
  Ruth (Nudd)...................... 485
  Sally 576
  Sally (Johnson).................. 398
  Samuel 484
  Sarah..........................483, 484, 485
  Sarah (———).................. 484
  Sarah Emeline................396, 487
  Sarah Jane...................487, 522
  Sarah (Rand)..................... 502
  Shua (Mason).................... 484
  Timothy 483
PERRIER, Abigail P. (Moulton)....... 578
  Daniel 578
PERRY, Abigail....................... 427
  George..................66, 457, 548, 561
  George N.......................... 342
  Mary (Drake).................... 342
PERVIERE, Abigail.................... 491
PETERSON, Martha W. (Foss)....... 347
  Paul 347
PETHICK, Lilla L..................... 559
PETTIGREW, Sarah (Downing)....... 336
  Timothy 336
PEVERLY, Betsey..................... 563

PHILBRICK-FILBRICK-PHILBROOK-
  PHILBRUCKE.
PHILBRICK.................64, 72, 144
——— Jenness..................... 490
——— (Randall).................. 493
——— (Shaw)..................... 488
——— (Trundy).................. 494
Abigail........143, 312, 332, 430, 445, 479
        489, 490, 491, 492, 493, 514, 574
Abigail (Brown)............313, 493, 421
Abigail (Locke).................... 489
Abigail (Marden)...............455, 490
Abigail (Perviere)................. 491
Abigail (Williams)................ 492
Adeline.....................491, 493, 504
Adeline E.......................... 493
Adeline M......................... 496
Albion..........................61, 178
Albion Reuben.................... 496
Alfred 64
Alfred Cheney..................... 497
Alice (——— Sanderson)........ 496
Angelina (Batchelder)........295, 496
Ann 489
Ann (Dearborn).................. 489
Ann E...........................494, 495
Ann (Gwinn)..................... 496
Ann (Knapp)..................... 488
Ann M............................ 108
Ann Matilda...................... 495
Ann (Palmer)..................... 488
Ann Roberts...................... 488
Anna.........................297, 490, 583
Anna (Perkins)................... 485
Anna (Towle).................490, 546
Annie 497
Apphia.........................488, 489
Arvilla F. (Jenkins).............. 494
Benjamin......274, 312, 490, 491, 518, 583
Benjamin P.................295, 491, 493
Benjamin Pitman..............493, 496
Benning 497
Bethia.........................488, 489
Bethia (Marston)................ 489
Betsey.....................389, 433, 491, 519
Betsey Brown..................... 491
Betsey (Jenness).................. 492
Betsey (Page)..................... 492
Betsey (Wells).................... 491
Betty (Jenness)................... 384
Byron 497
Caroline 495
Caroline A........................ 108
Caroline A. (Young)............. 495
Carrie.........................495, 497
Catherin 496
Charity 334
Charles B......................... 496
Charles C......................... 493
Charles Newell................... 496
Charles P......................... 491
Charlotte 494
Christianna 487, 492
Clara B. (Seavey)................ 530
Clara H. (Perkins)............... 497
Clara J. 453
Clarissa 493
Clarissa Jane..................... 495
Clarissa (Shaw).................. 495
Cornelius 496
Cynthia Ann (Odiorne)......469, 497
D 265
Daniel...64, 160, 172, 205, 220, 332, 455
       489, 490, 491, 492, 493, 494, 496
Daniel Dalton.................... 495
Daniel Webster....64, 139, 469, 494, 497

INDEX OF NAMES. 649

PHILBRICK, David..265, 278, 281, 492, 494, 496
David S............................ 495
David Smith....................... 495
David W........................... 280
Dolly (Grover).................... 490
Dorcas (Johnson)................. 489
E........................146, 504, 529, 539
E. B................................52, 181
Ebenezer........22, 24, 26, 27, 72, 87, 136
137, 160, 285, 288, 489
Edward 372
Edward P.......................... 494
Eliza 496
Eliza J. (——— Fogg)........... 496
Eliza (Jenness)...............392, 495
Eliza P. (Jenness-Fogg).......... 390
Elizabeth.........357, 464, 488, 489, 490
493, 500, 580
Elizabeth (———).................. 488
Elizabeth (Barron)................ 488
Elizabeth (Brown)................. 312
Elizabeth (Perkins)...........484, 489
Elizabeth (Rand)................. 490
Ellen...............................351, 495
Ellen R............................ 497
Elvina 496
Emeline...........................493, 496
Emeline A......................... 341
Emerson 491
Emily 494
Emily May........................ 497
Emma 464, 494
Emma Chase...................... 496
Emma L. (Brown)................. 497
Emmons B.............286, 291, 292, 331
495, 497, 532
Ephraim........92, 117, 174, 275, 276, 290
353, 364, 370, 407, 456, 469
488, 489, 491, 492, 494, 565
Estelle (Goss).................372, 494
Esther 488, 512
Esther (Dority)................... 495
Ethel (Bickford).................. 307
Ethel L. (Stone).................. 497
Ezra B............................496, 497
Fannie 495, 522
Frances S. (Barrett).............. 496
Frank.............................208, 395
Frank A....................117, 307, 495
Frank M........................... 494
Flora 533
Flora Belle........................ 494
Fred 494, 497
Freddy 497
George 494
George Clinton................491, 493
George F.......................... 493
George Oliver..................... 497
Georgianna (Pressey)............. 496
Hannah...401, 464, 488, 489, 490, 491, 580
Hannah (Locke)................... 490
Hannah E. (Mosher)...........463, 494
Hannah (Moulton)................ 489
Hannah (Perkins)................ 488
Hannah (White)................... 488
Harold 497
Harriet 491, 494
Harrison 494
Harry 496
Henry R........................... 496
Herbert 457, 494
Hester 489
Hiram 493, 496
Horace 495, 496
Huldah 525
Ida 494

PHILBRICK, Ida F.................. 321
Ida Florence (Marden).......457, 494
Ira 491
Ira P............................. 494
Irena 491, 493
Irena (Philbrick)..............491, 493
Irving 64
Irving Cheever.................... 497
Isaac 489
J. C.............................. 112
J. Curtis......................... 208
J. Harry.......................... 530
J. Newell........................ 208
James..............72, 254, 255, 276, 289
488, 489, 490, 491
James A........................... 496
Jane 488
Jane (———)...................... 489
Jane C. Benson................... 579
Jemima 575
Jennie May........................ 497
Jesse 177, 493
Jesse A........................... 491
John..........58, 164, 172, 290, 315, 488
489, 492, 495, 496, 526, 537
John C..................106, 117, 392, 492
Mrs. John C...................... 117
John Colby....................... 495
John Dearborn.................... 495
John Ezra........................ 497
John Ira......................... 493
John Tyler....................... 493
John Walbach..................... 491
John William..................... 495
Jonathan................35, 64, 140, 144
163, 166, 169, 170, 172, 173
205, 220, 255, 275, 284, 286
289, 290, 291, 313, 448, 455
488, 489, 490, 491, 493, 531
Jonathan Curtis...............493, 496
Jonathan P....................... 492
Joseph........21, 35, 45, 46, 61, 101, 135
137, 138, 140, 143, 144, 147
164, 172, 174, 176, 203, 217
265, 273, 277, 283, 284, 285
288, 289, 290, 402, 421, 463
484, 488, 489, 490, 491, 492
493, 494, 496, 532, 546, 583
Joseph Newell.................493, 496
Joseph P......................... 493
Joseph Woodbury................. 496
Josephine Marjorie............... 497
Joses...................58, 67, 72, 75
87, 88, 136, 161, 167, 170
177, 191, 192, 200, 201, 202
205, 276, 283, 288, 289, 464
489, 490, 491, 492, 543, 571
Josiah 344
Josiah W....................314, 492, 495
Julia Ann........................ 493
Katie A.......................... 493
Langdon 491
Lemira 494
Lester W......................... 496
Levi 490
Lizzie 496
Lizzie (Hill).................... 495
Lizzie N. (Breed)................ 494
Lizzie T......................... 493
Louisa 494, 495, 496
Lucretia (Catlin)................ 496
Lucy (Moulton)................... 464
Lydia 395, 433, 495
Lydia (Moulton).................. 495
Lydia (Watkins).................. 491
Lyman 491

INDEX OF NAMES.

PHILBRICK, M. (Woods).............. 493
  Manning 496
  Margaret (Godsoe)................. 491
  Margaret (Woods).................. 496
  Maria (Goodwin)................... 493
  Martha................386, 488, 496, 532
  Martha Ann........................ 493
  Martha F.......................... 495
  Martha (Wadleigh)................. 489
  Mary...............311, 356, 488, 489, 490
                     492, 493, 494, 496
  Mary (———)....................... 489
  Mary A. (Nutting)................. 493
  Mary Ann.......................... 492
  Mary Abby................493, 495, 531
  Mary Ann......................295, 493
  Mary Charlotte (Seavey).....497, 532
  Mary E. (Cummings)................ 496
  Mary (Elkins)..................... 344
  Mary Frances...................... 496
  Mary (Marden)................448, 491
  Mary (Neal)....................... 488
  Mary (Nudd)....................... 490
  Mary (Palmer)..................... 489
  Mary (Philbrick).............493, 494
  Mary S............................ 493
  Mary (Staples).................... 491
  Mary (Wedgewood).................. 490
  May (Powers)...................... 496
  Mehitable 488
  Mehitable (Dalton)...........328, 488
  Melissa (Jenness).............395, 494
  Mercy..........................330, 490
  Molly (Beck)...................... 490
  Moses 496
  Moses C........................363, 492
  Moses W........................... 495
  Nabby (Brown)..................... 312
  Nancy..........................491, 573
  Nancy (Woodman)...............492, 571
  Nathan 489
  Nathaniel 490
  Nellie (Hodgdon).................. 496
  Nellie M. (Dow)................... 497
  Nellie T. (Rand)..........496, 497, 512
  Newell.....................491, 493, 494
  O. P.............................. 280
  Olive 493
  Olive Rand (Locke)...........437, 494
  Oliver......................119, 208, 491
  Oliver B......................493, 496
  Olivia 494
  Olly 525
  Page 464
  Pamelia 494
  Pamelia (Gunnison)................ 494
  Patty B. (Knowles)...........402, 493
  Phebe..........................463, 489
  Phebe W. (Greening)............... 496
  Polly......146, 364, 491, 492, 503, 566, 583
  Polly (Page)...................... 492
  Polly (Randall-Varrell)...493, 518, 557
  Priscilla 534
  Prudence (Swain).................. 488
  Rebecca 496
  Reuben......31, 92, 140, 144, 160, 176, 204
              274, 289, 312, 384, 490, 491, 492, 583
  Roxanna 496
  Rufus W...................463, 492, 494
  Ruth..........................489, 490
  Sabrina........................414, 489
  Sally....................293, 490, 491, 492
  Sally (Brown)..................... 315
  Sally (Emery)..................... 493
  Sally (Smith)..................... 543
  Sally (Webster)................... 565

PHILBRICK, Samuel......265, 266, 488, 489
  Sarah (———)....................... 489
  Samuel Bickford...............493, 495
  Samuel E.......................... 494
  Samuel N.......................... 493
  Sarah.............172, 295, 311, 389, 456
                     460, 488, 489, 490, 492, 494
  Sarah A........................492, 495
  Sarah Adeline (Garland).....363, 492
  Sarah Ann.....................492, 494
  Sarah Ann (Brown)............314, 495
  Sarah Ann (Philbrick).......492, 494
  Sarah (Brown)..................... 495
  Sarah E........................... 493
  Sarah (Lamos)..................... 494
  Sarah (Marden)................455, 491
  Sarah (Nay)....................... 489
  Sarah (Smith)..................... 492
  Sarah (Webster)................... 492
  Sarah (Wells)..................... 491
  Sheridan 491, 494
  Shirley 497
  Silas 493
  Spaulding 494
  Stephen 490
  Susannah (Pitman)................. 491
  Thomas..............297, 328, 356, 487
                     488, 489, 492, 495
  Thomas II.......208, 280, 437, 492, 494
  Thomas W.......................... 579
  Titus..........................33, 490
  Tryphena (Marston)................ 489
  Tryphena......................490, 523
  Viana M. (Dalton) see Vienna
    (Dalton).
  Vienna (Dalton)...............331, 497
  Walter........................494, 497
  William.......................488, 492
  William C..................496, 497, 512
  Willie J 494
  Wilmar 497
  Woodbury 390
  Zacharia 489
PHILLIPS, Anna Belle (Marden)..... 454
  Edward 454
  L. Walter 175
  Lewis 174
PHINNEY, Ann...................... 418
  Betsey 419
  Elizabeth M. (Haley).............. 375
  William 375
  Love 419
PHIPPS 24
PICKERING, ——— (Fabyan)........... 498
  ——— (Furber-Mills).............. 498
  Abigail 535
  Abigail (Fayben).................. 498
  Abigail (Sheafe).................. 540
  Alice 498
  Anna (Trefethen).................. 550
  Benjamin 498
  C 134
  Deborah 377
  Elizabeth 498
  Ephraim 89
  Gee 498
  Hannah 527
  Horace 550
  James.........................260, 498
  John......................51, 246, 540
  John Gee 498
  John Lowe......................... 306
  Joseph 371
  Joseph W 347
  Levi 260
  Lydia.........................335, 580

INDEX OF NAMES. 651

PICKERING, Martha.................. 498
  Martha (Pickering)............... 498
  Mary 410, 498
  Mary (Berry)..................... 306
  Mary Jane (Goss)................. 371
  Mary (Janveins).................. 497
  Mary (Langdon).................. 410
  Mary (Thompson)................. 498
  Nichols 410, 498
  Patience 411, 498
  Polly 498
  Richard 498
  Sarah 498
  Sarah (Foss)..................... 347
  Temperance 498
  Thomas 497, 498
  William 498
PICKERMAIL, Maria................... 467
PICOT, Ellen M...................... 545
PIERCE, ——— (Randall)............ 578
  Annie (Knowles).................. 403
  Betsey (Shapley-Randall)......... 537
  Daniel 207
  Frank M.......................... 403
  Franklin 133
  George 410
  Joshua 24
  Margaret 428
  Mary (Langdon)................... 410
  Mary R........................... 479
  Olive K.......................... 579
  William........................537, 578
PIGOTT, Hannah Salter (Locke)...... 436
  Richard 436
PIKE, Flora May (Jenness).......... 394
  John 396
  Polly (Prescott)................. 578
  Robert 246, 485
  Samuel 394
  Sarah (Jenness-Norris)........... 396
  Sewell 578
PINKHAM, Sophia..................... 428
PIPER, David........................ 343
  Hannah (Crimble)................. 579
  John L........................... 105
  Mary 466
  Mary (Crimble)................... 578
  Noah 578, 579
  Polly (Edmunds).................. 343
  Susannah 548
PITMAN, Betsey (Locke).............. 430
  Dorcas 524
  Hannah 430, 517
  Joseph 430
  Susannah 491
PLACE, John......................... 383
  Joseph 263
  Lucy (Jenness)................... 383
PLAISTEAD 24
  Joseph 578
  Mary (Fitzgerald)................ 578
PLUMMER, Avery......................243
POMERIE, Leonard.................... 8
POOL, Angelina E. (Caswell)......322, 498
  Carrie E......................... 498
  Ethel V.......................... 498
  Ida M............................ 498
  John..........................280, 322, 498
  Lillie B.......................... 498
  Lizea 498
  Minnie E......................... 498
  Nellie 498
  Nellie G......................... 498
  Richard E........................ 498
POOLE, Mary Davis................... 394
POOR, Abigail Daniels............... 498

POOR, Betsey (Shapley)...........498, 537
  Daniel Sheafe.................... 498
  Eliza 498
  George 498
  John 309
  John R........................234, 235
  Judith 498
  Mary 498
  Nancy 498
  Robert........................498, 537, 583
  Sally 498
  Sarah (Brown).................... 309
POPE, Catherine..................... 577
  Sarah Ann (Jenness).............. 389
  William 389
PORTER, ——— (Wentworth)......... 499
  Allen 504
  Anna Trefethen (Rand)........... 504
  Caroline 499
  Charles 499
  Charles II.....................169, 499
  Elizabeth (Comstock)............. 499
  Eliphalet 499
  Emery (Moulton)................. 499
  H.............................157, 254, 255, 260
  Huntington.........65, 100, 101, 149, 156
    163, 164, 169, 205, 253, 498, 499, 573
  John 108, 499
  Louisa 499
  Maria 499, 579
  Martha R......................... 499
  Merinda P........................ 519
  Nathaniel Sargent................ 499
  Oliver 108, 499
  Olivia 499
  Samuel II........................ 499
  Samuel Huntington................ 108
  Sarah 170
  Sarah E.......................... 499
  Sarah (Moulton).................. 498
  Susannah (Sargent)............... 498
  William II....................169, 499
POTTLE 174
  Abby 530
  Levi 268
POURSEL, Phebe 583
POUTRINCOURT 3, 4, 5
POWELL, Esther (Garland)........... 356
  William 356
POWERS, see Poor.
POWERS, Elizabeth................... 583
  Judith 307
  Mary 441
  May 496
PRATT, Phinehas..................... 12
PRAY, Hannah.....................499, 500
PREBLE, Andrew Jackson............ 470
  Olive Ann (Odiorne).............. 470
PRESCOTT, Abigail................... 422
  Abigail (Marden)................. 449
  Ann 547
  Annah (Locke).................... 428
  Asa 449
  Benjamin 329
  Charlotte A...................... 577
  Hannah 433
  Jesse 263
  Jonas 265
  Jonathan 265
  Joshua 449
  Josiah D......................... 579
  Lucy A. (Batchelder)............. 579
  Mehitable (Dalton)............... 329
  Nancy (Marden).................. 449
  Polly 578
  Samuel 329

INDEX OF NAMES.

PRESCOTT, Sarah (Dalton).......... 329
 Timothy 428
PRESSEY, Georgianna................. 496
PRESTWICK, Maria................... 330
PRIEST, Frances.................... 443
PRIMERS, Thomas.................... 263
PRING, Martin.....................2, 228
PUDDINGTON, Robert.............126, 308
PULSIFER, Eleanor (Lang).......... 406
 Jonathan 406
PURRINGTON, I...................... 453
 Ivory T.......................... 579
 Susan S. (Marden)................ 453
 Susan T. (Marden)................ 579
PUTMAN 270
PYNCHON 474
QUIMBY, Becky...................... 515
 Elizabeth 515
 Dolly 402
QUONDY, Betty...................... 250
 John 250
QUINT, Alonzo H.................... 258
RADCLIFFE, Catharine............... 473
 Edward 473
RAITT, Alexander................... 212
RAMSDELL, Blake.................... 499
 Dexter 499
 Edna G............................ 499
 Edward 454
 Edward E.......................... 499
 Emerett E. (Marden)..........454, 499
 Fred 499
 Ralph 499
RAINSTEAD, George.................. 548
 Polly (Trefethen)................. 548
RAND..........72, 127, 135, 149, 204, 245, 252
 ―――― Carter..................... 502
 ―――― (Danforth)................. 501
 ―――― (―――― Grogan).......... 510
 ―――― (Norton).................. 507
 ―――― (Pottle).................. 507
 ―――― (Sanders)................. 514
 ―――― (Tarlton)................. 545
A. Y............................... 208
Aaron....131, 285, 291, 502, 504, 509, 572
Abby 506
Abby A.......................506, 508, 539
Abby M............................. 508
Abiel (――――).................... 512
Abigail..................304, 382, 500, 512
Abigail (Berry)................305, 506
Abigail (Marden).................. 513
Abigail (Trefethen)............... 512
Ada 511
Ada Philbrick..................... 508
Addie S........................... 509
Adelaide 514
Adeline....................504, 506, 507
Adeline (Philbrick)...........493, 504
Adeline (Rand)................504, 506
Adeline (Vennard)................. 504
Albert................107, 213, 506, 508
Aldana 507
Alice 508
Allen Porter...................... 506
Almeria 506
Alonzo 506
Amanda 508
Amanda A. (Downs).............338, 505
Amos............27, 60, 87, 88, 136, 139
    142, 160, 281, 506, 512, 513
Amos Seavey....................... 504
Ann 537
Anna....................508, 512, 513
Anna (Jenness).................... 508
Anna L............................. 506

RAND, Anna Trefethen............... 504
 Anna Yeaton (Jenness).......... 389
 Annie Emery...................... 511
 Annie Hodgdon.................... 510
 Aphia 512
 Arthur 510
 Asenath 508
 Atwell Yeaton............281, 509
 Augusta (Buker).................. 508
 Augusta Emma (Drake).......341, 506
 Augustus Yeaton.....108, 280, 338, 505
 Benjamin......................265, 512
 Benoni........................259, 266
 Bertha 508
 Bessie 511
 Bethia 500, 513
 Bethia (Rand).................... 513
 Betsey..................330, 424, 502, 553
 Betsey (――――).................. 514
 Betsey (Dow).................335, 504
 Betsey (Houston)................. 501
 Betsey (Jenness)................. 383
 Betsey (Tarlton)............513, 545
 Bickford 514
 Bickford Lang................279, 502
 Billey......68, 75, 290, 291, 500, 502, 505
 Billy.....................278, 376, 463
 Blake 341
 Blake II..................195, 286, 509
 Byron W.......................... 514
 Caddie 507
 Caroline.................386, 505, 513
 Caroline (Paul).................. 505
 Carrie A. (Drake-Foster).....342, 511
 Carrie J. (Fuller)............... 509
 Caty M. (Trickey)................ 504
 Charles.............68, 391, 513, 514
 Charles C........................ 315
 Charles Clinton..............504, 508
 Charles E........................ 509
 Charles Edward...............505, 509
 Charles F........................ 506
 Charles H................68, 287, 327
 Charles Henry...........496, 507, 512
 Charles M................291, 341, 506
 Charles Obed..................... 508
 Charles Wallis...............506, 514
 Charlotte (Batchelder)........... 505
 Christina.....................499, 506
 Christina (――――)............... 499
 Clara 508, 509
 Clara E. (Odiorne)...........469, 511
 Clara (Frisbee).................. 506
 Clara Maria (Dow)................ 336
 Clinton 513
 Cyrus 507
 Cyrus H.......................... 506
 Cyrus James...................... 507
 D 69
 Daniel.....69, 172, 276, 290, 501, 504, 528
 Daniel Fogg...................... 513
 Daniel W......................... 506
 David.....275, 276, 413, 501, 503, 514, 522
 David L..................503, 506, 572
 David Lang....................... 507
 Deborah (Burleigh)............... 503
 Deborah (Seavey)................. 418
 Dolly (Rollins).................. 501
 Dorothy (Bristol)................ 508
 Dorothy (Moses)..............463, 506
 Dorothy (Seavey).............504, 528
 Dowrst.................31, 59, 276, 308, 406
      500, 502, 583
 E. D............................. 280
 E. (Moulton)..................... 500
 Eben Watson...................... 510

INDEX OF NAMES. 653

RAND, Ebenezer.......................... 502
Edith C. (Foss).................350, 511
Edith Mabel (Trefethern).....511, 551
Edith P............................. 508
Edgar Otis.......................... 510
Edward......107, 108, 502, 505, 506, 514
Edward A........................... 505
Edward Stern....................... 509
Edwin B............................ 507
Edwin Reed......................... 504
Eldred 513
Eleanor Dow (Locke)..........435, 507
Eliza.........................459, 503, 565
Eliza J. (Yeaton) 505
Eliza Jane.......................... 505
Elizabeth........405, 490, 499, 500, 501
                504, 512, 571, 580
Elizabeth (————).................. 499
Elizabeth (Chesley)................. 514
Elizabeth (Cilley).................. 514
Elizabeth H. (Yeaton).........509, 572
Elizabeth J....................108, 362
Elizabeth (Jenness)...........389, 510
Elizabeth Martha................... 505
Elizabeth (Philbrick).............. 500
Elizabeth (Rand)...............501, 504
Elizabeth (Stevens)................ 506
Ella M. (Parker)..............506, 514
Ellen 508, 510
Ellen A............................ 394
Ellie Morrison..................... 502
Elvin..........69, 285, 287, 290, 291, 504
                509, 534, 564, 570
Elvira W. (Odiorne)...........469, 506
Elzader A. (Odiorne)............... 510
Emily 504, 570
Emily (Bell)....................... 506
Emily (Jenness)...............389, 507
Emily Jones (Foss).............350, 511
Emma 508
Emma J............................. 510
Emma Shaw.......................... 505
Enoch 502
Ephraim..........59, 142, 153, 160, 255
                500, 501, 543
Ernest 513
Esther........308, 368, 508, 512, 574, 583
Esther (Locke)..................... 504
Esther (Marden)................449, 504
Esther May......................... 511
Esther (Philbrick)................. 512
Etta J............................. 512
Eunice (Carter).................... 514
Ezekiel 514
Ezra 504
Ezra D............................. 508
Fannie 513
Fanny 512
Florence 507
Florence L. (Berry)...........302, 511
Florence (Remlele)................. 506
Florence W......................... 444
Florinda 170, 502
Frances Adelaide................... 513
Francesene M., see Francina M.
Francina M....................443, 509
Francis............70, 71, 127, 280, 499
Francis W.......................... 507
Frank.........................323, 395, 557
Frank H............................ 511
Frank P............................ 506
Franklin 506
George.....33, 141, 144, 205, 227, 500, 502
George Wallis...................... 505
Gilman 213, 508
Gilman J........................... 503

RAND, Hannah....66, 352, 353, 426, 450, 470
                499, 500, 501, 502, 506, 516, 583
Hannah B........................... 507
Hannah (Dolbee)................334, 501
Hannah (Jenness)..............500, 571
Hannah (Johnson)................... 503
Hannah (Lang)..................405, 502
Hannah (Locke)..................... 501
Hannah Parsons (Garland)....364, 504
Hannah (Pray).................499, 500
Hannah (Seavey).....501, 513, 534, 535
Hannah T. (Warren)................. 507
Hannah W. (Seavey)............504, 529
Harriet 513
Harriet (Mussey)................... 504
Harriett 401
Harriett J......................... 503
Harry.........................342, 504, 508
Harry O............................ 510
Harry Osmond..................510, 511
Hattie (Patten).................... 506
Helen 514
Helen A. (Fife).................... 510
Henrietta (Tower).................. 509
Henry S.......................506, 510, 550
Hepzibah 538
Herman O........................... 510
Herman Otis........................ 510
Hitty 501
Horace 508
Horace V........................... 511
Howard 64, 469
Howard S......................457, 509, 511
Ida 513
Ira...........................370, 503, 508
Irvin 511, 551
Irving N........................... 506
Isaac D....66, 106, 108, 132, 167, 168, 281
Isaac Dow.......................... 505
Isabel 507
Israel.....................31, 144, 273, 501
J. A............................... 280
J. Jenness...................68, 374, 457
J. Sullivan....................469, 506
James.......................501, 503, 504
James Alba......................... 336
James Alby......................... 495
James B.......................305, 506
James M.....................107, 374
James Moses..................506, 510
James O............................ 511
Jane Ann (Clough-Delancy)......... 327
Jane (Dently)...................... 508
Jedediah...67, 107, 164, 166, 170, 172, 208
            209, 350, 462, 502, 505, 509, 511
Jefferson 69
Jemima 418
Jeremiah 513
John....................69, 141, 144, 153
            254, 255, 256, 259, 262, 263
            273, 279, 499, 500, 501, 502
            503, 507, 513, 534, 535, 583
John Alonzo........................ 507
John G............................. 513
John Gilman........................ 513
John Howard...................505, 509
John I............................. 106
John Ira......................208, 363, 506, 510
John O............................. 545
John Oris.....................503, 507
John T........................107, 163, 166, 169
            172, 278, 290, 335
John Tuck..................66, 168, 502, 504
John Trueman 513
Jonathan 501
Jonathan J....................281, 288

INDEX OF NAMES.

Rand, Jonathan Jenness..........507, 510
Joseph.....31, 33, 35, 59, 68, 75, 139, 141
          142, 144, 160, 163, 164, 166
          169, 170, 172, 173, 176, 203
          205, 256, 261, 262, 273, 275
          276, 278, 286, 368, 418, 435
          449, 500, 501, 503, 507, 512
Joseph Jenness.................508, 510
Joseph P........................... 510
Joseph W.......................291, 350
Joseph William.............59, 510, 511
Josephine W....................... 506
Joshua...............27, 68, 69, 136, 141
      144, 146, 169, 203, 225, 260
      262, 273, 278, 449, 499, 500
      501, 504, 513, 534, 535, 583
Josie B. (———— Bartlett)........ 509
Julia Ann P....................306, 507
Julia Dodd (Spinney)............. 509
Kate 510
Kate M........................508, 559
Leonie S. (Drake)..............341, 509
Leroy Odell....................... 505
Letitia (Caswell)..............323, 506
Levi...................169, 501, 503, 507
Levi Moses........................ 502
Lizzie 510
Lizzie A.......................... 510
Lizzie (Rand)..................... 510
Lizzie A. (Rand).................. 510
Lizzie W.......................... 511
Lizzie W. (Rand).................. 511
Lotta S........................... 509
Louis Henry....................... 504
Louisa.........................504, 573
Louisa M. (Marden)...........457, 511
Louise 511
Louise (Hodgdon)................. 509
Lucy 512, 513
Lydia 499
Lydia Nora (Varrell)............. 557
Lydia (Storey)................... 504
Mabel H........................... 509
Mabel M. (Greggs)................ 514
Manning 505
Manning C.....................507, 545
Marianne 504
Martha.....................432, 502, 504
Martha A. (Marden) 507, 510
Martha A. (Willey)............509, 570
Martha Abby (Marden)........... 457
Martha Ann....................... 506
Martha (Batchelder)..........502, 514
Martha (Locke)................434, 501
Martha (Moses).................. 463
Martha S......................374, 506
Martin H......................302, 503
Martin Hickman................... 511
Mary..................358, 376, 380, 432
      499, 500, 501, 502, 503, 504
      505, 506, 507, 508, 510, 512
Mary Abbie....................... 504
Mary Abby.................506, 549, 552
Mary Abby (Philbrick)........... 495
Mary Ann......................436, 503
Mary (Bean)...................... 513
Mary C............................ 506
Mary C. (Homan)................. 508
Mary Emerett..................... 507
Mary Emma.................317, 318, 511
Mary (Hanson)................... 512
Mary Jane (Garland)............. 510
Mary Jane Wallis................. 502
Mary L. (Yeaton)................ 572
Mary (Leavitt)................... 512
Mary Lizzie...................... 511

Rand, Mary M..................... 460
Mary Moses..................499, 500
Mary O. (Trefethen)..........510, 550
Mary (Odiorne)................... 513
Mary (Rand)..................503, 503
Mary (Richardson)............... 513
Mary S. (Yeaton)................ 507
Mary (Salter).................... 522
Mary Salter (Trefethen)......... 550
Mary (Smith)............377, 500, 543
Mary T........................... 108
Mary (Tuck)...................502, 552
Mary Tuck........................ 505
Maryette 510
Mehitable..............344, 435, 512, 573
Mehitable C...................... 418
Mercy..................460, 513, 514, 525
Mercy (Palmer).................. 512
Merribah......................351, 500
Mical 500
Mildred 511
Mina 508
Minerva L. (Cutting)............ 508
Minnie (Doane).................. 506
Molly....................379, 512, 513
Moses.................501, 504, 529
Nabby 514
Nahum 504, 508
Nancy 376, 501
Nancy (Haley)................... 503
Nancy W. (Shorey).............. 507
Naomie (Sherburne).............. 502
Nathan 507
Nathaniel....22, 24, 26, 27, 31, 68, 71, 75
    135, 137, 133, 141, 142, 144
    176, 205, 261, 262, 264, 273
    288, 289, 499, 512, 513, 514
Nathaniel Marden.............503, 507
Nellie T....................496, 497, 512
Nora (Varrell)................... 511
Obed.....................389, 501, 508
Olive..................501, 503, 504, 512
Olive (Marden)................449, 503
Olive W........................... 507
Oliver 502
Oliver Porter.................502, 513
Olly 512
Patty 514
Patty L........................... 308
Patty Lang....................... 502
Patty (Moses).................... 502
Persis (Merriam)................ 508
Phebe 564
Philbrick 512
Philemon 500
Polly...................319, 401, 501, 513
Polly (Bean)..................... 502
Polly Jane Garland.............. 363
Polly (Philbrick)............491, 503
Polly (Salter)................... 503
Polly Zebudu..................... 503
Rachel.................238, 500, 513, 535
Rachel (Farnum)................. 508
Rebecca.......................462, 500
Reed V............................ 364
Reed Vennard..................502, 500
Remembrance (Ault).............. 499
Reuben..............500, 503, 506, 512
Richard......24, 72, 135, 138, 153, 160, 255
    261, 283, 288, 289, 345, 502, 512, 514
Rosamond (Jenness)...........391, 512
Rosilla (Green)...............374, 510
Ruth..................306, 500, 512, 583
Ruth (Philbrick)................ 489
Ruth (Seavey)................501, 535
Ruth (Tarlton)................... 513

INDEX OF NAMES. 655

RAND, S. Anzolette................ 505
Sally................145, 501, 512, 513, 570
Sally J. (Thomas)............507, 545
Sally (Rand)..................... 513
Samuel................22, 24, 26, 27, 31
   47, 68, 71, 75, 89, 134, 135
   137, 141, 144, 153, 160, 205, 208
   209, 255, 259, 260, 262, 264, 278
   334, 339, 347, 434, 499, 500, 501
   502, 504, 505, 507, 508, 512, 513
Samuel H....................68, 389, 491
Samuel Hunt...............501, 503, 507
Samuel M..............68, 290, 463, 502
   506, 510, 528
Sarah............369, 376, 499, 500, 501
   502, 503, 512, 513, 514
Sarah Abigail 513
Sarah Ann (Brown)..........314, 505
Sarah Ann (Goss)............370, 508
Sarah Ann (Stewart)............. 508
Sarah (Currier).................... 505
Sarah (Dowrst)................339, 500
Sarah Elizabeth.................... 508
Sarah (Fogg)...................... 513
Sarah (Foss)...................347, 502
Sarah G........................... 507
Sarah G. (Rand)................... 507
Sarah Jane........................ 508
Sarah Jane (Rand)................ 508
Sarah (Jenness)................... 395
Sarah (Marden)................... 503
Sarah (Mead)...................... 507
Sarah Olive....................... 508
Sarah (Page)...................... 472
Sarah (Rand)...................... 503
Sarah Smith 508
Sarah (Trefethen)................. 508
Sarah W. (Marden)...........453, 506
Serena M.......................... 507
Sidney (Lang)..................... 503
Simon 501, 503
Sophia (Brown)...............315, 508
Stephen............31, 140, 144, 153, 169
   172, 173, 205, 253, 255, 256
   276, 512, 513, 514, 545, 583
Stephen Dolbear.................... 502
Susan..........................436, 503
Susan E........................... 507
Susan (Otis)...................... 513
Susan P........................... 514
Susannah 512
Susannah (Goss)..............308, 501
Susie P........................... 325
Sylvanus 508
Sylvia 507
T. W.............................. 209
Tabitha 512
Temperance 500, 536
Theodore 501
Thomas.........22, 24, 26, 27, 67, 71, 127
   134, 135, 137, 138, 144, 170
   172, 173, 176, 177, 205, 209
   252, 253, 273, 285, 288, 314
   351, 383, 499, 500, 502, 505
   507, 512, 552
Thomas Brown................505, 509
Thomas J.....................472, 504
Thomas Jefferson.............503, 506
Thomas W...........67, 79, 108, 209, 285
Thomas William...............505, 509
Trundy..................172, 279, 502, 506
Veranus 505
Vienna J. (Leavitt)............413, 506
W. Alonzo......................... 508
Wallace 511
Walter H.......................... 512

RAND, Warren L.................... 506
Wesley Adams..................... 509
William.................26, 27, 59, 69, 90
   136, 256, 260, 262, 264, 453
   499, 504, 505, 511, 513, 514
William Bramwell.................. 508
William E......................... 506
William J..59, 102, 287, 290, 389, 506, 510
William S.....................493, 501
William Watson...............503, 506
Zebedee 501
RANDALL 72
———— (Baker).................... 518
———— (Carr)..................... 514
———— (Haley).................... 517
———— (McDonald)................. 517
———— (Pierce).................... 516
———— (Tibbets)................... 515
Ably Anna (Caswell)............. 517
Abigail........111, 338, 371, 514, 515, 517
Abigail (————).................... 517
Abigail (Philbrick).............490, 514
Abigail (Webster)............515, 565
Abigail (———— Whidden)......... 518
Abigail (Whidden)................ 518
Amelia 525
Amelia B.......................... 515
Anna Maria (Varrell)..........517, 556
Arthur 518
Augusta (Berry).................. 515
Augusta (Berry-Johnson)......... 306
Becky (Quimby)................... 515
Benjamin...............260, 516, 517, 524
   537, 560, 579
Betsey......................515, 516, 517
Betsey (Downs)...............339, 516
Betsey M.......................... 460
Betsey (Shapley).............516, 537
Betsey (Smith)...............516, 544
Catherine (————).................. 517
Catherine Elkins (Marston-Caswell) 458
Clara (Adams).................... 516
Daniel 515, 516
Deborah 515,517
Deborah (Yeaton).............516, 571
Dolly (Wendell).................. 516
Dorothy.....................515, 516, 538
Dorothy (Randall)................ 515
Edward............26, 127, 153, 255, 256
   259, 514, 515
Eleanor (Osgood)................. 514
Eliza Esther (Caswell)........... 517
Eliza G. (Caswell)............... 517
Elizabeth... 169, 321, 368, 385, 515, 565
Elizabeth (Berry)..........300, 515, 516
Elizabeth (Galloway)............. 515
Elizabeth (Marden)............... 301
Elizabeth (Quimby)............... 515
Elizabeth W...................... 515
Flora Ann........................ 518
Frank Waldron.................... 517
George..........31, 35, 141, 144, 259, 262
   273, 276, 297, 299, 300, 376
   399, 514, 515, 516, 518, 583
George S.......................... 339
George Saunders.................. 516
Gilbert Ira....................... 518
Gladys May....................... 517
Hannah................298, 303, 436, 493
   515, 516, 517, 518, 579, 583
Hannah (————)................514, 517
Hannah (———— Randall)........ 517
Hannah (Adams).................. 517
Hannah (Bragg).................. 517
Hannah (Locke)...............431, 517

INDEX OF NAMES.

RANDALL, Hannah (Marston) 514
  Hannah Olive (Locke-Lane) 405, 437, 517
  Hannah (Pitman) 517
  Hannah (Pitman-Randall) 517
  Hannah (Rand-Foye) 501, 516
  Harriet N. (Lear) 412, 517
  Horace 518
  Huldah 338
  Ira Gilbert 517, 557
  Jack, see George.
  James 24, 27, 38, 71, 134, 135, 259, 264, 518
  James Abner 517
  James Marston 514
  Jane G 517
  Jane (Locke-Brown) 315, 436
  Jessie M. (Lear) 517
  Job L 579
  Job Locke 517
  John 153, 255, 315, 375, 436, 514, 515, 517, 579
  John Cook 322, 518
  John Porter 518
  John W 412, 437, 556
  John William 405, 517
  John Y 501
  John Yeaton 516
  Jonathan 514
  Joseph 514
  Joseph Smith 516
  Joses 153, 255, 515
  Josiah 517
  Judith 537
  Judson 517
  Levi 565
  Levi D 276, 515
  Lizzie 544, 579
  Lizzie (Randall) 579
  Love 375
  Lovey Brackett 516
  Lucy 514
  Lucy J 375
  Lydia C 323
  Margaret 517
  Margaret (Tuckerman) 517
  Mark 69, 141, 210, 252, 255, 257, 259, 262, 289, 306, 490, 514, 515
  Martha Jane 323
  Mary 304, 324, 334, 376, 437, 446, 515, 516, 517
  Mary Ann 516, 518, 521
  Mary (Bragg) 579
  Mary (Downs) 337, 517
  Mary E. (Varrell) 518
  Mary Elizabeth (Varrell) 517, 557
  Mary (Foss) 515
  Mary H. (Caswell) 322, 518
  May Louilla 518
  May S 517
  Mercy 516
  Mercy Sewell 517
  Nancy 516
  Olly 515
  Paul 69, 111, 142, 160, 416, 417, 517
  Permelia 517
  Phebe (Drew) 514
  Polly 304, 306, 518, 534, 557
  Polly (Rugg) 516
  Prudence N 516
  Rachel 444, 515
  Reuben 147, 278, 303, 515, 516
  Reuben S 301, 516
  Richard 516
  Ruth Maria 518
  Sally 515

RANDALL, Sally (Johnson) 399
  Sally Johnson (Goss) 516
  Sally Johnson (Goss-Randall) 516
  Sally (Johnson-Randall) 399
  Samuel 146, 276, 515, 517
  Samuel B 544
  Samuel Berry 516
  Samuel Saunders 516
  Sarah 303, 304, 306, 385, 514, 515, 517, 560, 578, 583
  Sarah (Berry) 299, 515
  Sarah H 443
  Sarah Hannah 517
  Sarah J. (Baston) 517
  Sarah Jane 518
  Sarah Olive 516
  Sarah S 391
  Sarah (Saunders) 516, 524
  Sarah (Young) 515
  Stephen 514
  Susanne Lang 516
  Thomas 514
  William 60, 142, 147, 160, 169, 288, 337, 399, 431, 514, 516, 517, 583
  William B 516
  William Bates 515, 516, 571
  William Bunker 517
  William Monroe 517
  William O 517
  William S 458, 517
RANSON, Sarah 460
RAWDING, Fannie E. (Jones-Michie).. 400
  Fannie E. (Jones-Mitchie) 513
  Joseph William 518
  Robert J 400, 518
RAWLIN, Esther (Abbott) 579
  John 579
RAWLINS, Sarah (Philbrick-Sanborn) 489
  Thomas 489
RAY, H. F 441
  Ida L. (Locke) 441
  Mary (Locke) 434
  Nathaniel 434
REDDIN, George G 454
  Nettie Jane (Marden) 454
REDDING, John 517
  Mercy Sewell (Randall) 517
REDMOND 60
  John 28
  Mary (Locke) 422
  Tristram 422
REDWOOD, Joseph 334
REED 480
  Alden 419
  Martha (Libby) 419
REEDER, Deborah (———) 563
  James 563
REID, Abigail 347
  Arthur 566
  Elizabeth (Webster) 566
REMICK, Abby S. (Johnson-Mace) 399, 445, 519
  Addie 412
  Albert D 519, 520
  Albert L 446
  Albert M 520
  Amos 519
  Anna C. (Mace) 446, 520
  Bernice 520
  Betsey 518
  Betsey Brown (Philbrick) 491
  Betsey (Philbrick) 519
  Caroline (Fox) 519
  Charles M ...108, 286, 291, 318, 519, 520
  Clara Emma (Varrell) 519, 559

INDEX OF NAMES. 657

REMICK, David..........264, 291, 399, 445
                                           518, 519, 534
    Daniel L........................... 519
    Eliza A............................ 519
    Emily Blanche (Brown).......318, 520
    Esther Y....................440, 519, 520
    Esther (Yeaton)................519, 571
    Frances........................... 520
    George O......................519, 559
    George William.................... 519
    Hannah........................325, 518
    Hannah (Mow).................... 465
    Hannah (Varrell)..............519, 556
    Harold John....................... 520
    Huldah........................455, 518
    Isaac.....259, 276, 345, 518, 519, 566, 571
    Jacob............................. 571
    James F........................... 519
    Jane..........................347, 518
    Jane (Foss)...................345, 519
    John A............................ 520
    John S....280, 281, 287, 291, 519, 520, 531
    John Y........163, 170, 172, 276, 491, 519
    Joseph.............68, 277, 518, 519, 583
    Lizzie S.......................... 520
    Lydia Esther...................... 519
    Lydia (Varrell)...............519, 556
    Mabel............................. 520
    Mary.............................. 518
    Mary (Damrell-Drisco)............ 342
    Mary F. (Seavey)................. 531
    Mary (Floyd)..................... 519
    Mary (Lang)...................... 518
    Mary P........................... 578
    Mary Pauline..................... 519
    Mary T. (Seavey)................. 520
    May Blanche...................... 520
    Meribah.......................... 518
    Meribah (Smith).................. 518
    Merinda P. (Porter).............. 519
    Moses......................518, 519, 583
    Moses M.......................... 519
    Nancy.........................519, 583
    Sally............................. 519
    Sally (Paul)...................... 518
    Sarah............................. 518
    Sarah Eliza....................... 519
    Susan (Yeaton)................... 571
    Thomas.....................342, 518, 519
    Walter............................ 520
    William........................... 519
REMINGTON, Olly (Jenness).......... 387
    Polly (Jenness).................. 387
REMLELE, Florence.................... 506
RENDALL, see Randall.
REYNOLDS, Asa........................ 545
    Carrie M. (Jenness).............. 390
    Daniel............................ 268
    Hannah (Locke).................. 428
    Hannah (Tarlton)................ 545
    James............................. 390
    Winthrop......................... 428
RHODES, Edward...................... 508
    H. J.............................. 175
    Lizzie............................. 455
    Sarah Elizabeth (Rand).......... 508
RHYMES, Christopher................. 579
    Sarah (Hale)..................... 579
RICE, Elizabeth....................... 479
    Elizabeth (Garland).............. 365
    D. Hall........................... 385
RICH, Johanna........................ 566
RICHARDSON, Caleb................... 419
    Mary.........................392, 513
    Olive (Libby).................... 419
RICHMOND........................... 270

RIDER, Hannah (Matthews).......... 461
    Henry............................ 461
RIEB, Anna (Smith).................. 520
    Ernest............................ 520
    Ethel C........................... 520
    Florence.......................... 520
    Fred.............................. 520
    George............................ 520
    Patrick........................... 520
RIGGS, Aaron......................... 434
    Aaron L.......................... 439
    Martha Seavey (Locke).......... 439
    Patience.......................... 549
    Sarah (Locke)................... 434
RINDGE, Mary Ann................... 435
RING, Mary.......................... 574
RILEY, Elizabeth..................... 366
ROBERTS, Ann........................ 488
    Anna (Rand)..................... 508
    F................................. 508
ROBEY, Eliza......................... 574
ROBIE, Hannah P. (Seavey).......... 531
    Jeremiah H...................... 531
    John.............................. 359
    Lucy (Kenniston)................ 579
    Mary (Garland).................. 359
    Nathan........................... 579
ROBINSON, Abigail................... 521
    Asa........................337, 499, 579
    Asa C............................ 579
    Elizabeth......................... 356
    Elizabeth (Matthews)............ 460
    Elizabeth (Newton).............. 521
    Hannah (Randall)................ 579
    James......................337, 520, 583
    James Monroe.................... 521
    Jeremiah......................... 579
    John.................520, 521, 537, 579
    Jonathan......................... 270
    Lovey Brackett (Randall-Haley). 375
                                             516, 521
    Lovina........................520, 539
    Margaret......................... 520
    Maria (Porter)................499, 579
    Mary.............................. 583
    Mary Ann........................ 562
    Mary Ann (Randall)..........518, 521
    Mary B. (Downs).............337, 579
    Mary (Matthews)................ 460
    Mary (Page)..................... 579
    Mary (Shapley)...........521, 537, 579
    Mehitable........................ 520
    Nabby............................ 520
    Nancy (Knowles)................. 579
    Olive Haley...................... 521
    Peter............................. 579
    Phebe............................ 486
    R................................. 418
    Robert.............279, 337, 520, 579, 583
    Sally..........................521, 583
    Sally (Downs)................337, 520
    Sally (Downs-Downs).........337, 520
    Samuel.............375, 516, 521, 579
    Sarah............................. 323
    Sarah Elizabeth..............521, 555
    Tammy (Caswell)................ 579
    William.......................518, 521
ROBY, Elizabeth (Philbrick-Chase-Garland)............................ 488
    Henry............................ 488
    Huldah........................... 484
    Joanna........................... 343
RODGERS, Mary E.................... 461
ROGERS, W. T........................ 173
ROLLINS, ———....................... 108
    Anna (———).................... 521

658 INDEX OF NAMES.

ROLLINS, Dolly 501
   Elizabeth 568
   Henry 521
   John 265, 266
   Lydia 389
   Martha 521
ROSS, Elizabeth 463
   Sarah 416
ROTHWELL, Eliza 486
ROWE, Abigail 472
   Caroline 558
   Eliza Jane (Varrell) 558
   Frederick 556
   Jane (Libby) 415
   John 558
   Martha 578
   Mary (Varrell) 556
   Meribah 579
   Meribah (Rowe) 579
   Rebecca J 395
   Samuel 579
   William 558
ROWELL 175
ROYEN, see Ryan.
ROZZELL, Charles. 353
   Martha T. (Foye) 353
RUGG, ———— 521
   Elizabeth 577
   Judah Mace 521
   Judith (Mace) 579
   Polly 516
   William 579
RUMERY, Albert 327
   Elizabeth Rosamond (Clough) .327, 412
RUNDLET, Hannah (Gould) 373
RUNDLETT, George 264
   James 547
   Nancy 547
   Reuben 267, 268
   Sally (Towle) 547
   Solomon 267, 268
RUNNEL 267
RUNNELLS, Grace. 464
RUSSELL, Carrie S 570
RUSWICK, John 579
   Mary (Barker) 579
RYAN, James 256, 257, 260, 261
RYDEN, Hannah (Matthews) 521
   Henry 521
RYENS, see Ryan.
ST. CLAIR, Anna (Jenness) 391
   Ira 391
SALTER, Abiah (Webster) 522, 564, 565
   Albert 495
   Albert E 522
   Alexander 68, 75, 141, 145, 205
                     254, 256, 259, 262, 273
                     299, 521, 522, 564, 565
   Amy (————) 521
   Anna (Webster) 522
   Elizabeth 521
   Elizabeth (Sanborn) 521
   Fannie (Philbrick) 495, 522
   Fanny (Davis) 522
   Florence L. (Berry) 522
   Florence L. (Berry-Rand) 302
   Hannah (Dana) 522
   Huldah 522
   Jeremiah Webster 522
   John 75, 521, 522
   Joseph 522
   John 565
   Louise 522
   Lucy 360, 522
   Martha 579
   Mary 521, 522

SALTER, Mary Ann 522
   Mary (Berry) 299, 522
   Molly 521
   Polly 503
   Sally 412, 522
   Sarah 522
   Sarah (Libby) 418, 522
   W 302
   Webster 418, 522
SALTONSTALL, ———— 246
SAMPSON, Elizabeth Beverly (Lang). 408
   John 408
SANBORN, Abigail (Philbrick) 492
   Benning 387, 522
   Benning W 522
   Betsey 547
   Betsey (Wallis) 564
   Charles Richmond 522
   Daniel 378, 493
   Deborah 390
   Ebenezer 579
   Edward 564
   Elizabeth 314, 521
   Ella (Caswell) 323
   Enoch 521, 579
   Esther (Smith) 544
   Hannah 357, 577
   Hannah (Dalton) 330
   Hannah (Philbrick) 488, 489
   Hannah (Walker) 579
   James 547
   Jenness 522
   Jeremiah 544, 579
   Jewett 265
   John 28, 41, 263, 489
   Joseph 428
   Josiah 357, 522
   Josiah H 492
   Judith 385
   Levi 265, 266
   Levi Thomas 208, 487, 522
   Lowell 450
   Lucia 434
   Lucy (Hobbs) 378
   Martha 407
   Martha (Salter) 579
   Mary 427
   Mary (Barnes) 522
   Mary Carrie 522
   Mary Jane 522
   Mary (Locke) 428
   Mary (Marden) 450
   Mary S. (Philbrick) 493
   Nancy 544
   Nancy (Towle) 547
   Nathan 522
   Peter 522
   Polly (Jenness) 387, 522
   Rachel 309, 433
   Reuben 330
   Sally 407
   Sally (Page) 579
   Sally (Wallis) 564
   Samuel 160, 522
   Sarah 434, 522
   Sarah Jane (Perkins) 487, 522
   Sarah (Philbrick) 489
   Sarah T 418
   Simon 263
   Stephen 488, 489
SANDERS, Amelia 308
   Amelia B. (Randall) 515
   George 193
   John 193, 274, 490
   Mary 307, 327
   Robert 31, 141, 203, 273

INDEX OF NAMES. 659

SANDERS, Samuel............193, 515
 Tryphena (Philbrick)............ 490
 Tryphene 298
 William 273
SANDERSON, Alice (———).......... 496
SANDY, John.................... 212
SARGENT, Betsey.................. 575
 Hannah (Dalton)................. 329
 John 329
 Martha (Locke).................. 434
 Nat 334
 Susannah 498
SAUNDERS, ———,.................... 72
 ——— (Buzzell)................... 525
 ——— (Chatham).................. 524
 ——— (Goss)..................... 524
 ——— (Hall)..................... 524
 ——— (Manson)................... 525
 ——— (Wallace).................. 525
 A 68
 Abigail 429, 523
 Abigail (Locke).................. 434
 Amelia (Randall)................. 525
 Anna (Locke).................... 433
 Anna (Page)...............471, 523
 Betsey..................524, 525, 553
 Dorcas 537
 Dorcas (Pitman)................. 524
 Elijah 176, 525
 Elijah Robert 524, 525
 Eliza Ann........................ 524
 Elizabeth............523, 524, 537, 557
 Elizabeth (Berry)................ 524
 Esther 523, 571
 Frederick 525
 George........145, 176, 257, 471, 523, 524
 George Berry.................... 523
 Hannah.................434, 523, 524
 Hannah (Foss)...............345, 523
 Henry Shapley................... 524
 Huldah 571
 Huldah (Philbrick)............... 525
 Job 525
 John.........145, 148, 433, 523, 524, 525
 Levi Dearborn................... 523
 Martha 524
 Mary......146, 371, 460, 523, 524, 537, 540
 Mary (Berry).................... 523
 Mary (Foss)..................... 345
 Mary J........................... 387
 Mary (Locke)................424, 524
 Mary Mead....................... 524
 Mary (Saunders)................. 524
 Mercy 538
 Mercy Haines.................... 524
 Mercy (Rand).................... 525
 Molly 525
 Molly (Foss)..................... 525
 Nathaniel 524
 O. H............................. 525
 Olive 553
 Olly 523
 Olly (Philbrick)................. 525
 Patience 146
 Patience Locke.................. 525
 Reuben 434
 Robert..........145, 160, 176, 262, 273
  345, 424, 523, 524, 525
 Samuel........160, 176, 345, 523, 524, 525
 Sarah...........448, 516, 523, 525, 583
 Sarah (———)..................... 559
 Sarah (Kive).................... 523
 Sarah (Saunders)...........523, 524
 Tryphena 306
 Tryphena (Philbrick)............ 523
 W. H............................. 525
 William...................523, 524, 525

SAUNDERS, William S.............. 559
SAUTERAGE, Richard................ 137
SAVAGE, ———,....................... 296
 Charlotte 468
SAWYER, Anna Knox................. 525
 Edward 525
 Horace..................291, 393, 525
 Horace Russell................... 525
 Mary W. (Whidden).............. 525
 Mildred 525
 Susan M. (Jenness)..........393, 525
SAYMORE, Ann (Cutt)............... 579
 Henry 579
SCADGEL, Abigail.................. 525
 Benjamin..................68, 110, 525
 Christopher 135
 Hannah 525
 Mary....................355, 525, 575
 Sarah 525
SCAMEL, ———,....................... 264
SCAMMON, Elizabeth W............. 331
SCEREN, Molly..................... 427
SCHEDEL, or SCHEGEL, Benjamin.... 525
 Christopher 525
 Deborah (———)................... 525
 Dorcas (———).................... 525
 Jacob 525
 Mary 525
SCHIELE, Mary B................... 487
SCOTT, Abigail Sarah (Moses)..... 462
 Daniel O......................... 526
 Daniel P......................... 526
 Elizabeth 475
 Haven 526
 Sarah.........................329, 536
 Sylvanus 462
 Walter P......................... 526
SEARCY, ——— (——— Alton)...... 580
 Josiah 371, 580
 Lucinda (Snow-Goss).........371, 580
SEARS, Rebecca 356
 Thomas 356
SEAVIE, see Seavey.
SEAVEY, ———..........53, 61, 67, 72, 79, 149
 ——— (Ackerman)................. 529
 ——— (Berry).................... 529
 ——— (Fallen)................... 536
 ——— (Garland).................. 531
 ——— (Gerrish).................. 530
 ——— (Jenness).................. 529
 ——— (Leavitt).................. 531
 ——— (Smith).................... 534
 ——— (Stevens).................. 534
 ——— (Thomasine)................ 527
 ——— (Tilton)................... 537
 Aaron.....................153, 255, 535
 Abby (Pottle).................... 530
 Abigail............326, 360, 367, 527, 528
  529, 533, 536, 537
 Abigail (———)..........527, 533, 535
 Abigail A........................ 463
 Abigail (Gardiner)............... 535
 Abigail (Pickering).............. 535
 Abraham 534
 Adeline 532
 Albert Storer.................... 532
 Albert W....................494, 533
 Alfred....................61, 403, 529, 543
 Alfred V...........281, 341, 363, 531, 532
 Alina A.......................... 531
 Amasa 418
 Amos...68, 69, 72, 110, 131, 141, 145, 148
  160, 163, 205, 209, 210, 212
  219, 262, 273, 279, 283, 284
  286, 288, 289, 290, 340, 410
  476, 527, 528, 530, 532, 537

660 INDEX OF NAMES.

Seavey, Andrew P. 530
Angenette 532
Ann 416, 580, 583
Ann Elizabeth 336, 530
Ann (Seavey) 580
Anna 526, 527, 528
Anna P. (———) 569
Anna (Seavey) 527, 528
Anna T. 530
Anna Towle 529
Anna (Trefethern) 528
Annie E. (Smith) 532
Asa 529
Augusta O. (Moses) 463
Benjamin 22, 24, 26, 27, 134, 135
      136, 137, 339, 527, 534, 536
Betsey 368, 529
Betsey Brown (Garland) 360, 531
Betsey (Handley) 534
Betsey (Stevens) 530
Betsey (Webster) 529, 565
Caesar, see Wallis, Caesar.
Calivena E., see Calvinna E.
Calvin 529
Calvinna E. 318, 532
Carlton 534
Caroline 534, 535
Caroline L. 530
Caroline T. 456, 461
Caroline Theresa 530
Catherine 535
Cato 583
Charles 363, 530, 534
Charles E. 531
Charles W. 530
Charlotte 380, 531
Charlotte Ann 533
Charlotte Ann (Garland) 363, 533
Charlotte M. (Foss) 349, 533
Clara B. 530
Clara E. 469, 531
Clara Josephine (Drake) 341, 533
Comfort 534
Damaris 527
Daniel 31, 176, 177, 500, 535
Deborah 418, 528, 534
Dolly 527
Dolly (Foss) 536
Dorothy 504, 528
Dorothy (Parsons-Follett) 529
Eben 69, 457
Eben Leavitt 529, 532
Ebenezer 66, 176, 205, 273, 526
                   528, 529, 534
Ebenezer Wallis 529
Edward 291, 529, 531, 570
Edward E. 533
Edwin 534
Elijah 534, 535, 536, 537
Eliza 371
Eliza Ann 530
Eliza J. 530
Eliza J. (Seavey) 530
Eliza Jane 530
Eliza Mary Langdon 529
Eliza S. (Parsons) 477, 532
Eliza (Whidden) 531
Elizabeth 313, 320, 335, 339, 352
          382, 526, 527, 528, 533, 534
Elizabeth Ann (Lear) 412
Elizabeth (Ayers) 529
Elizabeth Fidelia (Garland) 363
Elizabeth (Fuller) 535
Elizabeth (Garland) 359, 528
Elizabeth (Langdon) 410, 527
Elizabeth S. 532

Seavey, Elizabeth (Weeks) 532
Ella May 533
Ellen 534
Ellen Tasker 534
Elmira A. 379
Emeline 530
Emily 530, 552
Emily C. 531
Emily C. (Seavey) 531
Emily (Seavey) 530
Emos 261
Ephraim ..101, 169, 277, 360, 527, 528, 531
Ervin J. 291
Eunice 332, 471
Everett Charles 532
Everett H. 533
Fanny 361, 528
Fidelia (Garland) 531
Flora Belle (Philbrick) 494, 533
Frances 534
Frances (Goodall) 532
Frances (Locke) 534
Frank H. 531
Frederick 531, 536
G 280
George 534
George H. 281, 533
George Henry 531
Gideon 528, 529
Gideon W. 537
Hannah 212, 353, 380, 387
        501, 504, 513, 526, 527, 528
        529, 534, 535, 536, 540, 567
Hannah (———) 526, 535
Hannah J. 530
Hannah M. (Jewell) 532
Hannah P. 531
Hannah (Philbrick-Walker) ...488, 526
Hannah (Pickering) 527
Hannah (Seavey) 527
Hannah W. 529
Hanson 349
Hanson W. 531
Harrison 530, 532, 566
Henry 402, 529, 533, 534, 535, 536
Henry Dow 534
Henry J. 534
Hepsibah 526, 536
Huldah 485, 537
Huldah (Locke) 424, 536, 537
Ichabod 536
Irvin G. 533
Irving J. 341, 531, 533
Isaac 35, 532, 534, 535, 536
Ithamar 533, 534
J. J. 531
James 22, 24, 26, 69, 71
       75, 135, 137, 141, 144, 145
       160, 212, 213, 219, 256, 259
       260, 262, 273, 283, 288, 298
       349, 410, 526, 527, 528, 529
       531, 534, 535, 548, 580
James E. 531, 533
Jeremiah 534
Jesse 529
Joanna 355, 535
John 35, 71, 75, 134, 203, 273, 488
      526, 527, 528, 534, 536, 580, 583
John L. 279, 281, 290, 528
John Langdon 528, 530, 532
John William 530
Jonathan 533, 534
Joseph 22, 24, 26, 31, 60, 61
        69, 135, 137, 140, 144, 146
        163, 170, 172, 225, 259, 262
        273, 528, 529, 534, 535, 536

INDEX OF NAMES. 661

SEAVEY, Joseph Jackson............, 412
  Joseph L...68, 75, 141, 144, 172, 359, 530
  Joseph Langdon............68, 110, 186
            411, 525, 527, 528, 531
  Joseph Mason..................... 535
  Joseph Oren...................... 533
  Joseph Whidden...........408, 529, 531
  Joseph Williams...............493, 531
  Joshua...................528, 529, 565
  Julia A. (Holmes)................. 532
  Lettis..........................305, 530
  Levi 534, 537
  Lizzie A.......................... 532
  Lizzie (Foss)..................349, 531
  Lizzie II. (Bebee)................. 533
  Lucy 536
  Lucy Wainwright................. 535
  Lyman..................169, 477. 530, 532
  M. Eva........................... 531
  Margaret.....................458, 534
  Maria (Libby).................... 418
  Mark 527, 535
  Martha...362, 388, 434, 527, 528, 532, 570
  Martha Adeline................... 531
  Martha Ann....................... 531
  Martha Ann (Philbrick).......493, 532
  Martha Elizabeth..............531, 561
  Martha J. (Webster).........532, 566
  Martha (Patten)................. 528
  Mary.............294, 316, 327, 468, 476
          526, 527, 528, 529, 530
          533, 534, 535, 536, 583
  Mary (———)...............533, 535
  Mary (——— True).............. 526
  Mary A........................... 530
  Mary A. (Drake).................. 533
  Mary Abby (Philbrick).......493, 531
  Mary Abigail..................... 531
  Mary Charlotte...............497, 532
  Mary F........................... 531
  Mary (Hincks).................... 527
  Mary J. (Drake).................. 341
  Mary Jane....................354, 531
  Mary (Kingman)..............402, 534
  Mary (Langdon)..............410, 527
  Mary Langdon.................... 476
  Mary Moses...................... 529
  Mary T........................... 520
  Mary (Trefethern)............531, 548
  Mary (Whidden).................. 529
  Mary (Willey)................531, 570
  Matty, see Martha.
  Maud E. (Wiggin)................ 533
  Mehitable..............307, 360, 418, 528
                533, 535, 573
  Molly 536
  Moses..........22, 58, 139, 142, 144, 160
          262, 424, 533, 535, 536, 537
  Nancy 536
  Nathaniel 135, 526
  Noah.....................135, 203, 536
  Olive................469, 529, 535, 536
  Oliver 530
  Oslow 527
  Otis 532
  Patience (Berry).........298, 534, 580
  Paul................68, 75, 141, 145, 262
            527, 528, 529, 563
  Peter 434
  Phudesy 536
  Polly 314, 528
  Polly (Randall)................... 534
  Priscilla (Philbrick).............. 534
  Prudence Perry (Marden).....457, 529
  Rachel Rand.................500, 535
  Rebecca 527

  SEAVEY, Ruth..........446, 501, 534, 535, 536
  Ruth (Moses).............418, 463, 534
  Ruth (Tarlton).................... 537
  Sally............370, 529, 534, 535, 536
  Sally (Locke)..................... 434
  Sally (Seavey).................... 534
  Samuel.........22, 24, 26, 27, 60, 87, 88
      134, 135, 137, 142, 153, 225
      255, 262, 265, 288, 369, 527
      529, 530, 533, 535, 536, 537
  Samuel Wallis................528, 529
  Sarah...............305, 457, 528, 529
            533, 534, 535, 536
  Sarah A. (Hatch)................. 530
  Sarah A. (Moulton).............. 533
  Sarah Adeline (Moulton)......... 531
  Sarah (Berry).................... 536
  Sarah D.......................... 530
  Sarah (Drake)................340, 530
  Sarah Elizabeth.................. 532
  Sarah H.......................... 531
  Sarah (Lang).................408, 531
  Sarah Lang...................... 529
  Sarah (Locke).................... 536
  Sarah Olive (Drake)..........341, 533
  Sarah (Scott).................... 536
  Sarah (Wallis)...............528, 563
  Shadrach 535
  Sidney 397
  Sidney Langdon.................. 530
  Sidney S.....................528, 530
  Sidney S. (Seavey)...........528, 530
  Simon 534, 535
  Solomon...................142, 160, 536
  Sophronia 530
  Stephen 526
  Susan 532
  Susan H.......................... 530
  Susannah (Kennison)............. 536
  Temperance 536
  Temperance (Langdon)........411, 531
  Temperance (Rand).............. 536
  Theodore 274
  Theodore J...................528, 530
  Thomas.........71, 127, 134, 526, 527, 536
  William...............18, 21, 22, 24, 26
      27, 31, 33, 69, 70, 71, 75
      78, 90, 126, 127, 134, 135
      137, 141, 145, 160, 205, 212
      256, 259, 260, 262, 265, 273
      276, 278, 284, 287, 288, 289
      290, 418, 463, 501, 526, 527
      528, 529, 530, 534, 535, 536
  William Harrison................. 532
  William J........................ 532
  William L........................ 530
  William Warren..............530, 532
  Winthrop 529, 537
  Woodbury......172, 208, 290, 493, 530, 532
SEAVY, see Seavey.
SELLERS, Abigail (Randall).......... 517
  Permelia (Randall)............... 517
SENTER, ———...................265, 270
  Sarah 566
SEVEAY, see Seavey.
SEVERANCE, Joshua..............267, 268
SEVEY, see Seavey.
SEWALL, Samuel.................... 243
SEWARD, Joanna.................... 349
SHACKFORD, ———.............248, 249
  Sarah (Rand).................... 513
SHANNON, Ann (Rand)............. 537
  Bettie 537
  Elizabeth 339
  John 537
  Nancy 404

INDEX OF NAMES.

SHANNON, Samuel..................... 537
   Thomas 537
   William 253, 537
SHAPLEIGH, Nicholas................. 16
SHAPLEY, ——— (Blaisdell)......... 537
   ——— (Leighton)................. 537
   Abby A. (Rand)................506, 539
   Abby Jane.......................... 539
   Abby Ruth.......................... 539
   Abigail (Parker)................... 539
   Adeline (Rand-Foye).............. 507
   Ann (Clark)........................ 537
   Ann (Gray)......................... 538
   Ann (Knowland)................... 538
   Apphia (Locke).................... 435
   Benjamin...................537, 538, 583
   Betsey............498, 516, 537, 538, 584
   Chalcedonia (———)............. 538
   David 539
   Dorcas 349
   Dorcas Pitman..................... 538
   Dorcas (Saunders)................ 537
   Dorothy (Randall)............516, 538
   Edward....................141, 537, 538
   Eliza..........................348, 538
   Elizabeth 384
   Elizabeth (Saunders).............. 537
   Elizabeth (Yeaton)................. 571
   Emeline (Jones)................... 539
   Emily 332, 539
   Frances Ann....................... 538
   George 146, 538
   George W.......................... 538
   George Washington................ 538
   Hannah 516
   Harriet E........................... 539
   Harriet T. (Gilman)................ 539
   Henry........141, 145, 256, 259, 262, 276
          300, 349, 537, 538, 539, 584
   Henry Carter...................... 537
   Henry J........................537, 538
   Hepzibah (Rand).................. 538
   J. H................................ 280
   James............516, 524, 537, 538, 583
   James Albert...................... 538
   James Hill 539
   John 537, 539
   John Palmer....................... 538
   Joshua 539
   Jotham 539
   Jotham Berry...................... 538
   Judith...............146, 148, 537, 538
   Judith (Randall)................... 537
   Lovina Robinson...............520, 539
   Margaret (Thompson)............. 539
   Maria (Haines).................... 539
   Martha (Langdon)................. 410
   Mary........................521, 537, 579
   Mary (Berry)...................... 538
   Mary Jane......................... 539
   Mary R............................ 539
   Mary (Randall).................... 516
   Mary (Saunders)..............524, 537
   Mercy 145
   Mercy Haines (Saunders).....524, 538
   Mercy (Randall).................... 516
   Molly (Berry)...................... 300
   Nancy (Blaisdell).................. 537
   Nichols 410
   Nora S............................. 539
   Olive 387
   Olive Jane......................... 538
   R. P................................ 280
   Rachel (Foss)..................347, 538
   Reuben............60, 146, 170, 516, 520
              524, 537, 538, 539

SHAPLEY, Reuel..................60, 361
   Reuel G.......................506, 539
   Robert....................108, 537, 538
   Robert P........................... 539
   Ruth 573
   Sally......................146, 537, 538
   Sally (Caswell).................... 537
   Samuel........170, 172, 276, 347, 538, 571
   Samuel B.......................... 539
   Sarah 537
   Sarah A....................301, 375, 539
   Sarah Ann 146, 538
   Sarah Caroline 538
   Sarah F. (Coleman).............. 539
   Sarah J. (Hill)..................... 539
   Semira 539
   Thomas 435
   William 507
   William H.......................... 539
   William Henry..................... 538
SHAW, Abiah 564
   Abial 309
   Abigail 332
   Abigail (Dalton)................... 330
   Abraham 265
   Addie S. (Rand).................. 509
   Andrew 579
   Bathsheba 305
   Betsey (Folsom).................. 579
   Clarissa 495
   Clarissa (Blake)................... 579
   Clarissa L. (Marston)............. 579
   David 265, 266
   Dearborn T........................ 579
   Edward 395
   Elijah 295, 579
   Eliza 574
   Emma 505
   Gilbert 263
   Jeremiah 241, 509
   Jerusha 422
   John 579
   Joseph 309
   Josiah 579
   Lizzie B........................... 393
   Mary..........................429, 434
   Mary (Nason)..................... 427
   Moses 330
   Rhoda (Dow)...................... 579
   Samuel 471
   Sarah 574
   Sarah (Batchelder)................ 295
   Sarah (Wells)..................... 579
   Susan (Page)...................... 471
   Zipporah J........................ 395
SHEAFE, Abigail...................... 540
   Edmund 540
   Elizabeth 540
   Elizabeth (Cotton)................. 540
   Hannah 540
   Hannah (Seavey)..............527, 540
   Henry 540
   Jacob.....................47, 75, 527, 540
   James 540
   John 540
   Margaret 540
   Margaret (Webb).................. 540
   Marion (———).................. 539
   Mary 540
   Mary (———).................... 540
   Mary (Sheafe).................... 540
   Matthew 540
   Mehitable 540
   Mehitable (Sheafe)................ 540
   Rebecca 540
   Sampson 58, 540

INDEX OF NAMES. 663

SHEAFE, Samuel..................539, 540
Sarah 540, 579
Sarah (Walton).................... 540
Thomas 539, 540
William 540
SHELDON, Eliza (Holmes)........... 579
Isaac 475
Kitteridge 579
Sarah 475
Sarah Warner...................... 475
SHEPARD, Comfort.................. 404
Comfort (Hobbs)................... 378
Elizabeth Lang (Berry)............ 305
John 378
SHEPPARD, Adeline................. 431
Betsey (Foye)..................... 352
Joseph 347
Olive (Foss)...................... 347
SHERBORN, see Sherburne.
SHERBURN, see Sherburne.
SHERBURNE, ——..............105, 134
—— (Warner).................... 541
Adeline 541
Andrew................259, 411, 541, 579
Anna 541
Anna (Perkins).................... 485
Catherine 468
David 263
Edward 541
Elizabeth...................410, 411, 441
Elizabeth (Langdon)............... 411
Henry.....................73, 137, 541
James Henry....................... 541
John....................127, 259, 541
Jonathan..............27, 135, 485, 541
Joseph (Mrs.)..................... 248
Love (Mrs.)........................ 73
Martha 541
Mary (—— Moses).............. 462
Mary Elizabeth.................... 450
Nancy (Perkins)...............485, 541
Naomie 502
Nathaniel 541
Noah 261
Polly (Cotton).................... 541
Rebecca (Gibbon).................. 541
Sally 334
Samuel 73, 541
Sarah 411
Sarah (Warner).................... 541
Susannah (Knight).............541, 579
Thomas 541
SHERWILL, Nicholas................... 8
SHIELDS, Abigail (Robinson-Brown). 521
Sarah 294
William 521
SHILLABER, Almira (Walker)........ 563
Rebecca 555
Robert 563
SHIRBORN, see Sherburne.
SHOREY, Nancy W................... 507
SHORTRIDGE 541
Ann 563
Esther (Dearborn)................. 541
Richard 541
Robert 541
SHURTLEFF, Barzilla............... 428
Dolly (Locke)..................... 428
SHURTLIEF, William.............27, 28
SHURTLIEFF, see Shurtlief.
SHUTE, Christina (Rand)........... 499
James........24, 26, 27, 68, 136, 137, 541
John..........................134, 527
Rebecca (Seavey).................. 527
Samuel 21
Sarah 541

SIDES, Andrew..................... 295
Mandana (Batchelder)............. 295
SIMES, Alexander......24, 26, 70, 136, 138
SIMMONS, Clara Ann (Jenness-Mason) 394
John 394
SIMONDS, Clark.................... 174
SIMPSON, John..................... 579
Martha (Langdon-Barrell)......... 411
Sarah (Sheafe).................... 579
SIMS, see Simes.
SINCLAIR, Charles A............400, 413
Emma I. (Jones)................... 400
Sarah (Hall)...................... 377
SKILLINGS, Lydia.................. 415
Martha 419
Sarah 417
SLEEPER, —— (Bean)............ 543
Aaron 541
Abigail (Coffin)..............384, 542
Alice (Moulton)................... 542
Amanda 542
Annie L........................... 542
Benjamin 541, 542
Charles B.......................... 61
Charles Benjamin.................. 542
Charles E.......................... 61
Charles Everett................... 542
Daniel 543
Edward D.......................... 542
Eliphalet.................170, 276, 384, 542
Elizabeth 483, 542
Emily (Garland)..............360, 542
Frank 542
Hattie F........................... 542
Jane 542
Jane B............................. 561
John 541
Joseph 541
Marion (Clough)................... 542
Martha Jane (Jenness).......395, 542
Martin V...................61, 395, 542
Mary...................542, 543, 567
Mary (Marston)................... 542
Mehitable (Crockett).............. 543
Molly (Jenness)...............384, 542
Moses 541
Nabby 543
Nancy 390, 542
Nancy (Randall).................. 516
Oliver.................222, 223, 224, 542
Richard 516
Richard Jenness............61, 360, 542
Ruth 584
Ruth (Tarlton).................... 542
Ruth Tarlton...................... 543
Sally (Berry)..................... 543
Sally (Brown)..................... 542
Sally J........................... 542
Sally (Smith)..................... 542
Sarah Ann......................... 542
Sarah (Berry)..................... 298
Sarah (Boardman).................. 542
Theophilus William................ 542
Thomas....61, 205, 276, 298, 541, 542, 543
Thurston......................140, 145
Tristram.............31, 61, 205, 262, 584
Tristram Coffin...........160, 343, 542
Trustram, see Tristram.
W 146
Walter 542
William..................61, 147, 169, 542
SLIGGINS, Hannah.................. 578
SLOOPER, Elizabeth................ 379
Sarah 554
SMALL, Nancy (Libby).............. 418

INDEX OF NAMES.

SMALL, Samuel 418
    William 180
SMART, Emily A. (Jenness) 395
    Emma 443
    Emma L. 543
    Fred L. 445, 543
    Martha A. (Mace) 445, 543
    Mary Watson (Garland) 365, 543
    Maurice H. 543
    Samuel 313
    Samuel G. 365, 543
    Sophia G. 324
    Sophia J. 324, 543
    William 395
    Wilmot Manning 543
SMARTT, Joseph 138
SMILEY, Sophronia 576
SMITH, Abigail 418
    Alice J. (Berry) 302
    Anna 520
    Anne (Garland) 359
    Annie E. 532
    B 573
    Betsey 146, 516, 544
    Betty 225
    Bezaleel 158, 164, 166, 169, 172, 173
    Caroline G. (Willard) 580
    Charles 341
    David 26, 27, 44, 45, 46, 50, 61
          135, 137, 140, 145, 160, 205
          262, 263, 273, 447, 543, 584
    Deborah 416, 543
    Deborah (Locke) 426
    Eben 540
    Eliza J. 486
    Elizabeth Anna 579
    Elizabeth (Hall) 376, 543
    Elizabeth Martha (Drake) 341
    Esther 544
    Esther (Parsons) 474
    Hannah 311, 543
    Israel 414, 543
    James W. 517
    Jane 437
    Joanna 543
    John 6, 228, 347, 544, 580
    John J. 281
    Jonathan 543
    Joseph 359, 474, 544
    Joshua 302
    Linda (Berry) 302
    Margaret (Felear) 544
    Mary 311, 377, 447, 500, 543
    Mary (Marden) 447, 543
    Mehitable (Shapley) 540
    Meribah 518
    Molly 455, 543
    Nancy (Garland) 359
    Nancy (Sanborn) 544
    Origin 243
    Patience (Foss-Newton-Butler) 347
    Ruth 581
    Sally 542, 543
    Samuel 31, 60, 376, 543
    Sanborn 265
    Sarah 333, 492, 508, 543
    Sarah (——) 543
    Sarah H. 578
    Sarah J. (Baston-Randall) 517
    Sarah (Libby) 414
    Simon 572
    Solomon 266
    Tamah (Yeaton) 572
    William 544
    Winthrop 266
SNELL, John 579

SNELL, Olive (Cate) 579
SNOW, Lucinda 371
SOMERBY, Harriett (Lang) 408
    Sherburne 408
SOULE, Adoniram 419
    Sarah Frances (Libby) 419
SPARHAWK 274
SPEAD, Elizabeth 366
SPEAR, Addie E. 544
    Adeline (Cook) 544
    Charles 454
    Charles W. 61, 210, 214, 520, 544
    Elva 544
    Harriett 352
    Lizzie S. (Remick) 520, 544
    Mary E. (Marden) 454
    Mary Frances 544
    Mary L. (Marden) 544
    Samuel B. 544
SPEARS, see Spear.
SPENCER, Robert 299
    Sarah (Berry) 299
SPINNEY, Julia Dodd 509
    Mary E. (Waldron) 580
    Matilda 407
    Samuel A. 580
SPRAGUE, Mary Frances (Clark) 326
    Seth M. 326
SQUIRE, Alice 544
    Eliza (Burnell) 544
    Frances 544
    John 544
STACKFORD, Joshua 356
    Nancy (Fuller) 356
STACKPOLE, Elizabeth G. (Hills) 378
    Elizabeth W. (Jenness) 389, 579
    Paul A. 378
    William 389, 579
STANDISH, Miles 12
STANLEY, Caroline Frances 482
    Ezekiel 579
STANTON, Mary (Yeaton) 579
STANYAN, James 217
STAPLES, Mary 491
    Mary H. 431
STARK, Lewis 469
    Mary Hannah (Odiorne) 469
STAUNTON, Elizabeth (Yeaton) 571
    John 571
STAVERS, Bartholomew 463
    Martha (Moses) 463
STEAD, Ann 458
    Anne 577
STEARNS, Eliza 399
    Isaac 268
STEBBINS, Mercy 475
    Sarah 475
STEPHENS, Alexander 389
    Alonzo 331
    Clara (Dalton) 331
    James 278
    Lucy Jane (Jenness) 389
    Nabby (Rand) 514
    Olive D. 459
STERLING, Sarah Ab'y (Odiorne) 469
    Thomas A. 469
STEVENS, Benjamin 259
    Betsey 530
    Charles 453
    Charles W. 281
    Elizabeth 506
    Georgianna M. (Marden) 453
    Harriet 561
    John 127
    Josiah 243
    Lydia 352

INDEX OF NAMES. 665

STEVENS, Olive D. 577
 Susannah (Haley) 243
 Thomas 133
STEWART, Sarah Ann 508
 W. H. 173
STICKNEY, Jane 357
 Sarah Elizabeth (Waldron) .. 560
 William 560
STILES, Dorothy (Dalton) 328
 Ebenezer 328
STILLMAN, Elias 78
STOCKBRIDGE, Isaac 263
STOCKELS, Elizabeth (Tucker) 579
 Robert 579
STODDARD, Augusta A 470
 Elizabeth (Lightford) 580
 Henry 572
 John 572
 Joseph E 580
 L. Jane (Yeaton) 572
 Madelaide M. Yeaton 572
STONE, Ethel L 497
 Sarah (Rand) 514
STORER, Hannah 411
 Mary (Langdon) 411
STOREY, Lydia 504
STRAW, E. A 208
 Josephine (Perkins) 487
 Parker 487
STREETER, Anna 366
STRONG, Elizabeth 474
 Elizabeth (Parsons) 475
 Mary (Halton) 475
 Ebenezer 475
STROUT, Adeline (Yeaton) 572
 Byron 572
STUBBS, Mary 422
STURTEVANT, Lucetta (Dalton) 330
 Ward C 330
SULLIVAN 263
 James 411
 John 257
 Martha (Langdon-Barrell-Simpson) 411
SWAIN, Benjamin 265
 George M 231
 Jeremiah 265
 Mary Ann 417
 Prudence 488
SWAINE, Benjamin 263
 Bethia 464
 Hannah 63, 381
 William 381
SWAN, Dorothy 328
SWEAT, Benjamin 268
 Thomas 266
SWEENEY, Francis 389
 Mary (Jenness) 389
 Rozanna 390
SWEET, Carrie (Philbrick) 495
 Frank 495
 Thomas 265
SWEETSER, Ida (Caswell) 324
 John 324
SWENSON, Agnes 544
 Anders 544
 Carl A 544
 Carrie W. (Lewis) 544
 Emilie 544
 Inez 544
 Louise 544
 Louise (Swenson) 544
SWETT, Benjamin 378, 466
 Elizabeth (Norton-Jenness) . 466
 Maria Salter (Caswell) 322
 Sarah 378

SWINSON, Annie 339
SYDENHAM, Catharine 474
 Hester 474
SYLVESTER, Fanny 417
SYMENS, Abigail 416
SYMES, Sarah 304
 Susannah 578
SYMMES, Ann 415
 Mehitable (Palmer-Dalton) .. 328
 Zechariah 328
TALLENT, Mary (Langdon) 411
TAPPAN, Moses 310
 Sarah (Brown) 310
TARLETON or TARLTON.
TARLTON, ——— (Rendall) 544
 ——— (Yeaton) 545
 Abby A 576
 Abigail (Brown) 545
 Anna M 442
 Benjamin 203, 545
 Betsey 513, 545, 580
 Catharine (Odiorne) 468
 Comfort 545
 Comfort (Cotton) 545
 Elias 23, 24, 203, 544, 545
 Hannah 545, 578
 Hannah (Ackerman) 545
 Hannah J. (Seavey) 530
 Harriett (Atkins) 580
 James 545, 580
 James N 530, 532
 John 203, 545
 Joseph 368, 545
 Katherine (Odiorne) 580
 Margaret 560, 581
 Mary 306, 383, 417
 Mary E. (———) 395
 Mery (Goss) 368, 515
 Mehitable 576
 Mercy 573
 Nathaniel 545
 Richard 203, 544
 Ruth 513, 537, 542
 S 280
 Samuel 276, 545
 Sarah A. (Hartshorn) 545
 Sarah Elizabeth (Seavey) ... 532
 Simon F 395
 Stedman 545
 Stephen 545
 William 545
TASH 270
 Clarissa 433
TASKER, Ellen 534
TATE, Hannah 422
TAYLOR, Bethia 358
 Ebenezer 145
 Edward 295
 Elizabeth (Jenness) 383
 Hannah (Brown) 311
 Hannah (Seavey) 529
 Helen W. (Batchelder) 295
 John 311, 357
 Jonathan 484
 Joseph 580
 Mary (Lovering) 580
 Mary (Perkins) 484
 Rhoda 474
 Sarah 357
 Sophronia (Lang) 409
 Thomas 409
TEMPLE, William 160
THING, Bartholomew 42
 James 330
 Lydia (Pickering) 580
 Lyford 580

666 INDEX OF NAMES.

THING, Mary (Dalton).............. 330
THOMAS, Alice....................... 545
  Ann 5C3
  Ann L............................ 545
  Ann Louise....................... 545
  Benjamin 580
  E 266
  Elbridge A....................... 545
  Elisha 265
  Ellen M. (Picot)................. 545
  George Augustus 545
  Hannah (Cushing)................. 580
  James..................208, 276, 355, 545
  John Saunders.................... 545
  Lois (Clarke).................... 545
  Mary (Ball)...................... 294
  Mary Elizabeth 545
  Mary (Saunders)...........460, 523, 545
  Olive 469
  Prudence (Marden)................ 450
  Sally J....................507, 545
  Thomas 545
  Trefethen J...................... 68
  William...............160, 460, 523, 545
THOMPSON, Amy...................... 346
  Benjamin 475
  Betsey (Seavey).................. 529
  David 266
  Eliza 574
  Elizabeth 475, 568
  Margaret 539, 406
  Mary 498, 577
  Olive 355
  Susanna 475
  David..........7, 8, 9, 10, 11, 12, 13, 14
         15, 16, 17, 18, 20, 73, 229, 265
  Mrs. David....................... 11
  John 12
THURSTON, Huldah (Perkins)......... 485
  Nathaniel 485
TIBBETTS, Edward Rendall........... 545
  Jacob...................70, 256, 299, 545
  Judith (Berry)..............70, 299, 545
  Mary 545
  Samuel 545
  Thomas 545
TIDY, Robert....................... 414
  Sarah (Libby).................... 414
TILTON, Asa........................ 404
  Betsey (Locke)................... 433
  Daniel 433
  Elizabeth 311
  Jacob 433
  John 265, 266
  Lucy (Lamprey)................... 404
  Lucy M. (Locke).................. 433
  Martha (Perkins)................. 484
  Sally 450
TINDALL, Martha F. (Philbrick)..... 495
  Richard B........................ 495
TITCOMB, Elizabeth................. 352
TITUS 212
TODD, Lydia........................ 560
  Sally (Grover)................... 580
  Samuel 580
TOOL, William...................... 281
TORREY, Alexis..................... 572
  Alfred W......................... 559
  Edith M. (Varrell)...........327, 559
  Lucina (Yeaton).................. 572
TOWER, Henritta.................... 509
TOWL, see Towle.
TOWLE 72
  ——— (Emery).................... 547
  Abbie 400
  Abigail 427
  Abigail (Brown).................. 312

TOWLE, Amos.....................490, 580
  Ann (Prescott)................... 547
  Ann 433
  Anna.....................457, 490, 546
  Anna (Norton)................466, 546
  Anna R........................... 320
  Benjamin..................357, 546, 547
  Benjamin Marden.................. 547
  Betsey 571
  Betsey (Sanborn)................. 547
  Betsey (Woods)................... 547
  Betty 546
  Charlotte 577
  Darius 580
  Dearborn 547
  Dolly 546
  Elizabeth 546, 547
  Elizabeth (Fogg)................. 547
  Elizabeth (Jenness)..........383, 546
  Elizabeth (Marden)...........455, 546
  Elizabeth (Philbrick)............ 580
  Esther 546
  Esther (Johnson)................. 546
  Fanny (Jenness).................. 386
  Gardiner G....................... 547
  George W......................... 123
  Hannah...................546, 547, 571
  Hannah Ely....................... 547
  Hannah (Locke)................... 432
  Hannah (Philbrick)...........490, 580
  Hannah (Yeaton)..............547, 571
  Hitty 485
  Huldah 298
  Isaac 580
  James....................312, 546, 547
  Jarius 339
  Jeremiah 546
  Job 546
  John.........................432, 546
  Jonathan..........31, 32, 60, 87, 138, 139
         140, 142, 145, 160, 255, 262
         288, 289, 383, 466, 546, 547
  Joseph.....253, 255, 329, 378, 422, 546, 547
  Joshua 309, 311
  L. Gordon........................ 547
  Lemuel 547
  Levi............141, 145, 262, 378, 425
                       455, 546, 547
  Lucy 546
  Lucy (Hobbs).................378, 547
  Lydia 577
  Maria 547
  Mary.........................378, 400, 546
  Mary (French).................... 547
  Mary (Locke).................425, 547
  Mary (Locke-Redmond)............. 422
  Matthias 547
  Mehitable 309
  Mehitable (Hobbs)................ 546
  Molly 373, 546
  Nabby 546
  Nancy 547
  Nancy (Rundlett)................. 547
  Nathan..............32, C0, 256, 262, 546
  Olive (Brown).................... 311
  Olly 546
  Perna 547
  Perna (Judkins).................. 547
  Rachel 429
  Rachel (Elkins).................. 546
  Rebecca (Garland)................ 357
  Rhoda 547
  Rhoda (Harvey)................... 547
  Ruth (Marden)................455, 546
  Sally....................320, 546, 547
  Sally B.......................... 578
  Sally (Downs)................339, 580

INDEX OF NAMES.

Towle, Sally (Lake).............. 547
  Sally (Wallis)................. 547
  Samuel....31, 140, 141, 145, 386, 546, 547
  Sarah 546
  Sarah (Brown).................. 309
  Sarah (Dalton)................. 329
  Sarah (Hobbs).................. 378
  Simeon 259, 262
  Simon..............145, 263, 265, 448
                        455, 546, 547, 571
  Sophia 560
  Susan 547
Townsend, George................. 371
  Mary 338
  Mary Ann (Goss)................ 371
Trafton, Alfred S.............451,549
  Emily (Trefethen-Hall)......... 549
  Rhoda (Marden)................. 451
Trask, Martha (Seavey)........... 532
  R. W........................... 532
Treadwell 213
  Daniel 207
  William Earle.................. 201
Tredick, Dolly (Locke)........... 437
  Edward 580
  Henry 437
  Jane (Trundy).................. 580
Trefathern, see Trefethern.
Trefethen, or Trefethern, or Tre-
  ferrin 72
  ——— (Partridge).............. 547
  Abby Grace..................... 550
  Abigail.................4C2, 512, 547
  Abigail (Locke)............421, 547
  Adeline 550
  Adeline P. (Locke)............. 437
  Adna (Nutter).................. 550
  Albert B...................549, 551
  Albert Bracket.............506, 552
  Alfred M....................... 549
  Alvedea H. (Clough), see Alvida
    (Clough).
  Alvida (Clough)............327, 551
  Ann M. (Clark)................. 551
  Anna..............528, 538, 549, 550
  Anna M. (Clark)................ 326
  Anne Louisa (Odiorne).......... 470
  Annie 551
  Annie L. (Odiorne)............. 552
  Annie O........................ 470
  Annie (Walker)................. 561
  Arthur Elwyn................... 551
  Austin 551
  Austin Wallace................. 551
  Benjamin Bailey............548, 549
  Bertha W. (Abbott)............. 552
  Betsey 548
  Betsey (Randall)............... 517
  Bob 289
  Carrie L. (Furlough)........... 552
  Charles 549
  Charles E...................... 294
  Charles Elvin..............550, 551
  Charles F.............451, 548, 550
  Charlotte 326
  Charlotte H.................... 550
  Charlotte (Jewell)............. 548
  Clara 550
  Clara I........................ 409
  D 280
  Daniel H....................... 561
  Daniel J..................548, 550
  David 549
  Deborah (Randall).............. 517
  Dennis C....................... 108
  Dennis Hill................549, 551
  Dorothy B. (Marden)........451, 550

Trefethen, Edith................. 511
  Edith Mabel 551
  Eliza Ann (Marden)..........451, 550
  Eliza Locke.................... 549
  Elizabeth (Locke).............. 436
  Elizabeth (Mason).............. 550
  Elizabeth (Tucker).........548, 553
  Ella M. (Maxwell).............. 551
  Ellen 549
  Elmer Balch 551
  Elvina Porter.................. 549
  Emily 377, 549
  Emily A........................ 549
  Emily (Seavey)................. 552
  Emma B......................... 552
  Everett 552
  Flora Ida...................... 550
  Florence 548
  Florenza 409
  Frances L...................... 549
  Frank......................550, 552
  Frank J........................ 551
  Frank Pierce................... 551
  Freddie Irving................. 552
  Frederick A.................... 549
  George Chester................. 551
  George Lercy..........550, 551, 566
  Gertrude 551
  Gilman D..............291, 550, 552
  Grace 551
  Grace E........................ 552
  Hannah 550
  Hannah C....................... 409
  Hannah Josephine...........442, 549
  Hannah L. Berry............299, 548
  Hannah L. (Garland)............ 549
  Hanson 549
  Hanson Hoit.................... 548
  Harriet (Keen)................. 549
  Hattie O....................... 552
  Henry.............276, 278, 547, 548
  Henry H........................ 550
  Herman 470
  Herman O...................551, 552
  Hiram 437
  Hope G......................... 550
  Horace 281
  Horace L.............326, 550, 551
  Izette 341
  Izette Morris.................. 549
  James Oren..................... 549
  Jane 550
  Jennie 551
  John 262
  John A.........70, 106, 147, 170, 172, 285
                          286, 290, 432
  John Adam..................548, 549
  John E......................... 70
  John Edwin..................... 549
  John I......................... 460
  John Ichabod...............549, 550
  Joseph..........147, 153, 255, 276, 278
                     290, 299, 547, 548, 551
  Joseph P..............287, 291, 451
  Joseph Parsons.............548, 550
  Josephine 550
  Julia 550, 552
  Julia Alice.................... 551
  Julia (Trefethen)..........550, 552
  Laura F...................342, 550
  Levi 549
  Levi B......................... 436
  Levi Berry.................548, 549
  Lewis W........................ 549
  Lizzie Wallis.................. 551
  Locada (Locke).............436, 549
  Louisa 550

INDEX OF NAMES.

TREFETHEN, Louisa R.............. 552
Louisa (Trefethern).............. 550
Louvia 548
Louvia (Trefethern).............. 548
Lucenna Jane..................... 377
Lucretia 547
Lydia (Berry)............298, 299, 548
Lydia M.......................293, 549
Maggie A. (Burchell)............. 551
Marcie Elizabeth................. 551
Margaret 547
Martha 367
Martha C. (Balch)................ 294
Martha Ellen (Balch)............. 551
Martha (Moulton)................. 549
Martha Semira................374, 549
Martin Percy..................... 551
Mary................479, 531, 547, 548
Mary (————).................... 547
Mary Abby (Rand)........506, 549, 552
Mary (Brown)..................... 548
Mary Elvira...................... 552
Mary Emily (Clark)..........326, 551
Mary G............................ 554
Mary Gilman...................... 552
Mary J............................ 549
Mary L. (Gilbert)................ 551
Mary (Locke).................432, 549
Mary O.......................510, 550
Mary Salter...................... 550
Maud 550
Nabby 548
Nancy 548
Nathaniel................276, 290, 548
Nellie 551
Nellie G........................t.. 550
Octavia 549
Oliver 549, 551
Oliver B......................... 552
Oliver Winslow...............327, 551
Olivia B. (Marden)..........451, 550
Patience (Riggs)................. 549
Polly 548
Polly (Lang)..................... 407
Ralph 552
Raymond Hall..................... 551
Robinson...........65, 103, 153, 255, 261
              262, 286, 289, 421, 547
Rozette (Webster)............551, 566
Ruhannah (Mason)................ 460
Ruth Mabel....................... 551
Sabrina 548, 566
Sabrina E........................ 550
Sabrina (Trefethen).............. 548
Salome 346, 547
Samuel 68, 451
Samuel A...............246, 549, 550
Samuel H......................... 551
Sarah 437, 508
Sarah E......................380, 549
Sarah (Moulton).................. 551
Sarah P.......................... 552
Sebastian 548
Sebastian J..................436, 549
Simon G.......................... 548
Simon Goss...................548, 550
Supply F...............180, 183, 326
Supply Foss..................549, 551
Susannah (Piper)................ 548
Susie E.......................... 551
Thaddeus R....................... 550
Wallis 552
Walter A......................... 550
Willard A........................ 552
William.........31, 66, 141, 145, 170, 257
          259, 262, 273, 275, 278, 290
          298, 299, 547, 548, 549, 553

TREFETHEN, William Henry Jackman 549
  Willie Marshal.................. 551
TRELAWNY 413
TRICKEY, Caty M.................. 504
  Eleanor (Libby)................ 414
  John 263
  Mary 366
  Susan (Ball)................... 294
  Zebulon 414
TROOP, Lydia..................... 352
TRUE, Betsey..................... 387
  Daniel 268
  Edward 268
  Joseph 267, 268
  Julia M........................ 338
  Mary (————).................. 526
  Polly 391
  Sally 391
TRUEWORTHY, John................. 314
TRUNDY, Jane..................... 580
  Sally 369
  Tobias...........153, 255, 259, 261, 500
TUCK, or TUCKE.
  Abigail 553
  Benjamin 358
  Bethia (Hobbs)................. 552
  Edward 488
  John..............240, 241, 243, 476, 552
  Joseph 553
  Josiah 406
  Judith (Gardiner).............. 552
  Love 552
  Love Muchmore.................. 552
  Mary 502, 552
  Mary (Dole).................... 552
  Mary (Parsons)..........240, 476, 552
  Mary (Philbrick)............... 488
  Richard 553
  Samuel 552
  Sarah (Garland)................ 358
  Sarah (Lang-Crockett).......... 406
  Thomas 553
TUCKER................88, 141, 145, 584
  Abigail 554
  Adeline 326
  Adeline J...................... 554
  Alfred 437
  Alvira (Locke)................. 437
  Betsey 435, 553
  Betsey (————)................ 337
  Betsey H. (Hayes).............. 554
  Betsey (Hall).................. 377
  Betsey (Rand).................. 553
  Betsey (Saunders).............. 553
  Charles 555
  Charles W...................... 554
  Daniel 554
  Edna Maud...................... 554
  Edward W....................... 554
  Elijah 261, 554
  Eliza S......................... 446
  Elizabeth................548, 553, 579
  Elizabeth Esther............... 553
  Elizabeth (Fernald)............ 554
  Elizabeth H.................... 553
  Elizabeth (Hall)............... 553
  Elizabeth (Lear)............... 553
  Elizabeth M.................294, 554
  Elizabeth (Moses)........463, 554
  Elizabeth Whidden (Perkins).... 486
  Ernest Albert.................. 554
  Esther 376, 377
  Florence Emma 554
  Grace 296
  Hannah (Yeaton)................ 571
  Harry 555
  James 553, 554

INDEX OF NAMES. 669

TUCKER, John............................ 553
John W....................208, 553
Joseph............145, 147, 337, 553, 554, 563
Joseph Parsons...................... 553
Joseph Wallis....................... 554
Madge Levia........................ 554
Mary................300, 345, 553, 554, 555
Mary (Archer)...................... 553
Mary Elizabeth..................... 554
Mary (Fogg)........................ 553
Mary Gilman (Trefethen).....552, 554
Mary (Mason)....................... 554
Mary (Wallis)..................554, 563
Michael W.......................... 463
Michael Wallis..................... 554
Nancy.............................. 554
Nathaniel..........31, 141, 145, 153, 255
                   259, 262, 377, 553
Olive.............................. 553
Olive (Saunders)..............523, 553
Rebecca (Shillaber)................ 555
Richard................153, 255, 553, 554
Sally.............................. 553
Samuel............................. 554
Sarah...................317, 416, 553, 554
Sarah (Slooper).................... 554
Stephen............................ 571
Susan A........................326, 554
Susannah 343, 553
Trefenna........................... 553
William............31, 176, 269, 275, 276
                   278, 523, 552, 552, 554
William W.......................... 554
Woodbury 554
TUCKERMAN, Margaret................. 517
TUCKESBURY, Ann..................... 434
TURNER, ——— (Seward)............. 554
Elizabeth 578
George Lester...................... 554
Hannah (Perkins)................... 554
John 554
Joseph 555
Lucy 554
Mildred Frances.................... 554
Norman Delbert..................... 554
Phillip Willard.................... 554
Sarah 554
William 554
TUTTLE, James....................... 343
Jane (Edmunds)..................... 343
Betsey (Morrison).................. 462
TWOMBLY, Isaac...................... 462
TYNG, Dudley A.................240, 241
ULRICH, Christine................... 480
UNDERWOOD, John..................... 127
UPHAM, E. Maria..................... 341
Joy Wilmot, see Tucker, John W.
USHER, Elizabeth Allen.............. 475
Frances 475
John 475
VARNEY, Elias....................... 431
Hannah (Locke)..................... 431
Harriett N. (Foss)................. 348
John 348
VARRELL, or VERRILL.
Abigail 295, 557
Abigail Locke...................... 559
Alma G............................. 559
Amy J. (Caswell)..............323, 559
Ann M.............................. 517
Ann Anzolette...................... 559
Anna 556, 557
Anna (Lang)...................406, 555
Anna Maria......................... 556
Annie M. (Burrell)................. 556
Benjamin..................323, 555, 556
Bessie 557

VARRELL, Betsey.........555, 557, 559
Betsey (Brown)..................... 558
Betty 557
Carrie Etta........................ 559
Charles Edward..................... 556
Charles F.......................... 559
Charles William...............555, 556
Clara Emma.....................519, 559
Clara Susan........................ 556
Clarissa 556
Clementina 558
Collista (Dotie)................... 555
Cordelia 558
Deborah...................406, 445, 556
Deborah (Bartlett)................. 555
Eddie II........................... 559
Edith 327
Edith M............................ 559
Edna 558
Edward............141, 145, 257, 259, 264
                 273, 276, 278, 300, 557, 580
Elbridge Gerty..................... 558
Eleanor (Norton)..........466, 555, 580
Eliza 577
Eliza E........................443, 557
Eliza Esther (Foss)................ 348
Eliza Foss......................... 558
Eliza Jane......................... 558
Elizabeth 386, 555
Elizabeth Mary..................... 557
Elizabeth (Saunders)............... 557
Elizabeth Saunders W. (Waldron) 559
Elizabeth (Waldron)................ 557
Ellen A............................ 558
Elsie Victoria..................... 556
Emma Eliza......................... 557
Ernest 559
Eunice 558
Eunice (Brown)..................... 558
Fannie E.......................555, 558
Forrest C.......................... 559
Frank 556
George A........................... 558
Gilman 442, 558
Gilman Henry....................... 559
Gilman N.......................280, 322
Gilman Nathaniel................... 558
Granville 556
Hannah.............467, 519, 555, 556
Hannah Elizabeth (Locke-Marden)...........................442, 558
Hannah Jane........................ 557
Hannah (Lewis)..................... 555
Harvey 558
Henrietta F. (Chickering)......... 556
Henry J............................ 555
Henry L........................453, 557
Herman 559
Hiram 558
Ida 557
Ida M.............................. 556
Inez W............................. 556
J. Winfield S...................... 323
Jacob 556
James T........................555, 556
Jefferson B........................ 558
John......35, 141, 145, 259, 262, 273, 406
         466, 555, 556, 557, 558, 580
John Albert........................ 558
John C............................. 556
John C. F.......................... 559
John J............................. 555
John Milkfield..................... 556
John Wesley........................ 558
Jonathan 164, 172
Jonathan W.................461, 557, 558
Joseph.........276, 278, 523, 524, 558, 559

INDEX OF NAMES.

VARRELL, Joses............... 559
  Kate M. (Rand)..........510, 559
  Kenneth Eugene............ 556
  Laura E...............558, 567
  Lilla L. (Pethick)........... 559
  Lizzie A................... 558
  Lorina 556
  Lulu M.................... 558
  Luther 556
  Lydia................519, 555, 556
  Lydia (——— Kien)........... 557
  Lydia Christina............. 557
  Lydia Nora 557
  Margaret (Muchmore)....... 555
  Maria (Norton)........466, 555, 556
  Martha 556, 558
  Martha A.................. 470
  Martha E.................. 409
  Martha (——— Hanscom)..... 558
  Martha Lang............... 558
  Mary............517, 555, 556, 557, 558
  Mary (Berry)............300, 557
  Mary (Berry-Mace) 445
  Mary (Caswell)..........323, 556
  Mary (Dearborn)........557, 580
  Mary E..................446, 518
  Mary E. (Matthews)........ 461
  Mary E. (Waldron).......... 559
  Mary Eliza................. 556
  Mary Elizabeth............. 557
  Mary Elizabeth (Mathes).... 558
  Mary H. (Lord)............. 555
  Mary (Hanson)............. 556
  Mary Jane................. 558
  Mary Jane (Marden)......453, 557
  Mary (Lang)............407, 555
  Mary O.................323, 555
  Molly (Berry-Mace)......301, 558
  Nancy 556, 557
  Nancy J. (Berry)........299, 556
  Nathan 556
  Nathaniel 555, 556
  Nora 511
  Orville F................510, 559
  Phebe Philbrick............ 559
  Polly (———)............... 493
  Polly (Randall)............. 557
  R. V....................... 280
  Rachel 557
  Rebecca 555
  Richard..........301, 445, 557, 558
  Richard F............323, 558, 559
  Richard Harvey............. 558
  Richard T.................. 493
  Richard Tucker............. 557
  Robert W...............285, 348
  Robert Waldron............ 558
  Robert Walter.............. 558
  Sadie (Campbell)........... 558
  Sally..............322, 555, 556, 559
  Samuel.........172, 276, 557, 558, 559
  Sarah 555, 557
  Sarah (——— Saunders)...... 559
  Sarah A. (Caswell).......322, 558
  Sarah Ann (Locke).......... 437
  Sarah E.................... 323
  Sarah O.................... 317
  Sarah O. (Locke)........... 557
  Sarah Olive................ 556
  Sarah (Saunders-Saunders)...523, 524
  Solomon.........141, 145, 259, 555, 556
  Thomas Ira................ 558
  Tryphena Philbrick......... 556
  Washington 407, 555
  William...........177, 273, 299, 466, 517
               555, 556, 557, 559
  William Dudley.........437, 557

VARRELL, William S............. 558
VAUGHAN, Elliot................ 201
VEASEY, Eliphalet.............. 264
VENNARD, Adeline.............. 504
  Fanny (Locke).............. 433
  Jonathan 433
  Mary 437, 577
VEREL, see Varrell.
VERHOEFF, F. H................ 444
  Margaret (Lougee)........... 444
VINCENT, Anthony............... 263
VIRGIN, Joel B................. 386
  Olive (Jenness)............. 386
VITTAM, Hannah.............303, 306
WADLEIGH, Elijah............... 524
  Martha 489
  Martha (Saunders).......... 524
WAIT, Sarah.................... 575
  Sarah Ann (Jenness)......... 386
  William 386
WALBACK, ———................. 412
WALCOTT, Catherine (Elkins)..... 344
  Edward 344, 457
  Eunice Abby (Marden)....... 457
WALDRON, Alfred A.............. 560
  Anna (———)................ 560
  Benjamin Franklin.......... 560
  Clarence 29
  Daisy 560
  Eliza (———)............... 560
  Elizabeth 557
  Elizabeth Foss..........346, 559
  Elizabeth P. (———)......... 560
  Elizabeth Parsons.......... 560
  Elizabeth Saunders W....... 559
  Emily (Rand)............... 570
  Eva Jane................... 560
  Franklin 107
  George 559
  Grace 560
  Hannah (Drown)............ 560
  Henry 560
  Huldah (Ladd)............. 559
  Isaac..............75, 170, 560, 564
  Jacob..................348, 560, 581
  John 560
  Jonathan B...........177, 346, 559
  Joshua Foss............559, 560
  Lois 560
  Lydia (Todd).............. 560
  Margaret (Tarlton).......560, 581
  Martha 560
  Martha (Lang)............. 560
  Martha (Melcher).......... 560
  Mary C.................... 560
  Mary E...............559, 560, 580
  Mary F. (———)............. 560
  Mary Jane (Wallis)......... 560
  Mary Jones (Wallis)........ 564
  Mina L..................... 560
  Nathan 570
  Polly W.................... 438
  Polly Westbrook............ 559
  Richard................18, 40, 560
  Richard H...........170, 172, 517
  Richard Harvey..........559, 560
  Robert 560
  Robert Saunders........559, 560
  Sally (Foss)............... 348
  Samuel Wallis.............. 560
  Sarah Elizabeth............ 560
  Sarah Jane (Baston)........ 560
  Sarah (Randall).........517, 560
  Shaw 560
  Sophia (Towle)............. 560
WALES, see Wallis.
WALFORD, ———.................. 153

INDEX OF NAMES. 671

WALFORD, Thomas............. 246
WALKER, ——........23, 136, 274
A. M...................... 195
Adelaide (Banks)............. 562
Albert M.........57, 65, 195, 209, 213
     287, 438, 531, 561
Alice J...................302, 561
Almira 563
Ann L. (Thomas)............545, 563
Anna (Cater)................. 563
Annie 561
Annie Julia (Foss)..........349, 562
Arabella Ringe (Locke)........ 440
Archie 562
Arthur 562
Augusta M. (Page)............ 562
Benjamin Franklin 561
Betsey 408
Betsey (Peverly)............. 563
Catherine (Beck)............. 563
Chalcedona 562
Charles 67, 454
Charles A..............291, 561, 562
Charles E.................... 440
Charlotte (King)............. 561
Christie (Foss).............350, 562
Clara A. (Marden)...........454, 562
Cora 561
Cora Belle (Jenness).........390, 562
Deliverance 577
E. Annie (Manson)............ 562
Edwin...............390, 561, 562
Edwin B..................... 195
Elbridge Thomas.............. 545
Eliza A...................... 298
Eliza Ann..........66, 225, 297, 561, 562
Ellen A. (McLawlin)........... 561
Ezra Howard................. 562
Fannie Grace................. 562
George 134, 135
George S........... 286, 350, 561, 562
George Storer................ 561
Gideon 563
Gilman 365, 562
Hannah 453, 579
Hannah Beck................. 563
Hannah (Marden)..........457, 560
Hannah (Philbrick)..........488, 526
Harlan (Manson).............. 562
Harriet A. (Dow)...........336, 561
Harriet (Stevens)............. 561
Helen S...................... 561
Hermon E.................... 562
Isabella 303, 562
Jane B. (Sleeper)............. 561
Jenness 561
Jesse M...................... 562
Jesse Merrill................. 561
John K..................545, 563
Jonathan T.....108, 162, 164, 166, 169 171
   173, 214, 286, 290, 291, 314
Jonathan Towle............... 561
Joseph 488, 526
Katie (Hamilton).............. 561
L. E......................... 195
Levi Henry................... 561
Levi T..............66, 286, 290, 336
Levi Towle................... 561
Lewis E..................214, 349
Lewis Everett............561, 562
Lila 562
Margaret (Anderson)............ 563
Margaret (Neil).............. 562
Martha Elizabeth (Seavey)....531, 561
Mary Anderson............... 563
Mary Ann (Robinson).......... 562
Mary Esther (Brown).......314, 561

WALKER, Mary W................ 563
Maud 562
Maud G...................... 377
Nancy 407
Nathaniel 563
Nathaniel M.........106, 163, 166
Nathaniel Marden............. 561
Nellie (Hobbs)............379, 562
Ralph 379, 562
Raymond 562
Samuel.......66, 131, 169, 170, 172, 173
   278, 289, 290, 457, 560, 561
Samuel J.................... 107
Sarah (Wright).............. 562
Susie Emma (Garland).......365, 562
W. C......................... 195
William................400, 561, 563
William C...............107, 214
William Chauncey............. 561
William J..........66, 195, 561, 562
WALINGFORD, ——............. 173
WALL, James................. 488
Mary (Philbrick-Tuck).......... 488
WALLACE, Abby Francette (Goss).... 371
Albert 419
Clarissa 433
Edwin G..................... 107
John 371
Julia E. (Libby)............. 419
William..............135, 137, 267
WALLER, Edmund.............. 473
Sarah 473
WALLFORD, Jeremiah........... 129
WALLES, see Wallis.
WALLIS, ——........27, 53, 68, 127, 149
—— (Comstock).............. 564
Abigail..................463, 563
Ann (Shortridge)..........541, 563
Appia 434
Benjamin 580
Betsey 564
Caesar..............212, 268, 269, 563
Caesar Seavey................ 584
Comfort................404, 564, 580
Comfort (Cotton)............. 580
Deborah (—— Reeder)......... 563
Deborah (Fuller)............. 580
Dorothy (Lang)............... 406
Ebenezer......31, 35, 58, 68, 110, 141
   145, 262, 273, 406, 528, 563
Elizabeth 388
Elizabeth (Parsons).......476, 563
Elizabeth (Rand)............. 580
Eunice 431
George.................134, 541, 563
Hannah..................450, 563
Jane 563
John 429, 564
Joseph 580
Margaret 563
Margaret (Fuller)............ 580
Margaret (McCleary).......... 563
Martha................563, 580
Martha L.................... 563
Martha (Wallis).............. 580
Mary.............294, 434, 554, 563, 564
Mary Jane.................560, 564
Mary (Locke)................ 429
Molly (Brown)............... 564
Moses 564
Nancy 564
Phebe (Rand)................ 564
Phillis, see (Phyllis).
Phyllis..........212, 268, 269, 563, 584
Ralph 563
Reuben 580
Sally 547, 564

INDEX OF NAMES.

WALLIS, Samuel..22, 24, 26, 27, 31, 35, 53, 58
    75, 90, 91, 135, 137, 141, 145
    160, 205, 207, 212, 259, 261
    262, 268, 269, 273, 283, 284
    288, 289, 463, 476, 563
  Sarah 345, 528, 563, 564
  Sarah (Moses) 463, 563
  Susan (Lucas) 564
  Weymouth 580
  William...22, 24, 26, 27, 71, 127, 134, 249
    250, 205, 268, 503, 564, 580
WALPEY, Joseph....................... 263
WALTON, Sarah........................ 540
  Shadrach 40, 127
WARD, Abigail (Fullerton)........... 580
  Cotton 340
  Eliza (Brown)...................... 314
  Emma Eliza (Varrell)............. 557
  John T............................ 557
  Joseph 64, 314
  Lydia 314
  Margaret 421
  Mary E............................ 442
  Samuel 260
  Sarah 333, 340
  Simon.......................50, 51, 580
WARNER, John W...................... 366
  Jonathan 47, 133
  Estelle (Garland)................. 366
  Abigail (Leavitt)................. 581
  Albert 508
  Samuel S.......................... 581
  Sarah 541
  Sarah Olive (Rand)................ 508
WARREN, A. K......................... 299
  Augustus 347
  Caroline 401
  Catharine (Foss).................347
  Eliza (Berry)..................... 299
  Hannah T.......................... 507
WASSON, Thomas....................... 262
WATERHOUSE, Dolly................... 402
WATERS, ———.......................... 253
  Mary (———)....................... 253
WATKINS, Lydia....................... 491
WATSON, ———........................... 69
  Alice (Clark)..................... 564
  Asa 432
  Clara E. (Locke).................. 442
  James I........................... 442
  John 564
  Mary 363
  Nathaniel 107
  Polly (Locke)..................... 432
  Ruth 464
  Samuel 564
  Thomas 135, 136, 160, 564
  Timothy 262
WATT, Anna Knox (Sawyer).......... 525
  Joseph 525
WEAR, Peter........................... 39
WEARE, D............................. 265
  Daniel 203, 265
  Ebenezer 421
  Mary 309
  Prudence (Locke)................. 421
WEATHERBEE, Harriet................ 436
WEBB, Margaret....................... 540
WEBBER, Huldah....................... 330
WEBSTER, ———.....................72, 135
  ——— (Brackett)................. 566
  ——— (Ladd)..................... 564
  ——— (Nowell).................. 566
  Abby 566
  Abiah........................522, 564, 565
  Abiah (Shaw)...................... 564

WEBSTER, Abigail........300, 447, 515, 565
  Albert G.......................... 330
  Andrew 421
  Andrew Gerrish................... 566
  Andrew Jackson................... 566
  Anna 400, 522
  Anne 565
  Archie 567
  Arvill (Johnson).................. 566
  Augustus Floyd................... 566
  Benjamin Franklin................ 566
  Betsey 529, 565
  Betsey (Clark).................... 325
  Caleb 564
  Charles Edward................... 566
  Charity 304, 564
  Daniel 566
  Daniel C....................... 550, 566
  David.......................565, 566, 580
  David Locke...................... 566
  Dolly 374, 565
  Dorothy (Chapman)................ 565
  E. (Macy)......................... 565
  Emily 566
  Emily C........................... 566
  Eliza (Rand)...................503, 565
  Elizabeth..............401, 455, 564, 566
  Elizabeth H. (Clark)............. 506
  Elizabeth (Randall)............515, 565
  Eunice (Nowell)................... 580
  Fanny 565
  Fanny (Conner).................... 566
  Frances M. (White)............... 566
  Hannah 389, 565
  Hannah (Grant)................... 565
  Hattie 567
  Jeremiah 172, 564
  Jeremy........102, 164, 170, 279, 503, 565
  Johanna (Rich).................... 566
  John.........31, 54, 75, 137, 141, 145, 176
    262, 273, 275, 289, 564, 565, 566
  John Gerrish...................... 566
  John H.......................208, 278, 325
  John Hobbs.....................565, 566
  Josiah........75, 136, 145, 160, 177, 227
    273, 288, 368, 428, 564, 565
  Laura E. (Varrell).............558, 567
  Levi Locke........................ 565
  Lizzie F. (Briggs)................ 566
  Lizzie (Josselyn)................. 566
  Mark 276
  Mark R................166, 170, 173, 408
  Mark Randall..................565, 566
  Martha........315, 339, 433, 468, 564, 565
  Martha D. (Dalton)............... 330
  Martha J.......................532, 566
  Mary 344, 565, 566
  Mary Ann (Lang)...............408, 566
  Mary Chatman..................... 566
  Mary E............................ 566
  Mary (Locke)...................... 227
  Mary (Philbrick).................. 492
  Mary S............................ 467
  Nathaniel 565
  Olive 565
  Orin 558, 567
  Patty (Goss)...................368, 564
  Polly (Philbrick)................. 566
  Prudence (Locke-Weare).......... 421
  R 266
  Richard........31, 35, 75, 105, 108, 141
    145, 170, 176, 259, 265, 269
    270, 271, 273, 276, 286, 289
    477, 492, 515, 564, 565, 566
  Roswell 566
  Rozette 551, 566

INDEX OF NAMES. 673

WEBSTER, Sabrina E. (Trefethern)..
  550, 566
Sally 565
Sarah.....227, 433, 449, 451, 492, 564, 565
Sarah (Dunn)..................... 566
Sarah L........................... 566
Sarah (Locke)..............428, 565
Sarah (Senter)................... 566
Susan (Johnson)................. 566
Thomas 564
Ursula 566
Warren P......................... 566
William.....................24, 135, 137
William Wallis.................. 566
WEDGEWOOD, Abby................ 567
Betsey 301, 567
Charles 567
David........67, 205, 209, 278, 279, 352
  387, 402, 542, 567, 584
David William..................... 567
E. S........................276, 319, 361
Eliphalet S....................... 567
Eliphalet Sleeper................ 567
Eliza G............................. 314
Emily 567
Gilman 567
Hannah.................330, 397, 567
Hannah (Brown)................. 567
Hannah ((Garland-Brown)........ 361
Hannah (Seavey)............528, 567
Hannah (Wedgewood)........... 567
Jonathan..........67, 205, 273, 274, 275
  276, 284, 289, 290, 348, 389
  431, 435, 502, 503, 528, 567
Lott 259
Mary...................383, 386, 490, 567
Mary (Marston)................... 567
Mary (Sleeper)..............542, 567
Polly (Jenness)..............387, 567
Sally Wallis....................... 567
Sarah 567
Sarah W........................... 437
WEED, George...................... 567
Mary (Whitten).................. 436
WEEKS, Abigail.................467, 568
Anna (Philbrick)................. 490
Betty 568
Bridget 578
Daniel 553
Elizabeth 532
Eunice 354
Hannah (Lang).................... 406
Hattie B.......................... 396
Helen A........................... 341
John......................255, 406, 568
Joshua..........48, 50, 160, 203, 263
  382, 568, 580
Josiah..................263, 490, 514
Louisa (Porter).................. 499
Lovina 302
Mary (Jenness)................... 382
Mercy (Rand-Colman)............ 514
Molly 568
Olive (Tucker)................... 553
Sarah.................459, 568, 577
Sarah (Jenness).................. 580
Sarah (Marston)................. 568
William 89, 499
WELCH, Daniel.................... 580
Elizabeth (Abbott).............. 580
Margaret 431
WELLS, ———— (Shaw)............ 568
Anna 568
Betsey 491
Deborah 568
Elizabeth 568
Elizabeth (Rollins)............. 568

WELLS, Elizabeth (Thompson)....... 568
Hannah (Brown)..................... 568
Hannah (Seavey).................... 526
Hiram 580
Isaiah 568
Jeremiah 568
John 568
Lydia V. (Green).................. 580
Molly 568
Moses 580
Olive 295
Olly 568
Patty 370
Polly (Merrill).................... 580
Priscilla (Brock)................. 568
Sally (Batchelder)................ 568
Samuel........33, 58, 139, 142, 145, 160
  203, 205, 262
  273, 526, 568
Sarah.....................491, 568, 579
Simeon 253, 568
Simon 205, 568
WENDELL, Abraham................ 581
Auburn 568
Charles 336, 568
Dolly 516
Elizabeth 299
Henry F........................... 463
John S............................. 486
Mamie (Dow)..................336, 568
Martha Jane (Perkins).......... 486
Mary B. (Moses).................. 463
Mary (Locke)..................... 435
Olive 568
Sukey (Gardiner)................. 581
WENTWORTH, Benning..........191, 202
Charles E.....................397, 568
Charles Sumner.................. 568
Charlotte 431
Gates 453
Hunking 201
John................22, 25, 133, 257, 258
Joshua 263, 270
Mary 436
Mercy 385
Minerva S. (Jenness).........397, 568
Sarah Ann (Marden)............. 453
WESTON, Thomas 12
WEYMOUTH, ————................ 127
Eunice 568
George 568
James 568
Samuel 568
Shadrach 160, 568
Thomas Cotton................... 568
WHARTON, Emily 396
WHEELER, Betsey (Tarlton)...... 580
Hunkin 580
Mary 474
WHENAL, Isabella (White)....... 570
Thomas 570
WHIDDEN, ———— (Gerrish)........ 569
—— (Gerrish-Seavey)........... 530
Abigail 518
Abigail (————)..............518, 569
Abigail (Seavey)................. 528
Alice J. (Jenness)...........392, 569
Andrew J......................... 569
Anna 569
Anna A............................ 363
Anna (Langdon).................. 411
Anna P. (Seavey)................ 569
Anna Partridge (Foss).......... 347
Betsey (Downs).................. 338
Betsey (Jenness)................ 391
Charles 392, 569
Charles H......................... 569

INDEX OF NAMES.

WHIDDEN, Charles S............60, 285, 291
  Daniel 569
  Data (Brown)..................314, 569
  Eliza 531
  Elizabeth 569
  Elizabeth Anna..................... 569
  Elizabeth (Berry)............306, 569
  Elizabeth (Langdon)..........411, 569
  Ellen A................................. 569
  Fanny 569
  Frances A............................ 569
  Frances P. (Foss).................. 580
  Goodman Brown.................... 569
  Hannah...............212, 518, 569, 584
  Hannah (Jones).................... 580
  Hannah L............................. 569
  Hannah (Langdon)...........410, 580
  Hannah (Marden).................. 450
  Hannah (Whidden)................ 569
  Harnett A............................. 569
  Horace 569
  James 406, 411
  John 338
  John H................................. 569
  Joseph 528, 569
  Joseph W........................306, 569
  Langdon 530, 569
  Mark 569
  Mary 529, 569
  Mary Ann............................. 569
  Mary (Heheir)....................... 569
  Mary W................................ 525
  Nettie 569
  Nettie R............................... 362
  Peggy Sherburn 569
  Rebeckah 448
  Richard 569
  Samuel............212, 314, 391, 410, 411
                                    569, 580
  Samuel H............................. 569
  Samuel S............................. 569
  Samuel Storer...................... 569
  Sarah 569
  Sarah (Johnson-Lang)........... 406
  Sarah L............................... 569
  Thomas 569, 580
  Thomas J............................. 347
  William 450, 569
WHIPPLE, William.................... 270
WHISTLER, Joshua.................... 474
WHITE, Abbott........................ 570
  Abigail (Berry)..................... 300
  Ada Emerett 570
  Augustus 349
  Crummitt 300
  Elizabeth (Jenness).............. 387
  Frances M........................... 566
  George 454
  George 570
  Hannah 437, 488
  Irving 570
  Isabella 570
  Joseph 411
  Josiah 265
  Mary 373
  Mary (Langdon-Tallent)........ 411
  Mary (Locke)..................421, 580
  Nathaniel 387
  Nellie 570
  Polly A. W. (Marden).......454, 570
  Rolla G................................ 570
  Salome 381, 421
  Sarah 334
  Sarah G. (Foss).................... 349
  Solomon 421, 580
  William 135
  Willie 570

WHITTEN, Anne...................... 578
  Mary 436
WHITTIER, Dolly (Brown)......... 311
  Richard 311
WIBIRD, Richard...................... 29
WIGGIN, Andrew..................... 42
  Benjamin 335
  Clara W.............................. 354
  David 259
  Hannah 580
  Hannah (Wiggin)................. 580
  John 581
  Lovina 574
  Martha 330
  Mary (Dow-Dowrst).............. 335
  Mary (Webster)................... 565
  Maud E............................... 533
  Noah 105, 565
  Sally H. (Marsh).................. 581
  Sarah A.............................. 575
  Stephen 580
WIGGINS, see Wiggin.
WILKES, John......................... 67
WILKINS, Charles F................. 379
  Mabel 444
  Sarah Eliza (Holmes).......... 379
WILLACY, Mary Jane (Page-Marden) 452
  William E........................... 452
WILLARD, Caroline G............... 580
WILLET, Alice......................... 302
WILLEY, Charles..................... 570
  Clarissa 353, 570
  Ellen 570
  Lucy (Lang)...................407, 570
  Martha A.......................509, 570
  Martha Ellen...................... 411
  Martha (Seavey)..............528, 570
  Mary 531, 570
  Samuel.....................105, 528, 570
  Sarah 473
  William 407
  William S........................... 570
WILLIAMS, Abigail................... 492
  Hannah G.......................... 354
  Jennie E............................ 442
  John F.........................205, 354
  Mary 364
  Peggy (Appleton)................ 580
WILLIAMSON, ————........230, 234
  George W........................... 281
WILLIARD, Ezra H................... 469
  Joseph 540
  Mary (Sheafe).................... 540
  Sarah Holbrook (Odiorne)..... 469
WILLIS, A.............................. 440
  Caroline (Locke)................. 440
WILLISTON, Joseph.................. 474
  Mary (Parsons-Ashley)......... 474
WILSON, Albert H.................... 570
  Alice G.............................. 342
  Bertha H............................ 570
  Hannah (Cragg).................. 570
  Helena 570
  Herbert C........................... 570
  Isaac 570
  Joel 175
  John 547
  Keziah 393
  Laura 303
  Perna (Towle).................... 547
  Rhoda F. (Page)................. 472
  Salome 393
  Samuel 472
  Susan (Seavey).................. 532
WILLSON, Cora D. (Babbitt)..... 394
WINFIELD, Elizabeth............... 418

INDEX OF NAMES. 675

WINGATE, ——............................ 260
Joshua 41
WINKLEY, Sarah........................ 410
WINTHROP, John........................ 9
WITCHER, Martin L..................... 434
Mary 385
Nancy (Locke)......................... 434
WOLCOTT, Abigail (Brown-Marden).. 315
E 315
WOLFE, James.......................... 254
WOOD, Minnie E........................ 341
WOODBURY, Carrie G. (Brown)....... 318
Walter 318
WOODMAN, Betsey...............360, 571
Betsey (Jenness-Rand).............. 383
Carrie S. (Russell).................. 570
Chauncy 570
Chauncy M........................286, 291
Elizabeth 574
Emery..........................287, 291, 570
Emery C............................... 291
Hannah (Jenness).............382, 383
Hannah (Jenness-Rand)............ 571
Harriet (Briard).................... 570
Jesse 428
John 570
Jonathan......205, 276, 383, 501, 570, 571
Mary 571
Mary Ann (Bickford).............. 570
Mary Elizabeth..................... 570
Molly (Locke)....................... 428
Nancy 492, 571
Nancy Ann........................... 570
Sally (Rand)....................501, 570
Sarah (French)...................... 570
Thomas 263
William 570
WOODS, Betsey......................... 547
M 493
Margaret 496
Sarah 435
WOODSUM, Helen....................... 437
WOODWARD, Eliza A................... 419
WORCESTER, James...............264, 268
WORMWOOD, Love (Fuller)........... 580
William 580
WORTHEN, Jane (Libby).............. 417
Samuel 417
WRIGHT, Hepzibah (Seavey)......... 526
Sarah 562
Thomas 526
WYMAN, Emery (Mason).............. 460
Frank 460
YEATON, ——— (Hayes)............... 571
Abba L................................ 574
Abigail (Bell)....................... 572
Abigail (Gaudy)..................... 572
Adeline 572
Anna 389, 571
Arvilla Augusta..................... 572
Betsey 297
Betsey (Brown)..................... 571
Betsey Drew......................... 571
Betsey (Towle)...................... 571
Charles William..................... 572
Deborah 516, 571
Dolly 572
Dorothy 468
Mary (Durgin)....................... 581
Eben 572
Eliza J............................... 505
Elizabeth 509, 571
Elizabeth (Brown).................. 313
Elizabeth H.......................... **572**
Elizabeth (Ham)..................... 571
Elizabeth (Rand).................... 571
YEATON, Esther.............403, 519, 571
Esther (Saunders)..............523, 571
Hepsibah (Bell)..................... 572
Hannah 547, 571
Hannah (Towle)..............546, 547, 571
Hitty 572
Hopley........................353, 571, 572
Huldah (Saunders).................. 571
Isaac 572
Jane (Mitchell)..................... 572
John...........145, 193, 267, 523, 571, 572
John E................................ 572
Jonathan 547, 571
Joseph......31, 141, 145, 160, 203, 262, 265
273, 313, 571
L. Jane............................... 572
Lavinia (Berry)..................... 306
Levi 571
Lovina (Berry).................304, 572
Lucie Adelaide...................... 572
Lucie Adelaide (Yeaton)........... 572
Lucina 572
Lucy 578
Lydia Ann............................ 572
Lydia (Foye)........................ 572
Lydia Stevens (Foye).............. 353
Madelaide M......................... 572
Mary...................398, 468, 571, 579
Mary L................................ 572
Mary (Mathews)..................... 571
Mary S................................ 507
Mary Sheaf.......................... 470
Merribah 571
Peggy 572
Philip 571
Polly 571
Rebecca (Bickford)................. 571
Richard 572
Ruth 572
Ruth (Grant)........................ 572
Sally 571
Salome (Lear)....................... 571
Samuel 571
Sarah..........................387, 571, 572
Sarah (Coochman).................. 571
Sarah Elizabeth..................... 572
Sarah (Yeaton)...................... 572
Susan 571
Susannah 571
Susannah (Lang).................... 571
Sylvester 572
Tamah 572
Towle 571
William..........31, 35, 141, 145, 257, 273
546, 571, 572
William F.......................304, 306
William Foye........................ 572
YULEE, ———............................ 480
YOUNG, Abbott........................ 457
Anna (Locke)........................ 436
Benjamin 265, 266
Caroline A........................... 495
Clementina (Varrell-Heath)....... 558
David 581
Emma Jennette (Marden).......... 457
Esther (Libby)...................... 418
Hannah 435
James............................451, 581
Mary A............................... 431
Mary (Marden)...................... 451
Ruth (Smith)........................ 581
Samuel 280
Sarah 515
Timothy 418
William 436, 558
YOUNGS, Joseph....................... 280